PRAISE FOR *JEWISH CULTURAL STUDIES*

"Simon J. Bronner remains the most elegant and insightful commentator on the complex and convoluted world of Jewish (no matter how defined) cultural production. One of the creators of Jewish cultural studies, his work has always been a beacon for all scholars and readers who are trying to frame questions about the Jews and the modern world, no more so in this age of COVID-19, where the Jews seem to be simultaneously perpetual victims as well as perpetrators. An important book for all scholars of 'out groups,' including the Jews."

—Sander L. Gilman, author of *Stand Up Straight! A History of Posture*

"In *Jewish Cultural Studies*, Simon Bronner caps a lifetime of research about Jewish life and lore with an original, provocative cultural perspective that changes the way people think about what Jews do, say, and feel. Breaking new ground for a fertile field of inquiry, it will surely inspire intellectual excitement and provide a basis for the ways that Jews are studied and understood."

—Haya Bar-Itzhak, co-editor of *The Power of a Tale: Stories from the Israel Folktale Archives* (Wayne State University Press, 2019)

"Based on immense scholarship, *Jewish Cultural Studies* problematizes the categories of ethnic, cultural, and religious, querying boundary maintenance, community construction, and the creation of distinctive Jewish culture and practice. With astute observation, Bronner probes the conceptual and literal, the rhetorical and ethnographic, and the historical and contemporary in this multifaceted exploration of Jewish culture."

—Amy K. Milligan, author of *Jewish Bodylore: Feminist and Queer Ethnographies of Folk Practices*

JEWISH
CULTURAL
STUDIES

RAPHAEL PATAI SERIES IN JEWISH FOLKLORE AND ANTHROPOLOGY

General Editor

Dan Ben-Amos

University of Pennsylvania

JEWISH CULTURAL STUDIES

SIMON J. BRONNER

WAYNE STATE UNIVERSITY PRESS
DETROIT

Library of Congress Control Number: 2020945635

ISBN 978-0-8143-4828-4 (hardcover); ISBN 978-0-8143-3875-9 (paperback); ISBN 978-0-8143-3876-6 (ebook)

Published with support from the fund for the Raphael Patai Series in Jewish Folklore and Anthropology.

Wayne State University Press
Leonard N. Simons Building
4809 Woodward Avenue
Detroit, Michigan 48201-1309

Visit us online at wsupress.wayne.edu

For Haya Bar-Itzhak of blessed memory (1946–2020),

friend and colleague from Haifa to Harrisburg

CONTENTS

PART III: NARRATION

PREFACE AND ACKNOWLEDGMENTS

This book is about contemporary Jewish culture and ways that it might be analyzed to uncover elusive issues of and needed answers to questions of Jewishness for both Jews and non-Jews. By "culture" I mean not only the aestheticized expressions of self, group, and nation in art, architecture, music, literature, legend, food, and speech, to name a few significant genres that I present in this volume, but also the symbolic beliefs and ideas, indeed worldviews and identities, that guide the way people think and act every day and ultimately their "frames of mind," one of which is feeling, if not evincing, Jewish qualities. I came to probe Jewishness through culture not in my scholastic studies as much as in my observations of the dizzying array of Jewish traditions swirling around me, first in Israel in my early childhood and then through personal and professional experience in the United States, Europe, and Asia, always mindful of being the offspring of Holocaust survivors and therefore constantly comparing Old and New World tradition, indeed prewar and postwar Jewish societies, and the attendant ways of thinking through the twenty-first century.

Like many young Jews, I was immersed as a student of Judaism in sacred texts, ancient history, synagogue practice, and institutional settings. I was rarely challenged to fathom the vast cultural diversity or social meaning of modern practices—religious and nonreligious—among people identifying themselves as Jewish. I sought to reveal Jewish culture at home and on the street by plowing the fields of folklore and ethnology and, later, media studies and modern historical approaches. To be sure, I came to appreciate the special association of Judaism with ancient tradition while recognizing its variability and evolving nature in modernity. By taking this analytical path, I often found that writers built artificial walls between folk and popular expression, past and present, and Jews and non-Jews, particularly those non-Jews belonging to other ethnic groups. The budding branch of Jewish cultural studies to which I have been given credit for growing arose as a collective effort to dissolve those boundaries while being sensitive to documenting and explaining varieties of social experience. The result, as the essays that follow demonstrate, is an interpretative reorientation toward the question of how and why one thinks Jewishly and feels and expresses Jewishness in culture.

Even in the contemporary American settings that mainly command my attention in this volume, one finds great variety and complex social relations to unravel. Methodologically, I am drawn to the use of ethnography and rhetorical analysis to locate patterns, processes, frames, and themes of events and actions identified as Jewish to discern what makes them appear Jewish and why. These tools facilitate documentation and decoding of repeated cultural scenes or frames for symbolic action and communication regarding the Jewish subject, whether that is by non-Jews or Jews. Toward the goal of explaining the meanings of such scenes and the cultural expression within them, I probably use psychological and historical interpretation more so than my fellow travelers in folkloristic and ethnological circles and more sociological, linguistic, and political perspectives than those in popular culture and humanistic studies. With the focus on culture, one cannot ignore religion in any discussion of Jewishness, but the approaches in the essays that follow tend to be about practices and performances in everyday life rather than about abstracted theology, and they take into account the influence of sacred texts and rabbinic thought from the past to the present. This is to all to say that Jewish cultural studies is an open field, an interdisciplinary venture that shares specific goals among its devotees, although their angles of vision vary greatly.

A primary concern in my charting of culture to explain thought and action—often leading to engaging variable identities in the course of one's life and activity that could be called Jewish and otherwise (such as the relation to many "host" societies)—is the dynamic between tradition and modernity. These are socially constructed concepts, to be sure, but they are very much a part of the dialectic that Jews particularly face in personalizing their views of what it means to be Jewish, especially in a place like the United States, which is associated often with novelty, individualism, and futurism—and remaking oneself. And there is no question that the situations I analyze and the perspectives I take draw especially on American

experience, where the tension between tradition and modernity is especially evident. Tradition is frequently used in the rhetoric of Judaism to emphasize the
authority of an unbroken chain from the ancient past, but in cultural studies tradition refers more to the use of variable repetition and precedent to bond people
together, provide stability, and guide creative expression. Sometimes conceptualized as a dualistic sense of community "we-ness," in the sense of being both
inwardly intimate and outwardly facing to the world, tradition stands relative to
but not apart from modernity in a usual thought process, or cognitive balancing
act, with pressure to embrace the fresh start and the individualized, often secular
path associated with the constantly changing, mediated, and massified society.

Modernity is a relative concept, often based on the idea that change improves
life through rationalized, secular science and technology and, subsequently, social
progress and intellectual enlightenment. Modernity implies a constant state of
transformation and vicissitude and, for many people, disconcerting uncertainty,
risk, and flux. If tradition is often characterized as a socially rooted we-ness, then
modernity represents a me-ness amid an expansive, mobile mass of people and
a worldview that embraces adaptation to the future rather than continuity with
the past. Although tradition is necessarily intertwined with modernity, it is often
associated with groupthink, whereas modernity is connected to individualism and
free volition, or the right to choose rather than submitting to the constraints of
the group and environment to which one is born. As a result, modernity often
implies mobile, divergent paths and people in response to the question "What
do you want to do (or be)?" rather than "Do you know what to do?" The first
individualistically oriented question can evoke an image of disorganization, dis-
cord, and conflict. And tradition is often invoked, particularly in Jewish culture,
to negotiate one's sense of belonging between continuity and change and to provide a basis for identity, connection, and creativity.

To my mind, essential to this dialectic between tradition and modernity is
what I call conceptualization, in addition to ritualization and narration. Underlying these categories are both intellectual and physical processes of cognition and
materialization, that is, rendering our anxieties with or attraction to Jewish identities socially visible through cultural expression. Such expression can be physical,
as in voluntarily eating matzo during Passover while others eat bread or laughing
knowingly and perhaps uncomfortably or protesting resentfully upon hearing a
Jewish joke. This kind of materialization draws attention to socially shared and
cognitively generated symbols while disguising and thereby raising the question

of embodiment—whether the Jewish body and mind are different to the point of being typified. Therefore ambivalence results from or is imposed on expressing Jewish selves as distinct for a sense of belonging, and in doing so, Jews take the risk of being exposed as othered—and are potentially stigmatized.

In part 1, "Conceptualization," I discuss the formation of beliefs and ideas in academic culture and in everyday domestic life. By contesting the modernist view of tradition as inflexible and the traditionalist attitude toward modernity as fundamentally detrimental to ethnic heritage, I show conceptually the inexorable tangle of continuity and change, tradition and modernity, and past and future in social reality. I thus address the processes of intellectual construction in addition to individual and social agency in Jewish cultural practice. In part 2, "Ritualization," I continue this exploration of agency with considerations of so-called traditional or traditionalized rituals and customs associated with Jewish identity and the ways that they have been adapted, created, and imagined in modernity. Processes of materialization might appear most evident in these discussions of ritual and custom, but they also inform theoretical discussion of other expressive actions of affirming or denying identity, whether hanging a mezuzah or singing a song. Finally, in part 3, "Narration," I do not just document Jewish texts but again identify and interpret actions of *narrating* as a symbolically expressive and cognitively significant practice in oral, literary, and political culture. I consider the special association of Jews with self-deprecating humor, often evident in the constructed genres of the Jewish joke and the mystical belief legend (often about miracle-working rabbis and holy places) to theorize about abstracted ideas of *Yiddishkeit*, Holocaust memory, assimilation, and public culture that are enabled through what appears to be parabolic narration between and about tradition and modernity. My hope is that the approaches, hypotheses, and theories emanating from the various case studies in this book will advance Jewish cultural studies and foreground Jewish culture on the street, in the home, and in the synagogue as well as in the halls of academe and heritage organizations.

Before writing this volume, much of my effort toward expanding Jewish cultural studies was in editing the book series on Jewish cultural studies for the Littman Library of Jewish Civilization. I revised and updated my texts from those books to reflect my present thinking and to create continuities among the chapters. For example, the first chapter on defining Jewishness includes new material from my presentation "The Jewish Problem in American Studies," which was battle-tested at the Society of Americanists meeting at Central Penn College, Summerdale,

Pennsylvania, in March 2019 and at the Academic Engagement Network conference in June 2020. I thank Brant Ellsworth, John Kasson, Joy Kasson, Charles Kupfer, Spencer Kent, Jay Mechling, and Michael Barton for their comments before I went to press. I also expanded my remarks as chair of a session appropriately titled "New Perspectives on Jewish and Israeli Folklore" at the American Folklore Society meeting in October 2019 and appreciated the lively interchange there between the audience and fellow panelists Dan Ben-Amos, Amy Milligan, and Tsafi Sebba-Elran. The epilogue in this volume has not been previously published and was inspired in large measure by illuminating Shabbat discussions with Rabbi Levi Brook and Rebbetzin Fraidy Brook of Chabad of Waukesha-Brookfield, Wisconsin, and previously from gatherings at Beth-El Temple (Conservative) in Harrisburg, Pennsylvania, in addition to Sababa (formerly Hebrew High) of the Jewish Federation of Greater Harrisburg. I thank them, Professor Ellyn Lem of the University of Wisconsin-Milwaukee at Waukesha, and Congregation Emanu-El of Waukesha (Reform) for being so welcoming to my Jewishness in my transition from central Pennsylvania to southeast Wisconsin.

I am grateful to Littman's managing editor, Connie Webber, and her partner, Jonathan Webber, at the Institute of European Studies at Jagiellonian University for the creative dialogue over the years concerning the growth of the Jewish cultural studies field. My work on media, mediation, and Jewish community that appears in the present book benefited from editorial collaboration on the introduction with Caspar Battegay to the last volume of the series, *Connected Jews* (2018). I carry through the inquiry I started there on Jewish response to social media and Internet lore in the chapters of the present book on telling Jewish jokes online and religious response to the use of digital devices during services. Influencing my revision here is the coronavirus pandemic in 2020 and its severe test of the social basis of Jewish culture and the often taken-for-granted meanings of in-person customs and storytelling.

The rise of Jewish cultural studies was influenced by the memorable conference "Modern Jewish Culture: Diversities and Unities," held in Wrocław, Poland, in 2008 and generously funded by the Rothschild Foundation Hanadiv Europe. I offer special thanks to Marcin Wodziński and Agnieszka Jagodzińska for hosting the truly global summit that fueled the movement. Back in the United States, I was joined by Sander Gilman, Matti Bunzl, Galit Hasan-Rokem, and Barbara Kirshenblatt-Gimblett in San Diego in 2006 on the first panel at the Association for Jewish Studies meetings to address the challenge of Jewish cultural studies.

Right up to the present, these colleagues have continued to generate new ideas and engage in dialogue at various meetings. It was clear then, as it is now, that we have different opinions on the directions for exploring the frontiers of Jewish cultural studies, but our open exchange was crucial to the field's development.

Another influential conference that affected my thinking was "Going to the People: Jews and the Ethnographic Impulse," held at Indiana University in 2013, organized by Haya Bar-Itzhak, Dov-Ber Kerler, Anya Quilitszch, and Jeffrey Veidlinger, and sponsored by the Robert A. and Sandra S. Borns Jewish Studies Program and the Dr. Alice Field Cohn Chair in Yiddish Studies. The "From Function to Frame" essay (chapter 4) derived from that invigorating experience. The conference, global in its reach, allowed me to connect particularly with other folklorists and ethnologists about method and theory in an expanded vision of Jewish cultural studies.

Within folklore and ethnology studies, I am grateful to the *Children's Folklore Review* and its masterful editor, Elizabeth Tucker, for encouraging my rethinking the bar mitzvah as an American rite of passage. Camille Bacon-Smith receives my praise for steering my presentation on inventing and invoking tradition in Holocaust memorials for the innovative journal *New Directions in Folklore*. Literary maven Mary Ellen Brown at the *Journal of Folklore Research* was immensely helpful in my work on writer Leo Rosten and his folk type of Hyman Kaplan. Trevor J. Blank, as editor of *Folklore in the Digital Age: The Emergent Dynamics of Human Interaction*, made valuable suggestions for the inclusion of my essay on Jewish jokes online. My revision for this volume benefited from an edifying exchange with the audience at my presentation on Jewish joking to the Museum "Jews in Latvia" arranged in 2018 by the Latvian Academy of Culture, where I was a resident scholar with support from the Baltic-American Freedom Foundation. I thank Nathanael Riemer, editor of *Jewish Lifeworlds and Jewish Thought*, for shepherding my original essay on Jewish naming ceremonies for newborn girls. Glenda Abramson, editor of the *Journal of Modern Jewish Studies*, provided welcome guidance on the Lieberman syndrome, and Tsafi Sebba-Elran, an editor of *Massoret Haya: Living Tradition*, nurtured my work and provided additional materials on the Remu grave legend for the present volume.

At the risk of omitting figures who deserve acknowledgment for their continued support of my scholarship in addition to their friendship, I want to single out some inspirations who have led me to this point. It has been my honor to work with and learn from Dan Ben-Amos, editor of the Patai Series in Jewish Folklore and Anthropology for Wayne State University Press. He is indeed responsible for drawing me to the impressive series and its goals to widely broadcast cultural analysis of Jewish experience. He has always been generous in sharing wisdom and encouraging my scholarship, even when I held views that were different from his. I like his often-repeated metaphor of us as toiling colleagues working in an academic kibbutz cooperatively toward the same goal and learning from our disagreements, several of which I lay out in my essays. Wolfgang Mieder, whose friendship I have cherished and who is another of those valued scholarly heroes with immense global knowledge in multiple languages, provided feedback on my initial book proposal. I never had to worry about Elliott Oring bluntly giving his opinion on my work, and I have prized his willingness to do so and his collegiality over the years. Amy Milligan and Matthew Singer are former doctoral students in Jewish cultural studies, now thriving in their academic careers, whose research and *chokmah* contributed to this volume. At home, Sally Jo Bronner can be credited for being equally honest and for improving my writing, and outlook, in countless ways. A cherished Hebraist, she provided assistance on the intricacies of Jewish languages, but I absolve her from any blame for my errors.

I am grateful to the University of Wisconsin–Milwaukee (UWM) and especially Provost Johannes Britz for supporting my scholarship while I served as Dean of the College of General Studies. Also at UWM, I appreciated the opportunity to schmooze with Joel Berkowitz and Rachel N. Baum, director and deputy director, respectively, of the Sam and Helen Stahl Center for Jewish Studies. Max Yela, head of Special Collections in UWM's Golda Meir Library, shared his extensive knowledge on Latin American Jewry and guided me to the library's myriad Jewish book treasures. Coming to Milwaukee gave me the opportunity to reconnect with Gary Alan Fine, James E. Johnson Professor of Sociology at Northwestern University, who is a font of great ideas. I am especially grateful for his reflections on the sociological theory of Erving Goffman and the symbolic interactionist school. Gary kindly let me sit in on his Ethnography Workshop at Northwestern, and I benefited from the experience as I completed this book. At Penn State, I profited from time in the library's special collections and was fortunate to be director of the Center for Holocaust and Jewish Studies, which allowed me to bring many eminent speakers to campus to edify the community and engage in scholarly dialogue.

This book is dedicated to Haya Bar-Itzhak, an eminent folklorist, former chair of the Department of Hebrew and Comparative Literature, and director of the Israel Folktale Archives at the University of Haifa. I had the privilege of directly receiving her wisdom when she was a Fulbright Scholar at Penn State

Harrisburg, where I taught for many years. She also involved me in various projects from which I always learned, including the *Encyclopedia of Jewish Folklore and Traditions* and a heady conference in Israel on Jewish community at the turn of the new millennium that sowed many seeds for the branches of learning I have pursued to this day. I extend a heartfelt *sheynem dank* to her for all she has brilliantly done and continues to do for tillers of the Jewish cultural studies field.

CREDITS (ALL ESSAYS BY SIMON J. BRONNER)

(Introduction) "The Chutzpah of Jewish Cultural Studies" in *Jewishness: Expression, Identity, and Representation*, edited by Simon J. Bronner, pp. 1–26. Oxford, UK: Littman Library of Jewish Civilization, 2008. Used with permission of the rights holder Liverpool University Press.

(Chapter 1) "Framing Jewish Culture" in *Framing Jewish Culture: Boundaries and Representations*, edited by Simon J. Bronner, 1–32. Oxford, UK: Littman Library of Jewish Civilization, 2013. Used with permission of the rights holder Liverpool University Press.

(Chapter 2) "Dualities of House and Home in Jewish Culture" in *Jews at Home: The Domestication of Identity*, edited by Simon J. Bronner, 1–42. Oxford, UK: Littman Library of Jewish Civilization, 2010. Used with permission of the rights holder Liverpool University Press.

(Chapter 3) "Media, Mediation, and Jewish Community" in *Connected Jews: Expressions of Community in Analogue and Digital Culture*, edited by Simon J. Bronner and Caspar Battegay, 1–44. Oxford, UK: Littman Library of Jewish Civilization, 2018. Used with permission of the rights holder Liverpool University Press.

(Chapter 4) "From Function to Frame: The Evolving Conceptualization of Jewish Folklore Studies" in *Going to the People: Jews and the Ethnographic Impulse*, edited by Jeffrey Veidlinger, 303–32. Bloomington: Indiana University Press, 2016. Used by permission of the publisher Indiana University Press.

(Chapter 5) "Ritualizing Jewishness" in *Revisioning Ritual: Jewish Traditions in Transition*, edited by Simon J. Bronner, 1–42. Oxford, UK: Littman Library of Jewish Civilization, 2011. Used with permission of the rights holder Liverpool University Press.

(Chapter 6) "Fathers and Sons: Rethinking the Bar Mitzvah as an American Rite of Passage." *Children's Folklore Review* 31 (2008–2009): 7–34. Used with permission of the Children's Folklore Section of the American Folklore Society.

(Chapter 7) "Jewish Naming Ceremonies for Girls: A Study in the Discourse of Tradition and Modernity" in *Jewish Lifeworlds and Jewish Thought*, edited by Nathanael Riemer, 211–20. Wiesbaden, Germany: Harrassowitz Publishing House, 2012. Used by permission of the editor Nathanael Riemer and publisher Harrassowitz Publishing House.

(Chapter 8) "Inventing and Invoking Tradition in Holocaust Memorials." *New Directions in Folklore* 4, no. 2 (2000). www.temple.edu/isllc/newfolk/journal .html. Used by permission of the New Directions in Folklore Section of the American Folklore Society.

(Chapter 9) "Structural and Stylistic Relations of Oral and Literary Humor: An Analysis of Leo Rosten's H*Y*M*A*N K*A*P*L*A*N Stories." *Journal of the Folklore Institute* 19 (1976): 31–45. Used by permission of the publisher Indiana University Press.

(Chapter 10) "Telling Jokes: Connecting and Separating Jews in Analogue and Digital Culture" in *Connected Jews: Expressions of Community in Analogue and Digital Culture*, edited by Simon J. Bronner and Caspar Battegay, 181–214. London: Littman Library of Jewish Civilization in association with Liverpool University Press, 2018. Used with permission of the rights holder Liverpool University Press.

(Chapter 11) "Attempted Desecration of the Remu's Grave and Its Punishment: A Holocaust Belief Legend among Yiddish-Speaking Survivors" in *Masoret Haya: Living Tradition*, edited by Tsafi Sebba-Elran, Haya Milo, and Idit Pintel-Ginsberg, vi–xxii. Haifa: Israel Folktale Archives, University of Haifa, and Pardes Publishing House, 2020. Used by permission of the Israel Folktale Archives and the University of Haifa.

(Chapter 12) "The Lieberman Syndrome: Public and Private Jewishness in American Political Culture." *Journal of Modern Jewish Studies* 2 (2003): 35–58. Used by permission of the publisher Taylor & Francis Ltd.

INTRODUCTION

The Chutzpah of Jewish Cultural Studies

Jewish cultural studies centrally places culture in an investigation of the socially shared ideas and identities, bodily actions and perceptions, and textualized and materialized expressions that are labeled Jewish. Objectively, the subject might be broadly called studies of Jewish culture, except that scholars often present concepts swirling about the label of "Jewish" that are not lodged in the cultural practices of Jews. The additional position, which might be called subjective in the sense of pertaining to attitudes, perceptions, and biases, considers the meaning of Jewishness as an idea, or a way of thinking, in different cultures, even those devoid of Jews. It includes not only the prejudices or affections of non-Jews but also representations by Jews themselves, some of which may indeed be outside their awareness. Such representations are important in the analysis of the ways that Jews view and differentiate themselves from other Jews and the means by which they distinguish and align their cultural profiles in relation to non-Jewish others. If studies of Jewish culture consider what Jews do, then the overarching concept of Jewish cultural studies takes in what is thought by and about Jews—and the idea of feeling Jewish, that is, Jewishness, in words, images, and things. The connection between the objective and subjective views is the quest for the meaning of being Jewish or representing Jewishness. A way to fuse the standpoints into a conceptual whole is for scholars to refer to the cultural—those matters that are *related to and constitutive of* culture.

I propose with the designation of Jewish cultural studies that Jewishness—or what people think of as Jewish, which may be distinct from the Jew or the things made by Jews—is revealed in the expressions of culture: speech, story, literature, art, architecture, music, dance, ritual, film, theater, and so on. In contrast to rarefied studies of the arts and humanities, cultural studies is especially concerned with the kinds of expressions that draw attention for their symbolic or parabolic content at the grassroots and therefore reflect or comment on social reality more so than aesthetics. Cultural studies expands the scope of culturally related matters from artistic questions to their social relevance in politics, health, environment, and economics. An implication of using "cultural" as a keyword, therefore, is to declare that culture is to be not only studied for the sake of aesthetic appreciation, as it traditionally has been in arts and humanities scholarship, but also viewed as crucial to the conflicts and tensions faced by societies and the individuals who compose and construct them. The addition of "Jewish" to cultural studies represents at this juncture not so much a new discipline as a location for existing work. For readers, it should be a common ground, a broad, fertile field, where intellectual connections and new understandings are created. With the emphasis on cultural matters on this turf, comparisons are naturally made to the guideposts set up by the scholarly movement called cultural studies, traced to the late twentieth century.

Readers will find, however, that Jewish cultural studies, as I outline it, is being mapped largely outside the academic departmental walls of cultural studies. Studies of culture have various homes, which usually slice off a piece of a subject—whether literature, film, music, or art—for their specialization. The effort in conceiving of Jewish cultural studies as a prime location for investigation is to be able to see culture as a whole panorama as well as a specific focus. A challenge to this endeavor is a legacy that has treated the modifier *Jewish* narrowly as a religious label. For instance, is it surprising that a publishing icon such as the sixteen-volume *Encyclopaedia Judaica* (1972) lacks an entry on "culture"? The classic *Standard Jewish Encyclopedia* (C. Roth 1959) also leaves it out, and *The Book of Jewish Knowledge* (Ausubel 1964) deals with it by referring readers to entries on various disciplinary strands, including art, Bible, folklore, language, and music.

Indicating a growing awareness of Judaism as a kind of heritage or social identity as well as a religion, writers of reference works since the late twentieth century have drawn attention to culture but have nonetheless struggled with defining what constitutes culture and how its study is conceived. Glenda Abramson, in her introduction to *The Blackwell Companion to Jewish Culture*, opines that of three signifiers that structure her reference work—"modern," "Jewish," and "culture"— culture is the most difficult to grasp, but she leans toward thinking of culture in terms of its components, particularly artistic activity (Abramson 1989, xii). David Biale's *Cultures of the Jews*, despite its objectivist title, promotes a subjectivist cultural history of the Jews. Admitting that "culture is an elastic term," Biale introduces the concept of meaning into a modern definition, which I will expand with attention to a theory of mind: "manifold expressions—written or oral, visual or textual, material or spiritual—with which human beings represent their lived experiences in order to give them meaning" (Biale 2002, xvii). In Biale's definition, culture becomes evident, and significant, because it is externalized and therefore materialized through repeated stylized expressions. It appears behavioral and often verbal rather than extending to sources in thinking in response to the social and physical environment. Biale also underscores that culture as a representation of experience is distinct from the experience itself.

Scholars are attracted to culture, therefore, because it channels reality or offers fantasy as a discourse on life. The meaning it holds is not just its documentation of an occurrence but its commentary on it, often elaborated with emotion and ideation. The expressions of culture, typically recognized by their characteristics of being aestheticized or performed, are therefore *symbolic* representations of experience. They stand for something, which is often different from the thing that they name. In folk speech the heart may represent life, love, centrality, enthusiasm, or compassion, and the Jew, especially in various expressive combinations (such as "a good Jew," "dirty Jew," and "Jewish Jew"), has various connotations, both positive and negative, that call for contextualization—and inquiry into the psychology of thinking by and about Jews—to illuminate their meanings. Because culture is shared among people, it often works to bind groups together and to distinguish them from others. It gives insiders a sense of belonging and outsiders a reminder of difference.

KEYWORDS OF EXPRESSION, IDENTITY, AND REPRESENTATION

At the heart of Jewish cultural studies is social psychological attention to the nature of expression, identity, and representation of communicative practices that are perceived or enacted to be Jewish and their rhetorical and ethnological analysis. *Expression* refers to observable and collectible items—words, images, and things—that people offer to others to communicate something about themselves. The importance of these items lies not only in their content but also in how they embed and materialize the beliefs and values of the giver. Accompanied by gesture and textured with style, words thus reflect the cultures in which people operate. Images are the way that people picture themselves and others, whether in a signature or a movie. People are surrounded by images in advertisements, photographs, and logos that they "read" for their message, see for their beauty, and critique for their representation (or stereotype). Things express the needs and feelings of their makers and users and can be viewed as props in social practices and ritual displays. In a variety of hands and across various landscapes, things enact culture for people to behold and interpret (Bronner 1986b, 2013; B. Brown 2004).

Identity shifts attention to the social and psychological functions of cultural behaviors that provide a sense of self or community. For Jews, with their prominent history of diasporization and victimization, a great diversity of identities have been acquired and discarded as they adapted to new times and places. Whereas studies written from a historical perspective frequently cover national traditions, from a cultural studies perspective attention is especially given to the situations of localized everyday life in which identity is negotiated and divided between public and private personas. Indeed, in response to the emphasis on broad religiosity in Judaica studies, Jewish cultural studies often deals with particularized cultural identity apart from religious affiliation. As a matter of identity, being Jewish does not necessarily mean professing religious faith but is revealed in what people do and how they think of themselves (or how others define them), whether in the street or in the synagogue. Practitioners of Jewish cultural studies ask how people calling themselves Jews, and even those who do not, convey Jewishness and how the larger non-Jewish worlds they inhabit perceive, symbolize, ritualize, materialize, and narrate their belonging.

Representation in Jewish cultural studies refers to symbolic communicative systems that mediate culture—in oral narrative, literature, and popular entertainment—often outside the awareness of participants (Bar-Tal and Teichman 2005, 177–207; Bronner and Battegay 2018, 13–22; Cheyette 1996; Schechter 2003). To actualize this concept, I analyze texts of a culture that are symbolically encoded by their creators and then variously decoded, or read for meaning, by audiences and communities. I uncover the significance of culture as an arena for meaning-making in the struggles among groups for the power to dictate the readings and images that a society favors. I also ask about the social and cultural structures that contain and constrict such readings and the traditions that allow for the forms they take or the texts they inhabit. From a psychological viewpoint, the texts of a given culture are locations in which to air and contest often troubling dialogues that are difficult to broach in everyday conversation and formal institutional outlets. The definition of culture that is used refers to an expressive or projective quality that draws attention to itself and is associative in identifying a people who relate to it.

Sensitive to the way in which meanings are conveyed through language and its social contexts, I should explain that the concern in Jewish cultural studies for the ordinary has multiple layers. It can shed light on the customs and traditions shared by people in their day-to-day existence to relate to the idea that culture is defined by expectations, often so ordinary that they do not need to be stated, of what is commonly done. Of great analytical benefit, the ordinary often signals what people believe, what they take for granted, and what they do un-self-consciously. Where actions are self-conscious, when culture is organized, or when communities are mobilized, ideas in discourse can be identified and analyzed. Indeed, cultural studies often looks at *extra*-ordinary instances, when cultural practices are problematized, contested, or complicated, to discern the forces that maintain or dissolve social conditions and to shed light on the intellectual construction of the ordinary.

Such conditions are especially important to signify in Jewish cultural studies because Jews are a diasporic people with a long history and a legacy of power struggles in the face of persecution who nonetheless maintain the practices that exemplify their Jewish identity in a variety of cultural contexts. Jews are also an exemplary case of an "ordinarized" group, in the sense that a precursor of cultural studies, Raymond Williams (1983, 71–72), described: a category essentialized by elites as *vulgus in populo*, or "common folk," meaning the unprogressive or incorrigible element of society. "Ordinary" indicates for intellectual consideration the way in which people and their beliefs constitute, in Williams's terms, "a generalized body of Others" (225–26). As a mode of inquiry that digs down for the various relative values held by different segments of society, cultural studies also seeks to discover the ways that "ordinary" can mean mainstream, popular, or normative. "Ordinary" can signify "us" rather than "them," or what one considers "sensible," "right," and even "decent."

In sum, Jewish cultural studies decodes meaning about Jewishness that is created and received by different groups in various situations. Representations of Jewishness emerge—or are suppressed—in such scenes and become cultural by virtue of the symbolic communication and action within them. Jews have a special position from which to comment on culture in such an analysis, because in their diasporic experience they have typically been part of, yet apart from, a dominant society. Thus they have occupied a liminal space in which they comment as both observers of and participants in the larger society while also being concerned for the maintenance and representation of their cultural differences. Because this space is viewed as unbounded, that Jewish commentary has often been viewed as incisive, bold, and even radical, pointing out implications that the participants are unaware of or unwilling to admit. Jewish cultural studies is hardly content to be descriptive, as is often implied by the rhetoric of "studies of Jewish culture" or even "cultural history." In staking out a location for explanation outside the awareness of participants, Jewish cultural studies has an edgy quality. Invoking a Jewish cultural expression, it has *chutzpah*.

THINKING WITH CHUTZPAH

What does the iconic Jewish word *chutzpah* mean? When used in speech—whether in English, Hebrew, or Yiddish—it draws attention to itself, as expression, identity, and representation. *Chutzpah* can make Jews cringe or crow, and many scholars have a similar reaction when they hear the phrase "cultural studies," because it carries the connotation of challenging assumptions and disrupting canons. Throw in "Jewish" and one might just recoil, as awareness of the tradition of critical inquiry into Jewish hermeneutics doubles the bite. On reflection, that observation could cause worry that analysts are slipping into stereotype, essentializing Jews as obtrusive. Yet American legal scholar Alan Dershowitz, for many readers the most public Jew they know, hardly shies away from chutzpah. In fact, he had the chutzpah to title one of his books *Chutzpah*, with the comment, "Notwithstanding the stereotype, we are not pushy or assertive enough for our own good and for the good of our more vulnerable brothers and sisters in other parts of the world" (Dershowitz 1991, 3). Calling for a post-Holocaust break with the old worldview that Jews were guests in host countries, Dershowitz brought out the irony that non-Jews associated Jews with chutzpah even though Jews themselves decried it. It is in that acquiescence, he brazenly asserts, that Jews find a reason for the diminishment of their cultural identity and visibility (Dershowitz 1997).

But wait. What about the supposedly Jewish trait of self-deprecation? Even an advertisement for the entertainment icon Jackie Mason—who is characterized as full of chutzpah and with a voice that he boasts sounds genuinely Jewish (with a slap at Jewish celebrities worried about being cast as "too Jewish")—hooks buyers with the pitch that he "blends self-deprecating humility with abrasive chutzpah to acutely dissect the differences between American Jewish and Gentile culture" (CD Baby 1991). Playing out in real life the fabulistic story line of the American-born son of immigrant parents who forsakes following the rabbinic line to go on the popular stage and make it in the modern age, Mason nevertheless adopted the role of the rabbi on the long-running television series *The Simpsons*, but in his Broadway shows he still reminds audiences that when he opens his mouth, they will know he is ethnically different. From that position, he trenchantly comments on the foibles of the goyim, literally "non-Jews" but also a metaphor for the dominant society, as well as on the peculiarities of "our people." Mason has penned a book instructing Jews "how to talk Jewish"—not necessarily because they have forgotten the language but because they have lost its flavor. Yiddish words used to be more "expressive," he says. As a man of words, Mason draws attention to the idea that the way Jews sound and are understood is central to their cultural identity.

Chutzpah naturally occupies a central role in Mason's book. He describes himself as someone who is "brazen, brash, and has the gall to tell you off even when you did nothing to him," but he makes that sound like a good thing (Mason 1990, 34). After all, against the background of repression and discrimination, the humor of chutzpah can be rendered as a projection, maybe a fantasy, of a survival strategy, a way to triumph over adversaries. Mason's explanatory narrative could even be read as a projective inversion in which the victim becomes the victimizer: "A guy with chutzpah takes out a gun and shoots you in the heart and then blames you for being in the wrong place at the wrong time." For it is Jews who are often told they are in the wrong place and time, wandering, as the Christian legend relates, looking for somewhere to rest and call home (see Dundes and Hasan-Rokem 1986). Mason realizes the significance of his expressions for the identities and representations they suggest. In fact, he inaugurated the Jackie Mason Lectureship in Contemporary Judaism at Oxford University in 1990, where he told the august gathering with self-deprecating humor, "If the lecturers all start talking like me, the English language will be wiped out" (Anderson 1990).

Yiddish writer and Nobel laureate Isaac Bashevis Singer, talking through his character Joseph Shapiro in *The Penitent*, was more philosophical than Mason about chutzpah. The story originally appeared in Yiddish in a daily newspaper read primarily by Jews with an Eastern European background, but when it came time to produce an English version, the translator (his nephew Joseph Singer) left the Yiddish term *chutzpah* in. Sure, it is often explained by the nouns "gall," "impudence," or "insolence," but it is usually considered untranslatable because it supposedly embodies an imponderable Jewish spirit. *The Penitent* illustrates chutzpah through a humorous story. Shapiro mulls over the idea of divorcing his wife, which leads him to muse, "It's a principle among today's men that the unjust are always in the right. Chutzpah is the very essence of modern man, and of the modern Jew as well. He has learned so assiduously from the Gentile that he now surpasses him" (I. B. Singer 1983, 129). Does Singer, speaking through Shapiro's character, mean, then, that chutzpah as a kind of arrogance is wrong, or that the unjust have been wronged? In a twist on the usual attribution, he seems to credit the dominant non-Jewish society of passing chutzpah on to modern Jews. "Modern" here appears to mean secular or assimilated, judging by the way Singer contrasts it to traditional Orthodox Jews (in the English edition *hasidim* is translated as "the pious Jews") who maintain an obvious material separation from "modern" Jews and non-Jews alike by adopting distinctive customs and dress: "The truth is that the element of chutzpah was present even among the pious Jews. They have always been a stiff-necked and rebellious people. Well, there is a kind of chutzpah that is necessary, but I won't go into that now" (129–30). Singer's implication is that Jews embody chutzpah in their everyday folklife rather than in their occasional speech or behavior. As the translator explains in a note appended to the story, Singer has a personal sympathy for chutzpah as the rhetoric of secular protest: "To me, a belief in God and a protest against the laws of life are not contradictory." With a dash of chutzpah, he elaborates, "If I were able to picket the Almighty, I would carry a sign with the slogan UNFAIR TO LIFE!" (169).

The Yiddish word *chutzpah* enjoyed a wide enough circulation in modern English to warrant an entry in the *Oxford English Dictionary* (OED), which defines it in negative tones as "brazen impudence." The earliest example to supply the OED's definition is British Jewish writer Israel Zangwill's use of the word in an essentialist characterization of Jews in *Children of the Ghetto* (first published in 1892), subtitled *A Study of a Peculiar People*. Like Mason's narrative, Zangwill's can be read as expressing a survival strategy. Zangwill's story depicts the condescension of a Jew named Levi toward his younger brother Solomon: "But it took a great deal to overawe Solomon, who, with the national humor, possessed the national *Chutzpah*, which is variously translated enterprise, audacity, brazen impudence and cheek" (Zangwill 1938, 77). The nation, or society, to which

Zangwill refers is Jewish, separated physically and culturally in a ghetto from the dominant English society. The spirit represented by chutzpah could be positively rendered to suggest the promise of integration into that society (symbolized as a melting pot in his 1908 stage play). But Zangwill looked down with disdain on the expression itself, probably because he had internalized the elitist opprobrium expressed toward a backward, "oriental" civilization by members of Western industrial society (see Zangwill 1938, v, ix; see also Kalmar and Penslar 2005). He associated these "despised words" with "superstitions grotesque as the cathedral gargoyles of the Dark Ages in which they had birth" (Zangwill 1938, v, ix). The words, including *chutzpah*, remained intact in the many translations of *Children of the Ghetto*, which circulated worldwide in languages including Dutch (1896), Hebrew (1901), German (1913), and French (1921).

Disavowing Yiddish as a legitimate language for the redemption of the Jewish nation, Zangwill, in an elitist and cultural Zionist polemic, reminds readers that "most of these despised words are pure Hebrew; a language which never died off the lips of men, and which is the medium in which books are written all the world over even unto this day" (Zangwill 1938, v). In other words, Hebrew for Zangwill is the pure literary language of art and "the rose of romance" from the Land of Israel; Yiddish expresses "the folk who . . . are children of the Ghetto," persecuted in and corrupted by European culture (ix). Even when linguists point out that *chutzpah* (rendered as *khutspe* in Uriel Weinreich's [1968] modern Yiddish orthography) in fact derives from Hebrew of late antiquity (*chutspah*), the popular perception remains that *chutzpah* is a Yiddishism and a way to express *Yiddishkeit* (a Jewish cultural sensibility generally but relating especially to Eastern European Jewish heritage) (Steinmetz 1986, 60–61). In believing in the untranslatability and abstruseness of *chutzpah*, English speakers of the word imply that the culture that it represents is distinctive, although many English dictionaries do indeed translate it. In contrast to its meaning in Hebrew or Yiddish, *chutzpah* in English often has a positive value of self-confidence or initiative, unless modified by "real," "unbelievable," or "the height of," in which case it negatively connotes effrontery (61). For instance, Norman G. Finkelstein blared *Beyond Chutzpah* in the title of his book critiquing Alan Dershowitz's assertions, thereby conveying the idea that Dershowitz's stance is unbelievable and idiosyncratic (Finkelstein 2005).

In English, use of *chutzpah* is not restricted to Jews, although its application by non-Jews can draw notice. When Italian Catholic Antonin Scalia, a justice of the United States Supreme Court, chastised the plaintiff in a decision (*National*

Endowment for the Arts v. Finley, 1998) for a "high degree of chutzpah," it drew commentaries from legal observers and Internet bloggers alike. Even before Scalia's reportedly groundbreaking use of the term in the Supreme Court, Alex Kozinski and Eugene Volokh (1993), writing in the *Yale Law Journal*, found that *chutzpah* had appeared in judges' decisions in a whopping 112 cases, mostly since 1980. They attributed its usage to the perception that Yiddish expressively underscores a point as no other language can, and *chutzpah* in particular needs no definition. In their words, Yiddish terms add spice to dry "American legal argot" (463), but there is also the implication that Yiddish is safe to draw on because it has become a classical language—much like Latin, which it has supplanted for legal flair. Yiddish, more than Latin, though, provides a folksy spin appropriate to a democratic society and implies a perception that Jews as an othered group are more expressive or demonstrative than the non-Jewish host society. Use of *chutzpah* may be appealing in legal decisions because of its connotation of shamelessly or intentionally defying norms, with an echo of the Jewish tradition of the legalistic interpretation of religious texts. Is the mainstreaming of *chutzpah* a sign or construction of the loss of ethnic difference, since, as Jackie Mason observed, few people, at least in popular culture, "talk Jewish"? And is chutzpah also significant in revealing how non-Jews "see Jewish," even when they are not aware that they are doing it?

Given that the word *chutzpah* has entered common parlance, I have frequently heard Jews scornfully mock its mispronunciation by non-Jews as a signal that their ethnicity cannot be appropriated, indeed displaced, along with the word. Jews in conversation with one another observe that non-Jews reveal themselves by the inability to utter the *ch* sound, found also in *challah* and *Chanukah*, or they share stories associated with chutzpah as a kind of esoteric folklore, usually showing that use of the word is highly contextualized. The subtext is that Jewishness is a birthright with local knowledge and a cultural continuity that cannot be mimicked.

More than giving definitions or pronunciations, Jews are wont to tell stories of chutzpah. They may sound humorous, but in that play frame they allow for serious considerations of the limits of intrusion, perhaps by placing the culprit in the role of trickster Jew, and questions of "outing" Jewish identity when Jews are not distinguished by dress and physical differences. Probably the most frequently cited narrative, again giving the word a legal context, describes the man who murders his mother and father and then asks the judge to forgive a poor orphan (Rosten 1982, 85). Renowned Jewish writer Leo Rosten liked to tell the story of the

Jewish businessman who is distraught because a huge crate of black brassieres has been returned. His partner tells him to relax: "What we can do is cut off the straps and sell them for *yarmulkes*" (85; see also chapter 9).

If Rosten's joke has a decided ethnic sensibility (or entrepreneurial stereotype) in it, the following story I have heard widely offers chutzpah as the strategy of the underdog or trickster.

> A little old lady gets on a crowded bus, then clutches her chest and says to the young girl seated in front of her, "If you knew what I have, you would give me your seat." The girl gets up and gives up her seat, then takes her magazine and starts fanning herself. The woman looks up and says, "If you knew what I have, you would give me that so I could cool off." The girl gives her the magazine. Several minutes go by, then the woman gets up and says to the bus driver, "I want to get off right here." The bus driver says she has to wait until he gets to the next stop, a block away. She clutches her chest again and tells him, "If you knew what I have, you'd let me off right now." The bus driver pulls over, opens the door, and tells her she can get off the bus. As she steps down he says, "Ma'am, I hope you don't mind my asking, but what is it you have?" And the woman says, "Chutzpah!"

Various analytical comments can be made on the text, such as the symbolic equivalence of *chutzpah* with "old" and "feminine," doubling the character's unlikelihood of holding power. The first person confronted is a girl, which in the narrative structure seems to be an easy mark. The more difficult challenge is the patriarchal bus driver, obviously in charge with his task of controlling the wheel. The literal vehicle for the story is the bus, indicating mobility, a microcosm of urban society, suggesting a competition among constituent social groups. What is first viewed as pathology turns out to be puckish impudence, thus raising the question that someone posing Jewish cultural studies queries, such as Sander Gilman, might call the materialization of the Jew in the body as a device of othering (Gilman 1991). In this story, unlike others invoking dialectal use of chutzpah, the term is a metaphor to live by. Instead of *talking* Jewish, the old woman is shown to be *acting* Jewish, with the conclusion that she *feels* Jewish (without ever stating that she is) as a strategy to triumph over those who view her negatively or render her invisible. Chutzpah is her way of drawing attention to herself. Further, the ending of the story raises a crucial question for Jewish cultural studies of whether one can read Jewish, or for that matter think in and with the idea of Jewish (Bial 2005; J. Boyarin 1996; Gilman 1996; for the concept of "good to think [with]" as symbolic material suggesting ideation outside the awareness of cultural participants, see the original context in Lévi-Strauss [1963, 89] and adaptations in Culler [2013], Garber [2012, 94–103], and Leach [1989]).

Rendered positively or not, *chutzpah* in the twenty-first century or the digital age has been used in popular culture to convey an unshakable Jewish spunk in the absence of material difference. Underscoring the point, the comedy musical group Chutzpah made a splash in the media by broaching the muting of Jewish intrusiveness, materially and musically, by making a comparison with African American ghetto youth, who receive ample mass-cultural notice or stereotyping. The three members of Chutzpah donned the garb associated with hip-hop rappers and belted out songs with such titles as "Dr. Dreck" ("feces," a play on the name of popular African American rapper Dr. Dre), "Chanukah's Da Bomb" (Black argot for something being the best or cool), and "Shiksa Goddess" (a phrase for a conspicuously non-Jewish woman as an object of desire for Jewish men). They also produced a film (later available on DVD) called *Chutzpah, This Is?* (2005), a parody of the 1927 film *The Jazz Singer* but with the main character being Master Tav, a cantorial student turned edgy rapper. Across the Pacific, *Chutzpah* (2000) is the title of an Australian animated short, again encapsulating Jewish identity, that challenges norms by featuring two aging lesbians. Sometimes chutzpah does not have to be encoded by producers into a title to represent Jewishness. For example, in case theatergoers did not recognize Wendy Wasserstein's Broadway play *The Sisters Rosensweig* as thematically Jewish, columnist Bill Marx titled his review "Queens of Chutzpah" (Marx 2005), and the *New York Times* unapologetically characterized Jewish comedian Alan King, upon his death in 2004, as a "Comic with Chutzpah" (B. Weber 2004).

PUTTING THE JEWISH IN CULTURAL STUDIES

So what does all this have to do with Jewish cultural studies? My intention in discussing chutzpah has been to pose questions of representation and identity that arise from symbolic cultural communication. To be sure, other cultural expressions in words, images, and things can illustrate the layers of meaning and psychological sources that become apparent as people invoke tradition and evoke cultural responses in various social contexts. I am drawn to the rich narrative and to the linguistic aspects of a word with meanings constructed in diverse contexts. A yet wider link is to an inspiration for cultural studies in the work of Raymond Williams, outlining what he calls "keywords," which are "binding words in certain activities and their interpretation; they are significant, indicative words in certain forms of thought" (Williams 1983, 15; see also Bennett et al. 2005; J. Boyarin and Boyarin 1997, vii–viii; Feintuch 2003). That is, everyday terms reveal ideas that are socially constructed and often contested. People vie to dictate how they are represented in relation to the other and especially in the conceptual terms that are considered essential to human existence: culture, society, tradition. On a behavioral level, key or loaded words signify the experience that people describe through a shared vocabulary: They categorize the environment, create divisions, and characterize experience, thus setting up a nexus of expectations that people think of as culture (Garber 2012). On another level of thought revealed by discourse, keywords refer to themselves as part of a rhetoric of persuasion and presentation. The words thus invite efforts, often socially and politically driven, to give them value and to guide the way that people think of themselves and others.

Since Williams sparked this inquiry into keywords in the 1970s, the vocabulary of culture has expanded to include many forms of expression that are considered critical for directing perception. Buildings, paintings, advertisements, films, jokes, and rituals are all symbolic representations meant to communicate ideas as much as they are modes of habitation or entertainment (Bartov 2005; H. E. Goldberg 2003; Hoberman and Shandler 2003; Kleeblatt 1996; Sachs and van Voolen 2004; J. E. Young 2000; Zurawik 2003). To be sure, recognizing the symbolic importance of cultural expression is not new. The social science of culture and tradition has been most notably pursued professionally for more than a century by folklorists, sociologists, psychologists, and anthropologists, before *cultural* became a term for a mode of inquiry (Bronner 1998, 141–83). Practitioners who use these labels continue to identify and interpret the workings of culture with attention to social forces, practices, and contexts. Often devoted to the gathering of empirical evidence in culture, these disciplinarians distinctively invoke cultural studies to explore the idea of culture as it is conceptualized in "ordinary" life and scholarship. Cultural studies is also an academic space to which analysts can bring popular-cultural evidence and objects closer to home (especially in modern complex societies), because traditional social science disciplines often call on scholars to detach themselves from their subject or choose topics that are unusual, even exotic.

Not to be ignored, the humanities have made an important contribution to the knowledge of culture with the identification of artistic modes, forms, and styles of expression, usually by exceptional individuals. Humanists often approach expression as a portal through which to capture emotion and reveal spirit—indeed, to comment on, if not elevate, the human condition. If it is not empirical or explanatory in the tradition of the social sciences, the humanistic mode of inquiry has been interpretative, offering meanings of the impressions made by artists and creators. But cultural studies advocates complain that the humanistic tradition has been prone to exalting uncommon, even unrepresentative, individuals in a culture for their genius rather than choosing persons valued for their relation to ordinary societies or communities and common practices. The humanistic search for sui generis creation rather than the process of creativity in everyday life means that emphasis is placed on production over consumption, writers over readers, performers over audiences, texts over processes. Another critique of classical humanities is the equating of culture with high art rather than viewing the ordinary and traditional as a site for creative or artistic communication.

In response to such issues of purview, cultural studies proposes to democratize, decolonialize, and diversify the arts that are part of culture. In this view, culture takes in, as the editors of the weighty tome *Cultural Studies* state, "the entire range of a society's arts, beliefs, institutions, and communicative practices" (Nelson et al. 1992, 4). Culture is often presented as a perspective that approaches material from a critical angle rather than as a disciplinary alternative within the humanities or social sciences. This modus operandi could be characterized as working from the inside out, as opposed to the conventional direction of coming from the outside and looking in, in the sense that the depth of experience of participants in a culture is valued (particularly in multiple, often overlapping, subcultures). Meanings are sought that are generated by different, sometimes discordant, voices as events unfold in human lives. Processes that set the multivocal tone, such as the formation of identity, the construction of collective memory, the fabrication of tradition, and the signification of imagery, attract comment (Du Gay et al. 2000; Hall 1997; Hall and Du Gay 1996). Power structures in which social hierarchies and cognitive categories operate are important to discern. Thus cultural studies can also entail asking a series of reflexive questions not posed from the detached position of the observer or the centralized vantage point of the elite. It intentionally charts the margins of a culture to find how the center is maintained. To bring out the relativism and fiction of culture, it asks what is *there*, to know what is *here*; it discerns rather than dismisses fantasies to better comprehend realities. Cultural studies typically identifies the multiple dimensions of culture and the different attitudes and motivations of its participants instead of reducing each culture to a single trait. Reflexively, it probes the idea of culture: how it is used, who shapes it, and why it means something.

In defiance of setting boundaries on their subject, many cultural studies proponents prefer to set out characteristics of inquiry. That perspective allows them to be more flexible in approach and responsive to the types of problems studied. For example, the editors of *Cultural Studies* refer to cultural studies theory as "sufficiently abstract and general that it can be moved [applied] to new contexts whenever it is helpful. It provides a way of describing the continual severing, realignment, and recombination of discourses, social groups, political interests, and structures of power in a society. It provides as well a way of describing the discursive processes by which objects and identities are formed or given meaning" (Nelson et al. 1992, 8). All told, there is a characteristic interpretative strategy in cultural studies of reading and observing expressions that reveal the various stakes of and identities in a culture (Shank 2001).

So why carve out a space for Jewish cultural studies when interdisciplinarity has already become commonplace in academic discourse? In announcing a "new Jewish cultural studies" in the late 1990s, Jonathan and Daniel Boyarin answered forcefully that, for starters, non-Jewish academics have consistently devalued Jewish cultural difference since World War II (J. Boyarin and Boyarin 1997). They stated a need for Jewish cultural studies to sight Jews on the academic radar and make possible a comparative ethnic perspective on culture. Other critics have also noted that the Jewish voice has been driven from or left out of the multicultural chorus, with the comment that since World War II many liberal academics have considered Jews inadequately racialized, problematized, colonized, or victimized to rate being featured on the public stage, with ethnicities such as Africans, Latinxs, Arabs, and Asians being viewed as more in need of advocacy (Biale et al. 1998b; Brodkin 1999; Gilman 2006; E. L. Goldstein 2006). Typically omitted from the curricular roster of programs for cultural studies and ethnic studies, Jewish studies typically stands on the margins of academic offerings or research into culture in departments for folklore, anthropology, psychology, and sociology, although Jewish studies could benefit the larger programs immensely if it was integrated (Morahg 1991).

One indication of what could appear to be ethnic erasure is that the hefty flagship readers for the field, *Cultural Studies* (Grossberg et al. 1992, tipping the scales at 788 pages) and *The Cultural Studies Reader* (During 1999; 624 pages), make no mention of Jews. This omission is remarkable, considering the importance of Jews in the extensive historiography of race, ethnicity, class, othering, and subculture (see Hart 2011; Patai and Patai 1989). The Boyarins caustically comment that the deafness of cultural studies to Jewish voices has resulted from the politics of Jewish identity in the academy. Because the bulk of Jewish studies majors are primarily Jews, the Boyarins argue, "Few outside of the Jewish community have imagined that anything they said was worth listening to" (D. Boyarin and Boyarin 1997, ix). The cultural terms by which many Jewish scholars have presented the variety of Jewish societies and traditions—readings of ancient texts and languages, philological methods of interpretation, and cross-cultural comparisons over a diasporic history thousands of years in the making—are alien to the conventional presentist, nationalist mode of cultural studies inquiry. Sander Gilman adds to the critique of cultural studies for alienating Jews and the Jewish subject by noting that, although cultural studies tends to situate its cultures in rooted settlements, the Jewish articulation of cultural meaning is often couched in terms of frontiers and movements as a result of the consciousness of dispersion and exile (Gilman 1999, 2003).

I would go further in stating that cultural studies, influenced by ideas of post-colonialism and orientalism, has often tended to frame Jewish groups as connected with imperial powers rather than as colonized or ghettoized subcultures affected by experiences of expulsion and Holocaust (Hirsh 2018; Said 1994). In the usually presentist mode of cultural studies, Jews are typically essentialized and stigmatized (e.g., as Zionist exclusionists) or stereotypically cast as assimilated suburbanites fusing with the power elite and white privilege. On the rare occasions that Jews are considered, the roots of Jews in the Middle East, the expulsion of Sephardim from Spain in 1492 and their subsequent Mediterranean presence, and the derogatory orientalist images of Jews in Europe in discussions of the cultures of imperialism are largely ignored or roundly dismissed in favor of a conspiratorial association with the power elite (see Mills 2000, 16; Wisse 2007).

Writing in *Orientalism and the Jews*, Ivan Davidson Kalmar and Derek J. Penslar find that a crucial turn in the perception of Jews occurred with the Balfour Declaration (1917), which committed the British Empire to the establishment of a Jewish homeland in Palestine. They comment that, as a result,

> the Jewish people became embroiled in imperialist intrigue, and the Zionist movement became from both the Western and the Arab point of view

an instrument of European imperialism. Such was the beginning of the end of the story of the Ashkenazic Jews as a target of orientalism, and was no doubt what [Edward] Said had in mind when he suggested that the Jews, unlike the Arabs, were able to escape the stigma associated with the label "Semite." (Kalmar and Penslar 2005, xxxv)

Other factors besides this historical moment can be cited, including the assimilationist view that Jews have lost their difference, physically and spiritually, or that Judaism has been reduced to an occasional religious faith rather than a deep cultural difference. One can also hear references in twenty-first-century academic conferences to the idea that Jews have become implicated, by their economic and intellectual success, in capitalist as well as imperialist intrigue, raising anti-Semitic images of the "rich fat Jew" (Gilman 1991). Arguably, then, Jews have not escaped a new form of anti-Semitism resulting from Western academic antagonism toward Israel or resentment of ascribed Jewish economic success, despite the fact that the concentration of poverty among older and urban Jews (e.g., 32 percent of Jews in New York City reportedly live in poverty), especially with close to half of all Haredim falling below the poverty line, remains a serious problem (Chesler 2005; Hirsh 2018; Hornstein 2019; K. I. Marcus 2015; Wisse 1992, 2007).

A PARABLE OF JEWISH EXPULSION

I faced this prejudice head on in my active participation as a teacher, writer, and researcher in ethnic studies covering various groups and in my work to integrate Jewish studies into American studies. I thought that through the late twentieth century Americanists welcomed Jewish studies as part of ethnic studies to represent the cultural diversity of the United States. In the eye-opening essay "Paradigm Dramas Revisited: A Brief History of American Studies as Reflected in *American Quarterly*," for the first issue of *SOAR*, the journal of the Society of Americanists, Jeffrey Meikle, the senior member of the Department of American Studies at the University of Texas, observed that by the early twenty-first century, "American Studies was becoming ethnic studies" (Meikle 2018, 31). Toward the goal of inclusion, all ethnic groups were being counted as part of the American mosaic, but Meikle noticed that American studies had taken a particular vision of which ethnic groups, defined as "subaltern" minorities, could took center stage to represent the culture of the United States. Meikle worried that this move amounted not only to a redefinition of the discipline but also to an assault on senior scholars, even if they had worked in ethnic studies: "The implication [was that] . . . ASA [American Studies Association] members whose scholarship did not reflect this ethnic, transnational turn [needed] to get with the program or get out" (26). Meikle referred specifically to Americanist David Nye, who asserted that anyone who did not focus on ethnic and racial minorities was being read out of the profession and, in the process, was indicted for discrimination or, even worse, racism in thematic, interdisciplinary work, even if that was not the case.

The question is left about the ASA's definition of ethnic studies and the groups that supposedly matter most in this intellectual turn and reframing of U.S. culture and society. Meikle found in a survey of the ASA's journal *American Quarterly* that articles on African Americans led the way, with 19 percent of all published essays in the journal; articles on Native Americans, Pacific Islanders, and Latinxs each represented 10 percent, and articles on Asian Americans came in at 6 percent. One might surmise that, rather than pursuing ethnic studies, the ASA's focus was on racialized ethnic groups, or "people of color," usually coded as "critical," "radical," or "intersectional" race studies. Yet groups such as Jews, Italians, and the Irish had been the subject of racial categorization and were notably absent in Meikle's results. He did not count any articles focusing on European Americans or, for that matter, religious groups, although they make up a large proportion of the United States population. Meikle found no participation by American Jews except for condemnatory remarks on their support of Israel (and in 2013 the ASA passed a resolution that was criticized as having anti-Semitic intent because of the society's endorsement of a boycott of Israeli academic institutions; see Bérubé 2015; Brahm and Romirowsky 2015; Musher 2015; Nelson 2019).

Checking Meikle's statistics, I used the JSTOR database to locate articles with "Jewish" in their title in twenty-year intervals since the founding of the *American Quarterly* in 1949. In the first period to 1969, only one article shows up (a literary critique of Jacob Gordin's *The Jewish King Lear*); two articles appeared from 1970 to 1990 (one on the Americanization of Tevye in *Fiddler on the Roof* and the other a historical look at Jewish American women through the 1930s); and only one article was published between 1991 and 2011 (a paper on the historical ties of Jewish secularism to liberalism). Yet Jewish studies had obviously grown nationally in American studies journals, judging from JSTOR's American studies category. In the first period, 62 articles appeared with "Jewish" in their title; the figure rose more than fivefold between 1970 and 1990 and almost doubled in the last period to 642. And much of that increase was due to work in Jewish folk and popular culture. So should Jewish cultural studies go its own way or join other interdisciplinary organizations?

The trigger for my questioning of the erasure of Jews from the American picture as intentional or as a by-product of the critical racial or intersectional turn was a pivotal incident in the historiography of American studies and where the field went in the twenty-first century. In 2001 the ASA was about to meet in Washington, D.C., on the theme of multiple publics and civic voices. Recognizing the neglect of the Jewish subject in American studies, including no presentations on Jewish studies for several years, ASA president Michael Frisch, with whom I worked on a previous program committee, encouraged me to organize a panel to raise a dialogue concerning American Jews in the ethnic landscape. Both of us recounted that in our graduate work Jews and African Americans were often presented through early American studies scholarship as the classic othered groups in America. Their situation through basic texts by Oscar Handlin, Irving Howe, and Salo Baron were springboards to discussion of American ethnic experience and the story of various social movements. So together with American Jewish studies luminaries Linda J. Borish, Hasia R. Diner, and Deborah Dash Moore, I proposed a panel titled "Multiple Publics, Varied Contexts: The Public and Private Jew in American Culture," and I asked Ted Merwin, a young faculty member in the Department of Judaic Studies at Dickinson College, to chair it, to underscore the presence of young new Americanists to the subject. The first two papers, on the rise of Jewish food and Jews in sports in the twentieth century, were historical, whereas mine, on the Joseph Lieberman campaign and Jewish political culture, was more ethnographic (see chapter 12).

Packrat that I am, I pointed out that in my collection of nondigitized ASA meeting programs, there had not been a single panel on a Jewish subject in five years (since 1996) and that one was a historical panel on Jewish ethnic identity at the turn of the nineteenth century, despite the fact that the ASA met in cities with significant Jewish populations and Jewish studies programs, including Detroit, Montreal, Seattle, and Washington, D.C. In that period, however, there were more than 30 panels with "ethnic" in their titles. To join Jewish studies and the Association for Jewish Studies, whose membership had grown since its establishment in 1969 to be even larger than the ASA's, to the discourse on ethnic studies, we approached the Task Force on Relations with Ethnic Studies Programs, Faculty, and Students with what we thought was a generous offer to put the task force's name on the session as a sponsor. The task force declined with the shocking exclusionary explanation, at least to us, that Jews did not constitute an ethnic group in their definition of ethnic studies. And we took the response to mean that the study of Jews was not legitimately part of ethnic studies or American studies. Or that we were better off being segregated into Jewish studies and the Association for Jewish Studies meetings.

In my experience, it was not a question, and chapters or sections on Jews were regularly part of textbook surveys of American ethnic groups. Panelists were aware of the effort to redefine ethnicity as a racial subject and to remove European American groups along with Jewish studies scholars from scholarly discourse on ethnicity and even intercultural relations. And for those who treated Jewish studies as a cultural rather than a religious topic, there was a feeling of a crossroads moment in organizing their subject within the frame of Jewish studies or national, transnational, and ethnic studies. In fact, 10 years earlier, a special issue of *Shofar*, which in its subtitle of *An Interdisciplinary Journal of Jewish Studies*, appeared equivocal or ambivalent by embracing interdisciplinarity, had the provocative title of "Are Jewish Studies Ethnic Studies?" In the introduction, editor Gilead Morahg did not come to a single conclusion. He noted that the ethnic studies movement at his home institution of the University of Wisconsin helped to establish a Jewish studies program and center and that ethnic studies majors had the option of taking courses in Jewish studies. Yet Morahg also reported faculty unease with the implication in his view that Jews constitute a "distinct ethnic minority in the United States" (Morahg 1991, 111). Following the line of this thinking, from the viewpoint of some American studies faculty members, Jews more properly characterized white privilege of the majority society. Acknowledging Jews as part of ethnic studies either connected them to disempowered groups who had been successful, or "model minorities," or else stereotyped them with the anti-Semitic trope of Jewish power and conspiracy.

Morahg (1991, 110) also pointed out some discomfort with the linkage to ethnic studies by Jews. One concern was that by emphasizing their contemporary role in American society, placing Jewish studies in the larger ethnic studies diluted Jews' historical and religious basis in classical civilizations. Second, according to Morahg, "In our world of discourse the term 'ethnicity' is often associated with skin colors and cultural characteristics that are very different from those of most American Jews" (111), and there is an intellectual suspicion of a field such as ethnic studies that appears to be more about politicized advocacy than scholarly analysis.

This discomfort relates to the philosophical connection of ethnic studies to multiculturalism that arose during the 1990s. Largely replacing the concept of cultural pluralism that was championed by Jewish American philosopher Horace Kallen (1882–1974), who argued that cultural diversity and national identity were compatible with one another, multiculturalism, in one of its most prominent forms, as described by American studies scholar Ronald Takaki (1993), advocated for the cultural sustainability of racialized communities that should not be pressured to conform to national political, linguistic, and social standards. That definition largely excluded Jews and their experience as ethnic. Renowned world historian Jonathan Sacks (2002) countered with the view that Jews constituted the ethnic group whose experience originally established the concept of social difference. I should not be misconstrued to be arguing against the altruistic vision of multiculturalism to recognize the persistence and tolerance of ethnically bound communities and the relativism of their traditions in a national polity. I am pointing out the cultural bias and redefinition of ethnicity that emerged. This conceptualization became codified in the passage of a law (AB 1460) in 2020 that requires students at the California State University system, the largest public university system in the United States, to complete an ethnic studies course to graduate. Over the objection of 90 education, civil-rights, and religious groups, including ethnic studies professors, ethnic studies was narrowly defined in the law by specifying racialized groups of Native Americans, African Americans, Asian Americans, and Latinx Americans rather than covering the concept of ethnicity (Dresner 2020; Parry 2020). The exclusionary ideological version of multiculturalism represented by the bill appeared to confine and stigmatize Jews from a former ethnic victimized position to a victimizing racialized category of an assimilated white elite. It essentialized or stereotyped Jews into a narrow image of descendants in late-nineteenth-century immigration from Eastern Europe, or what Seth Wolitz (1988) described in the *American Quarterly* as the Americanization of Tevye. Compounding this damaging picture was the association of Jews with colonizing Westerners against Easterners (Kalmar and Penslar 2005; see also E. B. Katz et al. 2017; Koffman 2019).

In confronting the issue of the perception of American Jews' ethnic role in the ideology of multiculturalism, a number of scholars made the connection to the nineteenth-century discourse on the so-called "Jewish question" or "problem" in Europe (Biale et al. 1998b, 4–5; see also Gilman 2006). The Jewish question was an issue because of the rising political paradox for nations embracing Enlightenment values of egalitarianism and emancipation. With the rise of antimonarchical cultural nationalism, Jews clamored for civil liberties within host countries or even for their own state based on a common linguistic-ethnic existence. Yet hostility to and marginalization of Jews in Europe remained at a political and social level. In fact, national leaders viewed Jews, who were supposedly unassimilable, as barriers to the development of new democratic nation-states. Debates raged on the problem with proposals that ranged from support for a Jewish state outside Europe to the relinquishment of religious observance in exchange for political emancipation (Bauer 1843; H. Mitchell 2008; Mufti 2007).

The connection to the American situation probably owes more to the civil rights movement and liberal progressive values than to an awareness of the European Enlightenment, although the precedent of the Jewish question continued to influence the marginalization of Jews in the United States and in some cases the erasure of the Jewish subject in American academe. The roots of ethnic studies in the United States can be traced to the alliance of Jews and African Americans in the civil rights movement and their linkage as disenfranchised minority groups. Yet that alliance was disrupted by multiculturalism, because of the perceived success of Jews economically and their supposed deracialized status as whites, notwithstanding the complexity of American Jewish identity, including an estimated 12–15 percent of Jews who are people of color (Dolsten 2019). Few American studies programs had a Jewish studies track; more common options were to study African Americans, Latinx Americans, and Native Americans. Jewish studies operated more freely but in the process became more siloed and marginalized outside American studies. Jewish scholars pursuing American Jewish historical and political topics found themselves ostracized in a different way: representing, not necessarily by their own choice, an establishment model that relied on self-actualization and assimilation. Many faculty members and students migrated to Jewish studies to rejoin religion and culture in a comparative ethnic study, because many American studies programs reflected a secular emphasis. Ironically, as a field, Jewish studies emphasized the diasporic, historical diversity of Jewish identity and the continued scourge of anti-Semitism. Yet often the intercultural connections were lost.

This parable of expulsion is repeated in other nation and area studies programs, and, in large part, Jewish cultural studies arose from a growing gap between nation and area studies on the one hand and Jewish and religious studies on the other. The resolution to de-ethnicize and thereby remove Jews from the American social mosaic undermines knowledge of the varieties of ethnic—and national—process in the United States and elsewhere. Even worse, it raises anti-Semitic tropes of attributing ethnic success to clannish, surreptitious power and conspiracy. The Jewish problem in American studies is also an Italian problem, an Irish problem, a German problem, a Catholic problem, a Protestant problem, a Mormon problem, a Mennonite problem, a New England problem, a European problem, a South Asian problem, and ultimately, to cite a classic title of American studies, a new American dilemma (Myrdal 1944; see also Beatty and O'Brien 2018). Underlying Jewish cultural studies is the desire not to wander in the wilderness alone but to generate issues and questions that can be applied to the thought and practice of cultural difference generally.

If cultural studies is often guilty of the omission or stigmatization of Jews and consequently of the Jewish subject, Jewish studies is frequently not exactly a cozy home either for Jewish cultural studies. By treating Jewish studies as part of the classics, curricula typically steep students in the biblical and talmudic periods with special attention to readings of sacred texts. The study of "Judaica" in this context equates Jewish identity with religion. The linguistic requirement is usually biblical Hebrew rather than the languages in which Jewish culture is secularly expressed or represented—Yiddish, Ladino, Russian, German, Polish, French, English, Arabic. When the contemporary scene is discussed, it is given a special designation of "modern," often with reference to political and social thought, such as the history of Zionism, rather than cultural genres (music, art, folklore) or groups (Hasidim, Sephardim, African and Asian Jewry). For instance, the huge *Oxford Handbook of Jewish Studies* (Goodman 2002), which covers 39 subjects in over a thousand pages, has no chapter on culture, and it discusses "Modern Hebrew Literature" in a separate section and relegates "Jewish Folklore and Ethnography" and "Modern Jewish Society and Sociology" to the back of the book. Academic curricula follow suit, such as the University of Wisconsin–Milwaukee's track in Jewish Cultural Studies within Jewish Studies, which underscores the modern and its distinction from "the foundation of Judaism": "Jewish Cultural Studies focuses on *modern* Jewish history, literature, film and politics, and does not require Hebrew language" (https://uwm.edu/jewish-studies/undergraduate; emphasis added).

To be sure, Jewish studies has evolved from its original emphasis on biblical and classical Jewish texts, and there has been a movement to include more contemporary perspectives, particularly with reference to the Great Wave of immigration in the late nineteenth and early twentieth centuries, the Holocaust and its aftermath, and the Middle Eastern context of the State of Israel. Yet I contend that, more than adding culture and contemporary practices as an afterthought, philosophically putting Jewish studies at the center of inquiry changes the analysis and understanding of Jewishness—and particularly the double consciousness of identity as something inherited and expressed from within one's community and from outside of it—in people's heads, in society and politics, and in education.

TOWARD A THEORY OF JEWISH CULTURE

In its formation, Jewish cultural studies often takes the form of a hybrid of Jewish studies and cultural studies, along with genetic relations to the social sciences and humanities, and, although it takes substance from these areas, like a hybrid it has characteristics that are distinct from the union of its progenitors. Following the inclusive range of cultural studies, Jewish cultural studies covers culture broadly in its local contexts, demanding a multilingual, multivocal comprehension and an admixture of behavioral sciences, especially social psychology. It gives more attention to the synchronic level of culture by ethnographically surveying contemporary groups and genres but contextualizes its subject more than cultural studies has in its diachronic reference to the ancient past. In addition, it delves into more folk and popular culture, particularly representations in the mass media, than classically oriented Judaica work does (Kirshenblatt-Gimblett 1998). Jewish cultural studies can also be said to open the definition of "Jewish" to what people do and feel, often outside the synagogue, rather than narrowly focusing on their faith. The texts of interest are also more broadly defined to include objects, images, gestures, and performances in addition to the written word, and the approaches integrate more social and behavioral sciences than the conventional rubrication of culture under the arts and humanities.

I do not imagine Jewish cultural studies fencing itself off, because as a spacious, evolving location for inquiry it works with, if not in, cultural studies and Jewish studies. For cultural studies the Jewish addition to the subject naturally includes commentary on culture generally, especially that of a dominant society. This is a function of Jewish diasporic experience, which involves a position that is typically part of yet apart from a dominant society. Thus Jews have occupied a liminal space in which they elucidate their distinctiveness as both observers of and participants in the larger society, with its similarities of expression and identity, while also being concerned for the maintenance and representation of their cultural differences.

Liminality is evident, for example, in the position that Jews occupy in theories of orientalism and postcolonialism, because they have historically been racialized, ghettoized, primitivized, colonized, othered, and rooted in "the Orient" while also being depicted within fine arts as cosmopolitan generally and European specifically. The processes of fragmentation and othering are also constantly under scrutiny in Jewish social processes given to schism and, especially, bifurcation (e.g., the opposition of Zionism to Orthodoxy or Hebrew to Yiddish). These processes are therefore viewed not only as a binary of Jew in relation to non-Jew but also within Jewish social structures themselves—for example, Jewish perceptions of Mizrahi Jews (in Hebrew *mizrahi* means "eastern" and by extension Jews from Arab countries), of ultra-Orthodox Jews known as *haredim* (from the Hebrew *charedi*, meaning "God-fearing"), of Beta Israel (from the Hebrew *beit yisra'el*, "house of Israel"), and of Jews of Ethiopian origin, also socially constructed, often pejoratively, as Falasha (from the term meaning "strangers" or "exiles" used by non-Jewish Ethiopians) and *habashim* (from the Hebrew *chabash*, meaning "Ethiopia"). Even within the Jewish self, there is often a dialogue between public and private persona, past and present, tradition and modernity. Thus the Jewish subject is often cast in psychological terms of a double consciousness in flux: citizen and Jew, public and private, ancient and modern, religious and secular.

Following postcolonialism, the ever-present sensitivity to Diaspora, movement, emancipation, frontier, and homeland in Jewish thought relates to the postmodern awareness in cultural studies of globalization and transnationalism as it crosses the boundaries of European-American nationalism. An issue of transnationalism—that cultural exchange and creolization can trouble politicized ideas of racial or cultural purity within the nation-state—is very much part of the Jewish historical experience. A social phenomenon within this sense of the past related to Diaspora is an ironic social immediacy, perhaps driven by a legacy of removals, for the discourse of heritage is often about a few generations rather than a tall family tree rooted deep in the soil of the nation-state. Cultural practice and synchronic social relations, relating children to their parents rather than to their ancestors, characterizes much of the presentation of Jewish cultural studies.

In the context of this social immediacy, as many Jews pursue the Jewish subject as scholars of Jewish cultural studies, critics or reformists frequently become involved in and editorialize—some may even say with chutzpah—about the conditions they observe. Perhaps this comes from the Jewish ethic of *tikun olam* (repairing the world), in which learning results in action for improving social welfare. Or perhaps it is a postmodern, counterdisciplinary move to shape research in terms of cultural criticism and intercultural relations. Consequently, the cultural politics of anti-Semitism, Zionism, self-hate, marginalization, invisibility, assimilation, Orthodoxy, intermarriage, genocide, hegemony, and capitalism are never far from the surface. Because the identity of Jewishness is often open to interpretation, a related discourse of Jewish cultural studies is on the authenticity of cultural practice and disputed claims to heritage, whether it is among the Lemba and Igbo groups in sub-Saharan Africa or the so-called crypto-Jews of the American Southwest (Bruder 2008; Guiterrez 2017). This discourse is also evident in the evaluation of Jewish revival, revitalization, and renaissance, constantly claimed throughout modern experience, whether set in the context of Lubavitch Hasidism with its "Mitzvah Mobiles" (drawing in Jews to vans to put on tefillin) and its Chabad houses (outreach centers aimed at college-age youth) or the klezmer music revival discussed in relation to the early-twentieth-century Jewish "national renaissance" in Poland and Germany (Berlinger 2010; Fishkoff 2003; Waligórska 2013).

For Jewish studies, Jewish cultural studies helps to contemporize and contextualize Jewish experience. It provides an angularity characteristic to a wide-ranging approach to culture, because it gets beyond the literal content of sacred texts to their symbolic, performed meanings as they are constructed and communicated in everyday and ritual practice or mediated by cultural expressions, from speech to film. Whether as the people of the printed book or the oral joke, Jews have a long and diverse history of cultural expression, although much of it is still in need of recovery (e.g., the historical records of displaced persons camps and the ethnography of adapted, mediated Jewish customs during the coronavirus pandemic) and the discovery of emerging performative patterns (e.g., adaptations of Jewish melodies and performative styles in pop music) (Battegay 2018; Isaacs 2008; Königseder and Wetzel 2001; Nierenberg and Goldberg 2020). Socially, Jewish cultural studies investigates not only the many forms of Jewish communities across the globe but also the frames of mind and identities that individuals encounter for themselves and temporarily create (e.g., distinctive discourse with your "Jewish friends," the yeshiva environment, or the Jewish summer camp). Jewish cultural studies can also inform the expansion of the Jewish subject in Jewish studies by taking into account what non-Jews do with it, how they represent it, and even how they identify with or reject it.

Theoretically, Jewish cultural studies invites many perspectives to arrive at a holistic vista of culture. But it is worth pointing out some prevalent sources of keywords and approaches in its interpretative practices. I would first place the big tent of communication over the field of Jewish cultural studies. An organizing principle of concepts of communication is that culture arises from the interaction of individuals who construct symbolic systems transmitted through expressions and mediated by social structures and contexts. With the emphasis on symbolic systems, analysts are concerned with the ways in which meaning is *encoded* (i.e., embedded by the creator or performer), *mediated* by the means of communication (whether speech, ritual, film, or concert), and *decoded* by audiences (Hall 1992). In this approach, one can discern multiple readings by participants in the cultural scene; these can be dominant (in accordance with the intentions of the creators or larger society), oppositional (contrary to the creators' or society's intentions), or negotiated (selected meanings from both dominant and oppositional readings). The point is that, rather than viewing culture as "superorganic," that is, as an inherited, stable force dictating behavior beyond the control of individuals (Kroeber 1917), symbolic communication or rhetorical theory implies that culture is constructed by participants with strategic, instrumental goals in various situations (Abrahams 1968). Culture is therefore what many cultural studies proponents call dynamic: It acts and reacts in relation to various forces present in a social scene (Toelken 1996). Indeed, in this view, culture is communication (Carey 2009).

Complementing the Jewish philological and hermeneutic tradition, I would argue, is the emphasis in communication theory on rhetoric and discourse. The key signifiers—whether in words, images, or things—that are used to encapsulate a position or people and to persuade others through repeated or ritualized messages indicate broader concepts of culture. These signifiers, which are often packed into expressions recognized because they draw attention to themselves as keywords or icons, relate to a complex web of associations, referred to as the signified meaning. As discourse, signified meanings are often contested and negotiated among participants, indicating the heterogeneous nature of society and the emergent character of culture. Whereas the classic Jewish philological interpretation would trace the history of a word's use, especially relating it to its original forms and subsequent variations, communication and rhetorical approaches call for scrutiny of a word *in use*, or its socially situated expression. The assumption is not made that someone Jewish always speaks or acts Jewish; instead, reference may be made to the cultural "register," "frame," "practice," or "performance" in which participants strategically enact a kind of communication that is appropriate to the immediate context (Bronner 2010b; Kapchan 2003; Nicolaisen 2006).

To get deeper into the underlying structures of everyday life, analysts may also refer to *praxis*, or behavioral patterns that take on symbolic qualities for a group—in other words, the way a community expects things to be done (Bronner 1988, 2012, 2019; Schatzki 2001). From an anthropological viewpoint, cultural practice might be construed as custom and ritual might be seen as a marker of social difference. Yet the keyword of *practice* in cultural analysis identifies repeated behaviors, which might not draw attention to themselves as ritualized or stylized action, and signifies cognition behind them. These behaviors often seem normalized or "everyday," but they embody influences, or intentions, of difference. Jews are particularly sensitive to such actions because of a dual legacy of maintaining their identity through selected religious practices and at the same time of being singled out, often pejoratively, by non-Jews for speaking, acting, looking—and thinking—"Jewish" in secular ways (J. Boyarin and Boyarin 1997; Eilberg-Schwartz 1992; L. Jacobs 1987). Such issues of identity based on the esoteric lore of and exoteric lore about Jews lead to questions of power relations between Jews and non-Jews and within Jewish society. Consequently, use of *praxis* implies analysis of the political ramifications of cultural practices, often outside the awareness of participants (Conway 2006; Traverso 2019; Wisse 2007).

In Jewish historiography, in addition to philological interpretation, scholars have also been attracted to sociological and psychological explanations, which they carry over to Jewish cultural studies. Using Freud's psychoanalysis as an analytical springboard or point of departure, many contemporary critics find embedded symbols in the expressions people produce that project or externalize often repressed, pent-up, or disturbing feelings and desires. These feelings and desires can be said to be sublimated, transferred, or projected. According to this view, the frame of play or performance for many expressions allows outlets, or "fictive planes," for the coping mechanism of projection in which anxieties and ambiguities are addressed. Although in a clinical context this theory is applied to individuals, in Jewish cultural studies the cognitive patterns drawn from readings of symbol-laden fictive planes are discerned in social groups. Informed by the lessons of cultural relativism and cross-cultural work by folklorists and anthropologists, psychoanalytically oriented researchers are careful to situate their symbolic analyses within a particular culture or scene that fosters or sanctions projective expression rather than to universalize meaning (Bronner 2005a; Dundes 1987b; Kirshenblatt-Gimblett 1975; E. K. Silverman 2016).

The roots of the related concept of projective inversion come from Freud's 1911 paper "Psycho-Analytic Notes Upon an Autobiographical Account of a Case of Paranoia," in which he posited that the repression of "I hate him" becomes transposed to "He hates me" (Dundes 1987b, 36–38). Alan Dundes (2007), who frequently applies psychoanalytic theory to Jewish cultural subjects, has argued that the label "projective inversion" is more appropriate than "transposition," because desires are not only externalized but also inverted. Freud's projection, in a Dundesian perspective, can be interpreted as the symbolization of "I hate him" in slurs or stories in which the object of hate is victimized. Dundes defines projective inversion this way: "a psychological process in which A accuses B of carrying out an action which A really wishes to carry out him- or herself" (Dundes 1991, 353). Dundes distinguishes this kind of transposition from the transference of feelings onto an external object, which he calls projection. Dundes's projection is a way of dealing with anxieties or bridled emotions and involves disguising the object in the external expression. Dundes especially discusses examples of projection in jokes, myths, and rituals—for example, Jewish American Princess jokes (expressing unease with the independence of women generally, symbolized in the stereotype of the self-centered Jewish daughter) and the Creation myth in Genesis (the appropriation of female procreative abilities in origin narratives of the male creation of the world) (Dundes 1987a, 1997b).

An example of Dundes's application of the Freudian concept of projection is the representation of Jewish murder in the blood libel legend, which by implication provides a source of European anti-Semitism (Dundes 1991). In the legend, Jews kill a Christian child to furnish blood for their rites (motif V361 in Thompson 1975). The story has been recognized as a shockingly and mystifyingly persistent anti-Semitic narrative among European Christians since the twelfth century (H. R. Johnson 2012; Teter 2020). The legend is frequently recounted as a true event, despite its inherent implausibility and the fact that consumption of blood by humans is forbidden in Jewish law (Genesis 9:4, Leviticus 3:17 and 17:12; see also H. R. Johnson 2012). Dundes purports to solve this puzzle of the story not jibing with the facts, and especially its coincidence around the Easter/Passover season, by pointing out in the narrative the projection of guilt onto another group and the projective inversion of Christians committing murder.

> For the commission of an aggressively cannibalistic act, participants in the Eucharist would normally feel guilt, but so far as I am aware, no one has

ever suggested that a Catholic should ever feel any guilt for partaking of the Host. Where is the guilt for such an act displaced? I submit it is projected wholesale to another group, an ideal group for scapegoating. By means of this projective inversion, it is not we Christians who are guilty of murdering an individual in order to use his blood for ritual religious purposes (the Eucharist), but rather it is you Jews who are guilty of murdering an individual in order to use his or her blood for ritual religious purposes, making matzah. The fact that Jesus was Jewish makes the projective inversion all the more appropriate. It is a perfect transformation: Instead of Christians killing a Jew, we have Jews killing a Christian! (Dundes 1991, 354)

This example highlights the psychological interest in explaining the thinking behind apparently irrational anti-Semitic prejudice toward Jews by non-Jews. Psychoanalytical approaches have also been applied to ideas of purported self-hatred by Jews and to the cognitive processes involved in maintaining ethnic difference under pressures to assimilate or from being surrounded by hostile groups (Gilman 1990). If irrational hate draws psychological inquiry, so too does enigmatic love, or even philo-Semitism, in the representation of Jews in romantic and revival movements.

Many students of culture describe cultural expressions as performances of social structure rather than of repressed anxieties, in an interpretative concept of socioanalysis. Intellectually, reverence (as well as citation) is often given to anthropologist Clifford Geertz's *Interpretation of Cultures* and his concept of "thick description" in an "interpretive theory of culture" that often hinges on events serving to enact and reinforce hierarchies and roles within a social structure. Representing interpretation through the analogy of a patient being diagnosed, Geertz was particularly concerned that interpretation would not be predictive in the manner of psychoanalysis. Instead, it would anticipate a specific situation. His interpretation gave special attention to "the meaning particular social actions have for the actors whose actions they are, and stating, as explicitly as we can manage, what the knowledge thus attained demonstrates about the society in which it is found and, beyond that, about social life as such" (Geertz 1973, 27). Geertz's use of *interpretation* refers also to his background in literary study, because he conceived of actions as "texts" that could be read differently by various observers and by the participants in a cultural scene. Therefore the possibility exists—and is even expected—of different, even simultaneous, meanings. These simultaneous readings are significant because they offer a way to assess the sources of conflict within a society by examining the oppositional meanings of the same events or texts.

Dualistic terms arise from the importance placed on the relationship of participants in a cultural scene to the meanings they construct and perceive. One pair is the distinction between *esoteric* and *exoteric*. Esoteric lore refers to texts that are told by members of a group about itself, whereas exoteric lore designates narratives told about a group by outsiders (Jansen 1959). Thus the blood libel legend told at Easter/Passover is often presented as exoteric lore by Christians about Jews, but it could be argued that the legend of the prophet Elijah enacted at the Passover seder is an example of esoteric lore. One might also, as Dundes (1991) points out, see conflicting symbolic readings of matzo: the socially constructed perception of it as corporeal, following the Christian experience of the Communion host, and the Jewish construction of it as experiential, with reference to the narrative of Exodus. A related distinction is the linguistic one between *etic* (from "phonetic") and *emic* (from "phonemic") categories (Dundes 1962; see also the related distinction between *analytical* and *ethnic* categories in Ben-Amos [1976]). Socioanalysis often looks for native categorization of expressions that are called emic and refers therefore to the way that participants in a culture name and order their shared knowledge, whereas etic approaches are those used by analysts to organize their material (Bronner 2005a, 31–41). Chutzpah can be called a native category for a type of behavior that fits into an ethical order, but judges have etically defined it as legal argot, thereby given it a distinct meaning.

Despite the synchronic or ethnographic orientation of Jewish cultural studies that draws on the legacy of Jewish folkloristics and anthropology, a historicism adapted from Jewish studies is apparent. One can occasionally find a comparative project to relate contemporary practices to sources of customs in the ancient period revealed in biblical and talmudic sources. Yet Jewish cultural studies characteristically does not assume a causal link to religious precept and looks to evaluate the different functions of similar expressions across time and space. In other words, similar content does not translate into similar meanings, and that is why expressions are contextualized in localized cultural practices and social interactions.

Jewish historical periodization, organized by pivotal events and intellectual movements, informs ideas of social change in Jewish cultural studies. Moving backward from the present, cultural processes are set in time against the backdrop of the emancipation of Soviet Jews, the founding of the State of Israel, the destruction of the Holocaust and the subsequent rediasporization, the Great Wave of immigration from Eastern Europe to the Americas, the eighteenth-century movements of the Haskalah (Jewish Enlightenment) and Hasidism, the expulsions from Spain and England, the Crusades and anti-Semitic agitation, the talmudic or rabbinic period, and the destruction of the Second Temple, among others. This periodization establishes processes of trauma, resistance, and resettlement that run through much of historical criticism and affect the Jewish preoccupation with questions of expression, identity, and representation as functions of Diaspora and homeland, traditionalism and modernism, piety and secularism in Jewish consciousness and experience.

Part of the challenge, or chutzpah, of Jewish cultural studies is to develop a post-Diaspora and postmodern vista by which to comprehend Jewish consciousness and experience (Aviv and Shneer 2005; Rebhun and Lederhendler 2015). This wide-angle, multifaceted view brings into relief the arrival of Jews and their cultures metaphorically and literally. Instead of recovering cultural practices that *came from* somewhere—with origins in Central and Eastern Europe, Spain and North Africa, ancient Israel, central Asia, or the Bible—it considers the locations and situations they *go to*. This cultural inquiry is not just the city or country in which Jews form intergenerational bonds but also the ritual space they create in the home and reception hall. For example, Jenna Weissman Joselit has made a case for a "singular" American Jewish culture that is unique in the Jewish world because of the ways in which the home, bar and bat mitzvah, and wedding were reinvented and configured to suit the split away from a synagogue-centered life and to a locus in the Jewish family (Joselit 1994). An implication of this post-Diaspora bearing is getting away from the correlation of urban or ghetto density with a culture of poverty to foster an individualistic, dispersed Jewish culture. Instead of approaching the Jewish arrival in suburbia and holiday resorts as the end of Jewish history, Jewish cultural studies maps the sites and occasions where brands of Jewishness are organized, packaged, and consumed (Bronner 2001; P. Brown 2002; Diamond 2000; R. L. Moore 1994). Defying stereotype, small-town and rural Jews in modern industrial societies deservedly draw attention for their long history and distinctive cultures (D. R. Weiner 2006; Weissbach 2005). As the rhetoric of "New Europe," "New South Africa," and "New Asia" announce breaks from the past, Jewish cultural positions within these reconfigurations beckon scholarly scrutiny (Gilman and Shain 1999; Webber 1994). For example, the places where Jews are from are incorporated into a Jewish imagination, part of heritage tourism, that Ruth Ellen Gruber describes as "virtually Jewish" in Poland, a location now largely devoid of Jews (R. E. Gruber 2002, 2014; see also Kugelmass and Shandler 1989; Shandler and Wenger 1997; Siporin 2014). Relevant to this consideration of narratives and images of Jews in imagination and memory, for example, in chapter 11, I follow the migration and changing symbolism of a legend from Kraków to places where Jews have gone, and in so doing contemplate the changing dimensions of Jewish culture and the studies used to explain it. Jewish cultural studies thus addresses Jews where they live and even where they do not; or, where they do not identify as Jews, it theorizes Jewishness as a significant praxis, projection, and concept.

The chutzpah of Jewish cultural studies is not in its effrontery but in its Jewish sensibility and sensitivity to meanings generated by cultural expressions. It serves to probe the ordinary Jewish subject for what it reveals of culture generally and the Jew specifically. Jewish cultural studies opens common ground where the Jewish subject can receive the analytical attention it deserves for an understanding of culture and for the extraordinary complexity of what it means to identify—and act and think with—being Jewish.

I

CONCEPTUALIZATION

FRAMING JEWISH CULTURE

Jews' awareness of a history of non-Jewish differentiation, and indeed discrimination, has affected a tendency to view identity as a binary of being either Jewish or non-Jewish. This perspective also presumes a total identity rather than the kind of behavior that could be called Jewish in selected situations or settings in response to the audience and the desire by participants to present themselves in a certain way, one of which might be Jewish. Sociologist Erving Goffman (1974) is often given credit for the view of identities being selected for presentation according to the context of such situations or settings; he referred to it as frame analysis. The reference to frames borrows from the concept of play frames introduced by psychological anthropologist Gregory Bateson (1955) to describe the construction of situations that support expectations of or allowances for stylized behavior and communication that are different from those outside the often intangible social frames. The frames imply a psychological shift and often a place to air or resolve problems, because the use of play invokes a liminal boundary between conscious and unconscious, fantasy and reality, and past and present (Bronner 2010b). Goffman expanded the idea of social frames from those in which participants invoked the idea of play to give license to often contentious communication, to ritualistic and work contexts. Although Goffman meant this view to entail people generally, the question subsequently arose about how participants with ties to ethnic and religious groups negotiate the myriad situations of modern life differently.

Such groups often face another boundary between the conscious and unconscious that sociologist W. E. B. DuBois (1903) called double consciousness. DuBois noted that, as a consequence of racial difference, African Americans distinctively identify as a group not only as one affiliates socially with other individuals but also by taking into account how outsiders view the group. Although applied to Jewish identity by later scholars, the idea of double consciousness is complicated by the vagueness of Jews' racialization, consideration of the differentiation of Jews to one another, and the ensuing problem of presenting or hiding a Jewish face to outsiders in light of the wide range of behaviors falling under the umbrella of "being Jewish" (see B. Kaplan 2012; Thomas 2020). The analysis of shifting strategies taken by Jews and non-Jews in relation to one another takes a different turn from a prevalent scholarly approach that presumes a continuous Jewish history in which Jews live out an inheritance from, and indeed are chained to, the past, usually defined in the biblical era. The view of shifting strategies involves recognition of Jewish agency and the negotiation of identities through processes of boundary maintenance, public presentation of self, and representation of cultural distinction through ritual enactments and customary practices.

The term *framing* refers to this agency, which is often responding to the situation or context in which Jews find themselves or where others do it for them. Instead of generalizing the perception of non-Jews and strata of Jews, frame analysts are careful to identify the outlooks of participants with different affiliations within various cultures (Bateson 1956; Bronner 2010b, 2011b; Erving Goffman 1974; Mechling 1983, 11–30). As with the selection of a frame around a painting representing a border that complements a symbolic image, in my fieldwork I found that Jews in various settings make decisions about where and how the picture of themselves will be displayed, and in so doing create a message about what is inside and outside the frame. The framing is material in the sense that images and their messages are contained in outward signs, such as dress, food, and customs, and set the group apart from others, like the edges of the picture. It is also social because the framing process of selecting appropriate behavior for a situation invites others to engage one another, whether informally or in organizations, to define their Jewishness as a form of communication.

To introduce the perspectives on framing Jewish culture, I offer examples that epitomize this turn toward Jewish agency in identity formation and then discuss the terms of framing, representation, and boundaries in more detail.

FRAMES

In cultural analysis frames more often refer to communicative strategies of organizing experience than to physical enclosures. Goffman underscored the often unspoken negotiation of socially constructed frames by participants in a cultural "situation" when he wrote, "I assume that definitions of a situation are built up in accordance with principles of organization which govern events—at least social ones—and our subjective involvement in them" (Erving Goffman 1974, 10–11). Although credited with promoting frame analysis, undoubtedly influenced by his experience in a family of Ukrainian Jews migrating to Canada in the late nineteenth century, he did not analyze many Jewish situations for his examples of frame analysis (Burns 1992, 8; Cuddihy 1974, 68; Fernandez 2003, 206–7; Erving Goffman 1963, 60, 114). Nonetheless, according to those who knew Goffman, he became interested in the problem of socially constructed frames through issues of Jewish identity and his negotiation of social interactions far from his Manitoba home. For instance, classmate Saul Mendlovitz, who shared a Jewish background with Goffman, remarked of their graduate school experience together at the University of Chicago, "Erving was a Jew, acting like a Canadian, acting like a Britisher. . . . He felt that he was Jewish yet didn't want to be Jewish. He wanted to be something else. He really wanted to be an English gentleman [in line with] the picture of him that he had in his head" (Shalin 2009). A central problem in Goffman's paradigm-changing approaches to social interaction was one of identity that could be appropriated and related through expressive acts of gesture and talk in selected settings.

Goffman never wrote about his childhood, but he was quoted as asserting that "being a Jew and a Russian Jew at that, explained a lot about me," which biographer Ronald Fernandez took to mean that "he was a perennial outsider, caught between his ancestry and the prejudices of the larger society" (Fernandez 2003, 206–7). Taking the analytical role of an observer looking in on someone else's culture, Goffman sought to be an insider looking out, and he developed theatrical metaphors for cultural behavior—stages and performances—to describe variable social roles, much as touring actors adapt to different physical settings and audiences. Mendlovitz indicates that Goffman "was very much into that observational stuff very early on," based on his concern for his fit as a Jew and a Canadian with different social groups on campus. Mendlovitz, who also had a self-impression of himself as an outsider in Chicago, recalls that as Jews, "Erving and I used to go to [ethnically mixed] parties and agree that we would exchange [thoughts on] what we had seen. He especially was interested in what we had seen and then he would take copious notes on that. . . . And we would then go over very carefully what the girl said to him, who was going off into another room, what was the content, how come there were no paintings on the wall, but it was a full range of ethnography and that kind of stuff" (Shalin 2009). In these settings, often populated by strangers, Goffman noticed that a standard part of dialogue would be the extraction of information such as birthplace, occupation, and ethnicity between individuals to figure out another person's identity and categorize what to expect socially from that person. Goffman was apparently concerned with what the label "Jew" meant to others and how that identity matched his own self-awareness. Even though Goffman was self-conscious about his Jewish background as a basis for frame analysis, as a professor he encouraged ethnographers, including his Jewish students, to avoid studying their own families or cultural groups so as to maintain an objective distance from the observed scenes.[1]

One can read a concern for the kinds of interaction between individuals who have a self-awareness of ethnic difference in Goffman's reference to "stereotype" in his groundbreaking study, *The Presentation of Self in Everyday Life*: "If unacquainted with the individual, observers can glean clues from his conduct and appearance which allow them to apply their previous experience with individuals roughly similar to the one before them or, more important, to apply untested stereotypes to him. They can also assume from past experience that only individuals of a particular kind are likely to be found in a given social setting" (Erving Goffman 1959, 1). Before Goffman applied the terminology of the frame, he used the looser terminology of "situation" to refer to a recognizable context—at least recognizable by participants—that drives the distinctive forms of expression and impression that people convey to one another. Goffman was interested in the attempts of individuals in modern everyday life to manage the many situations they encounter in heterogeneous society, often through symbolic communication in talk and action, to advance their own interests. A proposition Goffman advanced that drew consideration in scholarly circles was the idea that in these situations boundaries and connections were established through symbolic communication often embedded in artistic performances, including the use of proverbs, slang, and body language.

Goffman's microsociological approach attracted wide notice because of the implication that participants have agency in the formation of their social life rather than blindly following precedents of traditions or repeating fixed texts of lore in their expressive talk (Scheff 2006). He outlined an ethnographic goal of analyzing through observation whether the expressive and often ethnically inflected communication that occurs in a situation is dictated by the setting, often outside the awareness of participants, or is strategically guided by one or more figures in the frame. Setting up a frame socially is an attempt by interacting participants to gain social order by emphasizing connections among themselves and by moving potential conflicts to the margins or edges of the frame. Goffman declared that this constant negotiation of different social settings is a function of modern everyday life in which identities are open to alteration in response to conditions of high mobility, social diversity, and extreme individualism. He conceptualized modern society as one in which people are strangers to one another and consequently create social frames constantly to establish familiarity and construct an identity appropriate to the situation (see Kim 2002; Packard 1972; Sennett 1977). Identities are not shaped by family line or locality alone, therefore, but are flexible and overlapping. Modernity offers individuals choices for who they want to be or how they appear to other strangers, but with those choices comes the often difficult cultural work of formulating and managing their identities in various social relations on a daily basis. Forced into this role of presenting themselves and taking on the risk of rejection, individuals become actors to one another and learn from culture the dimensions of acts they can ply variously to communicate and impress others. To this sociological premise, other scholars into the twenty-first century have added historical and psychological inquiries into the experiences and drives that shape socially framed behavior, particularly in Jewish contexts where issues of stereotype, migration, boundary, and difference abound (Boustan et al. 2011; J. Boyarin and Boyarin 1997; Bronner 2012, 272–96; Bush 2011, 57–67; Heilman 2006; Prell 1989; Sklare 1993).

Some scholars prefer the terms *scenes* or *stages* to *frames* so as to emphasize the performative, presentational, and emergent nature of socially contextualized expressions in modern everyday life, but I maintain that those theatrical terms do not fully connote the repetitive patterns of cultural impressions that arise from daily and ceremonial encounters. For many visual ethnographers, the frame draws on the documentary operations of framing, centering, and focusing in photography and the interpretation provided by sequentially arranging images in a gallery or exhibition (Bateson 1956, 175–76; Bateson 2000, 186; Bateson and Mead 1942; Mechling 2004, 2009). In this view, the observer looks through a lens and identifies boundaries that will not be apparent to the subjects. The observer as analyst is able to variously center or arrange different activities in the shot as symbolically related. The analytical act of framing scenes and arranging them in a sequence of communicative acts captures a narrative and action that have bearing on the perception of the event from the perspective of the participants and assorted viewers.

Consequently, frames refer to the ways that insiders and outsiders comprehend activity as a deep cognitive structure in addition to viewing and strategizing what occurs behaviorally. The use of a frame does not imply a singleness of mind or society among participants, because, as a culturally derived construct based on precedent that has been adapted to new situations, the elastic social frame is open to negotiation and contention by participants (R. D. Abrahams 2005; Bronner 2010b; Fine 1983; Mechling 1980; Raspa 1991; Sherzer 1993).

Addressing the theme of framing Jewish culture, folklorist Steve Siporin (2014) offers a perspective on the mediation of ethnic identities in a cultural frame in his study of Pitigliano, Italy, known in the region as Little Jerusalem. Siporin finds this moniker significant because Pitigliano not only had a large Jewish population historically but also supposedly possessed an interreligious harmony. He describes a contemporary situation in which town leaders celebrate local Jewish experience toward the development of tourism around Jewish sites, although the town is almost completely devoid of Jews. Among the settings for social interaction of tourists with townspeople is the Ghetto Wine Bar and Caffè. Siporin notes that American tourists consider the use of *ghetto* in bad taste because of its allusion to a history of forced exclusion, but for many locals the shop's name and setting represent an occasion to recount narratives about the rescue of Jews during World War II and to promote good relations between Jews and non-Jews. Siporin uses the idea that tourists feel compelled to experience Pitigliano firsthand, even if the historical representations are inaccurate, as a sign of deeper messages at work: consuming Jewish foods to gain a sense of authenticity, listening to stories about the town's Jews to confirm the townspeople's affinity for Jews, photographing themselves against staged Jewish backdrops as theater, and participating in festivities that relate in this setting a subtext about post-Holocaust Italian identity. Siporin asserts that "from an early time the Jews of Italy brought the host (Italian) culture into their own Jewish frame to a degree probably unsurpassed elsewhere in western Europe" (Siporin 2014, 254–55). This observation leads Siporin to ask, "To what extent might non-Jewish Italians today be incorporating Jewish culture into their understanding of Italian-ness?" (255). His answer is that Italians have promoted a Jewish cultural revival as frames in which narratives and the nostalgic behavior they enact can salvage Italian identity.

Ethnographer Amy K. Milligan (2014) studies a frame occupied by Jews in an American small-town setting. All the participants identified as Jews, ranging from Conservative to ultra-Orthodox, but they came together in the single synagogue. They negotiated the kinds of practices that can bind them together not just spatially, in a physical building, but also socially into a single cultural frame. The congregants were forced to reconcile different levels of observance among them, and in so doing danced around the very definition of Orthodoxy and its connection to historic Jewish tradition. Part of that negotiation in this particular context was the creative adoption of some practices, such as using head coverings, which connected the women in the congregation as the bedrock of the synagogue and also aligned them with the head coverings worn as a sign of pietism by the "plain groups" of Amish and Mennonites in the area. Hair covering more so than other familiar markers of Jewish pietism materialized their joined identity but also allowed for variability, from using a snood at the liberal end to a *sheitel* (Yiddish: a wig or half-wig worn by some Orthodox married women to comply with the halachic requirement of modesty to cover their hair; see Goldberger and Steinmetz 2014). on the more conservative side. Hair covering by the women in the congregation situated their Orthodoxy and empowered the women as taking responsibility in the synagogue for the continuity of the group and its maintenance of traditions.

In these and other pathbreaking studies, scholars frequently refer to the cognition of the frame in terms of action (or act) and interaction. Using the frame as a key to the consciousness of what is reality and fantasy, everyday and ceremonial, and play and work, ethnographic observers and historical chroniclers focus their analytic lenses on the way that ordinary activities—such as handing, lighting, sitting, and standing—become culturally framed as significant symbols (the kind of symbols that elicit responses in the form of gestures and ideas from others) with props, names, or narratives brought into the situation to support different meanings held by organizers and participants (see Blumer 2004; Duncan 2002, 92–106; Mead 1967, 61–81; Musolf 2003, 72–93). A historical example that uses ethnographic principles of frame analysis is Marcin Wodziński's "The Question of Hasidic Sectarianism" (2014). Besides noting the widespread classificatory act by non-Hasidim of referring to the Hasidim as a "sect," which differentiated the Hasidim from Judaism in an attempt to curtail their influence in Polish civic affairs, Wodziński analyzed the significant symbolism in a ceremonial frame of the mourning shiva enacted by many Jewish parents when their children left home to join Hasidic courts. The metamessage of these staged funerary events was that taking up Hasidism amounted to a conversion to a non-Jewish religion and therefore Hasidism was not part of Judaism. Of significance in Wodziński's historical study is his innovative use of court records, diaries, and narratives to provide insights into not only the sequence of events but also the frames of social interaction that changed over time.

Wodziński places the loaded terms of *sect* and *cult* in the historical context of the relation of Jews to non-Jews in Polish public policy and even the attempt to criminalize Hasidic religious practice. In analytical terminology, the frame and context may appear similar. In his original formulation of the play frame, Bateson (1955) characterizes the frame as a perception of a setting in which interaction occurs from a context, or surrounding condition of an event. Bateson muses:

> We assume that the psychological frame has some degree of real existence. In many instances, the frame is consciously recognized and even represented in vocabulary ("play," "movie," "interview," "job," "language," etc.). In other cases, there may be no explicit verbal reference to the frame, and the subject may have no consciousness of it. The analyst, however, finds that his own thinking is simplified. If he uses the notion of an unconscious frame as an explanatory principle; usually he goes further than this and infers its existence in the subject's unconscious. (Bateson 2000, 186–87)

One can read in this statement a call for understanding the cognitive process that produces the frame as well as the social, historical, and cultural forces apparent in communication that affect the comprehension of the frame. Following Bateson, social theorist Jay Mechling offers that the use of a frame signals a scholarly turn away from "positivist and formalist epistemologies to an epistemology that sees reality as created, mediated, and sustained by human narratives" (Mechling 1991, 43). This emphasis on the process of narration and action (often in reference to gesture, play, and festivity) is especially discernible in Jewish cultural studies that depart from the conventions of literal readings of Judaic texts to assessments of expressions and impressions enacted in everyday life (J. Boyarin and Boyarin 1997; Bronner 2008).

Frame analysis takes into account the role of the observer or analyst in the perception of the function of the frame. Much as I have discerned the effect of Erving Goffman's Jewish background on the development of his ideas of impression management (and interestingly, on other notable scholarly contributors to this development, including Roger Abrahams, Richard Bauman, Dan Ben-Amos, Alan Dundes, Gary Alan Fine, Kenneth Goldstein, Barbara Kirshenblatt-Gimblett, and Elliott Oring),[2] a trajectory of the inquiry into framing is toward historio-graphic studies that question the impact of personalities and movements on the discourse of impressions that the public or scholarly community has about groups and their interactions. For example, in the context of Jewish cultural studies, Jon-athan Boyarin (2014) examined the relationship between anthropologists Paul Radin (1883–1959) and Stanley Diamond (1922–1991) and their conceptualiza-tion of otherness based on their own experiences in Jewish culture, even though most of their studies were about other groups. He used this inquiry to address a broader question of the avoidance of Jewish culture by Jews in the social sciences who were formulating concepts of ethnic difference based on social interaction rather than on racial classifications following a natural history model. He found paradoxes in the ways that these scholars framed the social problems that could be resolved by ethnography of non-Jewish groups, even as their perspectives on these groups were colored by their Jewish background or were intended to shed light on Jewish experience (especially the iconic case of anthropologist Franz Boas [1858–1942] discussed in his introduction; see also L. D. Baker 2004; Bronner 1998, 129–38; Diner 1977; G. Frank 1997; Glick 1982; Messer 1986; Morris-Reich 2008, 4–17). One paradox that Boyarin pondered in terms of the frame built around the continuity between non-Jewish and Jewish othered groups is that the arguments they advanced to demonstrate that Jews did not constitute a race were also used to show that they were artless or without a distinctive culture.

MATERIAL FRAMES: EXHIBITIONS

Framing Jewish culture as a rhetorical and material action related to the repre-sentation of ethnic difference is exemplified by a signature event in the annals of Jewish display: the Anglo-Jewish Historical Exhibition of 1887. The popular press hailed the exhibition, which displayed 2,626 objects in the majestic Royal Albert Hall in London, as a momentous achievement that triggered, according to the *Jewish Encyclopedia*, "a distinct revival of interest in the history of the Jews in England" and apparently elsewhere (C. Adler 1906, 509; M. Cohen 1888, 295). The idea of the grand event came from English-born engineer and art aficionado Isidore Spielmann, who in 1886 at the age of 33 proposed to journalist and Jewish civic leader Lucien Wolf, also of his generation, that a large exposition of histor-ical and artistic relics could have a profound salutary effect on the state of Jews in England (Wolf 1911–1914). Spielmann argued that placing Jewish documents in cases for public viewing and highlighting artifacts on pedestals would raise the importance, especially to non-Jews, of the breadth and depth of Jewish contributions to English civilization as participants rather than outsiders and would also freeze these items in time to encourage their analysis, particularly by Jews.

Recollecting the impetus for Spielmann's brainstorm, Ephraim Levine pointed to an obvious identity conflict within the young rising star that the act of literally framing and displaying Jewish cultural materials might resolve. Levine referred to Spielmann's "double allegiance" to both national and ethnic society with the assumption that the national devotion meant a Christian as well as a political affiliation (E. Levine 1924–1927, 234). He observed that in the assimilated Spielmann, "No man was more completely identified with England and all that English culture connoted." Yet in the face of a wave of Jewish refugees fleeing from persecution in Eastern Europe washing over English shores, Spielmann

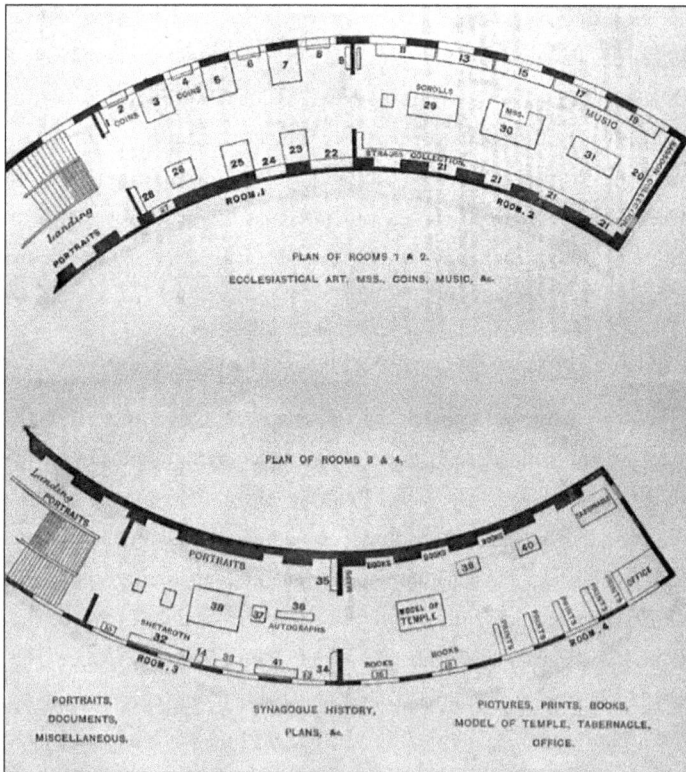

1.1. "Plan of Rooms" for displays in rooms 1–4 of the Royal Albert Hall, printed in Joseph Jacobs and Lucien Wolf's *Catalogue of the Anglo-Jewish Historical Exhibition, 1887, Royal Albert Hall* (London: W. Clowes, 1887), xxii–iii.

loudly called for "a well-organised community" (234) publicly promoting Jewish identity to transition the new arrivals. According to Levine, because at that time differences could be visibly discerned between native and immigrant Jews, Spielmann viewed the exhibition as an opportunity to show a long-standing tradition of Jewish integration with English society while maintaining ethnic variance, whether imposed from outside or within the community. Levine summarized Spielmann's paradoxical psychological profile as one of simultaneously "Anglicizing [i.e., assimilating] the foreign Jew in this country [England] and in protecting [or separating] him in other countries" (235).

Often mentioning the peculiar situation of Jews in host countries, curators guided by Spielmann contextualized sections of the popular exhibition for the primary attendees of non-Jews. In the introduction to the section "Jewish Ecclesiastical Art," Wolf and folklorist Joseph Jacobs wrote:

> Like the jargons of the Hebrew people, their manners and customs, their superstitions and other phenomena of their social life, their art is little more than a composite deposit of the contrastful impressions of a wide geographical dispersion, and of a varied and chequered history. . . . Whatever the normal artistic capacities of the Hebrew people, they must have been strongly affected, if not altogether transformed, by the stupendous catastrophe of the Dispersion, and the career of ceaseless wandering and misery which subjected them to the perplexing influences of ever-changing surroundings. (J. Jacobs and Wolf 1887, 83)

By this account, Jews sought a home in which they could thrive as citizens of the realm. Their cultural legacy need not separate them; it provided ingredients that could be mixed with the local environment into a joint identity. At the same time, Wolf and Jacobs recognized that differences existed between Jews and non-Jews in England, especially in worship rather than character, and they pronounced that Jewish distinctiveness should be respected and even praised as one of many constituent faiths in the nation. Exposing the historical anomalous position of Jews in England, the exhibition's curators arranged objects in a progressive order from medieval exclusion to modern inclusion. On the one hand, the exhibition was a call for preservation, especially as the organizers bemoaned the loss of physical remains of the Jewish "element" in England, but, on the other hand, it was a rhetorical act of framing Jews socially as worthy constituents within a larger

British culture. This act served to align Jews as a group among others within a host society and to establish the kinds of scenes or boundaries where Jews could establish their differences. More than providing a historical record of Jews in England, the exhibition was, in the organizing group's president F. D. Mocatta's words, "designed to alter this state of things," by which he meant that the ascription of artistic ability in the frames of the exhibition suggested that Jews had a vibrant living culture as well as a long historic legacy as a basis of their ethnic distinction (Mocatta 1887, 290).

Assessing the impact of the exhibition, Barbara Kirshenblatt-Gimblett underscored the significance of the display in launching the "Jewish plan" of organizing Judaica that would become standard in world's fairs and museums through the twentieth century. The arrangement was by ritual settings of synagogue, home, and person (life-cycle events), thus suggesting physically and socially bounded spaces in which Jews could express their difference. She interpreted the strategy as conveying a double consciousness of showing the discreteness of Jewish practices in confined instances while assuring Victorian visitors that Jews shared with non-Jews a national value system of fidelity to home, family, and faith (Kirshenblatt-Gimblett 1998, 85–86). Lest visitors imagine that Jews were estranged from the host country, Jacobs and Wolf included in the exhibition a framed written copy of the "Prayer for the Royal Family," placed, they emphasized, near the "Tablets of the Law" so that it could be read by the congregation (J. Jacobs and Wolf 1887, 96). In pointing out the especially lavish ornamentation of Torah scrolls, the curators observed more connections of Jews to non-Jewish faiths in England by noting that, although Jewish betrothal rings "bore a Hebrew inscription signifying 'Good Luck,' they rarely differed from the similar rings in vogue among the Gentiles" (83). In presenting a memorial for fallen Jewish soldiers who had served in British regiments, Spielmann told his audience, "This memorial stands here in eloquent testimony to the fact that British Jews are inspired by a love of King and country no less enthusiastic and no less devoted than that which animates their fellow-subjects. It testifies that in vindicating their claim to the same liberties and rights, they share an equal privilege of defending and of dying for the country which confers them" (Spielmann 1902–1905, 58). The design of the tablets drew attention to the difference of these soldiers "of the Jewish race and faith," as the words in memoriam stated, by having one tablet with their names in English and another translated into Hebrew surrounded by an elaborate Sephardic design.

More than a hundred years after the exhibition, museums built on the inspiration of Spielmann's urgency to display the evolving status of Jewish expressiveness. For example, to coincide with the publication of *Treasures of Jewish Heritage* (Burman et al. 2006), London's Jewish Museum proclaimed in 2006 a need drawn from the Anglo-Jewish Historical Exhibition to showcase the cultural worthiness of Jews with a demonstration of their artistry. The catalogue also continued the theme of dispersion among Jews to raise the question of whether a unified Jewish identity exists, no less an Anglicized one. Even more conspicuous in the twenty-first-century catalogue than the Anglo-Historical exhibition's reference in the nineteenth century to the plight of Jews from Eastern Europe is the challenge of creating a Jewish community and identity out of the diversity of Jews, who include immigrants from Asia, South America, and Africa in the United Kingdom. The curators declared that "the clothes, religious artefacts, photographs and other objects are characteristic of the widely divergent societies where Jewish people have lived over the centuries, ranging across Europe, Asia and North Africa. These objects embody the diversity of the community whose stories the Jewish Museum seeks to tell" (Burman et al. 2006, 187). The London Museum's exhibition questioned whether a singular Jewish cultural frame existed or whether Jewish identity depended on the geographic background of the Jews involved in myriad cultural scenes.

The lesson I draw from these exhibitions is not about museum techniques but about the agency of the acts of framing, bounding, representing, and exhibiting Jewish difference by Jews and non-Jews in both formal institutional and informal social contexts. Manifested materially in a public exhibition, ritual objects presented as communal possessions lead viewers to comprehend the cultural traits that compose an identity in everyday life in the bounded physical settings of the home and synagogue. Rhetorical acts of circumscribing, exhibiting, and representing identity can also be discerned in various social encounters between Jews and non-Jews and among Jews in which intangible frames referring to Jewish difference are enacted by participants. Indeed, the question arises whether these frames are in fact intentionally constructed or enacted outside the awareness of participants, especially when the boundaries of the frame emerge from an un-self-conscious change in behavioral action and mode of communication. In the absence of material walls separating Jews into ethnic zones or dress demarcating Jewish religious pietism, participants signal to one another a Jewish consciousness by using language and gestures meant to be esoteric. Physical context still comes into play because of the perception of where such encounters are appropriate—on the street, at work, in the market, at the theater, in a restaurant, in the synagogue, or at home—and with whom.

REPRESENTATIONS AND BOUNDARIES

The idea of strategically framing communication in selected situations, whether as an analyst or a participant, to demarcate social boundaries is common to the experience of many individuals who, by definition, operate with a double consciousness of a national association and a subcultural identity based on a supposedly foreign ancestry. The challenge of Jewish experience to this classical theory of ethnicity is the combination of diversity in the global Jewish experience, which comes out of a mobile diasporic rather than national ancestry, and the intersection of religion and race with locality. A statistical measure of this mobility relative to other religions is the 2012 study by the Pew Forum on Religion and Public Life. The study found that, by far, Jews have the highest level of migration among all faiths. It concluded that one-fourth of Jews alive today have left their birth country and now live somewhere else. In contrast, just 5 percent of Christians, 4 percent of Muslims, and less than 3 percent of other religious groups have migrated across international borders, according to the Pew survey (Pew Research Center 2012). Often there is an assumption that Jews reside in community with one another, as ethnic groups are expected to do, and yet they disrupt easy categorization because they mix and move in a socially heterogeneous workaday world or are capable of living in isolation as religious Jews. Whereas social difference is frequently tabulated by governments and neighbors by noting residents' consistency of appearance, language, and habits, Jews have not been easily separated by racial characteristics, despite anti-Semitic efforts to scientifically categorize Jews as an inferior, mongrel race (Gilman 1991; E. L. Goldstein 2006; Hart 2011; Patai and Patai 1989).

The issue of boundaries is prominent in Jewish studies because the mobility of Jews has led to the presumption that Jews always have neighbors whose animosity or friendliness to the idea of Jewishness and relations with Jews is constantly in question. Against this contextual backdrop, boundaries for Jews are frequently points of interface rather than separation (Bush 2011, 60–61). Although mobility and its association with personal freedom and socioeconomic enhancement are highly valued in modernism generally, Jews have especially embraced mobility as a test of their status because of historical associations with their movements being restricted or with being forced into slavery. Other social factors of boundary join with mobility in the highly publicized issue of marital choice and family formation, because of general demographic patterns in Europe and the Americas of relatively high intermarriage and late marriage rates. For example, in a survey of Jewish mobility in the United States, Sidney and Alice Goldstein commented, "If Jews marry at later ages, if more Jews choose not to marry at all, if marital disruption increases and if fertility remains low, conditions conducive to locational stability may continue to weaken so that even higher levels of longer-distance movement may result" (S. Goldstein and Goldstein 1996, 2). The discourse that this view opened is whether the demographic decentering of Jewish communities means the loss of Jewish identity. The Goldsteins are convinced that it does (317–31). Moving away from statistics to social observations, other scholars are not so sure. For example, Carole Fink, Ruth Gruber, and Diana Pinto have pondered the meaning of phenomena constituting a twenty-first-century renaissance of Jewish culture and renewal of Jewish identity in Europe (Fink 2010, 226–28; R. E. Gruber 2002, 68–69; Pinto 2006). However, this revival implies a challenge to or redefinition of the model of assimilation that leads to integration into mass society. Instead, the twenty-first-century model is one of intense Jewish action or expression enacted at pivotal moments and in designated or constructed spaces—physical and social—which suggests a social interactional perspective on frames as permeable limits, always under construction (S. J. D. Cohen 1999, 1–5; Lipphardt et al. 2008; Pinto 2006). Representation of occasions when Jewishness rises to the surface and needs enactment takes on more significance in such a social interactional model. Along these lines, Holly Pearse (2014) takes a Jewish cultural studies approach to note the ways that identity at points of interface relate to the question of consequences of Jewish mobility and how interfaith romance is expressed on movie screens for encoding filmmakers and decoding audiences. She views a historical change in screened representations from the assimilationist message of harmonious ethnic mixing in couples in an open democratic society to patterns of stress and strain in interfaith romances.

Ethnic theory often presumes minority status for the group in question (Sollors 1996), although another modern challenge has been the ethnographic and historical understanding of Israel as a Jewish-majority state whose residents nonetheless have perceptions of localized difference based on national and cultural origins, level of religious piety, institutional affiliation to a kibbutz or moshav, and even political orientation. A key to this modern diversity that links Jews in other national settings is the concept of situated identity, particularly set against cultural landscapes in urban and suburban spaces, forming "Jewish topographies" or "traditions of place" (Brauch 2008). Sociologist Herbert Gans was influential in developing a definition of situated identity out of his studies of an urban Italian neighborhood after taking on suburban Judaism (Gans 1957, 1962; see also Sklare and Greenblum 1979). He defined identity simply as "the sociopsychological elements that accompany role behavior" (Gans 1996, 434). His observation in a post-immigrant society beginning in the 1970s was that the

> ethnic role is today less of an ascriptive than a voluntary role that people assume alongside other roles. To be sure, ethnics are still identified as such by others, particularly on the basis of name, but the behavioral expectations that once went with identification by others have declined sharply, so that ethnics have some choice about when and how to play ethnic roles. Moreover, as ethnic cultures and organizations decline further, fewer ethnic roles are prescribed, thus increasing the degree to which people have freedom of role definition. (Gans 1996, 434).

Ethnic identity is expressed as action or feeling, or a combination of these, often in social situations or cultural spaces where the kinds of expression for identity are unconsciously perceived or overtly organized. This kind of identity is not an objective, historical category but subjective and modern in the sense that individuals claim an identity and work to reinforce it with participation in social events or expressive performances in selected cultural scenes or frames.

Not all scholars agreed with Gans that the influence of ethnic organizations had evaporated, that the options for creating identity were quite as limitless as he implied, or that assimilation was inevitable. For instance, writing generally on the "enigma of ethnicity," cultural geographer Wilbur Zelinsky noted the "virtually worldwide resurgence of fundamentalism" that suggests a total and often singular immersion in formal institutions and social structures (2001, 175). Within Jewish studies, Samuel Heilman, David Landau, and Jerome Mintz all observed in the 1990s the growth of ultra-Orthodoxy (whose adherents are known collectively by the emic term *haredim*) as a separatist movement bucking the creative ethnicity trend (Heilman 1992; Landau 1993; Mintz 1992). Landau editorialized that "the haredim, regarded only a few decades ago as a dying breed, have confounded forecasts of their demise. In their resurgence, they have proved that the dismissal of haredism as anachronistic may itself be an anachronism in the modern world" (Landau 1993, 334). In addition to fundamentalism, religious renewal and cultural revival projects that revolve around new Jewish priorities placed on the environment, spiritualism, or feminism have spawned intentional framing of group differences—from the larger secular society and between various stripes of Jews. Again, it appears that Jewish diversity complicates the understanding of ethnicity as boundary maintenance in relation to religion and culture.

Zelinsky speculated that rekindled religiosity was a side effect of globalization and a response to the shortcomings of modernization (2001, 175). Jews as a diasporic group are especially aware of varieties of tradition that demarcate the difference of Jews from host societies in a wide number of communities around the modern world. Every Jewish holiday, the popular press broadcasts recipes and customs not only in a descriptive sense of affirming Jewish diversity but also to suggest that traditions can be adapted to one's observance far from the original source or one's background (see Nathan 1994, 2004; Rose 1992; Uvezian 1999). Even representations of foods and holiday observances focused on Israel typically emphasize the many cultural communities with distinctive traditions (see Nathan 2001). Whether as a form of cross-cultural bonding or a response to assimilation, such diversifying practices lead past religiosity back to the concept of ethnicity and the questions raised by Spielmann concerning the consciousness of identity.

The alignment of Jewish identity with the concept of ethnicity has been notably reexamined, perhaps because the dawn of the twenty-first century brought forth heightened philosophical discussions about a break with the twentieth-century patterns of immigration and assimilation and a supposedly new postmodern age of cultural practices responding to transnationalism or "border crossing," localism and alternatives to suburbanization to restore community bonds, and interracial and interreligious relations. Introducing a Dutch conference on borders and boundaries among Jews in the Netherlands, Judith Frishman and Ido de Haan signaled a departure from past assumptions of binaries between Jew and non-Jew when they pronounced, "If identity is no longer to be regarded as something set but rather something that is subject to change and negotiation, then logically attention should be paid to the 'continuous construction, maintenance, or transgression of boundaries between ethnic and other collective identities'" (Frishman and de Haan 2011, 7–8). They sought to reexamine history in light of the view that "postmodernist historians have been turning their gaze to a wide range of identities once taken for granted, identities located on the border-lines between Jews and non-Jews as well as on those between one group of Jews and another" (8). A year earlier, a symposium titled "Boundaries of Jewish Iden-tity" (2010) sought to redefine a sense of Jewishness dictated by Jews' enemies or within the discourse of surrounding majorities. Similarly disputing the idea that Jewish identity is set or static, organizers Susan A. Glenn and Naomi Sokoloff called for an understanding of identity based on the "different social, intellectual, and political locations of those who are asking" (Glenn and Sokoloff 2010, 4). Much as Ephraim Levine speculated on Isidore Spielmann's motives for creating an exhibition of Jewish history and artistry that would affirm the place of Jews in England, so the "reflexive" analysis suggested by Glenn and Sokoloff looks to find the agents for the forging of Jewish identity in varied circumstances, especially by and for groups outside the mainstreams of Jewish life, such as the Lemba of southern Africa, Subbotniks of Ukraine, Kuki-Chin-Mizo of India, and crypto-Jews of the American Southwest. Yet another conference, "Beyond Boundar-ies," sponsored by the American Jewish Historical Association in 2012, agitated for reinterpretations of disciplinary divisions among scholars studying Jews and the difference between Jews and non-Jews in a postmodern ethnicity (American Jewish Historical Society 2011). With these trends in mind, I see a coalescing of discourse on a global scale, with Jewish cultural studies as an exemplary guiding structure for a problem-centered inquiry into the thinking behind the rhetoric of boundaries and the manifestation of difference in social life.

The reference to boundaries and borders suggests that much of the work of defining Jewish culture has been at the center of groups rather than at their bound-aries with other communities. The rhetoric of boundaries is meant to show that the lines of demarcation between Jews and non-Jews and between different groups of Jews are varied, negotiated, and mutable. From Jewish cultural studies, scholars find that the tenuous ethnic boundary defines the group, not the cultural forms it encloses (see Webber 2014). This concept builds on Gregory Bateson's suggestion that the social construction of a cultural frame in the absence of a physical bound-ary is a way for a group to handle paradox and tension in their situation, especially in the communication of play that allows transgressive behaviors or messages that subvert the society outside the frame (Bateson 2000, 184–92). Related to this idea that boundaries are constantly reconstituted in interethnic interactions is anthro-pologist Fredrik Barth's famous observation in *Ethnic Groups and Boundaries* that "cultural differences can persist despite inter-ethnic contact and interdependence"

(Barth 1998, 10), which he explained by pointing to the social construction of boundaries in societies where there is constant interethnic contact. In this view, identities in a modern context are not inherited but rather composed anew, in the sense of being enacted strategically in different social situations. The danger of this presentist perspective is that it does not take into account processes of heritage transmission through generations in daily life and the impact of historic events—such as the Exodus from Egypt, destruction of the Second Temple, erection of the Venetian ghetto walls, expulsion of Jews from Spain and the Spanish Inquisition, establishment of the Russian Pale of Settlement, the influx of Eastern European immigration to the United States between 1880 and 1920, and the Nazi implementation of the genocidal Final Solution and Holocaust between 1933 and 1945—on present-day thinking and collective memory. Several contributors to Barth's volume take up this challenge of assessing the influence of historical narrative and memory on awareness and reinterpretation of contemporary boundary maintenance and construction.

Jewish cultural inquiries have as their context an abundant number of references to awareness of boundaries in Jewish custom and sacred texts. The earliest biblical materialization of Jewish difference is the reference to an exclusive covenant with God by circumcising every male (Genesis 17:9–14). Although not visible to a public in the way that later evolving customs such as head coverings for men and women marked Jewish identity, circumcision became emblematic of a communally imposed celebration of difference (S. J. D. Cohen 2005; Glick 2005; E. K. Silverman 2006). Further into the Tanakh, one can hardly overestimate the impact of the Exodus story, to the present day, on holiday observances of Passover, politics, art, and ultimately worldview (N. M. Sarna 1996; Waskow and Berman 2011). Self-reflection on boundaries and identity is also evident every Purim; the memorable narrative of Esther involves a realization that the first figure to be named in the Tanakh as a Jew is Mordecai, who in his family line recounts an experience of exile and presumably diverse relations between Jews and non-Jews in different localities: "In the fortress Shushan *lived a Jew* by the name of Mordecai, son of Jair son of Shimei son of Kish, a Benjaminite. Kish had been exiled from Jerusalem in the group that was carried into exile along with King Jeconiah of Judah, which had been driven into exile by King Nebuchadnessar of Babylon" (Esther 2:5–6; emphasis added). Mordecai admonishes his adopted daughter Esther not to reveal her Jewish roots to King Ahasuerus and to blend in with the other maidens in the king's palace. Esther becomes queen, and when Haman issues a decree to exterminate Jews, Esther aligns herself with her culturally marked "people" and implores the king to countermand Haman's plan (Esther 7:3–4). Although Esther espouses what could be described as ethnic feeling, there is evidence of boundary markers of language in the narrative. The book of Esther relates that the king's scribes sent letters "to the Jews in *their own script and language*" (Esther 8:9; emphasis added; see Koller 2014, 65–78). Whereas Mordecai is clearly identified physically as a Jew, Joseph is not recognized by his brothers when they travel to Egypt (Genesis 41:1–44:17). A frequent question addressed in sermons on this *parsha* deals with assimilation and the maintenance of ethnic and family ties. One common interpretation is that Joseph was not recognizable to his brothers either as a family member or as a Jew because he had assumed the fashions and manners of the Egyptians (Schaktman 1998; Wildavsky 1993, 119–38). Nervous about the implications of this lesson for modern society, many interpreters claim that Joseph's invisibility was of his own doing or that his appearance had markedly changed with time (Schaktman 1998).

Other reminders of boundaries between the esoteric group and the outside world are ritualized and materialized. The weekly performed Jewish custom of the Havdalah blessing, or "distinction," emphasizes the division between the Sabbath and the ordinary weekday (see chapter 5). The Mishnah contains guidance about business dealings with non-Jews during the week that compels an awareness of boundaries. In *Abodah Zarah* Jews are prohibited from doing business with non-Jews for three days before and three days after "festivals of gentiles" (*Abodah Zarah* 1:1–3), and long lists of restrictions, often based on a binary between Jewish maintenance of cleanliness or purity and unclean or impure, follow. Although such business constraints appear anachronistic in the modern era, thinking about the divisions between purity and unclean states are evident in laws of kashrut, which also serve to identify boundaries between Jews and non-Jews (M. Douglas 1966, 30–41; Dundes 2002b, 75–88; Fabre-Vassas 1997, 138–60).

Judaism is replete with reminders of differences between men and women, and the compliance with practices revolving around these distinctions, such as women reading from the Torah and mixed seating in the synagogue, is often a basis for religious boundaries between the Reform, Conservative, and Orthodox wings. The extent of the *mechitzah*, literally "a partition" in Hebrew, that divides men and women in the synagogue is often negotiated and conceptualized as representations of observance. In some Orthodox synagogues, women sit in balconies or galleries, whereas in many congregations calling themselves Modern

Orthodox, the partition is symbolic, with men and women sitting on opposite sides of each other on the same floor. Conservative and Reform congregations usually forgo the division. The inclusion of the *mechitzah* in synagogue architecture derives from talmudic references to men and women being allotted separate space at festivities (*Middoth* 2:5; *Sukkah* 5:2). There is a symbolic connection of the *mechitzah* to identity formation because many liberal Jews view the abolishment of the partition as an embrace of egalitarian or Enlightenment ethics associated with the emergence of modern mass society. According to Meir Ydit, however, "Orthodox Jewry has come to regard the retention of the *mehizah* as a cardinal principle and as a mark of the preservation of the Orthodox character of the synagogue" (Ydit 1972, 1,235). This Orthodox character implies a visible announcement of a primary Jewish identity and continuity with historic practices based on the maintenance of boundaries (Sztokman 2011, 167–70; see also Heilman 2006).

Physical boundaries carry messages of exclusion that have launched a discourse about the importance of ethnic distinction for Jews that has been imposed by their enemies or that they have initiated for a sense of inclusion. Following the renewed attention to sources of border crossing in antiquity (see S. J. D. Cohen 1999), Samuel D. Gruber (2014) uses the term *selective inclusion* for Jewish strategic uses of physical boundaries in medieval Italy and the points of tension in spaces at the edge of boundaries between Jews and non-Jews, especially in performative festivities such as holidays and parades through public streets. He finds evidence of much more border crossing than had been thought to exist in medieval times and suggests that the process of cultural adaptation by Jews began early with cultural responses to liminal civic spaces. Moving into the modern period, scholars have argued about the persistence of outlooks by Jews as they move about or the persistence of historic boundaries, real or imagined, between Sephardic and Ashkenazic, Western and Eastern European, and American and Israeli heritages. For example, Charles Liebman and Steven M. Cohen opened their study of the Israeli and American experience by noting the disparity between the rhetoric of Jewish fundraising appeals declaring "We Are One" and the perception expressed in social encounters of a deep divide between American and Israeli Judaism (Liebman and Cohen 1990, 1–12). Zvi Gitelman (1998) posited that the national difference is not just between brands of Judaism but also in relations with the surrounding society. He observes that in Israel, Jews are easily defined by both cultural and political boundaries, but outside the Jewish state, the boundaries that once demarcated Jews are fading and the visible content that defined them is disappearing.

Yet Eliezer Ben Rafael, in *Contemporary Jewries: Convergence and Divergence* (2003), argues that in both Israel and the Diaspora Jews share multiple, localized "imagined communities," leading to self-awareness of various subidentities under the broad heading of Jewishness.

Sander Gilman has suggested that the modern metaphor of the frontier identifies a location where forces of change, confrontation, and accommodation dominate to displace the model of center and periphery in Jewish history (2003; see also Gilman and Shain 1999). This conceptual term is in line with the emphasis on social dynamics in the concept of the variable cultural frame where identity is formed and reconstituted through expressive acts. A border is usually construed as a demarcated line that is enforced politically or culturally (D. E. Johnson and Michaelsen 1997, 1–5). Boundaries are not always manifest and imply that differences exist on either side of them, even if the boundary areas are fuzzy. To Gilman, rather than serving as a geographic designation the frontier is an abstract concept that draws out the significance of othered perception and social interaction in the definition of identity. In his view, which emphasizes social dynamics of identities, the frontier "is the conceptual and physical space where groups in motion meet, confront, alter, destroy, and build. It is the place of the 'migrant culture of the in-between' as both a transitional and translational phenomenon, one that 'dramatizes the activity of culture's untranslatability,' according to Homi Bhabha" (Gilman 2003, 15).[3] This idea also follows from anthropologist Victor Turner's seminal idea of liminality, or a "betwixt-and-between frame," that sets off from reality on one side and fantasy on the other a position from which to evaluate the meaning of society through symbolic practices (V. Turner 1977, 1979, 1995; see also Deflem 1991). In a Jewish cultural context, Jews often take on liminal roles between insider and outsider and create impressions on holidays and in public civic spaces (such as the museums, exhibitions, and festivals described earlier) that, in their edginess, inevitably raise questions of the dimensions of identity (Biale et al. 1998a).

The divide between actual settlements on the landscape and communities that are imagined or formed temporarily in social encounters bears out the point that Jewishness that is not circumscribed physically is often an "illusion" perpetrated by participants and viewers to anticipate behavior (see Webber 2014, 34). Especially crucial to figuring out the reality of the illusion with regard to the significance of Jewishness to identity is answering the question of what difference being Jewish implies for the impression of a person or the community of which they are a part. Goffman, in *Presentation of Self in Everyday Life*, observed, "Information about the individual helps to define the situation, enabling others to know in advance what he will expect of them and what they may expect of him. Informed in these ways, the others will know how best to act in order to call forth a desired response from him" (Erving Goffman 1959, 1). For example, in exploring the attributes that expressing Jewishness or having Jewish identity ascribed to a person implies for expectations or perceptions of difference, anthropologist Jonathan Webber noted that the margins of social boundaries were blurred, because people on the edge of any culture have, or think they have, dual membership, dual citizenship, or ties of all kinds with people on both sides of the boundary. Such people may nevertheless present themselves, perfectly reasonably, as authentic members of the culture, even if they in fact live on the brim—just as there are people whose active membership in a given culture may have lapsed, even for several generations, but who for whatever reason subsequently return to the group and similarly present themselves as fully authentic members, producers, and consumers of the culture. The other possibility in this reexamination of boundaries is that people who navigate frequently at the brim, whether identified as Jewish or non-Jewish, develop a hybridized border culture that is an amalgamation of several identities (L. Kaplan 1997, 105–16; Paredes 2002; M. Weiner and Richards 2008, 112–15). At issue, for example, is how Jewish a Polish culture might be construed to be in light of Polish allo-Semitism (an ambivalent communication of both philo- and anti-Semitism), even in the absence of self-identified Jewish residents after the Holocaust (Z. Bauman 1998; R. E. Gruber 2002, 2014; Lehrer and Meng 2015; Orla-Bukowska 2014; Waligórska 2014). Another location that exemplifies this collapse of borders is the contemporary cultural label in global media representations and in American stereotyping of the "New Yorker," which implies Jewish sensibilities and cultural traits without differentiating them as such. Even the Anglo-Historical Exhibition in the nineteenth century could be interpreted as an attempt to show that English culture indeed incorporated rather than excluded a Jewish "ingredient," as the curators declared.

Whereas the question of Jewish difference within host societies was primarily stated in the twentieth century as a choice between ethnic isolation or integrated assimilation, Jewish cultural studies has expanded the twenty-first-century discourse on the social dynamics of Jewish identity. Jewish culture in this approach is not necessarily gained or lost but is used as a resource in the negotiation of identity. Cultural analysts locate texts and contexts that reveal the variety of human agency in boundary work as part of everyday life. A cultural agenda is to link Jewish identity to the physical and rhetorical processes of framing culture that establish often dynamic, if not paradoxical social relations among Jews and their various publics. Such processes typically include actions of boundary construction and maintenance between groups, representing and symbolizing meaning in cultural expression and exhibiting artifacts and behavior in an institutional as well as social context. Cultural analysts uncover this process historically, psychologically, and ethnographically in contemporary behavior to find explanations for the various manifestations in feeling and action of being Jewish over time and space. They also seek to explain, often in Goffmanesque terms, the motivations of agents, or framers, of cultural organization and analysis in addition to finding Jewish frames of reference.

DUALITIES OF HOUSE AND HOME IN JEWISH CULTURE

In this chapter, I address two related dimensions of the Jewish home: the physical and the metaphysical. Calling a house a home suggests an emotional connection that has been constituted by the shared history of the space and its occupants. When residents refer to a Jewish home, they are defining their domiciles socially as Jewish because their families live there, but a cultural question is how "Jewishness" is materially expressed to themselves and to others. For many Jews a mezuzah on the exterior doorway most clearly marks the Jewishness of the home, as it fulfills the mitzvah to inscribe the Shema, an important Jewish prayer, "on the doorposts of your house" (Deuteronomy 6:9). The mezuzah is usually an oblong or cylindrical case that holds a calligraphed Hebrew scroll; its external decoration and material vary and can be homemade, but the object is still recognizable as a mezuzah by its placement on the doorpost. The mezuzah is significant because it is the only Jewish artifact placed both outside and inside a Jewish home.

To grasp the idea of the dualistic and often paradoxical relationship of Jewish house and home and to gain a creator/user's perspective on the cultural agency of an object symbolizing home, consider the mezuzah shown in Figure 2.1, which draws analytical attention by its placement on a gallery wall rather than a doorpost. American artist Shelley Spector labeled her creation *Honor to Carry* for the 2008 exhibition A Kiss for the Mezuzah at the Philadelphia Museum of Jewish Art (M. Singer 2007). The piece shows artistic adaptation of traditional forms, reflecting what one of the curators called a modern attraction by Jews to mezuzot that "reflect their personality or the style of their home in addition to their commitment to God" (Agro 2007, 6). Some information on the mezuzah's function as a significant symbol is not apparent from the design of the object. The mezuzah is personally meaningful to Spector because it is made out of a cigar box owned by her father, relating to the parchment's text from Deuteronomy 11:13–21 to teach God's commandments to "your children . . . when you sit in your house and when you walk on the way and when you lie down and when you rise." *Honor to Carry* refers to Spector's Jewishness, of which she says, "It is an honor to have inside me something so ancient and spiritual"; like the mezuzah, she considers herself "a carrier of tradition, connecting the past to the future" (quoted in Holzman 2007, 8).

Inside the house, artifacts of home religious observance—often designated as specifically for Shabbat, Hanukkah, or Passover—are often displayed. They are described by families as markers of identity as well as items used for rituals. Because of their religious associations, these objects, including the mezuzah, are often categorized by collectors as Judaica, whether they originate in the synagogue or in the home, but this religious label can obscure the domestic context and use of objects as part of everyday material culture. For example, one might view the functions of the hamza for synagogue and home and interpret the transformation of its symbolic meanings from a protective amulet in Morocco centuries ago to a sign of Jewish nationalism, and transnationalism, on jewelry, key rings, and house decorations in contemporary Israel and elsewhere (see Sabar 2010).

Arguably, the symbolic home is central to the reproduction of Jewish culture and identity in the form of the chuppah, or wedding canopy. It has an architectural reference because of its temporary and ceremonial use as a representation of the home the couple will create. It literalizes the idea of the stability of home, symbolized by "a roof over our heads." In contemporary practice the chuppah has a cloth covering (often silk or satin) supported by four poles, sometimes held up by family members. It marks the sacred space in which the bride and groom stand, sheltering the couple while the marriage ceremony is performed; typically it remains standing throughout the wedding feast, which can last from one to seven days. In some Jewish communities the father of the groom has the responsibility of setting up the chuppah. The covering might be embroidered and adorned with flowers and green leaves, or it may be a tallit (prayer shawl) or adorned cloth, or several sewn together. Taking advantage of optical technology, couples can create customized chuppahs with photographs of actual homes, Jewish images, and other nontextile materials that are scanned and printed on fabric. Framing the wedding

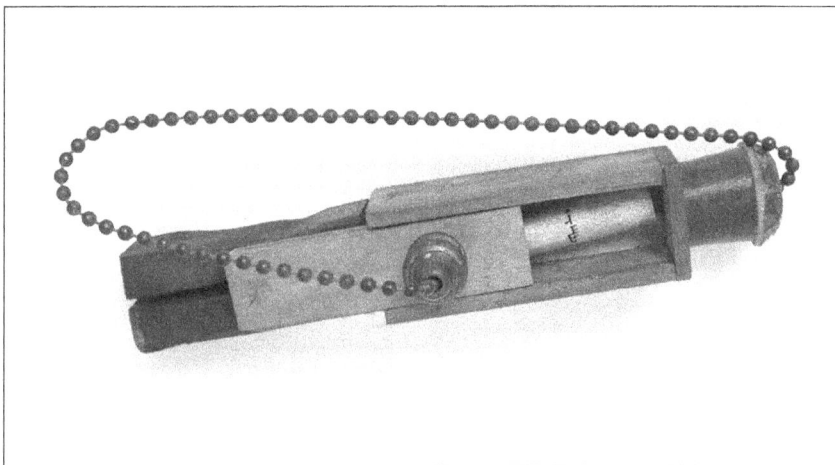

2.1. Honor to Carry, an open mezuzah that shows the *klaf*, or parchment scroll, inside, made by Shelley Spector. Photo courtesy of Shelley Spector.

ritual socially and physically, the chuppah in the twenty-first century invites creative variations that are personalized for the bride and groom. Traditionally, the chuppah is set up outdoors to represent a home on the landscape, although in contemporary practice it is commonly erected indoors. A historical connection exists between the chuppah and the ancient bridal bower, tent, or chamber where the couple consummated the marriage at the conclusion of the ceremony. It may also have ties to an old custom of spreading a cloth or protective screen around or over the couple to protect them from evil forces. More recognized is a symbolism of the chuppah representing the tent of the Jewish patriarch Abraham as a house "open on four sides" to welcome travelers. Rabbis often mention the chuppah, encouraging the couple to engage as householders in *hakhnasat orhim* (Hebrew: hospitality to strangers) and *hesed* (Hebrew: acts of love).

The chuppah also invokes the protective shelter of the home for a ritual inauguration of a Torah scroll. In this ceremony, religious and community leaders carry scrolls that are about to be installed in a synagogue, school, or other institution in an outdoor procession to the synagogue. Unlike the wedding, where the chuppah is stationary, in the inauguration ritual, pole holders walk while ensuring that the Torah holders are covered by the canopy. The procession is festive and usually accompanied by singing and dancing. Once in the institution, the scrolls are placed in the Torah ark after a short prayer service, and the service is followed by a celebratory meal (*seudat mitzvah*), as one might have after a wedding. In their messaging for such events, rabbis typically cite the housing symbol of the chuppah to emphasize that the Torah is central to Judaism. According to this imagery, the Torah is protected in a nurturing home of worship and forms a symbolic union between God and Jews, usually within a synagogue context rather than a family's domestic space. Distinctive in the Jewish ceremony is the procession of moving a home which conveys a message of mobility of special significance to Jews as a diasporic group.

The physical space of the Jewish house has often been overlooked in architectural study because of architecture's emphasis on form and typology rather than social process. The key material evidence in most architectural surveys is the form of the front elevation and the floor plan that constitutes the house type. This emphasis is evident in the standard reference work for ethnic architecture, the massive, 2,384-page *Encyclopedia of Vernacular Architecture of the World* (Oliver 1997). Jewish architecture is represented by synagogues in Central Europe, South India, and Sri Lanka and by community institutions of kibbutzim and moshavim (cooperative settlements or farms with different degrees of collective ownership), but no references can be found to domestic housing presently used by Jews. A brief mention is made of districts historically identified as Jewish, although Jews no longer live there, such as the San'ā Jewish quarter in northern Yemen, for which the author of the entry underscores the importance of typology by noting that the houses "represent a distinct typological group, although they are similar in many respects to the top-court houses found elsewhere in the country" (Varanda 1997, 1,458). This report emphasizing architectural form raises questions of contemporary adaptations that distinguish buildings as Jewish, such as the houses in San'ā "fitted with a top opening for the Feast of Tabernacles" (1,459). Arguably, Jewish identity is apparent from examinations of architectural details and social use, and studies of Jewish material culture have often stood apart with this instrumental attention in an approach that could be called contextual rather than formalistic, because the studies typically focus on the social and physical circumstances of Jewish everyday life, especially in relation to non-Jewish neighbors (Bahloul 1996; Golany 1999; Kroyanker 1984).

The study of Jews in the domestic sphere also stands apart from much of Jewish studies that affirms the synagogue as the ritual and physical center of Judaism. Often highly ornamented and visible on the streetscape, synagogues are artistically compelling and invite investigation by ethnographers as conspicuous public hubs of Jewish activity (Heilman 1998; Kravtsov 2008). Although synagogues are certainly important institutions in the Jewish world, Jewish homes are often underappreciated as physical and ritual centers, probably because of the prevailing assumption that modern Jews live in dwellings that have no distinguishing Jewish features or that they do not materially express their Jewishness outside the synagogue (Hubka 2003; Krinsky 1996; Sachs and van Voolen 2004). Yet the home in ethnological and folkloristic studies generally is viewed as crucial to the formation of cultural identity because of the intergenerational enactment of traditions and the lifelong construction of memory within its walls. Among the fields concerned for Jewish material culture, Jewish cultural studies can take the lead in consideration of the Jewish home as physical space in relation to other structures, such as the sukkah and synagogue, and as a social and psychological milieu in which selected objects play a major role.

The metaphysical or emotional aspect of the Jewish house is often expressed as "feeling at home," a sense of attachment and comfort in one's social and physical surroundings. That is hardly unique to Jews, but it arises often in Jewish discourse because of the Jewish experience of anxiety as a minority or immigrant community. Often the subject of literature and folklore and of the visual and performing arts, the emotional side of home has been problematized as "at-homeness in exile" in Jewish studies, highlighting tensions between different heritages, including that between the biblical promised land and later diasporic locations, such as the Pale of Settlement in Russia, from which Jews emigrated around the turn of the nineteenth century. The conventional Jewish historical narrative of expulsion, dispersion, and consequent exile provokes comment not only about where an emotional home is located but also about whether one can be "at home" in the Diaspora (Gilman 2003, 4–5). It is therefore common to hear the distinction between diasporic experience, as a peripheral or frontier heritage, and an ancient biblical homeland (or, to use a domestic metaphor, a historical cradle), with the presumption that on the frontier encounter and assimilation will lead to cultural exchange and loss (Gilman and Shain 1999; see also Sklare and Greenblum 1979). This version of Jewish exile from a historic center implies cultural linkage as Jews disperse. It suggests that Jews away from these historic cores still maintain a connection with, if not a longing for, the old country in the form of nostalgia or maintaining cultural traditions, rather than beginning anew by creating a singular Jewish culture.

A more decentered version of exile, which emphasizes the diversity of Jewish culture, refers to innovations in individual or domestic rituals that mark different brands of Jewishness in disparate locations (Gilman 2003, 6; Gould 2011, 2013; Ochs 2007). A scholarly manifestation of this decentered approach is the investigation of Jewish communities as independent, living traditions with their own discrete cultural histories (see Mikdash-Shamailov 2002; Shwartz-Be'eri 2000; Slapak 2003), and it is a major theme in works of literature, such as those from Brazil and Argentina examined by Rosana Kohl Bines (2010) and Mónica Szurmuk (2010), who reveal the tension between feeling at home in an unfamiliar new world and Jewish historical desires to return from exile to a biblical homeland.

Cultural historian Jenna Weismann Joselit is more forceful in her view of the discontinuity between life in the old and new worlds and between the synagogue and domestic life. In *The Wonders of America* she proposes an "independent sense" of a singular Jewish culture that was formed in the United States in the twentieth century. Family life in the home was a hallmark of this culture: "The community came together and coalesced around the ideal of a domesticated Jewishness in which the home and its inhabitants became the core of a modern Jewish identity" (Joselit 1994, 5; see also Joselit 2010). Walter Zenner provided a similar view of Jews from Aleppo, Syria. He was compelled to explain the distinctiveness maintained by members of the community as they dispersed because the group defied the scholarly expectation that assimilation would lead to cultural loss: "Rather than looking on the majority national community as the center into which one assimilates, each nation has many centers with which one may fuse or remain apart. In many though not all places, the Aleppan Jews have had the reputation for maintaining the home away from home" (Zenner 2000, 27; see also Sutton 1979). Zenner's analytical strategy is to demonstrate cultural diversification by highlighting distinct daily customs, typically in the domestic sphere, and contrasting them with the uniformity of following Torah. Summarized smartly by anthropologist Jonathan Webber, the strategy reflects "the anthropologist's idea of Jewish culture, in that it was about what people did and how they lived, and not necessarily about what people were supposed to do or how they ought to live" (Webber 2002, 324).

Extended beyond the anthropological emphasis on bounded, homogeneous groups to temporary groups in complex societies that self-consciously create identities for members through adaptive customs and material markers, the revisionist critique of the representation of exile points to exceptional situations in which Jewish minicultures arise. Examples that have attracted scholarly attention include Jewish summer camps and youth movements, kibbutz experiences for non-Israelis, Jewish community centers, and vacation communities that advertise themselves as homes away from home or as providers of an intense experience of Jewish belonging that one cannot get at home (Joselit and Mittelman 1993; D. Kaufman 1999; Richman 1998). Anthropologist Jonathan Webber's perceptive comment on the relationship between an emotional sense of at-homeness and *galut* (exile) is that "what happens at the level of assimilation, inconsistent though it may be, is not a reliable guide to the passions in people's heads. 'At-homeness in exile,' for example, can survive for centuries even after the people have left the country, as the poetry put out by Spanish Jews long after 1492 readily attests" (Webber 2002, 324). At-homeness therefore lies behind the rhetoric about the dual sources of yearning for homeland throughout modern Jewish history with reference to the roots planted by ancient residence in or experience with the old country. Zionism (based on the ingathering of Jews in Eretz Yisrael), complete with frontier metaphors of *halutzim* (pioneers) and settlement in "territories," exemplifies the historic homeland idea, and nostalgia for Jewish neighborhoods is evident in the mythologizing of certain places as "where we're from," such as the Lower East Side of New York, the East End of London, the Pletzl in Paris, and the Eastern European shtetl (Diner 2000; Kugelmass 1989; Polonsky 2005; Sternhell 1999).

In public discourse, such areas are often referred to nostalgically as the old neighborhood, and sometimes recovery projects are proposed to restore parts of them. For example, in the midst of the destruction of Jewish communities during World War II, the Yiddish Scientific Institute (YIVO) issued a call for a *muzey fun die alte heimen* (literally "a museum of the old homes" or, idiomatically, "of the old country"). The top priority, according to the call in the *heimische* language of Yiddish, was to collect "photographs of the external look of the towns, villages, homes, institutions, weddings and modes of entertainment," rhetorically linking the material and social aspects of community life, so as to "serve the present and future young generations who want to continue spiritually to lead a Jewish way of life." Referring to the disruption to intergenerational tradition associated with the domestic sphere, the organizers thought that the result of the project would be "a closer family connection between the parents and their first generation American children and also grandchildren" (YIVO 1944, 1).

If that call in 1944 looked back to a destroyed way of life, what about the establishment four years later of a new Jewish state in Israel? Israel appears to suggest a nationalistic model different from the diasporic model, but the regional situation is layered beyond the division between Arabs, Christians, and Jews. From an examination of the hamza, for instance, Shalom Sabar (2010) describes modern Israel as struggling to achieve Jewish unity out of multiple national ancestries, languages, religious differences, and beliefs absorbed by the nation-state (see also Bar-Itzhak 2005; Zerubavel 1995). Sabar traces the development of Zionism to embrace multiculturalism by the end of the twentieth century, particularly with the incorporation of Mizrahi groups (Jews from Arab, African, and Asian countries), to create a multicultural and multicolored social tapestry. He sees a sign of cultural change in the emerging popularity of the hamza in the home and on the street as an Israeli national symbol. On a local level, the display of the hamza, which has its roots in Morocco, at the entrance to the home has different material and emotional meanings. For Israelis of Moroccan descent it is connected to their heritage; for others it is connected to a post-Zionist Middle Eastern identity of joint Arab and Jewish creation. The hamza also implies Jewish reflections on Western ideas of Jews as "Oriental" and on the orientalism apparent in the predominance of Ashkenazic culture when Israel was founded—cultural categories that divide Eastern and Western Jews and affect the idea of at-homeness in the homeland (Kalmar and Penslar 2005). With its representation of the hand, it also psychologically suggests home-nurtured intimacy related to touch and the power of the hand to hold and construct.

INTERIORS AND EXTERIORS

The function of the synagogue as a house of worship implies that the home as a dwelling lacks religious significance. Yet the number of religious observances held at home in Judaism and the value placed on ethnic differences expressed in Jewish culture are reminders of the importance of the home not only in the way that Judaism is practiced but also in the way that being Jewish is experienced. At the start of the twenty-first century, amid concerns that public displays of Jewish identity were not as noticeable or desirable as they once were, Rabbi Andrew Goldstein emphasized the difference of a Jewish home in his popular children's book My Jewish Home (2000). The cover shows a generic single-family house, but, on opening the book, one reads, "When you knock on my door, you know mine is a Jewish home. There's a mezuzah on the doorpost. Now come inside." Goldstein identifies candlesticks and Kiddush cups as religious items in the home but also points to ordinary objects such as a bar mitzvah photo, Jewish cookbooks, and an Israel travel poster as signs of being Jewish. Not all the reminders are visual: "On Fridays when we bake challah, I can tell by the wonderful smell in the kitchen that ours is a Jewish home." He closes the book by asserting that "most important in my Jewish home are the people in it . . . my Jewish family." By its design and message, the book underscores that the exterior of the house is not noticeably Jewish except for the mezuzah, but a Jewish environment is constituted by the practices and social attachments inside.

Vanessa Ochs is an anthropologist who advanced the idea that domestic practices in home interiors signify Jewish attitudes and contexts. Beyond the ritual objects of Sabbath candlesticks and challah trays that fall into the commonly recognized category of "articulate objects"—props, she wrote, of Jewish observance that are displayed in the home—she refers to "Jewish-signifying" material culture, often not noticed as such by the residents, such as an abundance of books and food and "shrine-like displays of photographs," because they represent a Jewish value placed on *l'dor v'dor* (a Hebrew phrase meaning "from generation to generation"). She claims that piling up books and food "point[s] from one generation to another: family matters, love matters, keeping connections matters, increasing and multiplying matter" and is historically contextualized by middle- and upper-class Jews of the post-immigrant generations in the West as a response to an earlier culture of scarcity and restrictions on education in former Eastern European homelands (Ochs 1999–2000, 11).

Another category in which the Jewishness of the interior is constituted is in "ordinary objects transformed," a range of objects that could be found in any home but whose meanings and functions shift within the context of a Jewish home.

> A dish is a dish, but in a Jewish home where kashrut (the dietary laws) is observed, the dishes of a certain color or pattern placed in a particular and separate cabinet become and remain milchig (milk) dishes, and the dishes in another cabinet become and remain fleishig (meat). The telephone is a telephone, but when it's being used by a Jew who is checking on a sick friend who lives far away, it is a *klei kodesh*, a holy vessel used in the practice of *bikkur cholim*, the commandment to connect to the sick. All of the equipment one uses in house cleaning—cleansing powder, mop, Windex, Pinesol, vacuum cleaner—is just cleaning equipment. But in the Jewish home where Sabbath is observed by cleaning one's home beforehand, we

have again *klei kodesh*, holy vessels that create and point to the Sabbath, tangibly, experientially, and sensuously. (Ochs 1999–2000, 11)

Sociologist Solomon Poll (1962) referred to the practice of imbuing ordinary objects with Jewish values and thus incorporating them into religious identity as an important adaptive strategy of the Hasidim. It is hardly universal, though, among tradition-centered groups. Poll contrasted the Hasidic practice to the resistance of the Amish to technology such as the automobile. Unlike the Amish, according to Poll, "The Hasidim will not necessarily think of an automobile as a means of getting themselves away from the community and into the outside world, but rather as a vehicle that brings their children to study religion" (Poll 1962, 229–30). In the computer age, questions arise about the role of the computer in Orthodox Jewish homes and as a potential threat to traditional values. Giving a rare glimpse of Orthodox bloggers, religious studies scholar Andrea Lieber (2010) showed that differences of opinion exist within the various communities of which these computer diarists are a part. She understood that non-Orthodox scholars may be quick to dismiss the possibility of computers being transformed into Jewish objects in a traditional domestic interior.

Sociologist Samuel Heilman in his study of strictly Orthodox Jewry described his reaction to the home technology of Yisrael Eichler from the Belz court of the Hasidim.

Eichler sat at a computer workstation in the corner of his combination study and dining room. Next to the screen was a portable radio/tape unit along with files of papers, books, and clippings. The technology was the latest. This was not my grandfather; the scene before me resembled the view from my own desk! But Eichler's room gave off a series of alternate messages too. Holy books—*seforim*, as they were called—were one of its primary motifs. Along an entire wall of the room were shelves lined with bound seforim. . . . While in the past large libraries of sacred texts like Eichler's might have been found only in the possession of rabbis or a yeshiva, today even the most simple Jew could own a collection of books that his forebears could hardly imagine. Having seforim spoke volumes. These were not books for reading; they were tomes to study, tools for worship, and the visible symbols of an attachment to Jewish tradition. They were the literal props of every haredi home. Interspersed and sparkling amid the brown bindings and gold letters were the other props of a traditional Jewish home: Sabbath candlesticks, Chanukah menorahs, a Purim *megillah*, silver wine goblets, and a dish for dispensing honey on the High Holy Days. Eichler might be up-to-date with technology, but as his appearance and his other possessions showed, he was something far more traditionally Jewish as well. (Heilman 1992, 96)

Heilman draws a sharp contrast between the computer from his secular world and Eichler's religious one, but another interpretation is the computer's incorporation into the "traditional Jewish" interior as another tool to maintain Jewish identity.

The emphasis in Jewish museums, beginning in the nineteenth century, on displaying historic treasures and masterworks of Judaica, usually highly ornamented and articulate, has influenced the public understanding of traditional Jewish material culture (Kirshenblatt-Gimblett 1998). If architectural scholarship has underappreciated the Jewish home, history and art museums have been even less attentive to Jewish domestic life, which curators have tended to view as unworthy of display because it is ordinary and nonartistic (see, e.g., Altshuler 1983; M. Berger and Rosenbaum 2004; Burman et al. 2006; J.-M. Cohen et al. 2004). Museums of Jewish daily life are rare, because usually only synagogues, large public structures with spiritual symbolism, are considered worthy of preservation. One notable exception is the Lower East Side Tenement Museum established in New York in 1988. This museum includes a Jewish household among the apartments shown. Although tenements are not Jewish dwelling types, they were the characteristic abode for the majority of Jews who came to New York City during the Great Wave of immigration from 1880 to 1920. Part of the interest in walking through the dark, dingy apartment preserved in the museum is the contrast with dwellings thought to be more typically Jewish in old country villages or shtetls.

The folk-museum movement, with its nationalistic purposes, began in the late nineteenth century with Skansen, the Swedish open-air exhibition of buildings, but has rarely included Jewish environments, largely because the museums tended to promote the rural roots of a national culture rather than its ethnic components (Allan 1956; Bronner 2019; Michelsen 1966; Romanian National Committee 1966). Some indoor Jewish museums, such as the Jewish Museum of Belgium and the Irish Jewish Museum, purport to represent Jewish home life, often with room settings for Sabbath or holiday celebrations. The most active institution involved in ethnographic exhibitions depicting the daily life of whole communities is the Israel Museum in Jerusalem. This museum has an ethnographic department, and it has had a profound impact on promoting public appreciation for Moroccan and other underrepresented Jewish domestic arts and subcultural identities in Israel. Special exhibitions have been mounted for marriage contracts, amulets, and other domestic artifacts, but they have been displayed as works of art rather than for the way they fit into folklife or a traditional environment (Sabar 2000). Barbara Kirshenblatt-Gimblett has hypothesized that this tendency to depict Jewish culture with masterpieces of religious Judaica derives historically from nineteenth-century expositions in Europe in which Jewish exhibitors "framed the presentation of Jewish subjects in terms of art and civilization and secured for Judaism a central place in the history of religion" rather than a place in multicultural societies (Kirshenblatt-Gimblett 1998, 79).

Modern Jews setting up households have received help from an abundance of popular manuals since the early twentieth century, commonly referred to in cultural studies as handbooks, guidebooks, or advisers. A check of listings on Amazon.com, the world's largest bookseller, reveals more English titles for manuals for managing a Jewish household than for Christian or Muslim ones. This statistic may be a sign of more concern in Jewish culture for home observance, which often involves specialized procedures, or a need for more guidance in modern life, particularly for families living in non-Jewish neighborhoods. The home advisers often imply that, in the West, new families establishing households are distant from parents and grandparents, who in the past would have provided guidance on creating a Jewish environment. Subtitles of Jewish home manuals such as "A Guide for Jewish Living" create a duality between the synagogue, where one learns Judaism, and the home, where one lives as a Jew. For instance, Daniel B. Syme's *The Jewish Home: A Guide for Jewish Living* is introduced with the adage that "the synagogue makes Jews," but "a vibrant Jewish home is the seed-bed of Jewish culture, identity, and practice. A cardiac Judaism—'I feel it in my heart'—is grossly inadequate. Only a Jewish life that is knowledgeable and rooted in Jewish history and practice can be truly authentic" (Syme 2004, vii).

Directed usually at the new Jewish parent, the manuals underscore the need for a special intimacy in the home where Jewish identity can develop, unhindered by a national culture deemed different at best and oppressive at worst (Abramowitz and Silverman 1997; Bloom 2006; A. J. Goldman 1958; Blu Greenberg 1983;

B. D. Greenberg and Silverman 1941; Kitov 1963; Kolatch 2005; Olitzky and Isaacs 1993; Reuben 1992; Shendelman and Davis 1998; Syme 2004). Quoting a 1930s handbook that states that "the function of the home must therefore be to transmit a civilization, to provide for the continuity of a cultural inheritance as well as an ethnological one," cultural historian Jenna Weissman Joselit concludes, "Whatever the physical setting—the tenement of the pre-World-War-I era, the modern elevator apartment of the interwar years, or the suburban ranch house of the 1950s—the home played host to changing notions of Jewish domestic culture. As the intimate site of acculturation, home served a symbolic purpose as well" (Joselit 1990, 23). The symbolic purpose was to provide a modern Jewish identity, often creating a fortress of resistance to the cultural assault of the majority society, as well as food and shelter. The home was supposed to be the place where tradition would be passed on from one generation to another and where children were taught to be proud of their Jewishness and marry within the Jewish community.

Among the manuals that have become hallmarks of varying senses of Jewish at-homeness in different generations are *The Jewish Home Beautiful*, by Betty D. Greenberg and Althea O. Silverman (1941), *The Jewish Catalog*, edited by Richard Siegel, Michael Strassfeld, and Sharon Strassfeld (1973), and *Living a Jewish Life*, by Anita Diamant (2007). *The Jewish Home Beautiful* appealed to Jewish women as homemakers, but, more than that, it suggested social mobility from lower-class immigrant roots into middle-class America in its call for "gracious Jewish living." Through the book's many printings, the symbolic importance of the home as a sacred haven in a hostile diasporic environment was emphasized in the preamble.

> It was the Englishman's boast that his home was his castle. The outlawed, persecuted Jew could not make his home his castle; but he did more than that. He made his home his sanctuary. Because God had a great share in his little house, the Jew succeeded in transforming it into a great home. Because God was to be worshiped "b'hadrat kodesh," in the beauty of holiness, the Jewish home was to be holy and beautiful. (B. D. Greenberg and Silverman 1941, 17)

With the reference to the home as a castle, the writers, who demonstrated their table settings with fanfare in showy public demonstrations they called pageants, located the home as a Jewish sanctuary not just in Jewish neighborhoods but especially within non-Jewish environments as Jews moved into suburbs associated in popular culture with the white Protestant elite. The creation of table centerpieces and the placement of dishes and utensils thus became the fulfillment of mitzvot on one level and, on another, showed that being Jewish could be modern and fashionable (Milligan 2018). In its elaboration of Jewish-signifying objects, *The Jewish Home Beautiful* was not novel, but it articulated for a post-immigrant generation the sense of culture as refinement, with its elitist connotations. At the turn of the nineteenth century, this sense would prompt Jews to support the City Beautiful movement, which was intended to create separation from the lower class, who were widely perceived to be mostly "backward" or "superstitious" immigrants holding on to old-country traditions (Wilson 1994).

The Jewish Home Beautiful also assigned responsibility for the "keeping" of the Jewish home to women, connecting it to modernity while noting its traditional roots in the imagined Eastern European Jewish shtetl, much as the wildly popular musical *Fiddler on the Roof* later imagined an earlier heritage with the famous opening song lyrics of "Tradition" (lyrics by Sheldon Harnick, music by Jerry Bock, 1964):

> Who must know the way to make a proper home,
> A quiet home, a kosher home?
> Who must raise the family and run the home,
> So Papa's free to read the holy book?
> The Mama, the Mama! Tradition!

By the time of the staging of *Fiddler on the Roof* on Broadway, however, the depiction of women's confinement in the home so that Papa could be "free" was intentionally out of step with the feminist spirit of the times that challenged assignment of responsibilities for not only house maintenance but also guarding of Jewish tradition and difference (see Bronner 1998, 33–37; Fishman 1989; Nadell 2019, 233–62; Wolitz 1988). The representation of the home and the backdrop of hardscrabble houses of Jews living apart from non-Jews in the musical signaled a changing role of gendered space in the home and responsibility for maintenance of tradition in modernity. The framing of the production in the "old" world within the larger context of a modern urban landscape disconnected the heritage from the present and rendered it nostalgic.

Widely popular and written in the youthful, iconoclastic spirit of the countercultural *Whole Earth Catalog* of the late 1960s, *The Jewish Catalog* sought Jewish renewal through a more populist message. It rejected the elitist, materialistic undertones of the *Jewish Home Beautiful* with a call to get one's hands dirty, to experience a grassroots and more feminist do-it-yourself Jewishness. Instead of promoting a consumerist Judaism of manufactured goods, arbitrated by elite authorities, the writers encouraged Jews to make things for themselves from their own designs. It was a call to counter consumerism by engaging with Judaism firsthand. For the writers, the Jewish home was constituted by sacred objects, beginning with the mezuzah, but also including the *mizrah*, a wall hanging in any medium, placed on the eastern wall of a room to mark the direction of Jerusalem. The implication was that emphasizing the home in Jewish observance was crucial to ensuring Jewish continuity at a time when youth were rebelling against capitalism and the establishment.

First published in 1991 and revised in 2007, the popular *Living a Jewish Life* (which received more attention when its author, Anita Diamant, scored an international bestseller in 1997 with her novel *The Red Tent*), like most other manuals, carries the message that Jewishness begins at home. Unlike other manuals, however, Diamant gives biblical support to the ritual importance of the home in Judaism by writing that, with the destruction of the Second Temple in Jerusalem, the "Jewish home became the new center of Judaism" (2007, 15). Diamant extends the emphasis in *The Jewish Catalog* of encouraging engagement in Judaism by actively participating in hands-on projects rather than placing priority on Torah literacy in the synagogue. She defines the Jewish home not so much by ritual objects or home observances as by the values they express. More than *The Jewish Catalog*, *Living a Jewish Life* suggests that such expression can be individualized and invented in various ways. For example, in Diamant's view, a Jewish home can be characterized by hospitality. She extends the sacred obligation of *hachnasat orchim* (the bringing in of guests) to include having an extra room for guests and inviting an out-of-town visitor to the Passover seder. Following her advice, the sense of *hidur mitsvah*, the commandment to make an object used for ritual purposes as beautiful as possible, can be extended into everyday, secular Jewish life by, say, displaying a poster of the Hebrew alphabet illustrated with bright, funny pictures or hanging prints by Jewish artists such as Marc Chagall, Ben Shahn, and Chaim Gross (Diamant 2007, 19–20).

Many consumer catalogues in print and on the Internet support this cultural Jewishness. For instance, cover designs for *The Source for Everything Jewish* depict home festival or life-cycle celebrations and promote products that either thematize the home or are intended for home consumption. The opening page of the early spring 2006/5757 issue features a "Jewish Parents" lithograph in which an English-Hebrew biblical quotation encircles a message "honoring the Jewish home"; according to the blurb, "As is customary among Jewish parents, you have created a home filled with love and laughter, integrity and learning, compassion and generosity. Your home remains a loving environment rich in Jewish traditions and dedicated to peace, hope and respect for all people." In answering the question "Does the appearance of your Shabbat table need a little update?" the catalogue offers a challah board and knife made from a "patented, highly polished blend of Space Age metals," suggesting the integration of Judaica with modernism. As a consumer catalogue, *The Source for Everything Jewish* also encourages gift giving on home visits to other Jews, especially for the woman/mother of the house, as indicated by selections of aprons, jewelry boxes, "Woman of Valor" posters, biblical-heroine bookends, mother pins, and music boxes. Reminders of Israel as homeland abound, but one can also purchase a New York City skyline menorah and reminders of the Eastern European shtetl in Yiddish-tinged art, books, games, and recordings.

Home Jewishness often prioritizes the family in Jewish identity acquisition and emphasizes home as a location for social affiliation with other Jews. In the creation of family-centered events at home, such as a personalized naming ceremony for a girl (Simhat Bat), many Jews connect recent ritual innovations to traditional practices in the home, frequently associated with a maternal sense of nurturing (see chapter 7). Especially central in tradition is the Sabbath observance that inspires social bonding with family and guests. The traditional women's role of lighting the Sabbath candles and its symbolic importance in structuring time and ritual for Jews contribute to the maternal image of the home and the nurturing character of domestic Jewish culture. But home-based ritual extends beyond the celebratory; for example, mourning occurs there too, with the ritual process of sitting shiva and covering mirrors. Social support at home, including friends and more distant family bringing food for the mourners, is crucial to the process. Underscoring this connection is the identification of a home visit to the bereaved as a mitzvah.

Home is also a location for narrating Jewishness, especially evident in the tradition of conducting the Passover seder at home. The seder stresses the Exodus theme of finding the homeland after a period of wandering and the differentiation of Jewish houses to avoid the plague of death for the firstborn. From this narrative basis, many advocates of Jewish family life have called for organized efforts to revive storytelling on Jewish themes, even if those stories do not derive from the Torah or the Talmud (Blu Greenberg 1983; G. R. Maisel and Shubert 2004; Zeitlin 1997). Referring to such stories as "grandmother tales," a name that suggests continuity and domestication from one generation to the next and from the old culture to the new, folklorist Steve Zeitlin brings together traditional storytellers with parents and teachers to what he calls "a mythic version of my grandmother's kitchen table" (Zeitlin 1997, 17). It was a metaphor for "family life," he wrote, or memory socially enacted, evident in this quotation from a grandmother: "A table with people. Everything I remember, the events of my life, holidays and times of grief, news from the family, all the gatherings took place here at the kitchen table" (17).

For many households, Jewish identity is most commonly enacted through "kitchen Judaism": special dinners for holidays or social occasions or the consumption of Jewish dishes as comfort or heritage foods (Joselit 1994, 171–218; Kirshenblatt-Gimblett 1990). These meals are often remembered as occasions to talk and tell stories, to eat and enact tradition, and are associated with growth and social interaction, particularly for children (Reuben 1992, 75–108). *Arthur Schwartz's Jewish Home Cooking*, for example, equates the Jewish home with "Yiddish recipes" from Eastern Europe: "Food can connect us to our past. In fact, food is often our very last and only connection to our pasts, enduring long after the old language has been forgotten and other traditions have died. There's many a Jew, for instance, who identifies as a Jew mainly through his or her love of pastrami, or potted brisket, or chicken soup with matzo balls" (Schwartz 2008, vii). Ritualization of food for ethnic maintenance at special bagel and lox breakfasts or Israeli nights with falafel joins the meaning of food as sustenance to the maintenance of cultural vitality.

The symbolism of food and food-related behavior designated as Jewish is also evident in kitchen accessories and decorative items. In the *Source for Everything Jewish* catalogue, one can purchase a soup bowl with the words "Jewish penicillin" on it (referring to the therapeutic qualities of chicken soup), a romper with "Got Bagels" embroidered on it (a play on the nationally popular "Got Milk?" campaign by the California Milk Processor Board in 1993), a matzo ball candle, a coffee cup with "No Kvetching" printed on the side, and a kitchen apron with printed Hebrew letters arranged in the form of an eye chart (Figure 2.2). In this

2.2. Jewish American woman in her kitchen showing off her Yiddish apron bought from a consumer catalogue. Photo by Simon J. Bronner.

visual culture, designers depict a style of exuberant vocal interaction in Jewish dining that is associated with the intimacy and expressiveness of the Jewish home, as made famous by the split screen in Woody Allen's *Annie Hall* (1977) showing the contrast between the sedate behavior and refined dress and table setting of diners at a suburban Protestant repast and the noisy debates, coarse table manners, and informal attire at an urban working-class Jewish meal.

The significance of food as an ethnic marker is evident in the lively modern discourse on keeping kosher as a daily reminder of the differentiation of Jews and non-Jews. Yet Jews often discuss whether following dietary rules can be divided between practices inside and outside the home, especially in stories of crypto-Jews who maintained Jewish customs in the privacy of the shuttered house (J. L. Jacobs 2002; C. Roth 1941, 178–80). Special furnishings and physical alterations are frequently necessary to create a kosher home: designating separate cabinets for dairy and meat dishes and often redesigning the layout of the kitchen to include two separate sinks, countertops, dishwashers, and stoves: one for dairy and the other for meat (Appel 1978, 248–54). A widespread home practice is to distinguish sets of meat and dairy utensils using a color scheme, such as red for meat and blue for dairy (Kosher Kitchen 2008). For observant Jews who do not have daily access to kosher butchers, another kosher home marker is the addition of a deep freezer to store kosher meats delivered from large Jewish supply centers.

Building on the concept of kitchen Judaism, it is possible to view a twenty-first development of Jewish identity that could be called living-room Judaism. If kitchen Judaism suggests that identity can be gained in the private sharing of comfort foods associated with the old country and family lineage, living-room Judaism includes displaying objects to present a contemporary Jewish face to visitors and sometimes to construct family or ethnic shrines signifying the importance of Jewish continuity (Figure 2.3). Living-room Judaism also represents a setting for conversations on Jewishness, such as book displays and television watching that invite commentary on Jewish issues and values. Sometimes these knickknacks are referred to with the Yiddish term *tchotchkes*, suggesting that, although they may be ordinary objects, their assemblage is a Jewish practice. Tchotchkes are often small trinkets, related to family or community experience, often with a working-class connotation, and are distinguished from artwork hung on the wall or placed on a pedestal that incorporates more abstracted Jewish symbols into a modernist sensibility or style.

2.3. Modernist display in a living room that includes a decorated Shabbat plate. Photo by Simon J. Bronner.

The living-room metaphor might be seen as designating a transitional space, because the living room is part of the private house but is also public, in the sense that it is reserved for receiving guests. The living room implies a self-styled sense of Jewishness because the householder arranges objects to show a cultural personality. In living-room Judaism, residents manage identity to an extent by choosing what they want to reveal of themselves, their heritage, and their faith. For Emily Haft Bloom, author of *The Good Jewish Home*, "the true beauty of being a Jew is the freedom to choose how you wish to live your life" (2006, 9). Recognizing the do-your-own-thing sensibility of arranging objects to show a Jewish profile, Bloom responds with a traditionalist message in her twenty-first-century manual, declaring that "old traditions can enrich your family's life" (9). The addition of "good" to her title suggests that expressing Jewishness in the home is not a matter of decorating the domestic environment with Jewish material as much as creating what she calls a "template for existence" with ritual observance (8). It is a message echoed in another twenty-first-century manual, *A Handbook for the Jewish Home* (2005), by Rabbi Alfred J. Kolatch, who begins with life-cycle rituals and dietary laws to show the importance of a total Jewish life lived within a household devoted to and ordered for that purpose.

Jewish home manuals, especially those prepared by male rabbis, tend to rationalize the need for advice on domestic life because of the effects of modernization, including the increased secularism and individualism that have resulted in reduced synagogue attendance. One use of ethnographic studies of Jewish culture, however, is to test whether the display and consumption of Jewish symbols is actually compensation for decreased synagogue involvement. Various social and psychological correlations can be posited for the domestic environments that people create. Suzanne Rutland (2010) points to statistics showing that Australian Jewry, as a national culture, has maintained strong ties between home and synagogue, although Jenna Weissman Joselit (1994) observed that the emphasis on kitchen Judaism and living-room Judaism in American culture was a sign of the collapse of synagogue authority.

In my fieldwork in central Pennsylvania, I found that it was typical in Jewish homes to reserve a cabinet or bookshelf in the formal dining room for displaying Jewish-themed artifacts. I hypothesize that this strategy evolved because the formal dining room, apart from the kitchen space, is associated with holiday observances and the identity of the family unit. Placed in the formal dining room, Jewish-signifying objects invoke the heritage of the family with museum-like displays. The dining room can be used for many of the activities that are typical of both kitchen and living-room Judaism, and in many Western homes it is located between the kitchen and the living room. It is a place where guests are often present, and, as well as a table, it usually contains furniture such as a breakfront designed to display objects. The display of ethnic symbols contextualizes dining as a cultural event, even if no holiday is being observed. Some objects stand out and become conversation pieces. For example, in Carl Shuman's home, it is hard to miss his dining room cabinet (Figures 2.4 and 2.5). He belongs to a Conservative synagogue in Harrisburg, Pennsylvania, and attends regularly. He does not see himself as an artist but was driven to decorate his grandparents' cabinet with reminders of his children after they departed for college. He explains that it expresses his Jewish identity in his home and honors his family lineage. At the same time, it turns conversation to his children as questions naturally arise about its design. In a modern home without a focal point such as a hearth or parlor, it centers the house materially and binds the family to its ethnic identity.

With interiors decorated by Jewish families that showcase Jewish-signifying objects, it is easy to lose sight of the exterior facades that could be characterized architecturally as Jewish. Apartment blocks constructed for Orthodox Jews in Israel have sukkah balconies (i.e., the balconies are positioned in such a way that they are not overhung). Similarly, in London and New York, ground floor extensions are constructed with roofs that open on pulleys for the same purpose, and lofts are converted into additional bedrooms so that growing families can be accommodated without having to move away from a district with established communal institutions. Historian Irwin Richman argues that the bungalows in the Catskill Mountains of New York constitute a vernacular Jewish house type adapted from the British use of the Bengali bungalow as a "low house" or summer cottage (1998, 7). He points out that they differ in shape from the mainstream American image of the Californian bungalow with sloping roofs and eaves with enclosed rafters (see Lancaster 1985). The Jewish Catskills bungalow has a rectangular floor plan and a gable roof and is set on concrete or wooden piers rather than a foundation. The builders place the entrance at the gable end, which faces the garden (Figure 2.6). A front porch leads into the kitchen, and the bedrooms are in the back. Although parlors or living rooms were added later, the traditional pattern in Catskills bungalows was to have the kitchen serve as a socializing as well as a dining space. Customarily, Jewish bungalows were painted white with green trim and were built in clusters that came to be known as colonies. The term took

2.4. Dining room cabinet inherited from Jewish immigrant grandparents and decorated with Jewish motifs by Carl Shuman, Harrisburg, Pennsylvania. Photo by Simon J. Bronner.

2.5. Kiddush cups and other Judaica displayed in Carl Shuman's dining room cabinet. Photo by Simon J. Bronner.

hold because of the image of Jewish urbanites crossing a mountainous divide to reach tight-knit settlements amid rural non-Jewish environs. Although it became a self-referential term, the Catskills bungalow negatively suggested control by stranger-settlers of an indigenous community, and the structures stood in contrast to the regional architecture of New England–derived cottages with Cape Cod and upright and wing floor plans, often with Greek Revival ornamentation (Glassie 1968, 1–153).

Oral evidence shows that Catskills bungalows were perceived by an urban, immigrant generation as summer getaway houses similar to the garden houses outside the towns of Central Europe. The Catskills, unlike other mountain resort areas, welcomed Jews, and indeed many of the Catskill original boarding houses were owned by Jewish farmers who had rooms to rent for short stays. Perhaps this is why Richman claims that linguistically "bungalow is a very Jewish word to people who grew up in the New York City Borscht Belt sphere" (1998, 8). Although the word *bungalow* entered the American Yiddish lexicon for such a Catskills structure, the Yiddish term *koch-aleins* (literally "cook-alones") was

2.6. Bungalows in Kasimow's Bungalow Colony, Monticello, New York. Photo by Simon J. Bronner.

applied to rooming houses with a community kitchen: a uniquely Jewish phenomenon. Both frame structures were recognized as Jewish from their external appearance. They are examples of domestic structures that raise questions about the materialization of Jewish ethnicity in different locations, many of which are temporary and occupied in what appears to be an alien environment (Brauch et al. 2008; P. Brown 2002; Richman 1998).

Jews in Catskill mountain bungalow colonies lived temporarily in detached or semidetached homes with gardens between them. In places such as the Caucasus mountain range between Turkey and Russia, Jews built permanent homes that were tightly adjoined to one another for protection and mutual aid, particularly during the harsh winters. Their communities constituted the Jewish quarters of cities and towns (Figure 2.7). According to ethnographer Boris Khaimovich, most houses had closed courtyards, in which a sukkah was erected from *palas* (slit-tapestry kilim) rugs. Having a courtyard in which household tasks were shared was not unusual in the material culture of the Caucasus Mountains, but Jewish homes were distinguished by a veranda across the entire width of the facade with

2.7. Jewish neighborhood in Kuba, Azerbaijan. Photo by Michael Kheifetz, courtesy of the Center for Jewish Art, Hebrew University of Jerusalem.

separate balconies at the back (Mikdash-Shamailov 2002, 125). Houses typically had two rooms, one of which was reserved exclusively for guests in a culture that emphasized the importance of hospitality (Mikdash-Shamailov 2002, 126); they did not usually have their own kitchen. Liya Mikdash-Shamailov describes various seasonal and Sabbath preparation areas in the house.

> In the summer months, the vestibule, which contained an oven, functioned as a kitchen, and in the winter, food was cooked in an oven that stood in the corner of the room. On Sabbaths, use was made of an oven that was built in an alcove in a wall of the house, in which the heat was preserved during the whole day. Each house had a storeroom that contained supplies for the winter. (Mikdash-Shamailov 2002, 126)

One factor that the graphic rendering of elevations and floor plans cannot show is the economic standing of the owners, indicated by the number of rugs, often woven by the mistress of the house in a recognizably Jewish design, and the ornamentation of the copper vessels on the shelves (Khizghilov 2002, 151–57; Mikdash-Shamailov 2002, 126–28). In Vartashen, located in present-day Azerbaijan, a localized version of the Jewish house emerged, distinguished by its combination of unworked fieldstones and rows of flat bricks. Surveying the large, striking houses, Khaimovich observed that they had a characteristic interior plan with social divisions: "three rooms on the upper floor—one for the men, a second for the women and children, and a third for guests" (2002, 67). Jewish houses boasted large stone gates with carved wooden doors covered by an awning. Jews, here as elsewhere, knew where they stood in society ethnically and economically by exterior and interior benchmarks.

FEELINGS, PRACTICES, AND PERFORMANCES

Feelings of belonging to home are evident in Jewish languages. In Yiddish, *hoiz* (house) has the sense of property, whereas *heim* (home) is frequently heard in the positive attribute of *heimische*, meaning "pleasingly familiar," "cozy," "crafted," or "old-fashioned." *Heimische* is one of those Yiddishisms that have entered both English and modern Hebrew and that Jews have claimed as their own because it appears to express Jewish qualities that the workaday language cannot. One common use of the adjective is to lovingly identify a synagogue as homey rather than institutional, suggesting the social intimacy of the home as a model for Jewish practice. Although not entering English slang, *beytee* in modern Hebrew is also instructive for its dual meaning of "my home" or "homey," whereas the house is *bayeet*, but the invocation of the Yiddish word *heimische* in Hebrew conversation tells listeners that this place is familiar as well as comfortable. It marks the domestic space as intensely Jewish because it is nurturing, implying a maternal touch on a psychological level and as belonging to "us" with a communal, non-hierarchical connotation on a social level. By its coziness, it is inwardly directed rather than being open to the public.

Proverbs associated with Jewish culture underscore the role of home as haven for Jews. In Judeo-Spanish a common saying used to refer to the intimacy of a Jewish home is *Casa mio, nido mio* (My home, my nest) (Lazar 1972, 144). In Yiddish, sayings that allude to the value of home in the context of Jews' diasporic heritage are *Umetum iz gut un der heym iz beser* (It is good everywhere, but home is better) and *Voyl iz dem vos zitst in der heym* (Good for them who stay at home) (Kumove 1984, 121). The related idea of the Jewish home as protected space is communicated in the practice of the framing large *ketubot* (illuminated wedding contracts), typically in a living room for guests to see, so as to tie the domestic space to the family, in addition to displaying hamzas.

Although decorative displays of *ketubot* and hamzas have not been quantified in Jewish community surveys, sociologists have inventoried ritual practice at home in various communities. For example, a survey of New York Jews in 2002 showed that only 17 percent attended synagogue weekly, but 53 percent lit Sabbath candles at home, 88 percent lit Hanukkah candles at home, and 92 percent attended a Passover seder, also at home (Ukeles and Miller 2004, 129). The percentages for engaging in Jewish ritual practice at home were higher than those for attending High Holy Day services (40 percent) or belonging to a synagogue (43 percent). With regard to foodways, 28 percent of New York Jews claimed to keep a kosher home, compared to a national average of 18 percent (Ukeles and Miller 2004, 129).

The large Jewish population does not make New York unusual in its practices. Data from outlying communities also reveal the significance of the home in ritual practice. According to a United Jewish Community survey of Harrisburg, Pennsylvania, whose Jewish population is less than 1 percent of that of New York's, the top marker of Jewish identity is having a mezuzah by one's house door (87 percent; Bronner 1999, 320). The percentage of those lighting Sabbath candles is far lower than in New York, at 24 percent, but participation at home in a seder and Hanukkah candle-lighting is higher, 84 and 85 percent, respectively (320).

Across the globe, Jewish homes in Cochin, India, are also distinguished by mezuzot on doorposts but are additionally identified by carved oil lamps on their facades. A hollowed stone is inserted into the front of the house and the lamp is lit on the eves of Sabbaths and holidays (Slapak 2003, 111) (Figure 2.8). Cochin Jews celebrate Hanukkah in similar numbers to American Jews, but they have ceremonies unknown in any other Jewish community. Children burn an effigy of Bagris, Antiochus's second-in-command; the effigy is made of dry grass with salt added to amplify the crackling sound of the flames (92). Socializing at home in the Cochin Jewish community is especially important; hosts provide sweets, and people sing and dance, including a special women's dance for Hanukkah in which the dancers move around a circle, singing and clapping their hands (92).

Among European countries the Swedish Jewish community surveyed by sociologist Lars Dencik is among the smallest, but it has a high level of attendance at home seders (84 percent) and Hanukkah gatherings (83.8 percent) and of lighting Sabbath candles (47.6 percent) (Dencik 2002, 89). One might posit a correlation between Orthodox affiliation and observance of home ritual practice, but Dencik found that more than one-third of the respondents declared themselves "secular Jews" (only 3 percent said they were Orthodox). Yet more than one-third of Jewish residents reported observing kashrut to some extent. Dencik's explanation is that for Swedish Jews home practices of hanging a mezuzah or keeping kosher served as "a discreet marker of Jewish belongingness" rather than a sign of religiosity (89). In the Swedish context, "hardly any Swede would know what such a small sign on the door-post signifies, if they would notice it at all, whereas all Jews are able to 'read' it as a symbol signifying that behind these walls resides a Jewish family" (89).

Cultural patterns elsewhere raise the issue of local contexts so that the role of at-homeness in Jewish culture is not overgeneralized. For example, in Moldova, formerly part of the Soviet Union, surveys found that less than one-fourth of its 25,000 Jews lit Sabbath candles and only 30 percent lit Hanukkah menorahs. Compared to other national Jewish communities in Western Europe, participation in Passover seders at home was low (40 percent) and yet the public celebration of Purim was higher (54 percent). In the statistics for Passover observance, one can surmise the effects of repression of Jewish culture during the Soviet period, but why the popularity of Purim? Whether related to the Moldovan traditions of

2.8. Jewish residences with the synagogue at the end of the street in the Jewish section of Cochin (now Kochi), India. Stone oil lamps characteristic of such residences are visible next to the doorway on the left. Photo by Martin Hürlimann (1928, 59).

animated prespring festivals such as Mărțișor, or what Malka Korazim and Esther Katz call the priority of maintaining "Jewish culture and links to other Jews" in communal ways, Jewish identity in Moldova is performed at Purim, often with a festive meal as the primary feature (Korazim and Katz 2002, 163, 170). The public celebration of Purim does not have as many ritual requirements as Passover and is made appealing by the food and drink provided by the community. A change in this pattern may have been effected by the commitment of Chabad Lubavitch to Jewish education in Moldova, including the establishment of two Jewish day schools and publication of a monthly newspaper.

Moldovan Jewish heritage is one of many regional stories that emphasize arrival after exile and departure after catastrophe. The community traces its origins to Jewish merchants who came with the Roman legions in the first century BCE, and it was significantly expanded in the fourteenth century by a wave of immigrants who had been expelled from Hungary. By the end of the nineteenth century the community had grown to 225,000, and in the city of Kishinev Jews constituted 46 percent of the population of 110,000. The infamous pogrom in the city in 1903 is often cited as a catalyst for the migration of thousands of Russian Jews to the West and to Palestine. Later, Nazi brutality in ghettos and camps during the Holocaust destroyed many Jewish communities in Moldova, and most survivors did not return. This heritage has been thematized as one of wandering in several popular historical narratives, including *Wanderings: Chaim Potok's History of the Jews* (Potok 1978) and *The Wandering Jews* (J. Roth 2001).

With the wandering experience of exile and alienation as minorities in lands that others had previously settled, Jews idealize home ownership and permanence not just as a private domain but also as a sign of arrival, even liberation, whether politically longing for a homeland or socially constructing a domestic haven free of oppression from a non-Jewish host society and free of the pressure to conform to it. This construction of home in the Jewish imagination is especially evident in Jewish literature, where the search for home, physically and emotionally, became a central theme. Literary anthologies with titles such as *Writing Our Way Home* (Solotaroff and Rapoport 1992) exemplify the trope, but more general anthologies, such as *Who We Are*, edited by Derek Rubin (2005), and *The Oxford Book of Jewish Stories*, edited by Ilan Stavans (1998), show the tension between the ethnically distinct domestic and public personas in a non-Jewish host society as a driving theme for the drama created by Jewish writers. In the literature of personal reflections on the subject, the influence of childhood memories of Jewish home practice on sustaining one's ethnic identity as an adult stands out in memoires such as *I Am Jewish*, edited by Judea Pearl and Ruth Pearl (2005), and *Stars of David* by Abigail Pogrebin (2005).

In popular entertainment, dramas with global impact from twentieth-century popular culture—Tevye of stage and screen in *Fiddler on the Roof*, adapted from the Sholem Aleichem story, and Jakie Rabinowitz in the first feature-length talkie, *The Jazz Singer*—contrast the old-fashioned parental home as the center of Jewish tradition with the exciting, if rootless and shallow, modern world zooming children away by train. They also contribute to the image of the protective Jewish mother as an anxiety-ridden defender and designer of the Jewish home in the form of a bedrock of ethnic continuity challenged by worldly lures of intermarriage and popular culture. By the end of the show, one realizes that the certainty of this tradition has been severely challenged by modernization. In the Yiddish film version of *Fiddler on the Roof*, titled *Tevye* (1939), the last daughter to marry weds a non-Jew against Tevye's wishes and returns home after being exploited in her husband's environment. In the 1971 English film version of *Fiddler*, the couple stays together and joins Tevye's family in leaving Anatevka. In the Yiddish film version Tevye longs for the homeland of Palestine, whereas in the English version the family heads off to the United States, where he will be, as he sings, a "stranger in a strange place, searching for an old familiar face." "So what's a stove? Or a house?" he asks rhetorically. His answer is given in terms of belonging and memory, for he announces that he belongs in Anatevka, "underfed, overworked Anatevka. Where else could Sabbath be so sweet?" In the successful Yiddish stage revival in New York of the show in 2018, the writers offered contemplation of different Jewish choices as Chava and her husband head to Kraków, Yente goes to Israel, and Tevye journeys to the United States.

In the 1927 film version of *The Jazz Singer* with Al Jolson, the cantor's son, Jakie, returns home as Jack Robin after becoming successful in vaudeville. He serenades his mother, who embraces him. But she barely recognizes him in his posh attire after his five-year absence, and he in turn notices that his homey childhood portrait has been replaced on the wall with a generic landscape painting. His father, the cantor, representing the world of the synagogue, enters and banishes him for turning away from his Jewish roots, and Jack retorts that he cannot live in this sheltered world. To his mind, inside the home is old, whereas outside is new. Sensing the tension, his mother implores her husband, "Look, Yosele, supper is ready, and our son is home. Come, we should eat and be happy now" (Raphaelson

1935, 52). The serene setting of the home becomes a source of conflict because of the gulf between the identities inside and outside it. The father reminds Jack that in the home he learned to sing prayers, not "dirty music from the sidewalks" (50). Successful in the theater and adored by the public, Jack exclaims that he needs his *heimische* roots. He tells his father, "Why do you think I came home? I came home because I want to have your love again—that's why. I came home because I thought I could bring together all the things in my life that are dear to me, that made me happy from the time when I was a little kid til now—singing and playing in the streets—the East Side—shooting craps—baseball—my mama—my papa—the synagogue—and now my work in the theatre" (59). Yet after his father falls ill, Jack takes his place in leading the Kol Nidrei prayer on the Day of Atonement, and as a result he gains a hybrid identity, reconciling the New World and the Old World, modernity and tradition, home and synagogue.

The intergenerational conflict theme was not just an American story but was repeated in Yiddish films, such as *Dem khazns zundyl* (The Cantor's Son, 1937), and in fiction in the historical context of worldwide emigration from oppressed shtetls to new lands where the question arose whether Jews had finally found home. *The Jazz Singer* was updated in Hollywood productions of 1952 and 1980, and its influence is apparent in autobiographies posing the question of fidelity to tradition from one generation to the next, represented by the image of the *heimische* childhood home in such works as *The Ragman's Son* by Kirk Douglas (1988), *The Peddler's Grandson* by Edward Cohen (2002), and *The Rabbi's Daughter* by Reva Mann (2007).

Although the haven of home in imaginative literature by Jews is often drenched in romantic nostalgia, its symbolism as a Jewish space within a non-Jewish culture has also been used by non-Jews to promote anti-Semitism. Representative of this kind of literature is *The Jew at Home* by Joseph Pennell (1892). "Home" in this rhetoric is not the ethnic tradition providing nurture and comfort but a shadowy den for the preservation of "their superstitious customs, their habits, and their costume with the result that they intensified all those characteristics which in the end have made them so odious and have driven the Russians to get rid of them" (Pennell 1892, 9–10). The idea that Jewish practices behind closed doors are inscrutable to non-Jews helped to sustain the belief that they were uncivilized at best and dangerous at worst. That many of their ceremonies were quietly celebrated at home raised suspicions that Jews were hiding something sinister rather than practicing their spiritual faith. Written as exposés, such journalistic voyeurism implied that public legislation insisting on conformity to Christian values should extend to private life. In the constructed dualism of Christian and Jewish that matched the division between public and private, outside and inside the home, journalists such as Pennell drew portraits of Jews with a single brushstroke. The frontispiece to the book, drawn from sketches made in 1891 in the *Illustrated London News*, shows the racialized profile of a *shtreimel*-clad man with earlocks, scraggly beard, and protruding nose, looking out of place in a modern street scene. The implication is that something about their home life keeps Jews unwilling or unable to change. Pennell's warning to his fellow Christians was to "make him an Englishman or an American, break up his old customs, his clannishness, his dirt, and his filth—or he will break you" (10). Pennell offered his "glimpses" of clannish Jewish refugees from Russia setting up a new home in Austria and Hungary to show the Jew as "he really is"—cheerless and distressed. He predicted that wherever they went, whether in Baron Hirsch's colonization project in South America or responding to the call for a homeland in Palestine, Jews would be discontent.

From a cultural studies perspective one might interpret this view of eternal Jewish homelessness and the mystery of their home life as a manifestation of Christian belief in the wandering Jew. The belief stems from a legend that, as punishment for taunting Jesus on the way to the crucifixion, a Jew, sometimes identified as Ahasver or Ahasuerus (raising comparisons with the non-Jewish Persian king in the book of Esther), is cursed to walk the earth until the Second Coming, when he will be able to return to a flourishing Jerusalem and convert to Christianity (Anderson 1965; R. I. Cohen 2008, 150; Hasan-Rokem and Dundes 1986; E. A. Rappaport 1975, 80–93). In European literature and art, the mysterious racialized figure appears anachronistic in modern settings, with his long, flowing beard, outmoded, unkempt, and meager clothes, and cane. Documenting the iconography of the wandering Jew, art historian Richard I. Cohen draws attention to the impact of French broadsheets from the late eighteenth century that jump from a depiction of Christ on his way to Calvary to a contemporary scene of the *Juif errant* being met by townspeople as he tries to enter a city (R. I. Cohen 2008, 153–55; see also Knecht 1977). The racialized Jew in these prints epitomizes an outsider, set in contrast to residents and familiar characters (such as Cupid and Christ) by his dress, skin complexion, untamed hair, walking stick as a sign of frailty, and unhinged demeanor. Rather than being in transit to a destination as a traveler, he is in a constant state of exile and vagrancy, for he cannot return to the place he would call home (Figure 2.9). The literal gulf between his past and his present is especially evident in him wandering along the shore in front of a boat with furled sails, suggesting far-flung destinations. Of cultural significance is the Jewish reinterpretation of the legend, notably in the paintings of Marc Chagall, in which the shtetl figure with sack and walking stick is in imposed exile by what Cohen calls "callous pogroms and persecution, an experience that Chagall knew all too well from his own experience, as well as his family's" (R. I. Cohen 2008, 173).

2.9. Illustration of a wandering Jew tormented by Cupid in a story by John Leech for the London periodical *Once a Week*, April 14, 1860 (p. 338).

While the male figure of Ahasuerus is portrayed roaming over land and shore, women inhabit the domestic sphere, making it into a "proper home," as the lyrics of "Tradition" in *Fiddler on the Roof* avow. The home in *Fiddler on the Roof* is fervently guarded by the Jewish mother. Historian Joyce Antler has characterized the Jewish mother from biblical tales to European fiction as a strong, determined, family-bound, and loyal matriarch, raising her children, helping to sustain the family economically, and keeping the domestic flame of Judaism alive (Antler 2007, 15; see also Joselit 1994, 68–73). The shtetl guardian and the New World matriarch are united in the Yiddish-accented figure of Molly Goldberg, who maintained a Jewish home though her children were attracted to the trappings of modern life (Joselit 1994, 197). Molly leapt onto the radio airwaves in *The Rise of the Goldbergs* (1928), for which Gertrude Berg devised her character as a "*baleboste* of the airwaves" (*baleboste* is a Yiddish expression denoting a commanding wife devoted to maintaining a well-run Jewish home), and continued on Broadway in *Me and Molly* in 1946 and on network television in *The Goldbergs* from 1949 to 1956. Even for those who did not see this prototype of the domestic situation comedy, the image of a portly *yiddishe mama* who both nurtures children and takes charge of the home, embodied in Molly, is familiar in a host of films and television series (D. Weber 2005; Zurawik 2003). Antler offers the theory that, although rooted in the imagery of Jewish matriarchs, the hovering Jewish mother became fixed in popular imagination in the twentieth century because of the modernization of the Jewish man in relation to home. In *Fiddler on the Roof* Tevye longs to study in the synagogue and stays close to home to monitor his children's Jewish education. With the move out of the shtetl and the ghetto and into the suburbs, the theory holds, the man became the peripatetic worker and absent father. According to Antler, the Jewish mother "gained status because of her husband's default; so completely engrossed in business affairs was the absentee Jewish father that he neglected spiritual and cultural matters that had once been his province. Arising to fill this vacuum, the 'new matriarchate' assumed a position of 'executive leadership' in her home" (Antler 2007, 104; see also Gordon 1959, 59–61).

By the late twentieth century a new image, the spoiled, undomesticated, materialistic daughter who did not have the experience of the Old World to teach her Jewish preservation, burst onto the scene in jokes that appeared to epitomize the independent, unmotherly, selfish Jewish girl as combining the society-wide traits of feminism and consumerism. The "Jewish American Princess" had lost interest in sex, children, home—and Judaism—even though she is identified as

Jewish. She left home along with Dad, and a subtext of jokes based on the character is the disruption of Jewish continuity as a result. Whether alluding with the princess tag to a Disney fantasy or a feminization of the "A man's home is his castle" proverb (of concern in *The Jewish Home Beautiful*), the humor has given rise to various interpretations. For folklorist Alan Dundes, non-Jewish tellers used the Jewish American Princess to talk about the ascendancy of women generally, but to Jewish listeners the barbs could draw attention to ways that the supposedly Jewish parenting style of creating home as haven had the unforeseen consequence of undoing the relevance of Jewishness (Booker 1991; Dundes 1985; Medjuck 1988). Expressed imaginatively or pejoratively, the jokes force commentary on whether the characterization is indeed a distortion or a reflection of reality (Alperin 1989; Spencer 1989).

THE DOMESTIC SPHERE AND DOMESTICATION OF IDENTITY

A key word for understanding the Jewish home is *domestic*, because it demonstrates the various meanings attached to and constructed for the home. The term represents the intersection of both the material and the emotional dimensions of the home. The domestic sphere is the sheltered living space, often associated with family, women, and children, and it therefore raises dualities that often cut across cultures: the privacy or inside of the home against the publicness or outside of the street, the leisure of living space against the work of the business world, and the reproduction of heritage in the house against the production of goods in business. *Domestic* also connotes "tame" and "constructed" as opposed to the environment that is wild or natural. The domestic can simultaneously be construed as an escape from pressure outside its walls and as a restriction within a limited space. As a spatially organized sphere of activity, the domestic has been viewed as integral to modernization, because it supplanted the understanding of family as a largely temporal organization of kinship (George 2007, 90). As the root of "domestication," *domestic* raises the question of the processes that create the culture of the home. It suggests the dualism of the home being controlled from both the outside in and the inside out. That is, domestication implies an attempt at nationalistic control, emasculation, or "taming" of subcultural activities by external forces (as in the distinction between the domestic, meaning "national," and the foreign, meaning "international"). Yet the key word of *domesticity* alludes to the creation of a private proprietary realm through arrangement and alteration that can often counter the effects of the outside world. For cultural studies scholars, who often underscore the influence of social or intellectual construction, the domestic frame materializes symbolic messages built into the placement of walls, furniture, and objects. A connotation of domesticity is that it exudes harmony and serenity, and this state is imaginatively supported, or produced, by literature, art, and other expressive forms. But cultural studies scholars often ask whether this is an illusion that reinforces social constraint.

The connection of domestication with identity borrows from cultural anthropologists, who refer to "domesticated subjects" produced in the course of European colonial expansion (Pratt 1992, 4–5; see also Cieraad 2006). According to the prevalent anthropological view of colonial encounters with non-Western cultures, a master-subject relationship is created out of the contrast between supposedly primitive, wild natives, who are close to nature and presumed to be backward, isolated, and exotic, and the artifice of civilization, which the proprietary colonizers imagine will refine and tame indigenous people. A focus of cultural conflict is the colonizers' efforts to change home life, which is out of the public eye and difficult to regulate. Cultural forms, once taken for granted in an insular society, become agencies of resistance to and maintenance of ethnic identity in the domestic sphere. The natives may indeed alter and invent traditions so as to sustain their culture, although they often need to change them from public displays to private practices. Applied to ethnic groups in modern urbanized societies, the issue becomes one of majority and minority social forces, especially when the exoticism of a minority group is viewed with ambivalence—both as enriching the diversity or spirituality of a society and polluting it or inhibiting progress. A complicating factor is the lack of access to private property by minority groups and Jews are reminded of historic prohibitions on owning land and restrictions on where they could live.

In his sociological study of the Amish in American popular imagination David Weaver-Zercher advocates the use of domestication as an analytical concept because it "holds promise for describing the ways in which twentieth-century mediators and consumers have 'produced' the Amish. Less morally charged than the notion of exploitation, the concept of domestication nonetheless acknowledges the fact that, in the process of being mediated and consumed, the Old Order Amish have also been fashioned and refashioned to function toward particular ends" (Weaver-Zercher 2001, 12–13). The picture of this tradition-centered group struggling to maintain dignity and separation in the face of tourist fascination with their culture is complicated by the Amish's own cooperation with and their resistance to their image as traditional and bucolic (Bronner 2017b; Umble and Weaver-Zercher 2008). Especially symbolic is Amish control of opening their homes for communal dinners and the development of the quilt trade as signs of appealing domesticity. Yet they have encouraged commercial development of tourist areas away from their homes to preserve the isolation of their farmlands and to keep to themselves.

The Amish invite comparisons with the Hasidim, who are also separated by their dress and their limitations placed on technology in the home (see also chapter 3). The Hasidim will use modern stoves, but laws of kashrut followed by the Hasidim dictate alterations to interiors, including separate sinks, cabinets, and cooking stations for meat and dairy uses. Exteriors have not held the same symbolic status, but folklorist Gabrielle Berlinger (2010) suggests that the meshing of domestic and religious space with an externalized sign is key for at least one Hasidic movement: Chabad Lubavitch. This group erects buildings around the world on the model of the building that served as Lubavitcher rebbe Yosef Yitzhak Schneerson's home and as his successor Menachem Mendel Schneerson's office in Brooklyn (Figure 2.10). The inclusion of synagogue, offices, and domicile within the worldly Gothic revival style, originally designed in 1920 for non-Hasidic professional use, has become symbolically transformed by Lubavitch to represent the movement's integration of life and worship. The variations of other Chabad houses around the world and the use of the image of the facade to adorn various religious containers, such as *tzedakah* boxes and mezuzah cases, also denote an outward view of spreading Judaism rather than the inward insularity of other Hasidic courts. The distinctive Lubavitch practice of sending *shluchim*, or emissaries, often to remote locations, to promote Hasidism epitomizes this outward view, which draws on the inspiration of the urban village of Crown Heights in Brooklyn.

Berlinger notes the extension of spiritual significance from house of worship to home, and this symbolic transference is evident among both the Amish and the Hasidim, although the Hasidim have made more of a point of attaching religious importance to domestic objects. The Amish have resisted bringing media technology into the home, but Chabad Lubavitch will allow restricted use of the Internet and video equipment if it meets a religious purpose. The double consciousness implied by awareness of both long-standing Jewish tradition

2.10. Gothic Revival exterior at 770 Eastern Parkway, Brooklyn, New York, the world headquarters of the Chabad Lubavitch Hasidic movement. The building originally served as the home of Rabbi Yosef Yitzhak Schneerson, and his son-in-law and successor Menachem Mendel Schneerson, as leader of Chabad Lubavitch, had an office in the building.

and changeful mass-mediated culture is put into context by recent reexaminations of the definition of Jewish culture. Articulated by Jonathan Webber in his "Notes Towards the Definition of 'Jewish Culture' in Contemporary Europe," the modernity of Jewish culture contains two major contradictory assumptions: "One is that it is 'under construction' (in the postmodern sense); the other is that it already exists, and it is merely the task of the individual or the community to serve it up, promote it, and develop it" (Webber 2002, 320). It is not coincidental that Jenna Weismann Joselit's constructivist critique in *Wonders of America* is a result of her locating Jewishness in the home, where she notices contemporary trends to imbue it with designer artifacts and invented rituals.

Arguably, the dominant cultural narrative of Judaism as a tradition centered in the synagogue and rabbinic thought is the reason for the relative paucity of materials on Jewish home life. Neither of the standard reference works, *Encyclopedia Judaica* or the *Jewish Encyclopedia*, has entries on "house" or "home." What studies there are of the Jewish home are more likely to be found in literary bookshelves than in the architectural library. A remaining agenda is to represent different and often overlapping approaches to the material and emotional dimensions, both narrated and built. The task is to grasp the emotional dimension of home by describing everyday life and interpreting cultural practices, to bring out broader questions of the social and material aspects of the domestic sphere and the process of domestication and identity formation. Nonetheless, contemporary ethnographies and folklore collections focused on home are different from surveys, which often concentrate on peasant or exoticized settlements, such as the famed An-sky ethnographic expedition to the Jewish Pale of Settlement of 1912–1914, which followed the ethnological norm of seeking historical survivals and relics rather than interpreting contemporary practices (Gonen 1994; see my discussion in chapter 4). Often conducted *in* homes, interviews by ethnographers and folklorists have not generally been *about* at-homeness, although the scholarly concern since the 1960s for contextual explanations and the differentiation between folk culture and that generated by the mass media has produced a wave of work on ethnography "at home" (D. Miller 2001). Another development in the study of the home is an awareness that popular culture can influence public perceptions, even if it does not express realities. That is why many writers discuss the image of the Jewish home in such popular films and television shows as *Annie Hall* (1977) or *The Goldbergs* (premiering 2013).

Laura Levitt (1997), a feminist scholar who stresses the importance of home as a locus of Judaism, speculates that the rising use of domestic space for Jewish ritual has become more pressing as women increasingly step into analytical roles once reserved for men studying sacred texts. Levitt is especially concerned that feminist approaches restore the mother and children into the architectural conceptualization of the Jewish house, discussion of which has previously emphasized the construction of and provision for the house by men. She asks whether the feminist task is to disrupt the cultural assumption of women's place in the home or to analyze their influence outside it. Amy K. Milligan (2019a) picks up this theme by pointing out the connection of being outside the home with the maleness of worship movements, such as davening, and Jewish bodily adornment, including the wearing of tefillin, tallit, *kittel*, and tzitzit. She argues for the symbolic shift toward egalitarianism, when women take on the body practices of men. Yet she asserts that few Jewish men have adapted rituals traditionally ascribed to Jewish women's bodies in the home.

The two dimensions of home for Jews—physical and metaphysical—are integrally related because they structure social presence. Whether secure in one's house or feeling comfortable as a Jew in a country, invoking home is a way of saying that one's place in the present cannot be denied. In sum, the house as residence is a place to lay one's head, but home as an idea represents belonging (Kirschenbaum 1972, 158). Taking the vantage of the home and applying the concept of domestication, scholars can revise understanding of the lived and built past, and open new analytic possibilities for the future. The matter of domestic culture and its relevance to Jewish identity is one with which we should feel at home.

MEDIA, MEDIATION, AND JEWISH COMMUNITY

In this chapter, I grapple with the common assumption that, with each advancement in communication technology, media-driven popular culture has weakened ethnic-religious ties of community and has been especially detrimental to tradition-centered groups such as Orthodox Jews. Popular culture theorists have long asserted that the very notion of "popular" works against the survival of ethnic-religious groups who are socially interacting in locally bounded areas (Nye 1970, 6). Russel Nye, a leader in this school of thought, asserted that the idea of popular culture, associated with urbanization and industrialization, depends on artists and agents who exploit media and create cultural standards. He proclaimed that, to create for a mass audience made possible by communication technology, "the popular artists cannot take into consideration the individualities and preferences of minority groups." Nye explained that "since the popular arts aim at the largest common denominator, they tend to standardize at the median level of majority expectation" and that the objective of standardization typically cut out marginalized Jewish urban enclaves in the Diaspora (6).

Nye theorized that the process of popularization depends on a mass audience that consumes secularized cultural expressions, which became accessible in Western societies through communication media on a national and even global scale after the eighteenth century. To establish this audience, composed of strangers to one another, institutions and industries often function in the areas of entertainment to convince a populace, whose primary social frame of reference is the localized face-to-face community, that benefits accrue from consumption and communication through mass media rather than through localized, often oral conduits. These promised benefits might include more individual freedom and mobility coupled with diminished control by an elite class or local religious authorities. The advent of popular culture purportedly diminishes the need for public space and peer pressure, because consumers can make private choices about what and when information is consumed. Brokers for popular culture imply that the embrace of mass market products is progressive, in the sense of fostering change in the future by erasing the hold of elders and emphasizing imaginative, trendy options for gratifying the individualistic desires of urbanizing, modernizing youth. Whereas tradition holds that members of groups should follow practices and guidelines of the past, monitored by elders and conceptualized as "culturalism," texts and trends of popular culture generated by youth often emphasize breaks with tradition and community, in pursuit of determining one's own future path. In the Jewish liturgy, emphasis on continuity and community is expressed as *l'dor v'dor* (generation to generation) in the Kedushah (third blessing of the Shemoneh-Esrei prayer) and is extracted frequently as a guiding ethical saying in Judaism. Many Jewish community centers and synagogues also use the maxim "Do not separate yourself from the community," attributed to Hillel in the mishnaic tractate *Pirkei Avot* (Ethics of the Fathers).

The pitch to consumers to think and act globally and break from the past was not an easy sell. Conflicts among supposedly progressive and conservative factions arose in tradition-centered communities with the popularization of magazines, phonographs, and photography in the nineteenth century and particularly with cinema, radio, and television in the twentieth century. Considering the discussion in chapter 2 on *The Jazz Singer* (1927) and *Fiddler on the Roof* (1964) in the context of dualities of the Jewish home, I return here to these pivotal texts, familiar internationally in popular culture, and add comparative analysis of related Jewish content in the context of the process of mediation for Yiddish films, productions based on the diary of Anne Frank, and uses of Frank's image in memes.

I begin with *The Jazz Singer* because it stands as perhaps the most prominent historic symbol in film of a perceived conflict between accepting popular culture with assimilation or remaining loyal to tradition and Jewish ethnic community. Before its release, the Warner Brothers studio, which produced the movie, was associated with adventure films with decidedly nonethnic themes, featuring

Rin Tin Tin, "the famous police dog" (Hoberman and Shandler 2003, 78). Jews were not common characters in popular films up to that point, and when they did appear, they were usually unflattering characters from well-known literary adaptations, such as Dickens's *Oliver Twist* and Shakespeare's *Merchant of Venice* (L. D. Friedman 1987, 17).

Edison Studios, which dominated the film industry in the early twentieth century, was outright hostile to Jews as subjects, filmmakers, and cultural brokers. When Edison's white Protestant producers featured Jews, they intended to demean them to a popular Christian audience and to reinforce the image of a white Protestant majority at the heart of popular culture. As film historians Harry M. Benshoff and Sean Griffin point out, Edison Studios "featured grotesque stereotypes of Jews as hunchbacked, hook-nosed, and greedy cheats. Such subhuman depictions, found in films like *Levitsky's Insurance Policy* (1903) and *Cohen's Advertising Scheme* (1904), presented an image of Jews as money-grubbing and untrustworthy" (Benshoff and Griffin 2011, 65–66). One response to these depictions, Benshoff and Griffin surmise, was the creation of films made by and for Jews, particularly in urbanized ethnic neighborhoods, where immigrant Jews began breaking religious taboos on partaking in popular entertainment. Indeed, some cultural historians, such as R. Laurence Moore, counter Nye's account of immigrants swayed to a Christian-produced version of popular culture by arguing that urban entertainment was a "non-Protestant and ethnic working class accomplishment" (R. L. Moore 1994, 202). Religious historian Mark Massa defines the "ethnic working class" as primarily composed of Catholics and Jews who relocated during the global Great Wave of immigration between 1880 and 1920: "Catholics were far less important in crafting the twentieth-century mass-culture vision than second- and third-generation American Jews" (Massa 2004, 114; see also Buhle and Pekar 2007, ix; Schmalzbauer 2010, 259–60). A purported Jewish goal was to deracialize depictions of Jews, by characterizing them as ordinary citizens able to blend into mass society rather than by distinguishing and hence marginalizing them by depicting repulsive bodily features, clannish residence or vagrancy, and old-fashioned, even cultish dress. Yet in recasting or simply omitting their image through the media, assimilating Jews arguably lost their ethnic visibility and participation in a multicultural politics. According to many cultural critics, Jews hid or denied their ethnic or community identities in the name of subverting embodied stereotypes in popular culture (Brodkin 1999; Fingeroth 2007; Pearse 2008, 2014; Zurawik 2003).

The association of Jews with popular culture largely derives from their conspicuous involvement as producers in the early movie industry in the United States. Film critic Neal Gabler's best-selling book, *An Empire of Their Own: How the Jews Invented Hollywood* (1988), and the spinoff film documentary written and directed by Simcha Jacobivici (1998), drew attention not so much for its claim that the culture industry of Hollywood owed its existence to first- and second-generation Jewish entrepreneurs but more to the psychological interpretation that they were motivated by their alienation as Jews and immigrants. According to this view, Jewish studio moguls, in their quest to join the mainstream, created movies that, by appealing to the nonethnic "largest common denominator," in Nye's words, proclaimed their inclusion in society and endorsed assimilation. Yet at the same time, non-Hollywood Jewish producers sent out messages of ethnic persistence in silent films with Yiddish intertitles, such as *Mizrekh un Mayrev* (East and West, 1923), directed by the prolific Odessa-born Sidney Goldin (Samuel Goldstein) and featuring the budding Jewish star Molly Picon, who attracted young Jews in places such as the Lower East Side of New York City, despite religious prohibitions on moviegoing. Other metropolises with major Jewish districts in London, Paris, and Berlin gave rise to Jewish theaters that often spilled over into popular culture, but it was the Lower East Side that came to represent the Jewish imagination in the popular culture of the early twentieth century. Social historian Hasia Diner writes in her study of the Lower East Side in American memory that "pictures—moving ones—linked the immigrant Jews all over America and in eastern Europe through the neighborhood as a spatial icon" (Diner 2000, 144). She points out that films with their obligatory background shot of bustling street life forged a "constantly recycling diaspora culture" (144) because they played across North America to immigrant audiences and went back to Eastern Europe.

In addition to culturally connecting Jews across continents, the films contributed to what Diner calls "a cinematographic element to the inner Jewish debate" (Diner 2000, 145) about defining one's Jewish identity through a separatist religious community. The Yiddish New York films suggested the possibility of a cultural identity in a new urban maelstrom where people lived comfortably in an ethnically mixed social environment and retained continuity through Jewish cultural expressions of literature, drama, music, and food rather than through traditional dress and worship. According to literary historian Donald Weber, Jewish-made movies of this era "depict the combustible reaction of street versus home, English versus Yiddish (or 'potato Yiddish,' as the less than perfect rhetoric of *shund* [trashy] theater was derisively styled), of 'civilized' America and the nation's linguistically mongrel future. Out of that exhilarating encounter much popular culture in America was forged" (D. Weber 2003, 131).

Diner asserts the significance of popular culture arising out of and symbolized by the Lower East Side: "In that imaginary world made by the movies and other cultural products America emerged as a liberating land of opportunity yet one that shook the foundations of communal and familial coherence" (Diner 2000, 145). Flocking to theaters was the main source of entertainment for working-class Jewish immigrants in urban locales. The movies were more than cultural products in their ethnic language; they also had the psychological function of anticipating the future. Although many of the films were sympathetic to the bonds of heritage in the Old World, they typically showed America as a place to break the hold of ancient and apparently superstitious customs. Based on recollections of immigrant commentaries on the allure of ethnic stage and screen, Weber concludes that "audiences watched their deepest anxieties and desires literally enacted, displayed before their eyes" (D. Weber 2003, 131). Moviegoers tended to see the transitions to America and the apparently strange ways of popular culture as difficult—but inevitable. Thus for Jewish viewers the source of production and the setting in America advanced acceptance of popular culture as future-oriented and a sign of social progress.

With most public attention focused on culture industries of the United States, one should not overlook developments in other countries that were tied to creative endeavors of Jews, though not always successfully. Renowned Jewish artists, such as the director Ernst Lubitsch, worked for the major German production company Universum Film-Aktien Gesellschaft (UFA) before coming to the United States. Moreover, a long list of Jewish songwriters produced *Schlager* music (later this term became a loan word in other languages for a musical hit), and Jewish composers and cabaret singers populated the urban scenes of Berlin and Vienna in the 1920s and 1930s. Some of them—including the actor Kurt Gerron and the legendary comedian and cabaret artist Fritz Grünbaum— were murdered in German concentration camps. Others were able to escape to the United States or other countries and resume their careers. A prominent figure representing this transnational experience who affected the development of popular culture in both the United States and Germany is the composer Robert Gilbert (Robert David Winterfeld), who was one of the composers of the 1931 operetta *The White Horse Inn* (*Im weißen Rössl*). As a musical comedy, the show enjoyed international success with long runs in London, Paris, Vienna, and New York. Nazi officials denounced Gilbert's works and prohibited use of the material by other Jewish writers and composers. Gilbert managed to emigrate to New York, where he failed to find employment in English-speaking Broadway theaters. He continued to write in German, influenced by the "big revues, chorus lines, and dancing troupes" of Broadway musical comedy (Schlör 2014a, 2014b).

Gilbert connected to an émigré artist community through the publication *Aufbau*, founded by the German-Jewish Club in 1934 in New York. In that circle, he befriended and was influenced by writer Hannah Arendt, poet Heinrich Blücher, and composer Hermann Leopoldi (Schlör 2014b). Some of his Jewish countrymen, such as his former composer partner Werner Richard Heymann, went across the country to Hollywood to compose music for the studios (Heymann's musical film credits include *Ninotchka* [1939] and *To Be or Not to Be* [1942] under the direction of another German-Jewish émigré, Ernst Lubitsch; see Schlör 2016). Gilbert's lyrics for *The White Horse Inn* did not have explicitly Jewish content, but they reflected the show's theme of ethnic-class conflict between a privileged urban gentry and rural folk that results in a happy ending of a triple marriage representing social conciliation. Gilbert returned to Europe in 1951 (the same year that Heymann returned), where, according to cultural historian Joachim Schlör, "he came to play an important (yet forgotten) role in the translation and transfer of American popular culture to Europe" (Schlör 2014a). Gilbert was welcomed into the reviving postwar theater and film industry in Munich, where a German-language film version of *The White Horse Inn* (1952) was produced along with *The Forester's Daughter* (1952), which featured compositions by Gilbert. Revivals of the stage production of *White Horse Inn* continued to be popular throughout the 1950s and 1960s, and a new film version was released in 2013 as *Im weißen Rössl—Wehe Du singst!*

To be sure, the imaginary and real connection between Jews and the media was mostly located in the Los Angeles area, identified by the generic reference to Hollywood, because immigration to New York sharply declined during the 1920s with U.S. governmental efforts to stem the tide of East European Jews, among other racialized groups from Southern and Eastern Europe. Movies in the early twentieth century, as the main, technologically advanced popular entertainment (especially historically in the transition from neighborhood theater), sparked conversation—and debate—about the sustainability of Jewish community and tradition in a popular culture world generated out of or largely modeled on the creative industries of the United States (J. Barth 1982, 192–228). Because the finances and social capital to produce movies and television shows developed in different centers around the world, often with the intention of creating a distinctive popular culture within global regions and ethnic diasporas, textual and contextual analyses of language and performances in media productions involve not only aesthetic judgments but also cultural and political considerations. Thus German, Polish, and Russian productions of films on the Jewish experience are often couched within Holocaust histories and the relative absence of Jews in the present (Dorchain and Wonnenberg 2013; Gershenson 2008; Prawer 2007; Stradomski 1989). And when productions are adapted or distributed to new locations, commentaries often look for social and political reasons for changes. The popular Israeli television series *Srugim* (2008–2012) was the first to focus on religious nationalists in the Katamon neighborhood of Jerusalem, nicknamed "the swamp" for its dense population of unmarried religious Jews hoping to find spouses (S. Weiss 2016, 69). The title of the show refers to the crocheted skullcaps commonly worn by men in this group. When distributed to American audiences, who could watch it on the streaming services of Amazon Prime and Hulu, commentaries from Jews noted the connection of other Modern Orthodox communities to the dilemmas of young adults negotiating modernity and tradition. Non-Jews posted reactions that tended to overlook issues of community and nationalism and focused more on the love plot of religiously motivated young people. They interpreted the glimpse provided of this community as somehow representing Israeli daily life (S. Weiss 2016, 81–84).

Taken together, the different ways in which messages work with the media to convey ideas, embody values, and persuade audiences can be summarized as *discourse*. Often, scholarly analysis of discourse hinges on the use of keywords and the formation of stylized rhetoric, both verbal and visual, and their performance. Moving beyond linguistics into cultural studies, scholars frequently point to the contexts of texts, defining them broadly to include events, images, objects, and landscapes (Edwards 2017). A prominent model evident in the study of media productions with Jewish themes identifies the signs by which Jews and non-Jews identify or misidentify Jewishness. In addition, responses of individuals to media—in conversations on the street, in the home, in published reviews, and more recently in digital social media—indicate the perceived meanings of texts and the framing of figurative words or images as meaningful or iconic. Ultimately, the analysis leads to social and cultural perspectives on identity and the way that heritage is enacted in everyday life and informs a sense of self and community (Machin and Mayr 2015; Strauss and Feiz 2013). According to cultural historian Alan Trachtenberg, such heritage discourses are significant because they can determine behavior and affect social and political life as well as economic issues of production and consumption. They are "vehicles of self-knowledge, of the concepts upon which people act. They are also, especially in the public domain, forces in their own right, often coloring perceptions in a certain way even against all evidence. At the same time, figurative representations occupy the same social world as other forces, material and political" (A. Trachtenberg 1982, 8). In the Jewish world, discourse analysis is complicated further by representations in different ethnic-regional dialects and cultural products with esoteric audiences in mind and by the use of languages and images known widely in the host society. Symbolic readings are also made of ethnic keywords and images that enter into the popular domain, often acquiring new or multiple meanings when they do, such as chutzpah, bagels and lox, delis, and red string bracelets (Balinska 2008; Bronner 2008, 4–10; Merwin 2015; Teman 2008).

To demonstrate the analytical approach of discourse in popular culture, one can consider how a media production such as *The Jazz Singer* lifted the ethnic-religious symbol of singing Kol Nidrei at the beginning of the evening service of Yom Kippur into public consciousness. The play *Day of Atonement* by Samson Raphaelson, on which the movie *The Jazz Singer* is based, had a successful run on Broadway in 1926, but most film studios, leery of producing a movie perceived by the theatrical press to be a "Hebrew play," were not anxious to put the story on the screen (Hoberman and Shandler 2003, 78). Indeed, the reviewer for the *New York Herald Tribune* worried that the play would be unintelligible to non-Jewish audiences, largely on the basis of the esoteric knowledge of the significance of Kol Nidrei, an Aramaic declaration performed in the synagogue. The theater critic, noting a predominantly Jewish audience at the show, thought the play required an unusual "understanding of and sympathy with the Jew and his faith" (78).

The Warner Brothers studio, upon the advice of contract director Ernst Lubitsch, took a chance and bought the movie rights to *The Day of Atonement* with the idea of broadening the appeal with a new title that related to the popular culture phenomenon of jazz. Lubitsch related to the drama as a German-born son of a Russian Jewish tailor who was expected to continue in his father's business but instead left his family and home for the theater. The Warner (originally Wonsal) brothers consisted of Harry, Albert, Jack, and Sam, the Polish-born sons of a Jewish shoemaker. Sam was the first to venture into the film industry, after seeing Edison's *The Great Train Robbery* (1903), a short western. He was directly involved in the production of *The Jazz Singer*, although 25-year-old Daryl F. Zanuck, raised a Protestant in Wahoo, Nebraska, was given producer credits. Like the protagonist in *The Jazz Singer*, who has a love affair outside his faith after entering the entertainment industry, Sam married *Ziegfeld Follies* performer Lina Basquette, an American-born Catholic, much to the chagrin of the Warner family.

The background of the making of *The Jazz Singer* has been well covered by film historians, but the focus of Jewish cultural studies is the social and psychological processes by which cultural brokers and creative agents *encode* persuasive messages affecting public attitudes, patterns, and audiences and communities *decode* the production of media with broader, often political, ramifications. On a technological and organizational level, global histories credit the Warner Brothers production of *The Jazz Singer* with changing the film industry and heightening the international impact of motion pictures. Although the movie opened in only two theaters in 1927, less than a year later it was showing in 235 movie houses, resulting in the death of the silent film but not triggering a wave of big-studio-produced, ethnically themed films. According to film historian Ron Hutchinson, "an entire industry had reinvented itself more completely . . . than any industry in the world" (Hutchinson 1996). Yet Jolson's next role for Warner Brothers, in *The Singing Fool* (1928), while commercially successful, did not dwell on his Jewish background. The Warners' first all-talking full-length feature, *Lights of New York*, also produced in 1928, was an urban crime drama that, although set largely in New York, did not showcase Jewish content.

Working within a historical context, cultural critics usually point to Jolson's ethnic role as a breakthrough for Jews in the media. The film acknowledged a conflict between ethnic community and popular culture, threatening to displace centuries of tradition, but allowed that they could coexist. Did audiences view and hear it that way, especially because the 1920s ushered in a period of intolerance toward immigrants and minorities as well as youthful post–World War I enthusiasm for technological advancements (radio, phonograph, electrification) and modernization (Hing 2004, 62–70; Murphy 1964)? Cultural studies can illuminate the ethical and political message of *The Jazz Singer* and the way audiences decoded it in the midst of legislative measures to curb immigration and white Protestant efforts to establish a national culture in their image. The centrally conflicted figure in the movie is Jakie Rabinowitz, played by Al Jolson, a cantor's son growing up in an Orthodox Jewish household in New York. The cantor expects Jakie to continue the family tradition of singing in the synagogue. Jakie's father is horrified when he learns that instead Jakie is singing popular music in a club, and his father tries to suppress this worldly interest by beating him, which prompts the boy to leave home to pursue a secular stage career with the new music sweeping the land. In the modern fashion and demeanor he dons, Jakie appears transformed and his Jewishness appears to be lost in the process. Playwright Samson Raphaelson, who came from a New York Jewish family, cited a concert by Al Jolson that he thought sounded "cantorial" as the inspiration in glitzy California for his writing the play on which Jewish screenwriter Alfred A. Cohn in Los Angeles based his screenplay (Raphaelson 2003).

Al Jolson was born Asa Yoelson in Kovno, the son of a rabbi-cantor in present-day Lithuania. The children and mother immigrated to Washington, D.C., in 1894 to join Rabbi Yoelson, who had found cantorial work there. Asa's mother died in 1895, and to help with the family's finances, Asa found work in the local circus and sang popular songs, before moving on to neighborhood burlesque theaters. By the end of the first decade of the twentieth century, local theaters were being affected by the introduction of nickelodeons and, later, movies. Under the Anglicized name Al Jolson, the cantor's son made the transition to Broadway theater and movies, before embarking on *The Jazz Singer*. These roles did not invoke his Jewish background; in fact, Jolson became known for using blackface to frame Southern plantation songs that involved melodramatic performances and would not have been appropriate in restrained popular songs. Cultural critic Jan Stratton interprets these performances as aligning Jolson with rather than separating him from dominant American and, more generally, English-speaking understandings of race. By donning an African American costume, Jolson visualized himself as on the fringes of whiteness and became renowned for performance of the popularized, de-ethnicized "torch song" rather than as a racialized Jew singing in accented English (Stratton 2009, 13; see also Musser 2011; Rogin 1996; Romeyn 2008, 187–212; Whitfield 2008). As a fixture of popular culture and lacking visible public ties to the Jewish community, by the 1930s Jolson had issued 80 hit records and organized 16 national and international tours, making him the country's most famous and highest paid entertainer.

In *The Jazz Singer* Jolson, as the popular entertainer Jack Robin, returns after a five-year absence to visit his loving mother, who is still living in the traditional neighborhood. She barely recognizes him in his posh attire after the hiatus, and he in turn notices that his childhood portrait has been replaced with a generic landscape painting. In a scene that has synchronized sound, he shows her on the piano the difference between a mundane rendition of "Blue Skies" (composed by Irving Berlin in 1926) and a jazzed-up, or modernized, version. It is a core scene, translated into a sentimentalized image on the main poster for the movie (Figure 3.1). The choice of the song is undoubtedly symbolic; the recording from 1927 by Ben Selvin's Orchestra topped record charts (record Columbia 860-D). Both Selvin and Irving Berlin came from Russian Jewish backgrounds and were well known in American popular culture. The singer cheerily repeats the chorus line of "Blue skies smiling on me" to express his happiness at being in love, but in the context of the film he appears to use it to point to the freedom, upward aspiration, and unlimited possibilities outside the dark, traditional home, in the modern world characterized by popular culture. The song's sunny lyrics contrast with the father's entrance and order to stop playing "dirty music from the sidewalks" (Raphaelson 1935, 50). The cantor chides his son from turning away from his Jewish roots as Jakie, and the son, as the Anglicized Jack, retorts that he cannot live in this closed, sheltered world. To Jack's mind, inside the home is old and dark, whereas outside is new and bright. The father reminds his son that in the home he had meaning in his life, by learning to sing prayers and carry on the legacy of many generations.

However, after the cantor falls ill, Jack takes his father's role in leading the Kol Nidrei prayer on the Day of Atonement. Besides signifying the sacredness of the holiday in Judaism and atoning for past sins, the particular chant of Kol Nidrei represents the folk community, because of its inclusion in the liturgy by local custom rather than rabbinic authority (Benovitz 1998; Deshen 1979; Gershon 1994; Prosic 2007; Reik 1931, 167–219). Jack's return to his religious-ethnic roots and community does not signal an abandonment of the outside popular world that he had previously embraced, however. One encoded message is that Jews could strategically situate their identity privately rather than treat Jewish culture as a total experience paraded publicly. In the course of everyday life, Jack integrates into a secularized mass society and navigates freely with the cultural capital he has attained. On special occasions, he could return to his community for an intensive dose of tradition. Arguably, this reassuring mass-mediated message was more for a nativist American audience who felt that national culture was threatened by physically and religiously alien Jewish immigrants and who were worried particularly

3.1. Poster for *The Jazz Singer* (1927), showing Al Jolson, as Jack Robin, serenading his mother. The scene in the movie features Jolson playing a tame and jazzy version of "Blue Skies," composed by Irving Berlin.

about the possibilities of romantic ties between Christians and Jews, as depicted in the film.

George Jessel, who originally had been asked to play the role of Jack Robin, rebuffed the appeasing meaning of the story by telling his Jewish fans in 1928, "Since I owe my success in great measure to the Jewish public, and the Jewish public expects me to be loyal to it, I could not sincerely do the picture" (Jessel 1928; Merwin 2006, 119). Yet Jessel appeared in the original stage production, and, in films predating *The Jazz Singer*, he played another Old World Jewish character, Isadore Goldberg, who becomes acculturated to an Irish neighborhood and takes the name of Patrick Murphy, which helps him to prosper economically. When he develops an Irish romantic interest and his Jewishness is revealed, though, the Irish family objects (L. D. Friedman 1987, 106–8). Although the "Izzy Murphy" series of movies sends out a message about problems stemming from interethnic prejudices and stereotypes, it also values the Irish and Jewish immigrant communities as sharing nurturing, socially intimate qualities that will probably be lost in a modernizing society. The New York–born Jessel never let go of his Jewish persona in life or stage; he was associated throughout his life with Jewish characters in his stage and screen roles. He also recounted a father-son conflict regarding his life in the entertainment industry; his father opposed his work on the stage, and it was only after the father died that Jessel began his show business career.

In the Yiddish film *Dem khazns zundyl* (The Cantor's Son, 1937), Moishe Oysher plays Saul "Shloimele" Reichman, who leaves his rural Polish shtetl for New York's crowded, bustling Lower East Side and finds fame in the theater. Like Jolson, Oysher was born to a cantorial family in the old Russian Empire and immigrated to the United States, but he was more connected than Jolson with the Jewish community, as a practicing cantor and Yiddish theater actor. In the movie Reichman is drawn back to the shtetl for his parents' golden anniversary and ultimately chooses to stay within the nourishing environment of his family and his childhood sweetheart. In answer to "Blue Skies," Oysher, who in real life claimed to be the sixth generation in a line of cantors, sings "Mayn Shtetele Beltz" as he approaches the familiar village. In this song, composed specifically for the film by Alexander Olshanetsky and Jacob Jacobs, the we-ness of the shtetl is fondly recalled: "Beltz, my little town! My little town where I had so many fine dreams!" The diminutive suffix *-leh* added to the word *shtetl* not only marks its modest size but acts also as an expression of endearment. Eleven words in three verses carry the diminutive tag. In the final verse the singer couples *alt* (old) with *shtibl* (a little synagogue), implying that by being small, it is more sociable and loving. The Jewish marker of the Sabbath undergirds the specialness of the community. The song continues, "Every *shabbes* I would run to the river bank to play with other children under a little green tree," evoking the natural and idyllic life in the shtetl. Whereas the dank interior of the home in the *Jazz Singer* appears stagnant and unchanging, in contrast to the futuristic "blue skies," the image of the tree answers this charge with an organic life-cycle icon. Even if Jews decided to choose an assimilative path or not as a result of watching these films, they became profoundly aware, beyond the plot lines of romance and father-son conflicts, of larger themes about the fragile role of the Jewish community, often set against the power of media to normalize nationalist discourse.

Emanating from this example of brokered popular culture that drew attention to the Jewish situation as emblematic of both wider ethnic dilemmas and particularly the Jewish urban experience are questions about the impact of noncinematic media in other periods and places in the modern era. In focusing on the effects of popular culture in connecting and uncoupling Jewish social networks, primarily in urban environments, I am not diminishing the dramas of identity for Jews in small-town life, agricultural settlements, and Jewish "frontiers," such as regions in the Diaspora not usually identified with Jewish settlement. I caution against assuming that these locations have necessarily receded and are unaffected by popular culture. A number of scholars are concerned with their adaptation to media to enable Jewish lifestyles in new and changing areas for Jewish residence (see Gilman 2003; Libo and Howe 1984; Milligan 2014; Morawska 1996; Weissbach 2015). An example is the reliance on regional conventions and, increasingly, social media among international Jewish youth organizations devoted to "community service" and "identity development," such as the B'nai B'rith Youth Organization (BBYO) and United Synagogue Youth (USY), to give a sense of belonging to a coherent unit to youths from smaller communities (BBYO 2008). A cultural studies query investigates the kinds of relationships that arise through media in these and other Jewish community organizations and the way that outlooks on Jewish life are consequently affected. One can also inquire about ways that media productions not only *reflect* issues and narratives of the Jewish community and a mobile, multicultural society at large, but also *shape* actions and *project* anxieties, conflicts, and emotions. In the remainder of this chapter, I offer a guide to cultural processes that I consider analytically important to the ongoing negotiation or mediation of popular culture and its connection to modernity and Jewish community and to folk tradition.

TECHNOLOGY AND MEDIATION

The example of films in my previous discussion draws attention to the technology and the content of media arising in the twentieth century and their contribution to the creation of a mass society on the one hand and their effect on tradition-centered Jewish communities on the other. Writers often use the term *mediation* beyond its literal meaning of arbitration to refer to the signal, even interventionist, role of media in the way that people receive and communicate ideas in a mass society (R. Bauman 2010; Bel et al. 2005; Kember and Zylinska 2015). *Mediation* also refers to the push to advance media technology as a sign of progress and modernization. In this concept of technological mediation, emphasis is placed on devices that not only offer speed of communication but also socially and psychologically emphasize novelty, privacy, and self-actualization for individuals navigating in a mass society of strangers. In a mass-mediated society, individuals gain status for possessing the latest gadget that promises wider and instantaneous communication (Kiran 2015; Morley 2005: 212; Verbeek 2005). The modernization of such equipment is often exaggerated by a discourse in advertising and entertainment that ridicules the old-fashioned ways of community groups. Early in commercial phonograph recording, for example, a string of records featured sketches such as "Cohen on the Telephone," laughing at the difficulty experienced by Jews who spoke English with an othered ethnic or foreign accent when using popular technology such as the telephone (R. Bauman 2010; Merwin 2006, 24). The comic bit was first recorded in July 1913 by Joe Hayman in London for Regal Records and then released in the United States by Columbia Records. It reportedly sold 2 million copies and led to other performers, such as Monroe Silver, taking on the persona in various media (Murrells 1978, 10). For cultural critic Ted Merwin, the character's technological difficulties symbolized the "continuing perceptions of Jews as ethnic and racial outsiders" (Merwin 2006, 24), even as they became more visible outside their old enclaved communities.

To be sure, Jewish learning symbolically derives from a manual rather than mediated source: the Torah. A specially trained scribe (*sofer* in Hebrew) prepares Torah scrolls by hand. The scrolls are read aloud in the public religious space of the synagogue. The *sofer* prepares other documents of Jewish ritual practice, such as mezuzot (small parchment scrolls bearing biblical texts affixed to the doorposts) and tefillin (phylacteries used in daily prayer). These objects thus connect Jews by the symbolism of the hand in personal, small-scale contact, handing down or handing over knowledge in oral tradition (and the Oral Law) and their manual means of production. Reverence is given to the oral recitation of the Torah, and festivals such as Passover involve storytelling and singing that symbolically represent passing down traditions from elders to youngsters in small groups.

The synagogue has traditionally been a place to worship without media, especially on Shabbat, in keeping with the interpretation of the fifth commandment: "Remember the Sabbath day, to keep it holy" (Exodus 20:8). In the nineteenth century rabbis drew a line between prohibited mechanical media, such as magazines and photographs representing work, and potentially profane entertainment from the outside world and in the sanctuary, and acceptable printed books with religious material. With the growth of congregations, many synagogues added amplification systems in the mid-twentieth century, and a number of Reform and Conservative synagogues added screens to project prayer texts during services. In the twenty-first century some synagogues have gone further by live-streaming services with the justification of reaching homebound and institutionalized congregants. The use of and debate about media in the sanctuary accelerated during the global public health emergency caused by the coronavirus pandemic in 2020, when shelter-in-place orders forced congregations to decide whether to use Zoom and other platforms to broadcast interactional religious ceremonies from remote locations (Feldman 2020; Lavallee 2020). Orthodox synagogue leaders have mostly proscribed electronic devices in the sanctuary and on Shabbat, but a grassroots movement has arisen among some youth in the Modern Orthodox community who keep what they call half-Shabbos. They use personal devices to communicate through instant messaging and social media because of their view that digital practice constitutes communal socialization rather than *malakhah*, or "work" (Younger 2013). Indeed, a folklore has developed among Jewish youths with its own digital shorthand, such as "gd Shbs" for "good Shabbos" (Lipman 2011). The Jewish press reports opposition to this trend, which has been characterized as an "open secret in their schools and social circles." Some rabbis, while insisting that electronics are off-limits on the Sabbath, suggest that the problem is the dangerous addiction of youth to personal devices that makes it difficult to make the transition to the ritualistic restrictions and the shalom, or peaceful, out-of-time spirit of Shabbat. Yet some pious teenagers argue that texting uses a low level of electricity, and they avow that, just as religious books are allowed, using technology for religious purposes is not shameful (Lipman 2011).

Although ultra-Orthodox leaders have been known to denounce the use of smartphones and the Internet altogether, in recognition of their pervasiveness as a work tool they have accepted use of a "kosher" smartphone, modified in a way that controls the content, to restrict mediation by popular culture. Such phones are often accompanied by a certificate issued by a rabbi, attesting to the modifications. For example, the Google search engine is deactivated, and on some phones, even the ability to make and receive calls has been turned off; secular news and recreational sites are blocked. Digital banking, satellite navigation, and religious reading are allowed. The Haredim have a Rabbinic Committee for Matters of Communications that issues guidelines on the use of media (Jeffay 2013; see also Y. Cohen 2011). One issue has been limitations on the popular mobile application WhatsApp, which allows transnational communication, appealing to many ultra-Orthodox families and to business executives (Figure 3.2). Founder Jan Koum, a Jewish immigrant to the United States from Ukraine, was influenced

3.2. Averimi Wingut, co-founder of the Kama Tech start-up accelerator in Bnei Brak, Israel, displays his modified "kosher" smartphone, pointing to its black WhatsApp icon (bottom right corner), which indicates that the app cannot transfer or display images or participate in group chats. His company also produces an "ultra-Kosher cellphone" without Internet access. Photo by Nir Alon; Alamy Stock Photo.

by government surveillance in the former Soviet Union to design a communication tool that does not collect personal information (Reuters 2014). One "kosher" response has been to block transmission of images and disable group chats, in order to encourage community ties and privilege voice-to-voice connections.

In the Reform and Conservative movements, questions about using e-readers in the synagogue on Shabbat have arisen because of their similarity to books. Critics worry that the devices will tempt users to surf the Internet, represent the action of work in pushing buttons and turning pages, and constitute a prohibited *toledat kotev* (a derivative form of writing that is prohibited on the Sabbath) in the spiritual sanctuary; they are also concerned that these devices will simply distract congregants from worship (Boorstein 2013; U. Friedman 2010; Holzel 2013). Proponents answer with the need to use communication technology to attract youth, whose popular culture in the digital age of the twenty-first century is based on the screen rather than the printed page (Holzel 2013). Although many rabbis insist on keeping a wall of separation between popular culture and the premodern sanctuary of the synagogue, in the face of declining numbers of attendees at services, some innovative rabbis have invited congregants to use social media to interact as a religious community during worship. For instance, Rabbi Paul Kipnes of Los Angeles received a Techie award from the Union of Reform Judaism for making sermons interactive by inviting congregants to respond to the sermon. A Facebook page, Twitter handle, and mobile phone number appear on an enormous screen near the bimah, or central platform (A. Lewis 2012). In Miami Beach's Temple Beth Sholom, a Reform synagogue surrounded by reminders of hedonistic pleasure in a popular vacation destination, Rabbi Amy Morrison provides an alternative worship service for Jews in their 20s, attracted, she observes, by the temptations of the popular culture world. In a nod to the participatory, democratized nature of digital communication, she announces from the bimah that "texting will give you a voice in the service." She was willing to diminish her rabbinic authority to have her congregants socially as well as electronically connected (Alvarez 2012). An example is during the Mi Sheberakh, or healing, prayers, in which congregants who previously had been hesitant to announce the names of their ailing loved ones actively participated when the rabbi asked congregants to text names of those in need of prayer (Alvarez 2012).

In the same year that Morrison introduced the texting into her services, an audience of 42,000 *haredi* Jewish men rallied in Citi Field Stadium in Queens, New York, to hear warnings from rabbis of the dangers of the Internet to their families and societies and to receive admonishments to remove it from their homes. Mediation was evident, however, as another 20,000 Haredim crowded into nearby Arthur Ashe Stadium to watch on closed-circuit television screens and thousands more watched on satellite broadcasts in Jerusalem, Bnei Brak, London, and Antwerp (Ettinger 2012).

Although Satmar and Bobover Hasidic leaders steadfastly resist use of social media to get their message out to their followers, Chabad Lubavitch has a conspicuous Internet presence in emphasizing its global network (Shandler 2009, 230–74). Its website, Chabad.org, is also the title of its Facebook and Instagram accounts; it additionally has a smartphone app. The organization provides links to more than 15,000 videos on the website Jewish.tv, and the phone app includes over 3,000 videos on the life and teachings of the rebbe, Menachem Mendel Schneerson. In response to the question "Is the Internet evil?" Moshe Goldman on Chabad.org answers, "The status of every object is determined by the way it is used," and he notes that the Internet is "peerless in its ability to disseminate Torah information and values" (M. Goldman 2017; on religious use of earlier media technology, see Poll [1962, 228–30]). In keeping with the movement's emphasis on *shluchim* (emissaries who educate Jews about religious piety and Lubavitch worldwide), Goldman asserts that the Internet helps reach isolated Jews and youth on college campuses. Nevertheless, he requires the use of filters to restrict access to profane aspects of the Internet and to ensure limited use of the medium for work. Chabad encourages unmediated social gatherings at their centers, such as "Hakhel" meetings, named after the biblically mandated practice of holding assemblies in the Temple in Jerusalem every seven years. Chabad leaders describe them as a "a true celebration of Jewish community," owing to their face-to-face reinforcement of camaraderie and unity (Posner 2016).

A major challenge to the dividing line that many Jewish religious leaders placed between the unmediated sanctuary and the world around it was the COVID-19 pandemic in 2020. Particularly hard hit were Hasidic communities because of their emphasis on large ritual gatherings in urban spaces (Stack 2020). Whereas many Jewish community centers, along with Reform and Conservative congregations, canceled Purim celebrations in March 2020, ultra-Orthodox groups encouraged the festivals to go forward to maintain cultural continuity. As stay-at-home orders took hold during the spring of 2020, Reform and Conservative congregations quickly shifted beyond live-streaming to interactional Zoom broadcasts with no congregation members present. Many Orthodox rabbis held the line on virtual services but, in compliance with quarantine regulations, encouraged prayer at home. Chabad.org issued a statement that prayer via webcam could be considered only for weekday services but not on Shabbat and major Jewish holidays (Davidson 2020).

A central argument in whether to use media during the public health emergency was the interpretation of the minyan, consisting of ten adults who, according to the *Shulchan Aruch* (Code of Jewish Law), are gathered "in one place." The leading Israeli *rosh yeshiva*, Rabbi Eliezer Melamed, countered that the minimum requirement is for the adults to see each other (*Shulchan Aruch, Hayyim* 55:13–14) and that the optics of videoconferences count as viewing other people. The spirit of gathering as community, this position holds, is evident with mediation. Baruch Davidson (2020), writing for Chabad, was skeptical that a webcam image could replace a physical presence. He contended in legalistic terms that the original Hebrew phrasing of the talmudic text *bei asarah* (*Sanhedrin* 39a) literally translates as "a house of ten," implying that ten men must share an actual physical space.

The COVID-19 outbreak restricted Passover observances in April 2020, and many Jewish families resorted to videoconferencing platforms to simulate the traditional large social scene if they were not willing to narrow the meal to the nuclear family. Orthodox religious law normally bans electronic devices on festivals, but a 14-member panel of Sephardic rabbis in Israel produced a *posek*, or ruling, that videoconferencing was permissible to connect elderly relatives to their families because a health emergency existed and devices could help sick and older adults to assuage loneliness (Jeffay 2020). Israel's chief rabbis, however, advised that, though it was allowable to have a videoconference before the start of the holiday, electronics would desecrate the observance and therefore should not be operated (Bachner 2020; Lavallee 2020). The rabbinic prohibition notwithstanding, large numbers of Jews all over the world, out of sociocultural needs, organized virtual seders anyway to observe the holiday in quarantine. I participated in three of them, and a meta-discourse erupted at all of them on the meaning and significance of gathering virtually. The consensus was that, although videoconferencing did not displace the in-person experience of sharing the meal, reading together, and singing in unison, the mediation was especially important for a diasporic group like Jews, even if it tended to secularize the proceedings or limit socialized ritual engagement. At the events I attended, participants were in far-flung locations across many time zones in Israel, Europe, and North America (Figure 3.3). The content of the seders changed to accommodate the videoconferencing medium. The readings were condensed, the proceedings and dress became more casual, and synchronization with the meal was suspended. Indeed, I heard commentary on missing the sensual experience of dining together, and kibitzing (informal talk with a neighbor) around the ritualized table. Several participants expressed the view that when it came time in the virtual seder to drink wine, it felt like "drinking alone." The comment veiled an anxiety about being isolated as a Jew in locations where they did not feel socially connected to a Jewish community or have material reminders of public Jewishness.

Key elements that remained in the virtual seder were the recital of the Four Questions by the youngest child as a performance, and as one might expect, nervous humor surrounding and emphasis on the dipping of a finger in a cup of wine to represent the ten plagues. Hosts, usually the more observant of the groups, consistently invited participants to use the gallery view rather than a central shot of the seder leader to gain a sense of groupness (see Figure 3.3). The hosts hoped that being able to see everyone at once would foster singing in unison, but the effort could not be maintained. I could detect Zoom fatigue as side conversations at the different home screens ensued and remote participants

3.3. Screen shot showing the communicative and visual structure of a virtual seder connecting relatives during the COVID-19 pandemic. The observant Jewish hosts who prepared a Passover table were in Israel (second row from top, second from left), and others were in living rooms and offices. The participants were located in Israel, Europe, and the United States. One couple used a background of the Egyptian pyramids in line with the Exodus story. During the seder, participants wrote messages in the chat sidebar. Photo by Jonathan Gleich.

became easily distracted. At the end of the ritual portion, the discussion turned toward whether the videoconferencing would become a permanent fixture of holiday observance in the post-COVID era. The response was mixed, as many felt that the whole point of the holiday was to gather together in someone's home and connect as Jews and families in typically heterogeneous communities. Another view was that videoconferencing would be a permanent, if not preferred, tool for connection of Jews more so than other groups because of their diasporic spread.

My take on virtual seders is that a certain separation occurred between the media event of the seder to situate one's identity socially in family and culture and the religious observance and the spiritual experience it provides. Virtual seders during the pandemic also invited comparisons with other holidays that have outdoor customs, such as Purim and Lag b'Omer, and the consequent limitations of the media to replicating them online (Loschak 2020; Reich 2020). And I noticed increased use of the virtual meeting format to maintain interaction among community members, such as pre-Shabbat "gatherings" (avoiding the more bureaucratic term *meeting*) via videoconferencing, even by Chabad and other Orthodox leaders. Many Jewish leaders seemed to realize that the medium could enhance the oral traditional connections of community. As one Orthodox rabbi expressed at one gathering I attended during the pandemic, "I didn't realize how much I missed talking." He then posed the question to others of what they missed, and most cited the unmediated in-person social connection "in one place."

Analysts of mediation interpret the way that mechanical and electronic technologies shape the relations between humans, their communities, and their world. Researchers question how interventionist, democratizing, or deluding this process is, in which information is curated and distributed widely by faceless brokers representing the behemoth figure of "the media." Many cultural studies scholars credit the concept of mediation to translations of German Jewish philosopher Walter Benjamin's essay "The Work of Art in the Age of Mechanical Reproduction," originally published in German in 1935 (J. Lewis 2002, 92; W. J. T. Mitchell and Hansen 2010, 11). Benjamin addressed the social ramifications of industrially produced paintings on posters and prints and undoubtedly had in mind the mass production of artful propaganda posters that often took images out of their original context and used them to speak an overarching, master narrative.

In the churches and monasteries of the Middle Ages and at the princely courts up to the end of the eighteenth century, a collective reception of paintings did not occur simultaneously, but by graduated and hierarchized *mediation*. The change that has come about is an expression of the particular conflict in which painting was implicated by the mechanical reproducibility of paintings. Although paintings began to be publicly exhibited in galleries and salons, there was no way for the masses to organize and control themselves in their reception. (Benjamin 2007, 235; emphasis added)

In the original German, Benjamin used the adjective *vermittelt* (mediated) to describe art and to point out that all art is mediated but that changes in technological reproduction have altered the way in which art is encountered and deciphered.

Benjamin continued to compare this experience to film, which he saw as having a dual significance because of its technological advancement over the photograph and "the manner in which, by means of this apparatus, man can represent his environment" (Benjamin 2007, 235). He identified a modern age characterized by media devoted to mechanical reproduction on a mass scale that obviated the need to view the original object or congregate together in localized community. In addition, he theorized that moderns lived segregated lives in which they experienced the world primarily through media and that their worldviews were affected through narratives implied or explicitly broadcast in images.

These observations led to claims by cultural critics of the disturbing extent of individuals' alienation, and limitations on community resistance. Although Benjamin was concerned about the danger of authoritarian and nationalistic appropriations of media, the concept of mediation suggested that the interpretation of information for a consuming public was negotiated between public and private interests rather than imposed on a society. A case in point is the popular mediation of Sholem Aleichem's *Tevye der Milkhiker* (Tevye the Dairyman, 1894) into *Fiddler on the Roof*, first as a Broadway play (1964) and then a movie (1971), in the midst of an American ethnic revival during the 1960s and 1970s (Figure 3.4). Tevye, living in a shtetl in the Russian Empire, grudgingly accepts social changes as his daughters choose spouses, but he digs in his heels when Chava wants to marry outside their faith and community. For American audiences during this tumultuous period, the struggles of the interfaith couple for acceptance implied the need for integration and tolerance as a break with traditional social divisions of the past. The American translation of "tradition" on the stage was to be faithful

3.4. Men dancing together as women watch on the other side of a barrier at the traditional Jewish wedding of Tzeitel and Motel from the film *Fiddler on the Roof* (1971). The scene early in the movie is crucial to the theme of tradition's hold on Jewish heritage because Perchik, the teacher with revolutionary political leanings, steps over the rope to dance with Tevye's daughter Hodel. Ronald Grant Archive; Alamy Stock Photo.

to one's ethnic identity while joining in a diverse, progressive society. Whereas the Broadway play allows the interfaith couple to reconcile with Tevye and his family, the earlier Yiddish-language dramatic play *Tevye der Milkhiker* (1919) and the movie *Tevye* (1939), viewed primarily in Jewish neighborhoods, would have none of that. The distraught Chava, abused by her husband's non-Jewish family, abandons the unhappy union and begs forgiveness from her father.

Another difference between *Fiddler on the Roof* and the Yiddish production on which it was based is the explanation for Tevye's departure from his home. In the Yiddish movie the non-Jewish town council invidiously orders him out. In the play, the culprit is the state, represented by the police loyal to the tsar. To the American producers of *Fiddler on the Roof*, the anti-authoritarian theme must have appeared easier to swallow for post–World War II audiences than representation of the inherent vindictiveness of Christian neighbors. In the Yiddish-language play and movie, Tevye makes a choice in response to expulsion. Rather than remain in place waiting for the Messiah, he takes the initiative to go to the Holy Land so that he can live a traditional life basic to his beliefs (Wolitz 1988). But in *Fiddler on the Roof* his destination is the United States, and what he will face there is uncertain and worrying because of the implicit break with tradition and community. It is an omen of further pressures from modernization on community that his wife berates the children, "Stop that! Behave yourself! We're not in America yet!" In the last line, Tevye, who has already capitulated to his children's pressures to accept change, turns to the younger generation and quietly commands, "Come, children. Let's go," as though he knows that his Old World ties of the shtetl and its representation of community are lost forever (Bronner 1998, 35).

In applying the idea that popular culture is more likely to be mediated than folk or elite processes—that is, produced and channeled through media—cultural critics have noted that the romanticized images of the shtetl in the movie have come to represent Jewish Old World experience, as well as the roots of Western Jewish cultural values, even though many scholars have pointed out the limited and often misrepresented picture of diverse Jewish communities that these images present (S. T. Katz 2007; Polonsky 2005; Shandler 2014). The significance of this issue of representation relates to its social and psychological effects on individuals: Do non-Jews view Jews differently as a result of this representation, and conversely, do Jews view themselves in a light they did not before? As a further result, do attitudes toward heritage shift—perhaps, as some critics have claimed, from a focus on sustaining religion to a cultural connection to roots in the Eastern European Jewish experience (Estraikh and Krutikov 2000; Miron 2000)?

Many interpretative approaches in Jewish cultural studies contrast representations in media with reality, but to get answers to these questions, analysts explore the way in which mediation is a process of blurring boundaries between imaginative simulations and social reality. Following the ideas of French philosopher Jean Baudrillard, cultural critics often cite theme parks and futuristic urban environments as simulations of reality using popularized images (taken together as an "imaginary") that signify their own social world with a distinctive ideology, forming what Baudrillard called a simulacrum (Baudrillard 1994; A. A. Berger 2016; Kline 2016; M. W. Smith 2001). Baudrillard was especially taken with the power of Disneyland to produce a global popular culture that can be experienced outside as well as inside its confined space. Disneyland's Main Street, the primary gateway to its parks in Florida and California, in addition to Paris and Tokyo, is both a representation of an imagined pleasant past and a future devoid of ethnic communities. It projects a utopian mass reality based on a unified racial and environmental profile (Baudrillard 1994, 12–14).

Irus Braverman (2013) suggests that this model of constructing mediated space is evident for Jewish nationalistic, if not communal, purposes in Jerusalem's Biblical Zoo (officially titled the Tisch Family Zoological Gardens). It began in 1940 as a small children's zoo in the middle of a *haredi* neighborhood, with a religious mission to reenact animal scenes from the Bible. Relocating to larger sites, the zoo declared a conservationist purpose by invoking the symbolism of Noah's Ark. The zoo has evolved to become a top tourist destination in Israel with approximately 1 million visitors annually. It has been estimated that a third of its visitors come from *haredi* and Palestinian communities in Israel, and zoo directors point to the site as a "cosmopolitan" multicultural location for coexistence (Braverman 2013, 134–35). Ethnographers, however, have viewed it as an "intrinsically Jewish space, continuously substantiating the land's own identity" by eternalizing the biblical past in an understanding of the need for a Jewish national home (Braverman 2013, 137–38; El-Haj 2001, 18; see also Zerubavel 1995).

One issue that has generated commentaries on differences in the processes of mediation with different technologies is whether such environments result from the influence of the media (such as thrill rides based on popular movies and television) or constitute media themselves, by immersing audiences in a sight and sound experience of an eternalized past. In *Understanding Media* (1964), Marshall McLuhan famously labels films a "hot" medium because viewers do not exert effort to fill in the details of a movie image. He categorizes television as "cool" and potentially more capable of culture change because it requires more effort by the viewer to determine meaning. Critics have found this bifurcation simplistic but have built on McLuhan's questioning of the medium by which texts and images are broadcast as a message in itself (A. Jacobs 2011). McLuhan theorized that television would displace community programming in the United States because of the national broadcasting networks, in contrast to the regional reach of radio and the emphasis on the local area in print culture. Yet the availability of cable and satellite broadcasting has made possible channels devoted to ethnic-linguistic and special interest groups, including the Jewish Channel and Jewish Life Television. Nonetheless, advocates for media pluralism argue that these corporately owned channels force viewers into passive positions rather than encouraging them to be interactive and activist (Gray 2005). In the twenty-first century many Jewish organizations have launched Jewish film festivals to draw attention to the use of media to convey ethnic-religious issues that are lost in mainstream commercial productions (Figure 3.5). The festivals, often aimed at Jewish audiences while being public events, also imply a nonreligious identity of Jews; this identity is based on shared cultural rather than spiritual interests and arguably arose in the post–World War II era with the rise of television and suburbanization (Rocker 2015). Many adherents to a Jewish cultural rather than religious identity claim it as a result of immersion in popular culture, with visual representations of expansive, flexible Jewishness in film, television, and art. The move to a cultural identity can especially be discerned on the Internet, often hailed as a triumphant evolution from the "ghetto mentality" of secluded enclaves, based on oral tradition, to liberating image or visual culture (Bronner 2011a, 398–450; Rosen 2005).

The Internet is often imagined as the ultimate global, socially equalizing, and potentially homogenizing medium (Zukin 2005, 227–52). Developers hailed the

3.5. Carol Kane (left) in conversation with Jewish film-maker Aviva Kempner at the Washington Jewish Film Festival, in Silver Spring, Maryland, following a 40th anniversary screening of *Hester Street* (1975), based on Abraham Cahan's novella *Yekl: A Tale of the New York Ghetto* (1896). Kane received an Academy Award nomination for best actress for playing the role of Gitl, a Jewish immigrant who has trouble assimilating to life in New York. Photo by Ron Sacs, DPA Picture Alliance; Alamy Stock Photo.

Internet as vast and open and ultimately democratizing because it simultaneously allows users to produce and consume and therefore accords them more economic clout, as well as social power to shape the medium (Ritzer and Jurgenson 2010). The Internet also is perceived differently from other media needing professional production, because of the assumption that communication is instantaneous, participatory, and indeed placeless out in cyberspace. With the medium being portable and highly individualized, some critics worry that it portends the end of public space for community gathering and communication (Karppinen 2013; Nie and Erbring 2000; Sennett 2012). Although giving the primary impression that it goes beyond the capabilities of print, radio, and television to reach a global audience, the Internet also has facilitated small-scale "online communities" and simulated "chat rooms" for many individuals who do not have access to "real" ethnic spaces (Foster 1996; Norris 2004). It is possible with social media to localize as well as globalize these spaces by delimiting and even mapping members logged in within a geographic area. For the Jewish world, Ari Kelman finds that "the internet has given both younger and more marginal voices a platform for speaking, broadcasting, organizing, and creating their own communities while still participating in larger communal conversations" (Kelman 2010, 78; see also Golan 2015; L. Roth 2015, 204–6). The question is whether users shape the Internet as a pluralistic medium or are swayed by either corporate forces or the nature of the technology to become part of a homogeneous, de-ethnicized society.

Radio and arguably newspapers have a more localized connotation, as is evident in the framing of "Jewish media," such as the Yiddish-language *Jewish Daily Forward* newspaper and WEVD radio station in New York, as community outlets. The two are related because the newspaper appropriated the radio station in 1932, after it had been launched in 1927 by the Socialist Party of America. Many accounts of listening to the radio station are filled with nostalgia for a sense of *Yiddishkeit* coming over the airwaves to sets placed in cozy kitchens. With the slogan of "The station that speaks *your* language," WEVD identified itself as an ethnic radio enterprise with the aim of spreading progressive ideas to a Jewish audience. However, with a sharp decline in the number of Yiddish speakers and the rise of mass-market radio programming, in 1981 the Forward Association sold the station to Salem Media Group, a national corporation that changed the format to Christian content (Kelman 2009, 95–107). The *Jewish Daily Forward* survived by transforming into a Yiddish biweekly and English weekly print edition and by maintaining an online presence (Manor 2009). With many Yiddish readers coming from tradition-centered Hasidic communities, new Yiddish newspapers have arisen to represent local concerns. Nineteenth-century Hasidic leaders usually frowned on newspaper reading, but because the twentieth-century moral line prohibited the viewing of television and films, newspapers became more important as a medium of communication in Hasidic neighborhoods (Greenbaum 2010).

ANALOG AND DIGITAL CULTURE

With the advent of computer-assisted communication in the 1990s, cultural studies scholars posited a division of media into analog and digital technologies, with cultural ramifications (Maley 2011). It was possible to differentiate between analog and digital computational devices: Analog technology relied on continuous representations that approximated the source. Promoters touted digital devices as providing perfect, discrete representations (Haugeland 1981). One noticeable difference between digital and analog devices, however, was the tendency of digital devices to combine transmission that had previously demanded separate gadgets. Smartphones, for instance, included capabilities for video, photographic, audio, and textual broadcasting in a process that media studies scholar Henry Jenkins called "convergence culture" (2006). This not only portends a risk of information overload in need of curating by media-savvy agents, who flex their "cultural capital" to direct attention to a variety of online identities, including Jewish networks, but also blurs the lines between sender and receiver, documenter and subject, or in entertainment, performer and audience (Zukin 2005, 227–52). The instantaneity of the Internet seems to encapsulate and document the world in "real time." News, as it is transmitted instantly to a global or local audience, calls for popular response, often in the form of comments visualized as message threads that suggest the need to weave them into a coherent text, as in "textile" (Blank 2013; R. Frank 2011; Sagan and Leighton 2010).

Electronic transmission by means of the Internet raises questions about the kind of cultural practice on digital equipment that constitutes social engagement. The association of generations and periods with technology, such as the computer age and the iPod generation, implies that lives are structured by the technology that people own and use. These labels communicate that users harness tools for individualistic purposes; users are digital selectors, in that they can create multiple personas suited for different web events. People materialize digital power in everyday life by hanging equipment on belts, reminiscent of empowering gun holsters, by opening laptop lids like lifting a treasure chest lid or using a secret spy code unit, and by being called with disruptive sound effects, such as an attention-grabbing siren, that show off the importance of the devices. Whereas going to the mailbox by one's house is an occasional, labored activity, or what computer geeks derisively call going to get snail mail, the cyberculture instantaneous experience of checking and receiving mail is constant and intrusive, especially when engaging in instant messaging, with a rhetoric suggesting instant gratification. Accumulating messages and correspondents is valued. A challenge of this enlarged, atomized amount of information in digital communication is finding and virtually crafting connection.

Being disembodied in digital communication allows for role playing, speech play, visual representation, bricolage, and sometimes anonymity and supports elaboration of the self—and connection to a group—through expressive material. The frame requires some boundaries to manage risks in communication, and although limitations are policed and legislated, a regulatory tradition of folk law has arisen that governs transgressions, voiced in the slang of trolling, flaming, snarking, lurking, spamming, phishing, socking, and thread bumping (Millard 1997; Stivale 1997). In other words, the Internet opens up investigation not just of the texts it produces but of the behaviors it spawns that draw attention to themselves as repeatable *practice*, related to logging on, and that rhetorically become ingrained into culture as *praxis*—representations for generalizable action such as networking and connecting (Bernstein 1971; Bronner 1988, 2012, 2019; S. Johnson 1999; Lavazzi 2001).

One digital age practice that carries symbolic attributes of praxis is blogging, that is, self-publishing texts known as posts on a personal diary-style website. Blogging has been important in the Jewish world because it provides personal testimonies about Judaism as a lived religion and about feelings, or identities, of Jewishness in a mass society. Religious studies scholar Andrea Lieber noted the use of blogging by Orthodox Jewish women, often at the risk of censure by rabbis. She found that these women, who gained a wide audience for their prosaic accounts of apparently mundane activities, blogged "to overcome feelings of isolation and frustration with their lives and their communities" (Lieber 2010, 266). Rather than constituting feminist rebels, the bloggers, with aliases such as Fancy Schmancy Anxiety Maven, Chayyei Sarah, and Aidel Maidel, according to Lieber, sought social connection for support, even if some followers decoded their self-expression as a call for liberation of women from their communities.

Lieber suggests that, considering the psychology of digital communication in the context of their decidedly analog, tradition-oriented society, the blogging Orthodox women were "motivated by a therapeutic need through previously unavailable means to 'talk through' their internal conflicts in their writing and seek support from sympathetic readers" (266). The women who she interviewed constructed a virtual Jewish community of their own, a *veibershul* (Yiddish: literally, a married women's synagogue and, idiomatically, a religious women's gathering space outside the home). Lieber credits the blogosphere of the Internet for making this networking possible for isolated pious women. According to Lieber, in their "talk, without fear of judgment" (277), the everyday lives of the women are politicized, although politics is not consciously motivating them to blog (see also Grinspan 2005). Lieber suggests, however, that the traditionally observant women mask a political dimension in order to embrace, or even Judaize, the digital medium.

Talk of an all-encompassing digital age and digital culture constructs a binary with analog culture that merits closer scrutiny. In this binary, which privileges the advancement of digitization, a number of structural oppositions are implied between digital and analog: large-small, new-old, artificial-natural, formal-informal, electronic-manual, and discontinuous-continuous. The implication of this rhetoric is that thinking has shifted as the technology and culture have changed. Emblematic of the digital-analog difference is the clock. The analog version is understood by the positions of the hands on a dial that makes reference to the natural occurrence of lines and shadows formed by the sun and read by relative positions. *O'clock* thus signifies the position of an observer in the center with 12 o'clock considered straight ahead. The digital clock takes the observer out of the equation. Time is represented in exact numbers or language and can be received anywhere and in any form. Its display is continuous and does not represent position as much as a code. Analog is considered more interpersonal and tactile, because it can be equated with the process of sensation, which can be perceived directly (Gregory 1970, 162–66; Stewart and Bennett 1991, 24–29). Digital is conceived as artificial and visual and usually is depicted in alphanumeric symbols or icons framed in mechanistic rectangles in contrast to analog's naturalistic circles.

Digital comes from the Latin *digitus*, "finger," suggesting discrete counting, converting real-world information into binary numeric form. Analog contains reference to the Greek *logos*, "philosophizing meaning," which comes from the related senses of the word as "word" (or "say") and "reason"; an analog is an item in relative position to another. Further, the definitional strategy of holding up the face-to-face group and environmental context as vital to community shows analog thinking, because it is relational, emphasizing the immediacy and fragmentation of the social event or performance; use of automation in new technology, including the Internet, is digital, because it refers to placeless, faceless, aggregate data (see Bronner 2011a, 398–450; Bronner 2016; Dégh 1994; Drout 2006; Köstlin and Shrake 1997; Koven 2000). Analog culture, often attributed to the touch-oriented world of tradition, especially in premodern society, derives its meaning from sensory aspects of perception (Stewart and Bennett 1991, 28–32; Bronner 2013). Cultural practices are circumscribed rather than delineated. People derive significance from face-to-face encounters, because their appearance, what they do, and how they do it convey an encircled, functional reality (Stewart and Bennett 1991, 29). Thus storytelling in analog culture is an event defined not just by a text but by a physical setting and the perceptions between tellers and audience (Georges 1969; Oring 2008).

Digital culture emphasizes the representations of reality and the outcomes of messages. Thus digital culture may seem to connect more people, but it derives meaning less from social relationships and appearances than from textual similarities. Arguably, in an analog context, meaning is attached to immediately perceived events within a small group; it is more sensitive to the natural, immediate social context. Analog privileges the sturdy ground of solid turf, whereas digital values the outgushing action of fluid surf. Both analog and digital culture are capable of producing tradition through expression, but they may perceive it differently. Analog culture might be said to be relational and localized, with a high degree of sensitivity to experience, context, emotions, relationships, and status—within place. Digital culture relies on analytical, inductive thinking that transforms observable events into informational pieces linked in causal chains and categorized into universal criteria (Stewart and Bennett 1991, 41–42; R. A. Cohen 1969, 841–42; Jones 1971). The misplaced perception that the Internet is devoid of culture is a relational, evolutionary outlook, in which digital equals machinery that replaces the human capacity to emote and embody. Viewed operationally or analytically, however, digital culture, as represented by the Internet, is replete with construction and assemblage of multilayered messages into virtual, rather than natural, reality. One of those constructions is the binary itself, with the presumption that digital is preferred because it is more efficient and more cerebral than physical, leading to a certain illusion that the digital world is culture-free.

Viewing the Internet as daily practice rather than special performance raises the question of whether it structures perceptions outside users' awareness. This line of inquiry includes positing folk belief systems about Internet usage and its supposed global reach, classlessness, democratization, and gender neutrality (see Poster 2001; Wallace 1999). Expressed beliefs about the Internet are not always consistent. In the rhetoric of transmission, the Internet is frequently characterized in terms of its mass globalization and acquisitive individualism as well as its freedom and collectivity, even by its most avid or addicted fans. One can look for cultural expectations when logging on that affect the kind of traditions created online. Often negotiating between the expansiveness suggested by being on a *worldwide* web and a desire for more intimate social connections, users operating as secluded individuals often acquire online personas on different sites that accord identities, or simulations of them.

A prominent example of mediated social connection for Jews is the utility and "spreadability" of JDate, an online Jewish dating service, within a massifying digital society (Jenkins et al. 2013; Kelman 2010) (Figure 3.6). Founded in 1997 by Jewish digital media entrepreneur Yoav Shapira as a niche dating site modeled on Match.com, JDate announced its service as "the modern shidduch" (Yiddish: arranged marriage) intended "to strengthen the Jewish community and ensure Jewish traditions are sustained for generations to come" (JDate 2017). The emphasis on community continues with CEO David Siminoff's claim that JDate's success owes to "word-of-mouth" in "small [Jewish] communities" (OPW Interview 2006). The founders imagined that the site would be appealing to Jews looking for mates outside their immediate social circles or to Jews disconnected from Jewish networks (Hill 2013). As the site grew, however, non-Jews could also join, but they needed to indicate whether they were willing to convert. Reportedly, they were attracted by stereotypes of Jews as wealthy, kind, and family-minded (Hill 2013). Members could also state whether they sought heterosexual or homosexual relationships. By 2014 JDate boasted a roster of 750,000 active users per year and estimated that 20 percent of all single Jewish adults in the world had used JDate in a given year (Glassenberg 2014). Jewish civic leaders who had concentrated their efforts on communal institutions, such as Jewish summer camps and community centers, lauded the site for reversing trends toward intermarriage and loss of Jewish continuity (Glassenberg 2014).

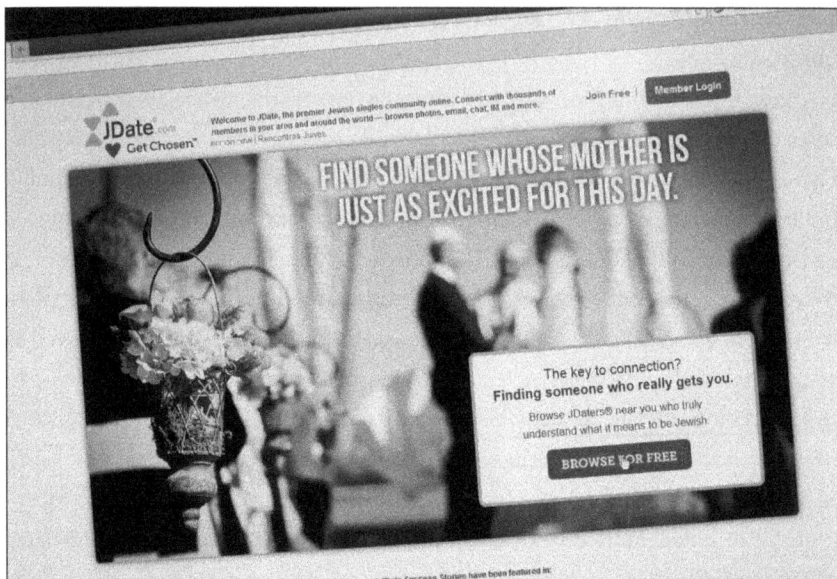

3.6. Screenshot of JDate.com, which self-identifies as a "Jewish singles community online." The rhetoric referring to the image of apparently assimilated Jews under a chuppah (wedding canopy) refers to the importance of Judaism passed down in the maternal line and the cultural representation of Jewish mothers pushing their children to marry within the faith. The trademarked phrase "Get chosen" has a double meaning of the biblical covenant of God with the Israelites (Deuteronomy 7:6) and the selection of potential mates online. Contributed by Maurice Savage; Alamy Stock Photo.

JDate spawned a major rival in JSwipe, an online dating application for smartphones modeled more on the popular non-Jewish-focused Tinder geosocial platform, which allows users to anonymously swipe profiles based on their photographs to discard or keep in search of a match. Although sharing components of non-Jewish dating sites, JSwipe contains esoteric reminders of Jewish culture, such as pop-up graphics of a bar mitzvah celebration when the user locates a match. After a trademark battle ensued between the two sites over software patent infringement of the "J" in their names, in 2015 Spark Networks, which owns JDate along with other dating websites, acquired JSwipe (Vaitsblit 2015). JSwipe's CEO voiced a conciliatory tone in declaring that together the sites have as their mission "strengthen[ing] the Jewish community through dating and marriage" (Vaitsblit 2015).

A more localized approach to connecting Jewish singles in the spirit of the traditional *shadkhan* (Yiddish: matchmaker) is evident in YentaNet, created by a rabbinic student in New York in 2014. Clients meet with volunteer matchmakers who interview them about their backgrounds rather than rely on online profiles (D. N. Cohen 2016). Even Chabad Lubavitch operates ChabadMatch.com specifically for members of the group worldwide. Joining enables Chabad *shadkhanim* to access the member's profile and work on arranging *shidukhim* (Hebrew: matches). Acknowledging modern mobility and work environments that often limit opportunities for faith-based courtship, many dating websites have adapted the Internet to facilitate the maintenance of Jewish households, although Jewish civic leaders nonetheless worry that these Internet-generated families will not coalesce in communities (Kelman 2010).

JDate, JSwipe, and YentaNet strike at the heart of Jewish continuity because they address the way that the community will reproduce itself *l'dor v'dor*. They indicate struggles in modern life to temper digital media as a tool for Jewish continuity rather than as a force undermining ethnic-religious identity. The idealization of the Internet as an untethered, unbureaucratized commons suggests that, although it is certainly viewed as postmodern in its transcendence of space and time, it can also be constructed on the model of the premodern community, raising comparisons to McLuhan's global village, governed by tradition rather than the nationalistic rule of law. Its folk malleability is one of the Internet's culturally expected, spreadable, and addictive features, although modern folklore also casts a shadow over it because of popular conspiracy beliefs in secretive corporate hegemony and invasions of digital natives' privacy (Bronner 2011a, 398–450; Etzioni 2015; Fenster 2008; Prensky 2012).

MASSIFICATION AND DOMESTICATION

Central to issues of the effects of media on Jewish culture is the question of whether the expansiveness of popular culture can work for or against maintaining Jewish communitarian ties. According to cultural historian Russel B. Nye, the rise of popular culture in the European Renaissance and early modern period resulted in "the incorporation of the majority of the population into society" (Nye 1970, 1), thus creating pressure to break the bonds of face-to-face community in favor of belonging to the mainstream on a large scale. Nye noted that the process of popularization at the expense of community accelerated with the mass industrialization and immigration of the late nineteenth century, particularly in North America. In Europe, urbanization and industrialization had increased dramatically, and migrations, often caused by wars, heightened the need for transmission of information across borders. Nye thought that in these social and historical contexts the cultural standards of the mainstream over time increasingly shifted to the urban middle classes, who had a political and economic interest in diminishing the hold of ethnic-linguistic communities on daily life and creating a commanding, de-ethnicized lingua franca of popular culture. Sociologists Richard A. Peterson and Paul DiMaggio articulated this outlook as a two-part "massification hypothesis": first, that the forces of modernization had significantly reduced cultural diversity and, second, that an increasingly homogeneous mass culture had emerged (Peterson and Di Maggio 1975, 498).

Analysts of massification frequently look to media as a driving force of modernization and gauge media's effects on diverse communities. These include assimilation into mass culture; adaptation of media for communitarian purposes, although possibly in a diminished or changed state; separation or unification of communities by tradition; and the domestication of ethnic-religious groups by the dominant society (see my definition of *domestication* in chapter 2). The movement of media as consumer entertainment into the home has informed the rise of the concept of domestication to account for changing social interactions associated with media. Domestication implies an attempt at nationalistic control, emasculation, or taming of subcultural activities by external forces (as in the distinction between domestic and public space). It can have a physical connotation, of a private refuge organized around a media entertainment center (such as the TV or family room or home theater in the dwelling, displacing the living room or the hearth, which were geared toward conversation), through arrangement and alteration to counter the effects of the boisterous outside world. These kinds of rooms and pastoral simulations of the lawn and backyard have been associated with the placidity and disconnection of suburbia (symbolized in the trope of the television-watching couch potato), which, as sociologists have noted, were a magnet for urban Jews in the second half of the twentieth century, a sign of socioeconomic success (S. Adler and Connolly 1960; E. L. Goldstein 2006; Gordon 1959; Rand 2001; Sklare 1979). Suburban enclaves often compensate for lack of public space and neighborly connection by featuring extra media in the home, including the idea of a television and computer in private bedrooms that enable individualism (Bronner 1983). For cultural studies scholars, who often underscore the influence of social or intellectual construction, the domestic is literally imbued with symbolic messages built into the placement of walls, furniture, and objects. A connotation of domesticity is that it exudes harmony and serenity, and this state is imaginatively supported or produced by media believed to avoid conflict and encourage passive consumption. Analysts often ask whether this is an illusion that reinforces social constraint.

Relevant to the question of illusion is Antonio Gramsci's Marxist critique that ruling classes exert political control by convincing the masses to take on the values of popular culture (Lears 1985; Pratt 1992, 4–5; see also Cieraad 2006). According to this theory, media become a powerful instrument to enforce the majority view because they transcend the borders of the home and become part of daily routine. Media create a standard of modernity by which ethnic-religious groups, depicted as antimodern or tradition-centered, appear subservient or inadequate. In many countries of Europe and the Americas in which this popularization process emerged, Jews constituted a major subaltern, urbanized ethnic-religious group. Using various forms of Jewish community as a prime example of a long-standing minority group, which in most societies is dominated by a majority media-controlling culture, analysts therefore theorize that Jews negotiate for access to media in order to become incorporated into national mainstream society, or even to resist it, and to intensify their localized community ties.

With media becoming central to modern industrial economies and politics, additional questions arise about media's role in othering and integrating Jews and their relation to other minority groups (S. B. Cohen and Koch 2007; Ethan Goffman 2000; Stratton 2009). In Jewish cultural studies, scholars tend to adopt a dual perspective of the way that Jews have been mediated by dominant society and how they have mediated themselves; the two often respond to one another. Such mediations historicize Jews as survivors from the ancient past who have not been able to progress, or they exoticize them as uncontrolled, unscrupulous "Orientals" amid more restrained, understandable, and refined Occidental moderns (Brodkin 1999; Brunotte et al. 2015; E. L. Goldstein 2006; Kalmar and Penslar 2005). Of significance is the way that media's form and content generated by Jews speak simultaneously to Jews and to images of Jews created by the dominant society (Bartov 2005; Erdman 1997; Jonathan Pearl and Pearl 1999; Shandler 2009).

The situation in Israel complicates the issue of mediation, because there Jews constructed a national mainstream and created a discourse on the broadcasting of Jewish cultural values in a multicultural society. Digging down to the local level in which Jews have formed tight-knit neighborhoods within large heterogeneous metropolitan areas, one might ponder how the popularization process affected enclaves such as the predominantly Hasidic areas of New York and Antwerp, in which religious leaders place limits on their group's access to media and yet direct publishing houses to address intragroup divisions. Some of these communications reach a Yiddish-speaking population in outlets around the world and create a transnational identity. Varieties of communications also can mark, if not reinforce, cultural diversity within the broad movements of Judaism, including the role of women, nonwhites, and LGBT individuals. And what about the role of converts and claimants to their "lost" Jewish heritage?

If these thorny situations force examination of localized practices that people engage in with media in different situations every day, they also connote contextual consideration of a broad set of beliefs that people hold about media technology and its ethnic-religious ties. The main belief with regard to Jewish culture is that Jews control national media, an anti-Semitic innuendo of Jewish diabolical conspiracy (Dershowitz 2011). If one uses psychoanalytic theory to analyze this phenomenon, are such accusations actually forms of projective inversion, in which Jews are accused of the very devious control to which they have been subjected (Dundes 2007)? Some historians claim that Jews were attracted to popular media because dominant groups considered the entertainment media industry unsavory or unprofitable and that Jews suppressed Jewish content in order to succeed (Benshoff and Griffin 2011, 65; see also Hoberman and Shandler 2003). Others note that the same democratizing process that allows for more Jewish connections, entrepreneurship, and expressions of Jewishness to be made in media also permits more anti-Semitic content to circulate. In any case, in the digital age Jews are not solely responsible for producing Jewish content. When the Jewish subject is culturally "cool," that is, popularized across groups, Jewish critics often worry that non-Jewish interpreters have domesticated Jews or stripped the texts of their Jewishness (Baskind 2007).

The Jewish editors of *Anne Frank Unbound: Media, Imagination, Memory* (Kirshenblatt-Gimblett and Shandler 2012a) note that Anne Frank never participated in her own fame, and yet, through innumerable works of films, radio and television broadcasts, and websites, she has become a global popular culture phenomenon, sometimes to the chagrin of Jewish critics, who find her Jewish experience muted and domesticated at the expense of an optimistic coming-of-age story (Figure 3.7). *Anne Frank Unbound* necessarily examines the Anne Frank phenomenon in the context of Jewish culture with attention to mediation—that is, motivations for and consequences of Frank's diary being translated, sung, dramatized, filmed, or rendered as a graphic novel or museum exhibition. Mediation

3.7. Scene from the movie *The Diary of Anne Frank* (1959) with the non-Jewish Millie Perkins portraying Anne Frank and Austrian American actor Joseph Schildkraut, whose family was Jewish, playing the part of Otto Frank. The movie was nominated for an Academy Award for best motion picture but did not win, though it received a Golden Globe Award that year for best film promoting international understanding.

does not simply reproduce or transfer its subject; instead, it produces something related to the source but also different—a new work (or practice or experience) (Kirshenblatt-Gimblett and Shandler 2012b, 7).

The editors of the volume did not anticipate, however, a further development: the use of Frank's image in a widely circulating meme, apparently with humorous intent, if not response. With textual labels superimposed over a smiling, carefree countenance, such as "I am sick of these Jewish jokes, Anne Frankly, they need to stop," the memes have been variously received on the global Internet as offensive or creative references to her youthful idealism or to her overwrought role in popular culture (Figure 3.8). Frank's read name has been turned into a pun for an oral pronunciation of "and frankly," suggesting on the one hand her attainment of iconic status and, on the other, her sharing of her private thoughts with the world. There is the suggestion that, because she did not intend for either to happen, the reality is different from the mediated message. The anything-can-be-said context of the open web appears to comment that corporate media has unduly sentimentalized or even censored the real Anne Frank. Visual evidence of this cynical attitude circulating on the Internet is the juxtaposition in a single meme of Frank's picture next to the famous quote "I keep my ideals, because in spite of everything I still believe that people are really good at heart." Below it is a frowning cat, symbolizing unruly, transgressive Internet visual culture, with the large caption in large capitalized yellow letters: "What a Dumbass."

One might argue that the Anne Frankly meme should not be interpreted broadly because of the difficulty of identifying the anonymous Internet encoders and their intentions. Users are clearly aware of the incivility of the memes, much as tellers and listeners are aware of the tastelessness of "sick" or "gross" jokes, which draw attention as metafolklore to the process of joking as much as to the content (Dundes 1987a; Sutton-Smith 1960). The memes intentionally defy the normal limits of good taste to comment on the social construction of politicized morality and receive response (other than laughter) from listeners and viewers (Bronner 1985). An example of this metafolkloric reference in the meme to the praxis of meming is one variable caption of "This Meme Is Offensive (or This Is Racist, or I Find This Highly Offensive), Anne Frankly, I Won't Stand for It." The wordplay of *frankly* signals that the encoder is saying something unsaid but which others are thinking and in which the no-holds-barred framing of the "open" line-crossing Internet is brazenly stated. The meme uses knowledge of Frank's supposedly secret musings to different ends than the ones on stage and

3.8. Anonymously created meme using Anne Frank's image circulating on the Internet in 2019.

film. Indeed, many images simply state "Anne Frankly," as though the meaning of the wordplay is self-referential.

Some posted memes superimpose Anne Frank's face on the image of Gene Wilder's sardonic character in *Willie Wonka and the Chocolate Factory* (1971) with the caption, "So Sick of All Those Jew Jokes, Anne Frankly, They Need to Stop." Another visual superimposition is of Anne Frank's face on the iconic image of Scumbag Steve, an annoying, mooching teenager, with the caption "Yo, Can I Stay in Your Attic for a Bit? Stays for 3 Years" (a variation of the common caption for Steve standing in a doorway with the line, "Hey, Man, Can I Crash at Your Place? Stays for 20 Years"; see Puglia 2019, 609–15). The question arises of whether the image of Anne Frank exposes her Jewishness to critique it or to mock the lessons of tolerance and social justice drummed into youth when reading or viewing adaptations of the diary—and the Holocaust generally. Most captions express a sick humor regarding the Holocaust that is intended to shock (see Dundes and Hauschild 1983). For example, extending the wordplay on Frank's naïveté, among the most common images generated by a Google search will be one with the caption, "I Did Nazi [not see] That Coming, Anne Frankly, I Don't Give a Fuck." In another reality check, sometimes the memes contain intentional misspellings to show that young Anne really did not write as well as she has been presented by the media. Or in response to the cultural universalizing of Frank's coming-of-age experience, captions will refer to contemporary expressions to create dark humor, such as "This Girl Is on Fire," "This One Time at Camp We Got So Baked (Gassed)," "I Had a Secret Door (Played Hide and Seek) Before It Was Cool," and "Gonna Go Outside, #YOLO." The last caption is a reference to the common Twitter hashtag for "You Only Live Once," which draws attention to wild youthful behavior or major life decisions or events. It is also a subject of wordplay as in the caption of "#Yolocaust," sometimes showing Anne with a "SWAG" hat, also a common hashtag slang term representing swagger or boastful arrogance. Perhaps as a critical comment on multiculturalism, or the attempt of Jews to be represented in it as a racialized, victimized group, the meme can also feature "The Real Anne Frank" with the image of an African American face superimposed on Frank's body or an altered image showing Frank with body piercing and close-cropped hair with the caption "Lesbianne Frank." Reinforcing the interpretation of racializing or revised metaphorization of Anne Frank is a series of captions having her utter contemporary slang, such as "Yo Dawg I Herd You Like to Hide," and "Oh No Jew Didn't. Anne Frankly That Pun Wasn't Funny at All. It Was Way Out of My Kampfort Zone." One might summarize, then, that the memes are not propagated by Jews but symbolize Jews, or at least a mediated iconic one, to comment on cultural difference.

From Budapest to Brooklyn and from the Holy Land to Hollywood, Jews connect with one another through media, and the practices and images that produce solidarity and division demand inquiry into rapidly changing ideas of identity, agency, community, and reality. Once restricted to information within earshot, Jews in the cyber age can instantly view events and Jewish cultural continuities and differences across the globe through constantly changing digital technology. For some Jews this development has not been to the social advantage of community because of the lack of physically being in touch and of a real localized space where people can congregate publicly as a group. Despite the availability of mediated face time, they might even claim that media has disconnected Jews from what is important: their lived religion. I maintain that to figure out the consequences and agency of media for Jewish culture, scholars need to look at home and in the synagogue and explore the expansive mediated world for ways in which people and institutions harness, tolerate, or resist media to form their sense of ethnic-religious social belonging in mass society. One needs to read images as well as texts for contextualized meanings and the way that the visual is put into social action. Whether on pages or screens, people create and respond to cultural links that both connect and separate Jews or develop and dissolve their Jewishness.

FROM FUNCTION TO FRAME

The Evolving Conceptualization of Jewish Folkloristics

The writings of S. An-sky (Shlomo Zanvil Rappoport, 1863–1920) may not have been the first words on Jewish folklore, but they were certainly among the most influential in raising the visibility of folklore. An important context for An-sky's work, of which he was well aware, was a contentious discourse that arose in the early nineteenth century regarding the stake that Jews held in modernity. Signifying a move in Jewish consciousness from a social connection based on ancient sacred texts and theology to more contemporary cultural expressions, An-sky's vision of folklore was not just about salvaging traditions in the wake of modernization but also a symbol for the perpetuation of Jewish identity and, ultimately, Jewish nationalism (see Gottesman 2003, 75–110; Rabinovitch 2005). An-sky invoked the notion of "expedition" rhetorically, associating it with geographic exploration, to suggest the comprehensive charting of traditions in Jewish locales as a way to gauge the viability of these roots as Jews modernized. The scouring of remote locales that were relatively untouched by industrial movements allowed An-sky to contemplate the evolution of Jewish customs into the present and their comparability to other remote Jewish corners of the world. Yet An-sky was making a powerful etiological statement in the presentation of stories and songs from the Russian Pale of Settlement as a special historic place and social space, that is, a font of *Yiddishkeit* defined for the intrepid ethnographers on An-sky's expedition as cultural Jewishness. Folklore from the Pale, particularly for a group without a country, emerged as the poetic soul for Jews elsewhere, and this was a quality to hail, rather than hide, for post-Enlightenment Jews.

By exposing beliefs, rituals, and craft, the ethnographers who ventured into the Pale bore the risk of confirming the stereotype of Jewish culture as primitive and stubbornly antiprogressive, but An-sky's team presented these traditions as the mother lode of authentic and valuable cultural ore out of which Jewish social consciousness was or could be forged. An-sky's ambitious project looked to Eastern Europe as the cultural source area of traditions that allegedly disappeared elsewhere with modernization. In addition, by inquiring into the role of oppression in the cultural progress of Jews, the expeditioners questioned how shtetl traditions could serve as the foundation of a new and often problematic Jewish identity then forming in industrial, democratizing societies.

Rather than view the traditions of the shtetl as backward or bizarre, An-sky took a cue from the Romantic nationalistic ideology of the Grimm brothers, Wilhelm (1786–1859) and Jacob (1785–1859), in celebrating peasant expression as folk artistry at the heart of sustaining national creativity and identity (Gonen 1994, viii). For Dov Noy (1920–2013), the American-educated, Polish-born doyen of Jewish folklore in Israel, An-sky "anticipated the basic precept of modern ethnography concerning 'ethnicity'—i.e., that a custom is Jewish even if its origin and language are not, provided that it is performed in a clearly Jewish context" (D. Noy 1994, xvii). Fellow Israeli folklorist Haya Bar-Itzhak additionally credited An-sky with coining the term *ethnopoetics*, which, in describing a group's own conceptualization of its aesthetic systems, became central to modern folklore studies (Bar-Itzhak 2010, 28). In the United States, Slavicist Gabriella Safran observed that "earlier than others, An-sky described folklore as the dynamic product of interactions among people and nations. He grasped that the stories people tell depend on who is listening, and he strove to vanish into the background as he heard them, to be indistinguishable from the people he was studying" (Safran 2010, 6).

Despite these tributes to An-sky for setting a theoretical course for the analysis of folklore as prime "dynamic" evidence of a subaltern ethnic group in the broader realm of culture, An-sky is noticeably absent from citations of folklore and ethnography outside the Jewish world. Much as An-sky suspected that his expedition was distinctive among the cultural forays of the time, An-sky, like his Jewish subject, was largely overlooked in academic social sciences, particularly in the study of Russian folklore.[1] Historiographies of field-inspired theory have emphasized both the regionalist study of Christian Northern European peasant societies, spurred by Swedish folklorist Artur Hazelius (1833–1901), and the evolutionist "English anthropological school" of George Laurence Gomme (1853–1916), Andrew Lang (1844–1912), Charlotte Sophia Burne (1850–1923), and Edwin Sidney Hartland (1848–1927) more prominently than An-sky's contributions (Cocchiara 1971; Dorson 1968). Some of the omission, or ignorance, of An-sky's expeditions might be attributable to the lack of reports in English, French, and German, but a more likely explanation is that the literary- and evolutionary-minded folklorists who dominated European cultural studies had difficulty with (and possibly prejudice against) the Jewish subject in their hierarchical framework for folklore as evidence of stages of social progress and cultural nationalism (Bronner 1998, 129–40).

Although Noy and Bar-Itzhak tried to publicize An-sky's contributions to their non-Jewish colleagues, they realized that the largest notice he received was from Jewish intellectuals who had an insider discourse about Jewish destiny. Noy and Bar-Itzhak addressed their fellow Jews to make the case that An-sky's lasting legacy was not so much in his literary or political work but in his representation of directly experienced folklore from the shtetl as the expressive lifeblood of a dispersed, assimilating people in need of a cultural transfusion. Even if An-sky's post-Holocaust audience did not accept some of his romantic notions of the shtetl, he provided a model of the Jewish cultural task ahead by identifying folklore in situ as a deep voice that could clearly benefit shallow moderns stripped of their heritage. Noy and Bar-Itzhak suggested that An-sky associated folklore with the everyday grassroots of culture, implying that it could be adapted and function in communities elsewhere.

Yet by organizing, in Bar-Itzhak's words, "the first fieldwork in the study of Jewish folklore that applied the research tools of modern folkloristics" (An-Ski 2010, 34), An-sky became problematic as a progenitor of folklore at the core of Jewish cultural and identity studies. Rather than giving attention to emerging practices and situated performances in modern everyday life, he appeared to have an archaeological obsession with the relict minutiae of the past in isolation (see Beukers and Waale 1992; Kugelmass 2006). An-sky still approached folklore as a relic of a bygone age surviving in remote locations. Later scholars, though, mined An-sky's materials to find new meanings in their expressive content and symbolism. The "modern" in Noy's ethnography and Bar-Itzhak's folkloristics was at bottom process oriented rather than product centered. Instead of romantically imagining the Jewish nation through its people in their home locales, as An-sky hoped, later scholars framed folklore in the processes of variable social interactions in a mobile, transnational society. Folklore, as a topic and a vision, was tied less to place and more to a portable, intangible heritage or even state, and projection, of mind. It defined a malleable, adaptable Jewishness that could be enacted on certain occasions, not an isolated, totalistic folklife.

The question I take up here in light of the reflection more than a hundred years after An-sky's campaign to yoke folklore and ethnography to dilemmas of Jewish identity is how and why the idea of folklore has evolved from a functional approach to the Jewish text or object to a frame of action. Both viewpoints arose under similar circumstances: the perceived decline of religiosity and isolation along with the threat of secularism and dispersal. Yet with the creation of a national state of Israel and the emergence of North America as a population and cultural center for Jews, the role of folklore as a vehicle for romantic nationalism changed. With a revision of the standard historiography of ethnographic continuity from An-sky that I present here, one also has to question whether folklore and the understanding of ethnopoetics still figure significantly in the conceptualization of Jewish sustainability in a fragmented, global Jewish culture. My purpose is to point out the continuities and disparities between An-sky's foundation and the American edifice, as it later arose, to theorize about Jewish identity as tradition in response to modernization. I argue that in this move of location and orientation was an abandonment of a nationalistic project to renew Jewish social and cultural solidarity in favor of a model that guided Jews as individuals to navigate through an unfamiliar world of strangers.

AN-SKY'S ETHNOPOETICS AND CULTURAL NATIONALISM

An inquiry into the uses of folklore in a philosophy of Jewish cultural action can begin with an examination of An-sky's essay on ethnopoetics, originally published in 1908 in the Russian-language collection *Perezhitoe* (Our Past). Two epigraphs set the tone for the essay. The first comes from the pen of Ilya Orshansky (1846–1875), known more as a lawyer and historian than as an ethnographer. Orshansky's claim to fame was as an activist for Jewish emancipation in Russia. The quote that An-sky used refers apparently to the limitations of history and the advantages of understanding identity through "a people's poetry," or folklore viewed as folk artistry: "A people's poetry depicts, vividly and in clear relief, the hidden inner world of national life, to which we are admitted neither by the pen of the diligent historian nor by the sharp eye of the chronicler" (An-Ski 2010, 34). The second epigraph is the talmudic directive "Go out and see what the people do" (BT *Eruvin* 14b). The original context of the phrase is in regard to arguments among the rabbis on the width of a post in an *eruv*. The answer from one rabbi was to learn from the people's customs rather than dictate a rule. Yet An-sky implied that this knowledge was hard to come by: "One may boldly say that there is no other people who speak about themselves so much and know themselves so little as the Jews do" (An-Ski 2010, 34). An-sky contended that Jews could be revealed, that is, their "inner world of national life" could be uncovered, through their customary expressions, or "people's poetry."

An-sky, who had achieved literary distinction in Russian as well as in Yiddish, pointed out that the Jewish intelligentsia, who were more occupied with recognition in the fine arts and humanities, had not helped unveil this inner world. Indeed, they appeared bent on separating from and hiding their cultural roots to achieve success. A new kind of study and student was necessary, An-sky maintained, to expose "matters of Jewish ethnography and folklore, that treasury of folk art which provides the only way to discover the Jewish national character and to penetrate to the depths of the worldview of the Jewish people and its ethnographic-cultural and moral lineaments" (An-Ski 2010, 34). The meaning he wanted to convey is evident in the rhetorical equivalence of ethnography and lore with art, suggesting that attempts to restrict Jewish cultural production to the elite level of "civilization" in Enlightenment discourse were misplaced. According to An-sky, this discourse compelled Jewish fine artists to abandon the richness of their traditions as a cultural resource and instead build on an essentially foreign heritage. Jewish fine artists, he argued, were not being true to themselves.

Looking to scholars who had previously worked with folklore, An-sky found models for action in the nineteenth-century Russian ethnographers Vladimir Dall, Lev Y. Sternberg, M. A. Krol, Vladimir Bogoraz, Pavel Schein, and V. I. Jochelson (An-Ski 2010, 35). But An-sky complained that, although they were of Jewish origin, they gave little attention to Jewish folklore or else devoted themselves to "savage and half-savage nomads" out in the remote Siberian tundra instead of the people of the western provinces of the Russian Empire. He also lamented that, although songs and proverbs had been collected in chronicles of

Jewish folklore, "no attempt has even been made to collect and record the folk-tales, legends, parables, spells, superstitions, and so on" (35). Taken together, these kinds of material could show the holistic fabric of the interrelatedness of Jewish culture, he thought, rather than isolating a particular thread. The urgency of this collection of texts for An-sky was due to the disappearance of folklore, which he compared to losing a treasure trove of art: "Every year, and even every day, the most precious pearls of folk art are being lost. The older generation, that which preceded the cultural revolution, is departing this world and taking with it to the grave a millennia-old heritage of folk art" (35). The cultural revolution to which he referred dates to the late nineteenth century, when Russia felt pressure to modernize, as its Western European neighbors had. The changes took the form of transitions from village life to industrialization and urbanization, which were sustained by an ethos of progress and innovation rather than by tradition and social intimacy. An-sky feared that the imposition of the majority culture would destroy Jewish culture.

An-sky blared in the essay what can be read as a call to cultural arms: "Our task today is to organize without delay the systematic collection of the works of folk art, of the monuments of the Jewish past, and to describe Jewish lifestyles over the generations. This task is not partisan, but national and cultural, and the best forces of our people must be mobilized and unified for it. The time has come to create Jewish ethnography!" (An-Ski 2010, 35). An-sky's definition of folk art was oral rather than visual: "tales, legends, songs, parables, superstitions, sayings, proverbs, and so on, produced by the people itself, as well as works that penetrated it and won great popularity" (40). He noted the common criticism that the Jews appeared "cultureless" because their folklore resembled the traditions of the host society (J. Boyarin 2014, 85–92), and he hypothesized that going to the people to see what they do would reveal "forms, character, and orientation" that are distinctively Jewish (An-Ski 2010, 51). He called for the analysis of European literary "motifs" that were rendered in folktales performed by Jews with a "different form and character." One example he gave was of the "hidden *tzaddik*" or *nister* replacing the fool of European märchen. An-sky declared that, although Jewish and European narratives were structurally similar, the function of the character was different in Jewish culture. The *nister* was depicted as a simpleton, the apparent butt of many jokes, but, An-sky pointed out, "When the time is ripe—generally when Jews must be saved from peril—he is suddenly revealed and turns out to be wiser than all the greatest *tzaddikim*, with total mastery not only of the entire

Torah but also of the arcane lore that only angels achieve" (61). An-sky generalized that, whereas in European folklore this and other motifs appeared against the
background of "material and physical might, in Jewish art they are shown against
the background and in the domain of spiritual power only" (51).

Suggesting a function of folklore not just as entertainment but potentially
as resistance to oppression and a parable of social reality, An-sky commented
that Jewish heroes fight with spiritual strength rather than physical power: They
"act not with the sword but through a word and the power of the spirit" (An-Ski
2010, 51). An ethnopoetics thus serves to identify from a group's perspective its
own "patterns, images, and terms," or, put another way, its folk aesthetics and
native classifications as sources of power. An-sky's concept of ethnopoetics is distinguished from the kind of poetics that looks for universal external—or what he
calls "superficial"—similarities and therefore emphasizes the uniformity of culture. The *ethno* in ethnography and ethnopoetics emphasizes the distinctiveness
of the group as conveyed in its artistic expressions, most vividly evident in the
collective folklore of people close to the land.

An-sky's social cause apparently came to him late (Lukin 1994, xiv). Earlier in
his Russian literary career, he claimed to have harbored a "hatred and contempt"
for Jewishness until he discovered in folklore "the beauty of the poetry that lies
buried in the old historical foundations and traditions" (Roskies 1992, 247). But
Jewish literary critic David G. Roskies wrote of this return to Jewish identity that
"far from being a pious act of self-negation, Ansky's was a Western sensibility
engaged in a highly self-conscious act of retrieval" (247). By seeking out the original versions of "old historical" poetic texts surviving in the present among peasants
uncontaminated by modernization, An-sky offered that his expedition would venture into a zone he recalled from his childhood as "the thick of Jewish life" (247).

Aware that some collectors in America such as Leo Wiener and Y. L. Cahan
had recorded Yiddish folk songs from Eastern Europe among Jewish immigrants
in New York, An-sky insisted in a letter to Chaim Zhitlovsky that "Yiddish tales,
legends, and the like must be collected among old folks who carry the past with
them in unadulterated form" (Roskies 1992, 257). That unadulterated form, he
believed, could be recovered only from the cultural source area of the Pale, which
presumably contained homogeneous, tradition-centered communities of Orthodox Jews. Roskies reflected that An-sky's emphasis on spiritual power in folklore
is a reckoning with, or remaking of, Judaism in his old age in the midst of social
and technological change. Roskies proclaimed that with An-sky's expedition in

1912, An-sky "turned the disparate remains of Jewish folklore and folk life into an all-embracing Oral Torah" (260). Thus An-sky established a paradigm for Jewish revitalization with a cultural rather than a religious turn. He epitomized the folkloristic stance for the twentieth century of insiders-turned-observers to confront the sacrifices they had made to assimilate and modernize. An-sky asserted that Jews needed to take responsibility for their own culture and use their studies of authentic folklore to shape the future instead of anthropologically or linguistically focusing on the traditions of "savages and half-savages" far removed from their experience and leaving often anti-Semitic non-Jews to dictate the narrative of the halted progress of the so-called Jewish race.

Dov Noy described this liminal folkloristic position in fieldwork in Jewish terms of the *meshulah*, or messenger-collector (others refer to the position as "new class" consciousness; see Bronner 2005b; Bruce-Briggs 1979; Mechling 1989): "A *meshulah*, unlike a *shaliah* (messenger), acts in total dedication to his mission, initiating original and individual steps and often displaying bizarre behavior, casting him in the image of an outsider" (D. Noy 1994, xvii). Noy noted that in An-sky's *The Dybbuk* (1914) the *meshulah* yearned for the coming of the Messiah but was paradoxically immersed in the materialism of modern life. Noy observed parallels with An-sky's situation and many of his followers in the folkloristic field (xvii). One weakness of this preoccupation with the spiritual, Noy claimed, was a relative neglect of visual tradition, although he pointed out An-sky's growing awareness of the material once out among the people on his expedition. Although not as comparative or visual as Noy would like for the future generation of Jewish folklorists working to preserve old identities as well as construct new ones, Noy asserted that An-sky holds "a distinguished place as a pioneer in folkloristics and ethnography" (xvii). For Noy's student Haya Bar-Itzhak, representing the next generation of Jewish folklorists into the twenty-first century, An-sky made too many sweeping generalizations and overrelied on textual evidence, but nonetheless she recognized him as "the keystone of Jewish folklore studies to the present day" (Bar-Itzhak 2010, 33).

JEWISH ETHNOGRAPHY IN RELATION TO THE ETHNOGRAPHY OF JEWS

As important as An-sky was to the long-term project of collecting folklore in constructing a comprehensive ethnography of Jews, his influence did not significantly extend to North America (Kugelmass 2006, 346). It was Franz Boas (1858–1942), a prominent anthropologist of Jewish background who arrived in the United States in 1884 at the age of 26, who established principles of cultural relativism and particularism in his folklore-based ethnography that were similar to An-sky's. From his teaching and leadership post in anthropology at Columbia University, Boas drew from African American and Native American folklore to encourage the replacement of the reigning paradigm of an evolutionary ladder that all cultures climb from savagery to civilization (Zumwalt 2019). Cultural evolutionists placed modern industrialized societies, devoted to science rather than superstition, at the top and relegated ethnic groups, such as Jews, to a "barbaric" stage on the lower rungs; they contended that the old "superstitious" traditions associated with Judaism had been displaced by progressive-minded Christianity. Instead of this hierarchical model based on notions of cultural superiority, Boas proposed a flattened heterogeneous model of many cultures that were relative to one another. Aware of the treatment of Jews as a darker, inferior, and outsider race, Boas maintained that his relativist model countered the racist undertone in evolutionary thought that connected biological differences to a cultural hierarchy from dark to white peoples. Facing resistance to his ideas and anti-Semitism from colleagues in the American Anthropological Association, he used the American Folklore Society and the *Journal of American Folklore*, which he edited from 1908 to 1924 (and influenced through 1940 with his students Ruth Benedict and Gladys Reichard at the helm), to expand his vision of culture as holistic, relativistic, and pluralistic (Liss 1995).

Boas's explanation of cultural similarities in different parts of the globe followed the historical experience of Jews in the Diaspora. He embraced folklore as primary cultural evidence to reveal the particular character of a group and the ways that cultural ideas move. For Boas, folklore comprised the tales and myths that revealed the specific values and history in a bounded group. Using folklore even more than linguistics or physical anthropology, he described cultures by their geographic spread and special conditions rather than by their level and type (M. Jacobs 1959; Reichard 1943). As editor of the *Journal of American Folklore*, Boas departed from An-sky's call for Jewish "insider" ethnographers by insisting on the anthropological stance of objectivity for ethnographers, who he thought should be outsiders to the cultures they observed. Thus Boas discouraged his Jewish students Paul Radin and Melville Herskovits from studying Jewish communities, but he nonetheless published in 1916 and 1918 the folkloristic documentation collected by Russian-born, Yiddish-speaking Jewish high school teacher Leah R. C. Yoffie (1884–1956) of Eastern European Yiddish-speaking Jewish immigrants. Although Yoffie noted in both articles that "the majority of their practices are common to the orthodox Jews in all the lands of the earth," she drew attention to the emergent lore of immigrants adapting to the particular conditions of urban St. Louis (Yoffie 1916, 413). For example, she collected the saying "Zie is azei dick wie die grobe blecherin" (She is as large as the tinner's fat wife) and commented, "This is a purely local St. Louis expression. About twenty years ago there lived on North Seventh Street a tinner whose wife was abnormally large. This simile is the result of that good woman's excessive girth, and is still used by Yiddish-speaking Jews in this city" (Yoffie 1918, 165). In contrast to An-sky's search for authentic lore of the remote past in isolated rural environs to salvage a disappearing culture, Yoffie declared the urgency of going into the cities where Jewish immigrants had settled to collect their folklore and get a sense of their continuity and change. With rhetoric of "inner life" and a "lack of knowledge" of Jewish culture, she declared, "Very little is known to most of us about the inner life of the people who have recently come to this country from other lands. There is a promising field for the scholar in the folk-lore of the immigrants in our large cities. This is especially true of the legends and customs among the orthodox Jews in our country" (Yoffie 1916, 413).

Boas, like An-sky, was concerned with religious and ethnic identity in a modernizing society associated with individual freedom, but Boas expressed more ambivalence toward the contribution of tradition to progress. Perhaps having in mind the tradition-centered Eastern European *Ostjuden* in contrast to the "liberal" Jews of Germany, he announced, "My whole outlook upon social life is determined, by the question: how can we recognize the shackles that tradition has laid upon us? For when we recognize them, we are also able to break them" (Boas 1938a, 202). Boas, then, was not calling for the preservation of tradition as much as for using its knowledge to enhance intellectual freedom and gain progressive enlightenment. In a rare reference to his Jewish upbringing, he used his father's example to make his point.

> My father had retained an emotional affection for the ceremonial of his parental home without allowing it to influence his intellectual freedom. Thus I was spared the struggle against religious dogma that besets the lives of so many young people. . . . As I remember it now, my first shock came

when one of my student friends, a theologian, declared his belief in the
authority of tradition and his conviction that one had not the right to
doubt what the past had transmitted to us. The shock that this outright
abandonment of freedom of thought gave me is one of the unforgettable
moments of my life. (Boas 1938a, 201)

For other public intellectuals, Boas's stands sounded revolutionary, and indeed,
Boas had publicly mentioned that he had been conditioned by "a German home
in which the ideals of the revolution of 1848 were a living force," referring to
unsuccessful protests of noble privilege and efforts to guarantee civil liberties
for Jews and other minorities (Boas 1938a, 201; see also Bronner 1998, 129–34;
Glick 1982).

As a result of his social and political stands, Boas frequently suffered anti-
Semitic and ideological attacks. Working in the same city as Boas, Brooklyn
Museum curator Stewart Culin (1858–1929) unleashed some of the most vitriolic
rhetoric against the Columbia professor. Embittered in the 1920s because of the
decline of museum evolutionism and fired up with Henry Ford's support of anti-
Semitic tracts such as the *International Jew* (1920), Culin implied that Boas's scholarship was a brand of Russian-inspired radical socialism inspired by a conspiracy
of international Jewry. He cited a council meeting of the American Anthropological Association in Philadelphia where members allegedly "were aligned, divided
into two parties, who separated and seated themselves on opposite sides of the
room. On one side were the Jews and the converts and supporters, mostly students of Franz Boas of Columbia University, and on the opposite side, their opponents. The Jews stood for Internationalism, and so proclaimed themselves. They
had succeeded in securing possession of this important association and used it for
their personal and political ends" (Bronner 1998, 133). Culin's Swiss-born colleague Adolph F. A. Bandelier (1840–1914) used an ethnic slur when he accused
Boas of clannishly relying on Jewish ethnographers composed of "some bloom-
ing youngsters and . . . a Sheeny from Russia." He viewed them as culturally
and academically ill-equipped because they did not live up to the standards of
Christian modernism. These "children of Abraham, Isaac and Jacob," he sarcastically wrote Culin, compose "the JEW speculating on the ignorance of others"
(Bronner 1998, 134).[2]

Beyond the ample evidence of ethnic prejudice by evolutionary anthropologists Culin and Bandelier against the very idea that supposedly "superstitious"

Jews could climb the intellectual ladder, Jews constantly faced in scholarly circles an evolutionist assumption that the persistence of ancient Judaism in modern industrial civilization showed the inability of Jews to progress. Evolutionists
often dismissed Jewish advancements in science as a result of deviousness to get
ahead and supported restrictions on Jews in education and organizations. Jewish counterclaims to scientific, literary, and cultural achievements on individual
merits challenged the consistency of evolutionary racial doctrine based on the
backwardness and ignorance of Jews stuck in a barbaric stage of progress (see Gilman 1996). Joseph Jacobs (1854–1916), an Australian-born Jewish scholar known
for his diffusionist folklore studies, presented results of an elaborate social study
that defied evolutionary predictions of cultural backwardness. In essays such as
"The Comparative Distribution of Jewish Ability" (1886), which built a case
for the claim of Jews as being "civilized," expressed ultimately in *Jewish Contributions to Civilization* (1919), Jacobs found that Jews showed a higher rate of intellectual ability than evolutionary doctrine predicted. In his prideful phrase, " 'Tis a
little people, but it has done great things" (Gilman 1996, 71).

Typical of the case for Jewish racial typology in cultural evolution is John
Sterling Kingsley's *The Standard Natural History*. Kingsley insisted on Jews as a race
at a "low stage of culture," characterized by ignorance, fanaticism, and superstition (Kingsley 1885, 472). Yet if an evolutionary racial classification based on
English Christian superiority placed Jews at a primitive cultural rung, Kingsley
had to explain the renown of highly regarded Jewish scientists, intellectuals, and
leaders such as British prime minister Benjamin Disraeli. Kingsley admitted, "A
Jew, it is true, can rise to be the premier of the British empire, but this is the
exception noted; here there was contact with other people. To see the Jew in all
his purity and the accompanying degradation, *we must visit those places, like southern
Russia, where they form whole communities*" (472; emphasis added). With this prevailing intellectual bias against the *shtetlekh* epitomizing the degradation of Jewish
culture in mind, An-sky's insistence on the folk artistry of the Russian communities and Boas's defiance of biological determinism bear the stamp of their concerns for Jewish emancipation resulting from an appreciation of the stigmatized
Jewish vernacular as valuable art. Although both An-sky and Boas viewed Jewish
folklore as material for a relativistic, liberating agenda, they were aware of the
vulnerability of Jewish folklore being used for racist purposes as a sign of social
backwardness. An-sky's response was to elevate and creatively adapt Jewish folklore as a national symbol. Boas's was to redirect Jewish concerns regarding racism

and anti-Semitism to distinctive non-Jewish native artistry in exotic locales. Even
if they had similar aims, it was Boas who ended up being more influential in creating a relativistic cultural awareness of ethnic tradition in modern life and in
positing rational functions for the persistence of folklore (Greenhouse 2010;
H. Lewis 2001; McGowan 2014).

Joseph Jacobs (who is notable in his roles as editor of the British journal *Folklore* as well as *Jewish Social Studies*) was one Jewish folklorist of the era who dealt
more with Jewish-Christian relations as opposed to Jewish folklore in isolation.
He openly ridiculed attempts by such renowned British folklorists as George Laurence Gomme and Andrew Lang to portray Judaism as a "savage" religion displaced
by Christianity and therefore to render Jews obsolete and necessarily "backward"
(Bronner 1998, 134–37; see also Dorson 1968). He mocked the Victorian folklorists by stating that, if that was the case, then the Christian mass of eating the
host was barbaric because it represents the savagery of cannibalism. He connected
Passover historically to Christian Communion but argued that Passover's meaning
could not be narrowed historically to the original commemoration of Exodus,
as the Victorians were wont to do. By ethnographically pointing to varieties of
customs attached to Passover in different Jewish communities, he maintained that
folk practices should be observed to determine how they functioned differently
according to the locale. He contended that, rather than being a survival of the
ancient ritual eating of unleavened bread as a historical commemoration, the consumption of the communal wafer in the Christian mass functioned to create holi-
ness through the belief in bodily transference. Years later, eminent folklorist Alan
Dundes, who had a Jewish background, went one step further, with a psychoanalytic interpretation that persistence of the irrational blood libel legend in the oral
tradition of non-Jews could be explained as a "projective inversion" of Christian
guilt over the symbolic act of eating human flesh. He contended that this guilt
was instead projected onto narratives of Jews killing a Christian child for blood to
eat in a wafer-like matzo instead. It thus was a legend with the function of reliev-
ing anxiety by Christians rather than an outgrowth of historical practices (Dundes
2007, 386–409; and see the discussion in the Introduction to this volume).

Jacobs, like Boas, was known as a diffusionist, and he made a major contribution to the use of folklore studies generally by recasting the meaning of *folk*,
arguably based on his Jewish experience. Reflecting a concern for diasporization,
Jacobs presented folklore not as an irrational survival of savage practices but as
a functional expression of tradition that spread with social movements and was

capable of producing new forms emerging in contemporary situations (Fine 1987). Resisting racial stereotypes, Jacobs characterized the "folk" not as primitives but as social segments of societies, "many-headed . . . and often many-minded" (Joseph Jacobs 1893, 234). Instead of portraying culture as a hierarchy with folk at the bottom and moderns at the top, Jacobs declared a relativist concept: "We are the Folk as well as the rustic, though their lore may be other than ours, as ours will be different from that of those that follow us" (237). In this conceptualization, Jewish folklorists were instrumental in shifting the use of *folk* from a noun for a remote group or lower level of culture to an adjective for a traditional process that marks, and indeed is needed by, all people. It could be collected in the city as well as in the country, among the elite as well as the peasantry, and even more significantly it could constitute individual agency of, rather than placing shackles on, as Boas lamented, one's identity.

THE RISE OF AMERICAN FUNCTIONALISM

With the devastation of the Holocaust in mind and with Jewish rediasporization renewing an ethnographic urgency to collect folklore in Israel and North America toward a revised picture of post-shtetl, modern Jewish culture, a landmark meeting in Chicago titled the "Regional Conference on Jewish Folklore," organized by the Association for Jewish Studies (AJS) at the Spertus College of Judaica, sought in 1977 to reflect on the progress of Jewish folkloristic work and query whether it represented a unified movement. The conference gave special attention to uprooted communities from Eastern Europe and North Africa in new locales, particularly in the United States and Israel, as destinations for Jewish refugees. The reference to "regional" in the title in relation to the national AJS belies its global importance. The conference's driving force, Dov Noy from the Hebrew University of Jerusalem, claimed it was the first Jewish studies conference outside Israel that was devoted explicitly to folklore. Noy went on to view it historically as the "cornerstone in the development of the academic study of Jewish culture as part of the field of Jewish Studies" (D. Noy 1980, xi). He implied that this interdisciplinary field was more hospitable than anthropology, religious studies, or literature to Jewish folklore broadly conceived and analyzed by Jews. Noy pointed out that in Israel, where folklore was a popular subject, Jewish folklore studies had been narrowly defined as a literary resource and its study was centered on origins of narratives in ancient texts. In the United States, there was an opportunity to integrate new developments beyond literature in Jewish studies and a greater acceptance in folklore studies of "fieldwork at home" than in anthropology.

To be sure, Jewish folklore since the nineteenth century had been previously discussed in scholarly meetings, including those of the American Folklore Society and the Association for Jewish Studies, but the Chicago conference conspicuously pushed for folklore as a separate ethnographic approach and a type of renewable, modern resource in Jewish studies. This concern for folklore as key evidence of a new interdisciplinary Jewish studies aiming to uncover cultural relationships was especially evident seven years after the AJS conference in the organization of the conference "Living Tradition: Jewish Folk Creativity and Cultural Survival," sponsored by the Center for Jewish Studies of the City University of New York and YIVO in New York City. The organizers of the New York City conference boasted that, because the AJS conference had been a regional one, "Living Tradition" was appropriately "the first national conference devoted to Jewish folklore" ("Conferences and Meetings," 1983–1984, 5–6). The conferences featured many of the same speakers who had initiated courses on Jewish folklore at Indiana University, the University of Pennsylvania, Harvard University, UCLA, and other prominent national universities. Reference to folkloristics emerged as a large umbrella under which to connect genres of narrative, music, and art and to confront big ideas about ethnic identity, the interrelationship of tradition and modernity, and cultural massification and sustainability. Folkloristics also seemed more welcoming to the idea of Jews studying other Jews, despite the anthropological questions of objectivity. Yet folkloristics was the product of scattered individuals rather than the kind of concentrated, comprehensive team project represented by the An-sky expedition. Still, by using fieldwork with outstanding tradition-bearers and varied cultural scenes, the participants in the conferences presented more of Jacobs's picture of a many-headed and many-minded Jewish culture than An-sky's ur-source of Jewishness in the shtetl.

These events of the 1970s and 1980s suggested to participants the beginnings of a cultural revitalization as well as an intellectual movement. It was a period of consolidation that led to a push for new ethnographic perspectives on contemporary Jewish culture. The perspectives countered the prevalent emphasis on ancient literary and historical foundations of Jewish civilization. In many ways, the movement took the An-sky expedition as its inspiration for this effort, although it wanted to be sure to present new ethnography not as a salvage operation but as an inquiry into the adaptation of traditional forms and the emergence of new ones. It also faced a lack of institutional support and contemplated whether such a movement could be sustained with individual endeavors rather than organized team projects. I maintain that the ethnographic approach to the Jewish subject, though not driven by a singular project, has cast the problem of Jewish culture as a paradox of identity out of the conflict of tradition and modernity and has challenged conventional categorizations of Jewish studies.

No longer amassing poetic material for a case for cultural nationalism, many conference participants observing Jews in the practice of traditions that were not isolated in time and place, and those analyzing "urban villagers" (such as the Hasidim in new modern settings) as folk societies problematized the supposed primary function of folklore to provide group maintenance. More of the issues at hand concerned the way that practices and performances of folklore constructed individual identities and projected anxieties about the relation of Jewishness to a dominant Christian society. Rather than treating popular culture as sitting on an opposite pole from tradition, more questions arose about the hybridization of folk and popular culture into ethnic symbols.

In the major theoretical move from positing functions of Jewish practices to situating behavior within frames of communication, ethnographers of the Jewish subject redefined culture as a process of representation and subjective organization of experience (Bronner 2013; Georges and Jones 1995, 289–93; Hasan-Rokem 2002, 969–72; Kirshenblatt-Gimblett 1998, 17–78). This is an old story in social sciences, but the narrative I propose that is new or revised is the uneasy alignment of folklore and ethnography in the emergence of Jewish studies. I contend that in the twenty-first century a new period of reconfiguration has been recognizable in which Jewish folklore and ethnography, viewed in the context of popular culture, merged into Jewish cultural studies.

With the theoretical shift to Jewish cultural studies came a different historiography that emerged from the study of Jewish folklore in the modernized, heterogeneous societies of Central and Western Europe rather than the isolated, homogeneous *shtetlekh* of Eastern Europe. For example, Dov Noy, in narrating 80 years of ethnographic progress toward the creation of a Jewish folklore field at the Chicago conference, credited Prussian-born Max Grunwald (1871–1953) rather than An-sky in Russia for setting the stage for later work. Reflecting on the achievements and tasks of Jewish folklorists from 1897, the date of Max Grunwald's publication of "Zur Volkskunde der Juden,"[3] Noy emphasized the instrumental use of folklore as an umbrella term to cover the spectrum of culture, including (1) names and oral aspects, (2) poetry, (3) belief and legend, (4) customs and folkways, (5) augury, and (6) material culture. Notably absent is music, which Noy aligned largely with musicology, although he included presentations on the ballad and Yiddish music to draw attention to the possibilities of folkloristic perspectives on music and song, much as had been done for British and American folk music (D. Noy 1980, 5–10).

Another factor in the integration of music into folklore studies came from the Yiddish world, where figures such as Vilna-born Yehudah Leib Cahan (1881–1937) promoted the linkage of folk narrative and folk song studies as part of *folksshafung* (Yiddish: folk creativity) and others worked with the broader concept of *folkloristik* (Yiddish: folkloristics) for the study of traditions (Cahan 1952; Kirshenblatt-Gimblett 1985). Still, the predominant approach of mining historical texts for references to folklore was evident in books such as Angelo S. Rappoport's *The Folklore of the Jews* (1937), Joshua Trachtenberg's *Jewish Magic and Superstition* (1939), and Theodor H. Gaster's *The Holy and the Profane: Evolution of Jewish Folkways* (1955), all of which appeared in the United States and Great Britain and were concerned with the origins of modern customs in pagan or ancient rituals. They owed much to Grunwald's stated aim of *Volkskunde*: to reach back from the present with folkloric evidence to find the roots of culture ("Rückwärtsschreiten zu den Wurzeln der Menschheit") (see Hödl 2002–2003, 56).

Noy, who had been a talmudic scholar, broke away from religious studies, literature, and anthropology by receiving a degree in folklore in 1954 from Indiana University and viewed folklore in the Boasian sense as a mirror of culture. Together with the anthropologically oriented Raphael Patai and literary scholar Francis Lee Utley, Noy spearheaded a volume titled *Studies in Biblical and Jewish Folklore* (Patai et al. 1960), published by Indiana University's Folklore Institute, to show new research by individuals calling themselves folklorists. Patai used the opportunity to reiterate a call he made in "Problems and Tasks of Jewish Folklore and Ethnology" in 1946 (in English; it appeared in Hebrew the year before), advocating for "the study of the folklore of *present-day* Jewish communities" receiving "the highest priority within the general field of Jewish learning" (Patai 1960, 11; emphasis added). The folklorists were agitating for a shift from an emphasis on the historic relics or survivals of Jewish beliefs to an ethnographic project analyzing the contemporary functions of Jewish customs in everyday life. Sensitive to the charge that Judaism as an ancient religion was superstitious and therefore anachronistic, the folklorists wanted to show the rationale behind, indeed the necessity of, Jewish folkloric production in the modern age. For example, Richard Dorson posited the need of an assimilated American generation to deal with their immigrant legacy in the formation of Jewish American dialect stories, and Beatrice Weinreich closed *Studies in Biblical and Jewish Folklore* by drawing attention to adaptations to modernity in her study of the Americanization of the traditional Passover seder stabilized through renderings of the Haggadah (Dorson 1960; B. S. Weinreich 1960; anthropologist Vanessa Ochs [2020] picks up this theme into the twenty-first century). By the time the Chicago conference came together in 1977, the peripatetic Noy was especially sanguine about the primacy of Jewish folklore as a key to unlocking puzzles of Jewish culture in multiple locations and about its connection to mass culture within the new interdisciplinary construct of Jewish studies. Noy challenged leaders of Jewish studies to alter their studies by questioning the conventional reliance in academe on literature and art and to inclusively consider cultural evidence presented by folklorists of ordinary people and their workaday worlds. The contemporaneousness of folklore was rhetorically conveyed by dropping "biblical" from the title of the publication of the conference, *Studies in Jewish Folklore* (Talmage 1980), and by its sponsorship by the Association for Jewish Studies.

Raphael Patai laid the foundation for the realignment of functionalism in a contemporary Jewish perspective by his assertion in *Studies in Biblical and Jewish Folklore* that, "as an anthropologist, one agrees with the anthropological definition[4] of folklore as 'dependent on oral transmission' and thus including 'myths, legends, tales, proverbs, riddles, the texts of ballads and other songs, and other forms of lesser importance, but not folk art, folk dance, folk music, folk costume, folk medicine, folk custom or folk belief.' But as a student of Jewish culture one knows that Jewish legends and tales can be studied only in the context of Jewish folk custom" (Patai 1960, 21). Patai's emphasis on the significance of custom as a context for analysis suggests that in Jewish culture, the function of tradition matters most because it explains the persistence of a variety of traditional material in terms of the social and psychological benefits it provides rather than a backward, stubborn, or superstitious character of a group of people. Explaining Jewish cultural scenes as rational responses to diverse social and cultural contexts held an urgency for many mid-twentieth-century anthropologists and folklorists willing to study their own culture. Yet it also carried over into analyses of other groups. Folklorist Roger Abrahams, who had Jewish roots and devoted a career to African American folklore, in the lead essay of the Chicago conference even asserted, "To the extent that we all study others that we may better understand ourselves, for me all folklore is, at least by refraction, Jewish" (R. D. Abrahams 1980, 14). For Abrahams, the concept of folklore as a key expression of culture shifted discussion of race to ethnicity and the capability of agency in the formation of identity.

SITUATING AND FRAMING JEWISH CULTURE

Discontent with functionalism arose across the social sciences during the 1980s because of skepticism about its capacity to serve as an explanation for cultural practice. According to Jewish folkloristic critics such as Elliott Oring (1976), functionalism often described unintended consequences of events rather than their causes. It also raised a psychological question of whether functions outside the awareness of participants constitute motivations by those participants to engage in cultural scenes. One could posit functions as factors contributing to the perception of an event rather than as a reason for behavior within the cultural scene. This criticism appeared to signal a general anti-psychological turn in ethnographic work, as scholars worked to validate the experiences of participants as reasons for engagement with culture (see Dundes 2005). The resulting move to variably interpreting the text of scenes rather than invoking scholarly authority to explain the actions of cultural practices led to a frequent assertion of multiple meanings coming out of a single event coupled with the charge that functionalism was reductionist because it relied on the analysis of an observer rather than of participants (see Ben-Amos 1993; Hufford 1995, 528). By decentering the ethnographer's viewpoint in an alternative to functionalism, there could be as many explanations as there are participants, because individuals brought their own perspective to an event. In historiography, one could speculate on the American connection to this view because of the popularity of performance analysis or post-structural ideas in individualistic societies related to the critique of functionalism. Yet judging from the contents of the *Jewish Folklore and Ethnology Review* through its run from 1977 to 2000, one might also conclude that Jewish folklore studies relied heavily on functionalist explanations of contemporary events. In advancing the symbolist position coupled with functionalism that participants have motivations and impulses outside their awareness, folklorist Alan Dundes especially urged scholars to use psychological analysis of both Jewish religious ritual and popular myths and legends that circulated among non-Jews about Jews (Dundes 2002b, 2007; Dundes and Hasan-Rokem 1986).

One methodological adjustment to functionalism was to ground it in micro-situations, many of which are not bounded in space but defined by individuals who form a cultural relationship that becomes apparent through stylized "performances" (Ben-Amos 1971; see chapter 5). Such situations went by the terms *cultural scenes* or *frames*, and scholars strove to study them in social "context," often attributing the character of performances in events to particular "situated" social interactions. Sociologist Erving Goffman, whose book *Frame Analysis* is a benchmark for this kind of study, underscored the often unspoken negotiation of socially constructed frames by participants in a cultural scene: "I assume that definitions of a situation are built up in accordance with principles of organization which govern events—at least social ones—and our subjective involvement in them" (Erving Goffman 1974, 10–11). According to those who knew Goffman, the problem of socially constructed frames was aroused by issues of Jewish identity and his negotiation of social interactions far from his Manitoba home (see chapter 1). A central problem in Goffman's paradigm-changing approaches to social interaction was identity that could be appropriated and related through expressive acts of gesture and talk in selected settings.

To be sure, this frame analysis is not a Jewish property. Yet I have observed a Jewish perspective of sorts through my editing of six volumes of the Jewish Cultural Studies series for the Littman Library of Jewish Civilization in which ethnographic essays often refer to the mobility and constructiveness of Jewish expression and representation.[5] In such essays the concept of what I would call the psychology of Jewishness as a cultural quality, rather than an anthropology of Jews and Judaism, appears to prevail. This approach is especially evident in confronting Jewish coding in digital communication, a medium that reduces ethnic affiliation on its surface but might also be harnessed to raise it (see chapter 3). Still, one could complain that, although this view of Jewishness as a framed cultural quality is applicable to the Jewish subject, it has not been fully integrated into Jewish studies as a whole, perceived as grounded in historicity and hermeneutic reading of texts. For instance, *AJS Review*, the journal of the Association for Jewish Studies, categorizes articles by historical periods, and the mission statement of the AJS refers to "Jewish Studies scholarship" rather than Jewish culture. Its starting point is "biblical and rabbinic textual and historical studies." Ethnography and folklore gravitate toward a separate development of Jewish cultural studies that has arisen as a new hybrid, distinct from both Jewish studies and cultural studies. Perhaps in reaction to the presumption that biblical and ancient sources dictate later behavior, this hybrid seeks sociological and psychological explanations that posit the *production* of tradition and culture prompted by individuals acting in agency.

The new configuration of Jewish cultural studies centered in ethnography and folklore declares analysis to be about what people think of as Jewish, which may be distinct from the Jew or the things made by Jews. It is revealed in the expressions of culture—speech, folklore, literature, art, architecture, music, dance, ritual, film, theater—that blur the boundaries set up in Jewish studies between Jew and non-Jew, past and present, folk and popular, modernity and tradition. Although growing out of modern American conditions, the orientation has driven a return to Eastern Europe, which is still recovering a disappearing past but more so in the twenty-first century at points of encounter and emergence, such as touristic zones, museums, camps, festivals, and representations and adaptations of tradition betwixt and between national and ethnic identities (see Bar-Itzhak 2005; R. E. Gruber 2002; Kugelmass 1989; Lehrer 2013). These points often invoke cultural memory suited to the occasion and surrounding social and political conflicts rather than exhibiting relict features of folklore as idealized "unadulterated" artifacts.

The shift from function to frame compels a reassessment of Jewish studies historiography toward the fabric of Jewish cultural studies out of the twisted strands of literature, sociology, and history. From the folkloristic side, one might draw lessons from the Jewish ethnology of Central and Eastern Europe to reassess the influence on the contemporary study of mobile, emerging ethnopoetics and cultural scenes of the evolutionary anthropology of the British Empire and the Romantic nationalism of the Grimms. In this historiography, one could expound on the transformation of the vessel of Jewish heritage molded out of the cultural clay of the shtetl or community into what I call the culturalism of Jewish identity molded out of occasions or frames for expression perceived as Jewish in a transnational, dispersed culture. This concept of culturalism locates the production of traditions that provide a sense of cultural identity in the absence or deterioration of institutions in a mass society devoted to handing down and often imposing values through folklore from one generation to the next (Bronner 2011a, 261–66; see also Bronner 2001; Cooper 2012; Fromm 2007).

The search for texts and objects is less about distilling the "pure" strains of the folk than it is about interpreting the meaning of folk process and behavior in the often murky and conflicted representations of Jewishness. This Jewishness is complicated in the framing of Jewish culture by considerations of overlapping or disruptive identities of gender, sexuality, age, family, region, body, and age. The objectives and objects of the culturalism trajectory depart in many ways from the social functionalism of twentieth-century European ethnographers and reflect the setting of ethnographers' sights on the future and the posing of questions of continuity and adaptability frequently in a multicultural environment. Just as An-sky reconstituted his religion with the folklore of the disappearing Russian shtetl, so have Goffman-inspired folklorists, cognizant of the foundation of ethnographic expedition to the cultural "homeland" (as a contrast to the Holy Land), reframed Jewish identity as mobile enactments of the situated ethnography of social and cultural interaction in contemporary culture. Although oriented to the process of the many-headed and many-minded Jews in the myriad cultural scenes of modern life, this development still builds on An-sky's invocation to "Go out and see what the people do."

II

RITUALIZATION

5
RITUALIZING JEWISHNESS

Setting the tone for a theme that pervades Jewish culture, the first question posed in the Mishnah (Oral Law) concerns the flexibility of Jewish ritual. The query in the opening tractate of *Berakhot*, "From what time may they recite the Shema in the evening?" is a starting point likely because it deals with a prayer that structures the day and defines the collective referred to as "they," or Jews. The opening question, followed quickly by the timing of the Shema in the morning, may seem to require a straightforward answer, but it elicits a raft of answers, including "the end of the first watch," "until midnight," and "the rise of dawn," with accompanying commentaries. Several of the replies refer to the "obligation" to recite the prayer ritually—that is, performed repeatedly according to a set order with an understanding of the essential symbolic role it has in daily life. The Mishnah does not specify that fulfilling this obligation need occur in a synagogue or special part of the home. The precept of the tractate is that Jews repeat the recitation daily and that this action is viewed as central to a Jewish life; its repetition in the morning and evening represents a pattern of living, marking time from beginning to end. The Mishnah offers the details of Jewish practices, but it also reflects on the meaning of traditions, such as reciting the Shema, with the explanation that, as rituals beyond the text that is spoken, they serve to protect people from sin. The implication is that the ritual's performance should have a function in a larger interrelated system of action and belief. Broadly speaking in this thinking, ritual structures and symbolizes a Jewish conduct of life. A major lesson from the exchange in the Mishnah is that, although Judaism follows a number of laws that are in response to God's commandments, religious practice is often subject to variation and open to interpretation. That propensity for variation also creates the possibility of debate and controversy over the appropriate or effective form to adopt.

Complicating the application of a social model by which Jewish practices comply with ancient scriptural dictates, even while leaving details subject to revision, is the fact that many people who call themselves Jewish do not recite the Shema twice daily or maybe ever. They may not recognize a scriptural basis to Jewish identity but nonetheless participate in customs that they perceive to set them apart as Jewish—observing holidays, lighting Shabbat candles, eating kosher meat, installing a mezuzah, to name some examples cited in Jewish social surveys (Sheskin 2001, 72–103). Jews might also define themselves by what they do not ritualize, such as holding bridal showers, bringing flowers to a cemetery, or eating pork. Beyond the concept that ritual negation, or prohibitions, mark social boundaries and draw attention to the distinctive cognate customs that the group holds, one might further include under cultural self-awareness identity-forming practices that have modern secular overtones or that are self-consciously created to provide new spiritual ceremonies (Boris 2008, 36–38; Bronner 2008, 16–18; Ochs 2007; Mitchell Silver 1998, 60–78; Whitfield 2007). For example, what about attending a Holocaust commemoration annually? Or performing an Israeli folk dance at a festival? Or doing a mitzvah by helping others on Mitzvah Day or other occasions? Or eating Chinese food and attending a movie on Christmas Eve? Or forming a Rosh Chodesh women's group that features a blessing over Miriam's cup? Or composing a script for a new commitment or naming ceremony (e.g., the Simhat Bat, which I discuss in chapter 7)? Answering yes in deference to different ways of constructing "Jewishness" might also bring to mind boundary-setting practices that suggest ethnic or intrareligious differences within the Jewish world, such as eating rice at Passover (a Sephardic custom), holding a Feast of Jethro (identified as distinctively Tunisian), or observing Simhat Cohen (a unique Indian Jewish festival commemorating the hereditary priests' day after Yom Kippur). If these examples suggest intentional constructions of ritual, what about expressive behavior that appears ritualistic and characteristically Jewish to observers but of which the transmitter may be unaware? For example, one might notice personal rituals suggesting Jewishness, such as reflexively uttering "Oy vey," starting a meeting late with the explanation that the convener operates on "Jewish time," or making excessive amounts of food at a social occasion with the declaration, "I'm a Jewish mother." Finally, what of self-consciously inventing or adapting ritual to fill a personal or community need, such as creating a menstrual or menopausal ceremony for women, parents holding a separation "chai ceremony" on the occasion of their children turning 18 and going away to college, or organizing an Irish Jewish seder in Boston and Dublin?

These kinds of questions, posed in modern discourse and ancient texts, about the source, perpetuation, adaptation, change, and invention of rituals representing Jewishness spin off ultimately from a central query in Jewish cultural studies: How and why do Jews repeat themselves? Jewish studies scholarship recognizes that the ritual process in Jewish tradition is manifestly a way that Jews define themselves and are defined by outsiders. More than a classificatory device, however, ritual can also be studied particularly in a Jewish context as a strategy for perpetuating peoplehood and the values that suggests. Scholars may psychologically encapsulate this idea of a people's collective outlook as a worldview, or they may sociologically consider the particular context that gives meaning to localized ritual texts. Whether looking inside the participants' heads or outside to social and historical conditions, in my frame analysis ritual is subject to change across time and space.

Methodologically, I pursue evidence of the loss and gain of customs for interpretations of the contexts, rationales, and worldviews that constitute versions of the Jewish experience. The religious component is one aspect of a broader process that people engage in to create Jewish associations; others may be in social situations where ritualized, repeated practices such as play, dance, drama, and narrative evoke Jewishness. In other words, in focusing their analytical lenses on the revisions of ritual practices, Jewish cultural studies scholars seek to explain the visions of life that Jews hold. This approach differs from a prior emphasis in Jewish studies on the origin and diffusion of customs, often treating ritual practices as surviving remnants from antiquity (see F. Cohen 1900; Grunwald 1923b; Joseph Jacobs 1890; Yoffie 1916). Jewish cultural studies usually examines ritual situationally, often as diverse, emergent social and intellectual constructions, rather than presuming it to be inherited as a limited set of scripturally derived practices. As such, the concept of ritual expands from religious rites that are shown to be remarkably persistent and stable to symbolized practices that are contextualized culturally and analyzed for their change. Scholars taking a Jewish cultural studies perspective approach contemporary secular discontinuity, controversy, and initiative as much as, if not more than, the conventional idea of long-standing religious continuity and survival. The lesson of Jewish cultural studies is not all that far, though, from the one drawn from the opening exchange in the Mishnah:

Traditionality of Jewishness correlates with the variability and even creativity of Jewish practice. Working in cultural studies, scholars can be especially concerned with rituals as expressive forms that have been incorporated rhetorically and strategically into a multilayered Jewish cultural system. This system is not singular but emanates from the immediate community and individuals who are engaging in a ceremony to the broader contributions or detractions from Jewish and non-Jewish worlds.

A precedent for an approach to the dynamism of Jewish ritual lies in the discourse about *minhag*, from the Hebrew for "custom," encompassing the dualism of scripturally derived rite and the adapted or invented postbiblical ritual (Chill 1979, xix–xxii; J. Tabory 1997, 466). In rabbinic writing, *minhag* includes the kind of prayer rituals discussed in *Berakhot* and the liturgical variations that developed broadly between Ashkenazic and Sephardic observances. It can also suggest variations of religious practices within localities and subcultures, including rites and festivals of Hasidic, Karaite, German, Polish, Yemenite, Ethiopian, Bukharan, and Italian Jews, to name a few prominently mentioned regional traditions (Raisin 1907, 79–123). *Minhag* can also refer to customs that arose from popular usage rather than those introduced by a rabbinic authority or taken from biblical writ. Customs often attach to a community or region, although they can also be extended to wide adoption, even becoming binding as rules or norms, such as men wearing head coverings and eating apples and honey on Rosh Hashanah. The concern in much of the discourse of *minhag* is not so much an explanation of the process of attachment as it is the appropriateness of the custom as Jewish law, especially its characterization as functional, primitive, or even heretical (Chill 1979, xx–xxi; Linke 1999, 12–15; J. Tabory 1997, 467).

The use of *minhag* in the Torah differs from its meaning in rabbinic discourse. Originally, *minhag*, from the Hebrew root for "driving," refers in the Tanakh to the way that Jehu, son of Nimshi, handles a chariot (II Kings 9:20). The figurative use of *minhag* came out of a collective, anonymously constructed meaning of practices that people have to identify themselves religiously and, presumably, to drive, or conduct, themselves through life. With the emphasis of Jews on following the traditions of ancestors, the concept of *minhag* allowed Judaism to be conceived organically as an evolving religion in relation to its cultural context (Gaster 1978, 3–5). In fact, the Mishnah comments on the priority of *minhag* in several places, such as the directive for Passover that "a person should not vary from *minhag* [in the sense of local custom] so as to avoid contentiousness" (*Pesahim* 4:1f). An oft-cited passage concerns the repetition of verses at Sukkot: "Everything follows the *minhag* of the locality" (*Sukkah* 3:11d). Not coincidentally, the passage underscores the rhetorical connection between ritual repetition and the idea of *minhag* becoming widespread or binding through long-standing social usage. Attempts to integrate these customs that have the quality of law have emerged since the Geonic period, most notably the *Shulchan Aruch*, a compilation of 13,602 *minhagim* by Rabbi Yosef Karo in the sixteenth century, including judgments on the savoriness of the customs (Chill 1979: xx–xxi; A. Davis 2006). Karo's text led to a host of published commentaries on the appropriateness of the customs or notice of *minhagim* from particular communities that were left out or misinterpreted (Raisin 1907, 111–23). In Poland Rabbi Moses Isserles's 1570 commentary titled *Mappah* was especially influential on Ashkenazic Jewry in respecting local folk customs as validating agency by common people for their everyday religious practice. Often quoted is Isserles's declaration that the "*minhag* is the law" (Baumgarten 2019, 96), which set off a centuries-long debate on the authority of communities to dictate and codify religious practice and decentralize Jewish identity (Joseph Davis 2002).

Concerned with showing non-Jews as well as Jews that Jewish practices held meaning for the present as a basis for judgment of traditions to be encouraged, works such as *Taamei HaMinhagim* (Reasons for Our Customs; 1890) by Rabbi Avraham Yitzchak Sperling (1999) became popular in the wake of industrialism and opened symbolic as well as historic associations for scrutiny. However, the corpus of Jewish customs was still limited to religious or synagogue ceremonies. For example, in translating Sperling's work into English in the late twentieth century, Rabbi Abraham Matts dismissed ethnic or nationalistic uses of tradition with the comment, "These ceremonial acts of course, are but the means to an end, namely the religious life. If they fail to achieve that objective, they are useless" (Matts 1968, 7). Also referring to Sperling's work to rationalize tradition, Shmuel Pinchas Gelbard called his compilation of customs *Rite and Reason: 1,050 Jewish Customs and Their Sources* (published in Hebrew as *Otzar Ta'amei ha-Minhagim*). His intention was to review "many practices [that] have fallen into disuse and, more importantly, many of the reasons and rationales given for them [that] have become tarnished by time" (Gelbard 1998, vii). The categories of ceremonies that fell under the rubric of *minhag* in these works were primarily historic: first, the ancient customs that had universally become integrated into Halacha; and second, customs practiced by specific communities (Gelbard delineates Ashkenazim, Sephardim, Hasidim, German Jews, communities in Eretz Yisrael, and Jews of

Jerusalem). Defensive about the social challenge to rabbinic authority that *min-hagim* emerging from popular usage represented, these rabbinic commentators reflected more on the codification of law than the analysis of Jewish cultural patterns (Ben-Menahem 1996, 431–32; Chill 1979, xx–xxi; Ginzberg 1955, 153–86). For example, Rabbi William Rosenau, in his lectures collected in *Jewish Ceremonial Institutions and Customs*, extolled the value of codes "framed to meet all violations of sanctity" as a bulwark against "a marked tendency in the Synagogue to de-rabbinize Judaism, by laying less emphasis on the forms and more on the spirit of the faith" (Rosenau 1903, 43, 11).

Even as codification strengthened a rule-centered religious tradition admin-istered by rabbinic authority, support for inclusion of *minhagim* in the codes also implied what Jewish historian Theodor Gaster called a "progressive" world-view in Judaism: "The Torah itself is dynamic, not static, unfolding itself con-tinuously throughout the ages" (Gaster 1978, 4). In calling for the interpretation of practices by successive generations, Gaster recognized rituals adapted in the present that gave power to the living rather than to the dead. He sanctioned and relativized the multiplicity of Jewish experience. This view is evident in the sum-mative Yiddish saying, "Minhag brecht ein Din" (Custom breaks a law) invoked by prominent rabbinic figures labeled liberal, such as Philip David Bookstaber, who brought in relationships of Jews to non-Jews in the Diaspora: "Rabbinic literature is very insistent upon the maintenance of 'custom' and, likewise, with equal insistence, careful to exhort the Jew to revere and honor the customs of oth-ers within his own community or of the community into which he may come as a visitor. So strong and so important are these 'customs'—yea—these 'mores,' that for no idle reason has the following phrase been made classic in Jewish life: '*Min-hag brecht ein Din*'" (Bookstaber 1939, 15; see also Chill 1979, xxi). A counterview expressed as an aphorism is "Custom is Torah," suggesting, in Joseph Tabory's words, a rabbinic "protest against slavish adherence to senseless or even objection-able customs" that arose in the postbiblical period (J. Tabory 1997, 466).

The discomfort that the concept of *minhag* raises is that, despite the appear-ance of social acceptance, the entrenched customs became subject to rabbinic derision, or worse, condemnation by non-Jewish society, as dated, backward, superstitious, and irreverent. The concept forces a judgment of religious value and risks divisiveness rather than offering an analysis of cultural practices. One such controversial ritual is *kapparah*, which is traditionally enacted before Yom Kippur. It involves waving a fowl above one's head three times accompanied by the declaration, "This is my substitute, this is my exchange, this is my atonement. This fowl shall go unto death, and I will go, and enter, into a good and long life, and into peace" (Rappoport 1937, 114–16; Stern 1987, 123–26; Unterman 1999, 164). The animal is then ritually slaughtered to complete the expiatory process. Mentioned beginning in ninth-century Babylonia and associated today primarily with Orthodox Ashkenazim, to the present day the custom has aroused various calls to abolish the practice, to make it compulsory in keeping with the atonement of Yom Kippur, to revise it, such as using money instead of the bird and then giving the money to charity, or to replace it with another *minhag* of *tashlikh* (Hebrew: casting off), for example, throwing crumbs into water to discharge sins. Objections to *kapparah* for centuries focused on its similarity to pagan sacrifice, cruelty to the bird, or its absence in Torah references.

In a modern twist to the debate over the ethics of *kapparot*, the animal rights movement got involved in 2008 with a widely publicized complaint from the People for the Ethical Treatment of Animals (PETA) that the chickens were abused before the staging of the ritual (Fishkoff 2008). The implication was that the humane tradition, and therefore difference, from mass society that Orthodox Jews claimed in its justificatory label of religious ritual was belied by actual practice. Rabbi Avi Shafran, director of public affairs for Agudath Israel of America, answered that rabbinic authorities had taken steps to prevent chickens from being treated without "the sensitivity to animals' comfort that halacha mandates." He further addressed the underlying objection from both Jews and non-Jews that "the custom itself is 'primitive.' " Calling the *minhag* "indispensable" for Orthodox Jews, Shafran cited the belief that "the day of ultimate reckoning may be upon us far sooner than we imagine, just as fish swimming freely in the water may find themselves captured suddenly in the hungry fishmonger's net—and that we dare not live lives of spiritual leisure on the assumption that there will always be time for repentance when we grow old." He argued on religious grounds that *kapparot* are "an opportunity for self-sensitization to our need for repentance." He counted himself as "modern" as the next person, but complained, "All too often we moderns tend to view ancient Jewish laws, customs and rituals as quaint relics of the distant past evoking, at most, warm and nostalgic feelings of ethnic identity. But, as a closer look at Kapporos and Tashlich suggest, there is a world of difference between Tevya's celebration of 'Tradition!' for tradition's sake [in *Fiddler on the Roof*] and the deep meanings that lie in the rites and rituals of Jewish religious life" (Shafran 2010; for further discussion of the representation of tradition in *Fiddler on the Roof*, see chapter 3).

An issue evident in Shafran's final comments, at least for cultural scholars, is that *minhag* does not discriminate between rites, rituals, initiations, ceremonies, and customs that suggest different cultural processes and generally excludes nonreligious practices. Much as the *minhag* compilations provide a rich source of centuries-old evidence of perceived "deep meanings" for Jewish cultural studies, ethnological distinctions are useful to objectify and broaden understanding of tradition as lived experience. Rituals typically draw attention to themselves as events condensed in time that are typically repeatable, structured, expressive, performed, and intentionally symbolic (Bronner 2004, 17–29; R. A. Rappaport 1992, 249; R. A. Rappaport 1996; Snoeck 2006). Examined as a process, ritual exaggerates and symbolizes relationships by putting them on display in an event that is separated from mundane activity; it is often viewed as framed "time out of time" in which participants and their audiences expect words and actions to be symbolically significant (see Bell 1992, 197–223; Beattie 1966, 65; Bronner 2004; Handelman 2006; Houseman 2006; Leach 1968, xiii, 524; Shepard 1973, 196; T. Turner 2006). Following this emphasis on ritual involving symbolic action and embodying social contract, anthropologist Roy Rappaport asserts that ritual is the "fundamental social act upon which human society is founded" (R. A Rappaport 1992, 254). Whereas custom is an activity that is performed with regularity and could include rituals, custom is commonly, as folklorist Richard Sweterlitsch notes, "a vast aggregate of human behavior" that is usually described as part of the ordinary routine in people's lives (Sweterlitsch 1997, 168). Ritual breaks everyday routine, creates a different space and time, and establishes an *extra*-ordinary action or symbol as a guide to daily practice (see R. D. Abrahams 1986). An application of this idea is evident in the so-called Lubavitch "Mitzvah Mobiles" (brightly colored vans) stationed in Jewish neighborhoods to relate Jewish identity to ritual acts. Yeshivah youths from the mobiles ask passersby if they are Jewish; if the answer is yes, they request the individual to engage in ritual to affirm it: putting on tefillin or reciting a blessing. Debra Renee Kauffman ethnographically observes that these repeated scenes convey the message that ritual observance, apparently out of step with everyday routine, actually defines daily living and personal identity. She finds it significant that un-self-conscious engagement with tradition in the ritual is essential to the disruption of Jewish self-awareness: "Dressed in their black suits and hats and with untrimmed beards, these recruiters offer no explanations for ritual behavior—potential recruits are just encouraged to act" (Kauffman 1991, 26). The actions are supposed to be transformative.

Ritual acts hold social attention and signal an expressive moment. Yet ritual is not necessarily un-self-conscious. Modern institutions and individuals often organize ritual by introducing, scripting, and staging symbolic events within a ceremonial frame (Belasco 2009; Ochs 2007; N. Rubin 2009; Ruttenberg 2009; Schwartzman and Francesca 2004). Rather than imagining that rituals are repeated by blindly following precedent, the idea of individuals and groups scripting and framing events as integral to communicating meaning through rituals introduces agency to the cultural process (Bronner 2010b; Handelman 2006; Mechling 1980; Sax 2006). Yael Zerubavel (1995) provides an example in her historical ethnography of ritual innovations, particularly the holiday eve bonfire of Lag b'Omer celebrations by secular Israeli youth. Conventional instruction related in the Talmud about the holiday refers to mourning for a plague that wiped out 24,000 of Rabbi Akiva's students during the counting of the Omer (*Yevamot* 62b). Further underscoring the Jewish tragedy commemorated during the holiday is a legendary interpretation that the students died as a result of Roman campaigns to destroy Judaism during the Bar Kokhba revolt in the second century CE, which actually ended around Tisha b'Av, falling on dates in July or August in the Gregorian calendar (Zerubavel 1995, 97). Beginning in the 1920s in the Yishuv, organizers of Lag b'Omer events occurring in April or May in the Gregorian calendar explained the significance of the bonfires as representations of the fires kindled by Hebrew "freedom fighters"; the organizers said that during the ancient revolt, the fighters, who were camping in the mountains, used bonfires to communicate with other rebel groups, informing them of movements by Roman legions (101).

Zerubavel points out that the ritual context of the Bar Kokhba revolt shifted from inclusion in Tisha b'Av as a grim fast day to a festive celebration, thus transforming lamentation over Bar Kokhba's ultimate defeat to a victorious moment relating to Zionist discourse of a struggle for liberation. The ritual of bonfire kindling takes on added significance because wood is a relatively scarce resource in the Middle East and because Israeli culture treats the planting of trees as a major patriotic act. The gathering of wood in the preparation for the ritual becomes a sign of empowerment for Israeli youth: "In the days preceding Lag ba-Omer, children begin to look for scraps of wood and carefully hide or protect their findings because of the harsh competition over a limited supply. Humorous Lag ba-Omer lore describes the parents' need to protect their furniture from their children's overly zealous efforts to find materials for the bonfire" (Zerubavel 1995, 102). The point is that the memory of the Bar Kokhba revolt is symbolically merged with the "zealous" spirit of the Zionist youth movement. Zerubavel finds that the ritual reinforces the symbolic continuity between the ancient fighters and Hebrew youth, and an added dimension is the frequent burning of an effigy in the bonfires of a leading enemy (Adolf Hitler during the 1940s, Gamal Abdel Nasser during the 1950s). The symbolic burning of villainous destroyers of Jews may have a precedent of burning effigies of the Jews' archenemy Haman on Purim, but in the new context it is introduced as a novel, festive component. Zerubavel concludes, "The themes of courage, success, and revenge have become central to the commemoration of the Bar Kokhba revolt, thereby blurring the memory of the massacre, destruction, and exile it brought upon the Jews" (102). Supporting the Zionist themes are songs and stories that narrate the redefinition of the holiday and highlight the bonfire as its central ritual observance (99).

The initiation is a type of ritual with special reference to transition of status, particularly from one life stage to another or from roles as outsider to insider, and for some Jewish commentators it is the main source of *minhagim* (M. Fox 1979, vii). Rites constitute another subset of ritual that imply religious or magical functions (Pentikäinen 1997, 734–35), but the concept of "rite of passage," introduced by Arnold van Gennep in 1908, suggests a specific tripartite structure for initiatory events that move through distinct phases of separation, transition (or liminality), and incorporation (or return) (Bronner 2008–2009; Myerhoff 1982; van Gennep 1960). In the analysis of Jewish experience, rites connote a sacred or magicoreligious connection to transformation, whereas ritual, as a symbolic form that expressively embodies social contract, can be secularized and objectified (Bell 1997, 61–90; Burkert 1996; Girard 1996; Pentikäinen 1997, 735; V. Turner 1967, 1969, 1982).

Ethnologists often refer to ceremony in conjunction with ritual to refer to an organized event, such as a commemoration requiring reverence or special attention (Bronner 2008–2009). A ceremony's defining characteristic is that it is a formal act or observance, although as a whole it may not exhibit the structure or sacred qualities of rites. Nonetheless, along with festival, celebration, and holiday as cultural genres, ceremony may contain a number of discrete rituals within it (V. Turner 1982, 22–23). Most broad of all the terms related to *minhag*, tradition represents precedence for actions or ideas or, more generally, stands for continuity with the past. It differs from laws and rules, however, by being socially constituted (its derivation from the Latin *tradere*, "handing down or over," suggests oral or socially informal exchange) rather than officially inscribed; it is often expressed culturally as norms or conventional knowledge (Bronner 1998, 9–72; 2009b; 2019, 64–84). Tradition is often coupled with ritual because both connote precedence and the repetition of localized social convention. They both feed the perception that the conduct of life—and the cultural norms, symbols, and expectations guiding it—is subject to variation, change, and innovation.

Jewish ritual among different ethnic traditions often stands out in many societies because of its deviation from prevalent national customs by working with a distinctive calendar (lunar), life-cycle milestones (e.g., circumcision, bar mitzvah), and source (ancient Israel). If rabbinic sources underscore the importance of custom to actualize Jewish belief in practice and frame Jewish identity as a totalizing experience, then a related argument is that popular literature implied the exoticism, anachronism, and clannishness of Jews with the assignment of their practices to the category of ritual (J. Boyarin 1996, 138–39; Bronner 1998, 132–37; Judd 2007; Moltke 1997). Recognizing the importance of distinctive rituals, particularly in museum displays, nineteenth-century Jewish scholars could appear defensive about characterizing Jews by their rituals because of the association of the genre with secrecy and even diabolicalness. Jewish writers often framed Jewish worlds instead as a civilization marked by artistic and intellectual contributions or as traditions and faiths comparable to other modern religions (Jeremy Cohen and Cohen 2008; Glick 1982; Kirshenblatt-Gimblett 1998, 79–130). However, the tendency to categorize Jewish practice as naturally ritualized is evident in the popular taxonomy of Jewish activities prefaced by the word *ritual* (bath, slaughter, head covering, dress, food, object, law) and in anti-Semitic literature (murder).

With the modern shift in defining ritual from an exotic event suggesting superstitious, controlled, or irrational content to a behavioral basis of organizing experience that all people engage in out of social and psychological necessity, scholars have applied a more neutral and expansive rhetoric of ritual involving "interaction," "framing," "social construction," and "identity." Introducing the field of ritual studies, Ronald L. Grimes observed that "much that would not have been regarded as ritual three decades ago now appears, either literally or metaphorically, to be ritual. Ritual can seem to exist in strictly circumscribed spaces (as if it were hiding in the corners of decrepit churches), and yet, almost magically, it can be everywhere, functioning as the very lifeblood of individuals and societies" (Grimes 1996, xiv). Emphasizing the repetitive framing of activity as connotative and patterned, the elastic and presumably less mystical notion of ritual is evident in treatments of practices not covered by the Mishnah, such

as new Israeli commemorations, summer campfire programs as identity renew-
als, Israeli youth embarking on backpacking pilgrimages at an expected time in
the life course, or descendants of Eastern European Jewish immigrants creating a
nosh (snack) associated with *Yiddishkeit* as a symbolic personal routine (Sales and
Saxe 2003; Kirshenblatt-Gimblett 1990; C. Noy 2006; Zarubavel 1995, 114–37).
Although the range of practices considered ritual has been broadened in this elastic
approach, which emphasizes process and context by unlocking ritual from religious and historical restrictions, key questions of ritual's capacity to structure and
symbolize experience emerge as paramount.

With process and context as the defining characteristics for ritual in a broader
view of framed, repetitive behavior, ritual becomes evident throughout daily
life and is critical to the principles that guide that living as cultural experience.
Instead of being represented as unthinking and limited to magicoreligious uses,
ritual broadly represents connotative knowledge and action. Epitomizing this
approach to ritual is the work of social scientists Victor Turner, Erving Goffman,
and Clifford Geertz. These figures at the forefront of a pivotal "interactionist"
ethnographic movement of the 1960s and 1970s placed ritual at the center of
cultural analysis, labeling the symbols set by ritual "paradigmatic," because ritual
embodied conflicts and paradoxes of the society and could be studied as bounded,
communicative scenes (Grimes 2006, 384–87). Other scholars in the movement
shared the application of a dramaturgical rhetoric of actors, stages, and audiences
to describe these scenes as examples of ritualized, symbolized "performance"
(Ben-Amos 1997; Bronner 1988; see chapter 4). The new analytical rhetoric suggested that participants, in their behavior and communication with one another
and to the audience, created meaning anew rather than inheriting a preset script.
Instead of separating the spoken word as text from the actions that delivered it,
they encouraged treatment of the whole scene as a cultural text that could be read
for symbolism and structure. From their work, a host of daily nonreligious activities drew analysis as ritual and interactive cultural text, including play, dance,
drama, and joking in modern industrialized societies (McCurdy et al. 2004;
J. Silverman and Rader 2005).

Twenty-first-century museum exhibitions at major institutions, such as the
Jewish Museum in New York, the Jewish Historical Museum in Amsterdam,
the Contemporary Jewish Museum in San Francisco, and the Philadelphia Museum
of Jewish Art, particularly of new artistic (and often abstract) interpretations of
"ritual objects," fueled interactionist thinking about ritual by public viewers

formerly accustomed to musing on historic Judaica suggestive of continuity from an ancient past (Belasco 2009; Contemporary Jewish Museum 2009; Sachs and van Voolen 2004; M. Singer 2007, 2009). In the exhibition *Wimpel!* Wrapped Wishes (2009) at the Philadelphia Museum of Jewish Art, which displayed artistic variations on the cloth binders encircling Torah scrolls (often on decorated sashes traditionally used by Ashkenazic Jews in the circumcision ritual of the Brit Milah), mixed-media artist Kym Hepworth explains her representation of the *wimpel* in *To Part No More* (Figure 5.1) as part of a wedding canopy with paradoxes characteristic of ritual: "Here, the house/birdcage motif represents continuity, security, and hope for the future. However, there are cracks in this foundation and the overall stability of the structure is threatened by the tension of entrapment and anxiety of abandonment" (M. Singer 2009).

Hepworth's construction represents the kind of creative reformulation of ritual about which Arnold Eisen, chancellor of the Jewish Theological Seminary, commented in a catalogue for the Jewish Museum's exhibit Reinventing Ritual.

> Ritual has made a comeback of late. After decades (indeed, centuries) of denigration in the West as behavior that is hopelessly stereotyped, formulaic, repetitive, and largely boring, after unceasing put-down as rote action that stifles creativity and innovation, or as legalism that inhibits genuine feeling, or as mere "ritualism" that stands in the way of true human relationship and blocks the way to authentic encounter with God—after all of that, we find ourselves in 2009 at a moment when ritual is once again receiving its due as an essential element of culture. . . . The abiding chutzpa of Judaism—its central claim that the world is not good enough and that we can make it and ourselves better, with God's help—imperceptibly inspires contemporary Jewish creativity and performance. (Eisen 2009, xi, xiii)

In his assessment of ritual's reinvention in contemporary Jewish culture, Eisen probably makes too much of the encounter with God and not enough of the agency that seeks to link postmodern individualism with reconnection to communication. Hepworth, in her manipulation of Jewish traditional symbols' continuity across rituals from the *wimpel* in birth to the wedding canopy, seeks to find continuity across the life course. Her display symbolically interacts with viewers to ask what they recognize as Jewish with ordinary, popular materials and whether they can pick those out as a basis of an identity that aligns or chafes at mass society.

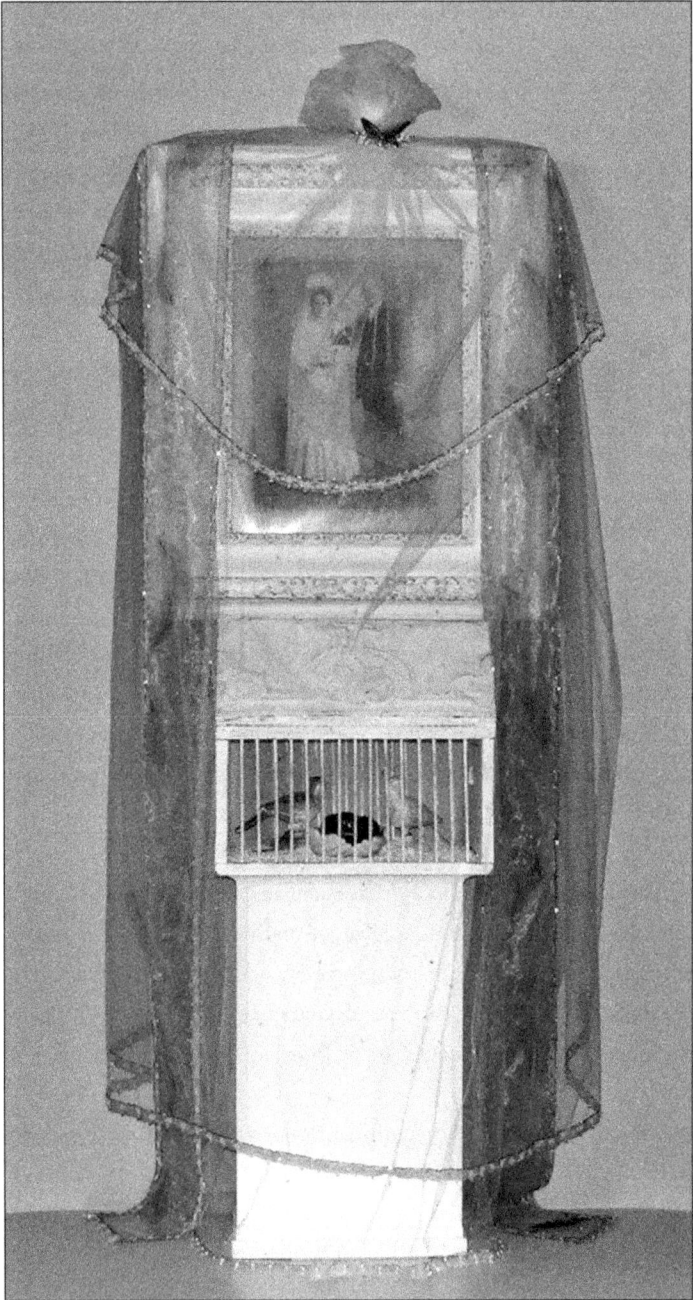

5.1. To Part No More, mixed media, by Kym Hepworth of Savannah, Georgia, featured in the exhibition *Wimpel!* Wrapped Wishes at the Philadelphia Museum of Jewish Art, 2009. Photo by Robin Miller; courtesy of Kym Hepworth.

The symbolic-interactionist perspective that could be applied to Hepworth's display owes much to the analytical work on Jewish ritual by Theodor Gaster and Raphael Patai, who, working in different parts of the Jewish world, drew out the importance of the performative context of the events and relationships to local societies (Gaster 1955; Patai 1960, 20–22; Patai 1983, 17–44). Gaster and Patai were concerned with the duration of traditions more than innovation, but they helped to promote the understanding of the process of ritualization as a social action strategically applied in various situations and countered the popular view of Jewish ritual as primitive or functionless (Grimes 1982, 133–59). For example, in *Thespis* (1961) Gaster linked Jewish ritual and myth to drama circulating in Middle Eastern communities about seasonal transitions. In *The Holy and the Profane* he insisted, "The Jews were not mere 'copycats' and did not borrow mechanically. The characteristic trait of Jewish folklore is a genius for infusing into originally 'alien' material a new and more spiritual meaning and significance born of their own distinctive heritage and tradition" (Gaster 1955, xi). Patai, meanwhile, declared the ethnographic priority for the study of Jewish culture: "The ethnologist working on a Jewish community has to take into account the special circumstances in which such a community lives," or, in other words, its local contexts and intercultural relations (Patai 1983, 27).

Other connections to the symbolic-interactionist perspective on ritual, art, and culture come out of research in Jewish ritual or theories contextualized by the ethnographer's Jewish background. For example, familiarity with the complexities of Jewish communities and ritual performances undoubtedly influenced Israeli American scholar Dan Ben-Amos's iconic processual definition of "folklore in context" as "artistic communication in small groups" (Ben-Amos 1971; see also Ben-Amos 1997). Ben-Amos was a contributor to a paradigm-shifting volume, *Toward New Perspectives in Folklore* (Paredes and Bauman 1972), that heralded approaches that focused on culture as performance. Another contributor to that volume was folklorist Roger D. Abrahams, who had a German Jewish background; Abrahams referred to rituals as enactments to be analyzed situationally and rhetorically (R. D. Abrahams 1980, 14; see also R. D. Abrahams 1968, 1972b, 1977, 2005). The processual orientation is evident in historical studies, too, such as Ivan Marcus's study of medieval Jewish rituals of childhood, in which he conceptualizes ritual broadly as "all conventional gestures that are routinely expressed in the life of a particular group" (I. G. Marcus 1996, 4; see also Geffen 1993; H. E. Goldberg 2003; I. G. Marcus 2004). For new cultural studies scholars, the Jewish subject, having been stripped of its physical, racial component, raises questions of boundary and identity maintenance, evident in anthropologist Harvey E. Goldberg's postracial questioning in his important twenty-first-century analysis of Jewish life-cycle rituals: "Can one speak of 'the Jews' in the absence of a centralized authority with the power to determine 'what Judaism is,' and when scholars writing about 'Jewish tradition' now recognize that they are dealing with phenomena whose contents and boundaries are fluid?" (H. E. Goldberg 2003, 11).

Often overlooked by both Jewish and non-Jewish commentators influenced by a preoccupation with difference and boundary maintenance is the way that Jews adapt or participate in local traditions and deal with the controversies that arise from hybridizing or acculturative processes. Indeed, one of the issues that arises in a broadened view of ritual revision is the way that shared or imported practices become Judaized, ethnicized, exalted, or stigmatized (R. D. Abrahams 1980). People who affiliate as Jewish or non-Jewish may perceive such practices to be Jewish, even though the structures and symbols are similar to those in non-Jewish culture (see Sharaby 2011). With the additional connection made between Jewish practice and ancient lineage, particularly the Middle East, emergent rituals—either socially constituted or individually composed and serving either nonsacred or religious purposes—may not receive the analytical attention they deserve for an understanding of Jewish identity. In sum, contextualizing changes and adaptations of ritual and conflicts and debates over ritual signify various transitions—between generations, among contemporary factions, between homeland and destination, between religious and secular functions, among sources of authority—that reveal the cultural experience people identify as Jewish.

Categories of Jewish ritual following symbolic-interactionist concerns for lived experience take on a different look and forms of analysis than the bifurcation of *minhag* into biblical and postbiblical custom and the engrossment in premodern sources (Eisen 1998, 8–10). By taking away the organizing principle of biblical source, rituals can be alternately summarized by cultural connection to contexts of (1) liturgy and prayer, (2) time and yearly cycle, (3) passage (or related to life course) and initiation, and (4) performance and practice. That is not to say that the sources of rituals in text and antiquity are immaterial; they have a strong bearing on the perception and enactment of rituals. A factor in the integration of text and context in analysis is the growth of Jewish field-based studies of the multiplicity of Jewish culture, defined as people conducted their daily lives at home and on the street as well as in the synagogue (Avrutin et al. 2009; Bronner 2010a;

Gonen 1994; Mikdash-Shamailov 2002; Shwartz-Be'eri 2000; Slapak 2003). In Harvey E. Goldberg's survey of ethnographic approaches to Jewish culture, he notes that "anthropology was suspicious in its formative period of attaching too much weight to written sources, or to the interpretations offered by literati of the rituals and mores of their own traditions" (H. E. Goldberg 2003, 6; see also Bronner 2006b; Hertzog et al. 2010; D. Noy 1980; Patai 1960). But disciplinary changes, including scholarly acceptance of group members studying themselves close to home, and the de-emphasis of racialization in cultural analysis encouraged more Jewish ethnography promulgated by Jews. Goldberg notes that these shifts endorsed Jewish cultural researchers' viewing of "texts as formative components in social life" while incorporating the "basic insight of social science that thought, speech, and writing often follow from behavior, rather than being the 'reason why' people do things" (H. E. Goldberg 2003, 6). Accordingly, Jewish cultural studies applies religio-historical and ethnological perspectives, but with a focus on questions of process, function, symbol, and constructed meaning. In asking how and why Jews repeat themselves, these scholars also query the ways that Jews revise and transform their worlds (Sax 2006, 474–76).

LITURGY AND PRAYER

Concern for textual sources is most evident in the ritual category of liturgy and prayer. This category comprises the forms of congregational and individual prayer, including the attire, gestures, and incantations, that ritualize the content of worship. Much of the attention to liturgy and prayer has been on the synagogue as an institutional context that frames the ritual components of services materially and socially (Elbogen 1993). The material aspects that signal ritualized behavior include the exterior of the synagogue, which sets it apart from domestic architecture, and, within the interior, the physical guides to practice, such as the expectations of expressive behavior around the ark, bimah, and Torah. Changing social contexts that have received attention for structuring synagogue practice—and for raising controversy over gender relations—include the constitution of the minyan (traditionally 10 adult males, 13 years of age or older) and the location of the *mechitzah* (Hebrew: partition). Noticeable as a sign of transition in ritual participation is the growing trend for women to wear yarmulkes, tallitot, and tefillin.

The connection between gendered ritual dress and gestures for prayer leads to consideration of the body's role in framing Jewish practice, and the negative perception of Jewish bodily practices by Christian standards of contemplative restraint. This might include the regard of the chevra kadisha for the deceased body in funerary rituals; the supposedly Jewish gesticulation of davening as a contrast to the constrained, kneeling devotion and pressing together palms in Catholic prayer; texts related to mitzvot for *niddah*, pregnancy, and childbirth (Wasserfall 1992; Weissler 1992); and the embodiment of the service as a male space (and, by extension, other spaces such as the *mikveh* as female locations) (Anijar 1999; Eilberg-Schwartz 1992; Gilman 1991; Konner 2009). Ritual as symbolic knowledge and action figures prominently not only in the gendering of Jewish liturgical practice but also in boundary maintenance between Jews and non-Jews and Orthodox and non-Orthodox Jews. This is especially evident in patterns such as the *ba'al teshuvah* movement (literally "masters of return" but, figuratively, individuals who have not been religious in their former lives but come to embrace Orthodox Judaism) that defy the modernist expectation that ritual observance declines with modernization. For example, in Debra Renee Kauffman's study of newly Orthodox women, identified as *ba'alat teshuvot*, one woman says:

> *I have found meaning in all this ritual* . . . meaning I have really had at another time in my life. Torah has so much to say to me as a woman. My feelings about myself as a sexual person . . . the family purity laws are so in line with me as a woman . . . it is commanded that I not be sexually taken for granted, that I have two weeks each month for myself. . . . It is mind-boggling to me to think that this wonderful Torah has known who I am as a woman for centuries. (Kauffman 1991, 45; emphasis added)

The speaker connects that meaning to *tzniut* (Hebrew: modesty) and suggests its ritual presentation of a bodily self as a strategy for boundary maintenance: "[*Tzniut* is] such a wonderful way of presenting oneself . . . it means modesty. It means you should present yourself as caring, soft-spoken, gentle, you know . . . in a feminine way. That's what orthodoxy is really all about. Tznius [Ashkenazic pronunciation] doesn't just apply to women; it's meant for all Jews. We are supposed to be separate, different, apart . . . different from a world that can do such things as a Holocaust" (Kauffman 1991, 45; see also P. E. Falk 1998).

Questions about the ritual texts of the congregational service include the selection and performance of prayers, often related to bodily gestures, such as the repetition of rocking on the balls of the feet during the Amidah and actions during the opening and closing sections of the various services to engage the ritual function of marking time (Ehrlich 2004). One example is the prevalent use of the Kaddish at the end of prayer services, because liturgical scholars point out that it was not part of the synagogue ritual (Eisenberg 2004, 394; Lamm 1969, 149–74). As Ronald Eisenberg notes, "The ancient custom of dismissing the assembly with the words of the *Kaddish* is still preserved in the *Kaddish de-Rabbanan* (*Kaddish* of the Rabbis), which is recited in the synagogue after communal study. However, instead of being uttered by the teacher, the *Kaddish de-Rabbanan* is now recited by those mourners who are in attendance" (Eisenberg 2004, 394). In the tradition of the *minhagim* compilers, Eisenberg notes the origin of the custom "out of the practice of honoring a deceased scholar, at the close of the seven-day shivah period," although cultural studies scholars may note, in the expected behavior of congregational response and the rhetorical importance of the Mourner's Kaddish in the service (and its relation to the *Yizkor* [remembrance] memorial service), a symbolic value placed on generational continuity as a key to reproducing Jewishness (Eisenberg 2004, 394; Lamm 1969, 153–61).

Indeed, the Kaddish is a ritual that carries over into home and individual practice, including the ritual lighting of a candle for *yahrzeit* (Yiddish: literally "time of year" and figuratively the memorial observance on the anniversary of the death of a relative) (Lamm 1969, 201–5; Syme 2004, 207–8). Rabbis often refer to the obligation of traditional personal prayers, such as the waking formula of Modeh Ani and bedtime blessings, as ritualizing Orthodox devotion. That suggests that common liberal practice is to omit these prayers, but the thanksgiving benediction of time in the Shehecheyanu (the first distinctive word of the blessing meaning "who has kept us in life") is often featured in coming-of-age events and in inventive ceremonies, such as Simhat Bat (see chapter 7), as a preface for newly composed blessings and recitations to frame joyous occasions (Cardozo 1982, 210; I. G. Marcus 2004, 106, 112; Wolowelsky 1997, 43–50).

Beyond the matter of content and agency of the text are performative issues that have arisen in the synagogue as context and liturgy as content. Since the early nineteenth century, the ritual framing device of music, especially accompanied by instruments or choirs, has raised debates about attitudes toward the sanctity of the synagogue in relation to music and, by extension, dance. In addition to spiritual and scriptural questions about the role of music and dance in the liturgy (and ritual specialists for them), their performance could be viewed as ethnic boundary markers provided by the Jewish liturgy, and the perception of their negation contributed to the view that Jews were not creative or modern (Gilman 2008). Jewish historian Jonathan D. Sarna notes that "questions concerning music in the synagogue have stood second only to questions concerning women in the synagogue as prime sources of disputation, dividing synagogues and sometimes even landing up in court" (J. D. Sarna 2003, 195). The two issues overlapped in the rise of a female cantorate as ritual specialists in the late twentieth century (Heskes 1997; Slobin 2002, 112–34), but well before that, many liturgical disputes between liberal and orthodox wings of Judaism were anticipated by controversies over the character of the music performed in the synagogue and, later, about the role of instruments, especially the organ, which was associated with Protestant churches. Music became a flashpoint for intra-ethnic disputes, according to Sarna, because "music was as tightly regulated as the synagogue ritual. Indeed, the music was inseparable from the ritual. Both were hallowed by tradition, what was called in Hebrew the *minhag*, the synagogue's ritual or custom as passed down from generation to generation" (J. D. Sarna 2003, 195). The symbolic upshot of the disputes was that, despite the hope that agreement on a musical standard in the liturgy would unite Jews into a common tradition, music, perhaps because of its performative ritual associations, came to represent the division of Jews from one another, and from non-Jews (J. D. Sarna 2003, 203; see also Judah Cohen 2009; L. A. Hoffman and Walton 1993; J. A. Levine 1989; Shelamay 1998; Shiloah 1992).

Outside the synagogue, various ritualized public commemorations after World War II in the Jewish world regularly included music and recitations for the victims of the Holocaust (Yom Ha-Shoah) (Figure 5.2), Israeli independence (Yom Ha-Atzma'ut), and reunification of Jerusalem (Yom Yerushalayim) (Flam 1992, 170–78; Handelman and Katz 1990; Schuman et al. 2003). Inside the synagogue questions arose whether memorialization of the major events could be incorporated into the *Yizkor* memorial service that recognizes martyrs or whether they necessitated a separate liturgical ritual. In the case of Israel Independence Day, blessings and gestures introduced into the service inside the synagogue provide a contrast to the parades, fireworks, fairs, and barbecues arranged for public celebration (Ward 2011). Although prayer books were generally slow to change, over time the impact of the Holocaust and the formation of the State of Israel precipitated some of the most noticeable changes in newly composed *siddurim* for all wings of Judaism (Harlow 1993).

5.2. At the annual "reading of the names" ritual in Harrisburg, Pennsylvania, a congregational member reads names while the rabbi sitting behind her oversees the event. During the 24-hour vigil the names of Holocaust victims are read continuously. The symbolic display includes the phrase "unto every person there is a name," which comes from a poem by Ukrainian-born Israeli writer Zelda (Zelda Shneurson Mishkowsky, 1914–1984); six candles, representing *yahrzeit* memorials for 6 million Jewish victims; and six plants for new life. Photo by Simon J. Bronner.

TIME AND YEARLY CYCLE

Ritual's function of marking time is particularly evident in many Jewish practices that reference daily, weekly, and yearly transitions. Ritual does more than structure quantities of time before and after framed events; it reassures participants that the ethnic ordering of time will be ever-renewing and infuses it with symbolic connections to nature and culture (Bell 1997, 102). Another symbolic division is apparent in the establishment of the Jewish weekly cycle between sacred and profane portions represented by Shabbat/Shabbos, or Sabbath, beginning the evening before, and the *shavua/voch* (Hebrew and Yiddish, respectively), or workaday week (Eisenberg 2004, 125–54; Linke 1999, 81–100). The relatively high number of symbolic components in the Havdalah (Hebrew: separation) ceremony to mark the shift from the Sabbath to the week indicates that the change is extreme. Entering the Sabbath takes less ritual complexity than leaving it, and consequently adult participation is higher for Shabbat services than for Havdalah services. Compared to other synagogue rituals, Havdalah provides a fuller sensory experience, a number of shared social actions, and several reminders of the interrelation of nature and culture. In addition to reciting a blessing over grape juice or wine, participants smell *besamim* (Hebrew: spices) in a decorative spice container as it is passed from hand to hand. Another blessing is recited as a special braided candle with more than one wick is lit. An important practice is to extinguish the candle's flame in the wine, so as to tangibly show that the candle was specially used for Havdalah. In many Jewish communities, participants further invoke the sense of touch and the magicoreligious power of the hand by consciously dipping a finger into the cup and transferring it to their eyes for wisdom or to their pockets for prosperity. The theme of separation from sacred time afterward might be emphasized with the singing of "Hamavdil Bein Kodesh L'Chol" (Hebrew: who makes distinction between the sacred and ordinary).

The theme of ritual separation in the Havdalah service is the inspiration for the growing home-based adoption of *chai* ceremonies to mark the transition of non-Orthodox Jewish American youth at the age of 18 to college (Danaan 2004). Teens in Jewish youth organizations are usually well versed in the Havdalah ritual because of it being a favorite festive feature of weekend conventions. In that context the ceremony becomes significant for youth as a gateway to jubilant Saturday night social activities. Teen group organizers might even be said to have appropriated the theme of separation from sacred time and reinterpreted the symbolic components to meanings of going out into the world with the social support of fellow Jews of their generation. In the celebrations after Havdalah, the teens from many locations emphasize a bond with one another and, at the same time, the coming-of-age traits of mobility and self-reliance.

Credit for the name and structure of the *chai* ceremony goes to Reconstructionist rabbi Julie Hilton in San Antonio in 2004, but before then Jewish families had organized other rituals of separation for their young adults with different names, such as *lech lecha* (Hebrew: leave!; adapted from the *parsha* of God telling Abraham to leave his native land) (FCCNN Administrator; Kram 2003; Pepperstone 2003). The label given to the Havdalah-based ritual by Rabbi Danaan derives from the numerological equivalence of the Hebrew word *chai* with 18 and its symbolism of luck and protection as well as literally representing life. Organizers follow the outline of a traditional Havdalah ritual and add responsive readings with messages of the parents releasing their children and the future college student entering a new exciting phase of life. The ceremony is followed by a festive celebration. Although parties are common for the student at high school graduation time, the *chai* ceremony is scheduled closer to the time the youth is about to leave for school, often after the mourning period of Tisha b'Av. Modern contexts for the rise of the ritual are the high percentage of offspring of Jewish parents, compared to offspring of non-Jewish families, who attend colleges and universities more than 100 miles away from home; relatively lower birthrates in non-Orthodox Jewish families that render the leave-taking of a young adult a more emotional experience; and in many locations, concern for anti-Semitic environments in colleges and universities (Pew Research Center 2013). With the ritual passage of the bar or bat mitzvah occurring early in one's teens (see chapter 6) and the high school graduation as a stepping-stone rather than a final ritual in Jewish American families, the Jewish framing of 18, a popular milestone of legalistic adulthood, serves to mark for many families cultural continuity of Jewish identity while also enabling separation.

Cultural critic Dietrich Harth notes the irony of rituals functioning to suspend time and yet to emphasize it "in order to establish that continuity of order called 'tradition' and that is meant to form a bulwark against the disintegration of community" (Harth 2006, 31). Scriptural connections to the ethnic organization of time have often been made mythologically from the creation of day and night in Genesis 1:1. In a form of metafolklore, Jews relate the Genesis narrative to the ritual start of Jewish holidays during the evening before the calendrical day. Other ritual periods take names from the time allotted for their completion: *shiva* and *shloshim* for practices of seven and thirty days of mourning, respectively. Yet as folklorist Jillian Gould (2011) points out, sitting shiva is a ritual that residents of Jewish senior care institutions deem flexible, particularly in the ritual mourning context of dealing with their own mortality. The alternative popular choice of three days as sufficient, despite rabbinic protests of this popular practice, indicates supplanting one ritual number with another. Three, as folklorist Alan Dundes has theorized, joins a quantity representing completeness (evident in the saying to begin on the count of three) to its magical associations in incantations (Dundes 1968).

In the ritual year, Rosh Hashanah, as the signal of the new year, explicitly marks time, but one can observe the work of ritual to continuously bring up a Jewish conception of time—past and present, suspended and real—enacted on other holidays. Purim, for example, is a time of ritual reversal: Participants revel in a lack of self-restraint customary in daily life and laugh at the sacred. Actors often publicly mock the rabbi in the performed skit (Purim *spiel*), and congregants may ritually kidnap him or her, followed by raising a ransom from the congregation. Yet in referring to a historic event involving Jewish response to oppression, Purim encourages contemplation of present conditions and, frequently, references to the Holocaust. The stage is literally set with the reading of the Megillah, and the scripted *spiel* (Yiddish: play) contains riffs of and costumes from contemporary popular culture (Figure 5.3). Folklorist Jean R. Freedman (2011) finds that the hilarity dramatizes in a play frame repressed conflicts about maintaining Jewishness while being assimilated into the accelerating modern world. She thus uses psychological ideas of projection to explain the revitalization of the Purim *spiel* as a strategy of ritualizing modern Jewishness. She finds in her ethnographic case study of a Washington, D.C., performance that the new *spiel* is not so much re-creation as it is re-visioning.

Whereas holidays such as Rosh Hashanah and Yom Kippur are universally recognized across Judaism, cultural studies attention can be drawn to distinctive ethnic practices in Jewish communities. An example of such a ritual synagogue

5.3. Performers from Foehrenwald, an international displaced persons camp in the American zone of occupation in Germany after World War II, in a Purim *spiel* with themes of combating anti-Semitism (Courtesy Linda Schwab).

celebration is Se'udat Yitro, which appears to be unique to Tunisian Jewry (H. E. Goldberg and Salamon 2011). It occurs on the Thursday of the week approaching the ritual reading of the *parsha* called *Yitro*, usually in January. Ethnographies indicate that the celebration has an association with another kind of time of the life cycle because it marks the first time that boys hear the reading of the Decalogue. Se'udat Yitro represents a subcategory of ritual in the yearly cycle that appears to be localized. Such rituals, including the previously mentioned Simhat Cohen and also the *sigd* of the Beta Israel Ethiopian community and the *mimuna* among Moroccan Jews (Goldberg and Salamon 2011), raise questions about the relationship of such rituals to local conditions and the perpetuation (or abandonment) of the rituals as communities relocate or experience new social and economic conditions. Such rituals often present puzzles for which pieces are missing from the historical record. In their cultural studies, Harvey Goldberg and Hagar Salamon (2011) find that the ambiguity of the ritual attracts conscious intervention and structuring by local rabbis, resulting in regional variation. They weigh the various meanings given by participants and chroniclers as rhetorically emphasizing Jewish time out of time, forming an overarching narrative of Exodus that creates peoplehood, relating a subcultural Tunisian heritage, or commemorating a religious coming of age. Instead of lamenting the inability to pinpoint a definite origin or spell out of a singular meaning, Goldberg and Salamon find that the vagueness surrounding the ritualized ethnic event and the variations it invites add to its attractiveness for participants.

Because many Jewish observances in the yearly cycle are intended to be conducted in the home, they invite a recontextualization by the gathered group—and constant renewal. In particular, cultural studies of Passover have focused on situated, variant readings of the Haggadah that are intended to convey social and political statements. An early model for the analysis of Jewish cultural adaptation and change in holiday ritual was produced by Beatrice S. Weinreich with data from probably the first systematic ethnographic questionnaire projects conducted by YIVO in 1928 and 1949. Weinreich reported that in the postwar period passages about the Holocaust were added to written Haggadot, in keeping with the memorial function of the seder. She also noted the invention in the 1920s of a "new tradition," the third seder framed as a secular ritual for Zionist and other political causes (B. S. Weinreich 1960, 355–60). But why would a group wanting, in Weinreich's words, "to renounce the religious content of Judaism" retain the seder model of Passover? The answer is in part that the symbolic overlay of secular practice drew more attention to their political cause as a Jewish movement; another factor was the appropriation of the freedom theme of Exodus for a nonreligious application. "The development of the Third Seder," she insightfully wrote, "is an interesting illustration of the 'de-dogmatizing' of a religious holiday, plus the selection of certain formal elements of traditional ritual (the use of a Haggada) coupled with the invention of new ritual. In this development, we see very clearly reflected the situation of those Jews who, though continuing to renounce the intellectual and practical (or instrumental) aspects of the Jewish religion, seem to feel a need for some of its emotional content" (362). David Shuldiner followed the third seder to the end of the twentieth century as a ritual of Jewish radicalism to represent a movement as much as a play on liberation (Shuldiner 1999, 119–40). Muky Tsur (2007) added the process of composing Haggadot to express a collective memory of kibbutzim in addition to the enacted outcome as a ritual process.

Rabbi Rebecca T. Alpert meanwhile reported the emergence of transgressive rituals in the first and second seders by lesbian Jews in the 1980s on the rationale that "there is as much place for lesbians in Judaism as for leavened bread at the Seder table" (Alpert 1989, 2). What began as a response to a remark at a public lecture became formalized as the "Crust of Bread at the Seder Table" midrash incorporated into Jewish lesbian Haggadot around the United States (2). For some groups who felt that placing bread on the seder plate was too great a transgression, alternatives negotiated within the symbolic grammar of the seder by participants included leaving an open space on the seder plate marked as *makom*, or a name for God that is without gender, and placing an orange on top of matzos or the seder plate to represent the role of homosexuals in Judaism (2–3). These precedents of ritual as intentional social action and the situated processual analysis of it as the strategic "invention of new ritual" influenced many scholars who examined not only the ritual function of marking time but also the representation in ritual of power relations and transformative intentions.

PASSAGE AND INITIATION

In the subset of rites of passage, rituals effect a transformation from one stage of life or social status to another. The changes that are marked by ritual may be conspicuous transitions, such as birth and death, that participants feel compelled to recognize, or else they are created through ritual, such as naming and consecration ceremonies. A processual question about both types is how the structure of these rituals facilitates passage. A psychological query is also raised about why people feel that passage needs ritual help and why some communities ritualize some status changes that others do not. An example is relatively modern haircutting ceremonies for boys, usually at the age of 3. Called an *upsherin* (Yiddish: to shear off) or *chalaka* (Arabic: haircut), the ceremony marks the beginning of formal Hebrew and Torah study, and cookies in the form of Hebrew letters, often covered in honey, are served to signify the sweetness of learning (Figure 5.4). Emphasizing a change in status from infant to student, the initiate will regularly wear a yarmulke and tzitzit after the ritual. The ceremony has not been universally adopted, but it is popular among the Hasidim, who particularly embrace the ceremony's symbolism of Torah study. Social construction of the ritual is evident in its home celebration, and many families hold it not on the boy's birthday but on the occasion of Lag b'Omer, conceptualized as the "scholar's holiday" and symbolically connected to the image of three as a quantity representing completeness, because it falls on the thirty-third day of the Omer. Families may design the ceremony to include family members and rabbis taking turns cutting the child's hair and making charitable acts with the hair, such as donating it for cancer victims or contributing money equivalent to the weight of the hair. Psychologically, the symbolism of cutting and the significance of shortening the hair to clearly distinguish the boy from the long locks of the girl come into question. Cutting as a ritualized action is symbolically associated with the previous rite of passage of circumcision in the Jewish life cycle, particularly among ultra-Orthodox groups concerned with the maintenance of ethnic boundaries (Bilu 2003). Amy K. Milligan (2017; 2019b, 49–62) describes the feminist adaptation of the rite to girls in the twenty-first century to mark a symbolic move toward egalitarianism by legitimizing female as well as male Hebrew education.

What is the relationship between constructing a life-stage passage and entrance into formal schooling? Marc-Alain Ouaknin and Françoise-Anne Ménager suggest that the immersion into books is symbolically consistent with the gendering of cutting rituals: "He goes from the maternal language, which is oral, to the paternal language, which is written. Hebrew also links writing to the paternal language in an extraordinary way. The word 'alphabet'—*aleph-bet* in Hebrew—is pronounced *av* and means 'father'" (Ouaknin and Ménager 2005, 48). In commentaries typically made by the boy's father at the *upsherin*, it is common to mention biblical allusions to human life as trees and to apply the prohibition on eating

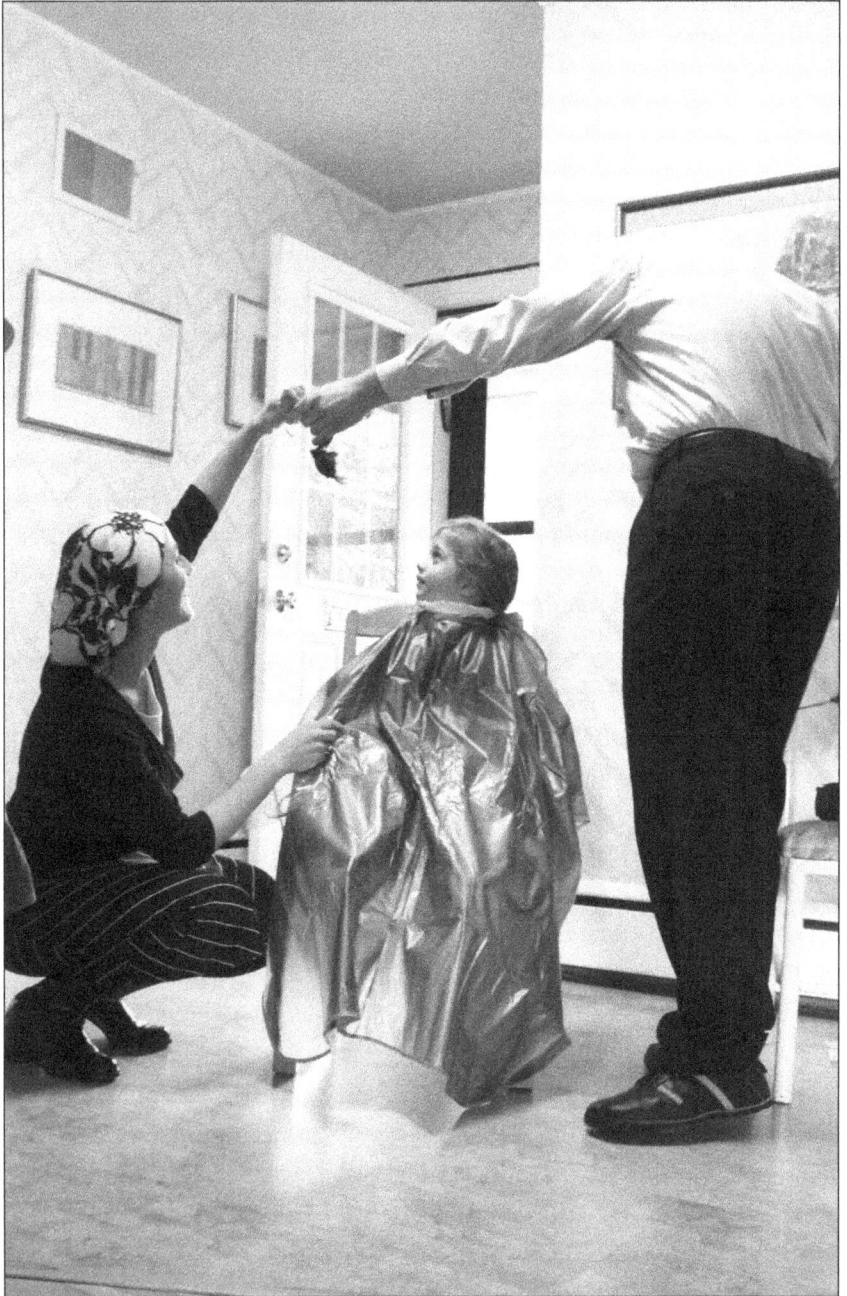

5.4. *Chalaka* ritual enacted by an Orthodox Sephardic family in Harrisburg, Pennsylvania, in 2009. The child's father cuts the hair while the mother watches. Family members and rabbis were called up to ritually cut a lock of hair. Photo by Simon J. Bronner.

fruit that grows on a tree for the first three years to cutting a child's hair (Leviticus 19:23). As a ceremony that usually is perceived to distinguish Orthodox affiliation from others, parents communicate in their staging of the *upsherin* a passage not only in age but also in piety. The child may echo this sentiment with the singing of a Hebrew song based on the biblical verse *Torah tzivah Ianu Moshe* ("Moses prescribed the Torah to us, an eternal heritage for the congregation of Jacob," Deuteronomy 33:4).

Many rituals condense a larger experience into a sequence of events that symbolize the desirability of the change or replace a real trauma with a manageable task that symbolizes the ability to overcome a challenge. Van Gennep (1960) suggested that life-cycle changes necessitated a tripartite structure representing entrance alone through ritual separation of the individual, symbolic completion of a task in a transitional phase, and status change with the support of a welcoming community (incorporation phase). The rites functioned to guide initiates and their communities in the expectations of transition. For example, van Gennep postulated that birth rites at the beginning of life emphasized incorporation into the community, whereas at the end of life, separation to move the deceased away from the community became central. In rites for the move from childhood to adulthood, when family responsibilities are especially significant, the liminal or transitional phase becomes prominent. Mircea Eliade (1958) elaborated that the symbolism packed into initiatory ritual represented an enactment of birth, death, and rebirth in an altered state, thus representing a fresh start in the new phase of life. Often in this process, the past life is stigmatized as profane and the new one is deemed sacred. To hold attention and lend symbolic significance to the event, paradoxes or conflicts of the society are often evident in the transitional stage, suggesting that emergence into the new status promises clarity and unity (Myerhoff 1982).

The complexity of rites of passage can be read as evidence of stress associated with the transition. Therefore the wedding is often elaborate and multi-episodic because of the perception that the move from being an individual to forming a union—and family—involves greater risk than other transitions in life. The special dress and number of attendants for the bride have been read in many ritual observances as conveying the meaning that the woman bears extra risk, especially if she is the one moving into the groom's family household (Bar'am-Ben Yossef 1998; Grossman 2001). At the end of life, the complexity of burial and mourning shows the strain that the loss of a community member, exalted in the status of deceased ancestor, places on the living left behind. Ethnographer Alanna E. Cooper (2011) compared mourning rituals of Bukharan Jews in Uzbekistan, Israel, and the United States. She looked at the evolution of what Bukharan Jews call a *yushva*, a Jewish mourning event that differs from sitting shiva. Unlike American and Western European mourning rituals, conducted as affairs that are relatively cut off from the everyday flow of life, among Bukharan Jews the *yushva* is tightly woven into the fabric of daily living. Despite changes in cultural life from Uzbekistan to Israel and the United States, the *yushva* has been a constant presence, and Cooper asked why it has endured while other rituals receded. She found that the *yushva*, which is a specific occasion for reflection on the past through spontaneous public oration, promotes contemplation about lost eras in communal life. In the ritual space and time that the *yushva* creates, ethnic Bukharan Jews have a renewable forum to cope with the imminence of change. Ritual, then, compensates for conflict in the society and for potentially creating tension and exhibiting contradiction.

Life-cycle rituals, such as the Brit Milah and the bar and bat mitzvah, have drawn cultural attention for defining ethnic affiliation, and yet they are also among the most contested of Jewish rituals for different reasons (Bronner 2008–2009; Shaye Cohen 2005; Glick 2005; Gollaher 2001; Mark 2003; Sabar et al. 2006; E. K. Silverman 2006). The more durable tradition is ritual circumcision (Schauss 1950, 11–62). In anthropological literature, circumcision has gained notice for being especially resistant to change and therefore bringing into question the symbolic importance of male genital alteration in ritual practice as well as a sign of Jewishness. Anthropologist Leonard Glick steps away from a typical cultural relativist position by arguing that parents do not have the right to "impose nonessential, irreversible surgery on him before he is able to decide for himself that he wants his genitals permanently altered" (Glick 2005, 280). He is puzzled by the fact that "practices mandated or sanctioned in the Hebrew Scriptures—animal sacrifice, slavery, polygamy, rites of purification"—have been abandoned but circumcision as ritual remains a pillar of Jewish identity in many locations, particularly in the West (281).

Glick's query about the choices and negotiations that occur between application of textual sources and modern practice is one that arises with other rituals. Worthy of comparison in connection to the discussion of structure and process is the bar mitzvah's relatively recent rise as a localized *minhag*, because unlike the Brit Milah, it is not prescribed in the Torah and has not become universally adopted in the Jewish world. The scholarly consensus is that as a religious ceremony it dates to local medieval German practices that diffused to Eastern Europe, but there it did not gain the elevated or standardized status now given it in Western Europe and the United States (I. G. Marcus 1996, 119–26; I. G. Marcus 2004, 82–123; Pollack 1971, 59–62). In the West the bar mitzvah gained notoriety in the twentieth century as a rare ritual for passage from adolescence into adulthood in industrialized societies and for its flexible, often individualized exhibition of material excess in the manner of a wedding for a family member considered by the host societies to be underage (Bronner 2008–2009; Joselit 1994, 89–118). The bat mitzvah for girls, also a growing phenomenon in the twentieth century, has similar functions and also draws attention to Jewish movements for gender equity. The kinds of interpretations heaped on the bar and bat mitzvah provide a benchmark for the meanings of the weddings and funerals perceived by different parts of society—Jewish and non-Jewish. Frequently interpreted sociologically as a sign of arrival for Jews as a minority group and the last opportunity to declare Jewishness publicly (in capitulation to the possibility of an interfaith wedding later), the rise of the bar and bat mitzvah has received psychological analysis as a ritual process involving ethnic status for Jews in a modern complex society in addition to the gendering of coming-of-age (Arlow 1951; Bronner 2008–2009; Judith Davis 2003; see also my discussion in chapter 6). For Jews, the bar and bat mitzvah is another ritual that brings into the open the tension between home and synagogue (especially with early rabbinic opposition to it) as well as different levels of acceptance and preparation by the various wings of Judaism (Sherwin 1990, 150; Spiro 1977). It also draws comparative ritual attention to characteristics of the wedding, such as lifting the honoree in a chair, festively showering the initiate (in the case of the bar and bat mitzvah, with sweets), and candle lighting by relatives.

Cultural continuity and change in Jewish wedding traditions, often in response to customs of the host society, have long been an issue in many countries, and legalization of same-sex marriage has raised additional questions of recognizing Jewish practices among gay and lesbian couples. Many Jewish wedding traditions make sharp distinctions between men's and women's roles (e.g., the Ashkenazic tradition of the bride circling the groom three or seven times and the groom smashing a glass under foot). Following her influential book *Inventing Jewish Ritual* (Ochs 2007) on modern ritual innovations, particularly in North America, anthropologist Vanessa Ochs (2011) addressed the rhetorical strategies evident in ceremonies adapted from heterosexual Jewish weddings and what she

calls the evolving tradition of "reconstructed" ceremonies that supplant the standard structure and symbolism with "liberal" homosexual values while still being
invested in Jewish tradition. Examples that she reports include a revised *ketubah* in
which both partners take a shared middle name and pledge to care for each other
instead of the groom caring economically for the bride. In lieu of a *bedeken* ceremony, in which the groom unveils the bride, the couple stare at each other and
write their own betrothal formula for the exchange of the rings, and at the end of
the ceremony each breaks a glass (Ochs 2011, 203). Ochs locates a longer timeline
for same-sex ceremonies in customs of commitment than may be apparent from
recent legalization and finds that marriage ritual over that period has been a central
arena where ethical battles over the compatibility of homosexuality with Jewish
law and identity have been fought (Alpert 1997; Balka and Rose 1989; Kaplan-
Mayer 2004, 11; Schwartzman and Francesca 2004, 58–60). The background for
ritual controversies over commitment and revised marriage ceremonies is community responses to the formation of separate gay Jewish congregations and the
acceptance of openly homosexual rabbis who are redefining and revisioning
the "normality" of Jewish sexual orientations and family practices (Eisenberg
2004, 58–61; S. Greenberg 2005).

PERFORMANCE AND PRACTICE

Many of the rituals described so far have audiences oriented toward a staged activity, be it in a ritual space of the bimah in a synagogue or the formalized dinner
table of a home seder. Roles are assigned and enacted, often by ritual specialists,
such as the rabbi and cantor, or by ordinary members of groups, such as the congregational mourner reciting Kaddish (see Heilman 1998; Sered 1992). Participants may not be aware of the function of performative roles and settings in the
ritual because of the cognitive tendency to separate ritual, considered meditative
or replicative, from theater, with its association of being artistic or individualistic
(Grimes 2006, 381). However, ritual draws much of its power not only from its
patterned repetition but also from its dramatic, affective quality. Rarely are ritual
scripts memorized; expectations of improvisation and adaptation rendered in a
personalized style within a sequenced order of events make performers out of
participants. Performance, in the sense of stylized actions that draw attention to
themselves, in contrast to mundane gesture and speech, also can act to signify an
ethical, symbolic message of fellowship and spirituality (Heilman 1987). If the

reciters of the Haggadah at Passover around the dinner table are unwitting performers, then the intentional staging of activities into ritual occasions, such as
dance festivals (Spiegel 2011) meant to be annual events and political street rallies
invoking Jewish holidays (Kelner 2011) normally observed at home or synagogue,
bring into analytic view the emotionally affective and socially effective theatrics
of ritual organized as a strategy of persuasion.

Organizers of staged events often do not promote them with the label of
ritual, even though they intend them to be ritualesque by engaging audience and
participants together in a shared purpose (Erving Goffman 1967, 5–45; Erving
Goffman 1974, 43–58; Handelman 2006, 571–78; Santino 2009). In the use
of ritual components, they often aim to elevate the event from fleeting entertainment or demonstration to momentous occasion. An example is the linkage
of ritual events of *hakafot* (dancing in circuits with the Torah) on Simhat Torah
with the exuberant street demonstrations to allow immigration of Soviet Jews
during the 1970s. Part of the political message was that the Soviet Union prevented Jews from ritually participating and rejoicing on the holiday. Besides the
rare use of demonstrative dancing in Jewish religious holiday observance, the Save
Jewish Jewry movement made a textual connection with the traditional holiday
invocation of *hoshiah na* (Hebrew: save us).

Organizers of staged events typically distinguish theatrical from ritual performance with the expectation in the ritual of a repeated, stylized sequence of events
that invites audience participation. The theatrical implies a unique statement of
artistry, whereas the ritual invokes tradition and socially shared purpose. With
the theatrical organization of ritual, it is possible to envision secular dramatized
rituals suggesting collective Jewish identity, whether in the staged performance of
klezmer music and a Jewish arts festival; regular storytelling at the kitchen table
or at a Jewish camping or scouting experience; a military induction ceremony at
the top of Masada and retirement rituals joined to secular observance of Hanukkah (N. Rubin 2009, 134–75); or organized pilgrimage tours, such as March of
the Living and Birthright Israel (Ben-Yehuda 1995, 147–62; Kelner 2010; Roginsky 2007; Sales and Saxe 2003; Saxe and Chazan 2008; Shavit and Sitton 2004;
Shevelev 1996; Slobin 2000; Zeitlin 1997; Zerubavel 1995).

Whereas ritual performance exaggerates the distance between everyday activity and staged action, ritualized practice draws attention to identity markers in the
structure of daily living. Guides to practice often identify activities in the worldly
realm that tie Jews socially and culturally. The rhetoric of "practice" implies

constant usage, but usage that is ritualized because it involves self-conscious patterning, especially in contrast to a modern world. A handbook such as *The Rituals and Practices of a Jewish Life* (2002) by Rabbi Kerry M. Olitzky and Rabbi Daniel Judson includes kashrut, covering the head, and Torah study under the rubric of practice. Other advisers dwell on dress and hair practices as keys to Jewish values of modesty, community, and devotion (P. E. Falk 1998; Schreiber 2003), and these cultural fashions commonly serve to signify and maintain sectarian boundaries and embodied pietism (Behrouzi 1991; Carrel 1999; Landau 1993, 32–40; Lowenstein 2000, 149–74; Milligan 2014; Yoder 2001, 144–46).

The cultural significance of practices is the way that in their patterned repetition they connote values to the practitioner and to the potential viewer. When actions take on collectively shared connotations, such as covering (of the head or legs), cutting (of hair and foreskin), and carrying (of objects on the Sabbath), in the context of systems of beliefs held by Jews, analysts may refer to them as "praxis" to identify their behavioral significance of forming a cultural paradigm (see Z. Bauman 1999; Bernstein 1971; Bourdieu 1977; Bronner 1988, 2006b, 2019; Milligan 2014; Wulf 2006; see also chapter 3). They may especially draw public and analytical notice when they symbolize ethnic and moral differences, such as the political controversy over bans on *shechita* (Hebrew: kosher slaughtering) in European countries (see Alderman 2008, 111–36; Judd 2007). If kosher slaughtering as a praxis draws critical attention, many less public practices are noteworthy of analysis because they present opportunities for personalizing and innovating meaning. Individuals may ritualize their Jewishness by having meals they recall from their forebears, leaving personal items besides rocks at a gravesite, adorning their yarmulkes with personal symbols, and producing creative works on a Jewish theme or beautifying ritual objects (*Hiddur Mitzvah*; see Splansky 2012). A processual question that arises from practices that skirt the line between ritual out-of-the-ordinary activity and the quotidian in everyday routine concerns how and why practices become ritualized, if they indeed are.

All told, my investigations show that ritual actions, from those steeped in ancient Scriptures to modern innovative festivals and ceremonies, are keys to the reproduction of culture and expression of worldview. Often overlooked as routine or dismissed as bizarre abnormality, ritual in its many forms, conflicts, and guises embodies experience that is lived, imagined, and even negated. For Jewish cultural studies, examining textual and contextual adaptations and innovations is especially meaningful for envisioning what is Jewish about Jewishness. The analysis of change in ritual content and the responses of both participants and nonparticipants to those changes is critical to illuminating the evidence of perception that has often been omitted from past documentation, mostly historical, of customs. With the understanding of perception, the derivation of meaning from ritual events—in liturgies, holidays, life-cycle events, and political rallies—can be discerned. Analysis also allows reflection on the uses of ritual and the context of tradition in everyday life set against the background of modernity and community. Jews are hardly alone in relying on ritual to provide them with an inventory of social meanings that have to be constantly negotiated, but as I will show in subsequent chapters in part 2, they are keenly aware of a duality of perception and enactment of ritual from within their community and from outside it. Jews know and embody themselves by their rituals. Whether or not they begin their day with the recitation of the Shema, they are aware of the importance of repetition—and variation—in Jewish thought and practice. The perceived malleability and diversity of Jewish rituals at home, on the street, and in the synagogue and the long legacy of Jews arguing over the propriety of their traditions are likely to be on their minds when they talk, and act, together.

FATHERS AND SONS

Rethinking the Bar Mitzvah as an
American Rite of Passage

The bar mitzvah draws popular and folkloristic attention because it is one of the few publicly recognized American rituals for entering adolescence. Popularly categorized as a Jewish folk tradition, the bar mitzvah is hardly a private affair. It is recognized, if not participated in, throughout the general population of North America as a result of being featured in popular films, television shows, and novels. Some of the notice for the bar mitzvah owes to depictions in the media of material excess. In addition, the bar mitzvah raises a social psychological question of the relatively early coming of age at 13 years old. The age is perceived as early in a modern American society characterized by an extended childhood and adolescence before adulthood. Elaborating on this critical coming-of-age issue, I propose that the folk sources of the bar mitzvah reveal a symbolism that suggests that the ceremony acts to resolve father-son conflicts. Further, in the American context both non-Jews and Jews have heightened the ceremony's importance, because the event represents public displays of or compensations for uncertain masculine status.

THE FOLK AND POPULAR LOGIC
OF THE BAR MITZVAH

The bar mitzvah is the coming-of-age ritual that everyone knows, in image if not in practice. Even if you have never attended the event, it is a safe bet that you have been exposed to it in popular television and film. Jonathan and Judith Pearl, discussing media portrayals of Jewish themes in *The Chosen Image*, claim that "of all the Jewish rites of passage depicted on popular TV, none has received more attention than the *bar mitzvah*" (Jonathan Pearl and Pearl 1999, 16). Since their book came out, the bar mitzvah has been dramatized or spoofed in popular movies such as *Keeping the Faith* (2000), *Glow Ropes: The Rise and Fall of a Bar Mitzvah Emcee* (2005), *Keeping Up with the Steins* (2006), *Sixty Six* (2006), *Knocked Up* (2007), *Two Lovers* (2008), *A Serious Man* (2009), and *Abe* (2019) and television series such as *Sex and the City* (2000), *Frasier* (2002), *Lizzie McGuire* (2002), *The Simpsons* (2003), *Entourage* (2005), *Unfabulous* (2005), *Naked Brothers Band* (2008), *American Dad!* (2009), *Black-ish* (2014), *Transparent* (2017), and *Alone Together* (2018). The bar mitzvah has been the butt of many jokes and cartoons among Jews and non-Jews alike, many of which concern the apparently young age, 13, when the boy is pronounced to be entering manhood or which question the Jewish boy's claim to manliness. For example, in the *Naked Brothers Band* episode "The Bar Mitzvah," wordplay is evident when a parent commands the bar mitzvah boy to join his friends with the Yiddish word *gey*, meaning "go," but the Americanized boy understands the word as questioning his masculinity for acting "gay." Related to this humor in a surfeit of comic graphics and mocking photographs is the common theme of discomfort for the boy in the fabled misfitting bar mitzvah suit (also the subject of barbs by television character Murphy Brown to her younger Jewish boss Miles Silverberg on the hit show *Murphy Brown* from 1988 to 1998). The humor depends on the perception that the Jewish boy is uncomfortable with or not ready for the commanding pose of an adult suit and mature authority over non-Jews.

The kind of bar mitzvah that commands popular culture attention is likely of non-Orthodox Jews, often called liberal or assimilated. In such satirical portrayals, viewers become aware of anxieties, not just for the bar mitzvah boy's relation to his faith or ethnicity but also for the modern consumer society of which he is a part. Depictions of the bar mitzvah in popular culture focus primarily on the party, because of the broader societal interest in modern materialism or parental indulgence that it raises, but contextualizing the celebration within traditional practices and symbols for the bar mitzvah boy leading up to and during the event sheds light on the inherited and invented meanings of the bar mitzvah. To get at these meanings, I examine more closely the folk cultural aspects of the event to explain its growing appeal since the mid-twentieth century.

The folkloric source of the bar mitzvah appears rooted in synagogue practice, but Patricia Keer Munro observes from its history that the ritual "developed from the needs of the people" (Munro 2016, 2). She asserts that by the late twentieth century the bar mitzvah displaced the wedding as the central Jewish American rite of passage, and "the ritual has changed how American Jews understand and engage with Judaism" (2). Along these lines, Jewish parents probably voice the attitude that the bar mitzvah is the most self-conscious expression of Jewishness in one's life and that it signifies entrance into what is known as religious majority: the ability associated with Jewish maturity to participate in a minyan (quorum of 10 adults for prayer), fast, and read from the Torah. Orthodox Jews may more clearly recognize the obligations that the bar mitzvah represents to Judaism to put on a tallit (prayer shawl) and tefillin (phylacteries), but the bar mitzvah in Orthodox communities does not have the conspicuous consumer display that it does among liberal Jews. For many Jews, the bar mitzvah signals a finality rather than a transition to another stage; it is an end rather than a beginning of religious participation. Historian Ivan Marcus, writing on the Jewish life cycle, observes that the bar mitzvah "can be seen as a finishing rite for many young Jewish adolescents. It moves the child from Judaism into the larger world possibly without any additional traditional Jewish rites until death, if then" (I. Marcus 2004, 123).

That a traditional ceremony would contribute to discontinuity rather than the continuity expected of rites of passage has been a concern not just of historians and ethnographers. American rabbis since the early twentieth century have complained about the use of the bar mitzvah to conclude synagogue attendance. For example, rabbinic philosopher Mordecai Kaplan, in his incisive tome *Judaism as a Civilization: Toward a Reconstruction of American-Jewish Life* (1934), criticized the "spiritual chaos" caused by "so casual a contact with Jewish knowledge" in short-lived attendance at a Hebrew school before the bar mitzvah (M. Kaplan 1994, 58). Although acknowledging that the Jewish educational focus on preparing for the bar mitzvah kept youth in Jewish schools, he advocated for a reorientation to signal entrance into a new stage of life or developing a lifelong commitment to Judaism (58–59). A later popularly known rabbi, Joseph Telushkin, renewed the complaint in *Jewish Literacy*: "While the bar mitzvah is intended to mark the beginning of a Jewish boy's adulthood, for non-Orthodox Jews it frequently signifies the end of his Jewish education" (Telushkin 1991, 612).

Surveys by Jewish organizations of their youth members verify that children perceive the bar mitzvah to be a conclusion to education rather than a transition to another stage. For instance, Barry A. Kosmin found that less than one-fourth of Conservative Hebrew school students showed a high score on their plans for attending synagogue monthly or more often after their bar or bat mitzvah (Kosmin 2000, 263). Despite the intentions of this minority, actual attendance was even lower, and this disengagement is typically blamed on teens focusing on secular high school studies and extracurricular activities with the support of their parents (Leneman 1993, 17–19; Sidlofsky 1993, 302). A higher percentage of boys have a bar mitzvah than girls for the bat mitzvah, and the boys report feeling pressure more intensely to disengage from religious activities in favor of weekend sports and social activities. Of the *b'nai mitzvah* students, girls who had a bat mitzvah were more likely to volunteer in the Jewish community and attributed more importance to being Jewish than did the bar mitzvah boys (Kosmin 2000, 253).

Although civic leaders often attribute the structure of American Hebrew school education as the reason for the rise of the bar mitzvah, rabbis and educators alike insist that Jewish education is geared toward wider goals and that the bar mitzvah ceremony involves an important (and to many civic leaders the most important) secular component. In light of the disappointing effects of the bar mitzvah on religious maintenance and coming-of-age transition, the most common alternative explanation is family socialization and the community networking it provides (Judith Davis 1995, 2003; Kennedy 2005; Munro 2016; Schoenfeld 1993b). Kosmin's statistics led him to consider that the continued appeal of the bar mitzvah, despite criticisms of it by rabbis for undermining their religious purpose and by civic leaders for being too materialistic and competitive, had to do with familial bonding, because of the uncertainty of holding a Jewish wedding in the life cycle of the boy. Basing his view on the observation that "for many couples it is the first major family and social event since their own wedding," Kosmin hypothesized that the bar mitzvah is a developmental milestone for the parents, who "must present themselves publicly in relation to their religious tradition to the most significant people in their lives—their family, colleagues, and social network" (Kosmin 2000, 236). This argument has merit because of the background of social and economic anxieties for many liberal Jews of, on the one hand, appearing integrated into the larger society and, on the other, validating their commitment to Jewish identity among members of their religious group (Keysar and Kosmin 2020). Yet a closer look at the ceremony reveals that the ritual portions of the bar mitzvah emphasize the relationship of the father and son rather than the whole family.

Related to the question of the bar mitzvah's modern appeal is its historical trajectory since the early twentieth century. Although popular culture may present the bar mitzvah as an ancient Jewish rite, its tradition is of relatively recent origin. Many scholarly observers have editorialized that its growth among the Jewish "people of the book" is remarkable, considering that there is no mention of the ritual in its sacred texts, the Torah or the Talmud. The term *bar mitzvah*, or son of the commandment, appears in the Talmud (*Bava Metzia* 96a) or a person subject to law, but it does not appear in reference to assuming religious obligations before the fifteenth century (Chill 1978, 315). The scholarly consensus is that, as a ceremony, the bar mitzvah dates to local medieval German practices that diffused to Eastern Europe, but it did not gain the elevated or standardized status there that it is now given in Western Europe and the United States (I. Abrahams 1958, 32; I. G. Marcus 1996, 119–26; I. G. Marcus 2004, 82–123; Pollack 1971, 59–62).

The key components of the *derashah*, or interpretive speech, and examination drew significant notice in eighteenth-century Italy, and it is likely that from there the ritual made some inroads into North African Jewry (H. E. Goldberg 2003, 90–91; Ouaknin and Ménager 2005, 335–39). Yet in the substantial Jewish communities of Yemen, the bar mitzvah did not develop at all (Ouaknin and Ménager 2005, 342–43). It is also noteworthy that in North Africa, religious majority could be reached any time the boy was ready, and among the Jews of India it occurred around 5 years old (H. E. Goldberg 2003, 92). The historical explanation of a German-Italian influence is often accompanied by speculation on the spread of bar mitzvah rituals as local imitations of Christian confirmation practices, whether out of interests of assimilation or modernization (I. G. Marcus 2004, 109–13; Schauss 1950, 120–21).

Well into the twentieth century, Judaism's rabbinic annals observed that the bar mitzvah was a fading tradition or that the rabbis should eradicate it because it challenged elite notions of Judaism (M. Silverman 1932, 329–31). For example, a leading authority for Orthodox Jewry in North America, Rabbi Moshe Feinstein (1895–1986), publicly declared, "If I had the power, I would abolish the *bar mitzvah* ceremony in this country. . . . It is well known that it has brought no one closer to study or observance" (Sherwin 1990, 150). For modern Jewish historians such as Jenna Weissman Joselit, the triumph of the bar mitzvah over this rabbinic resistance is an example par excellence of a singular American culture within the wider Jewish world. It demonstrates the ascendancy in the United States of the creative, upwardly aspiring folk interested in accommodating modernity over the elite hegemony of the ancients in the stodgy synagogue (Joselit 1994, 89–118).

Social psychological inquiries have underscored the way that the bar mitzvah involves the family and could be used therapeutically to link generations and create community (Judith Davis 1995, 2003; Kennedy 2005; Schoenfeld 1993b). Certainly the bar mitzvah can take on a different character depending on the family dynamic, but, after examining these findings, the unanswered question remains about the centrality of the father-son relationship, despite growing egalitarianism and feminization in Judaism. The social psychological interpretations positing a social bonding function are not that much different from the folk idea that the bar mitzvah is something that each family wants to make its own while still showing fidelity to tradition. Logically, the bonding is a consequence rather than a source of the ceremony (see my discussion of functionalism in chapter 4).[1] This folk view has been contrasted, particularly in religious literature, with elite pressures of rabbinic leaders to maintain the bar mitzvah's synagogue function of encouraging participation in the minyan (Kosmin 2000, 239–41; Liebman 1973, 42–87; Schoenfeld 1993a).

The implication of the functionalist analysis is that the bar mitzvah persists because it provides benefits to participants, but the bar mitzvah has raised conflicts in the Jewish community, and surveys affirm the tremendous pressures that preparation for the event arouses. For their part, folklorists and ethnologists have emphasized the expressive ritual components of the bar mitzvah as a Jewish version of global pubertal ceremonies. The bar mitzvah is cited most commonly in textbooks and reference works as a prominent coming-of-age "rite of passage" evident in Western industrialized countries (Haskell 1996, 410; McKeever-Furst 1992, 29; R. J. Smith 1972, 165; Spiro 1977). Folklorists and ethnologists are eager to include this example, probably because few public coming-of-age rituals exist in America and Europe to compare to the anthropological haul of so-called primitive puberty initiations that draw attention to themselves as exotic, sexually tinged practices of public transition to adulthood (Raphael 1988; Spiro 1977). The bar mitzvah lacks this sexual undertone, it seems, but it burst onto the American scene when industrialized countries were extending childhood and becoming aware of adolescence as a distinct stage of life (Russ 1993). This coincidence is apparent in the connection of the bar mitzvah to rites of passage, although a correlation cannot be established because of its premodern existence. The bar mitzvah, conceptualized as a rite of passage, shows folk tradition to be socially functional, presumably to mark passage from childhood into adulthood. Jewish educator Jack D. Spiro summarizes this view when he states, "The process itself may consume most of childhood, but the initiation rite is a form of 'cultural compression,' when all that is learned is compressed in the rituals. The compression itself focuses on the new roles that must be assumed by the initiate as he enters into the realm of manhood" (Spiro 1977, 394). For Spiro, this process is common among rites of all societies, but what is distinctive in Jewish culture is "the high degree of emphasis on learning, the paramountcy of knowledge and understanding" (399). Thus, he concludes, manhood is attained along with Jewish identity through the rite of passage, although Spiro has difficulty reconciling the "long, arduous intellectual process" of preparation with the relatively short "transition" phase on the big day.

A logical problem with the demarcation line for Jewish male passage is the fixed age of 13 years old. Biblical sources, for instance, cite 20 as a legal adult age and do not prescribe rituals for puberty. One can join the minyan without being bar mitzvahed, and one can celebrate bar mitzvah at other ages and localities. Jewish folklorist Hayyim Schauss hypothesizes that 13 became ritually significant not because of a developmental stage it marked but because "thirteen was a sacred number among the Jews in ancient times" (Schauss 1950, 113). He speculates that the designation of 20 for maturity was a later development, "when a more advanced legal system was in force among Jews" (113). If a sacred number was applied, however, it would probably be 18, after the mystical numerological equivalent of *chai* (consisting of the Hebrew letters of *het* and *yod*) for "living" (indeed, at bar mitzvahs today, common cash gifts are in multiples of 18 to signify good luck). And in fact, Rabbi Stuart Rosenberg (1923–1990), spiritual leader of Canada's Jews, writing in the influential journal *Religious Education* on the "right age for Bar Mitzvah," advocated for reforming the bar mitzvah tradition by holding it for boys at the age of 18 (Rosenberg 1965; see also discussion of the *chai* ceremony in chapter 5). Other liberal rabbis in the twentieth century tried to replace the bar mitzvah with a confirmation ceremony at 15 or 16, to keep children in Jewish education longer and to align it with an age perceived to be more of a coming-of-age period (as in the popular girls' celebration of Sweet 16), but the efforts have been largely unsuccessful (Joselit 1994, 105–30).

Looking to ancient sources for the entrenchment of age 13 in the Jewish ritual cycle, folklorist Theodor Gaster was concerned that correlation was difficult because neither a pubertal nor sacramental rite appears at age 13 in sacred texts. The age's cultural significance, he offered, was in being the traditional age for marriage in the ancient Near East (Gaster 1980, 68). The Mishnah, however, gives the expected age for marriage as 18, preceded by stages of study: "At five years the age is reached for Scripture, at ten for the study of Mishna, at thirteen for the fulfilment of the commandments, at fifteen for the study of the Talmud, at eighteen for marriage, at twenty for seeking a livelihood" (*Pirkei Avot* 5:25; see Hertz 1945, 101–3). In this interpretation, 13 is the appropriate age for understanding and enacting commandments in an educational life cycle, even though various rabbinic authorities have countered that the age is too young (Rosenberg 1965). Another possibility is the official periodization of 10 years after the haircutting ritual of *upsherin*, held at the age of 3, which ritually demarcates the beginning of the boy's Hebrew education. Rather than viewing a religious significance to the bar mitzvah because of the sacredness of the number, Gaster, as a historically minded scholar focused on the ancient golden age of Judaism, dismissed the bar mitzvah as a secular custom without meaning. He thought of it in the modern era as an occasion for a party without spiritual or developmental importance. Reflecting a common rabbinic attitude of "elite" Judaism, Gaster in his influential survey of Jewish folklife, disparaged the bar mitzvah as a sign of Jewish devolution of religious practice by concluding, "It confers nothing, imparts nothing, creates nothing; it merely celebrates" (Gaster 1980, 67).

Merely celebrates? What about bar mitzvah as a central Jewish rite of passage? Ivan Marcus hypothesizes that "in recent times, as Jews sought to mark the life cycle in ritual ways even in lives not otherwise filled with Torah observance, the bar mitzvah emerged as a rite of passage from Jewish childhood into adolescence and acculturation into the larger secular world, especially in American or Israeli life" (I. G. Marcus 2004, 123). The reference to a rite of passage declares the function of the bar mitzvah as moving from one stage to another, thought to be universally containing a structure of separation, transition, and incorporation by French folklorist Arnold van Gennep in 1908. It should be pointed out that, although van Gennep, as a scholar of religion, knew about the bar mitzvah, the event is totally absent from his foundational book *Rites de passage*, and in texts such as Gaster's and the *Encyclopedia Judaica* it is labeled a *ceremony* that is not about transition to adulthood as much as either a celebration of the conclusion of Hebrew education or a display of commitment to Judaism (Gaster 1980, 66–77; Z. Kaplan and Roth 1972). For psychologist Jacob Arlow the bar mitzvah also has educational more than developmental significance. He calls it an "ordeal by recitation," linking it to nineteenth-century educational tests establishing the authority of the patriarchal synagogue (Arlow 1951, 357). Spiro agrees, pointing out, "The boy is on trial, perhaps not the kind of trial involved in walking over hot coals. But it is an intellectual trial, no less traumatizing as he stands before relatives and authorities to demonstrate his skill, ability, and knowledge of Torah and Jewish law. 'It is, in essence, an academic degree'" (Spiro 1977, 397). Marcus observes that "there is a culmination in the bar mitzvah as well as a celebration of youth. It often is the end of a Jewish child's formal Jewish schooling, his or her graduation" (I. G. Marcus 2004, 122). Anthropologist Harvey Goldberg, in his comparative survey of Jewish rituals, surmises that this association with examination and graduation is grounded in the evolution of the bar mitzvah out of an educational context. In his view, the bar mitzvah replaced the common ritual of entering religious education with one to mark its end. Part of the rationale is that the transition at age 13 is one from elementary school to higher education of *bet ha-midrash*.

Part of the problem with the bar mitzvah as a rite of passage is the way that folklorist Arnold van Gennep's structural order for moving from one stage to another of separation, transition, and incorporation applies to the event. One would expect much transition in a coming-of-age practice, but the bar mitzvah involves an inordinately long preparation time, typically starting as early as 3 years old. The boy is not separated during the event and is not presented as liminal. His central task is to read a Torah portion and provide a speech rather than engaging in an initiatory act with male elders. As an incorporation, as sociologist Judith Davis noted, the bar mitzvah struggles to mark a change in status or passage to another stage. Adult privileges outside congregational life are not granted, and for most children, the bar mitzvah is something that parents plan for them. It is therefore in practice a milestone rather than an initiation.

I contend that meanings often exist outside the awareness of the participants that contributed to the bar mitzvah's spread in folk Judaism since the mid-twentieth century in Western Europe and the United States. My evidence comes from participation in a number of ceremonies, symbolic reading of liturgical texts, a survey of former *b'nai mitzvah*, and a content analysis of *derashah*, the interpretive bar mitzvah speeches the boys make. Using developmental psychology and historical context in the mid-twentieth-century crisis of masculinity, I provide a cultural explanation of why the bar mitzvah rose to its present status. I also look at the ceremony as an invented milestone tradition that deals with father-son conflicts as the boy wrestles with the uncertain status of his masculinity in a wider modern context.

PREPARATION, FASTING, SEPARATION, AND RECITATION

Jewish parents learn early in a child's life of the importance of the bar mitzvah. Most Jewish educators and synagogue administrators encourage participation in Hebrew school beginning with the Aleph grade, coinciding with kindergarten age, as preparation for the bar mitzvah by being able to read and chant biblical Hebrew, recite prayers, and participate in congregational life. The bar mitzvah is treated as a culmination of one's education, demonstrated by reading from the Torah and giving a speech (Figure 6.1). In the days before the bar mitzvah, no special events are planned, although in some communities the boy may wear tefillin all day, get his hair cut or shaved off, or fast.

The ritual fast for the boy usually occurs on the Yom Kippur before his bar mitzvah, and it is distinguished from the fasting he may do with adults afterward

6.1. Sephardic bar mitzvah ceremony, Brooklyn, New York, 1998. Photo by Simon J. Bronner.

by lasting until *chatzot* (midday as defined by Halacha, or practical Jewish law). Rather than being prescribed in the Torah, the transitional fast for the boy before his bar mitzvah on the Day of Atonement arose apparently as a folk custom in the modern period.[2] Fasting might be based on the examples of the father's obligations to train a Jewish child mentioned in the Talmud, which include partial fasting on Yom Kippur after the age of 9 (Shulem and Koenigsberg 2007). Yet Halacha calls for fasting as a commandment *after* the bar mitzvah, with special reference to the symbolism of pubic hair growth for maturity: "A boy of thirteen and one day who [has] brought forth two hairs" is considered adult "with regard to all of the commandments and must complete the fast as an obligation from the Torah, but if they have not brought forth two hairs then they are regarded as minors and complete the fast as a rabbinical obligation only" (Krieger 2006). The significance of the occasion of Yom Kippur for the fast on special occasions is that it symbolizes a death and rebirth, divesting individuals of their previous life (Linke 1999, 149). The fast and wearing the white robe that is traditionally donned on Yom Kippur and burial at the end of life will be reenacted, for example, on the wedding day along with the same confessional prayers that are said on the holiday and at a death bed. The process therefore ritually confronts mortality, which, according to clinical psychologist Stuart Linke, "returns us to our core values and enables us to perceive ourselves more deeply" (149).

On its surface, the ritual fast before the bar mitzvah appears to be preparation for the obligations that the boy will accrue after reaching the age of religious majority. Although fasting on Yom Kippur marks adult practice, the suffering it brings, even for the outcome of atonement, hardly could be considered a motivator to push on to the home stretch of bar mitzvah preparations, unless it is intentionally uncomfortable to metaphorically focus the bar mitzvah as an "ordeal," as psychologist Jacob Arlow contends (1951, 357). If so, then it is a risky metaphor of pain and hunger to impose, if, as Arlow argues, the period before the bar mitzvah "becomes the occasion for rebellion against the parents. The boy, for various reasons, may refuse to participate in the entire process and may repudiate his parents' authority as represented by the need to go through the Bar Mitzvah initiation" (356). But a symbolic rationale outside the awareness of the participants may be at work to explain why it is significant to fast (apparently in defiance of halachic authority) rather than perform other mitzvot after turning 13. One possible connection in religious scholarship is that the sacrifice of fasting is accepted as a purification rite and declaration of faith because it is followed by a joyous feast

(Farrell 1985). On Yom Kippur, fasting after the new year (Rosh Hashanah) is followed by an occasion for a social "breaking the fast." Occurring during the first Jewish month of Tishrei (from the root for "beginning"), the purifying fast marks a fresh start in the ritual year. Is a comparison being made between the enforced fast before the bar mitzvah and the bar mitzvah itself, in which the immaturity and irresponsibility of childhood are ritually replaced with adult religious obligations and encouraged by the festive meal?

If so, the comparison seems strained between the deprivation of food in fasting and the central recitation and discourse at the bar mitzvah ceremony. However, both actions do have something in common, in their attracting parental attention, and this clue may lead to an explanation of the tradition. My argument hinges on the symbolism of fasting in many religious contexts as the maternal provision of food pointed out by theorists of ritual (Dundes 2002a; Farrell 1985, 254). For example, anthropologist Eileen Farrell observes that fasting conveys a reference to birth or infancy in ritual time, because it "evokes the most primitive wish-fulfillment of all, the moment when the hungry infant regains its mother's breast" (Farrell 1985, 254). It is symbolically consistent, therefore, that fasting as a reminder of infantile dependence on the mother's sustenance is accompanied by prohibitions on adult male activities of shaving and "seminal pollution" (J. Trachtenberg 1939, 212).

With fasting often occurring during periods of mourning, representing, according to Theodor Gaster, "the state of suspended animation which ensues at the end of a life lease" (Gaster 1961, 29), it offers a separation from the mother that allows transition and growth. In other words, a previous state or life is being let go and a new one is being embraced. As with other symbolic practices, oral activity is associated with maternal attributes in the home (such as the Jewish folk term *mameloshn* for "mother tongue" or homey folk language). In contrast, synagogue practice involves patriarchal reading or codification (such as *Pirkei Avot*, literally "chapters of the fathers or patriarchs," or idiomatically as "Ethics of the Fathers," which is a significant tractate of the Mishnah composed by male rabbis). On Yom Kippur and other religious occasions where a connection to God is being made, part of that transition is making a transfer from the physical dependence on the mother to the spiritual guidance from the father (see W. R. Smith 1907, 51–53). Worshippers in the traditional Jewish liturgy thus speak of God in the central prayer of the Amida as "our God and God of our Fathers, the God of Abraham, the God of Isaac and the God of Jacob."

Even with revision of liturgies to reflect egalitarianism, the principle holds, as articulated by folklorist Alan Dundes: "If an infant associates feeling hunger pangs with the coming of an adult parent or parent-surrogate, then the adult who wants a deity to approach must clearly make himself hungry. Moreover, the hungrier he is, the more likely it is that the parent-deity will approach" (Dundes 2002a, 9). And that parent as authority will likely be patriarchal. Many midrashic legends underscore the idea that matriarchal intervention brings the patriarchal God closer. A popular narrated example is of the Jewish matriarch Rachel, frequently depicted as the compassionate mother weeping for her captured children, who, the midrash recounts, rises from her grave and begs for God's clemency for the Israelites driven into captivity. Rachel points out her self-abnegation, and there-upon God promises her the restoration of Israel (Rothkoff 1972, 1489). Rachel also shows up in modern wartime legends, protecting Israeli male soldiers from terrorist harm in campaigns outside their borders (Wagner 2009).

In line with the symbolism of fasting as separation from the mother to invite the father-deity, the feature of the pre–bar mitzvah fast begins to make sense. A question that is often posed about the bar mitzvah is how it acts as a coming-of-age ritual if the mother associated with childhood is largely absent from the supposed rite of passage. The answer is that the separation occurs before the cere-mony, beginning with the ritual fast, and the transition from physical dependence to spiritual awareness continues into the ritualized haircut and acquisition of tefil-lin. The task of the ceremony on the big day then becomes through reading and discourse to accentuate the role of the father-deity. Still remaining to be resolved is the relationship of the familial father, who had been an authority over and pro-vider for the boy. Indeed, during the ceremony, it is not uncommon, particu-larly in Sephardic ceremonies, for the father and son to carry the Torah together around the sanctuary, and then there is a moment for the boy to carry it himself. It appears that the rabbi and cantor can act as spiritual surrogates for the father and allow the boy to separate from familial paternity. Still complicating this ritualistic scenario connected to traditional cognitive categories held in Judaism is modern awareness of changing gender roles, especially in relation to the boy's understand-ing of "becoming a man," in which intellect in the Jewish ceremony rather than bodily strength is being used as a ritual measure of masculinity.

The ceremony begins with the boy going to the bimah (reader's stand) to recite standard blessings over the Torah that would be heard on any occasion the Torah is read. According to Spiro's ethnography of the event, "The boy separates himself from his mother, from his childhood, as he walks to the altar of the synagogue," where he is "wrapped in his 'tallit' and surrounded by the males who will read with him" (Spiro 1977, 398). Traditionally, women do not wear a tallit and do not participate on the bimah. The mother is a spectator, whereas the father takes a prominent position at the platform with his son. Unlike preparations for other readings of the Torah, the father recites a short prayer, *Barukh shepetarani meonsho shel zeh*, after the son's conclusion of the second blessing. This blessing is unique to the bar mitzvah; it is not said for the daughter at the bat mitzvah. The translation is "Blessed be He, who has now rid (or freed) me from the responsibility or punishment for this one." Rabbinic literature suggests two interpretations of this benediction, which is found in the Midrash (a compilation of commentaries on the Hebrew Bible), commenting on the phrase, "And the boys grew up" (Genesis 25:27). One is that the father was punished when his son sinned, for he failed to raise him properly, and the other is that the son was punished for the sins of his father (Nulman 1993, 91–92). Whichever interpretation one holds, the common thread is that the opening of the ceremony is thematized in relation to a father-son conflict. Unlike other blessings, the name of God is omitted from the prayer and the Hebrew word *patoor*, meaning "to exempt" or "to rid," conveys a negative connotation of vexation (Arlow 1951, 357).[3] With this connotation, Jewish historian Cecil Roth observed, the father's prayer declaring his freedom from responsibility for the boy "was considered an integral part of the celebration, *hardly less than the boy's own participation in the service*" (C. Roth 1955, 18; emphasis added).

The conflict resolution in the ceremony is for father and son to part ways, and at that moment the boy's teacher steps in to guide the boy in the reading, either the prophetic portion of the week (*haftarah*) or an entire biblical portion (the *sidrah*). Indeed, the father will often stand off at a distance at that point. Afterward, the boy presents a speech that discusses a point of Jewish law or interprets the weekly Torah portion (*parsha*). The speech is a narrative that typically follows a tripartite structure: (1) a standard opening of "Today I am a man," followed by an expression of gratitude to parents, especially the father, for having raised and educated the boy; (2) reference to biblical sources (a favorite in recorded speeches is the sacrifice of Isaac by his father) followed by its application to his own conduct or the society; and (3) a promise of allegiance to the Jewish community, often accompanied by an acknowledgment of the role of the religious leaders who helped him to become a bar mitzvah (Glazer 1928; Gruberger 1993; J. Katz

1931). At the conclusion of the speech, it is common among both Ashkenazic and Sephardic services for children in the audience to throw candies at the boy. Following the principle of sympathetic magic for ensuring growth in the future, the luxurious sweetness of the candy transfers to a prosperous future. Yet more than the contagious act of eating the candy, immersive dousing at the hands of others marks a social as well as age separation.

After the service, the parents host a *seudah mitzvah* (festive meal celebrating a commandment), and this has expanded into the bar mitzvah party, often held in a rented hall. Despite harsh criticisms of the party such as that voiced by Rabbi Abraham Chill—"The contemporary custom of celebrating the *bar mitzvah* with lavish and ostentatious parties has no basis in Jewish tradition and it is in fact contrary to the spirit if not the letter of Jewish law and morality" (Chill 1979, 316–17)—the secular celebration has grown and featured various themes geared to the boy's worldly interests. The party has often become tightly controlled by party planners, but an expectation among the bar mitzvah boy's male friends is that some pranking or even hazing will occur to torment the center of attention and provide a test of his toughness. This might include giving the bar mitzvah boy a wedgie or doctoring his food and drink. The boys may sit with the bar mitzvah on a dais, and frequently they initiate lifting the bar mitzvah on a chair in imitation of a wedding custom for the bride and groom. More sedate and official is the ritual lighting of candles by family members during the party.

Among the Sephardim, the donning of tefillin, or phylacteries, is featured in bar mitzvah practices, and families may hold a separate celebration before the bar mitzvah called Yom Tefillin. The tefillin are two cubical leather containers with attached leather straps. One is worn on the head (*shel rosh*), and the other is worn on the arm (*shel yad*); the thongs for *shel yad* are wrapped seven times around the arm, whereas the straps on *shel rosh* hang loosely behind the head and shoulders like hair strands. The cases hold parchments with four biblical passages, expressing four basic Jewish precepts: the law of tefillin, recognition of God's kingship, the unity of the Creator, and the exodus from Egypt (C. Roth 1955, 23). Betrothal is symbolized in the arm thong, which is wound three times around the middle finger while reciting, "And I will betroth thee unto me forever; yea, I will betroth thee unto me in righteousness, and in judgment and in lovingkindness, and in mercy. I will even betroth thee unto me in faithfulness; and thou shalt know the Lord" (Hosea 2:21–22). In keeping with the laying on of tefillin as a male rite, the Exodus story encased in the tefillin (Exodus 13:1–10, 11–16) opens with the commandment to consecrate to God "every firstborn male" and relates the promise of a "land flowing with milk and honey" promised to "your forefathers" (Exodus 13:1, 5). Indeed, the text signals a transference from a submissive state of slavery under Pharaoh in Egypt to a liberation with the guidance of Moses to the promised land. The bearded rabbi in the ceremony takes on the role of the teacher Moses, guiding his flock to be independent (Moses does not enter the land of Israel). The ceremony for Yom Tefillin also brings out the patriarchal correspondence between father and rabbi in their ritual placement of the tefillin on the boy before he does it himself (Figure 6.2). Typically, the father puts one of the cases on the boy's head, representing his education for which he was responsible, and the rabbi works the other case on the child's arm, representing his action (C. Roth 1955, 22). The boy may give a speech then as well as on the Sabbath, and he is blessed aloud by the adult congregation. A ritual practice that appears to reinforce the transition from father to teacher as patriarch is the boy walking around the assembly with his new decorated tefillin bag into which congregants would drop silver coins, which are then presented as a gift to the bar mitzvah boy's teacher (C. Roth 1955, 22).

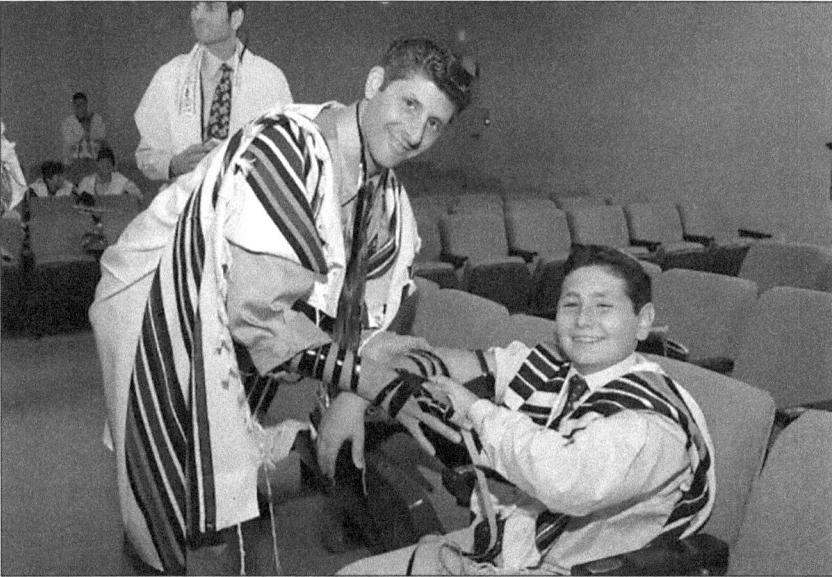

6.2. Yom Tefillin, a ceremony at which the father of the bar mitzvah boy ritually lays on tefillin with his son, Brooklyn, New York, 2008. Photo by Ronnie Habbaz; courtesy of Ronald and Adi Cohen.

The mother is usually involved in making arrangements for the event, and a modern tradition has been for her to weave or present a tallit to the bar mitzvah boy as a sign of nurturing by the praxis of wrapping. The significance of the tallit is that, after his thirteenth birthday, it can be worn on the Sabbath in prayer and thus represents his reaching religious majority. It is customary to have a formal photo portrait taken of the bar mitzvah boy in his tallit as a keepsake to distribute (Figure 6.3). The mother's role is what Judith Davis (1995) calls the traditional *balebosta*, translated from the Yiddish as the woman of the house with the implication that she has a managerial role to compensate for her exclusion from the ceremony. Her management has extended to responsibility for the boy's Jewish education, although the bar mitzvah ceremony conveys the frequent fiction that the father has been overseeing the boy's religious training (see Gordon 1959, 58–59). Nonetheless, at the bar mitzvah the father takes center stage with his son, until he is moved aside by the supervising rabbi and cantor.

RELATION OF THE BAR MITZVAH TO CIRCUMCISION, HAIRCUTTING, WEDDING, AND EXAMINATION

In its structure and symbolism, the bar mitzvah can be compared to four discrete traditions: bris (Yiddish; *brit milah* in Hebrew), or circumcision; *upsherin* (Yiddish), or the ritual first haircut; the Jewish wedding; and the final examination or dissertation. The comparison to the bris comes up in the discourse of the bar mitzvah because of its coincidence with the boy's birthday, which raises images of circumcision. Typical is a memoir I collected showing that the bar mitzvah was narrated in relation to the bris:

> I was constantly reminded that the bar mitzvah was the biggest event in my life after my bris. Since the bar mitzvah came around my birthday, my mother brought up her memories of the bris and how much I've grown. She's always sentimental, you know.
>
> My father would make a bad joke about it would be just as painful, besides telling me that another thing that's the same is that everyone will want to hold me. I did think it was funny when he said they're not talking about my pecker when they say, "My how you've grown."

6.3. Bar mitzvah studio portrait with objects identifying reaching religious majority: tefillin, book, tallit, and personalized tallit bag, New York, 1961. Collection of Simon J. Bronner.

More official charting of the Jewish boy's milestones typically involves the bar mitzvah's relation to ritual circumcision. For example, Cecil Roth, in the mid-twentieth century, declared:

> In the traditional Jewish scheme, there were three great festive occasions in a boy's life. There was the eighth day after his birth, when he was introduced into the Covenant of Abraham. There was the day when he was first initiated to study, being taken to synagogue, blessed by the rabbi, and given honey to lick from a slate on which letters of the Hebrew alphabet were written, as a token that the Torah should be sweet to his mouth all the days of his life. And there was the day when he was first considered legally bound to fulfill the obligations of Jewish law and practice, and could be regarded as a Bar Mitzvah, a "child of precepts." (C. Roth 1955, 15)

With the decline of honey licking to mark the start of study among modern liberal Jews, more attention has been focused on the continuity in the Jewish life cycle from circumcision to bar mitzvah.

Like the bris, the bar mitzvah is represented as an induction into faith and is prescribed in intervals of time: 8 days for the bris and 13 years for the bar mitzvah. The bris also centrally involves the father-son relationship, for the father gives the child to the mohel (Jewish ritual specialist in circumcision), who circumcises the child. Several college students who gave me memoirs of their bar mitzvahs mentioned that their friends often made references to the bris in their pranks. They made connections in their narratives to binding and cutting in the bar mitzvah suit and ritual haircutting, often accompanied by checking whether the boy has pubic hair despite the "damage" done by the circumcision.

Jewish religious advisers Marc-Alain Ouaknin and Françoise-Anne Ménager connect the importance of manhood to the head-shearing ritual (*upsherin* in Yiddish; *chalakah* in Hebrew) that many Orthodox communities observe for 3-year-old boys (Ouaknin and Ménager 2005, 46–48). An educational relationship exists because the boy is expected for the first time to go to school, where he will learn to read Hebrew. They find similarities between the attention in the haircutting ritual and the bar mitzvah (they could extend this comparison to the bris) to the trauma of loss and its provision of healing with cultural identity. Both rituals also are replete with reminders of masculinity. The short haircut distinguishes the boy from the long hair of the girl. According to Ouaknin and Ménager, the immersion in books is symbolically consistent with the gendering of cutting ritu-als: The boy shifts from the maternal language, which is oral, to the paternal lan-guage, which is written (48). Hebrew also links writing to the paternal language in an extraordinary way. Further underscoring study as intellectual gain to compen-sate for physical loss is a traditional gift in both rituals of a honey cake or sweets shaped like letters (48). In circumcision, haircutting, and bar mitzvah rituals, the boy acquires a new ceremonial garment. In the haircutting the boy gains a small tallit to wear as an undergarment, known as tzitzit (based on the commandment in Torah to wear fringes at the corners of garments and also meaning "hair"; see Ezekiel 8:3). Tzitzit, or braided fringes, are attached to the boy's tallit and are often used in the service to touch the Torah as it is carried around the synagogue.

In addition to the larger tallit conspicuously worn over the shoulders at prayer, the tefillin adds long strips of leather on the arm and head. The boy usually receives the gift of tefillin before the tallit. A common time to present the phylac-teries is 30 days before the bar mitzvah. This period is related to a monthly cycle in the Jewish lunar calendar and is commonly associated with a mourning period of *shloshim* (from the Hebrew for "thirty."). A mourning period is simulated for the passing of youth, and as in the ritual guidelines after burial, hair of the fam-ily mourners cannot be cut until after the mourning period (usually just before the bar mitzvah). "Laying tefillin," as the act is called, involves a form of binding, because leather cases attached to the leather straps contain Torah passages. Rabbis teaching the laying of tefillin will comment on the placement on head and arms as committing intellect and body to fulfillment of commandments. But there is also an important connection to the father-son relationship. The four passages from the Torah on the tefillin parchments are teachings the father will address to the child and relate to communicative skills: *Veamarta*, for "You will say"; *Veshinaneta vedi-barta*, for "You will repeat and you will speak"; and *Velimadeta*, for "You will teach" (Ouaknin and Ménager 2005, 161–62). Both tefillin and tzitzit are symbolically cut to show completion by going over the head and removing them after prayer (50).

A ceremonial connection to the circumcision at the bar mitzvah is the *wimpel* (from the German *Wimpel* for "flag" or "sash") (Figure 6.4), a decorated cloth on which the boy is circumcised and that is later used as a sash to bind the Sefer Torah (see my discussion in chapter 5).[4] The *wimpel* might be part of a custom at the age of 3 when the boy is toilet trained. The father gets an *aliyah* (invitation to the altar) and brings his boy with him to the bimah to wrap the *wimpel* around the Torah. Thought to be of German origin like the bar mitzvah, the decorated *wimpel* gains

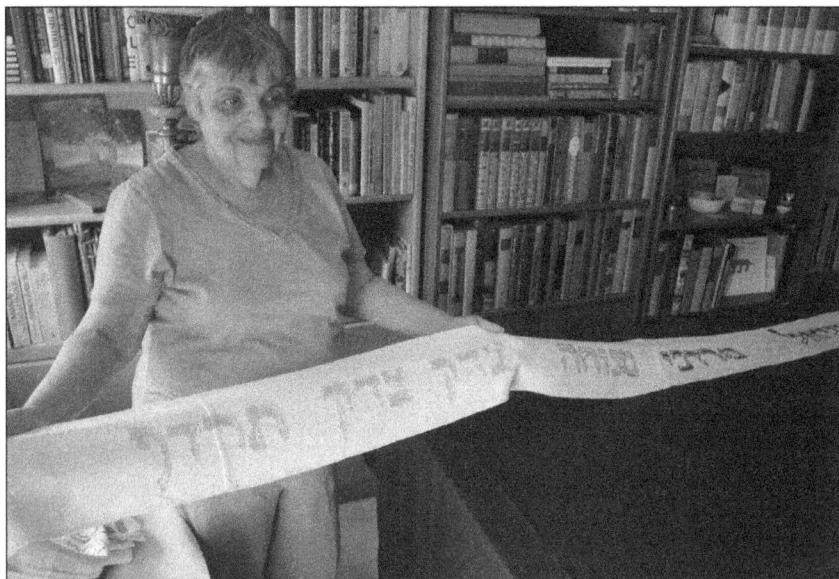

6.4. Judy Goldberg holding a *wimpel* that she made for a bris/bar mitzvah, Harrisburg, Pennsylvania, 2009. Photograph by Simon J. Bronner.

significance because it is was used to swaddle the baby boy at his Brit Milah and represents the covenant with a patriarchal figure, as the Hebrew blessing recited by the father reminds the gathered group: "Praised be Thou, O Lord our God, Ruler of the Universe, who has sanctified us by Thy commandments, and has bidden us to make him enter into the covenant of Abraham, our father." The group responds, "As he has entered into the covenant, so may he be introduced to the study of Torah, to the wedding canopy, and to good deeds." Based on this text, *wimpel*s are inscribed in Hebrew with the following message underscoring the patriarchal line: "(Name of child, called) son of (name of father), born under a good constellation on (day of week, date, month, year), may he (or may the Lord let him) grow to Torah, marriage, and good deeds." An artist might illuminate the text with related depictions of a Jewish wedding under the traditional canopy (chuppah); masculine animals such as the lion of Judah, eagles, and leopards;[5] and a boy holding up a Torah, commonly interpreted as a bar mitzvah scene (Eis 1979, 32; Hagen et al. 1984; Kirshenblatt-Gimblett 1977, 18–19; Lehnardt 2014). One way that the bar mitzvah is thematized in the father-son relationship is in the transfer of the *wimpel*. After the circumcision, the *wimpel* belongs to the father, but after the bar mitzvah, possession transfers to the son.

The bar mitzvah (exemplifying the commandment at the bris to "grow to Torah") and the wedding are linked in the custom of giving the groom an *aliyah* the week before his wedding to reenact the call to the bimah at his bar mitzvah. In a sign of readiness for marriage, the groom often donates his *wimpel* to his synagogue before the wedding. The covering of the chuppah is frequently composed of the boy's bar mitzvah tallit, and the bride will replace it with a larger tallit that she has woven or purchased for the groom (I. G. Marcus 2004, 117). The transfer of the tallit (at a critical part of the ceremony, both bride and groom are covered by the tallit to symbolize their unity) and the circling of the bride around the groom indicate readiness for sexual relations. Practices at the bar mitzvah suggest that the metaphor of the wedding is used to represent sexual displacement by immersion in books rather than sexual awakening. When the boy is called to the bimah at the bar mitzvah, he is identified as the "Bar Mitzvah Groom" and the Torah is the bride to which he is bound. According to Arlow's description, wedding and bar mitzvah are joined in the reading, because "throughout his recitation the initiate is observed intently as a young man on trial undergoing a very difficult examination. A sense of compassionate participation grips the audience, especially the boy's mother" (Arlow 1951, 357). The anticipation can be related to anxiety over sexually consummating a marriage; in this case the enactment is displacing the sexuality with potency in touching the Torah with a *yad*, a metal extension in the shape of a finger, and the oral performance. In the tefillin ceremony described previously, the boy places the *shel yad* on the arm and wraps straps that extend from it around the middle finger while saying verses referring to betrothal. Although 13 seems young to invoke the metaphor of marriage, Ouaknin and Ménager find evidence for its enactment as compensation for sexually "losing a part of oneself through the body" (Ouaknin and Ménager 2005, 46). They argue that "boys lose sperm (wet dreams and first masturbation)" at ages that "correspond closely to the time that the losses described above are first sustained" (46). Further, in the sympathetic magic of throwing candies at the bar mitzvah boy, an analyst could observe an ejaculatory praxis, resembling the showering of the bride and groom with fertility symbols of rice and shoes at a wedding (see Bronner 2017a, 33; Chesser 1980, 208; Crombie 1895).

Arguably, access to the Torah is unconsciously equated with access to a woman, which the father already possesses. Arlow hypothesized that organizing the ordeal as an examination is symbolically important because, "failing an examination, together with the humiliation which the student experiences, is often unconsciously equated with being castrated," and, from clinical cases, examiners are often identified with the father image of the oedipal phase (Arlow 1951, 365). To be sure, the bar mitzvah boy is expected to pass the examination by his male elders, but more than any other theme, memoirs mention performance anxiety about successfully completing the reading and speech under the watchful eye of teacher and father. The chanting for the reading is done by rote, and it is all the more challenging because of the absence of vowel aids to pronunciation. As Ouaknin and Ménager point out, "This means that to learn it, one has to accept being part of a tradition. One cannot learn this vowel-less text on one's own, even if one reads and speaks Hebrew fluently" (Ouaknin and Ménager 2005, 63). The process of tradition they are referring to involves an oral handing down of performative practices from male elder to the boy. In this way, the connotation of identity formation at the bar mitzvah is prominent, because more than a text is being chanted; tradition as a sustaining process for the group is being enacted—and honored.

A lesson of the boy's ordeal is that being part of the tradition is difficult and is administered by the synagogue patriarchy rather than the familial one. The following narratives, collected from young men who had experienced their bar mitzvah five to eight years before, exemplify these pervasive themes of performance anxiety and participation in tradition at the bar mitzvah.

> I was nervous beyond words. The cantor tried to calm me by telling me it was my special day, but that made me only feel worse. I felt that all eyes were on me and I could never be ready in time. I felt that my voice was going to crack at any moment. It's different from show and tell in school, because it was so formal and when I was reading, I was dwarfed by these older men who I thought were breathing down my neck.

> I think my mother worried about everyone coming and that the party would go well. It was my father who sweated the synagogue part, and I sweated the more he did, even though he didn't have to say much. That suit bothered me and my friends teased me about my get-up. Older relatives told me they remembered my father's bar mitzvah that was so wonderful and I felt that I had to live up to that. I think that's why I pushed to read faster than I should have. I don't think my sister had as hard a time at her bat mitzvah. There was totally more pressure on me.

I dropped everything as the time got closer so I could concentrate. I would have loved to have postponed it but that date was set. I was into sports and let that slide for the bar mitzvah. The rabbi told me that I would have the support of family to get me through, but I didn't know half these people. I felt that I was singing for strangers, which made me nervous. I think it was definitely worth it after everything, but I was a wreck before.

The tone of these narratives is borne out by Kosmin's survey, which showed that 51 percent of parents reported that the bar mitzvah dominated the life of the family during the year of preparation, but 97 percent still felt that the bar mitzvah "was worth the time and trouble involved" (Kosmin 2000, 235–36). Despite complaints that the bar mitzvah was time-consuming and nerve-racking, only 1 percent of the *b'nai mitzvah* wrote that it "was not worth the time it took" (235).

The bar mitzvah treats learning as a masculine attribute because command of the Torah is associated with male leadership and because the bearded rabbi signifies an especially learned man at a time when the boy is concerned with the growth of pubic and facial hair as a sign of maturing into manhood. These images are reinforced by cake toppers (a cake in the form of a Torah is commonly reported), a host of figurines often given as gifts that depict the tallit-covered hairless boy at the Torah or bimah under the tutelage of a bearded religious figure.[6] Arlow, however, did not believe that the bar mitzvah was effective in resolving oedipal conflicts because of the time lag between sexual maturity and heterosexuality sanctioned by modern society. He suggested that, as a result of the failure of the ceremony to ritualize puberty, the bar mitzvah boy chooses a number of psychological strategies, including channeling sexual and aggressive energies into study, rejecting the father by renewed submission to an exalted father image of God, or cessation of religious adherence to either join or rebel against his biological father (Arlow 1951, 364–68). Although the father is symbolically replaced in the bar mitzvah, the separation from and competition for the mother, characteristic of pubertal rituals, is not as apparent. What is manifested more than sexual competition is the celebration of the child's precociousness, evident in command of the "ordeal by examination."

Instead of performing independence for the boy, the bar mitzvah presents a paradoxical combination of separation and connection. The reading declares an early autonomy from education even as it joins the individual to a patrilineal tradition. The boy is not integrated into the community as much as he is forced to become self-aware of his own development and aspirations. Following the symbolic communication of the circumcision (*brit milah* is literally the "covenant of the word") of which he was unaware, and possibly the *upsherin* at which he begins immersion in the alphabet, the bar mitzvah shows his readiness for the world by a performance that draws attention to itself for what Ouaknin and Ménager call "creative combinations and recombinations of letters and words" challenging the linear structure of storytelling (Ouaknin and Ménager 2005, 63). The boy becomes conscious of the attainment of skills that will carry him into adulthood. Rabbis hope that the ancient source of the texts will remind him to commit to the synagogue, but the praxis of his "reading in bursts" (words bursting out into letters or into groups of letters, making other words and coming together into a new order) and exemption of his father allow him to detach (62–63).

HISTORICAL AND SOCIAL CONTEXTS FOR JEWISH MANLY DISPLAY

If the bar mitzvah is not effective as a sacramental or pubertal rite, its value as an ethnic commitment is questionable because of the decline of Jewish involvement after the event. If it is not particularly useful for coming of age or revitalizing Jewish identity and if parents complain of its exorbitant expense and material excess, then what explains its spreading popularity from the late twentieth century into the twenty-first? Joselit's thesis that the bar mitzvah became entrenched as a life-cycle celebration in which the family's economic success could be displayed and ethnic identity unhinged from synagogue life in the post-immigrant generation does not readily apply to a different set of social and historical circumstances for Jewish parents with only faint memories of the ghetto experience. And if there are traces of this motivation of status anxiety apparent in the suburban conspicuous consumption evident in renowned popular culture portrayals such as *Keeping Up with the Steins* and *Entourage*, then why did the synagogue component not disappear, particularly since prominent American rabbis held a negative or ambivalent attitude toward the bar mitzvah? The psychosexual connections of circumcision, examination, and wedding are strong in the ceremony, suggesting a developmental explanation, but is the ceremony working to resolve oedipal conflicts, considering that the mother plays a peripheral role by most accounts and that the separation that occurs is from the father rather than from the mother, as described in other coming-of-age processes?

With the rush to find a source in antiquity for the age of 13 as a Jewish ritual age, it appears that the modern symbolism of age 13 as the first year of adolescence, or the teen years, is being forgotten. The twentieth century, especially the years after World War II, was marked by the rise of teenagers as a separate, often troubled or rebellious age and marketing target. Many factors went into the creation of adolescence, particularly in North America and Western Europe, including the end of child labor and the rise of high school attendance and of status in popular culture. Wrapped up in the emerging image of the teen in the modern context of compensating for a lack of the provider role is the tough guy image of the adolescent relying on strength, competitiveness, and aggressive heterosexuality in preparation for economic and social independence. This image was coupled with the feminized, constricted, suited father of the 1950s vividly spread in iconic images such as the rebellious teen's father wearing an apron in *Rebel Without a Cause* (1955) and the domestication of the father-businessman in *The Man in the Gray Flannel Suit* (1956) (see Cross 2008, 95; see also Cohan 1997; Gilbert 2005; Gordon 1959, 57–64; Osgerby 2001; W. K. Young 2004, 30, 184–86). Against this background of changing views of age-based masculinity, the Jewish emphasis on learning as the basis of masculine identity caused conflicts with the dominant society, at least if the goal was to integrate into society. The Jewish body, as Sander Gilman has pointed out in his study of the European sources for this conflict, was defined as unsuited for military or strenuous work (Gilman 1991; see also Konner 2009, 144–53). Jews were known for brains rather than brawn (Gilman 1996). During the 1950s, Jews were notably absent from many cultural displays of teen masculine power, including music, motors, sports, and dance (Kimmel 1996, 277–78). In folk humor, Jews were smart but weak, and many jokes about the bar mitzvah boy underscored his inadequacy as a sexualized man (Ouaknin and Ménager 2005, 55).

If that pressure to show manly traits came from outside the Jewish community at a time when the bonds of the community began to unravel, from within the community, egalitarian ideas about the bat mitzvah began to take hold in the Conservative, Reconstructionist, and Reform wings of Judaism. The time of maturation for girls was originally defined a year earlier than for the boys, adding insult to injury, even though her ceremony was not thematized with any declaration of "Today, I am a woman." In the background of the Jewish boy's maturation is the growth of the image through popular sources of the overprotective mother who inhibits the Jewish boy's maturity and stays with him through adulthood

(Antler 2007). One should also not underestimate the psychological impact of Jewish circumcision as another internal conflict among Jews, because of the implication that it diminishes sexual aggressiveness and masculine identity (Glick 2005; Mark 2003; E. K. Silverman 2006).

Looking historically at bar mitzvah announcements, the theme of the bar mitzvah began to change from a subdued family ceremony of joining congregational life to the public celebration of manhood during the 1950s. It first becomes a theme of television sitcoms in the 1960s, usually representing a Jewish boy's anxiety about either going through the "ordeal by examination" or having missed an opportunity to have one (Jonathan Pearl and Pearl 1999). Many of the parties had as themes the interests of the boy, such as music, sports, and motors rather than religious subjects, and these interests along with displays of economic power were significant for culturally connecting to a normative, if not precocious hypermasculinity. For example, I asked boys who had gone through the bar mitzvah how they arrived at the themes for their post-ceremony parties. As the following narratives attest, it was a decision that they strongly wanted to control.

> If I left it to my parents, I'm sure they would have rented a boring hall and made it look like their wedding. I wanted a teen party and I wanted it to be cool. I was into cars and skateboards, so I got them to put it in an auto museum, which none of my buddies had done, and the centerpieces were dudes on skateboards. I told them that I would do all the traditional stuff for the synagogue if I could have the party that wouldn't embarrass me.

> My parents did ask me for ideas about the party, and I'm glad they did. I was worried that they would want too much of a family affair. The ceremony followed the law, and I wanted the party to be something that would be mine. I wanted to let go and impress my friends. It had to be about sports to save face after all the stuff I took about going through bar mitzvah lessons. There weren't too many Jewish signs, although my parents did want the candle lighting for the relatives. But I had a rock band, so the kids could get into it.

More than a celebration of the completion of the bar mitzvah, the party allowed the boys to show their connection to normative culture, especially to masculine pursuits of sports, recreation, and music. This was especially important because the boys recognized that, for the most part, their mothers made the arrangements for the party. With demonstrations of masculinity and maturity being important at the party, the ceremony is remembered in relation to the father's role. The components of the synagogue ceremony emphasizing the boy taking the father's role and the rise in status of the recitation as an ordeal were adapted into the declaration, "Today, I am a man." At several parties I attended, a competition between the father and son bubbled to the surface at the point when the parents and their son were lifted on chairs. The mother often acted fearful while the father rose up with aplomb, leaving the son to match his confidence. At a bar mitzvah reception in New York City, for example, the father positioned himself in the chair to ride it aggressively, and even sexually, like a bull rider (Figure 6.5). Considering the praxis of the bar mitzvah, one might easily construe this declaration as "Today, I am the father"—and I am better than he was. Competition for ownership of the event is evident in the idea that the successful bar mitzvah reflects on the status of the father, as shown especially in *Keeping Up with the Steins*. The early age at which the bar mitzvah occurred added to the ceremony's appeal for announcing the Jewish boy's claim to manliness if not legal maturity.

6.5. In this scene from a bar mitzvah reception in New York City, the father is lifted after his son in a chair in the style of a wedding custom. But in a symbolic distinction, the father positioned himself to "ride the chair like a bull." Photo by Simon J. Bronner.

Into the twenty-first century under the influence of the women's movement, questions of the proper masculine role taken by Jewish boys increased. Reports in books such as *Jew-Jitsu: The Hebrew Hands of Fury*, by Rabbi Daniel Eliezer and Paul Kupperberg (2008), along with satirical movies such as *The Hebrew Hammer* (2004) expressed a confusion about whether the answer to these questions would be to embrace knowledge as a source of social power or as a sign of diminished manliness. I contend that the bar mitzvah gained importance in what increasingly became seen as the most important phase of modern life and for a group that felt the most conflict in its definition of masculinity. Despite Theodor Gaster's avowal that the bar mitzvah imparts nothing, I find that its symbolism of circumcision, examination, and wedding is joined to modern meanings of masculine maturity. It is imperfect as a ritual of religious commitment, to be sure, but it has persisted and even spread in the modern context, not because of its signal of religious majority or adult obligations but because of its negotiation of adolescence for an ethnic group uncertain in American popular culture of its masculine identity and patriarchal continuity.

FEMINIZATION AND THE RITUAL BURDEN OF THE BAR MITZVAH

Having made an argument for linking the rise of the bar mitzvah to a crisis of masculinity for assimilating Jews in North America, I see signs that it is likely to enter a new phase as a managed, if not invented tradition. For instance, some of the connections to masculinity are undermined as the synagogue in the twenty-first century goes through what has been heralded as feminization, including female rabbis and cantors leading the bar mitzvah (Elyse Goldstein 1991; Marder 1996; Seidman 1997). Mothers are taking more of a role, and for my memoir writers concerned with their masculine image, that caused more rather than less distress. One compensation that several writers mentioned was taking more control of the party and infusing it with masculine themes, holding it at auto museums, on ski slopes, or in sports stadiums (Figure 6.6). Or the party exuded a sense of "coolness" in representation of a modern fashion and electronics rather than the process of tradition evoking continuity with Jewish identity. One bar mitzvah adviser touched a nerve by showing parents how to highlight their son's hip individuality in step with high style rather than collective tradition associated with sameness by offering *Mitzvah Chic: How to Host a Meaningful, Fun, Drop-Dead Gorgeous Bar or Bat Mitzvah* (G. A. Greenberg 2006).

6.6. Skateboarder centerpiece at a bar mitzvah held at an auto museum, Hershey, Pennsylvania, 2006. Photo by Simon J. Bronner.

A number of families view holding a bar mitzvah in Israel as a sign of religious devotion, but rather than departing from tradition, this practice fits into the trope of announcing manly attributes at a young age because of the image of Israelis as tough Jews. For example, a common post-ceremony activity is to go to Masada, the historic site where a small number of rebellious Jews held off legions of the Roman Empire. Many of the boys show their vigor by climbing up a steep path to the plateau, 1,300 feet high. In addition to this bar mitzvah trip, other activities feature creative ways to engage the boy with a strenuous and memorable experience. As the boys seek to declare their own identity, the fathers are frequently involved as the son's pal, engaged equally in sports and music rather than speaking as the authoritarian voice of the elders or sages (see Cross 2008). If my argument holds up, then, as the popular perception of Jewish masculinity changes to the point where it joins normative muscular manliness, the bar mitzvah will carry less of a ritual burden to show the development of the boy's mettle as well as his mind (see Brod 1988, 2004; Bronner 2005a, 34–36). The bar mitzvah is the tradition everyone thinks they know from popular culture as a sign of excess of mass culture generally, although assigned to Jews, but its folk cultural practice reveals an uneasy father-son relationship in a society that creates conflicts for the boy between brains and brawn as he declares at the age of 13, "Today, I am a man."

JEWISH NAMING CEREMONIES FOR GIRLS

A Study in the Discourse of Tradition and Modernity

A pivotal moment in modern Jewish cultural practice occurred in 1976 when Sharon and Michael Strassfeld, in their wildly popular *Jewish Catalog* series, spurred many readers to action by declaring, "With the new interest in Jewish feminism, many people have reassessed their needs and values and have written their own *brit* ceremonies. We include some of the many sent to us with the hope that they inspire other parents to explore the tradition and their own Jewish needs" (Strassfeld and Strassfeld 1976, 31). As the Strassfelds noted, they were not alone in issuing a call in the midst of the American women's movement of the time for ritual events to celebrate the entrance of a baby girl into Jewish communities, as is done for boys in the Brit Milah (see Reifman 1978). They chose their language carefully, retaining the reference to *brit* for covenant and avoiding the Yiddish *bris* or Hebrew *brit milah* representing a religious male circumcision. They appropriated *brit* as a generic term for all newborn rituals rather than gendering it. It was the Strassfelds' seven-page section provocatively titled "Oh Boy, It's a Girl!!!" that arguably catapulted the idea of baby naming rituals as *brit* ceremonies for girls in North America among liberal Jews. The Strassfelds' presentation of the ceremony followed their ideological "push for change" in the first volume in which they proclaimed, "Until women demonstrate that their needs as Jews are not being met and that they have valid reason to complain, nothing will be done; that is the nature of halakhah, which is basically a conservative institution" (R. Siegel et al. 1973, 254–55).

In the decades that followed, rituals for welcoming baby girls became more commonplace in the Reform, Reconstructionist, and Conservative wings of Judaism, and they made significant headway in Modern Orthodox communities. Commentaries by Jewish cultural critics typically referred to the female naming ceremonies as examples of extending the egalitarian or feminist revision of Jewish religious practices for the life course beyond the bat mitzvah (Nussbaum Cohen 2001; Reifman 1978; S. R. Siegel 2012, 2014). In making this move, questions of what to call the female naming ceremonies and their categorization in addition to the location and content of the rituals took on added importance and sparked considerable debate. For many feminist activists, the discourse around the ceremony's emphasis on women's control of ritual at the outset of life was especially significant as a counter to patriarchal hegemony in the synagogue.

The girls' baby naming presented a challenge to families and rabbis alike, because it is not exactly equivalent to the ritual tradition of boys' circumcision. The girls' ceremony does not involve genital cutting, and many critics did not want to venerate circumcision as a model ritual for entering a covenant with God (see S. J. D. Cohen 2005; Glick 2005; E. Tabory and Erez 2003). Mary Gendler (1974–1975), a clinical psychologist and prominent voice in the Jewish feminist movement beginning in the 1970s, advocated for a ritual rupturing of the hymen soon after birth, but the proposal did not receive wide support. More generally, the discussion of introducing welcoming ceremonies for baby girls generated a discourse of a feminist ritual model for Jewish practice that, in contrast to rites of passage for the Jewish life cycle, would be "fluid, open, and nonhierarchical" (S. R. Siegel 2012, 338; see also Plaskow 1991, 67). For example, instead of seeking alternative standard, highly structured synagogue-centered rituals in the manner of the bat mitzvah, many feminists sought to open rituals to flexible choice of content and creative personalization of the ritual actions. Indeed, the new scripted welcoming ceremonies set the stage for revisions or introductions of other home-based Jewish life-cycle events (S. R. Siegel 2012, 338).

The question of cultural meaning arises for "the Jewish tradition," as the Strassfelds underscore, in the different practices for girls and the names for them. If the female welcoming ceremony is not as dramatic and patriarchal as a "mark upon the flesh" in circumcision, can it effectively signal the worthiness and cultural expectations of the daughter as much as the son? What are the roles enacted for the mother as a symbol of the feminine in society and for the father and potentially the rabbi? And what stake does creative participation in the welcoming ceremonies have for parents and friends who do not identify as feminists? Beyond declaring the parents' joy in the birth of a daughter and perhaps an ideological foundation in feminism and modern liberal values, are there ethnic and denominational identities conveyed, much as there are in other Jewish home-based ritual practices? The significance of the answers to these questions is in the realization that bris and welcoming ceremonies are the first public display of Jewishness for the child and family. With the ritual entrance of another person into a local community and into a family, onlookers await signs of the path to be taken on the life course in the religious and secular worlds. The ceremonies are therefore hardly routine; they draw attention to themselves even more than the Brit Milah as performances designed by families of their position in modernity as well as Jewish tradition.

In this chapter, I propose that the ensuing meta-tradition of welcoming and naming ceremonies for girls—that is, commentary literally or symbolically expressed in the practices concerning the nature of and reason for the ritual—reveals a subsequent discourse about identities shaping modern Jewish culture. Although much of the scholarship on the ceremonies has focused on their feminist roots, my evaluation of scripts and observation of the ceremonies in North America and Israel covers the contemporary debates regarding the terminology to be used, the antiquity of the rituals, and continuity with denominational and national heritage. I view the contemplation of these issues as a struggle moving beyond gender issues to define modern Jewish life and its supposed tension with tradition. I hypothesize that the emergence of controversies over terms, age, and significance of the birth ceremonies for girls is more than a statement on women's roles in Judaism. It represents a projection of perceived contradictions between Jewish tradition and mass cultural modernity into an external, manageable form—a variable cultural practice—and location in the home that parents hope can resolve conflicts and paradoxes of their Jewish identities.

Parents distinguish the ritually framed welcoming ceremonies for girls from the synagogue practice of giving the father an *aliyah* at a Sabbath service shortly after the birth. In the synagogue ceremony, the father recites the Mi Sheberakh, a blessing for the health of the mother and daughter, and announces the name of the girl for the first time: "May the One who blessed our ancestors bless the mother (name spoken) and her newborn daughter, whose name in Israel shall be (name spoken). May they raise her for the marriage canopy and for a life of good deeds" (Diamant 2008, 124). The frequent absence of the mother along with the goal set from birth of marriage for the girl rankled many feminists. To be sure, at Reform and Conservative synagogues, both mothers and fathers can be called to the Torah and the mothers can recite the Birkat Hagomel, a blessing said upon coming through a dangerous experience. The importance of this blessing in Jewish feminism is that it traditionally offered a rare occasion for the woman to perform a mitzvah in a minyan. British Chief Rabbi Joseph H. Hertz, in his widely used *Authorized Daily Prayer Book* (1959), created a liturgical service with congregational responses around the mother's recitation to show the importance of the mother's role in Jewish religious continuity, but feminists nonetheless objected to the submissive tone of the narrative: "What can I render the Lord for all His benefits toward me? I will offer to you the sacrifice of thanksgiving and will call upon the Name of the Lord. I will pay my vows to the Lord in the presence of all His people; in the courts of the Lord's house, in the midst of you, O Jerusalem, Hallelujah" (Strassfeld and Strassfeld 1976, 37). To tie the service to a social celebration, synagogues typically encourage a celebratory Kiddush lunch in honor of the newborn.

Despite rabbinic efforts to recognize the joy of giving birth to a girl, by the early twenty-first century the trend among families was to hold a ceremony in the home or Jewish communal space (such as a community center). In the home the family exerts more creative control over the event and marks it as more of a social event related to a Jewish identity that is not exclusively religious. This appropriation of ritual for the family in the domestic sphere is contextualized generally in the United States by a historical shift in the twentieth century from community and synagogue institutions to the family and domestic sphere. Historically outlined convincingly by Jenna Weissman Joselit, the significance of this emerging American "domesticated Jewishness" is that the "home and its inhabitants became the core of a modern Jewish identity" (Joselit 1994, 6). Joselit points out that a key ethnic development of the twentieth century was the control families exerted over life-cycle rituals, with improvisation on tradition and, in the process, a redefinition of Jewishness as an emotional experience. Rather than viewing tradition as practices repeated from ancient Jewish scripture and sacralized in the synagogue, tradition as invoked in home-based ritual enactments became an evolving flexible guide drawn from contemporary culture that could be selected, altered, and personalized. According to Joselit, over the course of the twentieth century, "Familial and familiar, this brand of domesticated identity also emerged radiantly and triumphantly at key moments in the life cycle. Birth, death, adolescence, and marriage called forth displays of Jewishness seemingly unrivaled and unprecedented in their mix of emotionality, consumerism, pragmatism, and pageantry. These exuberant yet short-lived bursts of Jewishness even gave rise to a down-to-earth sense of the divine. 'The Jewish God,' insisted one observer, 'is a Household God'" (6).

If the centrality of family is a tie that binds modern Jewishness, then names given to the Ashkenazic ritual marking the beginning of life for a girl signal social division by affiliation, heritage, and ideology. The Brit Milah (or bris, in Yiddish) is standard terminology for the boy, but for the girl, families decide on the message and content of the ceremony from a variety of descriptors in Hebrew. These include *simhat bat* (joy of the daughter), *brit hayyim* (covenant of life), *brit kedusha* (covenant of sanctification), *brit bat Zion* (covenant for the daughters of Zion), *brit b'not Yisrael* (covenant for the daughters of Israel), *brit e'dut* (covenant of witnessing), *brit Sarah* (covenant of Sarah), *brit rehitzah* (covenant of washing), *brit mikveh* (covenant of immersion), *britah* (feminine form of *brit*), and *brit bat* (covenant for a daughter) (Diamant 2008, 122). Of these, *simhat bat* has emerged as the leading term for the ceremony, probably because of its celebratory tone, its avoidance of *brit* as a masculine term, and its evocation in the ritual imagination of a connection to the family-based *simha* or life-course party (187–91) (Figure 7.1). Another possibility is the linkage of birth, celebratory dancing, and marking of a new annual cycle at Simhat Torah. Debra Nussbaum Cohen, for example, draws attention to Orthodox Yemenite traditions of welcoming new babies into the congregation on the first Simhat Torah after their birth, "on the autumn holiday that celebrates the conclusion of the year-long cycle of reading the entire Torah and beginning it anew. The father or grandfather usually 'buys' a *hakafa*, or dance with the Torah, in the baby's honor, with the infant leading the procession around the block or the neighborhood" (Nussbaum Cohen 2001, 14). Dancing is not obligatory in the welcoming ceremonies, however, and most of the scripts for the event involve social recognition of adopting a Hebrew name and candle lighting.

The reference to *simhat* for joy of the daughter signals that as a female, the child will grow up to participate fully in Jewish life—and by extension be empowered in the greater society. According to anthropologist Riv-Ellen Prell, in line with a post-Enlightenment ideology of equal rights, the ritual announcement of participation

7.1. Naming ceremony identified as Simhat Bat in the family home with candle lighting and Kiddush, Harrisburg, Pennsylvania, 2000. Photo by Simon J. Bronner.

fits the modern American vision "of Jews as 'citizens' of their tradition" (Prell 2007, 5). Although referencing a Judaism in which gender determines Jewish rights and obligations, the naming ceremony paradoxically undermines gender as a principle for structuring social roles, because any cultural practice can be pursued and empowered by a citizen in the Jewish social body politic, regardless of sex (4–9). A way to contain this paradox is to ritually convey a flexible, integrating (rather than segregating) idea of tradition. Because of the presumption that Jewish tradition defined the male as following ancient scripture privileges, the content of the ceremonies often mentions rabbinic or folk sources that counter a view that girls were not entered into Jewish covenant.

One biblical text that is frequently cited in Simhat Bat ceremonies, particularly in introductions, is a verse that follows the change of Sarai's name to Sarah (Genesis 17:16): "And I will bless her and also give you a child [son] from her; and I will bless her and she shall be a mother of nations, kings of peoples will be of her." Religious studies scholar Rochelle Millen comments that in this verse "Sarah becomes a full partner with Abraham in the promise of the covenant. Since no rite is required of Sarah, she is subsumed under its aegis upon the transforming of her name" (Millen 2004, 74). By this interpretation, the Simhat Bat is not a weak imitation of the male circumcision rite marking the scions of Abraham but a ritual designation of Sarah's female descendants embodying covenant's meaning in the process of naming. A related statement of women being involved in the covenant despite not having a mark upon the flesh is in the Gemara's discussion of Zipporah (Exodus 4:25): "A woman should be classed among the circumcised" (Millen 2004, 74). Sarah frequently is venerated in welcoming ceremonies, including a special *brit ohel shel Sarah imeinu* (covenant of the tent of Sarah, our mother) that uses a scarf wrapped around the baby and handed to the mother to symbolize entering into Sarah's tent, a precursor to the *Ohel Moed* (Tent of Meeting, home of the *Mishkan*, which housed the Ark of the Covenant) and the *Beit Hamikdash* (Temple in Jerusalem) (*Genesis Rabbah* 80:16 on Genesis 24:67). After the baby passes to the mother or parents, the attendees recite, "May her mother and father rejoice and find delight in their daughter. Let her coming into the covenant of the tent be at a favorable time for God and for Israel." The parents then make no mention of aspiration to marriage when they announce, "May we find joy in this moment and pleasure in all that she becomes. May our tiny daughter grow to be great" (Diamant 2008, 148–49).

Such verses have not been universally received as justification for a ritualization of covenant for girls. Two years after the Strassfelds' call for changing Halacha, Rabbi Moshe Meiselman, a former principal of Yeshiva University High Schools of Los Angeles, declared the girls' welcoming ceremony, if not an overt defiance of Jewish law, then at least a thinly veiled mockery of it: "This ridiculous ceremony mocks the very concept of *brit*" (Meiselman 1978, 62). He explained, "A unilaterally executed covenant with God is, at best, a meaningless form of spiritual autoeroticism. . . . Talmud tells us that a woman becomes a member of the covenant automatically at birth" (62). The kind of "ritual creativity" represented by Simhat Bat in his view "should be discouraged." Invoking a notion of inherited tradition from an original source, Meiselman proclaimed that "God, and

God alone, initiates covenants," and he dismissed claims of inequality by noting, "A Jew does not view his Judaism as the cultural expression of a patriarchal society which imposes artificial sex-role differentiation on unwilling womanhood. Rather, Jewish law is the divinely given way through which each individual tries, in his own unique manner, to achieve closeness to the divine source. All human lives are equivalent in value, and no greater value is attributed to the masculine role than to the feminine" (Meiselman 1978, 62; see also Millen 2004, 83–84; Ochs 2007, 150–54; S. R. Siegel 2014, 116–17). To be sure, as Simhat Bat has evolved, it has less of a connection to Brit Milah and has moved increasingly from justification as spiritual transformation, or a rite equivalent to male circumcision, according to Halacha, to a custom (or *minhag*) effecting cultural integration. As custom, it appears more flexible and more personalized as well as centered in home and family. A sign of this differentiation is the timing of the ceremony, not on the eighth day after birth, as in male circumcision, but 15 days (for the period after *niddah*), 30 days (marking the lunar cycle and symbolically for renewal), or later (Nussbaum Cohen 2001, 44–49).

A customary precedent for a welcoming ceremony for girls, especially cited by Sephardic families, is Zeved Habat, or "gift of the daughter." Often traced to the seventeenth century in Italy, the ceremony derives its name from *Bereishit* 30:20. In the passage, Leah, after the birth of Zevulun and before the birth of Dinah, says, "Zevadani Elokim oti zeved tov" (God has granted me a gift). Participants sang special melodies and recited verses from the Song of Songs (Breger 2000, 3). In contemporary enactments, Psalm 128 and the priestly blessing of Birkat Kohanim may be added to the name-giving prayer in the form of a Mi Sheberakh that emphasizes the matriarchs.

> May he who blessed our mothers Sarah, Rebecca, Rachel and Leah, Miriam the prophetess, Avigail, and Esther the queen, bless also this darling baby. In happy augury may her name be called (speak name), daughter of (speak father's name). May he bless her to grow up in wealth, health, and happiness. May He give to her parents the joy of seeing her happily married, a radiant mother of children, rich in honor and joy to a ripe old age. May this be the will of God and let us say, Amen. (Nussbaum Cohen 2001, 203)

In a script for the Zeved Habat at the home of Abigail Gabriela Riemer Landres in Los Angeles in 2008, the parents printed in italics a meta-traditional commentary:

"For hundreds if not thousands of years, the traditional Sephardi siddur has included a liturgy for naming a daughter. Celebrating that part of Abigail's heritage, we draw upon its structure today" (Figure 7.2). Verses from the Song of Songs were recited by different family members (2:14 by the girl's father; 6:9 by the mother), and then the gathered crowd recited together, "The young women saw her and called her blessed; Queens and consorts praised her." A ritual enactment inserted into the ceremony was the following:

> Abigail's maternal grandfather, Daniel Riemer, will hold Abigail in a tallit worn by Abigail's paternal grandfather, Peter David Landres z"l, while Magdalena Urbanová and Juraj Urban, Abigail's maternal grandmother and great-uncle, themselves *Kohanim*, recite the text of the traditional blessing in Slovak and Hebrew.
>
> May God bless you and keep you.
> May God make God's face shine upon you, and be gracious unto you.
> May God lift up God's countenance upon you, and grant you peace.

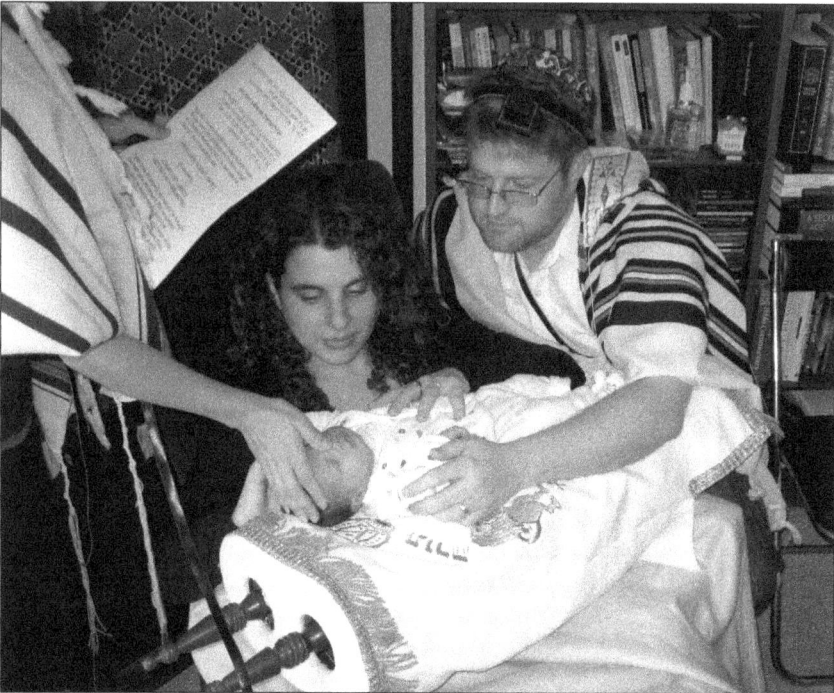

7.2. The Zeved Habat of Abigail G. R. Landres in Los Angeles, California, 2008. Courtesy Zuzana Riemer Landres and Shawn Landres.

The tallit ceremony links birth to coming of age in the bat mitzvah as well as marking family lineage. The parents printed a commentary in their script, for example, "God willing, we will merit to repeat this blessing for all the daughters of Israel, which comes from the Italian liturgical tradition, one of Abigail's many rich heritages, at her Bat Mitzvah." The names given to the child, as the script explained, honored her paternal grandfather and maternal great-grandmother. The ceremony concluded with a Kiddush and thanksgiving meal (seudat hoda'ah).

Landres's insistence that the ceremony is not invented or "new" stems from resistance to what he terms the "Ashkenazicentrism" of American Jewry. Concerned that the discourse of rituals in his planning for the event was "an Ashkenazic conversation with itself," he and his wife did not want to "puff up egalitarian bona fides," he said, but instead, show "a long and deep Sephardi tradition."[1] The Zeved Habat served not only to direct attention to Sephardic identity but also to disrupt an Ashkenazic-Sephardic binary by showing diversity within the family identity (Italian and Slovak). Another version of this use of the naming ceremony for ethnic continuity is in families with Balkan, Moroccan, or Turkish heritage, who make references to las fadas (probably deriving from the Spanish hadas, meaning "fairies"). Invoking the belief that a baby is blessed by benevolent fairies, the baby is passed from hand to hand among guests and showered with token gifts (sweets, coins, jewelry) and individual blessings (Breger 2000, 3; M. Klein 1998, 189; Nussbaum Cohen 2001, 13–14). Although a silver tray (silver, as well as garlic cloves and salt, ward off malevolent spirits) might have been used in the past, contemporary versions frequently use a pillow (sometimes colored red as a symbol of life and a counteragent to the evil eye).

Although much is made in the Sephardic celebrations of the continuity over time and place in welcoming ceremonies for girls, a Central European tradition that may be mentioned in modern home-based Ashkenazic ceremonies composed by parents is Hollekreisch (literally "Frau Holle's cry" in German), traced to the thirteenth century (Figure 7.3). It was not exclusively conferred on girls, but its performance at home and conferral of a name for the newborn drew attention in the effort to show precedents for modern-day welcoming ceremonies. Practices vary in the tradition, but often noticed is the ritual lifting of the cradle or bassinet three times with the accompanying cry, "Wie soll das Kindchen heissen?" (German) or "Wie solls pupele hasse?" (Yiddish) (What shall the child be called?) (Hammer 2005, 65). The enactment of the custom coincides with the mother's

7.3. *Hollekreisch* ceremony for a Jewish family of Alsace-Lorraine background in Jerusalem, November 2019. The children ritually lift the newly named baby three times in an infant seat instead of the traditional cradle. Photo by Michel Rothe.

rise from the birthing bed and gives the mother an important role in the ceremony that bestows a secular name and celebrates a new life. The mythological figure of Frau Holle in the name of the ceremony is not regarded as a Jewish character, but she may have been appropriated into the Jewish custom as an earth-mother figure who embodies both danger to and protection of life (Hammer 2005, 70; for discussion of the interpretations of the figure in folktales based on the commentary of Jacob and Wilhelm Grimm, see Grimm [2004, 1: 265–72], List [1956, 1960], Motz [1984], and J. B. Smith [2004]). The claim in commentaries of modern scripts referring to the ceremony with the Frau Holle figure is away from its superstitious nature and more toward its containment of the paradox of new life in the Jewish community. In the words of Jill Hammer, who contemplates what Holle holds for Jews in contemporary understanding, the ritual "honored birth as women experienced it: dangerous and necessary, painful and exhilarating, wondrous and sometimes tragic. Hollekreisch, while making reference to the Torah and other Jewish symbols, challenged the Jewish norm—birth ceremonies that honored male parentage and male covenant and ignored women—with a ritual that celebrated the emergence of life out of the womb, made the mother a central ceremonial figure, and recognized both girls and boys as members of the human community" (Hammer 2005, 81; for references to *Hollekreisch* in contemporary guides to girls' naming ceremonies, see Breger [2000, 4], Diamant [2008, 210–11], and Nussbaum Cohen [2001, 15]).

The naming ceremony, whether Sephardic or Ashkenazic, follows a sequential structure: (1) a welcome, often involving a song, inspirational message, or the Shehehiyanu; (2) blessings and/or readings by family members, often emphasizing thanksgiving; (3) presentation of the newborn and naming of the child; (4) ritualized actions, such as lighting candles, passing of the baby, immersion (metaphorically as in a *mikveh* rather than a baptism), foot washing, planting of a tree, wine drinking, or wrapping in a tallit or *wimpel*; (5) closing prayers or songs; and (6) Kiddush and festive meal (Bleich 1983; Wolowelsky 1997, 44–45). The sequence roughly follows the transformative ritual process of an initiate's separation, transition, and incorporation outlined by Arnold van Gennep (1960) in life-cycle rituals that facilitate passage from one stage to another. Predictably, the ritual composition of the naming ceremony coming early in life pushes the child toward incorporation (at the end of the life course, separation is emphasized), but arguably the girls' naming ceremony more than other comparable observances contains a number of transitional activities that indicate liminality, toward a resolution of paradoxes of integrating human and cultural experiences with biological destiny (Myerhoff 1982). That is, as a naming ceremony that does not clearly mark transformation physically or historically, it raises a number of uncertain relationships: Jews in relation to mass society, women to men in Judaism, tradition in modernity. To compensate, many scripts include commentaries on the intention of the parents in making ritual choices and the perceived meaning of practices and objects at the ceremony.

One script for a Simhat Bat at home, prepared by a couple affiliated with a Conservative synagogue in Harrisburg, Pennsylvania, prefaced the ceremony with "A Few Words of Explanation" intended to link the celebratory practices with a statement on identity drawn from the dizzying variety of ritual possibilities for inclusion: "In our version, we stress our gratitude for God's deliverance of this child to us, our reverence for tradition and the proud lineage of Jewish women before her, our hopes for her future well-being, and our reaching out to family and community for her sense of identity and feelings of support." For this family, references to the Holocaust and Israel, marked by homage to deceased ancestors and relatives transplanted to Israel, combined to point toward a future fusion of identities. One mark of that for the parents was a tree planting in their backyard coupled with a tree in Israel (Figure 7.4). The symbolism of planting a pine tree is drawn from a Jewish custom documented in the Babylonian Talmud: "When a baby girl was born, they planted a pine tree" (*Gittin* 57a).

For another family the key symbol that could resolve conflicted identities and dispersed family was water. Explaining the use of immersion in "Miriam's well," Yosef Abramowitz and Susan Silverman invoke a legend that God created this well of water to aid the Israelites for their journeying in the wilderness. The representation of the well in the ceremony becomes in their version of Simhat Bat a symbol "for the Jewish tradition and the wandering years in the wilderness are a metaphor for the physical and spiritual journey all of us must take" (the parents moved in various locations between the United States and Israel) (Abramowitz and Silverman 1997, 73).

Another issue is to balance the celebratory party with the solemnity of blessing for the child. Not a baby shower and not a liturgical service, the Simhat Bat has evolved to bring more declarations of family connection in a dispersed, mobile society. Guests coming from near and far often bring gifts to the ceremony, but the opening of the presents is usually not built into the public

7.4. Ritual planting of a pine tree for a baby girl by her cousins outside the family home, Harrisburg, Pennsylvania, 2000. Photo by Simon J. Bronner.

portion of the ceremony. The candle lighting, perhaps the most popular of the ritual actions selected by parents for the ceremony, recognizes family members and provides another link to a practice repeated at the bat mitzvah. One candle is placed for grandparents and siblings to represent family bonds (whereas Conservative rabbis relying on the revised manual of the Rabbinical Assembly *Moreh Derekh* [1998] insist on the candles at a bris ceremony symbolizing the seven days of creation), and the religious association of lifting the baby to touch her hands to a Torah scroll is added to the ceremony. Connected with the home location, tree planting may be explained as a custom in ancient Israel (pine or cypress for a daughter and cedar for a son), whereby the trees provide natural metaphors for Jewish identity (roots, branches, sturdiness) (Nussbaum Cohen 2001, 74).

The home is often staged with a deliberate arrangement of props. Parents enter into discussion about the way that these objects may stand for religious purposes, although I have found that the mother among heterosexual couples usually takes the lead in creative organization of the event and often feels ownership of the event. Parents may connect their own wedding to a chuppah erected in the home under which the baby is presented. Chairs may be designated as Elijah's or Miriam's. Elijah is a presence at every Brit Milah, and the figure is invoked at many girls' naming ceremonies as a guardian of young children. Debra Nussbaum Cohen notes that many parents replace Elijah's chair with one for Miriam as "a new interpretation of this tradition. Popular interest in Miriam has recently blossomed as feminist Jews look to unearth female role models from Jewish history and to expand understanding of these foremothers' roles. Just as a place for Elijah is a symbol of our hope for future redemption, a symbol of Miriam—a cup or a chair—represents our faith that the Creator will nurture and take care of us in the present" (Nussbaum Cohen 2001, 61). The Kiddush cup also can take on significance; some come with the explanation that it was the one used at the parents' wedding, but others are newly purchased or made and "will become hers when she gets old enough to sit at the table and sing along as the wine is blessed on special occasions" (60). Ironically, many Modern Orthodox celebrations downplay the religious representations and emphasize the readings to deal with an ambivalence toward the spiritual significance of the ceremony. Another way that the ceremony makes a public statement is the increasing effort to use the home-based ceremony to identify children of interfaith couples, gay, transgender, and lesbian partners, and adopting parents (sometimes separately identified as *brit immuts*, or covenant of adoption) as integrated into community life (Diamant 2008, 215–32; Ochs 2007, 21–24).

Ushered into American Jewish consciousness as a feminist statement on women's participation in Jewish life, naming ceremonies for girls have evolved into a triumph of a home-based folk Jewishness, if not a transnational family-generated creative practice heralded by the Strassfelds (Wolowelsky 1997, 44). The spread of the ceremonies launched a wider front to renew Jewish identity through revived and invented rituals. Introducing a special issue of *Contact*, published by the Steinhardt Foundation for Jewish Life to comment on "potential future tapestries of Jewish life in communities spanning the globe," Eli Valley asserted that "contemporary rituals open up new vistas for understanding and experiencing Judaism, and they reflect on the phenomenon of Jews empowering themselves to create and contribute meaningfully to the trajectory of Jewish tradition" (Valley 2010, 2). That trajectory has redefined tradition as a matter of personal choice, guided by precedents that families mold into an identity, and ritual events governed not so much by ancient text but by future aspirations. In so doing, though, participants, in a do-it-yourself mode of thinking to regain ethnic agency and meaning out of mass society and institutional life, risk bringing into view contradictions and paradoxes of identities held loosely together under the flexible rubric of Jewishness.

Beyond the egalitarianism and religiosity of men and women, the rituals at the beginning of the life course are forced to contend with the sustainability of living emotionally and culturally as a Jew in modern society. The discourse of the antiquity of such ceremonies signals a folk perception of a break with the past since the Holocaust and rediasporization of Jews after World War II. The content of ceremonies ritually bridges past and present to allow comment, a meta-tradition, not just on how one acts Jewish but also on how one thinks Jewish. Whether innovative or lasting, the content of the welcoming ceremonies that emanate from the likes of Simhat Bat, *brit bat*, and Zeved Habat is probably not as significant to the negotiation of social identity for Jews as the action of traditionalizing that is taken. The perception created in organizing the event that the family is taking social agency and transferring that path to the new life forces new questions of and attitudes toward ritualizing and sustaining Jewishness amid the decline of community in modernizing society.

INVENTING AND INVOKING TRADITION IN HOLOCAUST MEMORIALS

When ground was broken for the World War II Memorial on Veteran's Day in 2000 in Washington, D.C., a symbolic center and the capital of the United States, several speakers shared the hope that the structure would provide a sacred space that could become a backdrop for a ritual of remembrance. They hoped for the kind of ritual response that the Vietnam Veterans Memorial on the National Mall had inspired, and they privately worried that the memorial would go the way of the neglected sculpture for the Korean War (see Haas 1998). Pointing to the memorial, several elderly veterans expressed the wish that the "noble cause" they fought for would inspirit the memorial and move the site from being merely a symbolic text to a location for ritual pilgrimage.

In ritually breaking ground and expressing hopes and plans for memorials, especially for wars and tragedies, organizers confront a central problem of inventing and invoking tradition for public consumption. Although private ceremonies for individual deaths have prescribed customs of grief, according to ethnic and regional traditions, the process of constructing memorials meant for public display has less predictable responses. Because the purpose of public memorialization is more common on the landscape, memorial design, particularly for wars and tragedies that many citizens want to forget or erase from memory, struggles to create a location as well as an aesthetic for tradition.

Artists and planning committees can articulate the aesthetic purposes of designed memorials, but they have more difficulty predicting the cultural response, even if they try to strategize possible uses of their structures. A paradox that comes out of this thinking is the expectation that the markers will be, on the one hand, original, unique, outstanding—to name some common adjectives of praise for successful memorial art—and, on the other hand, able to invoke tradition to offer a space that is socially memorable and even iconic. It is a typical wish that the marker serve as a location for ritual return. As such, memorialization that forces issues of inventing and invoking customs and that renders markers meaningful is a test of the processes of the emergence, and indeed of the modernization, of tradition.

In this chapter, I focus on Holocaust memorials, because objectively they intrude on the landscape with remembrance of both a painful event and a troubling idea. Although the gravestone and cemetery bookshelf is abundant, historical precedents for edifices of genocide memorialization are not readily apparent. Some observers have an ethnic reference, whereas others have a human one. The Holocaust demands remembrance, educators for civil rights often announce, although its images call for something besides the common nation-state-municipality representations of soldiers, statesmen, and service professionals. For some, the disturbing images of the Holocaust need no reminder. For consideration of emergent traditions from a folkloristic perspective, Holocaust memorialization often has a special cultural location. Unlike the World War II Memorial, the Vietnam Veterans Memorial, and other "national" monuments, Holocaust memorials tend to involve more local knowledge and are less about heroism, because they transcend national commemoration and involve ritual grieving in and of various discrete communities and social groups (Gillis 1994; Rothman 1989).

When the issue was taken up in a major exhibition at the Jewish Museum the display was accompanied by a stirring set of essays under the title *The Art of Memory: Holocaust Memorials in History* (1994), edited by James E. Young, and by Young's insightful book *The Texture of Memory: Holocaust Memorials and Meaning* (1993). Young's contribution has been to show the ways that major monuments, such as those for the Warsaw Ghetto, the Dachau Concentration Camp, and the Birkenau Death Camp, have been used for political ends by the societies that erected and used them: "Through this attention to the activity of memorialization, we might also remind ourselves that public memory is constructed, that understanding of events depends on memory's construction, and that there are worldly consequences in the kinds of historical understanding generated by monuments" (J. E. Young 1993, 15). Young offers the hardly radical thesis that memorials remember the past to serve the present and, in the process, obscure the events of history in deference to political needs. With its typical message of suffering, injustice, and tragedy, Holocaust memorialization suggests intentionality, because the images it raises are meant to inspire by disturbing the calm of modern, typically progressive surroundings.

After World War II, designing memorials at major scenes of destruction raised the expectation of creating an artwork with moral and political messages for a historical event that is interpreted as unique, even aberrant. Informally, concentration camp survivors at Dachau, Buchenwald, and Bergen-Belsen arranged temporary memorial towers from the debris of dismantled barracks within days of liberation (J. E. Young 1993, 48). Official memorials sanctioned by cities and nations went up in Warsaw in 1948, in Berlin in 1952, in Mauthausen (Austria) in 1957, in Buchenwald in 1958, and in Dachau in 1965. Typically created by national government boards, the memorials in this early period tended to reflect national concerns, which were frequently at odds with the subcultural views of Jews and other persecuted groups. The often-stated theme of these memorials was for "victims of Nazi [or fascist] terror." For Jews, the memorials held the danger of, on the one hand, neglecting or misstating the root of their suffering and rise from survival and, on the other, signifying that they were singled out for extermination and lacked the bravery to resist. A reluctance to memorialize the Holocaust as heroless, detestable events could be discerned in the years after World War II. As rhetoric shifted to gaining lessons from an aberration of humanity, the possibility of shaping stone to pronounce meaning seemed more necessary (see Gottlieb 1990).

MONUMENTAL MEANING

The cultural scenes I present are not so monumental as the ones in Young's exhibition, but the processes involved offer views of the inspiration of meaning in artistic markers and the ways these structures become ritualized and traditionalized in separate cultural scenes. In these cultural scenes Jews organized to create markers, at first for themselves and later for a wider public. The first such scene is in the Jewish cemetery of Oświęcim, Poland, as a counterpoint to the infamous camp and synecdoche for the Holocaust of Auschwitz less than 2 miles away. The marker is a study of memorialization in a private, spiritual location where memorializers are distant from the site. The second scene is in the public location of Harrisburg, Pennsylvania, where Jewish memorializers conceived of a structure to engage non-Jewish city dwellers who had largely been insensitive to or untouched by the Holocaust. The significance of memorializing the Holocaust for a discussion of the invention and invocation of tradition is that it is a destructive event for which construction, indeed art and design, may seem antithetical. In concept a Holocaust memorial bridges humanity, but in praxis, it can bring out conflicts between perceptions of individuals and their communities separated by time and distance.

In the past, my approach to the meaning of things has been to describe artifacts in action, to analyze them as parts of cultural scenes where actors' roles can be identified and their behavior interpreted (Bronner 1986b). From these observable conditions, the workings of mind should be revealed. The perspectives, biases, and ideas that drive the ways that society and culture operate become apparent. I use the phrase *cultural praxis* to connote this attention to action, the human ability to form identity and extract experience from social activity. In my book *Grasping Things* (1986b), I used the double meaning of grasping as a physical and intellectual act to bring out the theme of the ways that self-knowledge derives from action. Even "things" had different levels of meaning: a specific physical reference and a general sense of life. When talking of the state of things, one summarizes existence, and some special symbolic things have the potential to condense experience and convey values in persuasive ways.

Befitting a consideration of material behavior, the kinds of things I previously considered were mostly items made for everyday use—tools, houses, foods—and, in deference to my folkloristic and historical training, I tended to look for behaviors—gravestone carving, architectural decoration, picnicking—associated with historical precedent. Many of these behaviors could be construed as fitting into the sphere of folk culture, and I tried to show the interplay of this sphere with a rising sphere of homogenizing mass culture. In the work leading up to this volume on Jewish cultural studies, I made less of a distinction between material and oral traditions and became more concerned for analytical purposes with the way people express and materialize their thinking, indeed their anxieties and conflicts, through ritualized practices (Bronner 2019).

The challenge I take up here is to consider the invention of tradition as a folk process within popular culture and for public consumption (see Bronner 1998). I shift from the intellectual consequences of action to the related but thorny issue of ways that intangible spirituality is both attained and referenced in ritual practice. The markers in question are created objects meant to be inspirited and also meant to inspire reflection, although the nature of that reflection for different actors and audiences can become controversial. This matter is complicated by the tensions between public and private purposes for memorials and the intense scrutiny and sometimes removal in the twenty-first century of memorials representing racism, colonialism, and disturbing histories of exclusion, in addition to the discourse raging of a monument culture on the control and materialization of meaning in the future for a past event, especially those affecting subaltern groups (Macaluso 2019; Upton 2015).

I also focus on Holocaust memorials for a subjective reason of my personal connection to the Holocaust identity in question. In *Grasping Things* and many of the studies in the present book, I play the role of an impartial ethnographer analyzing scenes with detachment to find meanings often outside the awareness of participants. In this chapter my perspective is gained as an insider to the process of creation. For questions of identity formation and ritualized public presentation, the subject of Holocaust memorialization became my object. Concerned with raising awareness of the Holocaust as my object through study as well as with advocacy for remembrance, I found myself questioning the processes of memorialization. The reflexive position that I assumed, and that more scholars are forced to consider as participants in the culture they seek to explain, according to anthropologist Barbara Myerhoff, takes "into account our role in our own productions" (Myerhoff 1992, 1) and results in subject and object fusing.

I grew up with the Holocaust as a child of Polish Jewish survivors of deadly ghettoes and concentration camps, and I listened to the special meanings derived from our family homeplace once called Auschwitz. There were stories but no things. It was a self-knowledge essentially devoid of shrines or markers, until public efforts largely during the 1990s created a landscape of memorials and forced a discourse on meaning in design that continued into the twenty-first century. In many ways, the memorials bespoke a lack of artifacts because of destruction during the war and the rapid rediasporization afterward. It was an identity strained by distance between several "homelands"—Poland, Israel, and the United States—and the issue of where memorialization, and indeed inspiration, is appropriate and for whom. If distance caused a strain on establishing an agreed-on collective meaning to events of a world away, it also enhanced the identity by allowing a mystification of reality (see R. E. Gruber 1994).

REMEMBERING JEWS IN OŚWIĘCIM, ALSO KNOWN AS AUSCHWITZ

The Jewish community in Oświęcim numbered between 7,000 and 8,200 persons, or more than half of the town's population, at the outbreak of World War II. Most of the Jewish population was engaged in trades and constituted an underclass in the region. Occupying Nazis pressed Jews into forced labor, my father among them, including working on what would later become the death camp across the Sola River. In 1941 the Jews were removed to Będzin and Sosnowiec and from there to concentration camps. After the war the community was not reestablished. All but one of the town's religious structures were destroyed, and few of the town's Jewish residents survived the war (estimated by the Auschwitz Jewish Center to number less than 200). Most of the survivors went to the United States and Israel, although some who fled to the Russian side (including an uncle of mine, originally believed to be dead, who reappeared 12 years after the war ended) were prevented from leaving the Soviet Union for many years.

My father's experience was not atypical. Liberated from the camp of Gross Rosen at the age of 21, he went back to Oświęcim to find relatives. He found that his parents were gone and his house occupied. He heard that two of his nine siblings were alive and sought them out. The three of them ventured to the American zone and landed in a displaced persons camp. Next they went to Weiden in Germany because it was the first outpost they found occupied by Americans. My father met my mother there and two weeks later they were married. With the creation of the State of Israel in 1948, my father, mother, and infant sister moved to Israel. My aunt went with her husband to the United States, and Uncle Max, the oldest of the family, remained in Weiden. I was born in Israel in 1954; my sister was born in the displaced persons camp in 1946.

With the discovery of another living brother in the Soviet Union in 1957, the only surviving woman in the family, who had since immigrated to Chicago urged my father to relocate to the United States to reunite as much of the family as possible. Although he knew no English and was concerned about finding employment, my father took my sister to the United States. He had not affiliated with the small Oświęcim Society in Israel because it was dominated by the pietistic segment of the community, which included a strong Bobover Hasidic influence. However, in addition to family help in America, he was aided by a working-class, Yiddish-speaking *Landsmanschaft*, or "hometown association," from the Oświęcim area, the mutual aid society of the Workmen's Circle, and a few concentration camp survivors from Gross Rosen who also relocated. As a survivor, he did not get much sympathy from American Jews, or the American public in general, until late in his life. He was not one for publicly relating his Holocaust experience, although during the 1990s he began to participate in ceremonies for Yom Hashoah, the commemoration instituted by law in 1959 by the Israeli Knesset. Yom Hashoah occurs after Passover with its Exodus theme and eight days before Israel Independence Day. The date often falls around the time of the Warsaw Ghetto Uprising to mark Jewish resistance to suppression. Originally, the Chief Rabbinate of Israel called for an annual memorial to the Holocaust on a traditional day of mourning in December. Before Jewish organizations in North America widely adopted the memorial day, my father created his own private ritual that he enacted at home in May every year to recognize his liberation. He downed a shot of schnapps, uttered "L'chaim," lit a *yahrzeit* candle, and silently contemplated his survival.

Plans in Israel for constructing memorials for the Oświęcim Jewish community did not emerge until the 1970s, when the opening of Yad Vashem's Hall of Remembrance in Jerusalem inspired memorial activities for the destroyed communities of Europe. Following the construction of the museum at Yad Vashem, the hall provided an epilogue to the suffering in the earlier drama of Europe. Politically, it pointed to Israel as the ultimate place of ingathering in keeping with biblical prophecy. It also held a social message of Jews forming community for themselves rather than wandering in the world and enduring pain.

In keeping with this theme, the small Oświęcim Society in Israel conceived of a memorial honoring the past in Tel Aviv Cemetery and the future in a newly planted forest near Jerusalem. The memorial in the cemetery contained human ashes brought from Auschwitz. On the memorial stone an ark with representations of a flame topped carvings of Torah scrolls. On the plot, six pillars holding lit flames, one for each million Jews destroyed, were surrounded by barbed wire. Some dispute arose over whether to use the Polish, Yiddish, or German name of the town on the stone. Religious leaders wanted to use the Yiddish name of Oshpitzin, whereas younger members wanted the German name of Auschwitz to draw the attention of visitors to the site. Using Yiddish would establish continuity with the Jewish life of Eastern Europe, whereas German projected a historical discontinuity. Finally, the designers decided that the Polish name of Oświęcim, written in Hebrew letters, should be prominent, with Auschwitz, also in Hebrew letters but smaller, in parentheses. Ceremonies featuring prominent

rabbis kindling each flame established the site as sacred in accordance with traditional burial practice. The ceremony turned into an unveiling usually meant for an
individual's headstone a year after the person has died. It became generalized for
all the townspeople of Oświęcim who did not survive the war. The site became a
sacred material presence mainly for survivors to mourn their parents before Rosh
Hashanah. At other times, the memorial is rarely visited.

Along with many other groups of Jewish survivors from Eastern Europe displaced by the Holocaust, the Oświęcim community in Israel sponsored a section
of the Martyrs Forest in the Judean Hills outside Jerusalem (Yaar Hakedoshim)
and placed a plaque in the Chamber of the Holocaust (Martef Hashoa) on Mount
Zion. The forest was intended "as a living memorial," reinforcing the connection
of land and state in Israel. The memorial related to Poland, however, in the sense
that the forested landscape that was being reproduced was essentially a Polish one,
a realization that became painfully clear in 1995 when thousands of acres burned
in the hot desert climate of Israel. The tree became an object of memory that
signaled growth of a new society out of Polish roots. The ceremony involved was
one of planting, as on Tu b'Shvat or to commemorate celebratory rites of passage,
such as a birth, bar mitzvah, and marriage. With no divisions between other sections of the forest sponsored by other communities, the overall sense is of a united
whole. It was not a site to be visited as much as a symbol of the return to and
prosperity in the original Jewish homeland.

Although many of the former residents of Oświęcim who settled in North
America followed these activities by purchasing a memorial book privately published in Israel in 1977, few had attended ceremonies for the events (Wolnerman
et al. 1977). Because of the small number of survivors from the town, an Oświęcim
Landsmanschaft did not form in the United States, although informal social gatherings formed in Los Angeles, Chicago, Miami, and New York. Despite the rise of
Auschwitz as a symbol of the Holocaust generally, the story of the town escaped
public notice and former residents did not appear to mind. Having a community
attached to the nearby death camp might suggest a normality and stability that
did not fit into the consciousness of the Holocaust as an aberrant event. For many
writers on the Holocaust, camps did not belong to towns; they were treated as
terror zones outside any moral community set historically in place (see Langer
1977; Rosenfeld 1980).

Because of memories of the Holocaust, most survivors of Oświęcim expressed
little interest in returning to the town or supporting efforts to reconstruct Jewish

sites. There were exceptions, who would appeal to the Jewish tradition of honoring the graves of family members. Jacob Hennenberg, living in Cleveland, Ohio, started collecting historical material on artifacts and photographs from his hometown of Oświęcim, and he returned frequently to the town. But into his 70s, he sought to take surviving stones of his grandfather from the cemetery to the United States to continue his tradition of saying a memorial prayer over the family grave. Two prominent families of Oświęcim—the Haberfelds and the Scharfs—who had settled in the United States and Canada, respectively, took significant interest in retaining Jewish memory in the town.

Little remained to save. The surviving religious structure had become a carpet factory. The cemetery had been destroyed, although stones remained scattered over the site. Some retired former residents who took trips to view the town once more came back with distressed reports of the cemetery's state. Anticipation of the visit of Pope John Paul II in 1979 to Auschwitz and a possible tour of the town initiated restoration activity in the cemetery. Stones once piled in one section were stood up in rows. The Haberfelds, now living in California, arranged to have a memorial built from portions of gravestones that could not stand by themselves. They designed a structure in the stepped shape of the ancient Temple in Jerusalem and contracted Polish laborers to build the monument (Figure 8.1). The stepped shape is reminiscent of monuments made of broken tombstones in the cemeteries of Siedlce and Sandomierz, Poland (J. E. Young 1993, 195, 198).

The Oświęcim memorial now stands in the center of the Oświęcim cemetery, although few visitors view it. The memorial is not visible to Poles from the street because it is hidden behind walls erected by the town to protect the cemetery from vandals. At the bottom of the memorial is a plaque honoring Rudolf Haberfeld, for whom no stone could be found. Rudolf, who died in 1921, had been president of the Oświęcim Jewish community. Mieczyslaw Kapala, whose father had worked for Jews, was caretaker of the cemetery through the 1990s and was not aware of the religious symbolism of the memorial. For him, it was a sign of family interest—since the name Haberfeld was widely known because of its bottling of spirits.

Another new structure, this one built by the Scharfs, went up in the Oświęcim cemetery with the help of the Poles (Figure 8.2). Kapala called it a family shrine, a mausoleum. The structure took the form of buildings usually reserved for *tzadikkim*—righteous and even miracle-working rabbis among the Hasidim. It was more than a shrine, however. Placed toward a secluded corner of the cemetery, the structure erected by the Scharfs provided a place to leave messages to the dead who presumably dwelled near the cemetery. For the Scharfs, the interior made it sacred, and its form reminded Oświęcim residents who came back to visit of a continued presence.

For Jacob Hennenberg, from Oświęcim, the need to mourn a material presence resulted in his taking his grandfather's stone out of the cemetery to New Jersey, where it was consecrated by a rabbi. To those who question the significance of the stone so far from its original site, he tells a story of looking for his grandfather's grave. Giving up the task, he said the mourner's prayer near the pile of stones when a ray of light shone on a stone and by his account, reflected into his eyes. He went to it and found his grandfather's inscription. This often-repeated motif of discovery and revelation in Holocaust narrative reinforces the homeland

8.1. Memorial structure in the Oświęcim Jewish cemetery, 1995. Photo by Simon J. Bronner.

8.2. Interior of the memorial built for the Scharf family in the Oświęcim Jewish cemetery. Photo by Simon J. Bronner.

as sacred ground meant to be left intangible while the tangible signs of growth thrive in a new land.

Closer to the Auschwitz camp, controversy erupted throughout the 1980s and 1990s over the landscape of death. In 1984 Jewish organizations objected to the conversion by the Catholic diocese of a two-story building at Auschwitz into a convent for Carmelite nuns. The building had been used by the Nazis as a storehouse for the deadly Zyklon B gas (which was used to exterminate prisoners brought to Auschwitz) (Rittner 1991). On the ritual occasion of the fiftieth anniversary of the Warsaw Ghetto Uprising in 1993, at which Prime Minister Yitzhak Rabin of Israel and President Lech Walesa of Poland were slated to speak, Pope John Paul II instructed the Catholic nuns to move out of the convent located on the perimeter of the camp (Perlez 1993).

The argument about the use of the building and its apparent erasure of Jewish memory, in addition to the Polish national context of Catholic-Jewish relations, spilled over into another controversy about the effect of commercialism on the spiritual framing of the camp site. Polish plans to develop a commercial strip in 1996 close to the camp to serve tourists raised protests from Jewish organizations, which insisted on respecting the area as sacred ground (Times Wire Services 1996). The strip was situated outside the 547-yard protective zone around Auschwitz, which was designated a special historic site by the Polish government in 1979. Fueling the debate over cultural memory was a demonstration of support for the commercial development by Polish nationalists with anti-Semitic messages. Although the developer shut down construction in the face of public pressure, four years later, another proposal by the company for a shopping center, this time connected more directly to the museum, was approved (JTA Staff 2000). It was inconceivable for many observers in the 1990s that a mini-mall with its modern exploitative taint of consumer culture should be built near the Auschwitz camp, much as it was equally unfathomable that a Jewish memorial would be built in the town of Oświęcim. Indeed, until then the town of Oświęcim hardly confessed any relation to the Holocaust in memorials or exhibits.

Yet changes in Polish governmental policies and a renewed effort by some aging survivors, ironically not connected to Oświęcim, resulted in one public overture to Oświęcim's Jews. In March 1998 the Polish government, following a new restitution law, gave a house and synagogue building to a 3-year-old organization calling itself the Auschwitz Jewish Center Foundation. It was the first communal property ever given back by the government to the Jewish community under the law. Thus Auschwitz, again as the symbolic center of the Holocaust, gained notoriety as the first expression of post-Communist Polish redemption. Plans for the buildings included restoration and creation of a Jewish museum and cafeteria to serve visitors to the Auschwitz-Birkenau concentration camp site. With only one remaining Jew in Oświęcim, the synagogue's oversight was given to the nearby Jewish community of Bielsko-Biała. The headline announcing the transfer in *Jewish Week* made sure to proclaim the ritual close to collective memory by blaring, "At Last, Kaddish in Auschwitz" (E. J. Greenberg 1998a).

The pattern of memorials for Oświęcim essentially provided settings and events for mourning the dead by saying of Kaddish at gravesites, in keeping with Jewish religious tradition. In the United States, survivors of Oświęcim typically light memorial candles at home for their deceased relatives and participate in ceremonies that reflect on Holocaust victims generally rather than for specific communities. At a gathering of Jews from Oświęcim in Los Angeles, several of whom were my relatives, I innocently asked about any efforts to create a more public memorial to specifically recognize the town's Jewish past. Their heated response made it clear that memorialization was separate from their memory of their prewar experience as a minority outside public culture. Holocaust memorialization for them was divided into its ethnic components, and the Jewish part was reserved for the private realm of the Jewish community. This led to a discussion of surprise concerning the boom in public Holocaust memorials in the United States. When I mentioned that I had been in Poland and saw many new public memorials to the Holocaust, I heard the response that those memorials were Polish. Public memorials in North America pleased, indeed surprised them, and, at the same time, disturbed them.

The experience with Oświęcim memorialization was fresh in my mind when I was called in 1992 by the Jewish Federation of Greater Harrisburg, Pennsylvania, to help with something of a social problem. In light of publicity given to the opening of the United States Holocaust Memorial Museum, a group of survivors who had lived for many years in Harrisburg pressed for a local memorial. Specifically, three survivors, all who had experience in public life, hatched the project to build a conspicuous memorial and museum to the Holocaust near the Jewish Community Center in uptown Harrisburg. The two oldest members of the group had vivid memories of Auschwitz and were frequently called to talk to area students. The youngest was involved politically in the city. I was called because, as an educational administrator, I seemed to the Federation board to be mindful of economic factors but also sensitive to design issues in a Jewish cultural context. Although board members were careful to honor the survivors, they generally found them unreasonably grand in their request. New resources for the community were scarce and the board had plans underway to renovate the community center. The rabbis in the city appeared cool to the project and their educational initiatives were oriented toward Israel.

I soon realized the difficult task to which I had agreed. Board members appealed to my professional sense by making appointments and addressing me as Dr. Bronner, whereas survivors called me on the phone and hailed me as Shimele, a diminutive, intimate form of my name in Yiddish ordinarily used in conversation of a parent to a child. I organized a committee with representation from the survivors and other segments of the Jewish community. The committee generated discussion of the philosophical meaning—its sense of being—that the memorial held. For the survivors, the project legitimized their experience in the community. Yet it became clear that the group was not unified. One prominent survivor wanted to memorialize the Holocaust with educational activities, but she was overruled with the opinion that the memory of the event required a physical thing to spark remembrance. An Orthodox rabbi hoped for an object of prayer, and younger members of the committee insisted on a public structure that spoke to the human lessons of the Holocaust for the present beyond the impact on Jews. Representatives from the yeshiva in Harrisburg hoped for a museum or educational program aimed at youth. The survivors steered the committee toward a focus on the memorial idea to perpetuate their presence in Harrisburg as much as to educate about the Holocaust. The Jewish Federation announced a competition for designs with a budget limit of $100,000.

The choice came down to a stark representation of concentration camp pillars and a more abstract design of silver shafts surrounded by barbed wire. The group was divided. The survivors and rabbi preferred the harshness of the pillars, whereas younger members of the committee liked the abstraction of the Holocaust in the second design. The survivors wanted a place to mourn death and a lost world, but others hoped for a sign of life and progress. As chair of the group, I suggested alterations of the second design to include historical information and the remembrance theme on the black stones surrounding the silver shafts. To compensate for this extra material and bring the project under budget, the cascading water and eternal light features of the original design were dropped. The idea narrowly passed, and it appeared that no one was fully satisfied.

Some of the older committee members complained that the message they wanted—"Never Forget!"—was not clear, and they wanted a structure that was more attention grabbing and even featured their personal stories. The contracted artist, David Ascalon, explained the sculpture's encoded meaning but failed to make an impression: "The element of 'Hope' is conveyed in the manner in which the stainless steel core reaches above the stranglehold of the Nazi 'snake.' It continues to grow and shows the redemptive hopes and the rebirth of the Jewish people through the establishment of the State of Israel, and the maintenance of 'Jewish Identity' and Jewish survival in the diaspora." To the contrary, the design seemed widely acceptable because of its lack of direct reference to Israel or the Diaspora.

When the committee made inquiries to the city about a location for the monument, the response was to move the structure closer to downtown along the

Susquehanna River, where other memorials to firefighters and war veterans stood. The mayor offered his support to the project as part of enhancing the attractiveness of the Susquehanna River green space. He publicly editorialized that "the need for this memorial could not have been fulfilled were it placed at the Jewish Community Center or some other more private place. This is a memorial that must belong to all, should be seen by all, should be understood by all. From this park, we can see upon a river, a river that has been a constant thread, a common link, from generation to generation, from one era to the next." His statement raised additional discussion within the Jewish community about the public component of the project.

The board became more enthusiastic about a project that would make the community more visible in the city. The survivors were not so sure, and they had something to point to when hearings at City Hall raised objections that spilled over into the letters to the editor of the city daily newspaper. Gay rights advocates protested that the memorial left out persecution of homosexuals, and some African American spokespersons used the occasion to complain of the lack of historic markers honoring African Americans in the city. In response, designers of the memorial shifted the justification for the memorial to honoring survivors of the Holocaust who had settled in the city, much as the nearby war memorials honored soldiers from Harrisburg. The wording also changed to recognize that Jews were the "primary" victims and the intent of the memorial was to warn against "racism and prejudice" wherever it is found. At that point, Kurt Moses, the leader of the survivors group called for a reconsideration of Jewish Federation support for the memorial, but the president of the Federation continued to press for the memorial as a civic project. The survivors complained to me that they had lost control not just of the location of the memorial but of the representation of their experience.

A serious threat to construction of the memorial occurred when environmentalists challenged the addition of memorials on the riverside. They opposed the project in the City Council, complaining that the river, a natural wonder, was becoming obstructed by too many memorials. The natural space in their view had become industrialized by memorials rather than factories and questioned whether several war memorials were still relevant, calling for an ecological "peace promenade." Although the City Council declined to remove memorials, members agreed to halt permits for memorials after the Holocaust structure was completed. Publicly relieved that the city supported the project, representatives of the

Holocaust memorial project privately fretted about undertones of anti-Semitism in opposition to the project.

A site was eventually prepared north of existing memorials, a location that placed it closest to city synagogues and away from the city center. The rabbis became more involved as plans were made for the groundbreaking. "A Song for Ascents," Psalm 121, became the theme for the event, and the closing was a cantor's rendition of "God Bless America." The keynote speech was given by the mayor. Although survivors were given seats of honor toward the front, they were not accorded time at the podium. After the event, Kurt Moses complained to the Holocaust Education Committee about the management of the program, especially when press releases issued for the event did not recognize the survivors' involvement in the original concept of the memorial. As the structure came closer to completion, survivors hoped to give the site a sense of the sacred and offer themselves a moment to be heard. The Holocaust Education Committee arranged for a more elaborate ceremony with Jewish rituals to consecrate the structure. Two rabbis were given time to give remarks, followed by a statement from Kurt Moses, an Auschwitz survivor. The survivors then stepped en masse to the sculpture to unveil it much as one would uncover a gravestone in Jewish tradition (Figure 8.3). The ceremony closed with a cantor's rendition of "El Molay Rahamim" (God Full of Mercy/Compassion), a memorial prayer usually recited at the Jewish burial service.

The site has since been used only for an annual ceremony sponsored by the Jewish community on Yom Hashoah in April. With the death or disability of most survivors in the early twenty-first century, the ceremony features children of survivors and the reading by the writer of a winning essay in a Holocaust education contest. An event that was added to increase attendance was to use the location as a ritual send-off for Jewish participants in the March of the Living program who were leaving to visit Holocaust sites in Poland (Shevelev 1996). Parents and friends came out to support the teenagers and heard the coordinator of the trip speak of the ritual connection between preserving the memory of the Holocaust in the Harrisburg structure and going to Poland to witness memorials at the site of destruction. She intended the narration of the event to bolster Jewish identity rather than to appeal to the wider Harrisburg community.

The March of the Living event and other commemorations at the memorial attract little notice in the press, and the site did not become the center for reflection that its designers had hoped for. It nonetheless turns a few heads from passersby on any one day, more so than nearby statues for firefighters and soldiers,

8.3. Ceremony for unveiling the Holocaust Memorial, Harrisburg, Pennsylvania. Photo by Simon J. Bronner.

in my observation. Park officials often have to chase skateboarders from the site, and other passersby use its seats to view the river. Its significance has been greatest to the survivors who gained recognition for their participation in their adopted community. Many in the survivors group still felt dissatisfied with the memorial standing away from the Jewish community, and, partly in response, Kurt Moses helped organize an annual Kristalnacht commemoration by the survivors group in November, featuring the lighting of candles away from the memorial at the Jewish Community Center. Adding to the survivors' distress was visible deterioration of the structure, which needed additional fundraising to repair.

Memorials to the Holocaust have become especially symbolic of resolving the meaning of survival from guilt to triumph, from the unimaginable to the comprehensible. It is part of the reason that many Holocaust memorials offer more resistance to our senses than other monuments in the landscape of remembrance. It is also a reason that designing the meanings to be imparted presents more of a challenge for viewers and creators; there seem to be few givens beyond some recurrent motifs of barbed wire and Jerusalem stone.

RITUALIZING AND TRADITIONALIZING MEMORIALS

The appeal to sacred tradition in Oświęcim's graveyard memorial debatably created a collective, if private, understanding of its meaning, although its distance created a problem of alienation from the action of mourning centered on a site. The memorial in Harrisburg lacked this communal aspect, but it provided a backdrop for occasional performance of identity in a multiethnic city. Indeed, Harrisburg's memorial needed signs to inform what it was about. It needed confirmation of its Holocaust reference. Oświęcim's did not; it relied on memory of response to a long series of past tragedies. Harrisburg's reinforced the singularity of an event in organizing the future. In fact, it took on more organizational ways of creating the object, whereas Oświęcim's was more communal and in many cases personalized. The tales of these two cities and their memorials are sketches of the varieties of Holocaust landscapes that emerged with increasing frequency during the 1990s and evolved in meaning through the twenty-first century as survivors passed away.

Why did so many Holocaust memorials arise during the 1990s? In recognition of 50 years since the end of the war, the 1990s became the great decade of memorials for the events of World War II. A milestone had been passed that prompted many institutions to reflect on history. In the wake of Vietnam and the rise of human rights rhetoric, a new sensitivity in the United States was evident in memorialization that recognized victims. The thinning of Holocaust survivor ranks added an emotional element to the proceedings as years passed. The memorials were their preview of their own funerals and markers that their struggle to overcome adversity and come to the United State mattered. Many of the memorials reflect less on the past than the announcement of triumph over history. The future-directed spires and upward reaching hands are among the most common symbols of public vindication, but I suspect that efforts will increasingly turn from markers to museums. Still, the move from historical memorialization to cultural education appears difficult for communities and their Jewish civic leaders.

The realization of multiple, contested meanings of the monuments for the survivors, American-born Jews, environmentalists, homosexuals, and politicians has caused a shift from the emphasis on historical memorialization to programs that leave less of the lessons open to interpretation. By the end of the 1990s, more views could be heard similar to the strongly worded editorial in the *New Jersey Standard* that called memorials the "latest Jewish battlegrounds." It asked whether the "craze" toward memorialization "isn't . . . a bit of idol worship with big-giver egomania thrown in for good measure" (Tobin 1998, 49). The newspaper argued, "Rather than looking to monuments or statues to commemorate the Holocaust or to celebrate our community history, let us instead invest in our children and their education. If we must choose—as I fear we must—between schools and museums, then let the choice be for Jewish education" (49).

The monument building will continue so long as a need is felt to tangibly provide an inspiring edifice to bridge the distance between the socially troubled present and the hidden atrocious past, to lay to rest through ritual and tradition the memory of many ancestors not given burial, and to belatedly announce the arrival and triumph of survivors. Moving from private to public purpose, traditionalizing of memorials has widened the meaning of Holocaust markers for a postmodern social vision. During the 1990s, Holocaust memorials were instrumental in bringing out before the public the wider discourse of human rights and ethnic pluralism set against the integrity of nation-states. Harrisburg's memorial had this meaning ascribed to it, but it arguably was not successful in having this message conveyed, maybe because the public traditions surrounding it were not convincing. The invention of Oświęcim's memorial invoked more continuity with the historical precedent of Jewish tradition, but the loss of community made it inaccessible as a ritual location.

As types of parables, objects made and used are not meant to be understood by all. The morals of the objects may come from connection to other objects and people and their perceived location in tradition. The marker is artificial, fictional and true, like the parable, and equally designed to persuade and hold emotional as well as practical meaning. It is formed from customary modes of life that can be analyzed and compared as praxis. It has a presence that causes response and resistance. It announces its meaning in the ways that people act toward it and the manner in which it is performed, traditionalized, and ritualized. The degree of influence that people bring to the object or that objects hold over people in these social frames may be less the issue than the process of transformation that turns ideas into icons.

III

NARRATION

THE YIDDISH ACCENT AND CULTURAL POLITICS OF ORAL AND LITERARY HUMOR

Leo Rosten's H*Y*M*A*N K*A*P*L*A*N Stories in Context

In modern Jewish American literature, much of which is centered on the immigrant experience and the negotiation of Old World pietistic tradition and supposedly secularizing modern America, Leo Rosten (1908–1997) drew renown in popular culture with his evocative brand of humorous literary narratives about Jewish immigrant Hyman Kaplan. Introduced in 1936, Rosten's Hyman Kaplan character was also featured in 1968 in a Broadway musical (Rosten 1936, 1937, 1938; Zavin 1968). The social scientist Rosten suddenly stepped into the literary limelight, even more so when his Hyman Kaplan books were named finalists for the prestigious National Book Award. Much of the attention was on the memorable character of Kaplan; from across the Atlantic Ocean, philosopher Isaiah Berlin called Kaplan "one of the great and enduring characters in English literature" (Weisberg 2008). Yet after the 1980s, with the sweep of multiculturalism, critics and professors who were considering using Rosten's narrative in classes regarded the lessons of Kaplan's ethnic and educational experience out of step with the temper of the times, embarrassing, and even antagonizing (Shiffman 1999, 2000).

My task in this chapter is to unravel the combination of oral and literary techniques coming out of Rosten's bilingual immigrant background that made his work appealing through the decades. I also explore the social agency Rosten strategically employed by manipulating these techniques, reflecting his own experience of selective assimilation, to use humor to take a centrist political stand about the promise and problem of American pluralist society. Finally I look at the markedly different reception for Rosten's work during the 1930s, 1960s, and early twenty-first century.

THE STRUCTURE OF ACCENTED ORAL AND LITERARY COMMUNICATION

I begin this query with the search for a structural basis to the connection between oral and literary communication. In humorous oral genres of jokes, riddles, and anecdotes, to name a few, a structural concept of incongruity is operative. For example, folklorist Elliott Oring commented that "humor involves the linking of disparate cognitive categories and their associated attitudes in some appropriate way, that is, humor is based upon the creation and perception of an appropriate incongruity" (Oring 1975, 151). In other words, expectations are determined by the cultural milieu in which the story is told and the social situation in which the narration occurs. Incongruity refers to the violation of that expectation in a creative or elaborate manner. Further, if the audience or teller cannot understand the references and images because of cultural differences, less humor is perceived, or in Oring's terms, there is an *inappropriate* incongruity.

Consider the following example of an *appropriate* incongruity in a narrative offered to me in an upstate New York bar by a female acquaintance.

> A woman got on a bus to Boston and saw two of her lady friends. She asked them, "What are you going to Boston for?" One of the ladies replied, "We're going to the docks to get scrod." The woman replied, "I always wondered what the past tense of that word was."[1]

In this joke *scrod* is confused with the past tense of *screw*, offering an opposite meaning from the hearer's expectation. The explicit reference to the women as "ladies" and the association with prudish behavior also heightens the incongruity. In addition to this structural component, certain cultural-contextual cues are necessary to determine whether the story is to be apprehended as "humorous." First, if the allusion to the colloquial use of the word *screw* is to work, the teller assumes a familiarity of scrod's association with Boston. Second, and more subtle, is the assumption that the listener is aware of English past-tense forms. The cognitive understanding of these cultural references makes the joke an *appropriate* incongruity. Yet beyond the structural frame that identifies a joke, the content that is risqué and suggests symbolic decoding is at work and important to the function of narrating in this setting.

Significantly, studies of humorous literature refer to incongruity with attention to writing style but frequently omit issues of contextualized symbolism and decoding that are central to cultural analysis (Leacock 1938; Pirandello 1974; L. D. Rubin 1976). To literary critics, creative writing often connotes elite or original qualities, and they therefore introduce artistic qualifiers to the concept. For example, Stephen Leacock argues that humor is the "incongruities of life, and the artistic expression thereof" (Leacock 1938, 3). Louis D. Rubin Jr. states that humor consists of "the contrast, the incongruity between the ideal and the real; in which a common, vernacular metaphor is used to put a somewhat abstract statement involving values—self-definition, metaphysical—into a homely context" (L. D. Rubin 1976, 257). Rubin exposes the fallacy of this thesis, however, when he writes, "The highest accolade we give to a humorist is when we say that even so he is a 'serious' writer" (256). Such an attitude equates oral with primitive, denies the reflection of values in oral narrative, and denies any thematic structure to oral narrative. Moreover, the attitude underscores a literary bias that fails to consider the utilization of incongruity in both oral and written media. For a fuller cultural perspective, I turn to a consideration of Leo Rosten's Hyman Kaplan stories to analyze the symbolic and processual issues in Jewish literary presentation as well as structural and stylistic continuities and disparities of oral and written humorous techniques.

HISTORICAL AND CULTURAL CONTEXT FOR THE ENCODING OF LEO ROSTEN

Rosten's background explains his familiarity with Jewish culture, immigrant acculturation, and American education—central elements of his writing. Rosten was born to Jewish parents in 1908 in Łódź, Poland. At the age of 2, he came with his parents to the United States. Raised in Chicago, Rosten was bilingual (English and

Yiddish) and honored his heritage later with several books on the Yiddish language, although he did not speak English with the noticeable Eastern European, supposedly "broken" accent of his parents (Rosten 1968, 1982, 2001). Indeed, much of Rosten's writing is about the integration of Yiddish in American English; for example, *Hooray for Yiddish* carries the subtitle *A Book about English* (Rosten 1982). With this work, Rosten implied a positive contribution of often denigrated immigrant Jews from Eastern Europe like his parents while assuring non-Jewish readers that their goals were to become integrated into "modern" American society, if not fully assimilated (Rosten 1976, xix).

Rosten did not attend college to become a writer; he had aspirations to become a lawyer. Aware of his ethnic background in relation to the rise of a pluralist society, in 1932 he entered the Graduate School of Political Science and International Relations at the University of Chicago. In 1934 he was admitted to the London School of Economics and Political Science and earned his doctorate in 1937. To support his studies, he took a position as an English instructor in Chicago; he taught a night class in English to immigrants, an experience that became the basis for the Hyman Kaplan stories. Rosten sent his first story, "The Education of H*Y*M*A*N K*A*P*L*A*N," to the rather unethnic literary magazine *The New Yorker*, because he heard that it paid writers handsomely and he needed money for medical bills (Weisberg 2008). Immediately setting the story apart is the rendering of the character's name with stars between letters. Kaplan used the stars in his written assignments as his signature statement of self-confidence, which set him up in contrast to the struggling, self-doubting immigrant characters of Jewish-American literature such as Abraham Cahan's David Levinsky and Anzia Yezierska's Sara Smolinsky set in the Lower East Side of New York City of the early twentieth century (Bronner 1997; Sternlicht 2004). Kaplan was announcing with his stars that as far as he was concerned his dialect and immigrant status were not a problem. He was comfortable with the heritage and language he brought from the Old World to the United States and despite the efforts to correct him, it was the straight arrow of the teacher who needed adjustment.

Fearing the disapproval of the Social Science Research Council, which was funding his doctoral studies, if it discovered that he was "committing humor" (Rosten 1976, xi) for his fiction, Rosten used the genteel sounding pseudonym of Leonard Q. Ross (with a possible allusion to the *New Yorker*'s founding editor Harold Ross in addition to a clipping of his last name). Reflecting in the 1970s on his sources, Rosten pointed out that he used the setting but not the texts from his experience of the 1930s: "Are the Kaplan stories true? (I certainly hope they ring true, though they never happened.) How many of the hundreds of malapropisms, massacred idioms and outrageous 'jokes' did I actually hear from the mouths of my pupils or read in their bizarre compositions? (Four.)" (Rosten 1976, xi).

Rosten, then, used conventional techniques, stylistic devices, and humorous themes to make his stories "ring true" rather than redacting specific items of oral humor. Instead of referring to the structural incongruities of humor, Rosten defined his humor as deriving from his characters. He called it "the affectionate communication of insight" and allowed for social issues to come through in his statement that he strove to bring out the "carnival and the tragedy of living" (Rosten 1976, xv).

After the first volume of his stories, *The Education of H*Y*M*A*N K*A*P*L*A*N*, was published in 1937, Rosten concentrated on his scholarly studies and put Kaplan on hiatus until *The Return of H*Y*M*A*N K*A*P*L*A*N* in 1959, and *O K*A*P*L*A*N! M*Y K*A*P*L*A*N!* (a play on Walt Whitman's famous extended metaphor poem "O Captain! My Captain!") a revised combination of the two earlier works, in 1976. The title of the original compilation carries a reference to the classic autobiography *The Education of Henry Adams*, winner of the 1919 Pulitzer Prize, which chronicled the dramatic change in the American twentieth century from the view of a member of an elite New England family of old colonial stock (Adams 1918). Just as Henry Adams reflected seriously on the inadequacy of his education to deal with rapid industrial and social changes, so too did Rosten use humor to comment on the rising immigrant generation represented by the dialectal shift in language. Kaplan confronts a frazzled teacher with the pastoral name of Parkhill, whom Rosten describes as "the product of Anglo-Saxon ministers from New England" (Rosten 1976, x). In contrast, Rosten identifies himself as "the child of Ashkenazic knitters from Lodz" (x). Parkhill attempts not only to instruct Kaplan, who Rosten remembers partly as a student he taught and who reminds him a lot of himself, about the nuances of the English language, but also to Americanize him according to apparently white Protestant standards.

The underlying theme of Kaplan's situation concerns the adjustment of Old World immigrants and their customs to the New World. Rosten steered speculation away from himself by generalizing that his "stories" were about "the hopeful immigrants to our shores who try—so movingly, so clumsily—to master the elementary yet baffling elements of the English tongue" (Rosten 1976, ix). He mentions "Jewish students" in linguistic rather than cultural terms: They "wander through bewildering gorges trying to arrest their habitual interchange of vowels—each of which they can easily enunciate yet treat as musical chairs" (xvii). He explains his "mesmerization by language" to "the fact that my mother tongue was Yiddish, so my youth was spent in mental shuttlings between 'the Robin Hood of languages' and English" (xviii). He describes an ethnic experience defined by language as he communicates with his parents and their friends and his own "cronies of the street" (xviii). Thus Rosten made the distinction between the official institutional culture of America and the unofficial ethnic society and his literary effort through what he calls storytelling to bridge them.

Yet as literary critic Dan Shiffman notes on the historical context in which Rosten worked, "The Hyman Kaplan stories play into a troubling tendency within American pluralism, one that relies on an *appreciation* of diversity—rather than meaningful acceptance of linguistic and cultural differences—as a way to underscore the resiliency and supremacy of Anglo values" (Shiffman 1999, 100). Arguably, Rosten mutes Kaplan's Jewishness and channels it into a generalized immigrant status. The linguistic differences of the reader's presumed standard English and Kaplan's malapropisms bring attention to the process of modernization, defined as becoming an assimilated American, albeit one who is recognizable broadly as an ethnic, rather than speaking from the singular identity of a Jew.

The historical context for Rosten in 1936 taking a centrist, defensive posture to the cultural-linguistic identity of immigrants in modernizing American society was the economic depression, which caused disillusionment with the American promise of prosperity and progress. Weighing undoubtedly on Rosten's mind, as someone born outside the United States to Eastern European Jewish parents, was the earlier imposition of immigration restrictions during the 1920s, at which time the flow of Eastern European Jews, who largely populated America's northern industrial cities, stopped (Daniels 2004, 27–58; Dinnerstein 1995, 78–104; Gurock 1998). The restrictions, which especially affected racialized immigrants from Eastern and Southern Europe, reflected a reaction of intolerance after a supposedly progressive era when social change toward a pluralist society was hailed. According to historian Paul L. Murphy, this backlash, evident in political calls for a "return to normalcy" (i.e., harking back to nineteenth-century values of nativism and Victorian sensibilities), which resulted in increasing antipathy toward Jews, Blacks, and Asians during the 1920s, "despite its surface prosperity and supposed gaiety and exuberance, was characterized by waves of public intolerance seldom felt in the American experience" (Murphy 1964, 61). The economic downturn of the 1930s heightened white Protestant resentment toward immigrants from Eastern and Southern Europe and resulted in exaggerations in the press and popular belief of their connections to radicalism, impoverishment, and disease (Kraut 1994; Marinari 2019; Marinari et al. 2019; Markel 1999; Michels 2012).

After putting the character of Hyman Kaplan on the shelf during the 1930s, Rosten brought back him back more than twenty years later with *The Return of H*Y*M*A*N K*A*P*L*A*N* (1959) when immigration and the promise of a pluralist society once again were part of political discourse. Reversing the preference through a quota system in the Immigration Act of 1925 given to Northern and Western Europeans over Southern and Eastern Europeans, the Immigration and Nationality Act of 1965 amid the civil rights movement was viewed as a progressive attempt to end discrimination based on an individual's place of birth (Chin and Villazor 2015; Orchowski 2015). Yet it also raised renewed concerns about the ability of the United States to absorb and educate stigmatized "foreigners" who were not anxious to learn English and assimilate. The rise in immigration, including Yiddish-speaking Jewish survivors of the Holocaust from Eastern Europe, also prompted creative productions on the ethnic-linguistic identity of descendants of the earlier Great Wave of immigration (Jacobson 2006). Rosten's Hyman Kaplan character, framed in a narrative of confrontation between an old and a new country, found new audiences amid these historical developments.

By the 1960s, when the Kaplan character appeared on stage in addition to print, more readings of his saga drew meaning from a conflict between traditionality, drawn from the Old World, and modernity, represented by the teacher as the symbol of the new future-oriented American. This dual theme is conventional, being found in both oral and written forms. Comic qualities of the theme, for example, are displayed in the following oral joke.

> An immigrant turned to a man he thought looked Jewish and said, "Verstehst Yiddish?" (Translation: "Understand Yiddish?") The other man nodded. The immigrant then asked, "Vat time is it?" (with inflection.)[2]

This story is an example of a structural incongruity between what is expected, namely Yiddish, and the corrupted form of English that is used instead. The ambiguity of acculturation alluded to in the narrative creates an opposition between Old World and New World and between traditionality and modernity. A similar technique is found in literature; for example, Montague Glass wrote the following in his Potash and Pertmuller stories.

> "What that 'R.S.V.P to residence of bride'?" Abe Potash asked.
>
> Morris reflected for a moment.
>
> "That means," he said at length, "that we should know where to send the present to."
>
> "How do you make that out?" said Abe.
>
> "R.S.V.P," Morris replied, emphasizing each letter with a motion of his hand, "means 'remember to send vedding present.'" (Glass 1911, 283)

Not only is there a misunderstanding of American wedding customs, but there is also an incongruity based on the understanding of RSVP's conventional meaning by the majority culture and its surprising interpretation. The ending carries a blunt ring of truth (or pointed satire of genteel society achieved through humor).

The consistent theme found in Rosten's stories concerns the failure of communication in the classroom, and it implies not only wider access to education by immigrants but also the institutional need to instruct or, rather, indoctrinate the dialect-speaking foreigners into an abstracted white Protestant–based Americanism. Incongruity between real and ideal is intrinsic and is a common ploy in the frame of fictional classroom situations and naturally charges them with humor. Given such conventional themes, one might ask, How does Rosten structure the content of his narrative and use the sociopolitical American context within one particular story, such as "The Education of H*Y*M*A*N K*A*P*L*A*N"?

DECODING HYMAN KAPLAN'S NARRATIVE

One apparent structural pattern that invites a query into the sociopolitical context of the Hyman Kaplan narrative is the building of several small humorous incidents climaxed by a longer episode in the conclusion of the story. Rosten establishes a structural pattern to quickly introduce the humorous situation and its characters. He thereby incrementally trains the reader to perceive the linkage of dialect, immigration, and education. He treads carefully at the beginning because he does not want to depict Hyman Kaplan as an angry, radical immigrant but instead as one who embraces the progressive promise of America. Rosten presents the teacher, Mr. Parkhill, as the superior authority, but by the end Parkhill becomes unnerved by Kaplan's confident exuberance and personalized, if not ethnicized, version of speaking and living in America. The humor of the climax is thus an appropriate incongruity, whereas, if it were isolated, it might not be understood by a segment of Rosten's literary audience or, at the very least, might not be considered funny. Contributing to the final display of humor are repetitions of humorous episodes containing incongruities, establishing an expectation of the type of content and form to come. The strategy of incrementally building a story to establish a climax is accepted as conventional in both folklore and literature (R. D. Abrahams 1972a, 80).

Each of the humorous incidents in the whole of the narrative displays a recognizable structure. Every action is couched between an introduction and a closing; the incident, or episode, contains a reflection of description that moves the action to a *calm* level. Similarly, folklorist Axel Olrik states that oral epics do not "begin with sudden actions or end abruptly" (Olrik 1965, 131). Referring to folktale, myth, legend, and folk song, he suggests that they naturally begin with calm, move to excitement, and return to calm. In Rosten's writing a similar pattern appears. For example, the opening episode of "The Education of H*Y*M*A*N K*A*P*L*A*N" (Rosten 1946) describes the problem of a written exercise for the immigrants in an understated tone. The text is thus enhanced by the contrast between the *action* of the exercise and the narrator's *description* of the exercise.

Interestingly, Rosten uses a written exercise apropos of the literary medium for his humorous vehicle. The visual image of the written exercise would be hard to reproduce orally, but similar effects could be produced. For example, Monroe Silver, a comedian of the pre–World War II era, recorded the following bit as part of an oral monologue: "Oy, what a picnic. Everyone was there: Mr. Katz, Mr. Lyons, Mrs. Wolfe. It was a regular menagerie" (Monroe Silver 1919). Silver, like Rosten, refers to the incongruity between the animal cat and the name Katz. As opposed to Silver's quick-fire delivery, Rosten follows his dialect text with the relative calm of Mr. Parkhill's restrained dialogue. This framework functions to increase the humorous content in a variety of ways. First, it makes the humor relative to the calm passages. Just as any one joke out of context often does not appear funny, the juxtaposition of several texts without intervening passages has a similar result. By bringing the reader back to a calm level, the text becomes more incongruous and therefore more humorous. Second, the sequence of closures and introductions forms a continuity between episodes. The connection is established by referring to theme and character development. In the fourth episode of "Education," the introductory section opens with "Mr. Kaplan was an earnest student. He worked hard, knit his brows regularly (albeit with that smile), did all his homework, and never missed a class. Only once did Mr. Parkhill feel that Mr. Kaplan might, perhaps, be a little more *serious* about his work. That was when he asked Mr. Kaplan to 'give a noun'" (Rosten 1946, 517).

The description of Kaplan's efforts continues from the closure of the previous episode, "Mr. Kaplan had overreached himself." In these sections, Rosten implies the theme of limitations of assimilation and symbolically renders the immigrant as sharing the frustrations of being a subordinate student, one who has to learn a new way to live as well as speak (Shiffman 2000). Stylistically, an incongruity is again established by the emphasis on *serious*. When Mr. Parkhill asks for "another noun," Kaplan replies *seriously*, "Another door," achieving a greater comic effect than an intentional retort. The incongruity exists between the ideal and real, serious and literal, teacher and student. This technique recurs as well in conversational genres. For example, a common reply in oral tradition to the demand "Say something," is "Something."

In his humorous texts, Rosten uses the stylistic devices of the question–surprise answer, dialect humor, misused language (play on words), misinformation, and hyperbole. The question–surprise answer device uses the technique of the "riddle-joke," defined by Jan Harold Brunvand as "an item which is question-plus-answer in structure which replaces the usual obscure logic of the true riddle with wit, punning, special information, or some other tricky humorous device" (Brunvand 1972, 15). The riddle-joke works less as a puzzle and more to create a social or linguistic incongruity, as in "What is a Jewish nymphomaniac? One who does it once a month." The incongruity is formed by exaggeration and the relative meanings of the word. The joke is humorous to non-Jews because of the thematic characteristic that portrays the supposed insensitivity and probably selfishness of the group through a supposed deficiency of its women, who are actually perceived as a threat by the majority culture. Brunvard notes a similar function in the riddle-jokes he collected and adds that examples often are "based on the idea of the group's inability to cope with some aspect of the modern world" (15). Consider, then, Mr. Parkhill's question in "Education": "Who can tell us the meaning of 'vast'?" Kaplan "rose radiant with joy. 'Vast!' It's commink fromm direction. Ve have four diractions: de naut, de sot, de heast, and de vast" (Rosten 1946, 518).

The confusion of *west* and *vast* is the linguistic incongruity here; the application of dialect is not the basis of the humor but rather the catalyst of expectation, making the incongruity appropriate. Rosten concurred with this view when he wrote, "Dialect creates plausible deception, persuasive flows of expectation which must be outwitted by surprising and amusing pay-offs" (Rosten 1976, xv). Symbolically, the direction of the west is the direction of immigration from Europe to the United States and the equivalence of this movement with *vast* suggests wider opportunity in the new land.

The expectation of Parkhill's comeuppance in "Education" is also increased by question *strategies*. Absent in Rosten's humor are purely wrong answers to questions; rather, he uses the following:

(1) Question → correct answers → wrong conclusion (five instances)

(2) Question → wrong attempt → another wrong attempt (two instances)

(3) Question → right answer to the wrong question (one instance)

In the first case, the repetition of correct answers establishes an expectation that is contradicted. This strategy is evident in Kaplan's statement, "Fife Prazidents United States us Abram Lincohen . . . Hodding Collitch, Judge Washington an' Benjamin Frenklin" (Rosten 1946, 517). I witnessed a similar strategy in a humorous story told by interpreters at Fenimore House, the site of James Fenimore Cooper's cottage, in Cooperstown, New York: "A couple told the guide, 'We're so excited; we've seen the homes of Washington, Jefferson, and Jackson—and now we're at President Cooper's.'"[3] This story forms an incongruity by repeating correct references, which leads the listener to expect a logical conclusion, but the result instead is a surprise or incongruous parallel (or opposition). And in the context in which the story is told, the structure and content serve to highlight the reputed simplemindedness of tourists, thereby raising the prestige and importance of the interpreters. In his stories, Rosten characterizes Hyman Kaplan as the wise fool with an abundance of information and misinformation, and the distinctions between the two often become blurred and ambiguous, thereby heightening Rosten's humorous vehicles.

In the second case, the establishment of a wrong answer sets up the expectation of a subsequent correct answer. The violation of that expectation in the form of an appropriate incongruity is the basis of humor. Thus Kaplan defines *vast* as a direction; on his second try he exclaims,

"Aha! . . . You minn 'vast,' not"—with scorn—"'vast.'"

"Yes," said Mr. Parkhill, faintly.

"Hau Kay!" said Mr. Kaplan. "Ven I'm buyink a suit clothes, I'm get-
tink de caut, de pents, an' de vast!"

This humorous statement would not have been possible without the establishment of the cultural clue of dialect, but it is not "funny talk" that creates humor
but rather the stylistic strategy and the structural incongruity of the statement.
Reinforcing the idea of *vast* as opportunity is the materialization of prosperity
in the purchase of the vest. Dialect acts to provide a sense of character for the
reader and, more significantly perhaps, to imitate orality. The reader naturally
falls into the habit of pronouncing the phonetic symbols for the dialect, pronunciation that is based often on the reader's firsthand experience with ethnic contexts.
The phonetic spellings add another dimension to the dialect not generally found
in the "dialect-joke" (Brandes 1983; Bronner 2006a; Dorson 1948, 1960; Nusbaum 1979). Consider Kaplan's utterance of "Lincohen"; the spelling not only
indicates the pronunciation, but also points to an alteration of a Jewish name.
Such a modification is also made on the dignified name of Shakespeare to form
the Judaized "Jakespeare" in another Kaplan story (Rosten 1937, 129–40).
Indeed, the manipulation of names is a common humorous practice, one Rosten even plied on the refined-sounding "Mr. Parkhill" to become the ignoble
"Mr. Pockheel" in one dialectal utterance (Rosten 1946, 520).

Mr. Parkhill is the butt of humor when he answers correctly to a wrong
question—the third case. Oral tradition contains many examples of this structure.
One clichéd routine begins, "Have you got a match?" answered by, "Yea, my ass
and your face" or "Me and Superman." In "Education" Kaplan takes advantage of
an invitation to ask questions of the teacher to say, "Vat's de minnik fromm . . . a
big department." Parkhill proceeds through a sedulous explanation of American
department stores and then carefully asks the class, "Is that clear now?" But in
Kaplan's counterexplanation, Rosten achieves the humorous climax.

I'm hearink it in de stritt. Sometimes I'm stendink un de stritt, talkink to a
frand, or mine vife, min brodder—or maybe only stendink. An' somvun is
pessink around me. An' by hexident he's givink me a bump, you know, a
poosh! Vell, he says, "Axcuse me!" no? But sometimes, an' *dis* is vat I minn,
he's sayink "*I big de pottment!*"

Mr. Parkhill studied the picture of Abram Lincohen on the back of the wall. (Rosten 1946, 520)

Rosten uses the device of repetition, associated with oral performance, to underscore the structural incongruities of this episode ostensibly about the immigrant misunderstanding of American department stores and their accessibility to working-class immigrants. Clarifying statements such as "Is that clear now, class?" only serve to widen the gap between the ultimate answer and the original question. The repetition of Parkhill's explanation of a department store also reinforces the logic of Parkhill's thinking. When that logic is juxtaposed with Kaplan's logic, the resulting incongruity facilitates humor by shedding light on Kaplan's misinterpretation and Parkhill's similar failure. The acceptance of this failure is evident to the reader in Parkhill's silent reflection on the transformation with immigration of the patriotic "picture of Abram Lincohen."

Final actions involving reversal of roles are also familiar in oral performance. A typical story concerns the Jewish immigrants who send their Yiddish-trained son to Yale University for the study of English. They meet his professor and are struck by the professor's perfect enunciation and grammar. When they visit the boy a year later, they ask the professor how their son is progressing in English. He replies, "Oy, is poifect!"[4]

THE CHARACTERIZATION OF MR. PARKHILL AND HYMAN KAPLAN—AND AMERICAN PLURALIST SOCIETY

Rosten's characterizations of Parkhill and Kaplan as coming from different worlds are exaggerated, perhaps even stereotyped to create a polarity. Literary critic Constance Rourke (1931) claimed that American humor derives from the magnification of character types who come from hardscrabble or lowly background and, as a result of a supposedly uncouth upbringing, are ill-mannered, boisterous "ring-tailed roarers." Readers familiar with the American scene recognize Hyman Kaplan's association with the stereotype, or folk type, of the Eastern European Jewish immigrant as coming from a peasant background and often appearing ignorant, as depicted famously in the iconic staging of *Fiddler on the Roof* (premiering on Broadway in 1964), and yet Kaplan's Jewishness is not explicitly stated. To be sure, stock characters in popular culture such as "Abe and Mawruss," "Cohen on the Telephone," and "Abie the Agent" employ the devices of Yiddish dialect and mispronunciation of English (R. Bauman 2010; Popkin 1952; Shiffman 2000, 52). Kaplan, however, lacks the negative attributes of stinginess and swindling common to the other Jewish characters. Kaplan does not display the full stereotype, but some readers may perceive humor because of a cognitive extension of Kaplan's persona. Stylistically, the extremes of characterization set up incongruities in the story. Once again a strategy used by Rosten matches one of Olrik's epic laws; Olrik's Law of Contrast requires the actions and characteristics of individuals other than the protagonist to be "antithetical to those of the protagonist" (Olrik 1965, 135). Indeed, Kaplan stands in marked contrast to Parkhill in disposition, background, education, and culture, but he is not on an equal plane. Clearly Kaplan is in a subordinate position and is expected to change his ways.

The confusion of words with multiple meanings, homonyms, and exotic spellings has traditionally been a source of humor. The manipulations of English by foreigners is an especially pervasive theme but often with the implication of ostracizing the immigrant speaker as ignorant and undesirable. English contains sounds alien to other languages, such as the *th* sound in *think* and the *wa* sound in *water*. Yiddish, for example, does not contain these pronunciations (thus often replacing *v* for *w* and *t* or *d* for *th*). Similarly, English spelling puzzles many nonnative speakers because of its questionable logic, and thus the corruptions of spelling produced in vain attempts frequently appear in Rosten's stories as humorous vehicles. Laughter at the difficulties of transcribing the sounds of words to their appropriate spellings is not simply limited to immigrants but is also found in narratives of children and rustics in cartoons, films, and oral tradition. For example, in Bel Kaufman's *Up the Down Staircase*, the teacher asks students to write their reaction to the question, "What did you get out of English?" One humorous reply is, "What I got out of it is Litterature and Books. Also some Potery, And just before a test—a doze of English. Having Boys in class distracks me from my English. Better luck next time" (B. Kaufman 1964, 74). Like Rosten, Kaufman (1911–2014) was a Jewish immigrant who based her novel on her teaching experiences in an urban environment. The literary challenge for Rosten is the reader's cognition of malapropisms as a sign of backwardness with an ethnic sensibility that arouses sympathy for the likes of Hyman Kaplan.

Although spelling humor is more prevalent in literary forms than in oral tradition, because of the need for visual images to perceive the humor, one should not assume that such humor is not found in oral tradition (see Bronner 1978).

Children, for instance, have the parodied spelling bee in which they playfully offer *sweat* for *sweet*, *shore* for *sure*, and *fucks* for *fox*.[5] Although parodies of spelling and grammar are not limited to Jewish characters in folklore and literature, the use of nonstandard forms by Eastern European Jews takes on added significance because of the special characteristics of Yiddish. Jewish psychologist Theodor Reik (1962, 203) noted that Jews were auditory rather than visual in everyday communication. He compared the impressions and memories of ancient Greek society, of which Jews were a minority, and found that the Greeks loved colors and forms and that the Jews preferred sounds of words and sentences. Another interpretation is that Jews relied on face-to-face oral communication because of their minority status.

The practice of wordplay is facilitated by experience with Semitic languages, because words in such languages often have two opposite meanings and can *simultaneously* imply a certain statement and its opposite. Indeed, Kaplan replies to Parkhill's explanation of *department* by saying, "Simms to me it's used in another minnink" (Rosten 1946, 519). Grammatically, Eastern European Jews have had problems with English syntax because of their training in the commonplace source of Old World learning, the Talmud, which treats punctuation and sentence structure casually. In fact, the melody of sentences can indicate punctuation and sometimes even meaning in these sacred texts (Reik 1962, 205). In modern life, certain inflections punctuate a sentence and change its meaning regardless of punctuation. Hence a statement such as "Everything should be all right now" can be negatively answered depending on the style of the delivery. Although literature cannot adequately indicate the inflections and kinesthetics of oral deliveries, Rosten uses this limitation to his advantage when he disguises the meaning of "I big de pottment" at the climax of "Education." Chances are that when read orally with the proper stresses, the incongruities would not be as apparent as they are on the printed page, but the previous uses of dialect, altered grammar, and nonstandard spelling in the story set up an expected narrative pattern that produces an appropriate incongruity. Rosten's familiarity with Yiddish and his English educational experience were probably responsible for the combination of characters and situations that satirized the English language and its inculcation.

Although Kaplan struggles with the standard English language, he conveys the self-assuredness and persistence of Jews, despite external pressures. The following traditional Eastern European Yiddish narrative, adapted by Rosten in *The New Joys of Yiddish* (2001, 170–71), is indicative of this theme of Jewish pluck.

When you tell a peasant a joke he laughs three times: once when you tell it, once when you explain it, and once when he understands it.

When you tell a land-owner a joke he laughs twice: once when you tell it and once when you explain it—he'll never understand it.

When you tell a military officer a joke he laughs once—when you tell it. Because he won't let you explain it and of course he doesn't understand it.

But when you tell a Jew a joke, he tells you that he's heard it already— and besides *you're telling it all wrong.* (N. Katz and Katz 1971, 216)

Such self-assuredness, especially with regard to normative truth, is found in "Education" when the narrator tells the reader, "It was obvious that Mr. Kaplan . . . would not compromise with truth" (Rosten 1946, 519). Just before Kaplan is about to give his explanation of "I big de pottment," Kaplan's "smile was broad, luminous, transcendent; his manner was regal" (520). Indeed, before his statement, the narrator declares, "The originality of his spelling and pronunciation . . . flourished" (517). This allusion to Kaplan's (and by association Jews') persistence allows Rosten to continue the Kaplan stories because the audience is prepared to accept, perhaps even tolerate, Kaplan's self-assuredness. If Kaplan's audience cannot accept his characteristics of persistence and self-assuredness, then Kaplan probably cannot be a vehicle for the incongruities of language and acculturation.

In sum, Rosten uses techniques that are usually associated with oral tradition: repetition of conventional themes, polarity of characters, linear plot, calm openings and closings, and employment of dialect. Nonetheless, Rosten is a *writer* in his Hyman Kaplan stories, not a raconteur, and his creative behavior in his experience and aspirations in the sociopolitical context of the 1930s affected his centrist stand between nationalistic assimilation and ethnic maintenance in a pluralist society. Beyond a literary criticism noting the techniques using the written medium—such as reflection, description, and characterization—Jewish cultural studies encourages a move beyond structural and stylistic analysis to a symbolist evaluation of Rosten's writings with oral tradition and its sociopolitical meaning of the time in mind. In the sweep of literature meant for Jews and literature intended for a popular non-Jewish audience, the academic distinctions between oral and written media are often misleading, because the devices of humor crosscut both oral and literary forms of expression. So as not to overstate my argument, let me caution that I am not claiming that Rosten's stories are necessarily reflective of the whole spectrum of modern literature, Jewish American or otherwise; rather, I use his stories to illustrate some of the cultural politics of framing Jewish characters for a popular audience and demonstrate the way that more than serving as a literary technique, the narrative structure employing dialect symbolizes a uneasy position between cultural separation and national assimilation. In the post-immigrant Jewish society of the twenty-first century in the United States, the message of Jewishness in the Hyman Kaplan stories appears less pointed, but the issues of what it means to be American and ethnic remain. Even if the literary Jew is not in the twenty-first century the essential transnational immigrant figure, Jewish cultural studies nonetheless contributes to the multilayered meanings and uses of narrative with an oral Yiddish accent and stars presented with immigrant flair in writing as they relate generally to a mobile, pluralist society.

10
TELLING JOKES

Connecting and Separating Jews in Analog and Digital Culture

Noticing in the 1990s that the behavior of "playing on the computer" (often perceived by office managers as "misusing" the computer) primarily involved sharing jokes, folklorist Paul Smith dubbed the computer "The Joke Machine" and predicted the exponential growth of its humor-generating function. This label implied that the computer was more than a storehouse of information. If the Internet merely provided a cabinet to file one's favorite joke, it would not brandish the expressive, interactive features or community-building functions of folklore that frequently lodge as commentary on popular culture. However, more than being a reproductive medium and then becoming more of a home appliance and later mobile device, the computer fostered the creation of new material that, in Smith's words, could exist only "within the machine" (P. Smith 1991, 274; see also Foote 2007; W. S. Fox 1983; Jennings 1990, 120–41). Users at home and at work manipulated images and adapted texts, often commenting on the technology and inviting social feedback that distinguished the humor as "computer lore" (Bronner 2009b; Bronner 2011a, 398–450; Preston 1996).

Why joke in and around the machine? Smith implied that it is natural for humans to appropriate new technology for folkloric transmission, and he drew an evolutionary pattern of user-controlled media from the typewriter to the photocopier, fax machine, and computer. Yet the high volume of traffic on the Internet and the creative, interactive forms therein suggest that something more is at work (and play) on the computer. In its personalized consumer version, the computer promises more self-reliance in a growing culture of modernistic individualism, but at the same time it risks alienation and corporate mass cultural control over individual users and appears to threaten social interaction in traditional communities. As a result, I contend that joking became associated with digital transmission for several reasons: First, it emotionally and psychologically responds to anxieties concerning diminished human control and competency for users; second, it signals for them an intimate social connection that questions a dominant corporate order; third, it creates symbols that provide or project a satisfying transgressive or aggressive effect; and fourth, its brief and often visual form adapts well to the physical screen frame.

The Internet is also appealing for enabling cultural agglomeration without the user being publicly visible. Users can usually amass news of their communities without confronting them physically and, at the same time, investigate cultures from around the world without being intrusive or noticed by those groups. Yet some computer lore, taken out of context or reframed with the productive capacities of the computer, can be disturbing to the communities that generated them. A prime example is ethnic joking, typically meant in oral tradition to be shared privately between one person and another.

Just twenty years after Smith made his observations, a Google search of "jokes" resulted in an astounding figure of 329 million hits, which clearly indicates a development well beyond the adaptation of lore transmitted by fax machine or photocopiers. Most of the Internet sites were lists of texts and cartoons arranged by category, and among the most common jokes were those identified as "Jewish jokes" or "Jew jokes." For the most part the jokes were about Jews rather than jokes provided by Jews, and they fit the characterization of Jewish humor as deprecating material related to the characteristics and characters of Jewish life, often deriving from the legacy of persecution in Eastern Europe and the immigrant experience in countries in the West (see Ziv 1998, 12).

Although jokes about Jews were especially conspicuous as ethnic humor in Europe and the Americas in the late nineteenth and early twentieth centuries, the extent of Jewish sites in the twenty-first century, as the Internet became a global phenomenon, is still surprising. One cause for amazement is the perception of Jewish jokes as "period pieces," related to their historical association with mass immigration in the early twentieth century rather than to the assimilation of the twenty-first century. Part of that association for Jews of Eastern European background was the incorporation of joking into Jewish wedding and festival traditions of the *badkhn* (Yiddish: jester) and uses of jokes in everyday life to mock and protest non-Jewish suppressive authority (Krasney 2003; Levitan 1911; Lifshits 1930; Ravnitzky 1922).

With the emphasis in the discourse of the twentieth century on the effect of joking in oral and print circulation, questions remain for the twenty-first century about the role of technological mediation, such as, What happens to the characterization of Jews as agents of joking when the category of "Jewish jokes" goes online in such a massive number of sites? More than 25 million hits come back from a Google search for "Jewish joke," and many websites, such as Old Jews Telling Jokes (www.oldjewstellingjokes.com), Jewish Jokes (www.jewishjokes.net), and A Word in Your Eye (www.awordinyoureye.com) are devoted exclusively to the Jewish joke as a genre. The number of hits for Jewish jokes is the largest among ethnic-religious categories, apart from racialized "Black jokes" and "Chinese jokes" (receiving 42 million and 46 million hits, respectively), and the figure has grown steadily since Smith's early inventory of ethnic jokes as an integral part of computer lore. An indication of the pervasiveness of Jewish jokes in my Google search is that the number of sites coming back as "Jewish jokes" or "Jew jokes" amounts to double the number of sites listed for Polish, Irish, Catholic, and Mexican jokes combined.

Once pronounced dead (or at least out of oral circulation) by Jewish public intellectuals such as Irving Kristol (1951), Jewish jokes abound on the Internet, in citation if not in performance. Does that mean that the jokes are enjoying a second, more robust life in digital culture than in oral tradition or photocopied lore? Broadly speaking, this query provides a basis for theorizing not only on the representation and expression of Jewishness in mass society but also, more generally, on the shift of narrative communication in the twenty-first century from analog culture (face-to-face, oral, corporeally based) to digital (reliant on mediated communication by individual users) (see Blank 2009, 2012; Bronner 2009a; Bronner 2011a, 398–450; Howard 2011; Jenkins 2006; Puglia 2019; Turkle 2011). Indeed, what happens in the move from a back-slapping rendition of a joke in person to a text read on an Internet site, or from an inside joke to a video gone viral in emails and downloads?

One answer to the question of the ubiquity of Jewish jokes on humor sites is that the texts are essentially archived and then selected for oral reenactment or private amusement. Readers can imagine a process by which the texts are extracted from their performative social contexts and are posted, as though the webpage were an enormous bulletin board for passersby to browse. In this view the Internet is a massive storehouse rather than a stage for performance or a folk frame for play "just among ourselves." In an archival transformation (or what some may see as a conversion experience), many webmasters take pride in or show their technological mettle by making available historic or formerly analog forms in long digital lists. Another slant is that the Internet transforms folkloric genres by providing a different communicative medium and a novel play frame. From this perspective, digital media are not simulating or stirring a face-to-face inter-active context; instead, they are redefining the social setting and reorganizing the cultural frame, thus allowing users to create a fresh expressive form.

Although it is tempting to lump Jewish jokes together with the ethnic humor that pervades the Internet, Jewish jokes are distinctive because of their special connection to Jewish culture derived from Eastern European heritage, their his-torical association with oral and print forms, and the scholarly presumption that they should not grow in digital culture because of their association with oral per-formance in Jewish community contexts (Oring 2016, 129–46, 165–81; Wisse 2013). Rising in oral tradition with the mass immigration from Eastern Europe in the late nineteenth century, Jewish jokes enjoyed immense popularity on the stage and in print in the early twentieth century. With the assimilation of subsequent generations, the repression of material that could be twisted into anti-Semitic barbs, and an aversion to self-degradation, American Jews especially discouraged the circulation of Jewish jokes. With their heavy reliance on Yiddish terminology and references to the immigration period, Jewish jokes were often contextual-ized and consequently distanced as old, "classic," or relic humor (see Biro 2001; Eilbirt 1981; Minkoff 2005). Although many of the jokes were reportedly told by Jews to one another and were enjoyed as a form of ethnic bonding, many Jews became uncomfortable when they went public in print, especially on the global Internet. If one accepts the view that Jews are symbolic targets for ridicule and marginalization in host societies, either because their social difference needs to be reinforced as they integrate or because their minority status raises suspicion among members of the dominant society, then the jokes inevitably raise the ques-tion of whether stereotyping and racism are evident.

As a minority group in a dominant Christian context, though not easily distinguished by physical difference, American Jews both championed and were victims of humor that commented on their alleged physical differences and social aspirations. Jewish jokes, many critics thought, demanded, more than other types of ethnic humor, symbolic decoding with knowledge gained from being in a Christian-dominated society (Fischman 2011, 48). When presented by Jewish humorists, the jokes were usually intended for Jews to poke fun at themselves, but Jews increasingly expressed concern that the narratives appeared malicious when told outside the group. A counterargument is that the Internet deflates the prejudicial impact of ethnic humor by rendering it in mummified form.

I maintain that digital culture has made Jewish jokes visible, if not audible, by recontextualizing them from esoteric folk culture into an exoteric memory piece.[1] Just as oral practice can signal a baleful or benevolent intent, so does the Internet have an open "design," a visual frame for interactive discourse that affects the projection of anxiety and consequent communication of meaning on the fictive plane of humor.

THE FORM OF THE JOKE, JEWISH AND OTHERWISE

For the comparison of analog and digital versions of jokes to be valid, I should first establish that the forms are equivalent. Jokes usually take the form of brief fictional narratives and are usually told as though they are happening in the present day. Complicating this description is the proliferation of joking questions (also called riddle-jokes) that are often included in lists of jokes on Internet humor sites and in oral performances. For instance, listed as a "Daily Jew Joke" on a Facebook community page is "What do you get when you lock 2 Jews in a room?" with the answer, "3 opinions."[2] It can also be rendered as a proverb by stating a condition and a result: "Two Jews, three opinions" (Telushkin 1992, 17). If "Jews" structurally constitutes a motifeme (a unit of action that is a variable building block of a plot or linguistic sequence), then other groups could conceivably fill the slot, as in a light bulb joke with the formulaic question "How many (group) does it take to screw in a light bulb?" (Dundes 1962, 1981). Yet a Google search for "two three opinions" comes back with hardly any variations of "two Jews, three opinions," suggesting a Jewish rhetorical frame. Even results such as "two lawyers, three opinions" and "two economists, three opinions" refer to the primary use of the phrase in a Jewish context (Michaels 2006; Michaelson 2006).

In uttering the saying or spinning a story around "two Jews, three opinions," the question arises whether the characterization of Jews is deprecatory inside as well as outside the play frame of humor. The Internet can be a location to offer a textual interpretation of the characterization that denotes a metafolklore of the Jewish joke—a traditionalized narrative that comments on a tradition. Although folklorist Alan Dundes suggested the term *metafolklore* in a predigital age for oral literary criticism, the expectation of commentary, often interactive, on the Internet invites an expansion of metafolkloric discourse (Dundes 1966). For example, under the title of "two Jews, three opinions," a rabbi online shares the following narrative.

> A new rabbi comes to a well-established congregation. Every week on the Sabbath, a fight erupts during the service. When it comes time to recite the Shema prayer, half of the congregation stands and the other half sits. The half who stand say, "Of course we stand for the Shema. It's the credo of Judaism. Throughout history, thousands of Jews have died with the words of the Shema on their lips." The half who remain seated say, "No. According to the Shulchan Aruch (the code of Jewish law), if you are seated when you get to the Shema you remain seated."
>
> The people who are standing yell at the people who are sitting, "Stand up!" while the people who are sitting yell at the people who are standing, "Sit down!" It's destroying the whole decorum of the service, and driving the new rabbi crazy. Finally, it's brought to the rabbi's attention that at a nearby home for the aged is a 98-year-old man who was a founding member of the congregation. So, in accordance with Talmudic tradition, the rabbi appoints a delegation of three, one who stands for the Shema, one who sits, and the rabbi himself, to go interview the man. They enter his room, and the man who stands for the Shema rushes over to the old man and says, "Wasn't it the tradition in our synagogue to stand for the Shema?"
>
> "No," the old man answers in a weak voice. "That wasn't the tradition."
>
> The other man jumps in excitedly. "Wasn't it the tradition in our synagogue to sit for the Shema?"
>
> "No," the old man says. "That wasn't the tradition."
>
> At this point, the rabbi cannot control himself. He cuts in angrily. "I don't care what the tradition was! Just tell them one or the other. Do you

know what goes on in services every week—the people who are standing
yell at the people who are sitting, the people who are sitting yell at the
people who are standing—"

"That was the tradition," the old man says. (Zauderer 2011)

"This is a joke," the rabbi affirms at the story's conclusion, but he connects
the fiction of the joke to a disturbing reality with the metafolkloric comment
that "Jews tend to fight with each other, especially with regard to matters religious, and how they establish one breakaway synagogue after another." The
rabbi narrates the joke in the present and frames it as a distinctively Jewish type,
but it has been traced to a nonethnic precedent in the nineteenth century with
the rabbi being replaced by a judge (Raskin 1992, 14–17). To be sure, the rabbi's narrative strategy is to engage his presumably Jewish readers with a story,
but he also acknowledges it as a way to deal with what he calls a "troubling
issue." He expects to arouse commentary on the issue with the story, because
"recognizing that problems exist is the first step in the healing process—not only
between husband and wife, but within the entire Jewish community as well"
(Zauderer 2011).

On the blog Two Jews Three Opinions, a nonrabbinic blogger visualizes the
joke by using photo editing software to create and subsequently post an image
showing the backs of two Orthodox Jews (identified by full beards and dark
skullcaps). The blogger put in English call-outs that viewers would read from left
to right, as one would read an English sentence, rather than the Hebrew, which
would be scanned from right to left. The first one states, "It's a valid point but I
must disagree." The second shows a cloud above a man who states, "But you're the
only one who has spoken so far." The blogger further clarifies that the intent of
the blog is to "provide fun, healthy and constructive debate about Jewish issues"
(Brad 2008). The reference that might be lost on non-Jewish viewers is the association of Orthodox Jews with an agonistic learning style called chavruta. Literally
meaning "companionship" in Aramaic, chavruta idiomatically refers to study partners, usually in a yeshiva, who analyze and debate religious texts. The implication of the cartoon, though, is that this style extends into daily life. The blogger
features the image's joke to promote feedback, indeed heated argument, over a
broad array of topics. Instead of seeing the screen as something to be passively
read, he encourages viewing the frame established by the "two Jews, three opinions" image as highly interactive.

The shared characteristic between riddle-joke, narrative, and image humor is the presence of a punchline. According to folklorist Elliott Oring,

> The punchline is a device that triggers the perception of an appropriate incongruity. It reveals that what is seemingly incongruous is appropriate, or what is seemingly appropriate is incongruous. In any event, the recognition brought about [by] the punchline must be *sudden*. The punchline must bring about an abrupt cognitive reorganization in the listener. As such, the punchline is not a necessary element of humor but a literary device that characterizes the particular form of humor we label "joke." (Oring 1992, 83)

(See also Oring 2016, 16–32.) I would add to Oring's characterization that the punchline can be a visual device as well as a literary one. In the image on the Two Jews Three Opinions blog the picture establishes that Jews are talking without a narrative stating so. An incongruity is set up by the first Jew apparently arguing with another person, but the punchline is that he is arguing with himself.

In the riddle-joke the punchline is the answer to the question that brings an unexpected or incongruous statement. The twist is often wordplay. In the visual material more common in digital culture, the convolution is conveyed visually by an incongruity either between what is seen and what is read or between the fiction of the composed image and its reality. Understanding the punchline, or "getting" the incongruity of the joke, depends on a shared, typically unstated cultural understanding of the references in the text or image (Correll 1997). Although some strict structuralists might view the production of humor mechanically as the setup of the incongruity, my point for further analysis is that the cultural analysis of texts relevant to their social contexts suggests a perceptual psychology used to unpack meanings, discern symbolic projections, and to identify processes of enactment. When a punchline falls flat and the teller responds with the apology of "I guess you had to be there," there is an indication that participants in the play frame do not relate to the joke in the same way. If the listener or reader mutters, "I don't get it," more than a miscomprehension of the structural incongruity is implied. The suggestion is that the joke is not relevant (or is even repulsive), and this situation raises questions about social perceptions and psychological factors often wrapped around the joke.

Both analog and digital cultural forms of jokes have punchlines, but a difference in ritualization can be discerned in oral performances. Someone might say, "I've got

a joke for you," at a place and time that the teller and listener perceive to be appropriate. Setting up a joking frame on a fictive plan outside everyday time signals a
play on forms, an expectation of symbols and associated references, and a ritualized
sequence of narration and punchline that often invites comment or a reversal of listener and teller (see M. Douglas 1968, 370). The content also needs to be considered
appropriate or the references understood for it to be effective. If participants in a
play frame perceive the joke as a genre with the expectation of being brief, biting,
and funny, the joke will be contextualized in the moment for teller and listener, and
the separation in time and place as joking will allow for reordering or subversion
of reality. According to anthropologist Mary Douglas, "Social requirements may
judge a joke to be in bad taste, risky, too near the bone, improper, or irrelevant.
Such controls are exerted either on behalf of hierarchy as such, or on behalf of values which are judged too precious and too precarious to be exposed to challenge"
(M. Douglas 1968, 366). All jokes, she observes, express the social situations in
which they occur: "The one social condition necessary for a joke to be enjoyed is
that the social group in which it is received should develop *the formal characteristics of a
'told' joke*: that is, a dominant pattern of relations is challenged by another. If there is
no joke in the social structure, no other joking can appear" (366; emphasis added).

If the joke is not *told* online, then is it, perceptually, a joke? On the Internet the poster of the joke is probably not aware of a listener, but nonetheless the
poster uses the design of the page to render the joke appropriate or to implicate
an audience. With most sites providing space for comments and ratings, the user
expects a response, but it is fair to say that online the joker has more opportunity
to joke and more leeway to post questionable material. The anonymity or disguise
allowed by the new medium encourages broader participation because the risk of
rejection is reduced. Thus jokes posted online still depend on a contextualized
appropriateness within the design of the electronic page. In print, in the spate
of joke books that appeared during the early twentieth century, and later on the
Internet, attention shifts from oral delivery to textual form.

An indication of the anxiety caused by the status of the Jewish joke is humor
about its definition. Richard Raskin calls defining the Jewish joke a "risky enterprise" and cites an attempt to draw ethnic boundaries in the metafolkloric statement, "A Jewish story is one which no *goy* [Yiddish: non-Jew] can understand and
which a Jew says he has heard before" (Raskin 1992, 181). Implying that the text
of the joke is not as significant a marker as the response of the listener is another
joke, typically set in Eastern Europe, that associates Jews with joking.

You tell a joke to a peasant and he laughs three times: when you tell it; when you explain it; and when he understands it. A landowner laughs only twice: when he hears the joke and when you explain it. For he can never understand it. An army officer laughs only once: when you tell the joke. He never lets you explain it—and that he is unable to understand it goes without saying. But when you start telling a joke to another Jew, he interrupts you: "Go on! That's an old one," and he shows you how much better he can tell it himself. (Friedlander 2011)

(For variants, see N. Katz and Katz 1971, 216; Olsvanger 1965; Raskin 1992, 181; Rosten 2001, 170–71.) The story set in Eastern Europe raises a question of whether the Jewish joke is historically defined by the Jewish Old World and immigrant experience, not only by its content but also in reference to the typical location in which it was delivered (Jason 1967, 49). In other words, as a performance, is Jewish joking a reenactment from the view of tellers of what Jews in shtetls might have done, or is it a modern urban practice that connects Jews who feel caught between their distant heritage and the assimilative pressures of a mass society that appears to diminish the functions of community?

As a type, the Jewish joke can be told or posted by both Jews and non-Jews, but there is typically a reference to a Jewish character or behavioral trait with roots in Eastern Europe. Writing in a folkloristic journal, Ed Cray tried to broaden the experience that informs Jewish jokes with the assertion that the joke is "one which intrinsically deals with the Jew and one which would be pointless if the Jewishness of a character were removed" (Cray 1964, 344). For sociologist Christie Davies, the key to the distinctiveness of the Jewish joke type is one of social boundaries that can be expressed positively or negatively and, for that matter, orally or online: "Jewish jokes are unique in the way in which they refer explicitly to the problematic nature of the boundaries of a people and focus on the blurring of this boundary not by similar or related outsiders but by assimilating insiders" (Davies 1990, 309). The trouble with this perspective is that it does not address the perception of the joke's content or transmission. For example, Fernando Fischman connects South American Jewish jokes (*chiste judío*) with their North American cognates by identifying key components of "a humorous narrative whose dramatis personae are Jewish and act according to socially shared stereotypical images—the Jewish mother, the greedy businessman, the stingy Jew" (Fischman 2011, 48). Of significance to the perception of the historicity of the jokes is Fischman's observation that the tradition bearers he interviewed generically classified the jokes as being of immigrant origin. The label "Jewish joke" in this perspective suggests an emic category of an orally delivered deprecatory, humorous narrative, whether told by Jews or non-Jews, deriving from Jews' immigrant experiences of the late nineteenth and early twentieth centuries.

DEAD OR ALIVE? OBSERVATIONS ON THE VITALITY OF THE JEWISH JOKE

Noting the rapid rise of the Jewish joke in the nineteenth century as a distinctive historic genre, *Commentary* editor Irving Kristol was one who proclaimed its demise, boldly declaring, "What we call Jewish humor is Yiddish humor" and "with the wiping out of the Yiddish-speaking communities, the creative source of this humor is gone" (Kristol 1951, 433). The American-born son of Yiddish-speaking immigrants from Eastern Europe, Kristol assumed that the Jewish joke was esoteric knowledge; it was a lore shared privately among Jews. This is not to say that the Jews stopped telling jokes, but to Kristol, in post-immigrant America neither Jews nor jokes should be defined by the lore of the Eastern European shtetl. Formerly, he claimed, "the European Jew, achieving self-consciousness in the Enlightenment, found himself at the point of intersection of faith and reason, in a comic situation he could only master with a joke" (436). From Kristol's mid-twentieth-century vantage point, Jews had moved past arguing for their place in civilization and had joined modernity. In this agenda, Kristol responded to Sigmund Freud's early-twentieth-century categorization of the Jewish joke as "stories created by Jews and directed against Jewish characteristics" (Freud 1960, 111). Unlike Freud, who thought that Jewish humor was unusual because the narrator is the object of mockery rather than an "other," Kristol reflected that American Jews no longer wrung their hands over the distressful "Jewish situation." Instead, he observed that Jews used humor as Americans generally did, to confront the challenges of modernization.

When Kristol suggested the end of the Jewish joke, he referred to the passing of the standard comic folk type of the bearded, backward Jewish immigrant on the vaudeville stage and in many joke books published in the late nineteenth and early twentieth centuries (see Erdman 1997). Along with Jewish civic and religious leaders, he disapproved of material that moved from private conversations among Jews to public consumption and misinterpretation. Well before Kristol's famous column, the Central Conference of American Rabbis (CCAR), in 1912, objected to the publication of the fast-selling publication *Hebrew Jokes*. In its *Yearbook* the CCAR reported that it "entered a strong protest, requesting the discontinuance of the publication and sale of the book, because of its vilification, and insisted that the jokes are not harmless fun, but dangerous libels. We regret to state that the firm in a letter received March 13, 1912, replied that it was at a loss to understand our criticism, and it assigned the conventional excuse of holding the Jew in high esteem, and of making him 'the target of the same good-humored raillery as the Scotchman and Irishman'" (W. S. Friedman 1912, 107).

The CCAR's Committee on Church and State observed "a large national movement" featuring the "Jewish Comedian," often a non-Jew spouting jokes in a costume lampooning the Orthodox Jewish immigrant from Eastern Europe. Often the theme of the jests concerned Jews involved in business as peddlers or merchants trading with non-Jews. The committee declared, "We are not super-sensitive, but our pride must resent the burlesquing of the Jew, of his religion or traditions" (W. S. Friedman 1912, 103). Although recognizing that Jews had told such jokes among themselves, the committee bristled at the mockery of Jews in the popular culture movement of Jewish jokes related on the stage and in print.

If not accused of being "supersensitive" to ethnic teasing at the turn of the twentieth century, the same Jews who laid claim to a long folkloric tradition of the self-deprecating jest were accused of being humorless. The chief rabbi of the British Empire, Hermann Adler, responded in 1893 to the public criticism of French historian Joseph Ernest Renan and Scottish philosopher Thomas Carlyle that Jews lacked the capacity to laugh and create witticisms (H. Adler 1893, 530). The sources he gave for the placement of Jews among civilized groups with a humorous repertoire was not in the earthy material of the Yiddish speakers from Eastern Europe but rather in the ancient texts of the Midrash, a genre of compila-tions of homiletic teachings on the Hebrew Bible (530–31). Adler recognized wit conveyed by Jews in Yiddish, but he noted that the humor was more esoteric and couched in the primitive "vernacular," presupposing "a very accurate knowledge of the Bible—ay, even of the labyrinthine intricacies of the Talmud—in order to be fully appreciated. And when once you attempt to explain and to interpret, all the sparkle and effervescence of the witticism are irretrievably lost, and the savor thereof is like unto that of a bottle of champagne that was uncorked yester-night" (531). Adler maintained to his non-Jewish audience that Jews use humor as a tool of survival of a downtrodden people: "I would rather liken [humor] to the weapon which a beneficent Maker has provided his feeble creatures, whereby they have been enabled to survive in the fierce struggle for existence" (530–31). Although he cited examples of such British Jewish figures as Moses Montefiore and Abraham Solomon contributing wit that entered into popular culture, Adler thought that humor in Yiddish stayed within the Jewish community (537).

The Yiddish language, and especially the Yiddish "accent" in a host country's language, represents the expressive inflection of Jews as distinct from non-Jews, and for many immigrants it signifies amusement and a sense of community (Fischman 2011, 47–49; see my discussion in chapter 9). In nationalist corners, however, immigrants' linguistic influence on English represents a threat to a social vision of racial and religious domination, and educators often denigrate the folkness of the Yiddish accent by calling it "broken" and "guttural" (with an allusion to the dirty street) and declare that the language is not a language at all but rather a "jargon" or "mongrel" form of communication. Yiddish expression, particularly its humor, has also embarrassed some religious leaders, such as Hermann Adler, who wanted to show the contribution of Jews to modern Western civilization in the form of fine arts and literature. Adler called Yiddish "that strange degeneration and uncouth blend of the two languages [Hebrew and German]" (H. Adler 1893, 531). Older civic leaders, many from German backgrounds, viewed use of Yiddish among immigrant Jews from Eastern Europe as a sign of insurmountable minority or ghettoized status that created a wall of separation between Jews and popular or mainstream British and American culture.

Yet reporters have also noticed the mixture of ethnic and popular culture on stage and screen. In 1913 Viola Paradise reported in *Survey* magazine that the typical Jewish immigrant went to the theater for amusement, where he or she "hears Yiddish jokes and songs and American popular music, and she marvels at the wonders of the moving-pictures" (Paradise 1913, 701). The historical association of Yiddish with the immigrant generation led to the presumption that, as Jews became assimilated and lost their inflection in the second and third generation, Yiddish humor would fall away in favor of the de-ethnicized popular culture of the host society.

Despite the predictions of the demise of the Jewish joke by the mid-twentieth century, exoteric forms of humor identified as Jewish jokes enjoyed great popularity in oral circulation and print during the boom of ethnic jokes in the midst of the 1960s and the civil rights movement (see Blumenfeld 1965; Dundes 1971). Besides being reported in folkloristic field collections (see Baker 1986; Barrick

1970; Cray 1964; Dundes 1997a), a spate of mass-market books such as Larry Wilde's *Official Jewish Joke Book* (1980), Blanche Knott's *Truly Tasteless Jokes* (1982), and Julius Alvin's *Gross Jokes* (1991) flew off bookstore shelves. Much of the content of these texts was not about the schlemiels (awkward, unlucky persons) and *schlimazels* (inept persons) of Kristol's Yiddish humor, but the narcissistic, spoiled Jewish American Princesses and their doting, neurotic mothers of an assimilated post-immigrant generation (Dundes 1985). The theme of a group using commercialism to advance themselves despite social prejudice and physical obstacles became channeled into queries of the impact of success on ethnic identity and social relations, epitomized by the nonnormative family and sexual mores. The new topics also included more comparisons to African Americans, with whom Jews were connected as persecuted minorities (Boyer 1993). Moreover, the structure of the civil rights era texts appeared different. Instead of the joke being related as an episodic story, the new forms offered a humorous answer to a question, such as the opener of the "Jewish" chapter of *Truly Tasteless Jokes*: "What's the Jewish version of foreplay? Half an hour of begging" (Knott 1982, 19).

Although the "Tasteless" books suggest that jokes were being silently read as relics of an earlier era, Henry Eilbirt, in *What Is a Jewish Joke?* insisted that the printed Jewish joke was still "an orally told genre." He argued that placing jokes on a printed page did not destroy their fundamental orality: "When we read them, we are really listening to them in our heads" (Eilbirt 1981, 5). Folklorist Dan Ben-Amos countered that Jewish jokes, like many folkloric forms, are performed and therefore depend on physical delivery and an appropriate social context; they are "communicative events" (Ben-Amos 1973, 122). The social context to which Ben-Amos refers is an encounter between teller and listener in which Jewish identity is shared. Compilers of Jewish joke books from the 1960s and 1970s drew their materials from oral tradition, but unlike the earlier period, they did not rely solely on Jewish tellers. Placing the jokes on the printed page encouraged a suspension of the social frames in oral performances. The selected jokes were those that did not need knowledge of the biblical and talmudic contexts that Hermann Adler thought was essential to a vernacular Jewish humor. No longer framed as a communicative event "just between us," the printed joke drew more cognitive attention to the meaning of words rather than to the contextualized inflected delivery or identity of the teller. Seeing the joke in print gave the text a fixity and permanence that it did not have in oral tradition. As reading material, the jokes encouraged individualistic, silent consumption.

The ambiguity of cultural effect as Jewish jokes moved from esoteric to exoteric expression became especially evident in the research of folklorist Alan Dundes, who documented the burgeoning technological mediation of Jewish humor through the fax machine and photocopier. Together with Carl R. Pagter, Dundes identified cartoons and texts distributed through the technology of reproduction that in the corporate "paperwork" empire appeared to contain more anti-Semitic sentiments, or at least relied on Jewish stereotypes, particularly on commercial associations, as ethnic icons to convey their humor (Dundes and Pagter 1978). For instance, Dundes claimed that the Jewish American Princess cycle did not consist of a Jewish joke per se but that it used the symbol of the Jewish female to reference mainstream American society's anxiety over the effects of consumerism (Dundes 1985). Dundes in fact identified the "begging" joke as a joke told by Jews, but he differentiated their poking fun at "the alleged proclivities of Jewish women, either the Jewish mother or the Jewish wife" from what he called anti-Semitic folklore, or the ethnic slur of Auschwitz and other Holocaust jokes that Jews eschewed (Dundes 1997a, 20).

Along with other analysts, Dundes also implied that the primary transmitters of jokes generally and of ethnic jokes specifically were men, and he further speculated that technological mediation by technology such as the fax machine, often managed by women, allowed females to express more "complaints about the males with whom they live" (Dundes 1997a, 94; see also C. Mitchell 1985). In popular culture, the tendency toward insulting or transgressive humor by women and the spread of the joking context to non-Jews became evident in the fame accorded to edgy Jewish stand-up comics, many of whom were women (Antler 2010; Del Negro 2010; Epstein 2001, 253–69). Their coarse use of sexual references and insults appeared to go over the line of genteel or Gentile propriety for humorous effect. The humor performed in nightclubs and on comedy records countered the image of self-deprecating Jewish humor with a post-immigrant aggression. In the digital age, the computer "joke machine" further altered the significance of gendered performance by removing or disguising the identities of posters. What appeared to rise in importance with anonymity of posters was the transgressive act of joking and the textual focus on the content of, and response to, the joke.

Online posters often leave clues in their monikers to their identities or the identities that they want others to perceive. One psychological statement is the assumption of Yiddish labels such as *shmendrick* (neurotic bumbler), *kibitzer* (busybody), *noodnick* (nag), and *payats* (clown) to emphasize effectiveness as a joker. This association with Old World Yiddish characters (and, later, Jewish comedians such as Jerry Seinfeld, Rodney Dangerfield, and Woody Allen) derives from the characterization of joke telling as a distinctive Jewish trait (Dorinson 2015). Echoing the sentiment of humorist Leo Rosten (1968), folklorist Elliott Oring (1983) interpreted the purported Jewish reliance on humor in everyday discourse as a turn from characterization of Jews in religious terms as the ancient "people of the book" to a modern secular classification as "people of the joke." This ascription raises the possibility that the modern post-immigrant popularity of the Jewish joke comes from the perception that Jewish jokes or Jews who tell them are supposed to be funny, at least in part because they have a background of an outsider's struggle out of which they lampoon the disrespect and uncivil responses they receive. The Jewish persona can be perceived to set up a play frame in a workaday world. Although this perception underlines an ethnic difference, objectifying Jews as consumable entertainment, it nonetheless tethers Jews more closely to mainstream society as a group that shares in the everyday experience of a good laugh (see C. Miller 1993; Spalding 1976, xv; Telushkin 1992, 19–20).

Behind the attribution of joking as a Jewish trait is the view that, with many Jewish material culture and religious practices fading from view in twentieth-century America, joke telling became a primary marker of Jewishness. Although assimilated, Jews could disclose their ethnicity through the esoteric and linguistic references in jokes or their fondness for telling jokes. With the idea of the Jewish joke being lodged in the topical context of European immigration to America and, to an extent, in Western Europe, the modern Israeli experience was difficult to fit into the self-deprecatory, mobile world of the Jewish joke. Some commentators claimed that "Jewish humor got lost in transit to Israel" or at least that Jewish humor in Israel, as part of a majority, nationalistic culture, is not self-aimed and universalized (Nevo and Levine 1994, 126; Saper 1993, 81; see also Telushkin 1992, 173–84). Their argument is that Israeli humor is nationalistically based rather than being associated with Jews globally.

In sum, the Jewish joke in its narrative form can be identified through at least seven thematic criteria:

1. A historical reference in humor to the experience of Eastern European or Yiddish-speaking Jews (see N. Katz and Katz 1971; Spalding 1976, xiii–xiv; Ziv 1998).

2. The use of humor to deny harsh conditions and to find advantage in disadvantage (H. Adler 1893, 530–31; Eilbirt 1981, 277–78; Spalding 1969, xiv).

3. The delineation of what is special about Jews in contrast to others, often stressing the uniqueness of Jewish society and culture, including reference to Jewish communal characters (turned into folk types) such as the *rebbe* and *rebbetzin* (Yiddish terms for an esteemed rabbi and his wife, respectively), the *chazan* (cantor), and the *shames* (synagogue sexton). The distinctiveness of Jewish society also is conveyed with reference to religious traditions, such as the bris (circumcision), reciting the Shema, and synagogue worship (see Cray 1964, 335–43; Oring 2016, 165–81).

4. The criticism by Jews of other Jews, often with the implication that Jews could criticize themselves better than anybody else (see Spalding 1969, xvi; Telushkin 1992, 17).

5. The use of humor as a kind of parable to elucidate a moral and teach a lesson. Related to this use is the textual or intellectual content of the joke related to the cerebral or inconspicuous nature of Jewish character. In Kristol's view of what Jewish jokes are *not*, for instance, Jewish humor contains "no pranks, no slapstick, no practical jokes— nothing that reduces the spiritual and human to the mechanical" (Kristol 1951, 433).

6. A propensity for using joke telling to manifest social differentiation, particularly of the branches of Judaism such as Orthodox, Conservative, and Reform. In this view the fact that Jews tell jokes about each other demonstrates not so much self-hatred as the internal segmentation of their society (Ben-Amos 1973, 129).

7. A concern for stereotypical Jewish attributes or collective cultural personality such as answering questions with questions, concern for money, argumentativeness of Jews among themselves, and a propensity to joke (Nevo and Levine 1994, 127). Folk types of community characters such as the *yenta* (talkative female busybody), *shlimazl*, and *schlemiel* mark esoteric versions of Jewish traits, whereas in exoteric versions the identification of the Jew (often in contrast to other ethnic types of the "Black man" and "Chinaman") signals behavioral stereotypes.

Although the emphasis in oral performances of Jewish themes had been on the historical context of immigrant and merchant life, the rise of print versions of Jewish jokes influenced a referential move to the last theme of stereotypical Jewish attributes or collective cultural personality. An implication of this move was that Jews were in fact less recognizable as an assimilated group in host countries. The play frame of the jokes, especially when contextualized by popular culture, appeared to mock Jewish foibles and implied the maintenance of a Jewish identity defining individuals and the solidity of their community. In so doing, the jokes raised the question of whether "Jewish" was in fact a significant ethnic or even racialized category of modern life.

In the nineteenth century Jewish advocates were concerned that a purported lack of humor among religious Jews discredited them from being part of an advanced civilization. Efforts in print and on stage were made to promote an ethnically distinctive humor among Jews to merit joining progressive, modern countries (Oring 1992, 116–21). In the twentieth century a collective humorous tradition associated with the past could be read as a sign of integration, but it ran the risk of fueling stereotypes that erected barriers between Jews and non-Jews. Scholars pointed out the decline of the Jewish joke as more than a loss of *Yiddishkeit* (Ashkenazic-based "Jewishness"); they correlated this decline with Jewish mobility out of separate communities and the subsequent loss of Jewish social bonds (Golden 1965, x; Telushkin 1992, 125–41; Zeitlin 1997). Jewish civic leaders still worried about the persistence of anti-Semitic humor, but they also postulated that with the increase of tolerance for or deracialization of Jews in middle-class society, the Jewish joke would go the way of stigmatized blackface minstrelsy (see R. Rubin and Melnick 2006, 17–48; Telushkin 1992: 21–25). The remoteness of the Yiddish-speaking community from Eastern Europe also contributed to the erosion of the dialect story, a mainstay of the post-immigrant Jewish generation. However, for many observers, the dialect joke was not Jewish anyway because its reliance on the immigrant malapropism could be located among many groups (Brandes 1983; Bronner 2006a). These signs could be read to mean that the Jewish joke engine would stall on the global superhighway of the future-oriented Internet in the twenty-first century. Instead, posting of Jewish jokes by all measures has accelerated in digital media (A. A. Berger 2006, xii; Davies 2011, 4; Schachter 2008, x; Serracino-Inglott 2001).

Jewish humor, even for the unassimilated Orthodox Jew, is hardly remote or esoteric on the Internet (Heilman 2006, 184). With a quick search, millions of jokes can be obtained. Although true for humor generally, the *Jewish Daily Forward*, the largest American Jewish newspaper, saw fit to feature a news story on the growth of sites for Jewish jokes. "From riddles and one-liners to satires and comic strips," the article proclaimed as news, "the Internet's trove of Jewish humor goes on and on." E. B. Solomont, the author of the article, viewed the trend positively with the comment, "This is instant gratification at its best, funnies at your fingertips" (Solomont 2005). Nonetheless, he was careful to note that sites such as Bangitout (www.bangitout.com) constituted "a place where Jews can laugh at themselves." The jokes selected to exemplify Bangitout, as in other sites such as A Word in Your Eye (www.awordinyoureye.com), referred to revealing Jewish identity in popular culture: "How do you know you are at a Jewish Thanksgiving meal? Leftover vegetable kugel [baked casserole usually with potato] is suddenly titled 'stuffing.'" According to the *Forward*, the "Jewish Humor Yahoo! Group" (groups.yahoo.com/groups/JewishHumor) was especially adept at poking fun at modern Jewish life (with reference to Jewish education, the joke is reported, "Did you hear about the synagogue having problems with mice? The rabbi bar mitzvahed them and they never came back"; for context see chapter 6), and one could note larger issues referenced, such as the recession at the time (an exemplary joke was "'Why did the man getting an *aliyah* [a ritual honor in synagogue] say his name was Sarah bat Moshe?' He's having financial trouble and put everything in his wife's name'").

The Jewish Telegraph Agency (JTA), the main international Jewish news agency, also took notice of the transmission of Jewish humor on the Internet but expressed greater worry about whether this humor in an open, public medium would be perceived negatively. The digital age story pointedly raised the question, "What is the line between lighthearted parody and wicked satire? Between being 'good for the Jews' and 'bad for the Jews'?" (A. Klein 2009). Although not a new question aimed at non-Jewish appropriation and even Jewish production of humor for a wide audience, the query took on a new immediacy because, according to the JTA article, in the twenty-first century, "people hang out . . . on Web sites." Rather than the image of the silent reader taking in a joke book, on websites users produce and consume and the result is often folkloric. An indication of the interactive folk process is in the response to the circulation of one video based on jokes about Jews eating Chinese food on Christmas. When asked for the source, a viewer commented, "Oh, my cousin from Argentina got it from his uncle in Israel who sent it to his doctor in California" (A. Klein 2009; see also Blank 2007).

I now turn my analytical attention to the placement of Jewish jokes on websites in the twenty-first century, where users in digital culture live, work, and play. I answer the questions raised by the journalists who noticed people connecting anew to Jewish jokes online.

THREE SITES OF THE JEWISH JOKE IN DIGITAL CULTURE

Whether or not the Jewish joke continues to be told in the twenty-first century, it is arguably more evident than ever before because of the global visual medium of the Internet. A key feature of the Internet in digital culture is the ability to retransmit material without necessarily taking the role of "teller." The forwarding, retweeting, or reposting of humor allows for a distancing of the teller from the material (R. Frank 2009; Hathaway 2005; Perz 2009). Users might even reinforce this transmittal objectivity with the introductory comment (or subject line) of "FYI" (for your information) or "Thought you'd be interested." Although the computer eases the process of transmittal mechanically by taking away the pressure to perform, the question remains: Why do so many users choose Jewish jokes to transmit, especially non-Jews who after all constitute the vast majority of computer users? One possibility is that the perception of Jewish jokes as historical artifacts or nonracialized material takes away the stigma of joke texts for some users. For many users, Jewish jokes are not as highly charged as other major sources of ethnic humor in African American and Chinese material. One could also point to symbolic reasons for their circulation: Many of the attributes of characters in Jewish jokes are visible in commercial culture (such as an obsession about money), feminization (in the roles of the Jewish mother and the Jewish American Princess), and the witty or creative individual struggling in a dominant society (see R. L. Baker 1986, 148–55; Dundes 1985; Foxman 2010; Reik 1962, 66–74).[3] These characterizations relate to the mass culture, which acts as a foil for many computer users working within a transgressive play frame. In choosing the Jewish joke, users can project their concerns about massification, represented by the computer, to an external source that is relevant to their status. Indeed, many websites for Jewish jokes differ from earlier print sources by having fewer references to the shtetl folk types and more references to the ordinary figure in a larger society who feels unjustly marginalized.

Even if this symbolic explanation holds, the spread of Jewish jokes online still seems curious in light of predictions of the decline or obsolescence of the defensive, self-deprecating Jewish joke and dialect story. Often torn from a performative context, Jewish jokes online convey ambiguous meanings (even more than in books, which have connections to an author or editor). As folklorist Elliott Oring points out, a website for humor is more like an archive than a repertoire or event, but it is an influential one because of its visibility in digital searches (Oring 2003, 129–30). Oral tradition operates editorially; jokes become transformed or eliminated from a repertoire (139). In a face-to-face communicative event, jokes frequently invite a comeback and a narrative exchange. Jokes can be customized and selected for specific social conduits. In oral tradition, observers have assumed that the lines between anti-Semitic or exoteric lore could be clearly distinguished from esoteric or Jewish humor. Online, many joke sites labeled "Jew jokes" are actually hate sites, and others are presented in conjunction with ethnic humor sites (Billig 2001; Weaver 2011). The division appears to signal a new era and definition for the nonperformative Jewish joke.

To identify varieties of the frames or designs used for Jewish jokes in digital culture, I discuss three renowned Jewish joke sites in an effort to identify patterns in online communication of ethnic humor and Jewishness. With digital culture it is prudent to contemplate not only the intentions of a Jewish joke, if that is what the genre can be called, but also the response of a remote and disembodied viewer. A broader thesis than Freud's self-deprecation postulate based on the Jewishness of the joke tellers needs to be tested in online communication—especially because of the uncertain relation of narrators to their subject and the removal of context in drawing attention to a text or image.

One analytical strategy is to adapt anthropologist Gregory Bateson's contribution of frame theory to explain transgressive play (Bateson 1955, 1956). According to frame theory, the Jewish joke online can be viewed as metacommunicative by referring to an inherent paradox of its framed or stylized play, characteristic of structural incongruity; messages in the play frame deny the very rules that make play possible. People listen to jokes because they accept the idea that the material is located in time and place within reality, but they will subvert that reality in the end. The fragile play frame is especially critical for jokes because the action of joking is often interpreted as offensive and aggressive, or at least risky. As I have previously discussed, Internet sites foster metafolklore because of their interactive and visual features and therefore use metacommunication to provide a discourse of meaning in the absence of a "real" material and social context.

In the physical frame of the computer screen, Jewish jokes online are arguably not about the Jewish joke. As metamessages, they use the ambiguity of the Internet frame to question Jewish joking and ultimately Jewishness as a category between reality and fantasy. Frames are constructed by social actors who cognitively establish boundaries or symbolic oppositions of allowable "play" and "not play." When the stylized actions of a group are challenged, the frame can be used to ask whether or not this is "play" and to confront the need for and meaning of the play in relation to behavior outside the frame (see Bronner 2010b, 2011b; Mechling 2008, 2009). The Internet poses this kind of challenge because the actors involved may be invisible to one another and do not constitute a group in the usual sense, or because the ability to restrict a frame within the Internet's openness presents an obstacle to social construction.

For the purposes of a frame analysis, I proceed from the most textual to the most contextual of popular Internet sites featuring Jewish jokes. The website Jewish Jokes was the top-ranked Jewish joke site retrieved from my Google search. The compiler is anonymous, but the site conveys its Jewish context by its welcoming rhetoric of "Shalom," its traditional "Hanukkah blue and white" color scheme, and a variety of Jewish networking links, including the Jewish online dating and social networking sites JDate, JSwipe, JewishSingles, and JewSchool. Whether as an editorial statement or a sign of Jewishness, the prominent image next to the welcoming message is of a bearded, tallit-wearing man beckoning the viewer with his index finger in one hand and a scissors in the other. When I asked a college-level class what this figure represented, my Jewish students recognized him as a mohel, a ritual circumciser, whereas the non-Jews thought of him as an "old country" stereotype.[4] The difference was significant because the Jewish students interpreted the figure as signaling that the site contained insider jokes relating to *Yiddishkeit*, whereas the non-Jewish students anticipated stereotypical or anti-Semitic material, especially related to the traits of financial stinginess and bodily difference. Gender was not as much a predictor of perception as religious-ethnic identity.

Under the "add a joke" tab, the site invites password-protected members to contribute jokes and then subjects the texts to ratings. The joke tellers therefore are identified, although they can use monikers that disguise their ethnic background. In the listing of the latest jokes, Jewish references can be discerned from screen names such as "moish" (a Yiddish nickname for the Jewish biblical patriarch Moshe or Moses), "funnyJew," and "alte kaker" (Yiddish: old shit; idiomatically, a geezer). Other participants' identities remain masked through less revealing handles such as "Tony," or "chihuahualady." Still, viewers scrolling through the lists get the impression that overall these are Jewish jokes from Jews. The preestablished categories for humor listed in alphabetical order are: "American Jewish," "Blue-Ish Jewish," "British Jewish," "European Jewish," "Food," "General Jewish," "Health," "Israeli," "Jewish Mother," "Rabbi," and "Yiddish."

The website Jewish Jokes presents a user-influenced voting forum that displays the site's top 10 rated jokes on a scale of 1 to 5 (with 5 representing "very good" and 1 standing for "very poor"). The only perfect score is surprisingly not awarded to a joke in narrative form. It goes to a humorous image deriving from *The Simpsons* that depicts a scene of Krusty the Clown (born Herschel Shmoikel Pinchas Yerucham Krustofsky, the son of Rabbi Hyman Krustofsky on the Lower East Side of Springfield) walking his dog through his old neighborhood, which also happens to feature store windows that advertise for the barber—"Fantastic Schlomo's: Payos Trims Two for One" (referring to the "two for one" bargain rhetoric for an ultra-Orthodox Jew who has earlocks, or *payos* in Yiddish)—and a grocery store bearing an advertisement for "I Can't Believe It's Not Trayfe [nonkosher food]" (a parody of a commercial advertisement for the margarine I Can't Believe It's Not Butter). All the other jokes given a rating of 4 are narratives involving Jewish denominationalism, Jewish figures such as rabbis, or Jewish/non-Jewish relations, often in an Old World context. Many of the low-rated jokes are in the Israeli category. For example, the lowest rated joke required esoteric information on the double meaning of *falafel* as food or as pips on a soldier's uniform: "There are two Israelis in the front of a car and an American in the back. One Israeli says to the other, 'Look at that man and his falafels.' So the American says, 'Falafels, where? I am hungry.'" Needing esoteric explanation of Hebrew slang, the joke falls flat. The content of the joke indicates a low-context frame because the knowledge necessary to appreciate the humor does not permeate the social conduit. The site distances narrator and viewer by not allowing comments on individual jokes, but it implies that humor can be key to social networking by facilitating the emailing of posted jests "to a friend" and receiving jokes by email.

In 2017 Jewish Jokes went offline without warning, but A Word in Your Eye increased in popularity, with 15,686 monthly unique visitors, according to data monitoring on SitePris.com. Like Jewish Jokes, A Word in Your Eye has a rhetorical reference to its Jewishness with its welcoming message of "Mazeltov, you have arrived at the best website available today for funny Jewish jokes and funny Jewish humour (humor). On this website you'll find Jewish laughs galore." The addition of "Jewish laughs" after mentioning "Jewish jokes" and "Jewish humour" implies that the material comes from Jews rather than mocking or deriding Jews. The home page screen is multicolored but contains no visual icons. The site has the look of an archive with enumerated sets of jokes. However, unlike Jewish Jokes, A Word in Your Eye has a clear backstory and moderator behind its production. The site began in 2000 when David Minkoff, a Jew from London, established the site to share "what I feel are the best Jewish jokes around." He claims oral sources for his jokes, including schoolmates, family, friends, co-workers, the changing rooms at the Maccabi football club,[5] friends at his Israeli dance class, and his rabbi. As of June 2019, the site contained more than 2,900 jokes organized into 171 sets of jokes under the categories "Jewish Jokes," "Naughtier Jewish Jokes," "Kosher Lateral Thinking," "Material for Speeches," "Jewish Jokes for Children," and "Non-Jewish Jokes."[6] With the framing device of designating Jewish jokes by what they are not, one notices that the three sets of Jewish jokes mostly concern modern institutions or situations, such as finance, education, marriage, and health. A few are about priests to act as a counterpoint to the rabbi jokes contained under the rubric of Jewish jokes.

The conceptualization of humor in A Word in Your Eye, based on an imagined Jewish tellers' evocation of laughter, also brings up another rhetorical strategy in the presentation of the jokes online. Minkoff insists that the jokes' selection be made on the basis of their funniness, but he couches them in nostalgia for a past world of *Yiddishkeit*. From the site, Minkoff published two joke books with the Yiddish interjection of "Oy!" as the hook in the book titles: *Oy! The Ultimate Book of Jewish Jokes* (2005) and *Oy Vey: More! The Ultimate Book of Jewish Jokes, Part 2* (2008). His introduction in the first volume nostalgically connects the Jewish joke to life in the Jewish community and a past age: "I grew up in a Jewish household (my father was a kosher butcher and poulterer) so I was surrounded by Jewish culture. I started collecting jokes from the age of thirteen. Don't all boys get a book on Jewish customs and folklore as one of their Bar Mitzvah presents (as well as umbrellas, a *siddur*—or prayer book—and fountain pens)?" (Minkoff 2005, ix). Minkoff's pride in the number of jokes compiled on the site denotes the value of the Jewish label while also representing the relic nature of its community in modern life.

More than Jewish Jokes and A Word in Your Eye, the website Old Jews Telling Jokes takes advantage of the visual quality of the Internet's capability of uploading and subsequently streaming. The site contains videos of Jews over 60 years of age telling jokes. Although not all the jokes are about Jewish topics, they associate Jews with being funny because of their heritage, culturally induced delivery, or collective personality. Animated tellers set against a plain white background are introduced by klezmer music associated with *Yiddishkeit*. Belying the site's modern media look, however, is the notion that the prime transmitters of the Jewish joke are old people, presumably representing a past golden age of *Yiddishkeit*. The performers are presented in contrast to digital natives, who are assumed to be young, assimilated, and cosmopolitan rather than ethnic and nontechnologically oriented (see Prensky 2010). The aged performers often inflect their stories with a Yiddish accent and conclude with a laugh track, thereby reinforcing the Jewish joke as a product of nostalgia.

The producer, director, and editor of Old Jews Telling Jokes is Sam Hoffman, who garnered notice with directorial credits behind such mass-market hits as *It's Complicated* (2009), *The Producers* (2005), *School of Rock* (2003), *The Royal Tenenbaums* (2001), and *Dead Man Walking* (1995). Hoffman describes the twenty-first-century beginnings of the site in his hometown of Highland Park, New Jersey, with twenty of his father's friends and relatives. Emphasizing the narrative of the Jewish joke, he cast people he thought could "tell a good story." Hoffman decided that no joke teller could be younger than 60 years old because he "wanted a lifetime of experience to infuse these jokes" (S. Hoffman 2010, viii). He filmed individuals in technologically advanced studios in Los Angeles and New York City. Within a year, he claimed that the jokes had been seen 6 million times and had gone viral, which, he had to explain to the predigital tellers (labeled "digital immigrants" by Prensky [2010]), was a "good thing." Implying the metamessage of the Jewish jokes within the play frame, Hoffman notes that on the archival, instantaneous Internet, the videos represent the performative memory of Jewish jokes. According to Hoffman, Jewish jokes as old jokes "get passed around and around, sometimes for decades. The jokes themselves become time capsules, revealing the fears and anxieties and celebrating the joys of all aspects of life, including its end" (S. Hoffman 2010, viii). In Hoffman's book describing the success of the website, he proceeds from the topics of the Jewish mother and coming to America rooted in the Great Wave of Eastern European Jewish immigration from the 1880s to 1924 to modern situations of the suburbs and retirement in Florida. The last two situations exemplify the representativeness with Jewish symbolism of a broader pattern of commercialism, individualism, and modernization.

As though to question the vibrancy of Jewish culture with the fading of the Jewish joke, Hoffman ends his book with jokes about death. An exemplary joke in Hoffman's collection refers to the transition of authentic Jewish artifacts to nostalgia in the post-Jewish context. Considering that the title of the site is Old Jews Telling Jokes, the opening line is startling: "The old man is dying." It continues:

> He calls his son into his bedroom. "Sammy," he says, "I can smell all the way up here that your mother is downstairs in the kitchen, baking rugelach. You know that your mother's rugelach is my favorite thing in the world. I'm sure that this will be the last thing I'll ever eat. Would you please go downstairs and get me some?"
>
> Sammy leaves the room. Five minutes go by. Ten minutes.
>
> Fifteen minutes later, Sammy returns to this father's bedroom. Empty-handed.
>
> "Sammy," the old man says, "where's the rugelach?"
>
> "Pop," Sammy says sheepishly, "Mom says they're for after the funeral." (S. Hoffman 2010, 225)

In another telling of the story that demands more Jewish esoteric knowledge by the audience, the *rugelach* are for the shiva (seven-day period of mourning) (see Lowitt 2006; Platt 2011; Rozakis 2007, 92). The food is associated with Eastern European cuisine, and the joke uses this detail for the significance of nostalgia as the younger generation contemplates the passing of Sammy (in oral versions the character is often rendered as the *zayde*, or grandfather). The old man, and his *Yiddishkeit*, is a thing of the past. His pleasure in eating *rugelach* has been transferred into a symbol by the dominating Jewish mother of the New World for the broader society. The mother reverses the expectations of evoking memory with a future orientation characteristic of modern culture.

In one joke featured at the close of Hoffman's book, the text appears to make a reference to the listing of jokes on the Internet. The joke raises the question of whether an archived joke still has life. In the metamessage of a joke about jokes, folklorists will recognize a migratory narrative adapted for a Jewish, or modern, context.

> This guy goes to prison. He's very scared. The first day he's eating lunch, and when lunch is over he sees one of the inmates get up on the table and

say, "Thirty-two!" and everybody in the whole place laughs. And then he says, "Sixty-eight!" and people are roaring. The new prisoner says to the guy next to him, "What's going on?" The guy next to him says, "Well, you know, we've all been here so long, we've heard all the jokes. We've memorized them, so we don't have to retell them. We just say the number, and people remember it, and then they laugh." Well, this guy just thinks that's terrific. So he spends the entire next year memorizing and practicing all of the jokes. He's finally ready and he gets the nerve to try it. He stands up on the table and shouts, "Fifty-five!" Dead silence. He can't believe it. He thinks for a moment and says, "Seventy-four!" Again the room is completely still. The other inmates stare at him. He starts to panic. So he picks the surefire one. He says, "One hundred and three!" Nothing happens. He goes back to his seat. He says to the guy next to him, "What happened? What went wrong?" The guy says, "Well, some people can tell a joke, and some people just can't." (S. Hoffman 2010, 237)

(See also J. Barth 1987, 70–72; Dundes 1989, 34; M. Miller 2010.) One might question how this narrative is a Jewish joke if there is not a single reference to a Jew or a Jewish object. I have collected variants of this joke with the punchline/ motifeme of "some people can tell a joke, and some people can't" in other socially contextualized settings (such as a hunting camp or university dormitory). Indeed, the joke emphasizes the importance of oral delivery, but placed within the context of "old Jews telling jokes," it additionally questions the passing of a Jewish community in which "we've all been here so long, we've heard all the jokes." The "new guy" cannot replicate the fantasy of the jokes or the reality of their experience in community. The website constructs a play frame on the site with old Jews, who are presumed to be funny, to create symbolic distance between old and new and therefore to create a paradox of a figure being connected to a group while being disconnected from its heritage. The new guy can recall the action but cannot maintain its practice.

Simcha Weinstein, author of *Shtick Shift* (2008), thinks that the Jewish joke of yore may be gone because of its struggle with the past need to disguise one's Jewish identity. In his view, a "twenty-first century humor" has emerged with the Internet that honestly and often brutally declares narrators' Jewishness as an attitude rather than as an appearance, belief, or practice. Referring to Jon Stewart and Sacha Baron Cohen as popular, edgy performers who do not tell Jewish jokes but act "Jewishly," Weinstein claims that these "performers are firmly rooted in reality—or at least a twisted sense of reality that includes themselves in their parody of anti-Semitism. All very post-modern" (S. Weinstein 2008, 33). Considering that the Jewish joke originally appeared as a response to oppression, in the context of the digital age Weinstein asks, "What happens when the oppression largely disappears?" Weinstein's claim is that Jewish humor with its shtick (style of performance or distinctive content) of neurosis from the burdens of being rich and famous projects anxieties of being American. Jewish success is narratively used to reference the paradox of America being the wealthiest and most powerful nation in history while Jews suffer at home and abroad. This pattern of symbolizing Jews as success-oriented Americans may have been presaged by the Jewish American Princess joke and the comical figure of the nervous, feminized, nebbish Jewish male as commentaries on American consumerism and feminization (Dundes 1985).[7]

A way to categorize the paradoxical perception of the Jewish joke's metamessage in emerging digital play frames of the twenty-first century is in the concept of allo-Semitism. The term emphasizes perception of otherness, from the Greek root *allos*, "other," rather than citing either hostility toward or adulation of Jews. Referring to a repeated process of symbolizing Jews that suggests a compulsion, allo-Semitism deals with often puzzling combinations of hate and admiration in expressive culture. Sociologist Zygmunt Bauman characterizes the consumption of apparently playful material about Jews as affectively ambivalent, especially in a modern environment of tolerance, meaning that, although use of the material can show either positive or negative emotion that is "intense and extreme," it contains evidence of the opposite (Z. Bauman 1998, 143–44; V. Weinstein 2005, 497–98). According to Bauman, the emerging psychology of allo-Semitism refers to the "practice of setting the Jews apart as people radically different from all the others, needing separate concepts to describe and comprehend them and special treatment in all or most social intercourse—since the concepts and treatments usefully deployed when facing or dealing with other people or peoples, simply would not do" (Z. Bauman 1998, 143). The possibility in this usage is that "the Jew" in the postmodern or digital age becomes a cognitive category for a nonracialized other, a type close to or actually part of the normative culture, but one that needs differentiation from or at least projection onto the category of "the Jew" from one's own social and economic anxieties about a differential identity within mass culture.

The dark side of projecting Jews as a broadly American malaise on the open, unregulated, and uncensored web is apparent in the use of joke sites by white supremacist hate groups to criticize moral decline and multiculturalism in America. The explicitly hateful Jew Jokes site at https://nazi-lauck-nsdapao.com is sponsored by the neo-Nazi NSDAP (the Foreign Organization branch of the neo-Nazi National Socialist German Workers Party) based in Lincoln, Nebraska. In making the rhetorical move from "Jewish" to "Jew" in its adjective for the jokes, the site is establishing the Jew as a racial type possessing physical differences rather than an ethnic background. The site emphasizes joking questions similar to those found in *Truly Tasteless Jokes* (Knott 1982), but they are framed in a succession that follows more traditional racial slurs, such as "Why is the rhinoceros jealous of Jews? Jews have bigger noses." They may also include propagandistic, anti-Semitic messages, such as "What caused the Jew's biggest problem? The greatest man who ever lived, Adolf Hitler." The site verifies Elliott Oring's (2016, 129–46) contention that humor may appear on the Internet, but its enactment or performance is not an unconscious sublimation of aggression as is often interpreted in oral tradition; instead, such humor is in fact deliberately and consciously used to exaggerate hostility (Oring 1992, 41–57). The play frame and its metamessages of paradox break down in hate group sites because their design rarely mentions laughter or a concept of a fictive plane. Unlike the other sites, Jews are depicted not as integrating into society but as being in need of removal. According to rhetorical critic Simon Weaver, the racist site operates on the logic of exclusion and segregation, based on the observation of threat (Weaver 2011, 421). More paradoxical is the arrangement of jokes around the observation of integration and inclusion, such as on the website Old Jews Telling Jokes, that rhetorically use allo-Semitic strategies of simultaneous inferiorization and aggrandizement to bring out the difference of the otherwise hidden minority group.

Not all humor sites are as overtly anti-Semitic and exclusive as the Jew Jokes site, but many do manipulate their presentation in popular search engine results by framing their sites' content as humor to lure in visitors and incite racial hatred. An exemplar of the humor of hate is Racist-Jokes.com, set against a solid black background. The site's home page prominently displays its proud slogan: "The face of Hate on the 'net'!" Like the Jew Jokes site, Racist-Jokes.com again concentrates on joking questions and cartoons with stereotypical icons to "spread the hate," as its banner declares. The home page leaves little doubt about the illiberal agents of its creation when it clearly states that their provision of "jokes based on race" is due to the fact that "we're racist" (Weaver 2011, 418). The jokes are not categorized by content, but by group—"Jews," "Arabs," "Gooks," and "Spics." In addition, a strong theme of homophobia runs through much of the content, along with support for what Simon Weaver categorizes as "the hard right, white power, neo-Nazism and the Ku Klux Klan" (Weaver 2011, 418). Trying to normalize the site's content, the designers include a traffic rank of over half a million visitors spread across the globe. These "visitor counters" rhetorically reinforce the acceptability of visitors perusing the profane content on the website. Moreover, a high visitor count also helps to validate the site's existence by creating an illusion of popular authority regarding its contents' acceptability as a legitimate storehouse for controversial or hate-inspired joke repertoires.

APPROPRIATING THE JEW IN DIGITAL JEWISH JOKES

My survey of popular sites with Jewish joke content demonstrates the ambiguity of the Internet when dealing with humor. Sites often simulate the presence of a Jewish narrator to evoke an esoteric experience, even as the texts tend toward an exoteric understanding of the material. Being in an open cyberspace, however, such sites still appear to struggle with the potential for conveying stereotypes to an audience that may not share the same frame of reference. One way that such sites often deal with this virtual dilemma is to couch Jewish jokes as nostalgia for a past era and people. Without the Jewish narrator and in the absence of narrative, the Jewish joke online appears unsublimated and contemporary. Hence it is clearer in conveying anti-Semitism on hate group sites and even on normal humor sites that decontextualize jokes as metafolklore about American or modern conditions. Online, Jewish humor often comprises jokes without Jews and arguably is not about Jews. In contrast to Sigmund Freud's view of "stories created by Jews," the Jewish joke online engages the transgressive qualities of cybermodernity and signals a change in the Jew as cultural symbol in the twenty-first century from forms consistently expressed in the nineteenth and twentieth centuries. Jewish joke sites display the paradoxical features of allo-Semitism by appropriating the figure of Jews full of *Yiddishkeit* and implicating them as the everyman lost in postmodern mass culture, a dumpy or neurotic character who is both revered and reviled.

Psychologist Theodor Reik, who elaborated on Freud's ideas on Jewish projection of self-degradation in humor (Freud 1960), theorized a psychology of

Jewish joking based on Jews' isolation in society and their wish for integration. Reik observed that many joke tellers intentionally operate in the region "between fright and laughter" to deal with difficult subjects (Reik 1962, 233). In a compact play frame, the effective joke evokes unconscious alarm, which is weakened by sharing social anxiety (equated with feelings of guilt) with the listener by the time the punchline rolls around. Reik speculated that the "intensity of response" to Jewish jokes, at least among Jews, owes to the "severity of Jewish moral notions, by the strict inhibitions and suppressions induced by religious education" (234). More than other jokes, he contended, Jewish jokes presuppose a "certain emotional solidarity." In other words, the modifier of Jewishness suggests communal connection in the midst of the alienating or individualizing forces of modernization (see Spalding 1969, xiv). In Reik's psychological take on oral performances of esoteric Jewish humor, "the telling of Jewish jokes also has the unconscious aim of cementing the bond that was originally founded on certain common values, and on the awareness of the Jewish isolation within the nations in which they live" (Reik 1962, 236). Countering Kristol's disdain for Jewish jokes gone public, Reik was of the opinion that Jewish jokes spreading to widening circles of non-Jews should be read as social progress, because possession of the jokes in their play repertoire meant that boundaries had been broken down. Reik hypothesized that attitudes of self-hatred represented a "masochistic-paranoid attitude" as a result of a concealed desire of Jews to suffer (so as to remain a community, which was at the root of Jewish humor) (227). With assimilation and social progress, Reik predicted, self-deprecatory humor would disappear (see Booker 1991; A. Falk 1993; Gilman 1990).

The explosion of Jewish jokes in digital culture plays out a process in which non-Jews appropriate Jewish jokes because of what psychologist Patricia Wallace describes as their provision of "socioemotional thaw" to the isolating "chill" of individualized, often alienating work on the computer (Wallace 1999, 18–19; see also Bronner 2009a; Bronner 2011a, 398–450; P. Smith 1991). Jewish jokes are not alone as expressive material in this process, as folklorist Paul Smith observed at the dawn of the digital age, but the symbolism of Jewish jokes regarding secluded, enervated individuals who negotiate between integrating into a large society and retaining a sense of membership in a group is psychologically compelling in response to the anxieties of a growing digital culture. To be sure, Jewish jokes online still can serve the purposes of bigotry and hostility, but the dominant frame for digital play refers to the symbolic acquisition of Jewishness as a way to access membership of a group in a commercial mass culture. The Internet has also facilitated the visualization and the virtualization of Jewish identity for Jews troubled by a loss of community. Jewish jokes, with their socio-emotional reference to *Yiddishkeit*, have reemerged online even more than on the street or stage to address the trade-offs of assimilation and commercial success. Despite Kristol's obituary, the Jewish joke in the twenty-first century has not yet been laid to rest.

SPARKS FROM THE GRAVE

A Holocaust Belief Legend Among Yiddish-Speaking Survivors

I'll tell you what people say. The Nazis went to burn the shul by the Remu's grave [located behind the Remu Synagogue, Kazimierz, outside Kraków, Poland]. But the sparks blew back, they got scared and left it alone.

—Told by Ed Dunietz, Polish-born Holocaust
survivor, in Harrisburg, Pennsylvania, 1993

As a child of survivors overhearing stories of a Jewish Poland that no longer exists, I became aware that the belief legends narrated the past disruption of their lives and projected their anxieties about the future. The telling of the belief legend prompted dialogue on their predicament and how they should move beyond the tragedies of the past. However, rather than passing down stories to my cohort and me, the survivors kept the verbal exchange about their homeplace among themselves. They imagined that the localized legend had references that others outside their experience would not understand; there were not lessons to convey, as is common in more historical testimonies. Belief legends, often told in private informal settings, function to elicit narrative response in their own frame of liminal time and place between the past and present (Bronner 2011a, 36–39; Bronner 2016; see also Halina Goldberg 2016; Nicolaisen 1984).

A setting that often prompts legend telling and expressions of belief is the *Yiddishe vinkl* (literally, a "Jewish corner"), in which Yiddish speakers, mostly Holocaust survivors, gather occasionally to socialize. Their rhetorical use of *vinkl*, with its privatized connotation, is one indication that their self-identification is framed differently from other Jews because of their experience and their cultural association with Yiddish language and a subaltern feeling of *Yiddishkeit* (Bronner 2001). After *vinkl* meetings, when tea and cakes are customarily served, the participants frequently tell legends that, on the one hand, recall the past and, on the other, question their significance to life today. Consider one such narrative frame I recorded in 1993 that was used by speakers to discuss the bridge between their tradition and the present: A group of Yiddish speakers had gathered in the dining room of Polish Holocaust survivor Ed Dunietz in Harrisburg, Pennsylvania, after a formal *vinkl* program of readings in the living room. Ed had placed a tantalizing array of pastries, fruit, tea, and coffee on the table, and the move to the dining room signaled the start of informal conversation among the members. Everyone in attendance, except for me, had been born before World War II. Several had been in concentration camps or had escaped to Russia from Poland during the war.

Leo Mantelmacher, who was born in Poland but had not been back since the liberation, pressed Ed to describe his trip there the month before. Ed, born not far from Kraków, had been hidden for much of the war. "Did you go to Kazimierz?" Leo asked. The question implied the specialness of this section of Kraków as a Jewish place. Ed nodded and described what seemed to him an astounding development: Jewish tourism in downtrodden Kazimierz. A museum had been created from the old synagogue, and a restaurant featured Jewish and Russian entertainment. His tone softened when he talked about the Remu synagogue. The name Remu was familiar to all of Ed's listeners. *Remu* (*remah* in Hebrew) is the Yiddish pronunciation of the initialism RMI, for Rabbi Moses Isserles, the renowned talmudist rabbi (born in Kraków in 1525 or 1530; died on the eighteenth of Iyar, or Lag b'Omer, in 1572).

In 1553 the Remu built a small synagogue in Kazimierz to memorialize his wife, who had died in 1552 at the tender age of 20. A cemetery lies beside the synagogue, and its major attraction is the Remu's grave in front of the synagogue wall (Figure 11.1). Before World War II it was a pilgrimage site for Jews from every part of Poland, who visited the grave of the wonder-working rabbi on the holiday of Lag b'Omer. Although the holiday is officially the thirty-third day of

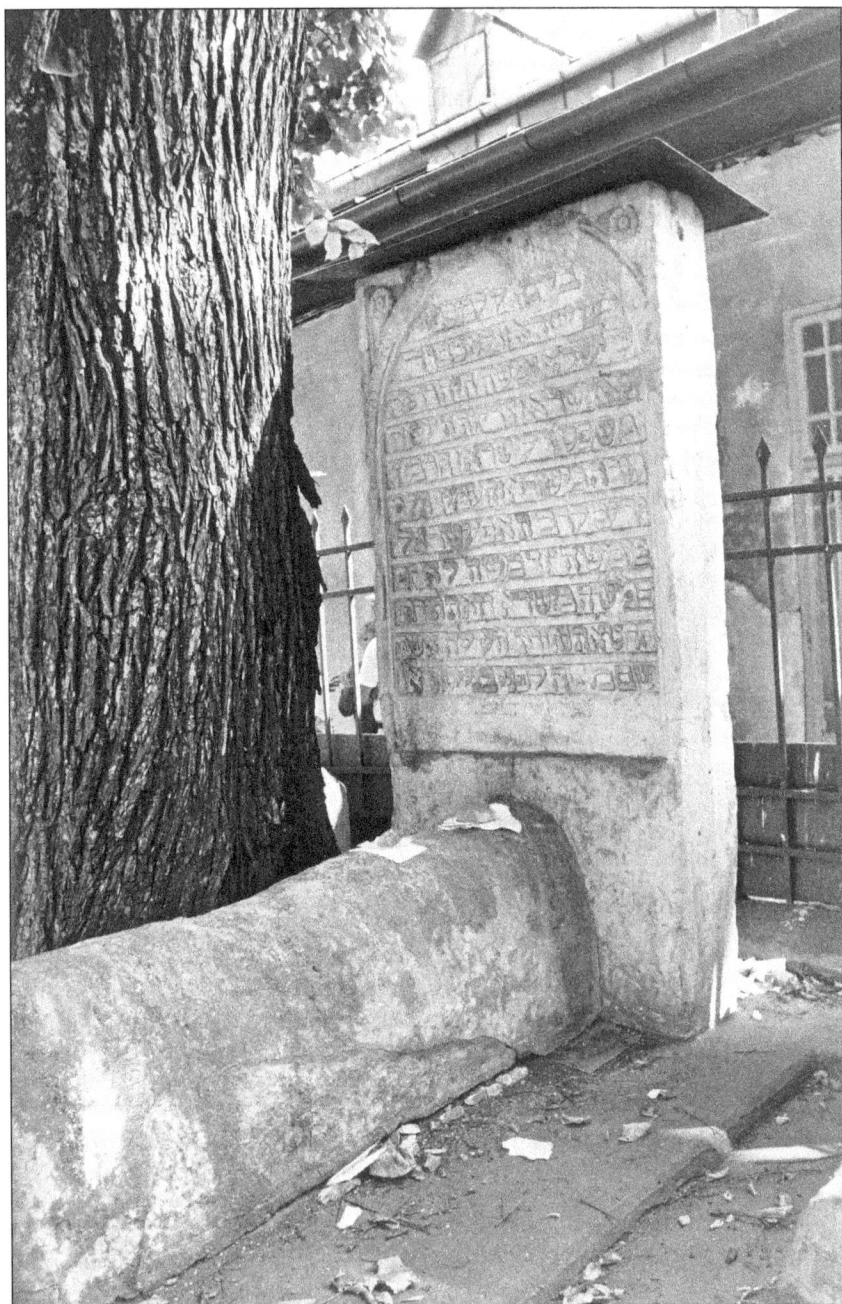

11.1. The grave of the Remu next to the synagogue bearing his name in Kraków, Poland. Photo by Simon J. Bronner.

the counting of the Omer (the period from the second day of Passover until the holiday of Shavuot), it is known colloquially as a "scholar's festival" by talmudic students and is marked by merrymaking, including the lighting of bonfires (Finkelman 1999; Zerubavel 1995, 96–113). The holiday coincides with the anniversary of the Remu's death, and pilgrims to his grave leave written wishes there.

"It's still there? The Nazis didn't destroy it?" Leo asked incredulously. "That's right," Ed replied. He knew that many of his listeners could recount stories of the destruction of synagogues, cemeteries, and yeshivas in their hometowns in Poland, so he felt the need to explain the survival of this structure revered by Jews (see Bar-Itzhak 2001, 134–58). "I'll tell you what people say," he said in Yiddish. "The Nazis went to burn the shul by the Remu's grave [the stone is situated next to one wall]. But the sparks blew back. They got scared and left it alone." The liminal characteristic of the belief as between fact and fiction, as well as between here and there, sets up a narrative frame that places the group in a different reality from the present. The image of burning is particularly emotive because of its suggestion of total annihilation (with the synagogue as the symbol for the continuity of the Jewish community) and cultural incineration with references to burnings of sacred books and structures.

"Dos iz a mayse," Leo said dismissively, as he tried to disrupt that liminal context. By *mayse* he meant an intentionally fictional narrative. "No, that's what the people there say," Ed repeated in his defense. "A legend," someone else interjected in English. "Nisht emes" (not true), Leo blurted out. Leo was irritated because the discussion had deviated from the hard facts and numbers of the Jewish catastrophe. Ed turned from the issue of whether it was true and impressed on Leo the importance of belief. "If you were there," Ed challenged, "you would feel it was a magical place." Then a lively argument ensued about the ruthlessness of the Nazis, with Leo taking the position that they would have destroyed the structure, and anything Jewish, if they had wanted to. Others were not so sure. Or else they did not want to discount a host of legends about the magical powers of wonder-working rabbis in Poland (see Bar-Itzhak 1990). "Maybe it is a *mayse*," Ed finally offered, and he emphasized in Yiddish, "Die geshichte bringt mir a sach wichtigkeit . . . bedaitung" (the narrative has importance, meaning, for me). His choice of *geshichte* implied a matter of immediacy, a matter Ed referred to as *richtig epes* (something real or meaningful).

It was not the first time I had heard the story told as a *geshichte* (narrative) and witnessed the argument that followed. In Los Angeles that same year, I attended the regular Sunday brunch hosted by Henry and Lola Bornstein, my uncle and aunt, for Yiddish-speaking Jews from Oświęcim, Poland (Oświęcim is the Polish name; in Yiddish the town is called Oshpitzin, and in German during World War II, Auschwitz). The conversation drifted, as it had many times before, to wartime Poland. My aunt sighed when she said to me, "No matter how we start off—the weather, taxes, traffic—the talk always comes back to the Holocaust. We're still trying to figure out how Auschwitz happened to Oświęcim" (see chapter 8). At one brunch, my aunt recounted her experience in Kraków after leaving the smaller town of Oświęcim during the 1930s. Her daughter asked, "Was Kazimierz *frum* [religious] then?" She acknowledged the Hasidic presence and recalled the pilgrimages to the Remu grave. "The Nazis cleared out the old quarter," she said, and some of her family members had been caught in Kraków. Her husband, Henry, piped in that it was "incomprehensible" that the Remu synagogue survived. "You know why it remained?" he asked in his typical cue that a story was coming. "I tell you. It was said that if the stone was touched, then your family would mysteriously die or disappear. So the Nazis were scared."

"You know, I heard that too," Nathan Littner, also from Oświęcim, replied, "but I thought the Nazis tried to burn it, but the fire flew back at them." One guest at the brunch was a Yiddish speaker from Romania; he emphasized the importance placed on burning the synagogue among the Nazis in his town, and he found it strange that they would spare the Remu structure. This led to an excited conversation about the Nazi destruction of Jewish sites in Poland. Some attributed the Nazis' actions to senseless cruelty, whereas others saw a method in their madness. Accentuating the devilish traits of the Nazis, Nathan remarked that they were "superstitious, into occult," and could have been scared by the curse.

When I made a query about the legend over the Internet, I received a note from Kraków resident Jonah Bookstein. He recalled that a Jew in the city had explained to him that the Nazis were aware of a curse on vandals of the grave: "When the first Nazi refused [to vandalize the grave] because he was scared (he had been told by a Jew the power of the Rabbi [Remu]), a second Nazi stepped up. He swung at the *matzevah* [Hebrew: gravestone] with a sledgehammer which bounced off the stone and hit him in the head. He was killed instantly" (Bookstein 1995). The significance of the story is the local awareness that stones around the Remu's grave were destroyed, and the cemetery was in disarray after the war. Historian Earl Vinecour has commented, in fact, that "*miraculously*, the only tombstone to survive the war totally unimpaired was that of Rabbi Moses Isserles"

(Vinecour 1977, 22; emphasis added). Part of the miraculousness of the grave, besides its towering size, its position right next to the eastern wall of the synagogue, and its elaborate inscription, is the boastful Hebrew phrase connecting the Remu with Moses himself: "From Moshe until Moshe, there was none like Moshe. May his soul be bound in the bond of eternal life."

My Internet query also produced an incredulous reply, similar to Leo's at the *vinkl*. In his message to me, Bernard Sussman of Washington, D.C., underscored his displeasure upon hearing the legend. He drew my attention to the work going on at the concentration camps in the region: "It is very probable that all the energies and facilities of the German troops in the area were devoted to the extermination camps, with nothing left over for pointless gestures such as desecrating a cemetery that Jews couldn't see anymore." What especially bothered him was the supernatural motif of the story: "This 'legend' about a Remu Stone supports the sympathetic notion of those poor ignorant, sentimental Nazis, so easily frightened by ghost stories, like little children; can't really hold them responsible for the Holocaust. That's why I am very unsympathetic to such 'legends.'"[1] He could not explain, however, why the Remu's stone survived when the rest of the cemetery was in disarray. He believed the stone's survival stemmed "partly from its superior construction and partly from the veneration of the spot which may have been known (if imperfectly) among local Christian Poles."[2]

Moshe Weiss, a Bobover rabbi who grew up in Oświęcim, made a connection of the belief about the Remu grave to synagogue legends when he recounted, "Legend has it that the Nazis spared the Remu Synagogue after being told that it was a holy place inhabited by the spirit of a holy man, and should they attempt to burn it down, they would fail in their mission" (M. Weiss 1994, 38). Weiss offered the narrative to emphasize the spiritual importance of the Remu, and he recounted other legends about the great wonder-working rabbi. One included a commentary on German destructiveness: "There is also another popularized story about a wedding celebrated on Ulica Sheroka near the Remu Synagogue until late one Friday afternoon. The rabbi implored the guests to end the festivities lest they violate the Sabbath. When the guests went heedlessly on their merry-making, the rabbi placed a curse on them. According to one account, they all died; another version has it that they were swallowed alive. In any case, after the Sabbath a fence was installed around the entire area. This fence remained standing until the Germans invaded Krakow and destroyed it" (M. Weiss 1994, 38; see also Grözinger 2010, 63; Seifter 1996, 43).

Jacob Seifter, a Jewish Oświęcim resident who immigrated to Cleveland, Ohio, wrote that the folk logic connecting the legends of the synagogue and the *Khasene Beysakvores* (wedding cemetery) is that the "ghosts did not have far to go" (Seifter 1996, 36). For Jacob Hennenberg, born in Oświęcim in 1924, the story of the ghosts is explained by a connection to the fierce pietism and magical power of the Remu.

> This story is told about the Kraków Rabbi Remu. He went to the syna-
> gogue on Friday and saw a wedding in progress. He ordered the party to
> stop the music because of the nearing of sabbath. They refused. He then
> said a prayer and the whole wedding party sunk in the ground. That space
> is still there surrounded by a fence. Last year [1992] I saw the place myself.
> The Germans didn't destroy it. This is the *Khasene Beysakvores*.[3]

Without saying that the Remu legend actually happened, Hennenberg verifies its possible veracity by noting the special powers of the Remu.

A Polish Catholic tour guide related the legend of the wedding ghosts in the fenced-in area by the Remu synagogue when I visited the site, but she did not relate the story of the Remu grave. Jacob Seifter, in the Oświęcim *Yizkor Bikh* (Jewish memorial book) (Seifter 1977, 355–61), refers to the spiritual, or magical, quality of places such as the Remu synagogue for Jews in that area as *epes tsoiber-haftes*, or "the essence of magic" (see Bronner 1996, 30). For many survivors from the region, Kazimierz symbolizes old Jewish Poland, and the Remu synagogue is its spiritual center. The legend of the Remu grave, as far as I can determine, mainly circulates among Jewish survivors of the Holocaust from western Galicia, which includes Oświęcim, Będzin, and Kraków. It is not a story that their children have inherited.

Yet folklorists can discern details about the desecration of holy places in the narrative that appear in migratory folktales, particularly in Europe. Using the standard reference of the motif-index of folk literature compiled by folklorist Stith Thompson (1975), one can locate magical motifs such as Q556, Curse as punishment; Q558.14, Mysterious death for desecration of holy places; and D1299.2, Magic sepulchre; but there appears to be a special relationship in the legend of the Remu grave to Jewish cultural perceptions of the synagogue as a synecdoche for the community. Haya Bar-Itzhak, in her study of Polish synagogue legends, notes the ubiquitous fear of fire in wooden shuls (Yiddish: synagogue, with the implication that the building centers the Jewish community) as the destruction of the sacred. She recounts several legends in which synagogues are rescued from fire by birds who extinguish the flames with the beating of their wings. She has collected several examples of synagogues miraculously able to withstand bombardments by foreign military forces, such as Russians during the eighteenth century (Bar-Itzhak 2001, 149). However, she reports that narratives of destruction rather than deliverance during the Nazi period are a sign of a lost Jewish world. Nonetheless, Bar-Itzhak recognizes the spiritual strength of the structures: "In post-Holocaust legends dealing with events during the Holocaust, the synagogues' uncanny endurance returns in a slightly different incarnation: the Germans must use an extraordinarily large quantity of explosives to blow up a synagogue" (149).

Folklorist Dan Ben-Amos identifies a pattern in Jewish desecration narratives of sacred persons, places, and objects exacting vengeance for a lack of faith or an attitude of contempt toward Jews. He associates this pattern as tale type 771 (Israel Folktale Archives), Desecration (sacrilege) punished, mostly in tales from Arab lands (Ben-Amos 2011, 146; see also Ben-Ami 1998, 70, 89, 202 [tales and legends 2.1, 2.2, and 2.3, which concern the tombstone of Rabbi Abraham Awriwer, whose *hillulah* is also celebrated on Lag b'Omer], 217 [tale 12.5], and 234–35 [tale 22.1]). The structure of the tales proceeds typically from desecration to punishment and finally to expiation through prayers, remorse, conversion to Judaism, demonstration of respect, renovating a shrine, or lighting candles at the grave site. Often the punishment is paralysis, fright, or death, although it might be symbolic, such as continuous micturition for a vandal who urinates on a scroll or the loss of hands for a thief of sacred objects. Yet the Remu grave desecration story does not involve expiation, and it is this missing component that likely elicits narrative response in the manner of the legend.

If the Remu legend as a historical narrative about the Holocaust derives from traditional Jewish themes of cemeteries and synagogues as magical sites, wishes fulfilled by saintly *tzaddikim* (righteous individuals who are often said to have spiritual powers), and Poland as the storied old country, more can be said in colonialist terms of the "vengeance from the grave" trope in the "curse of the pharaohs," also known as the "mummy's curse," which might suggest a connection to Jewish desecration narratives in Arab lands. The belief legend in a curse for outsiders who desecrate a sacred place is connected to archaeologist Howard Carter's discovery of the tomb of Tutankhamun in the Egyptian Valley of the Kings in 1922. Probably influenced by the British nineteenth-century literary fascination with mummies as scary bogeymen who exact revenge after being unearthed by colonialist discoverers, the King Tut legend claims that team members connected with excavation of the tomb died under mysterious circumstances soon afterward (Stephens 2001). The theme was the basis for Hollywood films such as *The Mummy's Tomb* (1942), in which a mummy kills an archaeologist after a high priest has vowed revenge on the men who entered the tomb years before (Lant 1992, 104). Interest in the curse remained through several blockbuster King Tut exhibitions in the early twenty-first century, and the documentary *Curse of King Tut* (2006) aired on American television on the History Channel.

No empirical evidence suggests that the mummy's curse legend popularized during the mid-twentieth century is a direct antecedent of the Remu legend. Nonetheless, its structural similarities suggest some symbolic equivalences between grave and tomb, saint and pharaoh, and ancient site and sacred space in the narratives. Especially notable is what Antonia Lant (1992) calls the twentieth-century "cult of the ruin" in mummy narratives, in which connections are found between contemporary and ancient civilizations, even though the moderns assume that the ancients are physically and culturally dead. In the movies the curse often follows the archaeologists from Egypt to modern-day America; in *The Mummy's Tomb*, for instance, the mummy travels to the unlikely location of New England. The insult added to injury, or the life force given to the ancient mummy, is shown to be the use of modern tools, such as electric lights and recording equipment. Following this line of inquiry, a subtext implied by tellers in America can be discerned in the Remu legend concerning the continuity of medieval Polish *tzaddikim* and religious piety in modern life in a new place. Tellers seem to be asking, Are they, and the tradition they represent, to be left behind with the Holocaust, or do they still have a place, even if they let us down? The reference to these elements, after all, is an esoteric knowledge that needs contextualization. The legend, then, is not just about the Holocaust but also about the disjuncture of Jewish tradition.

A remaining structuralist question is the symbolic equivalence of Nazis and British archaeologists. Both are presented as violating sacred ground for irreligious reasons that are shown to be exploitative—anti-Semitism by the Nazis and scientific colonialist inquiry by the archaeologists. Both are blinded by their obsessions and suffer personal tragedies for their more public triumphs. Both have a colonialist implication because they represent forces involving, in Edward Said's words, the "implanting of settlements on distant territory" (Said 1993, 8). Significantly, both represent orientalized groups, for Jews as Hebrews were referred to as "Orientals" in European literature (Kalmar and Penslar 2005; Said 1994). Moreover, Yiddish speakers were also derided as backward *Ostjuden* (Eastern Jews), a reference to their primary location in Eastern Europe. Both Jews and Egyptians were racialized or "othered" as inferior by Western imperial powers. In the legends, their domination is shown by references to modernity, whether warfare or science, which allows the displacement of their Eastern roots. But the stories remind listeners of the fearsome spiritual force and the often neglected wisdom in those ancient or traditional societies.

I am not discounting the impact of the Nazi dramatis personae as genocidal evil in the Remu legend, and whereas the imperialist archaeologists may have had good intentions, they were exploitative by venturing into areas where they had no place. They intruded as outsiders into a realm of tradition. Arguably, different psychological processes are at work. In the Remu legend, wish fulfillment for vindication is coupled with guilt about survival; the storyteller's vantage point is that of the minority. In the mummy's curse, guilt is also apparent, but the raconteur is a member of the colonialist majority and is worried about the consequences of tampering with spiritual forces and ancient tradition that his or her own culture has denied. This may explain why, in the popularized King Tut legend, the othered mummy is a monster instead of being a wonder-working saint in the expression of the collective self.

The Remu grave belief-legend can create controversy when it is told because of public sensitivity about relating the hard facts of the Holocaust. As my experience shows, there may even be attempts to suppress the telling of the story. But as Ed Dunietz related, the narrative is important for survivors to tell because of the *bedaitung*, the "meaning," which he rhetorically used to underscore their break from the Polish Jewish past. In the manner of legend, rather than the fictional folktale, the narrative serves to connect consequences to actions in real-life places considered to be mysterious or culturally liminal zones. It is not a ghost story, although it suggests a protective spirit and a reference to rabbinic veneration in Polish Jewish culture. This is significant, given the common discourse among Holocaust survivors about the role of God in combating evil. Leo Mantelmacher's denial of supernatural motifs is part of his bitterness at Orthodoxy for promising divine intervention. Bernard Sussman's protest of the legend represents resistance to the characterization of Nazis as blameless Germans.

For the tellers whom I heard relate the legend, the point of using it much like a parable rather than offering a factual conversation in everyday praxis was to draw a lesson to the self, if not the audience, to find vindication, because justice can never be served. By presenting the legend as an explanation of how the grave endured, they question how they miraculously survived. By not stating directly that a ghost or divine intervention was involved, the legend invites commentary on the persistence of Polish Jewish lives and traditions. Again, without directly including the details of Nazi crimes against humanity, the narrative challenges listeners to contemplate whether murder and destruction will go unpunished. The miraculous rabbi figure symbolizes the power of righteousness taught in Judaism, which seems ineffective against weapons. Set in the cemetery, the belief underlying the story raises images of wholesale death, and the key action of destroying a stone attached to a venerated rabbi, an object of pilgrimage, gains significance as the ultimate desecration.

The expression of belief might be heard in Freudian terms as a form of wish fulfillment through magic, but as legend, it questions whether fulfillment can be achieved. Frustrated that they cannot avenge the deaths of loved ones, tellers frequently relate variant punishments that affect the Nazis' families, just as the survivors' families have been disrupted by premature death at the hands of Nazi brutality. In some stories there is a reciprocal relationship between the deed—hitting the stone—and the consequence—being hit—but more often, the justice rendered appears to go beyond the moment. A curse acts to affect generations afterward and to move beyond the perpetrators to all their accomplices. The swing of the hammer not only applies extra destructive power but also creates an image, at least in the survivors' memory of old Europe, of often fearsome, blackened, and bulky blacksmiths who harness fire (hammers appear frequently in the iconography of contemporary hate groups; see SPLC 2006).

Sparks and flames as punishment are particularly apt because of the connection between veneration of the Remu and the lighting of bonfires on Lag b'Omer, with its association with Jewish mysticism and pilgrimage, but even more so, they are signs of mass destruction in Holocaust iconography, such as synagogue burnings. The narrator's intentional use of "sparks" triggers in his listeners awareness of Hasidic rhetoric and philosophy of "divine sparks" embedded, according to anthropologist Ayala Fader, "in a coarse surrounding husk which a Jew may liberate through his holy purpose/intention and by adaptation" (Fader 2007, 3). Thus a believer can have a magicoreligious outcome from an ordinary or popular form (Fader gives the example of a Lubavitcher composer adapting a Pepsi commercial for prayer and meditation). Summoning fire is often considered a divine power and is gendered as a masculine strength in war (Thompson 1975, Q552.13, Fire from heaven as punishment). The Remu grave belief-legend is ultimately a story of power and triumph for the vanquished. The introductory phrase "I heard it said," though, casts some doubt on the supernatural source of the action and invites listeners to comment in a liminal narrative frame between reality and fantasy on historical vindication on one level and belief in divine protection on another.

The Remu legend also deserves consideration as a statement or a question of Poland's position in Jewish sacred space. The holy places of Israel are venerated as pilgrimage sites, and for Polish Holocaust survivors, stories of the Remu invite commentary on the significance of their religious legacy in Eastern Europe. The old age of many synagogues and the representation of generations in cemeteries are reminders of Jewish persistence in the Polish landscape, but not necessarily in Jewish memory. Kazimierz, however, is a fitting legendary context for Holocaust survivors because of one unusual feature: It has two synagogues that date back to the sixteenth century or earlier. Although the Polish government's official guidebook notes that "the 15th century synagogue in Cracow, one of the oldest in Poland, miraculously escaped destruction," it was Remu's later one that gave rise to legend, probably because of the renown of the Remu himself. Polish historian Michał Rożek observes in his guidebook, "Moses Isserles is regarded by Jews as a miracle-worker. They come to his grave on pilgrimages from all over the world and leave notes with requests round the matzevah. Nowadays, [a] special metal box for the requests has been put on the grave. Rabbi Remuh's intercession eases suffering and hardship of everyday life and the belief in his might works wonders" (Rożek 1991, 71).

At the *vinkl* I attended, the Yiddish-speaking Jews raised in Poland indicated the special roles of synagogues and cemeteries in religious ritual as centers of spiritual activity and in narrative as belief centers of the activity of spirits. Synagogues and cemeteries are related because spirits from the cemetery often gather in synagogues as "spirit congregations," according to frequently collected legends from Eastern Europe (Seifter 1977; Sherman 1992, 76–77; J. Trachtenberg 1939, 62; B. S. Weinreich 1988, 348). Cleveland resident and Holocaust survivor Jacob Hennenberg related to me in 1995 the following narrative of a spirit congregation.

> I remember hearing a legend as a youth about the Great Synagogue of Oświęcim. It was told that there were ghosts inside. Going home from *cheder* [religious school] I had to pass the Great Synagogue, and I became

scared sometimes when it was an especially dark night. According to the legend, when someone passed the synagogue, the ghosts could call you to the Torah and you had to go in. The whole city knew the legend that one time this happened and some people walked by at night, and the doors of the Great Synagogue opened. The lights went on and the people were ordered to go in backwards and to say the "Brucha" [blessing] and walk out the same way.

As with other tellers, Hennenberg distances himself from the belief by using the rhetoric "it was told," although he indicates that he was affected in the Polish setting by being "scared." The legend expresses for him the power of faith in the Polish Jewish social structure that was disrupted in the new setting of America.

Jewish folklorist Joshua Trachtenberg devotes a full chapter in his classic study *Jewish Magic and Superstition* to the "spirits of the dead," most of whom, according to tradition, dwell in synagogues and cemeteries. Whereas the Jewish cemetery is an unclean place, as indicated by the ritual cleansing of one's hands upon leaving the grounds, and a place apart from life, as shown by the traditional absence of flowers and plant growth, it may also be a site for magical beseeching. Trachtenberg points out the custom of visiting deceased relatives and scholars to request their intercession to avert evil on earth. Indeed, the Remu grave site is a place where people leave written notes with prayers and wishes (*kvitl*). Cemeteries, Trachtenberg observes, are places to visit on certain occasions so "that the dead may beseech mercy on our behalf" (J. Trachtenberg 1939, 64–65). Befitting the power of spirits of the dead, grave inscriptions in Ashkenazic tradition became elaborate and, in the case of renowned scholars and *tzaddikim*, their graves became shrines. Folklorist Dov Noy (1954) identifies the perception of the meaningfulness of the grave in Jewish culture with the talmudic motif of "Return from dead to punish disturber of grave" (E235.6). Ben-Amos (2011, 146) points out the precedents of biblical narratives that involve punishing domineering individuals who threaten or rob sacred objects (1 Kings 13:4–6; 2 Maccabees 3).

That the spirits did not provide protection or return to punish Nazi destroyers of graves and synagogues is one of the running commentaries that pepper many conversations among Jewish Holocaust survivors. The Remu legend as a narrative of belief may have triggered the arguments I recounted here because it features magical intervention through Jewish spirituality, whereas many survivors report feeling disenchanted with religious faith. If survivors often contest the supernatural content of narratives about the Holocaust, they are nonetheless drawn to the often personalized stories about lost communities and notable figures. There is a sense conveyed in their reminiscences that their communities lie outside history, especially in relation to the settings of the concentration camps. Therefore, in memorial books and oral gatherings, they use narrative to signify their experience. For example, reflecting on her collections of narratives from Holocaust survivors, Haya Bar-Itzhak notes, "The survivors' sense of commitment to their dead and their community produces a sense of obligation to tell their stories and that of the community, which includes the story of its synagogue" (Bar-Itzhak 2001, 155). She gives as an example a narrative collected in Israel that recalls the glory of the Jewish synagogue on the Polish landscape and laments its destruction.

> The ancient synagogue in our town was built more than 900 years ago. They built it over a period of several years but were unable to finish it. Suddenly a Jew appeared from far away. No one knew who he was or where he had come from. He pledged to the community leaders that he would complete the synagogue. When the construction was complete the man abruptly disappeared. The next day the congregation found all the money the community council had paid him for his work in a corner of the synagogue. People said he was none other than King David, may his merit defend us and all Israel, who built this splendid synagogue, for it was impossible that normal flesh and blood, a *gevayntlikher mensch* [common man], could build such a glorious holy place. I myself cannot believe that I ever merited to see with my own eyes this remarkable and magnificent synagogue, which had all the hues and colors of the sun and the moon and the rainbow. And when I remember and call to mind the Great Synagogue, the ancient synagogue in our town, which was destroyed by the Germans, may their name be blotted out, then my eyes shed tears because the enemy has overcome; my sighs are many and my heart is sick. (Bar-Itzhak 2001, 155–56)

Although the teller is removed from the place of the synagogue, it is important to narrate the structure to give "a spiritual and theological seal of approval to the community's presence in Poland" (Bar-Itzhak 2001, 156). King David as a dramatis persona is ancestral; he is the greatest king and hero of Israel and is aggressively powerful. The Remu legend also provides an ancestral reference to somewhere the narrators have been, and it assures listeners that even if Jews are now most visible on the Polish landscape as graves, they are still protected from opponents. Bar-Itzhak contextualizes the telling of miraculous events in a post-Holocaust setting, far removed from Poland, as narrative efforts to tell about survivors' self and community with the themes she identifies as "destruction, eulogy, and lament" (156).

Yet when I heard the Remu stories, they offered less separation from the past than the destruction stories that Bar-Itzhak summarizes. The Remu narratives certainly refer to the annihilation in the Holocaust and the separation of pre- and post-Holocaust experience. They also offer a parable of Jewish persistence. And whereas Bar-Itzhak heard in her tellers' performances an editorializing about Jewish revival in Eretz Yisrael (Hebrew: the land of Israel), I understood from the commentaries on the Remu story a connection to the Diaspora. I heard the Remu narrative most often from Yiddish speakers who still felt some sense of connection, culturally and religiously, to their Polish Jewish past. The locations and characters in the story were significant, for they represented in the speakers' minds the oldest Jewish section with the most ancient synagogues and the most revered religious figures. Yet it was not uncommon for listeners to counter these stories with narratives that echoed Bar-Itzhak's theme of final destruction from which one can never return. Folklore thus acquires *wichtigkeit*, or "weighty importance," because it is a strategy of memorializing the dead and at the same time commenting on the new cultural milieu of the living. Arguments over its content are often about whether closure can be achieved, whether Poland can be left behind, or whether it still holds significance as a Jewish place to which tellers feel compelled to relate.

The attachment of the post-Holocaust narrative to the Remu is not incidental. He has attracted a host of legends set in the pre-Holocaust period, and the location of his synagogue and grave in the vicinity of the most notorious region of the Holocaust—Auschwitz and Płaszów—adds to his post-Holocaust significance. That his synagogue was built as a memorial to his wife, who died prematurely, is significant for its relation to Holocaust victims who died prematurely. Offering Hasidic tales of the Holocaust, Yaffa Eliach writes, "As I walk down the streets of Cracow I feel as if I am stepping on the dead. Each cobblestone is a skull, a Jewish face. Cracow's violated synagogues are habitations of ghosts. Cracow, the first Jewish settlement on Polish soil, the center of Jewish creativity, of law and Hasidic lore, is now a town with virtually no living Jews. Only a handful remain here, more dead than the clouds above Auschwitz and neighboring Plaszow" (Eliach 1988, 210).

In pre-Holocaust legendry the Remu has an additional connection to mysticism and legends of supernatural power because he was renowned for studying Kabbalah and commented on magical powers (Shulman 1991). Although he could be critical of unlettered people who engaged in mystical speculation, the Remu wrote on the roots of magical arts from God and nature and observed that material things can be endowed with occult virtues and powers (J. Trachtenberg 1939, 20–21; Unterman 1991, 101–2). Beyond the Remu's association with magic, he was also the codifier, sometimes called the Maimonides of Polish Jewry, and was known for his commentaries on the folk customs of Ashkenazic Jews in a positive light unlike other rabbis who derided community practices and beliefs in favor of an elite standardized vision of Jewish law. He thus represented an advocate for ordinary people carrying on with their lives as a Jew in Poland.

The Remu and his grave occupied a special place because of his stature as a *tzaddik*, or miracle-working rabbi. Yiddish folklorist Y. L. Cahan collected a legend in Poland concerning a poor man who asked to buy a plot near the Remu's grave because of its magical association. The caretaker took the man's money but buried him in a different plot, far from the Remu. The dead man's ghost appeared in the caretaker's dreams and disturbed him. After consulting with a rabbi, the caretaker honored his promise and reburied the man near the Remu. Mysteriously, the grave of the buried man collapsed in on itself (Cahan 1938, 152–53; see also B. S. Weinreich 1988, 338).

The Remu's saintly role is significant, according to Bar-Itzhak, because, whereas "the divinity . . . is an amorphous force in Judaism, the saint serves as a means of religious identification for the members of the community who are unable to identify with the divine force or can do so only through the saintly mediator" (Bar-Itzhak 1990, 207). Thus the poor man in Cahan's story seeks a place near the Remu. Frequently, a key feature of such legends about Jewish miracle-working rabbis is the saint as a hero who offers passive but profound resistance to persecution. The saintly hero uses spiritual or intellectual power to act for a people who are apparently powerless to combat violent attacks themselves. There can be a range of legendary explanations of resistance, from Rabbi Akiva Ben-Yosef's martyrdom, which inspired an insurrection against the Romans, to Yemenite Rabbi Shalom Shabazi's turning from his plowing to destroy the governor's palace. In the latter narrative, which Bar-Itzhak uses as an example of the Jewish saint's legend, "The governor, who was secretly plotting to deal unjustly with the Jews, saw the great power of Shabazi and recanted, and abandoned the wicked plot he had intended to carry out" (209).

The Remu legend combines reference to the saintly intervener with the pre-Holocaust legend of place. Like many pre-Holocaust narratives of synagogues connected to the place legend, it brings out the "uniqueness, beauty, and sanctity" of community and its religious center (Bar-Itzhak 2001, 134). It also locates a shadowy, extra-religious realm of belief connected to life in Poland. It offers an experience of a specific location. But in its post-Holocaust context, the story relies on a memory of place and the realization of a community's destruction. Its reference to the Nazis is not unique or final, being only one of many parables of Jewish persistence in the face of persecutors from the Romans to the Crusaders. The legend of the Remu's grave is a contested narrative, however, when the Holocaust is offered as a historical finality that marks the rise of a new Jewish identity. Its countering version is as much a narrative of explanation as the Remu legend is. The *bedaitung* in both cases comes from the struggle of memory. Not meant to be passed on to youth, the Remu story is told in conversation among elderly Yiddish speakers to record a connection to spiritual resistance, if not continuity with a younger generation.

THE LIEBERMAN SYNDROME

Narrating Jewishness in American Political Culture

Weeks after the 2000 U.S. presidential election between Al Gore and George W. Bush, the outcome was still uncertain. The ultimate winner depended on the result of the contested vote count in the state of Florida, home to the nation's third largest population of Jews. Much of the speculation in Florida centered on the impact that Gore's vice presidential running mate, Joseph Lieberman, a self-identifying observant Modern Orthodox Jew, would have on the substantial Jewish vote in southern Florida, especially when election officials revealed that many votes in Palm Beach County, home to one-third of all of Florida's Jewish voters, were disqualified (Reisner 2000). Although American political observers assumed that Lieberman would boost Democratic chances of winning in Florida's vote, the Democratic campaign managers worried about the negative effect of lingering anti-Semitism in the nation's heartland, which would sway voters away from the Gore-Lieberman ticket. Political insiders voiced concern about the choice of Lieberman even before Gore named him as his running mate. Ed Rendell, chairman of the National Democratic Committee, who identified himself as Jewish, responded to rumors about the breakthrough of a Jewish candidate on the national stage by saying, "[If] Lieberman was Episcopalian I think he'd almost be a slam dunk, [but] I don't think anyone can calculate the effect of having a Jew on the ticket" (Foltin 2001, 148). But calculate pollsters and columnists did, and

questions about Lieberman's political influence and the significance of his Jewish
background raged throughout the year. Over and over, commentators across various media publicly speculated on the "Lieberman factor," which was code for
public response to his Orthodox Jewish identity, and they provided narratives of
potential scenarios in which conflicts between piety and executive responsibilities
might come into play (C. Smith 2000).

Promotional literature pointed to Lieberman's religious faith to underscore
his morality (Singular 2000). Voters' perception of Lieberman's candidacy could
be described both as the response of a national Christian majority to Jewish identity and, alternatively, as a Jewish response, as a minority group, to the challenge
of a public, political Jewishness. I argue that Lieberman's presentation of himself
as religiously and publicly Jewish turned the "factor" of a public Jew to a narrated
"syndrome" of conflicted identity for American Jews. In rabbis' sermons, in oral
circulating folklore, and in editorials in the Jewish press, the theme leaped uncomfortably to the fore.

NARRATING PUBLIC AND
PRIVATE JEWISHNESS

The timing of the verbal wrangling at the dawn of a new century and a new
millennium, when there was much speculation about the fragile future of American Jewish culture, was not lost on most speakers and writers. For example, consider this poignant sermon from Reform rabbi Richard Agler, speaking on Rosh
Hashanah weeks before the election in the heart of Florida's voting battleground.
Titling his sermon "On Faith—Public," the rabbi expounded on the racialized
theme of "passing" to his congregation.

> For decades, and longer, in the U.S., the conventional Jewish wisdom has
> been symbolized by a phrase that we almost never utter, but have somehow
> all internalized: "try to pass." And we can see why we don't say it, we prob-
> ably try not to even think it. It's ugly. It's disgraceful. It's self-denying. But
> we have to admit, it's part of what most every American Jew does. "Try to
> pass." Not to stick out. Not to identify too publicly, too obviously, with
> who and what we are. Not to be, as the other infamous phrase has it, "too
> Jewish." And we understand why. It hasn't always been easy to get through
> American life as a Jew. Our neighbors haven't always been so enlightened

on the subject. And we've spent no small number of hours on psychologists' couches because of this denial of self identity. . . . We understand this
too: Even though America is supposed to be the melting pot—"Give us
your tired, your poor, your huddled masses yearning to breathe free, the
wretched refuse of your teeming shore, I lift my lamp beside the golden
door." Even though a nice Jewish girl wrote that and it's on the Statue of
Liberty, it was only half the deal. The other half, never stated, certainly
not so eloquently and not inscribed on any statues, was: if you want to
get much past the lamp and door and into the living room, you'd better
leave the "wretched refuse" business outside. Clean yourself up, look like
an American, speak like one, live like one. In other words, "pass." Don't be
"too Jewish." And we did, and we have, and we've done as well and better
than other group that has come to these shores in the process. You *vant* to
be a real *Yenkee*? Then pass. (Agler 2000)

The dialect ending of this passage generalizes to the American Jewish experience the master narrative of the great wave of Yiddish-speaking immigrants who
came from Eastern Europe around the turn of the twentieth century and
who encouraged professional success in later Americanized generations (see chapter 9). Yet with the turn of the twenty-first century, the question raised by the
rabbi and by Lieberman is how much of that public display of ethnic identity
should be sacrificed for the American promise of success. If the worry politically
was that the appeal of Jews appeared too particularistic to a general American
audience, then Lieberman offered during the campaign an odd connection—at
least to many Jews with a liberal political tradition—to the politics of a more public role for religion often espoused by the Christian right.

Indeed, the two surprises of the election were arguably the accolades, especially from Christian conservatives, for Lieberman's campaign and the conflicted
reception from Jewish organizations. Much of the news of Lieberman's candidacy was not anti-Semitic responses, as many Jewish organizations feared, but
the question of assimilated passing in public and a private persona for Jews.
During the campaign, Lieberman became a lightning rod, not just for denominational questions about the consistency of his religious observance but, even
more divisively, for his stance on the challenge to the traditional Jewish separation of publicly acting American and privately assuming an ethnic we-ness
(Shribman 2001).

Lieberman called generally for a necessary public role for religion and specifically for more assertive ethnic display of Jews and connections with other faith-based groups, including Christian conservatives. In folklore recycled in rabbis' sermons and recirculated around the dinner table, in columns of Jewish journals, and in pronouncements from Jewish organizations, the social divisiveness became increasingly apparent through the campaign, even if ultimately in the voting booth Jews held firm to their traditional Democratic voting pattern.

In the years before the 2000 election, Jewish organizations were still buzzing about the 1990 National Jewish Population Survey that found declining Jewish affiliation in the United States (S. Goldstein 1992). The survey attracted great attention from Jewish media and organizations because comprehensive demographic studies are rare in America; information from the U.S. Census is not helpful because it does not track religious affiliation, and other surveys have the daunting challenge of defining Jewishness as well as locating and counting Jews of secular and religious stripes (S. Goldstein 1992, 78–82; J. R. Marcus 1990). Following on the heels of the previous national profile in 1970–1971, called the National Jewish Population Study, the 1990 survey caused a stir by pointing to a high rate of intermarriage, which raised concerns for the sustainability of Jewish identity in new generations, and a dispersal of the Jewish population, which indicated a positive trend toward more geographic and social mobility for Jews but also a fear of losing the sense of a tightly knit Jewish community.

Sparking anew the dialectic over who is a Jew, the 1990 survey reported that in 20 years identification with secularism had increased, and the rise was especially dramatic among younger generations. The survey found that 20.3 percent of the Jewish population identified as secular Jews; the median age for secular Jews was 29.9 years, whereas for religious Jews it was 39.3 years. Surveying the practices of Jews, the 1990 study found that secular Jews were not likely to be synagogue members, go to Israel, fast on Yom Kippur, or belong to Jewish organizations, but they identified culturally (in appreciation of literature, food, music, and arts), ethnically (i.e., they socialized with other Jews), or emotionally. With fewer foreign-born Jews associating with Jewish immigrant "homelands" present in the population, a trend toward Americanization was apparent. Americanization suggested an increasing integration into American society, and a resulting primary identification with American culture rather than with "being Jewish." In sum, the 1990 survey showed that Jewish identity had become more fluid and fragile than had been supposed previously. In the American Jewish press and in Jewish organizational work, "identity" and "continuity" became keywords to focus on at home for the suddenly unsure future of American Jewish ethnic life.

A question about those organizations affecting Jewish identification is whether they are religious (usually thought of as a private association) or political (considered part of public life). The split between public and private life has been a widespread response since the nineteenth century to the apparent need to gain acceptance by the dominant Christian society to achieve commercial and social success in modernizing America. With this split, one could succeed in civic life in a predominantly non-Jewish society while retaining a Jewish identity, albeit privatized. Since the 1990s, however, a growing Modern Orthodox movement challenged this notion and called for revitalization of Jewish community and ritual practices without the stigma of a ghetto image (Berman 2001; Eleff 2016). Referring to the ability of other ethnic-religious groups to locate social standing in a diverse or multicultural society, many Modern Orthodox leaders called for a more public profile for Jewish identity, one that would be comfortable in the middle-class suburban enclave, in which Jewish practices would be accommodated and the psychological pattern of ethnic self-hatred for a marginal status would be broken. Tying Lieberman's candidacy to this movement, one rabbi observed, "We've seen a profound change in attitude, so that we can be both Jews at home and Jews in the street" (Foltin 2001, 150). A conflict between the approaches to maintaining Jewish continuity could be discerned in the demographic evidence from the late twentieth century to the early twenty-first century: The two fastest growing wings of Judaism were the divergent poles of Orthodox and Reform (Pew Research Center 2013).

It is the struggle to reconcile public and private roles in modern American Jewish identity that is at the heart of what I call the Lieberman syndrome. The condition epitomized by Joseph Lieberman's labored explanation of himself as a participant-citizen in the American polity despite his Orthodox Jewish belief and practice brought together an intricate group of signs, some may say symptoms, that collectively showed unease about the changing role of Jews and Jewishness in American civic life. It is at bottom a worry about being public with ethnic display. The *Jewish Forward* described the concern in the tamer language of the "Lieberman Balancing Act," one highlighting tensions between faith and politics, for Lieberman was repeatedly accused of sacrificing political centrism and religious traditionalism at the first hint of trouble (Eden 2000c). Amid the celebration by Jews of an ethnic breakthrough into politics was a deep angst about the diminishing meaning of being Jewish and the fragmentation of the formerly predictable public Jewish vote. Drawing on responses in the Jewish press and polling data, my inquiry related to Jewish cultural studies is to ask how and why, in addressing political culture, Lieberman's campaign narrated and thereby shaped the discourse on the future of public and private Jewishness in American culture.

Although Jews have been governors, senators, and U.S. representatives since the nineteenth century, the Roosevelt administration of the New Deal is often acknowledged as a catalyst to the heightened involvement of Jews in political life and public service. The overarching theme of this political history is that Jews did not seek or were excluded from prominence in government until the last third of the twentieth century. Political analyst L. Sandy Maisel, in the preface to *Jews in American Politics*, concluded that "the Jewish politician, even the Jewish appointed official, was the exception, not the rule. Other immigrant groups—the Irish and the Italians, to be sure—used politics as a means for social advancement. The Jews, by and large, did not" (L. S. Maisel 2001, xii). Writing an introduction to the book, Joseph Lieberman stressed the "public" aspect with which Jews should engage in their religious experience: "I hope this volume will help inspire a new generation of American Jews . . . to dedicate themselves to *public* life and *public* office. A hundred years ago, while some ethnic groups, such as the Irish, thrived in politics, Jewish Americans were not particularly involved in *public* life. This disengagement was strange because of Judaism's emphasis on the individual's responsibility to the community" (Lieberman 2001a, xxi; emphasis added).

Elected in 1989 to the Senate, Joseph Lieberman was the first publicly Orthodox Jew in the history of that body, and his candidacy for vice president raised for public scrutiny the issue of whether his Orthodox observance of the Jewish Sabbath would interfere with his public duties. The strain of this potential conflict represented a central theme of American Jewish identity: maintaining a communal identity while integrating into a society perceived as uncomfortable with many of its values, or at least cultural practices. The irony in this struggle for the preservation of communal identity is that the group's political culture of acceptance encouraged, as Arthur Goren pointed out in *The Politics and Public Culture of American Jews*, support for "the American promise of reward, recognition and acceptance for the deserving individual" (Goren 1999, 13). A split tended to occur between the private and the public Jew. The public Jew joined, in Goren's words, a "higher cosmopolitan fellowship," except for special public events "that marked some auspicious occasion in the life of the people"—mass meetings and rallies, parades, pageants, and other public displays that enabled the participants to affirm a collective identity (7).

The development of a "culture of organizations" beyond the synagogue in the social programming of Jews reinforced this occasional public expression of Jewishness coupled with private commitment. Support for Israel and the many philanthropic organizations devoted to it were one cornerstone of this public culture. Combating anti-Semitism and promoting civil rights for all minorities, particularly through the work of the Anti-Defamation League and the American Jewish Committee, constituted another. If this public activity appeared political, the reference to politics would often be muted. The *American Jewish Yearbook*, begun in the late nineteenth century, did not feature a section on politics until the 1960s, and one of the few conferences devoted to Jewish political culture occurred at the late date of 1989, with a focus then on Eastern Europe (D. D. Moore 1991). As Eli Lederhendler pointed out in his review of modern Jewish politics for *The Modern Jewish Experience* (1993), Jewish cultural history has a rich background, whereas political studies, basic to the diplomatic histories of other groups, is a new field because of the traditional Jewish discomfort with involvement in American politics as practicing Jews.

Narrative humor in American Jewish folklore, often serving the function of expressing peculiar conflicts and dilemmas of Jewish life that may be psychologically troubling, communicates a discomfort with national politics because it requires a public profile. Here are two versions of a common joke told by Jews since at least the 1960s that received new life during the Lieberman campaign.

> The first Jewish President invites his mother to come to Washington for Rosh Hashanah. "But how will I get there," she moans, "It's such a long trip." With frustration, the President replies: "Don't worry, mother, I'll send a limousine to get you in Brooklyn, Air Force One will fly you down here, and then a helicopter will bring you from the Air Force Base right to the lawn of the White House." The truth is, she doesn't want to go, so

she tries to think of more excuses. "You're so busy; what will I do after services, when you're talking to all those generals and senators?" The President, now exasperated, replies childishly: "Look, mother, you've gone to my brother's house every year since I've been in office. I want you to come here for Rosh Hashanah this year. I promise, barring national emergency, that I will take the whole day off to be with you and the family." Finally, mother relents. She will go to the White House for Rosh Hashanah. A week before the holiday, one of her friends asks her about her plans for the holiday. "I'm going to be with my son and his family," she says. "Which one?" her friend asks eagerly. "The doctor?" "No," she sighs, "the other one." (Block 2000)

Many years ago, a story was making the rounds about the first Jewish person elected to the Presidency of the United States. The most significant obstacle that President-elect Schwartz seemed to face was a mother who didn't want to leave North Miami Beach for the January inauguration in Washington D.C. With much coaxing and encouraging, Mrs. Schwartz relented, and took her place at the inauguration seat between the Secretary of Defense and Secretary of the Treasury. As her son approached the lectern, preparing to be sworn in by the Chief Justice of the Supreme Court, Mrs. Schwartz turned to the Secretary of State and whispered, "Do you see that young man up there? His brother is a doctor!" (Smason 2000).

One may read in these humorous narratives the incongruous conclusion that Jews, or the folk type of the overprotective Jewish mother often associated with the older immigrant generation, consider the doctor preferable to the eminent position of president of the United States. One might further comment that the doctor provides success *and* privacy, whereas the president may appear too public or *goyishe* (taking the manners of the non-Jewish host society). Lieberman himself engaged in self-deprecating humor that made reference to the public perception of a Jew not belonging in politics. On talk shows during the campaign, he regularly liked to quip that he would advocate a policy of a "matzo ball in every soup" instead of the clichéd promise of a "chicken in every pot" in Republican Herbert Hoover's presidential campaign of 1928 (Halloran 2000; Millman 2000).[1] Lieberman also joked that Air Force Two might be renamed Air Force Two Sets of Dishes and suggested, tongue-in-cheek, new slogans for the national ticket: "Gore-Lieberman: No Bull, No Pork" and "With Malice Toward None and a Little Guilt Toward Everyone" (Halloran 2000). The incongruity of the humor was the idea of normative American institutions taking an ethnic turn. One commentator for the *Jewish Forward* complained, "Mr. Lieberman's Borscht Belt, lox and bagels clowning treats Judaism as a collection of neuroses and idiosyncrasies" (Troy 2000, 9). He preferred to have Lieberman run as the best candidate and not the best Jew for the job and ironically cited a traditional Jewish story to make his point.

> The first Jew appointed to a Cabinet post was Oscar Straus. In an oft-told but probably tall tale, shortly after President Theodore Roosevelt appointed Straus to be Secretary of Commerce and Labor almost 100 years ago, Jewish leaders feted Straus and Roosevelt at a banquet. Telling the crowd just what it wanted to hear, Roosevelt thundered: "I didn't appoint Oscar Straus because he is or isn't a Jew, I appointed him because he is the best man for the job!" The president turned to the venerable, and hearing-impaired, German-Jewish banker Jacob Schiff to confirm the story. "Dot's right, Mr. President!" Schiff is said to have exclaimed. "You came to me and said, 'Chake, who is der best Jew I can appoint Secretary of Commerce?'" (Troy 2000, 9)

The fear is there in this telling that Jews give the appearance of being no different publicly but that privately they are regarded as distinctively Jewish and uncomfortable with presenting themselves as being called out by non-Jews for their Jewishness (and associated stereotypes). In reference to Lieberman, the Gore campaign frequently made the point that Lieberman's religion should not be an issue in how people vote or how the vice presidential choice was made, but comments made by Lieberman himself revealed that it had indeed become an issue.

RESPONDING TO AN ORTHODOX JEW ON A NATIONAL TICKET

The central theme in studies of American political culture—of the traditional split in public organizational causes and private search for meaning, often secular—provides the context for the worried reaction of the premier national Jewish newspaper, the *Jewish Forward*, to the announcement of Lieberman's selection to the Democratic ticket. Although the headline reporting Gore's choice of Lieberman for vice president declared that Jews were "electrified," a rare front-page editorial on August 11, 2000, as the campaign was gearing up for the traditional post–Labor Day push, nervously commented, "Many of us would rather understate the event" ("Vice-Presidential Values," 2000). The question is, then, Why, if the choice is of such great magnitude? The editors' explanation was that "the ambivalence is understandable. Jews have long preferred to downplay their successes, for fear of invoking the evil eye. Pragmatically, we seek a low profile in society, so as not to attract hostile attention. For all our achievements, one never knows when the Cossacks will come. A Jewish Vice-President could be just the spark needed to ignite the flames" (*Forward* Staff 2000). The editorial made reference to fear of pogroms in the Russian Pale of Settlement that caused many Jews to immigrate to America from 1880 to 1924, when the United States government, in an action that many historians viewed as based on anti-Semitism, imposed quota-based immigration restrictions on Jews from Eastern Europe (Marinari 2019).

Earlier during the primary season, a front-page column by Seth Gittell (2000) in the *Jewish Forward* speculated that Gore could easily pick Senator Diane Feinstein of California or Senator Joseph Lieberman of Connecticut. Feinstein had been on Walter Mondale's short list of vice presidential candidates in 1980, but Mondale backed away from making the choice of a self-identifying Jewish woman (Gittell 1998). Although Feinstein had been ahead for the vice presidential spot on the paper's scorecard, Gittell reported that Lieberman was closing fast. Lieberman had lobbied Jewish newspapers with a letter stating, "Vice-President Gore is a leader the Jewish community can count on to encourage tolerance and equality" (Gittell 2000). The paper was impressed that Gore had once offered up his parents' Capitol Hill apartment to Lieberman so that the Sabbath observer did not have to spend a Friday night on a camp bed in the Senate gym. Lieberman's political stands discomforted the paper, however. He opposed clemency for Jonathan Pollard, favored school voucher programs, antagonized the organized labor lobby, and challenged the traditional Jewish line in the stand on separation of church and state. If he was not the paper's choice for symbolizing Jewish political culture, he nonetheless forced consideration of Jewishness in public life for Jews and non-Jews alike.

Although Gore publicly claimed that Lieberman's religious background had no bearing on his choice of a running mate, he must have considered the implications. Previous national presidential aspirations of Jewish candidates Milton Shapp in 1976 and Arlen Specter in 1996, both from Pennsylvania, did not play well in the Iowa and New Hampshire primaries, but speculation ran high in the Gore campaign that Lieberman could help in the potential swing states of Florida, Illinois, and Pennsylvania. Some insiders worried that Lieberman would be a liability in Michigan, which had the nation's largest Arab American population (Gore ultimately took the state in the election). An NBC News/Wall Street Journal poll taken before the 2000 conventions revealed that overall 92 percent of the public would be accepting of a Jewish candidate (released September 18, 2000). Yet, even though this number was seen as a sign of improving attitudes toward the public roles of Jews, the same poll revealed the highest percentage of negative responses among Black and Latinx voters (12 percent and 19 percent, respectively), and they were considered core constituents of the Democratic coalition. Despite the lack of a national Jewish political candidate up to that point, 15 percent of the population felt that religious Jewish organizations had too much power, perhaps offset by the 31 percent who thought that religious Christian organizations had too much influence on government and politics.

Looking at exit polls in political history leading up to the 2000 election, religion and ethnicity were not guarantees of backing from a candidate's ethnic group. In 1960 a higher percentage of Jews than Roman Catholics voted for John F. Kennedy, and in 1988 more Jews than Greeks voted for Michael Dukakis, a second-generation Greek American (Shapiro 2001, 199). The presumed solidly liberal Jewish vote, representing those identifying themselves as Jewish in voter exit polls, went for Democratic candidates, but shapers of the Democratic coalition were concerned about the lasting effects of Republican Ronald Reagan's and George H. W. Bush's inroads among Jews in national elections. From a high of 90 percent of the Jewish vote for Democratic candidate Lyndon Johnson in 1964, candidates George McGovern (1972), Jimmy Carter (1976, 1980), Walter Mondale (1984), and Michael Dukakis (1988) could never top 67 percent of the Jewish vote. In a comparison of voting trends since 1916, one can see the Jewish vote becoming mobilized for Democrat Franklin Roosevelt in the 1930s and holding steady until the Eisenhower campaigns of the 1950s and a prolonged period in the Reagan-Bush years of the 1970s and 1980s (see Table 1).

TABLE 1. Jewish Voting Patterns in Presidential Elections, 1916–2000

* became president as result of election

Year	Democratic candidate and percentage of Jewish vote	Republican candidate and percentage of Jewish vote	Other candidate and percentage of Jewish vote
1916	W. Wilson* (55)	C. Hughes (45)	
1920	J. Cox (19)	W. Harding* (43)	E. Debs (38)
1924	J. Davis (51)	C. Coolidge* (27)	R. La Follette (22)
1928	A. Smith (72)	H. Hoover* (28)	
1932	F. Roosevelt* (82)	H. Hoover (18)	
1936	F. Roosevelt* (85)	A. Landon (15)	
1940	F. Roosevelt* (90)	W. Willkie (10)	
1944	F. Roosevelt* (90)	T. Dewey (10)	
1948	H. Truman* (75)	T. Dewey (10)	H. Wallace (15)
1952	A. Stevenson (64)	D. Eisenhower* (36)	
1956	A. Stevenson (60)	D. Eisenhower* (40)	
1960	J. Kennedy* (90)	R. Nixon (10)	
1964	L. Johnson* (90)	B. Goldwater (10)	
1968	H. Humphrey (81)	R. Nixon* (17)	G. Wallace (2)
1972	G. McGovern (64)	R. Nixon* (34)	
1976	J. Carter* (64)	G. Ford (34)	
1980	J. Carter (45)	R. Reagan* (39)	J. Anderson (15)
1984	W. Mondale (67)	R. Reagan* (31)	
1988	M. Dukakis (64)	G. H. W. Bush* (35)	
1992	W. Clinton* (80)	G. H. W. Bush (11)	R. Perot (9)
1996	W. Clinton* (78)	R. Dole (16)	R. Perot (3)
2000	A. Gore (79)	G. W. Bush* (19)	R. Nader (1)

The basis of the Democratic coalition was an appeal to labor interests, civil rights, and urban renewal that affected Jews as one of many disenfranchised, mainly urban ethnic groups; in addition, Jews influenced the party to have a strong foreign policy stand on support for Israel. Democrats usually backed the separation of church and state, which was important to Jews, whereas Republicans were associated with Christian conservatives calling for prayer in the schools, school voucher programs supporting religious schools, and government support for faith-based charities. But Reagan Republicans made a pitch to a growing number of business-class Jews that free-market economic policies would be in their interest, and they challenged the assumption that Democrats would unconditionally support Israel, particularly during the Clinton campaigns of 1992 and 1996. Republicans often insisted that they stood for religious tolerance and a civil society that had eroded under the Clinton administration. George W. Bush's campaign featured prominent Jews who had been Reagan aides, such as senior adviser and spokesman Ari Fleischer, policy director Joshua Bolten, and foreign policy advisers Dov Zakheim, Richard Perle, and Paul Wolfowitz (Donadio 2000). A host for the Republican convention was Pennsylvania senator Arlen Specter, who identified as a Jew. These aides and host, however, did not make public avowals of their religion as Lieberman did. Although the convention prominently featured Blacks, women, and Latinxs as speakers, the alliance between Blacks and Jews in the Democratic Party appeared to unravel as reports of African American anti-Semitism grew and Jewish organizations and Jewish candidates such as Lieberman criticized affirmative action policies (Brooks 2002).

Conventional political wisdom held that the vice presidential choice should offer regional balance on the national ticket, especially to bring in states with a large number of electoral votes. Since Walter Mondale chose Geraldine Ferraro as his Democratic running mate in 1984, the first woman to run for national office for a major party, political analysts have speculated that the vice presidential slot could also be used to appeal to women and minorities, and in 2020 presidential candidate Joe Biden chose Kamala Harris as the first woman with an African American and South Asian background to run for vice president on a national ticket. Reportedly, none of the prospects on Biden's short list identified as Jews, although Harris's husband was Jewish. During the 2000 presidential campaign, African American activist Jesse Jackson's name was floated as a possible running mate for the Democrats and Colin Powell came up as a candidate for the Republicans (George W. Bush later selected him as secretary of state). In response to the media's reporting of Black and Latinx anti-Semitism and disappointment in Lieberman's nomination, several African American leaders publicly announced that the choice of Lieberman was significant as a nod to American minorities generally (Buchanan 2000; Duke 2000a, 2000b; Jordan 2000). Jesse Jackson, who years earlier had been criticized for uttering an anti-Semitic slur, said at a news conference after the Lieberman nomination at his Rainbow/PUSH Coalition headquarters, "Let the nation rejoice. The tent is getting bigger and better. Gore rejected a pattern of discrimination that has limited the political opportunities of minorities." Jackson was a minister who frequently cited religion in his own political campaigns, and he emphasized, "As Americans, whether Catholic, Jewish, or Protestant, we live in our faith, and we live under the law—the Constitution. Senator Lieberman has remained true to this standard" (Buchanan 2000).

In an interview with a radio station oriented toward an African American audience in September 2000, Lieberman expressed words of respect for Nation of Islam leader Louis Farrakhan, who had been under press scrutiny for stirring anti-Semitism among Blacks, and offered to meet with Farrakhan on racial and religious conciliation. Even though this gesture was seen as a continuation of the outreach to the Black community that he had begun at the Democratic convention, Lieberman's remarks drew responses of outrage from many Jewish organizations. The American Jewish Committee proclaimed that "by virtue of his statements and his extremist positions, . . . he has not earned a place at the table in terms of discussions of race relations or public policy" (Foltin 2001, 155). One of those statements was Farrakhan's assertion that as a Jew, Lieberman could not be trusted to be loyal to the United States in a conflict with Israel. Many African American audiences were concerned about Lieberman's past criticism of affirmative action, and Lieberman cited his civil rights voting record and assured Black organizations that he would support Gore's positive proposals for continuing racial preference programs. Facing cool reactions from African American audiences, Lieberman turned to the common ground of advocating for a more public role of religion in American life when he spoke to Black organizations.

That Lieberman would not hold back on setting religion as paramount in his thinking was evident from his first public statements after the nomination. Appearing with Gore in Nashville the day after Gore called him with the offer of being on the ticket, he told the audience:

> I ask you to allow me to let the spirit move me as it does to remember the words from Chronicles, which are to give thanks to God, to give thanks to God and declare his name and make his acts known to the people, to be glad of spirit, to sing to God and to make music to God and most of all, to give glory and gratitude to God from whom all blessings do truly fall. Dear Lord, maker of all miracles, I thank you for bringing me to this extraordinary moment in my life. (Foltin 2001, 152)

Essentially an English version of the traditional Shehechiyanu prayer recited on special occasions, Lieberman followed these comments with his acceptance speech at the Democratic convention, clearly referencing his Jewishness in an American context. He thanked the nation for allowing one of its Jewish sons to have the opportunity to run, and he compared the acceptance of his grandparents by American Christian neighbors with the experience of his wife's parents, who were Holocaust survivors. Apparently asking for tolerance of his beliefs among the nation's youth, Lieberman was answered with standing ovations. The speech opened with the question, "Is America a great country or what?" and concluded with "Only in America" (Foltin 2001, 150).[2] Lieberman's Jewish wife, Hadassah, had preceded him at the podium and had connected her husband's religious beliefs to the American values of "family, faith, congregation, and neighborhood" (150).

A Newsweek poll released on August 10 suggested that having Lieberman on the ticket convinced 49 percent of Americans that Gore "is a man of faith and strong moral values." Other polls reported that the majority of Americans thought that Lieberman would help Gore. Jews at the time were not so much of a factor in this rise because they already were surveyed as predisposed to supporting Gore. What was it, then, that the public thought of Lieberman? A Fox News poll conducted shortly after the selection (August 9, 2000), asked, "In discussions with your friends and co-workers about (Al) Gore's selection of Joseph Lieberman as his 2000 Vice presidential running mate, what is usually the first thing that comes up about Lieberman?" The leading answer with 26 percent was simply "He's Jewish," followed by 20 percent noting, "He was the first Democratic Senator to criticize Clinton during the Lewinsky scandal" (for Lieberman's role in condemning fellow Democrat Bill Clinton in the Lewinsky scandal, see Busby [2001, 106–10]). Only 14 percent picked "his position on the issues." In fact, although few voters could identify Gore's religion, 64 percent knew Lieberman's (Gallup Poll, August 24, 2000).

It should be noted that the polls did not always agree on whether Lieberman's Jewishness would be a significant factor in the election. A poll on August 9 by Fox News revealed a disturbing 17 percent of the public choosing "less likely" to the question, "Do you think people you know will be more or less likely to vote for the Gore–Lieberman ticket because Senator Lieberman is Jewish?" A Time/CNN poll found that those Americans feeling a negative effect amounted to 3 percent. The same poll revealed higher negative numbers when people were asked about "the people in your area"; 15 percent responded they would be less likely. That figure suggests that respondents were hesitant to admit their own prejudices but suspected others of being less tolerant.

After the initial bounce for the Gore ticket that some media commentators said was caused by Lieberman's qualities as an honest and personable candidate, the gap in the polls between Gore and Bush tightened and questions were raised anew about the influence of Lieberman's public Jewishness on the electorate. A month after the selection of Lieberman, 17 percent of Americans considered Lieberman's religion and religious beliefs a "problem" (NBC News, September 18, 2000). Even after the election, disputes about the interpretation of exit polls concerning the Lieberman factor still raged. It was alternately reported that Lieberman did not add as many votes to the ticket as predicted among Jews or that he helped make Florida much closer than predicted (Foltin 2001, 155).

Besides these questions of the public perception of Lieberman's Jewishness, there were queries of his practices and beliefs that differed from other candidates. Surprising many pollsters, Lieberman's influence on foreign policy regarding Israel did not loom as large as expected. An NBC News/Wall Street Journal poll reported that national registered voters a month into the campaign rated the following statements of concern about Lieberman in this order:

- 14 percent: He does not believe in Jesus Christ as Lord and Savior.
- 10 percent: He will be too close to Israel on foreign policy.
- 10 percent: He brings too much religion into politics.
- 6 percent: I am worried that the Jewish establishment has too much influence on the Democratic Party.
- 5 percent: As an Orthodox Jew, he will not do work on Saturdays.

If Lieberman's lack of acceptance of "Christ as Lord" caused concern among Christians (the Time/CNN poll had the figure at 40 percent as "concerned" compared to 42 percent who were "not at all concerned"), his standing on Orthodoxy ironically pleased them. An ABC News/Washington Post poll revealed that 51 percent had a more favorable view of Lieberman, knowing he was an observant Orthodox Jew (16 percent felt less favorable and 34 percent had no opinion). These figures show that Lieberman's public stance on religion struck a responsive chord among voters who viewed a stronger role for religion in public life as an answer to the perceived problem of moral decline and increased incivility in American society. Nervous about the extreme-sounding label of "Orthodox," however,

Lieberman's aides early in the campaign promoted the candidate as "observant" rather than "Orthodox," even though Lieberman was a board member of the Union of Orthodox Jewish Congregations of America (Yudelson 2000).

But what of the differences between Jewish and Christian practice, such as Sabbath observance on Saturday, professed by Lieberman? Although Lieberman's Sabbath observance was the subject of many newspaper articles, the public response varied. Answering the question "If Joseph Lieberman were to become Vice-President, would you be very concerned, somewhat concerned, not very concerned, about . . . the possibility that he would not be able to fulfil some of his duties because they occurred on religious holidays or the Jewish Sabbath," 33 percent of respondents were either somewhat or very concerned in a Time/CNN poll (August 9, 2000), and 11 percent were somewhat concerned or concerned a great deal in an ABC News poll (August 7, 2000). If Lieberman did not dress "Orthodox," wear a head covering, or have a beard, the public awareness of Jewish difference was his Sabbath observance, and it was this difference that tested voter tolerance. This observance became more important to non-Jews as a sign of Jewishness than it did for Jews.

And the Jewish response? The American Jewish Committee asked a sample of Jews in its annual survey of Jewish opinion for 2000 about approval of Gore's "choice" of Lieberman: 90 percent affirmed. Significantly, the survey did not ask about his public stands on integrating faith into civic life. Yet the survey included other queries that could be interpreted as going against Lieberman's cause. Asked whether an increased emphasis in America on separate group identity divides or enriches society, 63 percent thought it would divide. In the 2001 survey the question was reworded to ask whether immigrants should be encouraged to blend into American culture by giving up some important aspects of their own culture, or whether they should be encouraged to maintain their own culture more strongly, even if that means they do not blend in as well. Probably reflecting the master narrative of the immigrant experience from Eastern Europe, the response was 59 percent encouraging immigrants to blend in, to 31 percent to maintain their own culture. Further evidence of this assimilationist stance is that 68 percent in the poll opposed government aid to parochial or other religious schools, although a Modern Orthodox initiative in the 1990s was the establishment of Jewish day schools and support for governmental voucher systems to support parents' costs.

Lieberman's public notoriety could have been an influence on political poll responses by Jews during his national campaign. From 1999 to 2000, a

7 percent increase occurred in the number of respondents identifying as Democrat. And after declines for some years in the number of individuals saying that being Jewish was "very important" in their lives, corroborated by the 1990 National Jewish Population Survey, the figure climbed from 57 percent to 59 percent. The highest proportion of "qualities" considered most important to Jewish identity, however, remained steady: "Being part of the Jewish people" at 45 percent, as opposed to 16 percent for "religious observance" and 21 percent for "a commitment to social justice." It was apparent from the survey that a shift was occurring in political culture from public concern for Israel abroad and anti-Semitism at home to more private consideration of the effects of intermarriage and the decline in Jewish education on Jewish identity. To be sure, for some, the public and private realms of these issues are simultaneous. But consider the rise in responses to this question: "In your opinion, which is a greater threat to Jewish life in the USA today—intermarriage or anti-Semitism?" (see Table 2).

TABLE 2. Responses by Jewish Americans to the Question "In your opinion, which is a greater threat to Jewish life in the USA today—intermarriage or anti-Semitism?"

	2000	1999
Intermarriage	41%	32%
Anti-Semitism	50%	62%
Both equally	7%	5%

The dramatic rise in the view of intermarriage as a threat to Jewish life is further evidence of the shift in discourse on Jewish identity from one of combating social obstacles to one of Jewish continuity and community. Lieberman stepped into this fray when he sparked a controversy in the Jewish press by claiming that his religious belief did not prohibit interfaith marriage. The *Jewish Forward* saw it as another example of Lieberman's balancing of faith and politics. His answer, the newspaper reported, shot "a hole in the Jewish community's chief plank in the fight for continuity, while angering many of those who admire the senator's fidelity to *halakha*, or rabbinic canon law" (Eden 2000c).

Jewish response along denominational lines to Lieberman's campaign brought out internal divisions within Jewish political culture that had not surfaced so heatedly previously. The American Jewish Committee survey for 2000 had asked, "Do you think that tensions between Orthodox, Conservative, and Reform Jews in the United States today are a very serious problem, somewhat of a problem, or not a problem at all?" Outdistancing all other responses was "Somewhat of a problem" with 55 percent; 13 percent thought it was a "very serious problem," and 30 percent thought it was "not a problem at all." The survey counted 10 percent of its sample Orthodox, 31 percent Conservative, 31 percent Reform, 2 percent Reconstructionist, and 25 percent "just Jewish," an umbrella category for nonobservant, unaffiliated Jews who nonetheless identify ethnically as Jewish. Voter polls, however, lump religious identities into broad categories of Protestant, Catholic, Muslim, and Jew, so one has to consult interviews, sermons, and denominational publications. My first conclusion from looking at this evidence is that Orthodox Jews were far more critical of Lieberman's Judaism than Conservative and Reform Jews. But the matter of public identity complicates the response and eventual conclusion, for Orthodox spokespersons were also more approving of Lieberman's faith-based policies than Conservative and Reform Jews and certainly more than those who were "just Jewish."

The first denominational response to Lieberman's nomination came from Reform Judaism. Representing the nation's largest Jewish organization, the Religious Action Center of Reform Judaism made sure in its statement to say that Lieberman was the best choice, not just the Jewish choice, but it also recognized his symbolic importance to Jews and other minorities: "For the first time, our children can look at a candidate for the second highest office in the land and see themselves. And we are confident one of the messages in Senator Lieberman's selection—that every American child can believe that, some day, he or she might be President—will be heard clearly, especially in other minority communities" (Religious Action Center of Reform Judaism 2000). Although Reform Judaism gave the most unequivocal approval for Lieberman, in the congregations the question inevitably arose about the implications of Lieberman's Orthodoxy on Reform answers to issues of Jewish practice. Reform Rabbi Barry H. Block in San Antonio, Texas, said bluntly to his congregation shortly after the nomination, "Don't we squirm a bit, as we read about Senator Lieberman? . . . As America learns about Jewish practice, how many of us have felt the need to defend our own Sabbath observance, or lack thereof, to our newly educated Christian friends?" (Block 2000).

Observing Lieberman's adherence to Sabbath restrictions, Block noted that "freedom from the strict limitations of an Orthodox Sabbath might have been

among the greatest motivations for the growth of American Reform Judaism."
Yet many Reform rabbis recognized Lieberman's flexibility on other matters,
such as wearing a head covering, shaking hands with women, and tolerance of
intermarriage, and so Rabbi Block and others gave an endorsement to Lieberman
for living "every day of our lives, with meaning, with integrity, and with faith."
Many Reform sermons interpreted the importance of Lieberman's nomination as
the signal of a new era for Jewish identity. In New York City, for instance, Rabbi
Serge A. Lippe told his congregation, "America, my parents and grandparents
believed, could learn to accept individuals who were Jews, but the price would be
a closeting, a privatization, of our Judaism. And they were probably right, in their
day. But this is a new day, a New Year, and even if this is only the first year of a
new decade by our Jewish calendar, for America this is the beginning of a new era,
a new century, and a new millennium" (Lippe 2001).

The Orthodox Union (2000a) released a statement to the press on August 7,
2000, praising Gore's choice of Lieberman for its basis of talent and integrity
rather than religion. It mentioned the Union's work with Senator Lieberman
on key issues of support for Israel, education reform, and morality in the media.
Other Orthodox spokespersons took more negative positions on Lieberman's
public representation of Orthodox doctrine, and the Union scrambled to restrain
them. Rabbi Mordechai Friedman, of the Union of Orthodox Rabbis, characterized the senator as a traitor for his opposition to the release of Jonathan Pollard,
and the Union condemned his "violent speech" while reaffirming its support
for Pollard's release (Orthodox Union 2000b). The Union joined the United
Synagogue Movement (Conservative) and Agudath Israel of America (Orthodox) in challenging Lieberman's statement on September 20, 2000, that Judaism
does not ban intermarriage. The Union of Orthodox Rabbis, issued a statement
on October 5, with the election a few weeks away, calling on Lieberman not to
appear on the eve of Yom Kippur before the Human Rights Campaign, which
advocates for homosexual rights (Union of Orthodox Rabbis 2000). Another
Orthodox group, Jews for Morality, which opposes homosexuality and abor-
tion, ridiculed Lieberman's Orthodoxy as "counterfeit—ad hoc, ad-lib, a-la-
carte Judaism" (Jews for Morality 2000a). The organization supported a staged
excommunication of the senator by a New York Torah court, the Beth Din (Jews
for Morality 2000b).

Some Modern Orthodox rabbis countered by allowing a range of practice
within Orthodoxy that runs from lenient to stringent interpretation of religious

law. Rabbi Barry Freundel of Kesher Israel, where Lieberman worshipped in Washington, D.C., told an inquiring *New York Times* reporter, "'Modern' means . . . a religious imperative to engage the modern world, the secular world and to take that which is of value in that world and make it part of our world" (Goodstein 2000). The rabbi downplayed Lieberman's need to show his Jewishness by wearing a *kippah*: "He has never wanted to be the Jewish senator. He has wanted to be the senator who happened to be Jewish, and wearing the *kippah* would change the perspective. If you met someone wearing a *kippah*, the Jewishness is immediately on the table. That is not how he wanted to be known" (Goodstein 2000). In his statement, the rabbi pulls back Lieberman's representation of unabashed ethnic display.

Rabbi Aaron Goldscheider, of Etz Chaim Synagogue in Jacksonville, Florida, called Lieberman the "perfect Jew," because "he represents a Jew who can keep his commitment to the faith and still be a part of the world" (Maraghy 2000). Wanting to support Lieberman but not advocate for his religious compromises, Agudath Israel of America, the political wing of Orthodox Judaism, proclaimed, through its director of public affairs, "He's running for Vice president, not Chief Rabbi. Therefore, there might be some things we would consider not thought out from a religious perspective, but we're not here to critique his religious life" (Goodstein 2000). Jewish comedian Jackie Mason and lawyer Raoul Felder, however, answered in the *Jewish World Review* that on both politics and religion, Lieberman "has flipped over more times than a mattress in a hotbed motel" (Mason and Felder 2000). Seeing his inconsistencies in religious observance as indicative of his political compromises on recognizing Jerusalem as the capital of Israel, they sarcastically declared, "Senator Lieberman, who wraps his religious beliefs around him like a flag, apparently subscribes to a new form of Judaism. There is Orthodox Judaism, Conservative Judaism and Reform Judaism. Senator Lieberman belongs to a new sect: Selective Observant Judaism" (Mason and Felder 2000).

The United Synagogue of Conservative Judaism did not issue a statement on Lieberman's candidacy, but its vice president was quoted as saying, "Many committed Conservative and Reform Jews will see this as a very positive empowerment. The fact that Lieberman makes Sabbath observance a priority will resonate well beyond the political" (A. L. Goldman 2000). He echoed the sermons of many Conservative rabbis who commented on the compatibility between Lieberman's brand of Orthodoxy and the spirit of Conservative Judaism. The Conservative movement's magazine *Moment* was also surprisingly silent on Lieberman's campaign, but columnist Michael Berenbaum observed a generational difference of viewpoint among Conservative Jews.

> Older Jews were somewhat hesitant, afraid of the backlash they've come to expect when a Jew becomes too visible, afraid that the good news about the battle against anti-Semitism is not quite as good as we have been led to believe. Middle-aged Jews, on the other hand, were jubilant. Lieberman's acceptance as a candidate for Vice president mirrors their own experience in the workplace and in the community. And my 20-something children wonder, What's the big deal? Full acceptance of Jews is the reality they have experienced from birth. (Berenbaum 2000)

The middle-ground split to which Berenbaum refers was statistically documented in the 2001 American Jewish Committee survey, which asked respondents whether they agreed or disagreed that virtually all positions of influence in the United States were open to Jews. Although 59 percent agreed, 40 percent still felt that many positions were not open to Jews, and this response may explain some of the sensitivity to Lieberman's public ethnic display. Reasserting the centrist position of public display, Conservative Rabbi Arthur Rulnick of Woodbury, New York, sermonized on Rosh Hashanah:

> Joseph Lieberman's success . . . challenges not only the Jewish assimilationists, but at the other extreme, separatists like the Hassidim. Joseph Lieberman's life shows that one can be a devoted Jew even while fully engaging in public life and that one can fully engage in public life while maintaining the traditions that have kept the Jews together and a holy people for three millennia. (Rulnick 2000)

Even though a single organization did not claim to represent the views of "secular" or "cultural" Jews, Michael Steinhardt, chairman of the Jewish Life Network, penned a strong opinion column titled "Giving Voice to a Secular Majority" in the *Jewish Forward* on September 15, 2000. Reviewing the statements from Jewish religious organizations, he expressed outrage that "Gentile Americans seem more comfortable with a Jew in the West Wing than do Jews themselves." While praising Lieberman's strong sense of self-identity, which gets away from the past fear of anti-Semitism, and avoiding public ethnic display, he was concerned about

Lieberman's religious definition of that identity: "We must reorient and revitalize our philanthropy and communal infrastructure to reflect the fact that American Jews are secular, integrated, accepted in American society and determined to remain that way" (Steinhardt 2000; see also Posen 2000).

More than any other issue in the campaign, the extent of Lieberman's Sabbath observance in line with "Orthodoxy" went to the core of the conflict between private and public ethnic display. Referring to the polarization of American Jews about religious observance, Larry Yudelson (2000), writing an opinion column in the *Jewish Forward*, offered that Lieberman represents a convergence of the secular and religious in a twentieth-century evolution of Orthodoxy—"Sabbath observance without militant ideology." He advocated Lieberman's flexible combination of faith and engagement with the modern world. The essay ignited a firestorm of letters to the editors of the paper. From an Orthodox writer came a swipe at spoiled, assimilating Jews: "If, for decades, the Conservative movement's Jewish law committee has seen fit to engage in '*halachic*' hijinks in order to spare suburbanite Jews the inconvenience of a long walk to synagogue on Shabbat, one can only wonder what sort of dispensations it would offer Mr. Lieberman" (Kobre 2000). Another letter writer reminded readers that the fervently Orthodox faithful achieve success in America as doctors, lawyers, and business people (Goldschmidt 2000). From the other side came a stand "against his injecting religious rhetoric into the public square" (Nord 2000; see also Zwiebel 2000).

Rather than stress pietistic separation, Lieberman emphasized engagement with modern American society. "He's about as Modern Orthodox as you can get," said Rabbi Haskel Lookstein, leader of Congregation Kehilath Jeshurun in New York City. He explained, "He is a genuinely religious, observant man, and nevertheless, he is very much committed to modern American life in its best expression" (Eden 2000b). If pietistic Jews questioned Lieberman's consistency with Orthodox practice, a large number of Jews told pollsters that they were concerned about his public stance linking religious faith to Jewishness. A survey conducted by the Philadelphia-based Center for Jewish Community Studies indicated that non-Jews were twice as likely as Jews to approve of Senator Lieberman's references to God and scripture. Although 84 percent of Jews were pleased that Lieberman had been nominated for vice president, a significant percentage, 55 percent, were unhappy that he was a "religious Jew" (Foltin 2001, 151).

In his campaign, Lieberman helped stir the politics of religion that many Jews feared from the religious Christian right. Even the mainstream American press began to notice that Jewish organizations criticized Lieberman after statements about the importance of religious values in public policy decisions and public expressions of faith in civic life. The criticism quietly began in response to Lieberman's book *In Praise of Public Life* (2000), in which he advocated government support of faith-based organizations as an effective way to treat many social problems. Aligning himself with advocates of prayer in the school, Lieberman wrote, "It is true in our public ceremonies and places where courts and officials have repeatedly prohibited expressions of faith, thus mistaking the Constitution's promise of freedom of religion for a policy of freedom from religion. That has deprived America of one of its greatest sources of strength, unity and guidance" (Lieberman 2000, 145).

After his selection by Gore in August 2000, Lieberman was embraced by Christian television evangelist and former presidential candidate Pat Robertson and appeared on August 27 at the Detroit Fellowship Chapel, where he was quoted as saying, "As a people we need to reaffirm our faith and renew the dedication of our nation to God and God's purpose" (Eden 2000a). The Anti-Defamation League (ADL) of B'nai B'rith dispatched the next day a forceful letter of protest: "We feel very strongly that appealing along religious lines, or belief in God, is contrary to the American ideal. The First Amendment requires that government neither support one religion over another nor the religious over the non-religious." The ADL concluded, "As this campaign unfolds, we urge you to keep in mind that public profession of religious beliefs should not be an elemental part of this or any other political campaign" (Eden 2000a). The *Jewish Forward* joined the ADL's criticism in a September 1 editorial and added that Lieberman was going against the "two-century-old commitment to church-state separation" of the Democratic Party and its Jewish heritage ("Editorial," 2000).

Despite the criticism from Jewish organizations of Lieberman's stands on loosening church-state separation, some conservative Jewish spokespersons felt that the Jewish organizations were still too soft on Lieberman. Implying that Jewish organizations were hesitant to criticize a Jew and a Democrat, Michael Medved, writing in the *Wall Street Journal* on August 11, accused Jewish organizations of a double standard when it came to religion and politics. He questioned why liberals were upset when Bush, as governor of Texas, signed into law the observance of Jesus Day but did not object when during Lieberman's introductory he invoked the name of God no fewer than ten times, offered a religious prayer, quoted from the Bible, and referred to Gore as a "servant of God Almighty" (Medved 2000). Lieberman did not relent, however, and polls showed a rise, as the campaign continued, in the number of Americans who felt that Lieberman was spending too much time talking about religion (Foltin 2001, 151).

The *Jewish Forward*'s editorial of August 18 implied that the discourse on religion and politics was about more than quotations of "God" or stands on school vouchers. It implied a fundamental cultural shift in the balance of private and public ethnic expression as a key to integration into American society. The newspaper pronounced that Lieberman's campaign toppled "a great many myths" and "none has fallen harder, nor more jarringly, than the sturdy notion of Judaism as a private affair. . . . For the foreseeable future, Judaism is everybody's business. It is about time" ("Into the Light," 2000). The editorial complained, "We have, many of us, internalized a stunted, *privatized* notion of Judaism, restricted to the home and synagogue, stripped of its civil values and divorced from society" ("Editorial," 2000; emphasis added). The crucial observation was:

> By choosing a running mate whose Jewish belief and practices are central to his *public* identity, Vice-President Gore has forced the *public* role of Judaism into general view. Suddenly, everyone is talking about it, writing about, trying to understand what it means. Journalists who are Jewish, but have never before written about it, are suddenly forced to examine the meaning of Orthodoxy, the importance of the Jewish vote and the danger of latent American anti-Semitism. Across America, Jews are re-examining their identities as members of the American Jewish community. ("Into the Light," 2000; emphasis added)

The editorial writers did not take a stand, however, on whether the path of identity would include a turn toward public avowal of religion as part of the explosion of the privatization myth in the striving for acceptance and integration. Barely a year earlier, the newspaper had observed, "American Jews are increasingly expressing their Jewish identities in religious, education and family activities rather than in Israel-related, communal and philanthropic pursuits of an earlier generation" (Kessler 1999). The newspaper called this movement the new "personalization" and "privatization" that stresses personal authenticity over communal norms.

AFTERMATH OF THE ELECTION AND CONTINUATION OF THE SYNDROME DISCOURSE

After the 2000 election, Lieberman's role in the Jewish cultural debate became even more forceful in advocacy for Jews affirming religion in public life, amid speculation that he would be a candidate for the presidency in 2004. In March 2001 he gave his first major speech on religion and politics after the election at the Pew Forum on Religion and Public Life. He sounded keynotes that would be repeated in many public appearances through 2001: that the founding of the country is based on the intersection of religion and politics, and in the twenty-first century more than ever, the lawful space for faith in public life needs to be increased (Lieberman 2001b). Acting on this principle, Lieberman broke with his party in supporting President Bush's program for greater involvement of faith-based charities in social services ("Lack of Faith," 2001). He also alarmed Jewish organizations with his call for lowering the "high wall" of separation between church and state. He was especially public on television religious programming after the tragic events of September 11, 2001. On the Sunday morning broadcast of October 14, for example, he appeared on the widely broadcasted *Hour of Power*, hosted by the Reverend Robert H. Schuller, and made pronouncements that touched particularly on his integration of religion and American culture. Schuller commented, "My dream is that this is a historic moment when all religions change their roles and see themselves as human bodies to carry out the love of God on earth," and Lieberman replied, "I share that faith and it is a particularly American faith. It is no accident when members of Congress gathered at the Capitol the song we sang was 'God Bless America.' That goes back to the very founding of our country, these were people of faith, when as you know, coming across the waters, they were creating a New Jerusalem."

Lieberman appeared intent on severing the connection between religious devotion and political conservatism, as Eleanor Brown observed in the *New York Times* on August 30, 2000, and in so doing, blurred the Jewish position on advocacy of a moral or civil society in which religion plays a public role. In his vocal complaints against Hollywood for setting a poor ethical model, Lieberman sided with Christian conservatives while backing liberal secularists on the need for social tolerance. Brown noted, "In the last few decades, the debate about religion in public life has been unable to move beyond a divisive standoff between religious conservatives and liberal secularists who are overwhelmingly hostile to public displays of religiosity" (E. Brown 2000). Lieberman had "revived the public debate," she wrote, and showed a way through the Jewish tradition of reuniting morality and political liberalism. Although in 2000 Lieberman rose to the top for the first time of the *Jewish Forward*'s list of influential Jews, in recognition of his national exposure, the paper's editors wondered in its 2001 list whether he really reflected Jewish shifts in political culture ("The *Forward* 50," 2001). Or perhaps his experience in 2000 is a reminder of the difficulty of categorizing an increasingly complex and fragmented Jewish identity.

In a feature in the *New York Times Magazine* on Lieberman's future national role, James Traub observed that, while Lieberman was pronouncing to Jewish audiences that "you don't have to hide who you are in order to be successful in America," he was in fact a poster boy for assimilation. In Traub's words, he is "an all-American—that is, Christian—character, earnest, hokey, friendly and sincere as all get-out. He is religiously Jewish and ethnically Fifties" (Traub 2001). Elsewhere, Traub elaborated that Lieberman redefined morality closer to the private avoidance of sin than to the public perpetuation of social justice, "the great watchword of the temple and of the entire Jewish milieu" (Traub 2000).

Lieberman emerged from the 2000 campaign bruised from campaign controversies, especially criticism from Jewish organizations, and yet he was more ubiquitous in the national spotlight. In the weeks following the election, he drew press for his continuation of the fight to challenge the Florida vote counts. After the Supreme Court decision on December 12, 2000, that effectively sealed the victory for George W. Bush as president and Richard Cheney as vice president, Lieberman spoke to the Senate and expressed his gratitude to Vice President Gore for having named a "Jewish-American" to a national ticket for a major party. Lieberman concluded with a biblical flourish by citing a theme from Psalm 30: "So today, as some of us weep for what could have been, we look to the future with faith that on another morning, joy will surely come" (Foltin 2001, 158).

While polling did not specifically query the Jewish vote, Lieberman's chances in a 2004 primary run were a matter of active speculation in the Jewish press, and such commentary had two significant implications: Jews were empowered as never before to go after the ultimate prize of the presidency, and if they were to, their avowal of Jewishness was likely to be under scrutiny by Jews and non-Jews for different reasons. For many Jews, the question of Jewishness had several layers, including considering Jewish identity on secular or religious grounds, responding to concerns for the future Jewish identity and continuity in the face of rising rates of intermarriage and geographic dispersion, confronting anti-Semitism that a Jewish public presence attracts, and evaluating the kinds of appropriate public ethnic display as a Jew in a predominantly Christian society. For many non-Jews, questions of the candidate as an "outsider," religion's role in public life, loyalty to Israel, and relations to other ethnic groups were at issue.

Looked at broadly, reports in the American Jewish press after the 2000 election on the implications of a presidential run by a Jew for public ethnic-religious display joined an intellectual discourse that was exploring ways to repair a weakened Jewish identity. Telling, for example, was the choice of Samuel Freedman's *Jew vs. Jew: The Struggle for the Soul of American Jewry* during the election year for the National Jewish Book Award and the bestseller status of such books as Alan Dershowitz's *The Vanishing American Jew: In Search of Jewish Identity for the Next Century* (1997) and Elliott Abrams's *Faith or Fear: How Jews Can Survive in a Christian America* (1997). Indeed, sensitive to the theme of Freedman's book (on conflict between secular and religious definitions of Jewish identity that threatened to rip apart American Jewry close to his interests), Lieberman felt compelled publicly to comment on *Jew vs. Jew*: "There emerges a provocative picture of the Jewish community in America that has both flourished in the unprecedented freedom and acceptance this country has provided and been divided and diminished by that freedom" (S. G. Freedman 2002).

Lieberman touted America's promise rather than its prejudice, but an ambivalence or psychological conflict is still evident between the achievement of success held up as the American dream, and the sacrifice for this ambition of the performance of ethnic-religious identity and a sense of community. Thus at least two narratives of American political culture can be related to the Lieberman syndrome of 2000. For Jews, the Jewish press reported, Lieberman's rise to national prominence signaled the most pronounced challenge to the traditional private-public split in Jewish identity in American society, a challenge that heightened a discourse already begun in the 1990s. Lieberman's idealistic interpretation of his campaign is that it shows that the forces of anti-Semitism have been beaten back to the margins of society, but for Jews it raised questions of the ways that Jews were defined (Lieberman 2001a). It brought up issues of the acceptance of Jewish diversity among Jews themselves. Begun with an appeal to the unity of American Jews, it quickly revealed their divisions, before they apparently mobilized behind the Democratic choice at the end of the campaign.

By 2008 Lieberman was again in the national spotlight, but this time on the Republican side. He won re-election for senator in 2006 as an Independent candidate, but when he was installed he sat with the Senate Democratic Caucus. However, at the 2008 Republican National Convention, he endorsed fellow Senator John McCain for president, and he stopped attending Democratic leadership meetings. McCain recounted in his memoirs that he decided at the end of July 2008 to choose Lieberman to be his vice presidential running mate (McCain and Salter 2018, 51). McCain did not mention Lieberman's Jewish identity as a factor; he wrote that a McCain-Lieberman "national unity" ticket "would send a clear message of change" (50). McCain's advisers warned him against the idea because Lieberman's positions on social issues appeared to be left of McCain's and because of the fear of alienating the Republican conservative base. McCain heeded the advice and went with Sarah Palin but later wrote that he regretted the decision (52). The attraction of Lieberman to the Republicans was prompted by concern among Jewish organizations of shifts in Democratic support of Jewish issues. Lieberman, as the most visible political Jew, was asked in 2019 if the Democratic Party was "anti-Jewish," as then President Donald Trump had declared, with the added

12.1. United States Senator Joseph Lieberman with Republican presidential candidate John McCain at the Western Wall, Judaism's holiest site, in Jerusalem, March 19, 2008. After the election, McCain wrote that he regretted not picking Lieberman for his running mate in the 2008 presidential campaign. UPI Photo by Debbie Hill/Alamy Stock Photo.

comment that a Jewish exodus from the Democrats was occurring as a result (Frazin 2019). Lieberman replied that it was not but that "it has members who say anti-Semitic things" (Frazin 2019). Lieberman did not run for re-election for his Senate seat in 2013, but Trump considered him for the position of FBI director in 2017.

The question of public Jewishness shifted in Trump's administration to his son-in-law Jared Kushner, an unabashedly Modern Orthodox Jew, appointed as a senior adviser in the White House. Aides to the president pointed to the presence of Kushner as a defense against Trump's purportedly anti-Semitic views and statements (Chozick and Seligson 2018). Once again, undue influence of a Jewish lobby came into media commentaries on the Trump White House, as it had in the Gore-Lieberman campaign, in addition to the public presence of Jews in the political arena. In a replay of the Lieberman syndrome, Kushner's role apparently caused divisions in the Jewish community (Chozick and Seligson 2018). *New York Times* reporters Amy Chozick and Hannah Seligson interviewed Ethan Tucker, the stepson of Joe Lieberman who is also a rabbi and president of the Hadar yeshiva in New York. He responded to the divided reception of Jared Kushner and Ivanka Trump in the Jewish community with the comment, "I don't think people generally honor people they feel were accomplices to politics and policies they abhor" (Chozick and Seligson 2018). The reporters concluded that the debate was not a political one but a cultural issue: "Talk to enough Jews about Mr. Kushner and Ms. Trump, and you begin to realize that the couple has become a sort of Rorschach test, with defenders and detractors seeing what they want to see as it relates to larger rifts about Jewish *identity*" (Chozick and Seligson 2018; emphasis added). Apparently the conflicts of public and private Jewishness that came out into the open during the Lieberman campaign have not been resolved.

To be sure, several candidates on the Democratic side in the primary race for the 2020 presidential election had a Jewish background: Senator Bernie Sanders, Mayor Michael Bloomberg, and Los Angeles Mayor Eric Garcetti. But no one received more questioning about a connection to Judaism than former Starbucks CEO Howard Schultz, who mulled an independent run for the presidency. Quickly after announcing his interest, reporters pressed him on the role of his Jewish faith. His answer was consistent: "I'm not running as a Jew; I'm running as an American" (Ratcliffe 2019). In his reply, Schultz made a separation between what he observes at home and how he approaches the public political arena. When asked by Scott Pelley on the popular television newsmagazine *60 Minutes* "What effect do you think being Jewish would have on your campaign?"—a question not posed to other potential candidates—Schultz answered in terms of the acceptance of non-Jews for Jews in America: "I have great faith in the goodness and kindness of the American people" (Pelley 2019). He joined being a Jewish politician to American pluralism and the American dream: "Nobody ever had to lecture us about diversity. We lived it" (Wilner 2019).

I know something about his living context because we were high school classmates in the late 1960s at Canarsie High School in Brooklyn. The Canarsie section of southeast Brooklyn at the time was a relatively new destination for Jews. It had been primarily known for its Italian American settlement and was removed from the more commercialized, bustling sections of Flatbush and Borough Park that were home to Orthodox Jewish schools and businesses we would call *frum* or pietistic. Once undesirable because it sat on marshland by Jamaica Bay, Canarsie became a landscape of quieter connected row homes (duplexes, they were called) rather than cramped apartment buildings (see Rieder 1985). The locale for the Jewish migrants epitomized a pluralistic vision of fitting into America publicly as assimilated individuals of white immigrant background, along with others, while privately, or occasionally, being able to maintain a Jewish identity. The parents who brought us to Canarsie appreciated, though, reminders, or materialization, of Jewish culture in the new environment—knish bakeries, Hanukkah displays, and mezuzot on doorways—while worrying, illiberally, sociologist Jonathan Rieder observed, that they would be accused of being ghettoized or racialized, as were the former Jewish neighborhoods of Brownsville and East New York (see Rieder 1992). It did not surprise me, then, that Schultz was not willing to give public notice of his "level of observance and the extent of his activity in the [Jewish] community" (Wilner 2019). Like Lieberman, he did not wear a *kippah* or sport Jewish symbols on his clothing in public and was averse to being stigmatized for his Jewish difference while also using it to shape his worldview. Unlike Lieberman, however, Schultz did not define Jewishness as inherently religious.

The Jewishness of political candidates in 2020 came to the fore in bickering between Michael Bloomberg and Bernie Sanders. Bloomberg referred to Sanders's experience on a kibbutz with the jab that, although he was not the only Jewish candidate running for president, he was the "only one who doesn't want to turn America into a kibbutz" (Dovere 2020). At a presidential debate, Sanders shot back by pointing out, in answer to a question on Middle East policy, that he was the only candidate on stage who had lived in Israel, but he stopped short of claiming a Jewish identity. Castigating Sanders for a lack of support for Israel and denying his Jewishness (Sanders publicly referred to his Jewish father as a "Polish immigrant"), Bloomberg made direct appeal to Jewish voters by lighting public menorahs and sprinkling his speeches with Jewish references. With questions circulating about support for his candidacy among Jews, Sanders in October 2019 addressed the national conference of the liberal organization J Street, which works to influence policy toward Israel. In a historic public statement regarding the evolution of the reticence of Jews to be politically involved nationally that I have called the Lieberman syndrome, Sanders told the Jewish audience, "I am very proud to be Jewish. I look forward to being the first Jewish president in the history of this country" (Dovere 2020).

For the non-Jewish American public, Lieberman and the political figures who followed him epitomize growing acceptance of Jews as a culturally mainstream character in the American drama of reforming values in a civil society, even if they are not included in the racialized American multicultural mix. The idea of this new American faith is a moralistic rather than a religious identity. Further, it seems that by playing this card, Lieberman was joining himself (and the traditionally marginalized Jewish persona) to Christian causes to be part of mainstream society. The interpretation read from the voting booth is that Americans viewed Lieberman, and others affiliated Jews, as representative of a new American faith based on the restoration of moral values. With that interpretation is the new realization for Jews that public and private roles of Jewishness in American political culture have yet to be reconciled.

THE SHLEP OF
JEWISH CULTURE

The chutzpah of Jewish cultural studies I have claimed owes in large measure to the notion that Jewish culture is a distinctive and weighty shlep. That is, as a result of a long history and wanderings around the globe, Jewish culture appears or is viewed by Jews as perplexingly complicated and fluid, with innumerable locations, multiple languages and practices, inscrutable ancient and modern texts, and both secular and religious manifestations. The multivalent tapestry of Jewish culture seems to run counter to the conventional academic view of culture as a singular community rooted in place. It troubles the divide between Culture and culture, with the former representing upper-class refinement. In practice, Jewish culture simultaneously evokes the vernacular of the home and community and the formality of the synagogue; it is often stigmatized from the outside and open to criticism from within, and, maybe most significantly or fatalistically, it is a continually threatened influence that cannot be easily denied or hidden, even though Jews and non-Jews try to suppress or minimize it. It is capable of being revered and reviled and, in its analysis, often raises judgment—about its appropriateness for modernity, its role in history, its distinction from and continuity with other ethnic-religious experience, and its aesthetic, intellectual, and ethical worth. To hear and view expressions of Jewish culture is to recognize that it paradoxically provides comfort and pain to its members. It is amazingly persistent and yet patently fragile.

My metaphorical use of *shlep* is not meant to be negative, nor does it exclude Sephardic, non-European, and other Jewish cultural identities in what might appear to be an Ashkenazic brush stroke of Jewish culture and its studies. *Shlep* enters into conversation among Jews of various stripes to describe situations in which they have an obligation to fulfill a duty and undertake an arduous journey. As a noun, *shlep* might refer to a yeoman, unprivileged, or ordinary existence in contrast to the anti-Semitic stereotype of Jews as elite power brokers. On one level it expresses for Jews a repeated obligation rather than initiative, often with the implication that it is their fate to constantly shlep (in Yiddish, a drawn-out ordeal translates to *oysgeshlept*), to be responsible to others or to an encompassing superorganic force. Earlier in this book, I observed that part of the psychology that links the bar and bat mitzvah to the innovative wedding is that they are shleps materialized in the time and the lengths taken by the organizers and participants. An expectation, Jewish guilt if you will, is conveyed to be present at the event. Moreover, the weight and sustainability of Jewish culture are evident, if only symbolically, in the special ritual frame created at those events and destinations. For example, a common joking reference to the *eruv*, which religious studies scholar Charlotte Elisheva Fonrobert calls "one of the most peculiar ritual systems that the rabbis of the Mishnah and the Talmud instituted," is the "magic schlepping circle" (Fonrobert 2005, 9, 27). It is not just that the *eruv* allows for literally carrying items within its boundaries but that it provides figuratively the weight of history and tradition by unifying a community that has "particular importance in a diaspora situation" (28–29).

Whether pressured to constitute a minyan, overly protect their children, or marry within the faith, Jews figuratively carry on and use expressive speech as a synecdoche for culture, to fathom their identity to themselves and others. The code-switching represented by *shlep* to an ethnic language certainly makes a social minority connection, but it also offers, in the connotation of persons carrying out the task or embarking on a trip by themselves, consideration of being on one's own with choices to make while carrying hefty cultural baggage. In conversation, *shlep* signals to another Jew a shared understanding of their othered lot in life or diasporic heritage, and the question is raised of why the need or compulsion exists to express as a cultural trope the Jewish character of one's errand. And for that matter, the additional query can be posed of how non-Jews respond to or adapt it. *Shlep* apparently was taken as a fighting word when on a London train non-Jews triggered by its imprint on a book bag verbally abused a Jew to get out of the country "with the other Yids" (Pitimson 2016).

To be sure, *shlep* might be heard on the lips of non-Jews and even in the press, but usually with the literal meaning of carrying something heavy or far, maybe with a tinge of colloquial humor. Jews usually view it, if subconsciously, with deeper layers of meaning that invite commentary about their cultural practice and legacy. For example, was it humor, politics, or Jewishness that inspired popular comedian-activist Sarah Silverman to go public by featuring the Yiddishism in an online video called "The Great Schlep" a month before the 2008 American presidential election? The video endorsing Barack Obama was produced by the Jewish Council for Education and Research, a political action committee. To the consternation of many Jews that was not all that different from the reaction to Jewish jokes online that I documented in chapter 10 (Brostoff 2008; see chapter 10), "The Great Schlep" with its play on Jewish stereotypes attracted a whopping 7 million viewers in its first two weeks of circulation. Echoing a theme of inescapable Jewishness, Silverman told a *New York Times* reporter in relation to the use of *schlep*, "I have no religion. But culturally I can't escape it, I'm very Jewish." Silverman's tongue-in-cheek message to Jewish grandparents living in the swing state of Florida was to vote for Obama or else their grandchildren will withhold visits to them. She reached out to older viewers, she said, "because of my Jewy-ness" (Itzkoff 2008). The video inspired a crowd-sourced website by the Jewish Council for Education and Research for "Schlep Labs" (thegreatschlep .com) aimed at creatively stirring the Jewish vote through media narratives for Obama with the theme that Jews should relate to him because of his minority status and insinuations hurled at him (e.g., that he is a secret Muslim). Their insider message to Jews was, "We're not afraid of doing the work, because we're Schleppers." The Yiddish definition of a *schlepper* as an ignoble tramp or beggar was adapted in the website to mean admirable hard workers, but still with the implication that they were necessarily mobile to fulfill their mission as Jews.

William Safire (born Safir), the famous presidential speechwriter of Jewish background who was renowned for his "On Language" column for the *New York Times*, singled out *shlep* as a special case of Yiddish loan words in English (Safire 2007). He contemplated its linguistic appeal because of its comical relation to others such as *schlub*, *schlump*, *shlock*, and *schmuck* and identified its origin from Low German (*sleppen*) via Yiddish for dragging or hauling something. Noting its novel appearance in the early twentieth century in some prominent newspapers such as the *Wall Street Journal* and the *Washington Post*, Safire opined on its Jewishness as an esoteric term rather than as another loan word that found its way into popular journalism or political talk. He was not about to use it in a public speech, maybe because it also connoted foolishness and even masochism in association with the *schlemiel* (Birner 1984). Safire is hardly alone in attributing a noble ordinariness to *shlep* connected to the daily round of work in everyday life with some reference to the "old country" (Apple 2006). Although to Safire the words in the phrase "ordinary shlep" appeared redundant, Safire (2007) underscored in cultural psychological terms that "*schlep* has a greater connotation of exasperated weariness on the part of a person clumsily trying to cope with an unwelcome burden." Yet *shlep* is often communicated in the context of a necessary responsibility, a cultural force, and social difference, especially for mothers with the matrilineal pressure to carry on Jewish traditions (A. Cohen 2014). For men, there is the hardly insignificant issue of their ritual circumcision, "a covenant for all generations to come" (Genesis 9:12; see Glick 2005). After all, commentators have written, Jews are diasporic, often downtrodden shleppers who "shlep around" the world, raising images of the wandering Jew (Chabad.org Staff 2019).

One might protest that the wandering Jew theme derives from a Christian legend with anti-Semitic overtones and is not properly part of Jewish culture in the sense that use of culture implies that beliefs and practices grow out of social production in place. Yet scholars have argued that the wandering Jew theme has Jewish roots in biblical narratives of Noah and Moses and, to some extent, was co-constructed with variations in Jewish and non-Jewish narratives in Europe (see Geller 1992; Hasan-Rokem and Dundes 1986). This multiperspective view of culture suggests another complication of Jewish cultural studies: It is as much what people think or believe about Jews as it is about the things that Jews do. This cultural consideration of cognition and belief does not draw universal conclusions, but it relies on the diverse social and physical contexts and situations in which Jews might or might not be present but whose conceptualization, ritualization, and narration are nonetheless invoked and materialized. This might be evident in anti-Semitic as well as philo-Semitic folklore and sometimes in the gray area in between (which Polish sociologist Zygmunt Bauman [1998] calls allo-Semitism).

I thought of the Semitism question when I was confronted with feeling detached from a Jewish community upon attending Indiana University in the decidedly Christian stronghold of Bloomington, Indiana (although I benefited from great professors of Jewish studies). I had a classmate who announced to me that I was the first Jewish person she had met. I replied that she probably had encountered Jews but was not aware of it. "It's not as if we have horns, you know," I said. She smiled and quipped with a southern drawl, "That's not what my daddy says." After I thought about her half-kidding remark, I continued the conversation on another occasion. She was obviously defensive and simultaneously in denial about the anti-Semitic folklore of Jews having horns, representing their connection to Satan, and about acknowledging its reality in her childhood home in rural Christian Arkansas (see Bertman 2009). She clearly looked to find Jewish difference to make sense of the othering with which she had been raised. Yet the distinction was hard to fathom not only because it was not physically embodied but also because she was confused by the relation of ethnicity to religious identity. She could understand the theological basis in the worship of Jesus but had a more difficult time with the idea of Jews as a culture. In many ways, she could be said to express her conflict in allo-Semitic terms.

The politically tinged debate in the twenty-first century over the inclusive rhetoric of "Seasons's Greetings" and "Happy Holidays" instead of emblematizing the majority culture in "Merry Christmas" further raises issues of allo-Semitism and implications of Jewish cultural studies because it deals with intercultural relations beyond the differences of Jewish and Christian groups. Thumbing his nose at multiculturalism, President Donald Trump in 2017 took credit for legitimizing the use of "Merry Christmas" in public declarations on the national stage in support of the Christian right (McGinley 2017). Without mentioning Jews, the stance most conspicuously alienated them, for Trump did not suggest appending "Happy Hanukkah" to wishes for a "Merry Christmas." The Jewish social response in many locales, particularly at the behest of Chabad Lubavitch, was to hold public menorah lightings to match ballyhooed Christmas tree lightings (*J.* Correspondent 2010) (Figure E.1). The matter of whether a public menorah lighting on government property is legal went up to the Supreme Court in 1989 in the case of *County of Allegheny v. ACLU*. Although the high court had earlier declared that the display of a creche violated the principle of separation of church and state, it ruled that the menorah as a cultural symbol did not promote religion (Green 2015). Although that reasoning seems strange to students of religious studies, it recognized the social symbolism of the menorah as equivalent in wintertime in a predominantly Christian country to the Christmas tree. Culturally, a relatively minor religious holiday had been elevated and transformed into a consumer phenomenon (Plaut 2012). In response to the trend, a number of Jewish commentators criticized the trend and the idea of public Jewish celebration as an ineffective way to "negotiate the twin, competing pressures of ethnic tension and assimilation" (Green 2015).

E.1. Standing behind a media backdrop in a public ceremony in 2019, a Chabad Lubavitch rabbi invites the audience to hold up their cellphones with the flashlight feature on to symbolize Hanukkah's meaning of light in the darkness at the Glow in the Dark Chanukah Celebration on the first night of Hanukkah at a shopping mall before Christmas in Waukesha, Wisconsin. Photo by Simon J. Bronner.

So did the rise of Hanukkah compared to other cultural practices epitomize an assimilationist victory or affirmation of ethnicity for Jews? The answer is largely couched in worries about whether the expression of Jewish culture is inwardly about ethnic solidarity or outwardly about combating anti-Semitism. A turning point in this public discourse, and not coincidentally a spark for the Jewish cultural studies movement, is another Supreme Court case: *Shaare Tefila Congregation v. Cobb* (1987). After vandals painted a synagogue with anti-Semitic slogans and symbols, the congregation pressed charges of racial discrimination against the defendants even though they are "part of what today is considered the Caucasian race." According to the Court, civil rights legislation was "intended to protect from discrimination identifiable classes of persons who are subjected to intentional discrimination solely because of their ancestry or ethnic characteristics."[1] Although providing civil rights protection to Jews because the motivation for discrimination was "racial animus," the ruling shifted identification of Jews to ethnic ancestry, based largely on cultural rather than religious grounds (N. Cohen 1988).

The ruling in the *Shaare Tefila Congregation* case frequently arises in investigations of the ethnic, racial, and religious status of Jews to which Jewish cultural studies has been especially critical in addressing. In the aftermath of the case, when Jews and Jewish culture were largely omitted from an increasingly racialized and politicized ethnic and multicultural studies, Jewish cultural studies, as I pointed out in chapter 1, worked to reconceptualize Jewish life and lore in terms of situated Jewishness. A political turn in this discourse that filtered down to the hallowed halls of academe and civic organizations occurred in 2019 when President Trump at Hanukkah time signed an executive order ostensibly to protect Jewish university students from discrimination. The wider implication of the order that made headlines was that in recognizing Jews as one of America's minorities, it perceived their social status as a nationality (Kampeas 2019). It brought the role of Israel, and the relation of diasporic Jews to it, into public discourse, with the partisan announcement that the Democratic Party, known for holding the allegiance of most American Jews, was the "anti-Israel, anti-Jewish party" (Lesniewski 2019). To this the Senate minority leader Charles E. Schumer, who is Jewish, retorted with an ethnic flourish that Trump had "redefined chutzpah" (Lesniewski 2019). Schumer's Jewish cultural credentials were evident, according to the *New York Jewish Week*, because he "shlepped" to Albany several times a month to work as a low-paid entry-level assemblyman (E. J. Greenberg 1998b). Assigning Jews legal status as a nationality does not make it so in culture, and that is part of the challenge for Jewish cultural studies to investigate.

Looking back on the different roads I have taken to analyze Jewishness, I see merit but also difference in the anthropology, history, literature, and sociology of Jews and the hybridized emergence of Jewish cultural studies. Jewish cultural studies has the chutzpah to get at the ways that Jews think and how they act. Its multiperspective view includes the perception by and of Jews and non-Jews as well as their reality. Jewish cultural studies takes an angular approach to the choices that Jews make, or reveal these choices as Jewish, in various situations, the interplay of belief, narration, practice, and ritual, and the sense of tradition and modernity to which they and their identities respond. Rather than marginalize culture as incidental, Jewish cultural studies gives it a central place to analyze symbols and metaphors that are used to confront the anxieties, paradoxes, and meanings of living and feeling Jewish. Locating Jewish culture is a shlep, to be sure, but the journey will be as revealing as the location.

NOTES

1. FRAMING JEWISH CULTURE

1   Renowned sociologist Gary Alan Fine recalled that, when he inquired about studying a Jewish wedding, Goffman emphatically told him with a Jewish inflection that "anyone who studies their own family is a schmuck." He told this anecdote as part of his delivery of the Francis Lee Utley Memorial Lecture, "The Folklore of Small Things: Tiny Publics and Realms of Local Knowledge," at the American Folklore Society annual meeting, October 2010.

2   Most of these figures were participants in the pathbreaking volumes *Toward New Perspectives in Folklore* (Paredes and Bauman 1972) and *Folklore: Performance and Communication* (Ben-Amos and Goldstein 1975), which advocated for a social-interactional approach to culture. Of these figures, Alan Dundes, Barbara Kirshenblatt-Gimblett, and Elliott Oring have been the most involved in applying attention to Jewish frames, although Roger Abrahams, known primarily for studies of the African American experience (another outsider group), contributed the lead essay on the definition of ethnicity from a Jewish perspective to *Studies in Jewish Folklore* (Talmage 1980) and Richard Bauman wrote on his grandparents' rendering of Yiddish folklore in "Y. L. Cahan's Instructions on the Collecting of Folklore" (1962), "The Collecting of Proverbs" (1963), and "Signing at Cross-Purposes" (2019).

3   Gilman cites Bhabba's *Location of Culture* (1994, 224) for the source of his quotation. Bhabha's challenge of boundaries is apparent in his postcolonial ideas on hybridization and the emergence of new cultural forms from multiculturalism. See Bhabbha (2006) and Huddart (2006).

4. FROM FUNCTION TO FRAME

1   It should be pointed out that, despite the celebration of An-sky in Jewish folkloristic circles, he is rarely cited in histories of folklore studies in Europe. Giuseppe

Cocchiara's 703-page *History of Folklore in Europe* (1971) omits any reference to him, although it claims to cover folkloristic scholarship broadly in Russia. Y. M. Sokolov has the chapter "Problems and Historiography of Folklore" in *Russian Folklore* (1971), but it also makes no mention of An-sky. No citations of An-sky appear in *The Study of Russian Folklore* (1975), edited by Felix J. Oinas and Stephen Soudakoff, giving the impression that the study of Jews in Russia was separate from the study of Russian Christians.

2   Letter from Adolph Bandelier to Stewart Culin, January 16, 1912 (Stewart Culin Papers, Brooklyn Museum). The previous quotation of Bandelier comes from his letter to Culin on January 16, 1912, also from the Stewart Culin Papers. Culin's comments on the American Anthropological Association meetings comes from his undated typescript "The International Jew" (Stewart Culin Papers, Brooklyn Museum).

3   Grunwald subsequently published the journal *Mitteilungen zur Jüdischen Volkskunde*, the organ of the Gessellschaft für Jüdische Volkskunde (Association for Jewish Folklore), begun in 1897 in Austria. An endowed chair in folklore at the Hebrew University in Jerusalem was named for Grunwald (1871–1953). See Grunwald (1923a, 1923b), Müller (1999), D. Noy (1982), and Schrire and Hasan-Rokem (2012, 331–32).

4   Patai cites the definition of folklore as "verbal art" from the work of American-born Africanist William Bascom (1912–1981); see Bascom (1953, 1955).

5   See the Jewish Cultural Studies website at https://www.liverpooluniversitypress.co.uk/series/series-12814/ and Bronner (2008).

6. FATHERS AND SONS

1   For the logical problem of social functionalism analyzing consequences rather than causes, see Oring (1976) and Bronner (1986a, 74–88; 2006b).

2   Evidence for the Yom Kippur fast before the bar mitzvah as a folk custom is found in online groups such as Imamother: Connecting Jewish Mothers (www.imamother.com). The question of whether to allow children to fast is frequently discussed. Among Orthodox members, there is reference made to "the three fasts" (out of seven Jewish fast days) that are ritually done by the bar-mitzvah-to-be: Yom Kippur (Day of Atonement, usually occurring in September or October), Tisha b'Av (usually held in July or August, remembering the tragedies of the Jewish people), and Ta'anit Bechorim (the Fast of the Firstborn, commemorating the saving of the firstborn in Egypt from plague, observed the day before Passover in March or April). On September 10, 2008, for instance, "1st" from Israel posted this query: "I am looking for the reason/source behind the custom of the fasting the 3 fasts before bar or bat mitzvah. Do only

people from certain backgrounds do this, where does this custom come from? Is there a basis for it? I always learned that children under bar/bat mitzvah age should not fast the whole day. Once they are at the age of chinuch, they can be encouraged to fast for a few hours in the morning (and at night 9 av and yom kippur). And then that when they do eat, it should only be what is necessary, not indulging on junk food and continuous snack." I recorded seven replies, none of which proposed any textual sources, and rabbis who were cited in the thread were mixed on whether to follow the custom. Shalhevet from Israel wrote on the same day, "Our rov says not to do it," whereas ChossidMom replied on October 2, 2008, "My son who will be Bar Mitzvah a couple of weeks after Succos should fast this Yom Kippur, according to the rav," even though he "says it's a bunch of baloney. . . . He said there is absolutely no source for this." The other replies referred to doing it, although they did not know the rationale: "we did—but I have no idea why" (greenfire, September 10, 2008); "My father holds by it. He told me the reason but of course I forgot" (flowerpower, September 10, 2008); "I never heard of 3 fasts before, but one I did. My parents always said to fast one fast before also only if you can" (cuteson, September 10, 2008); "I did, as a kid! I grew up in a modern orthodox community, and my whole circle of friends were really machmir on that one. (Then again, we made fasting into a competition—'how long did YOU fast?' 'What did you break YOUR fast on,' etc.)"

3 The rhetorical use of *patoor* in regard to release from manly obligation is still apparent in modern Hebrew usage in Israel, where it refers to an exemption from military duty.

4 Ruth Eis states that, although the sashes are referred to as "Torah binders" in English, "the correct name is *wimpel* (f.), an old German word for cloth or veil, related to the Middle High German *bewimpfen*, to cover, to conceal. Typically, they are made from the cloth which covers the new-born male during the circumcision ceremony" (Eis 1979, 11)

5 Ellen Frankel and Betsy Platkin Teutsch, in *The Encyclopedia of Jewish Symbols* (1992, 40) trace the frequent presence of lions, leopards, eagles, and deer in ceremonial Jewish objects to the Mishnah (*Pirkei Avot* 5:23), which commands, "Be as strong as a leopard, as light as an eagle, as swift as a deer, as brave as a lion to do the will of your Father in heaven."

6 See, for example, the cake toppers at the website Magic Mud (http://www.magicmud .com/Judaic%20a%20shots.htm; accessed December 28, 2008). It offers personalized bar mitzvah cake toppers and figurines at the bimah. Another site shows a figurine with the bearded rabbi overlooking the bar mitzvah boy, titled "Bar Mitzvah–Father and Son Figurine" promoted by Liorel Art from Israel (stores.ebay.com/Art_From_Israel_Figureines -Sculptures_WOQQFsubZ2100394).

7. JEWISH NAMING CEREMONIES FOR GIRLS

1   Correspondence from Shawn Landres to Simon J. Bronner, July 28, 2010. For a discussion of Ashkenazicentrism or Ashkenazi-normativity in a multicultural context, see Iny (2003, 96) and Ruttenberg (2001, 179).

9. THE YIDDISH ACCENT AND CULTURAL POLITICS OF ORAL AND LITERARY HUMOR

1   Collected from Elizabeth Sharpe, of Geneva, New York, by Simon J. Bronner on November 19, 1976, in a bar in Cooperstown, New York. Sharpe learned this joke from her mother.

2   Collected from Stephen Kornhauser, of immigrant Jewish background, from the Bronx, New York, by Simon J. Bronner on August 3, 1977, in Cooperstown, New York.

3   I heard this story from three guides when I was an interpreter at the Fenimore House museum during the fall of 1975.

4   Collected from Stephen Kornhauser, of immigrant Jewish background, from the Bronx, New York, in Cooperstown, New York, on August 3, 1977.

5   I remember this form of wordplay from my youth in Brooklyn, New York, during the 1960s. In addition, Jeffrey Gleich, an 8-year-old boy from Great Neck, New York, described this speech play to me on April 15, 1977.

10. TELLING JOKES

1   I use the concepts "esoteric" and "exoteric" in this chapter in the sense suggested by Franz Boas of a cultural process involving the movement of specialized knowledge within a community (esoteric) to a dominant society (exoteric). See Boas (1902, 1938b). William Hugh Jansen's (1959) problematic usage of the terms refers more to relative expressive content: esoteric as a group's folklore about itself and exoteric as a group's folklore about other groups. See Bronner (1986a, 109–10).

2   This particular joke can be found in the "Off-Topic" forum on "I'm not a racist, that's what's so insane about this" at the Civilization Fanatics Center (https://forums .civfanatics.com/threads/im-not-a-racist-thats-whats-so-insane-about-this.225199/ page-4, posted by jeps on June 2, 2007; accessed August 15, 2020).

3   An indication of this thematic shift is a relative absence of six jokes identified as "classic" in Richard Raskin's *Life is Like a Glass of Tea* (1992). With the exception of the Jewish mother joke (taken from Wilde's *Official Jewish Joke Book* [1974]) in Raskin's

list, the classic jokes involve religious themes of rabbinic characters questioning the relationship of humans to God. Raskin cites publication histories of the individual jokes but does not chronicle their circulation on the Internet.

4 *Mohel* is a Hebrew-Yiddish term for a specialist trained in the practice of Brit Milah (circumcision for boys eight days after birth, as specified in Genesis 17:1–4). The anxiety over circumcision and the view that the bris (Yiddish: circumcision) is a distinctive mark of Jewish identity have led to a large number of jokes in Jewish tradition and may constitute the reason for the website using the figure as a symbol for Jewish humor generally. For example, the website A Word in Your Eye has a separate page for "bris, circumcision, mohel jokes" (http://tinyurl.com/87k7bb). The naughtier versions are visually represented in red type, in contrast to the tamer jokes in black. Jewish students also thought the Yiddish pronunciation of the figure sounded funny: *moyel* (perhaps because it sounds similar to the English mole or a Brooklyn accent pronouncing "girl" as "goil"; a comic song title, for example, is "I Lost My Goil to a Mohel and Now I'm All Cut Up"). Most of the jokes involve wordplay, such as the confusion of "castration" and "circumcision," or variable meanings of "cut" and "tips." For example, riddle-jokes that were familiar to my Jewish students were, "Why did the mohel retire? He just couldn't cut it anymore," and "Why did the rabbi want to be a mohel? The tips were good." One mohel joke about the Internet requires esoteric knowledge: "What is the proper blessing to recite before logging on to the Internet? *Modem anachnu lakh*." One Jewish context for this joke is the reference to many blessings for everyday activities in Jewish tradition. Another is the familiar blessing of gratitude from the Amida prayer, which begins *modim anachnu lakh* (we shall thank you). In relation to my thesis about commentary in the jokes about commercial mass culture, the replacement of *modem* for *modim* represents the replacement of God with the machine in modern digital culture.

5 Maccabi football clubs are Jewish soccer organizations. They take their name from the Maccabees, a nickname for the Hasmonean Dynasty who rebelled against the Seleucid Empire to take control of Judea in the second century BCE. For an example of a London Maccabi football club, see http://www.londonlions.com (accessed August 31, 2017).

6 The site was active in the period I checked, between December 2010 and January 2012. In that time Minkoff added 140 texts and included a banner stating "The 135th set of Jewish jokes was added on 22nd December 2011." The site was still live in 2019 but the last set of Jewish jokes (cited as the 171st set) was last added on November 26, 2015.

7 The demasculinized Jewish man as a nebbish (Yiddish: a fearful, scrawny, or unfortunate person) is often portrayed as dominated and intimidated by women, although

he might be intelligent. In the modern American context, the Jewish nebbish is often equated with the technological or educated nerd. See Brod (1995) and Desser (2001, 278).

11. SPARKS FROM THE GRAVE

1   Bernard Sussman, Washington, D.C., correspondence with Simon J. Bronner, March 9, 1995.

2   Bernard Sussman, Washington, D.C., correspondence with Simon J. Bronner, March 13, 1995.

3   Interview with Jacob Hennenberg by Simon J. Bronner, Cleveland, Ohio, 1993. For background on Hennenberg, see Hennenberg (1995) and http://jacobhennenberg.com.

12. THE LIEBERMAN SYNDROME

1   The original advertisement, placed by a member of the Republican Business Men Inc., in support of Herbert Hoover's candidacy for president stated "A Chicken for Every Pot"; see National Archives (2019).

2   Some commentators wondered whether the phrase "Only in America" was a reference to the quotation often attributed to Yogi Berra after he was informed that Robert Briscoe, the mayor of Dublin, Ireland, visiting New York City was Jewish. See Rulnick (2000).

THE SHLEP OF JEWISH CULTURE

1   *Shaare Tefila Congregation v. Cobb*, 481 U.S. 615 (1987). https://supreme.justia.com/cases/federal/us/481/615/ (accessed December 25, 2019).

REFERENCES

Abrahams, Israel. 1958. *Jewish Life in the Middle Ages*. New York: Meridian Books.

Abrahams, Roger D. 1968. "Introductory Remarks to a Rhetorical Theory of Folklore." *Journal of American Folklore* 81: 143–58.

———. 1972a. "Folklore and Literature as Performance." *Journal of the Folklore Institute* 9: 75–94.

———. 1972b. "Personal Power and Social Restraint in the Definition of Folklore." In *Toward New Perspectives in Folklore*, ed. Américo Paredes and Richard Bauman, 16–30. Austin: University of Texas Press.

———. 1977. "Toward an Enactment-Centered Theory of Folklore." In *Frontiers of Folklore*, ed. William Bascom, 79–120. Boulder, CO: Westview Press for the American Association for the Advancement of Science.

———. 1980. "Folklore in the Definition of Ethnicity: An American and Jewish Perspective." In *Studies in Jewish Folklore*, ed. Frank Talmage, 13–20. Cambridge, MA: Association for Jewish Studies.

———. 1986. "Ordinary and Extraordinary Experience." In *The Anthropology of Experience*, ed. Victor W. Turner and Edward M. Bruner, 45–72. Urbana: University of Illinois Press.

———. 2005. *Everyday Life: A Poetics of Vernacular Practices*. Philadelphia: University of Pennsylvania Press.

Abramowitz, Yosef I., and Susan Silverman. 1997. *Jewish Family and Life: Traditions, Holidays, and Values for Today's Parents and Children*. New York: Golden Books.

Abrams, Elliott. 1997. *Faith or Fear: How Jews Can Survive in a Christian America*. New York: Free Press.

Abramson, Glenda, ed. 1989. *The Blackwell Companion to Jewish Culture: From the Eighteenth Century to the Present*. Oxford, UK: Blackwell Reference.

Adams, Henry. 1918. *The Education of Henry Adams*. Boston: Houghton Mifflin.

Adler, Cyrus. 1906. "Sir Isidore Spielmann." In *Jewish Encyclopedia*, ed. Cyrus Adler, 11: 509–10. New York: Funk & Wagnalls.

Adler, Hermann. 1893. "Jewish Wit and Humour." *Eclectic Magazine of Foreign Literature, Science, and Art*, n.s., 57 (April): 530–38.

Adler, Rachel. 1998. *Engendering Judaism: An Inclusive Theology and Ethics*. Boston: Beacon Press.

Adler, Selig, and Thomas E. Connolly. 1960. *From Ararat to Suburbia: The History of the Jewish Community of Buffalo*. Philadelphia: Jewish Publication Society of America.

Agler, Richard D. 2000. "On Faith—Public." Congregation B'nai Israel of Boca Raton, September 30. http://www.cbibo-ca.org/rda/000930.html (URL inactive, accessed November 1, 2000).

Agro, Elizabeth. 2007. "Mighty Mezuzot: An Obligation with Style." In *A Kiss for the Mezuzah*, ed. Matthew Singer, 6–7. Philadelphia: Philadelphia Museum of Jewish Art.

Alderman, Geoffrey. 2008. *Controversy and Crisis: Studies in the History of the Jews in Modern Britain*. Boston: Academic Studies Press.

Allan, Douglas A. 1956. "Folk Museums at Home and Abroad." *Proceedings of the Scottish Anthropological and Folklore Society* 5: 91–121.

Alperin, Mimi. 1989. "JAP Jokes: Hateful Humor." *Humor: International Journal of Humor Research* 2: 412–16.

Alpert, Rebecca. 1997. *Like Bread on the Seder Plate: Jewish Lesbians and the Transformation of Tradition*. New York: Columbia University Press.

Altshuler, David, ed. 1983. *The Precious Legacy: Judaic Treasures from the Czechoslovak State Collections*. New York: Summit Books.

Alvarez, Lizette. 2012. "Synagogue Uses Texting to Reach Young Members." *Seattle Times* (September 17). http://www.seattletimes.com/nation-world/synagogue-uses-texting-to-reach-young-members (accessed September 19, 2017).

Alvin, Julius. 1991. *Gross Jokes*. New York.

American Jewish Historical Society. 2011. "Call for Papers: 2012 Biennial Scholars' Conference on American Jewish History." H-Judaic Discussion Log, September 9. http://www.h-ne.org/~judaic (URL inactive, accessed June 6, 2019).

Anderson, George K. 1965. *The Legend of the Wandering Jew*. Providence, RI: Brown University Press.

Anderson, Susan Heller. 1990. "Chronicle." *New York Times* (September 19). https://www.nytimes.com/1990/09/19/style/chronicle-374890.html (accessed November 26, 2006).

Anijar, Karen. 1999. "Jewish Genes, Jewish Jeans: A Fashionable Body." In *Religion, Dress and the Body*, ed. Linda B. Arthur, 181–200. Oxford, UK: Berg.

An-Ski, S. 2010 [1908]. "Jewish Ethnopoetics." In *Pioneers of Jewish Ethnography and Folkloristics in Eastern Europe*, ed. Haya Bar-Itzhak, 34–74. Ljubljana: Scientific Research Center of the Slovenian Academy of Science and Arts.

Antler, Joyce. 2007. *You Never Call! You Never Write! A History of the Jewish Mother*. Oxford, UK: Oxford University Press.

———. 2010. "One Clove Away from a Pomander Ball: The Subversive Tradition of Jewish Female Comedians." *Studies in American Jewish Literature* 29: 123–38.

Appel, Gersion. 1978. *The Concise Code of Jewish Law*. New York: KTAV.

Apple, Sam. 2006. *Schlepping Through the Alps: My Search for Austria's Jewish Past with Its Last Wandering Shepherd*. New York: Ballantine.

Arlow, Jacob. 1951. "A Psychoanalytic Study of a Religious Initiation Rite: Bar Mitzvah." In *The Psychoanalytic Study of the Child*, vol. 6, ed. Ruth Eissler, Anna Freud, Heinz Hartmann, and Ernst Kris, 353–74. New York: International Universities Press.

Ausubel, Nathan. 1964. *The Book of Jewish Knowledge*. New York: Crown.

Aviv, Caryn, and David Shneer. 2005. *New Jews: The End of the Jewish Diaspora*. New York: New York University Press.

Avrutin, Eugene M., Valeri Dymshits, Alexander Ivanov, Alexander Lvov, Harriet Murrav, and Alla Sokolova, eds. 2009. *Photographing the Jewish Nation: Pictures from S. An-Sky's Ethnographic Expeditions*. Waltham, MA: Brandeis University Press.

Bachner, Michael. 2020. "Israel's Chief Rabbis Say Passover Seder Can't Be Held via Video-conference." *The Times of Israel* (March 31). https://www.timesofisrael.com/israels-chief -rabbis-say-passover-seder-cant-be-held-via-videoconference/ (accessed May 9, 2020).

Bahloul, Joelle. 1996. *The Architecture of Memory: A Jewish-Muslim Household in Colonial Algeria, 1937–1962*. Cambridge, UK: Cambridge University Press.

Baker, Lee D. 2004. "Franz Boas Out of the Ivory Tower." *Anthropological Theory* 4: 29–51.

Baker, Ronald L. 1986. *Jokelore: Humorous Folktales from Indiana*. Bloomington: Indiana University Press.

Balinska, Maria. 2008. *The Bagel: The Surprising History of a Modest Bread*. New Haven, CT: Yale University Press.

Balka, Christie, and Andy Rose, eds. 1989. *Twice Blessed: On Being Lesbian or Gay and Jewish*. Boston: Beacon Press.

Bar'am-Ben Yossef, No'am. 1998. *Brides and Betrothals: Jewish Wedding Rituals in Afghanistan*. Jerusalem: Israel Museum.

Bar-Itzhak, Haya. 1990. "Modes of Characterization in Religious Narrative: Jewish Folk Legends About Miracle Worker Rabbis." *Journal of Folklore Research* 27: 205–30.

———. 2001. *Jewish Poland Legends of Origin: Ethnopoetics and Legendary Chronicles*. Detroit: Wayne State University Press.

———. 2005. *Israeli Folk Narratives: Settlement, Immigration, Ethnicity*. Detroit: Wayne State University Press.

———. 2010. "S. An-Ski (S. Z. Rapoport), the Ethnographer of the Jews and His 'Jewish Ethnopoetics.'" In *Pioneers of Jewish Ethnography and Folkloristics in Eastern Europe*, ed. Haya Bar-Itzhak, 27–33. Ljubljana: Scientific Research Center of the Slovenian Academy of Science and Arts.

Barrick, Mac. 1970. "Racial Riddles and the Polack Joke." *Keystone Folklore Quarterly* 15: 3–15.

Bar-Tal, Daniel, and Yona Teichman. 2005. *Stereotypes and Prejudice in Conflict: Representations of Arabs in Israeli Jewish Society*. Cambridge, UK: Cambridge University Press.

Barth, Fredrik, ed. 1998 [1969]. *Ethnic Groups and Boundaries: The Social Organization of Culture Difference*. Long Grove, IL: Waveland Press.

Barth, John. 1987. *The Tidewater Tales: A Novel*. New York: Putnam.

Bartov, Omer. 2005. *The "Jew" in Cinema: From* The Golem *to* Don't Touch My Holocaust. Bloomington: Indiana University Press.

Bascom, William. 1953. "Folklore and Anthropology." *Journal of American Folklore* 66: 283–90.

———. 1955. "Verbal Art." *Journal of American Folklore* 68: 245–52.

Baskind, Samantha. 2007. "The Fockerized Jew? Questioning Jewishness as Cool in American Popular Entertainment." *Shofar* 25: 3–17.

Bateson, Gregory. 1955. "A Theory of Play and Fantasy: A Report on Theoretical Aspects of the Project for the Study of the Role of Paradoxes of Abstraction in Communication." In *Approaches to the Study of Human Personality*, by the American Psychiatric

Association, 39–51. Psychiatric Research Reports 2. Philadelphia: American Psychiatric Association.

———. 1956. "The Message 'This Is Play.'" In *Group Processes: Transactions of the Second Conference*, ed. Bertram Schaffner, 145–242. New York: Josiah Macy Jr. Foundation.

———. 2000. *Steps to an Ecology of Mind*. Chicago: University of Chicago Press.

Bateson, Gregory, and Margaret Mead. 1942. *Balinese Character: A Photographic Analysis*. New York: New York Academy of Sciences.

Battegay, Caspar. 2018. "The Jewish Atlantic: Diaspora and Pop Music." In *Connected Jews: Expressions of Community in Analogue and Digital Culture*, ed. Simon J. Bronner and Caspar Battegay, 109–30. London: Littman Library of Jewish Civilization in association with Liverpool University Press.

Baudrillard, Jean. 1994. *Simulacra and Simulation*, trans. Sheila Glaser. Ann Arbor: University of Michigan Press.

Bauer, Bruno. 1843. *Die Judenfrage*. Braunschweig: Friedrich Otto.

Bauman, Richard. 1962. "Y. L. Cahan's Instructions on the Collecting of Folklore." *New York Folklore Quarterly* 18: 284–89.

———. 1963. "The Collecting of Proverbs." *Western Folklore* 22: 271–72.

———. 2010. "'It's Not a Telescope, It's a Telephone': Encounters with the Telephone on Early Commercial Sound Recordings." In *Language, Ideologies, and Media Discourse: Texts, Practices, Politics*, ed. Sally Johnson and Thommaso M. Milani, 252–76. London: Continuum.

———. 2019. "Signing at Cross-Purposes." In *Contexts of Folklore: Festschrift for Dan Ben-Amos on His Eighty-Fifth Birthday*, ed. Simon J. Bronner and Wolfgang Mieder, 47–58. New York: Peter Lang.

Bauman, Zygmunt. 1998. "Allosemitism: Premodern, Modern, Postmodern." In *Modernity, Culture and "the Jew,"* ed. Bryan Cheyette and Laura Marcus, 143–56. Stanford, CA: Stanford University Press.

———. 1999 [1973]. *Culture as Praxis*. London: SAGE.

Baumgarten, Jean. 2019. "*Sefer Haminhagim* (Venice, 1593) and Its Dissemination in the Ashkenazic World." In *Minhagim: Custom and Practice in Jewish Life*, ed. Joseph Isaac Lifshitz, Naomi Feuchtwanger-Sarig, Simha Goldin, Jean Baumgarten, and Hasia Diner, 83–98. Berlin: De Gruyter.

BBYO (B'nai B'rith Youth Organization). 2008. *The Jewish Community's Guide to Understanding Teens: A Compilation of Research on Teen Trends, Tween Trends, and a Special Study on the Impact of BBYO on Alumni*. Washington, DC: BBYO.

Beattie, John. 1966. "Ritual and Social Change." *Man*, n.s., 1: 60–71.

Beatty, Aidan, and Dan O'Brien, eds. 2018. *Irish Questions and Jewish Questions: Crossovers in Culture*. Syracuse, NY: Syracuse University Press.

Behrouzi, Nitza. 1991. *Head Adornment: Festive and Ceremonial Headdresses*. Tel Aviv: Eretz Israel Museum.

Bel, Bernard, Jan Brouwer, Biswajit Das, Vibodh Parthasarahti, and Guy Poitevin, eds. 2005. *Media and Mediation*, vol. 1. Thousand Oaks, CA: SAGE.

Belasco, Daniel. 2009. "Chopping Noodles: The Art of Jewish Practice." In *Reinventing Ritual: Contemporary Art and Design for Jewish Life*, ed. Daniel Belasco, 1–45. New Haven, CT: Yale University Press.

Bell, Catherine. 1992. *Ritual Theory, Ritual Practice*. New York: Oxford University Press.

———. 1997. *Ritual: Perspectives and Dimensions*. New York: Oxford University Press.

Ben-Ami, Issachar. 1998. *Saint Veneration Among the Jews in Morocco*. Detroit: Wayne State University Press.

Ben-Amos, Dan. 1971. "Toward a Definition of Folklore in Context." *Journal of American Folklore* 84: 3–15.

———. 1973. "The 'Myth' of Jewish Humor." *Western Folklore* 32: 112–31.

———. 1976. "Analytical Categories and Ethnic Genres." In *Folklore Genres*, ed. Dan Ben-Amos, 215–42. Austin: University of Texas Press.

———. 1993. "'Context' in Context." *Western Folklore* 52: 209–26.

———. 1997. "Performance." In *Folklore: An Encyclopedia of Beliefs, Customs, Tales, Music, and Art*, ed. Thomas A. Green, 630–35. Santa Barbara, CA: ABC-CLIO.

———, ed. 2011. *Folktales of the Jews*, vol. 3, *Tales from Arab Lands*. Philadelphia: Jewish Publication Society.

Ben-Amos, Dan, and Kenneth S. Goldstein, eds. 1975. *Folklore: Performance and Communication*. The Hague: Mouton.

Benjamin, Walter. 2007. "The Work of Art in the Age of Mechanical Reproduction." In *Illuminations*, by Walter Benjamin; trans. Harry Zohn; ed. Hannah Arendt, 217–52. New York: Schocken.

Ben-Menahem, Hanina. 1996. "Postscript: The Judicial Process and the Nature of Jewish Law." In *An Introduction to the History and Sources of Jewish Law*, ed. N. S. Hecht, B. S. Jackson, S. M. Passamaneck, D. Piatelli, and A. M. Rabello, 421–38. Oxford, UK: Clarendon Press.

Bennett, Tony, Lawrence Grossberg, and Meaghan Morris, eds. 2005. *New Keywords: A Revised Vocabulary of Culture and Society*. Malden, MA: Blackwell.

Benovitz, Moshe. 1998. *Kol Nidre: Studies in the Development of Rabbinic Votive Institutions*. Brown Judaic Studies 315. Atlanta: Scholars Press.

Ben Rafael, Eliezer. 2003. *Contemporary Jewries: Convergence and Divergence*. Leiden, Netherlands: Brill.

Benshoff, Harry M., and Sean Griffin. 2011. *America on Film: Representing Race, Class, Gender, and Sexuality at the Movies*, 2nd ed. Hoboken, NJ: Wiley.

Ben-Yehuda, Nachman. 1995. *The Masada Myth: Collective Memory and Mythmaking in Israel*. Madison: University of Wisconsin Press.

Berenbaum, Michael. 2000. "Who Owns the Holocaust?" *Moment* (December). http://www.momentmag.com/archive/dec00/feat1.html (accessed January 15, 2001).

Berger, Arthur Asa. 2006. *The Genius of the Jewish Joke*. New Brunswick, NJ: Transaction.

———. 2016. *Understanding American Icons: An Introduction to Semiotics*. New York: Taylor & Francis.

Berger, Maurice, and Joan Rosenbaum. 2004. *Masterworks of the Jewish Museum*. New Haven, CT: Yale University Press.

Berlinger, Gabrielle. 2010. "770 Eastern Parkway: The Rebbe's Home as Icon." In *Jews at Home: The Domestication of Identity*, ed. Simon J. Bronner, 163–87. Oxford, UK: Littman Library of Jewish Civilization.

Berman, Saul J. 2001. "The Ideology of Modern Orthodoxy." *Sh'ma: A Journal of Jewish Ideas*, February 1. https://www.bjpa.org/bjpa/search-results?search=The+Ideology+of+Modern+Orthodoxy (accessed June 22, 2019).

Bernstein, Richard. 1971. *Praxis and Action: Contemporary Philosophies of Human Activity.* Philadelphia: University of Pennsylvania Press.

Bertman, Stephen. 2009. "The Antisemitic Origin of Michelangelo's Horned Moses." *Shofar* 27: 95–106.

Bérubé, Michael. 2015. "Boycott Bubkes: The Murky Logic of the ASA's Resolution Against Israel." In *The Case Against Academic Boycotts of Israel*, ed. Cary Nelson and Gabriel Noah Brahm, 128–33. Detroit: Wayne State University Press.

Beukers, Mariëlla, and Renée Waale, eds. 1992. *Tracing An-sky: Jewish Collections from the State Ethnographic Museum in St. Petersburg.* Amsterdam: Joods Historisch Museum.

Bhabha, Homi K. 1994. *The Location of Culture.* London: Routledge.

———. 2006. "Another Country." In *Without Boundary: Seventeen Ways of Looking*, by Fereshteh Daftari, 30–35. New York: Museum of Modern Art.

Bial, Henry. 2005. *Acting Jewish: Negotiating Ethnicity on the American Stage and Screen.* Ann Arbor: University of Michigan Press.

Biale, David. 2002. "Preface: Toward a Cultural History of the Jews." In *Cultures of the Jews: A New History*, ed. David Biale, xvii–xxxiii. New York: Schocken.

Biale, David, Michael Galchinsky, and Susannah Heschel, eds. 1998a. *Insider/Outsider: American Jews and Multiculturalism.* Berkeley: University of California Press.

———. 1998b. "Introduction: The Dialectic of Jewish Enlightenment." In *Insider/Outsider: American Jews and Multiculturalism*, ed. David Biale, Michael Galchinsky, and Susannah Heschel, 1–16. Berkeley: University of California Press.

Billig, Michael. 2001. "Humour and Hatred: The Racist Jokes of the Ku Klux Klan." *Discourse and Society* 12: 267–89.

Bilu, Yoram. 2003. "From *Milah* (Circumcision) to *Milah* (Word): Male Identity and Rituals in the Jewish Ultraorthodox Community." *Ethos* 31: 172–203.

Bines, Rosana Kohl. 2010. "Samuel Rawet's Wandering Jew: Jewish-Brazilian Monologues of Home and Displacement." In *Jews at Home: The Domestication of Identity*, ed. Simon J. Bronner, 217–40. Oxford, UK: Littman Library of Jewish Civilization.

Birner, Louis. 1984. "The Shlemiel and the Shlep: A Psychoanalytic Note on Two Masochistic Styles." *Modern Psychoanalysis* 9: 179–89.

Biro, Adam. 2001. *Two Jews on a Train: Stories from the Old Country and the New.* Chicago: University of Chicago Press.

Blank, Trevor J. 2007. "Examining the Transmission of Urban Legends: Making the Case for Folklore Fieldwork on the Internet." *Folklore Forum* 37: 15–26.

———. 2009. "Toward a Conceptual Framework for the Study of Folklore and the Internet." In *Folklore and the Internet: Vernacular Expression in a Digital World*, ed. Trevor J. Blank, 1–20. Logan: Utah State University Press.

———, ed. 2012. *Folk Culture in the Digital Age: The Emergent Dynamics of Human Interaction.* Logan: Utah State University Press.

———. 2013. *The Last Laugh: Folk Humor, Celebrity Culture, and Mass-Mediated Disasters.* Madison: University of Wisconsin Press.

Bleich, Judith. 1983. "The Symbolism in Innovative Rituals." *Sh'ma* (December 23). http://www.clal.org/e112.html (URL inactive, accessed January 30, 2011).

Block, Barry H. 2000. "Senator Lieberman and the Sabbath." Temple Beth-El, September 8. http://www.beth-elsa.org/be_so908.htm (URL inactive, accessed November 1, 2000).

Bloom, Emily Haft. 2006. *The Good Jewish Home: How Old Traditions Can Enrich Your Family's Life*. New York: MQ Publications.

Blumenfeld, Gerry. 1965. *Some of My Best Jokes Are Jewish!* New York: Kanrom.

Blumer, Herbert. 2004. *George Herbert Mead and Human Conduct*, ed. Thomas J. Morrione. Walnut Creek, CA: AltaMira.

Boas, Franz. 1902. "The Ethnological Significance of Esoteric Doctrines." *Science* 16: 872–74.

———. 1938a. "An Anthropologist's Credo." *The Nation* 147: 201–4.

———. 1938b. "Mythology and Folklore." In *General Anthropology*, ed. Franz Boas, 109–26. Boston: D. C. Heath.

Booker, Janice L. 1991. *The Jewish American Princess and Other Myths: The Many Forms of Self-Hatred*. New York: Shapolsky.

Bookstaber, Philip David. 1939. *Judaism and the American Mind in Theory and Practice*. New York: Bloch.

Boorstein, Michelle. 2013. "Should Observing the Jewish Sabbath Mean Switching Off the Internet?" *Washington Post* (September 13). https://www.washingtonpost.com/local/2013/09/13/121e7118-1bd2-11e3-8685-5021e0c41964_story.html?utm_term=.adb0d8eeccad (URL inactive; accessed June 9, 2019).

Boris, Staci. 2008. *The New Authentics: Artists of the Post-Jewish Generation*. Chicago: Spertus Press.

Bourdieu, Pierre. 1977. *Outline of a Theory of Practice*. Cambridge, UK: Cambridge University Press.

Boustan, Ra'anan, Oren Kosansky, and Marina Rustow, eds. 2011. *Jewish Studies at the Crossroads of Anthropology and History: Authority, Diaspora, Tradition*. Philadelphia: University of Pennsylvania Press.

Boyarin, Daniel, and Jonathan Boyarin. 1997. "Introduction: So What's New?" In *Jews and Other Differences: The New Cultural Studies*, ed. Jonathan Boyarin and Daniel Boyarin, vii–xxii. Minneapolis: University of Minnesota Press.

Boyarin, Jonathan. 1996. *Thinking in Jewish*. Chicago: University of Chicago Press.

———. 2014. "Trickster's Children: Genealogies of Jewishness in Anthropology." In *Framing Jewish Culture: Boundaries and Representations*, ed. Simon J. Bronner, 77–96. Oxford, UK: Littman Library of Jewish Civilization.

Boyarin, Jonathan, and Daniel Boyarin, eds. 1997. *Jews and Other Differences: The New Cultural Studies*. Minneapolis: University of Minnesota Press.

Boyer, Jay. 1993. "The *Schlemiezel*: Black Humor and the *Shtetl* Tradition." In *Semites and Stereotypes: Characteristics of Jewish Humor*, ed. Avner Ziv and Anat Zajdman, 3–12. Westport, CT: Greenwood.

Brad. 2008. "National Revelation and National Redemption." *Two Jews Three Opinions*, Weblog, November 25. http://tinyurl.com/2Jews3OpinionsBlog (accessed October 24, 2017).

Brahm, Gabriel Noah, and Asaf Romirowsky. 2015. "Anti-Semitic in Intent If Not in Effect: Questions of Bigotry, Dishonesty, and Shame." In *The Case Against Academic Boycotts of Israel*, ed. Cary Nelson and Gabriel Noah Brahm, 75–84. Detroit: Wayne State University Press.

Brandes, Stanley. 1983. "Jewish-American Dialect Jokes and Jewish-American Identity." *Jewish Social Studies* 45: 233–40.

Brauch, Julia, Anna Lipphardt, and Alexandra Nocke, eds. 2008. *Jewish Topographies: Visions of Space, Traditions of Place*. Aldershot, UK: Ashgate.

Braverman, Irus. 2013. "Animal Frontiers: A Tale of Three Zoos in Israel/Palestine." *Cultural Critique* 85: 122–62.

Breger, Jennifer. 2000. "Historical Precedents of Welcoming Ceremonies for Girls." In *The Orthodox Jewish Woman and Ritual: Options and Opportunities*, ed. Jennifer Breger and Lisa Schlaff, 3–5. New York: Jewish Orthodox Feminist Alliance.

Brod, Harry. 1988. *A Mensch Among Men: Explorations in Jewish Masculinity*. Freedom, CA: Crossing Press.

———. 1995. "Of Mice and Supermen: Images of Jewish Masculinity." In *Gender and Judaism: The Transformation of Tradition*, ed. T. M. Rudavsky, 279–93. New York: New York University Press.

———. 2004. "Jewish Men." In *Men and Masculinities: A Social, Cultural, and Historical Encyclopedia*, ed. Michael Kimmel and Amy Aronson, 441–43. Santa Barbara, CA: ABC-CLIO.

Brodkin, Karen. 1999. *How Jews Became White Folks and What That Says About Race in America*. New Brunswick, NJ: Rutgers University Press.

Bronner, Simon J. 1978. "Pictorial Jokes: A Traditional Combination of Verbal and Graphic Processes." *Tennessee Folklore Society Bulletin* 44: 189–96.

———. 1983. "Suburban Houses and Manner Books: The Structure of Tradition and Aesthetics." *Winterthur Portfolio* 18: 61–68.

———. 1985. "'What's Grosser than Gross? New Sick Joke Cycles." *Midwestern Journal of Language and Folklore* 11: 39–49.

———. 1986a. *American Folklore Studies: An Intellectual History*. Lawrence: University Press of Kansas.

———. 1986b. *Grasping Things: Folk Material Culture and Mass Society in America*. Lexington: University Press of Kentucky.

———. 1988. "Art, Performance, and Praxis: The Rhetoric of Contemporary Folklore Studies." *Western Folklore* 47: 75–101.

———. 1996. "Epes Tsoiberhaftes: The Rhetoric of Folklore and History in Jacob Seifter's Memoirs of Auschwitz." *Yiddish* 10: 17–46.

———. 1997. "Consumer Culture and Ethnicity in the Literature of Realism during America's Gilded Age." *Kansai American Literature* 34: 59-71.

———. 1998. *Following Tradition: Folklore in the Discourse of American Culture*. Logan: Utah State University Press.

———. 1999. "Cultural Historical Studies of Jews in Pennsylvania: A Review and Preview." *Pennsylvania History* 66: 311–38.

———. 2001. "From *Landsmannshaften* to *Vinkln*: Mediating Community Among Yiddish Speakers in America." *Jewish History* 15: 131–48.

———. 2004. "'This Is Why We Hunt': Social-Psychological Meanings of the Traditions and Rituals of Deer Camp." *Western Folklore* 63: 11–50.

———. 2005a. "Menfolk." In *Manly Traditions: The Folk Roots of American Masculinities*, ed. Simon J. Bronner, 1–60. Bloomington: Indiana University Press.

———. 2005b. "Plain Folk and Folk Society: John A. Hostetler's Legacy of the Little Community." In *Writing the Amish: The Worlds of John A. Hostetler*, ed. David L. Weaver-Zercher, 56–97. University Park: Pennsylvania State University Press.

———. 2006a. "Dialect Stories." In *Encyclopedia of American Folklife*, ed. Simon J. Bronner, 307–10. Armonk, NY: M. E. Sharpe.

———. 2006b. "Folk Logic: Interpretation and Explanation in Folkloristics." *Western Folklore* 65: 401–34.

———. 2008. "The Chutzpah of Jewish Cultural Studies." In *Jewishness: Expression, Identity, and Representation*, ed. Simon J. Bronner, 1–26. Oxford, UK: Littman Library of Jewish Civilization.

———. 2008–2009. "Fathers and Sons: Rethinking the Bar Mitzvah as an American Rite of Passage." *Children's Folklore Review* 31: 7–34.

———. 2009a. "Digitizing and Virtualizing Folklore." In *Folklore and the Internet: Vernacular Expression in a Digital World*, ed. Trevor J. Blank, 21–66. Logan: Utah State University Press.

———. 2009b. "The Problem and Promise of Tradition." *Levend Erfgoed: Vakblad voor Public Folklore and Public History* 6: 4–11.

———. 2010a. "The Dualities of House and Home in Jewish Culture." In *Jews at Home: The Domestication of Identity*, ed. Simon J. Bronner, 1–40. Oxford, UK: Littman Library of Jewish Civilization.

———. 2010b. "Framing Folklore: An Introduction." *Western Folklore* 69: 5–27.

———. 2011a. *Explaining Traditions: Folk Behavior in Modern Culture*. Lexington: University Press of Kentucky.

———. 2011b. "Framing Violence and Play in American Culture." *Journal of Ritsumeikan Social Sciences and Humanities* 3: 145–60.

———. 2012. "Jewish Naming Ceremonies for Girls: A Study in the Discourse of Tradition." In *Jewish Lifeworlds and Jewish Thought*, ed. Nathaniel Riemer, 211–20. Wiesbaden: Harrassowitz.

———. 2013. "The 'Handiness' of Tradition." In *Tradition in the Twenty-First Century: Locating the Role of the Past in the Present*, ed. Trevor J. Blank and Robert Glenn Howard, 186–218. Logan: Utah State University Press.

———. 2016. "Toward a Definition of Folklore in Practice." *Cultural Analysis* 15: 6–27.

———. 2017a. *Folklore: The Basics*. London: Routledge.

———. 2017b. "Popular Culture and Media." In *Pennsylvania Germans: An Interpretive Encyclopedia*, ed. Simon J. Bronner and Joshua R. Brown, eds., 441–68. Baltimore: Johns Hopkins University Press.

———. 2019. *The Practice of Folklore: Essays Toward a Theory of Tradition*. Jackson: University Press of Mississippi.

Bronner, Simon J., and Caspar Battegay, eds. 2018. *Connected Jews: Expressions of Community in Analogue and Digital Culture*. London: Littman Library of Jewish Civilization in association with Liverpool University Press.

Brooks, Matthew. 2002. "Voters Singing Battle Hymn of Republicans." *Jewish Forward* (August 2), 7.

Brostoff, Marissa. 2008. "Jackie Mason vs. Sarah Silverman." *Forward* (October 8). https://forward.com/news/israel/14343/jackie-mason-vs-sarah-silverman-02637/ (accessed December 25, 2019).

Brown, Bill, ed. 2004. *Things*. Chicago: University of Chicago Press.

Brown, Eleanor. 2000. "Lieberman's Revival of the Religious Left." *New York Times* (August 30), A27.

Brown, Phil, ed. 2002. *In the Catskills: A Century of the Jewish Experience in "The Mountains."* New York: Columbia University Press.

Bruce-Briggs, B., ed. 1979. *The New Class?* New York: McGraw-Hill.

Bruder, Edith. 2008. *The Black Jews of Africa: History, Religion, Identity.* Oxford, UK: Oxford University Press.

Brunotte, Ulrike, Anna-Dorothea Ludewig, and Axel Stähler, eds. 2015. *Orientalism, Gender, and the Jews: Literary and Artistic Transformations of European National Discourses.* Berlin: De Gruyter.

Brunvand, Jan Harold. 1972. "The Study of Contemporary Folklore: Jokes." *Fabula* 13: 1–19.

Buchanan, Andrew. 2000. "Jesse Jackson: Nation Should Rejoice About Lieberman." Beliefnet, August 8. http://www.beliefnet.com/story/36/story_3650_1.html (accessed November 1, 2000).

Buhle, Paul, and Harvey Pekar. 2007. "Introduction." In *Jews and Popular Culture,* vol. 1, *Movies, Radio, and Television,* ed. Paul Buhle, ix–xiv. Westport: Praeger.

Burkert, Walter. 1996 [1983]. "The Function and Transformation of Ritual Killing." In *Readings in Ritual Studies,* ed. Ronald L. Grimes, 62–71. Upper Saddle River, NJ: Prentice-Hall.

Burman, Rickie, Jennifer Marin, and Lily Steadman. 2006. *Treasures of Jewish Heritage: The Jewish Museum London.* London: Jewish Museum.

Burns, Tom R. 1992. *Erving Goffman.* New York: Routledge.

Busby, Robert. 2001. *Defending the American Presidency: Clinton and the Lewinsky Scandal.* New York: Palgrave.

Bush, Andrew. 2011. *Jewish Studies: A Theoretical Introduction.* New Brunswick, NJ: Rutgers University Press.

Cahan, Y. L. 1938. *Yidisher folklor: Filogische shriftn fun YIVO.* Vilna: YIVO.

———. 1952. *Shtudyes vegn yidisher folksshafung.* New York: YIVO.

Cardozo, Arlene Rossen. 1982. *Jewish Family Celebrations: The Sabbath, Festivals, and Ceremonies.* New York: St. Martin's Press.

Carey, James W. 2009. *Communication as Culture: Essays on Media and Society,* rev. ed. New York: Routledge.

Carrel, Barbara Goldman. 1999. "Hasidic Women's Head Coverings: A Feminized System of Hasidic Distinction." In *Religion, Dress, and the Body,* ed. Linda B. Arthur, 163–80. Oxford, UK: Berg.

CD Baby. 1991. Advertisement for *Brand New* by Jackie Mason. CD Baby website, www.cdbaby.com/cd/jackiemason2 (accessed December 7, 2006).

Chabad.org Staff. 2019. "What Does 'Schlep' Mean?" Chabad.org. https://www.chabad.org/library/article_cdo/aid/3920923/jewish/What-Does-Schlep-Mean.htm (accessed December 24, 2019).

Chesler, Phyllis. 2005. *The New Anti-Semitism: The Current Crisis and What We Must Do About It.* San Francisco: Jossey-Bass.

Chesser, Barbara Jo. 1980. "Analysis of Wedding Rituals: An Attempt to Make Weddings More Meaningful." *Family Relations* 29: 204–9.

Cheyette, Bryan, ed. 1996. *Between "Race" and Culture: Representations of "The Jew" in English and American Literature*. Stanford, CA: Stanford University Press.

Chill, Abraham. 1979. *The Minhagim: The Customs and Ceremonies of Judaism, Their Origins, and Rationale*. New York: KTAV.

Chin, Gabriel J., and Rose Cuison Villazor, eds. 2015. *The Immigration and Nationality Act of 1965: Legislating a New America*. New York: Cambridge University Press.

Chozick, Amy, and Hannah Seligson. 2018. "Are Jared and Ivanka Good for the Jews?" *New York Times* (November 17). https://www.nytimes.com/2018/11/17/style/ivanka-trump-jared-kushner.html (accessed June 22, 2019).

Cieraad, Irene, ed. 2006. *At Home: An Anthropology of Domestic Space*. Syracuse, NY: Syracuse University Press.

Cocchiara, Giuseppe. 1971. *The History of Folklore in Europe*, trans. John N. McDaniel. Philadelphia: Institute for the Study of Human Issues.

Cohan, Steven. 1997. *Masked Men: Masculinity and the Movies in the Fifties*. Bloomington: Indiana University Press.

Cohen, Anne. 2014. "Forget Uber—Let Jewish Moms 'Schlep' You Around." *Forward* (November 25). https://forward.com/schmooze/209854/forget-uber-let-jewish-moms-schlep-you-around/ (accessed December 24, 2019).

Cohen, Debra Nussbaum. 2016. "Matchmakers Make Comeback in Age of Tinder and JDate." *Forward* (February 14). http://forward.com/sisterhood/333501/matchmakers-make-comeback-in-age-of-tinder-and-jdate/ (accessed June 9, 2019).

Cohen, Edward. 2002. *The Peddler's Grandson: Growing Up Jewish in Mississippi*. New York: Dell.

Cohen, Francis L. 1900. "Folk-Song Survivals in Jewish Worship-Music." *Journal of the Folk-Song Society* 1: 32–38, 52–59.

Cohen, Jeremy, and Richard I. Cohen. 2008. *The Jewish Contribution to Civilization: Reassessing an Idea*. Oxford, UK: Littman Library of Jewish Civilization.

Cohen, Judah M. 2009. *The Making of a Reform Jewish Cantor: Musical Authority, Cultural Investment*. Bloomington: Indiana University Press.

Cohen, Julie-Marthe, Jelka Kröger, and Emile Schrijver, eds. 2004. *Gifts from the Heart: Ceremonial Objects from the Jewish Historical Museum, Amsterdam*. Amsterdam: Zwolle Amsterdam.

Cohen, Max. 1888. "Maimonides Library." *Menorah* 4: 293–97.

Cohen, Naomi. 1988. " 'Shaare Tefila Congregation v. Cobb': A New Departure in American Jewish Defense?" *Jewish History* 3: 95–108.

Cohen, Richard I. 2008. "The 'Wandering Jew' from Medieval Legend to Modern Metaphor." In *The Art of Being Jewish in Modern Times*, ed. Barbara Kirshenblatt-Gimblett and Jonathan Karp, 147–75. Philadelphia: University of Pennsylvania Press.

Cohen, Rosalie A. 1969. "Conceptual Styles, Cultural Conflict, and Nonverbal Tests of Intelligence." *American Anthropologist* 5: 828–56.

Cohen, Sarah Blacher, and Joanne Barbara Koch, eds. 2007. *Shared Stages: Ten American Dramas of Blacks and Jews*. Albany: State University of New York Press.

Cohen, Shaye J. D. 1999. *The Beginnings of Jewishness: Boundaries, Varieties, Uncertainties*. Berkeley: University of California Press.

———. 2005. *Why Aren't Jewish Women Circumcised? Gender and Covenant in Judaism*. Berkeley: University of California Press.

Cohen, Yoel. 2011. "Haredim and the Internet: A Hate-Love Affair." In *Mediating Faiths: Religion and Socio-Cultural Change in the Twenty-First Century*, ed. Michael Bailey and Guy Redden, 63–74. London: Routledge.

"Conferences and Meetings." 1983–1984. *Jewish Folklore and Ethnology Newsletter* 6: 5–6.

Contemporary Jewish Museum. 2009. *New Works, Old Story: 80 Artists at the Passover Table—The Dorothy Saxe Invitational*. San Francisco: Contemporary Jewish Museum.

Conway, Janet M. 2006. *Praxis and Politics: New Approaches in Sociology*. New York: Routledge.

Cooper, Alanna E. 2011. "Rituals of Mourning Among Central Asia's Bukharan Jews: Remembering the Past and Addressing the Present." In *Revisioning Ritual: Jewish Traditions in Transition*, ed. Simon J. Bronner, 290–316. Oxford, UK: Littman Library of Jewish Civilization.

———. 2012. *Bukharan Jews and the Dynamics of Global Judaism*. Bloomington: Indiana University Press.

Correll, Timothy Corrigan. 1997. "Associative Context and Joke Visualization." *Western Folklore* 56: 317–30.

Cray, Ed. 1964. "The Rabbi Trickster." *Journal of American Folklore* 87: 331–45.

Crombie, James F. 1895. "Shoe-Throwing at Weddings." *Folklore* 6: 258–81.

Cross, Gary. 2008. *Men to Boys: The Making of Modern Immaturity*. New York: Columbia University Press.

Cuddihy, John Murray. 1974. *The Ordeal of Civility: Freud, Marx, Lévi-Strauss, and the Jewish Struggle with Modernity*. New York: Dell.

Culler, Jonathan. 2013. "Lévi-Strauss: Good to Think With." *Yale French Studies* 123: 6–13.

Danaan, Julie Hilton. 2004. "Chai Ceremony." *Ohalah*. https://ohalah.org/resources/chai-ceremony/ (accessed August 2, 2020).

Daniels, Roger. 2004. *Guarding the Golden Door: American Immigration Policy and Immigrants Since 1882*. New York: Hill & Wang.

Davidson, Baruch S. 2020. "Will the Synagogue Ever Go Virtual? Why A Skype Minyan Is Not Okay." Chabad.org. https://www.chabad.org/library/article_cdo/aid/1783077/jewish/Will-the-Synagogue-Ever-Go-Virtual.htm (accessed May 8, 2020).

Davies, Christie. 1990. *Ethnic Humor Around the World*. Bloomington: Indiana University Press.

———. 2011. *Jokes and Targets*. Bloomington: Indiana University Press.

Davis, Avraham. 2006. *Kitzur Shulchan Aruch*, 3 vols. Lakewood, NJ: Israel Book Shop.

Davis, Joseph. 2002. "The Reception of the 'Shulhan 'Arukh' and the Formation of Ashkenazic Jewish Identity." *AJS Review* 26: 251–76.

Davis, Judith. 1995. "The Bar Mitzvah *Balabusta*: The Mother's Role in the Family's Rite of Passage." In *Active Voices: Women in Jewish Culture*, ed. Maurie Sacks, 125–41. Urbana: University of Illinois Press.

———. 2003. "Mazel Tov: The Bar Mitzvah as a Multigenerational Ritual of Change and Continuity." In *Rituals in Families and Family Therapy*, ed. Evan Imber-Black, Janine Roberts, and Richard A. Whiting, 182–216. New York: Norton.

Deflem, Mathieu. 1991. "Ritual, Anti-Structure, and Religion: A Discussion of Victor Turner's Processual Symbolic Analysis." *Journal for the Scientific Study of Religion* 30: 1–25.

Dégh, Linda. 1994. *American Folklore and the Mass Media*. Bloomington: Indiana University Press.

Del Negro, Giovanna P. 2010. "From the Nightclub to the Living Room: Party Records of Three Jewish Women Comics." In *Jews at Home: The Domestication of Identity*, ed. Simon J. Bronner, 188–216. Oxford, UK: Littman Library of Jewish Civilization.

Dencik, Lars. 2002. "'Jewishness' in Postmodernity: The Case of Sweden." In *New Jewish Identities: Contemporary Europe and Beyond*, ed. Zvi Gitelman, Barry Kosmin, and András Kovács. Budapest: Central European University Press.

Dershowitz, Alan M. 1991. *Chutzpah*. Boston: Little, Brown.

———. 1997. *The Vanishing American Jew: In Search of Jewish Identity for the Next Century*. Boston: Little, Brown.

———. 2011. "Do Jews Control the Media?" *HuffPost* (May 25). http://www.huffingtonpost.com/alan-dershowitz/do-jews-control-the-media_b_753227.html (accessed October 24, 2017).

Deshen, Shlomo. 1979. "The Kol Nidre Enigma: An Anthropological View of the Day of Atonement Liturgy." *Ethnology* 18: 121–33.

Desser, David. 2001. "Jews in Space: The 'Ordeal of Masculinity' in Contemporary American Film and Television." In *Ladies and Gentlemen, Boys and Girls: Gender in Film at the End of the Twentieth Century*, ed. Murray Pomerance, 267–82. Albany: State University of New York Press.

Diamant, Anita. 2007. *Living a Jewish Life: Jewish Traditions, Customs, and Values for Today's Families*. New York: HarperCollins.

———. 2008. *The New Jewish Baby Book: Names, Ceremonies, and Customs—A Guide for Today's Families*, 2nd ed. Woodstock, VT: Jewish Lights.

Diamond, Etan. 2000. *And I Will Dwell in Their Midst: Orthodox Jews in Suburbia*. Chapel Hill: University of North Carolina Press.

Diner, Hasia. 1977. *In the Almost Promised Land: American Jews and Blacks, 1915–1935*. Westport, CT: Greenwood.

———. 2000. *Lower East Side Memories: A Jewish Place in America*. Princeton, NJ: Princeton University Press.

Dinnerstein, Leonard. 1995. *Anti-Semitism in America*, 2nd rev. ed. New York: Oxford University Press.

Dolsten, Josefin. 2019. "Jews of Color Are Chronically Undercounted, Researchers Find." Jewish Telegraphic Agency, May 30. https://www.jta.org/2019/05/30/united-states/jews-of-color-are-chronically-undercounted-researchers-find (accessed June 4, 2019).

Donadio, Rachel. 2000. "With Diversity on Dais, Republican Convention Gives Key Role to Jews." *Jewish Forward* (August 4), 1, 10.

Dorchain, Claudia Simone, and Felice Naomi Wonnenberg, eds. 2013. *Contemporary Jewish Reality in Germany and Its Reflection in Film*. Berlin: De Gruyter.

Dorinson, Joseph. 2015. *Kvetching and Shpritzing: Jewish Humor in American Popular Culture*. Jefferson, NC: McFarland.

Dorson, Richard M. 1948. "Dialect Stories of the Upper Peninsula: A New Form of American Folklore." *Journal of American Folklore* 61: 113–50.

———. 1960. "Jewish-American Dialect Stories on Tape." In *Studies in Biblical and Jewish Folklore*, ed. Raphael Patai, Francis Lee Utley, and Dov Noy, 111–76. Bloomington: Indiana University Press.

———. 1968. *The British Folklorists: A History*. Chicago: University of Chicago Press.

Douglas, Kirk. 1988. *The Ragman's Son: An Autobiography*. New York: Simon & Schuster.

Douglas, Mary. 1966. *Purity and Danger: An Analysis of Concepts of Pollution and Taboo*. London: Routledge & Kegan Paul.

———. 1968. "The Social Control of Cognition: Some Factors in Joke Perception." *Man* 3: 361–76.

Dovere, Edward-Isaac. 2020. "Two Jews Walk into a Presidential Primary." *Atlantic* (January 26). https://www.theatlantic.com/politics/archive/2020/01/bloomberg-and-sanders-embrace-judaism-not-each-other/605503/ (accessed May 11, 2020).

Dressner, Stacy. 2020. "Groups Call on Newsom to Veto Ethnic-Studies Bill." *CT Jewish Ledger* (August 18). http://www.jewishledger.com/2020/08/groups-call-on-newsom-to-veto-ethnic-studies-bill/ (Accessed August 24, 2020).

Drout, Michael D. C. 2006. "A Meme-Based Approach to Oral Traditional Theory." *Oral Tradition* 21: 269–94.

Du Bois, W. E. B. 1903. *The Souls of Black Folk: Essays and Sketches*. Chicago: A. C. McClurg.

Du Gay, Paul, Jessica Evans, and Peter Redman, eds. 2000. *Identity: A Reader*. London: SAGE.

Duke, Lynne. 2000a. "American Jewish Congress Welcomes Mfume's Condemnation of Anti-Semitic Remarks of NAACP Dallas President Following Designation of Lieberman as Vice-Presidential Choice." American Jewish Congress, August 9. http://www.ajcongress.org/pages/RELS2000/AUG00_05.htm (URL inactive, accessed November 1, 2000).

———. 2000b. "Some Blacks' Harsh Comments About Lieberman Stir Old Tensions." *Washington Post* (August 20), A2.

Duncan, Hugh Dalziel. 2002 [1962]. *Communication and Social Order*. New Brunswick, NJ: Transaction.

Dundes, Alan. 1962. "From Etic to Emic Units in the Structural Study of Folktales." *Journal of American Folklore* 75: 95–105.

———. 1966. "Metafolklore and Oral Literary Criticism." *Monist* 50: 505–16.

———. 1968. "The Number Three in American Culture." In *Every Man His Way: Readings in Cultural Anthropology*, ed. Alan Dundes, 401–24. Englewood Cliffs, NJ: Prentice-Hall.

———. 1971. "A Study of Ethnic Slurs: The Jew and the Polack in the United States." *Journal of American Folklore* 84: 186–203.

———. 1981. "Many Hands Make Light Work or Caught in the Act of Screwing in Light Bulbs." *Western Folklore* 40: 261–66.

———. 1985. "The J.A.P. and the J.A.M. in American Jokelore." *Journal of American Folklore* 98: 456–75.

———. 1987a. *Cracking Jokes: Studies of Sick Humor Cycles and Stereotypes*. Berkeley, CA: Ten Speed Press.

———. 1987b. "The Psychoanalytic Study of Folklore." In *Parsing Through Customs: Essays by a Freudian Folklorist*, by Alan Dundes, 3–46. Madison: University of Wisconsin Press.

———. 1989. *Folklore Matters*. Knoxville: University of Tennessee Press.

———. 1991. "The Ritual Murder or Blood Libel Legend: A Study of Anti-Semitic Victimization Through Projective Inversion." In *The Blood Libel Legend: A Casebook in Anti-Semitic Folklore*, ed. Alan Dundes, 336–78. Madison: University of Wisconsin Press.

———. 1997a. *Cracking Jokes: Studies of Sick Humor Cycles and Stereotypes*. Berkeley: University of California Press.

———. 1997b. "Madness in Method Plus a Plea for Projective Inversion in Myth." In *Myth and Method*, ed. Laurie L. Patton and Wendy Doniger, 147–59. Charlottesville: University Press of Virginia.

———. 2002a. "The Psychoanalytic Study of Religious Custom and Belief: Ritual Fasting, Self-Mutilation, and the *Deus Otiosus*." In *Bloody Mary in the Mirror: Essays in Psychoanalytic Folkloristics*, by Alan Dundes, 3–15. Jackson: University Press of Mississippi.

———. 2002b. *The Shabbat Elevator and Other Sabbath Subterfuges*. Lanham, MD: Rowman & Littlefield.

———. 2005. "Folkloristics in the Twenty-First Century (AFS Invited Presidential Plenary Address, 2004)." *Journal of American Folklore* 118: 385–408.

———. 2007. "The Ritual Murder or Blood Libel Legend: A Study of Anti-Semitic Victimization Through Projective Inversion." In *The Meaning of Folklore: The Analytical Essays of Alan Dundes*, ed. Simon J. Bronner, 382–409. Logan: Utah State University Press.

Dundes, Alan, and Galit Hasan-Rokem, eds. 1986. *The Wandering Jew: Essays in the Interpretations of a Christian Legend*. Bloomington: Indiana University Press.

Dundes, Alan, and Thomas Hauschild. 1983. "Auschwitz Jokes." *Western Folklore* 42: 249–60.

Dundes, Alan, and Carl R. Pagter. 1978. *Work Hard and You Shall Be Rewarded: Urban Folklore from the Paperwork Empire*. Bloomington: Indiana University Press.

During, Simon, ed. 1999. *The Cultural Studies Reader*, 2nd ed. London: Routledge.

Eden, Ami. 2000a. "Lieberman Speech Stirs Ire in Crucial Democratic Group: Jews." *Jewish Forward* (September 1), 1, 5.

———. 2000b. "Orthodox Solon Sending Country to 'Judaism 101.'" *Jewish Forward* (August 11), 1.

———. 2000c. "Slips in the Lieberman Balancing Act: Intermarriage Gaffe Highlights Tensions Between Faith, Politics." *Jewish Forward* (September 29), 6.

"Editorial: Separation and the Senator." 2000. *Jewish Forward* (September 1), 8.

Edwards, Jason A. 2017. "Rhetorical Criticism." In *Encyclopedia of American Studies*, ed. Simon J. Bronner. Baltimore: Johns Hopkins University Press. http://eas-ref.press .jhu.edu/view?aid=806 (URL inactive; accessed June 9, 2019).

Ehrlich, Uri. 2004. *The Nonverbal Language of Prayer*, trans. Dena Ordan. Tübingen: Mohr Siebeck.

Eilberg-Schwartz, Howard, ed. 1992. *People of the Body: Jews and Judaism from an Embodied Perspective*. Albany: State University of New York Press.

Eilbirt, Henry. 1981. *What Is a Jewish Joke? An Excursion into Jewish Humor*. Northvale, NJ: Jason Aronson.

Eis, Ruth. 1979. *Torah Binders of the Judah L. Magnes Museum*. Berkeley: Judah L. Magnes Memorial Museum.

Eisen, Arnold M. 1998. *Rethinking Modern Judaism: Ritual, Commandment, Community*. Chicago: University of Chicago Press.

———. 2009. "Preface." In *Reinventing Ritual: Contemporary Art and Design for Jewish Life*, ed. Daniel Belasco, xi–xiii. New Haven, CT: Yale University Press.

Eisenberg, Ronald L. 2004. *The JPS Guide to Jewish Traditions*. Philadelphia: Jewish Publication Society of America.

Elbogen, Ismar. 1993. *Jewish Liturgy: A Comprehensive History*. Philadelphia: Jewish Publication Society.

Eleff, Zev. 2016. *Modern Orthodox Judaism: A Documentary History*. Lincoln: University of Nebraska Press.

El-Haj, Nadia. 2001. *Facts on the Ground: Archaeological Practice and Territorial Self-Fashioning in Israeli Society*. Chicago: University of Chicago Press.

Eliach, Yaffa. 1988. *Hasidic Tales of the Holocaust*. New York: Vintage.

Eliade, Mircea. 1958. *Rites and Symbols of Initiation: The Mysteries of Birth and Rebirth*. New York: Harper.

Eliezer, Daniel, and Paul Kupperberg. 2008. *Jew-Jitsu: The Hebrew Hands of Fury*. New York: Citadel Press.

Encyclopaedia Judaica, 16 vols. 1972. Jerusalem: Encyclopedia Judaica.

Epstein, Lawrence J. 2001. *The Haunted Smile: The Story of Jewish Comedians in America*. New York: Public Affairs.

Erdman, Harley. 1997. *Staging the Jew: The Performance of an American Ethnicity, 1860–1920*. New Brunswick, NJ: Rutgers University Press.

Estraikh, Gennady, and Mikhail Krutikov, eds. 2000. *The Shtetl: Image and Reality—Papers of the 2nd Mendel Friedman International Conference on Yiddish*. Oxford, UK: European Humanities Research Center, University of Oxford.

Ettinger, Yair. 2012. "Behind the Scenes of the Ultra-Orthodox Anti-Internet Rally." *Haaretz* (May 22). http://www.haaretz.com/jewish/news/behind-the-scenes-of-the -ultra-orthodox-anti-internet-rally.premium-1.431796 (accessed October 24, 2017).

Etzioni, Amitai. 2015. *Privacy in a Cyber Age: Policy and Practice*. New York: Palgrave Macmillan.

Fabre-Vassas, Claudine. 1997. *The Singular Beast: Jews, Christians, and the Pig*, trans. Carol Volk. New York: Columbia University Press.

Fader, Ayala. 2007. "Reclaiming Sacred Sparks: Linguistic Syncretism and Gendered Language Shift Among Hasidic Jews in New York." *Journal of Linguistic Anthropology* 17: 1–22.

Falk, Avner. 1993. "The Problem of Mourning in Jewish History." In *The Psychoanalytic Study of Society*, vol. 18, *Essays in Honor of Alan Dundes*, ed. L. Bryce Boyer, Ruth M. Boyer, and Stephen M. Sonnenberg, 299–316. New York: Routledge.

Falk, Pesach Eliyahu. 1998. *Modesty, An Adornment for Life: Halachos and Attitudes Concerning Tznius of Dress and Conduct*. Gateshead, UK: P. E. Falk.

Farrell, Eileen. 1985. "The Poetics of Renunciation: Form and Content in Ritual Fasting." *Journal of Psychoanalytic Anthropology* 8: 249–64.

FCCNN Administrator. 2001. "Jewish Ritual Celebrates Passage to College." *Brainerd Dispatch* (August 10). https://www.brainerddispatch.com/lifestyle/health/3406330 -jewish-ritual-celebrates-passage-college (accessed August 4, 2020).

Feintuch, Burt, ed. 2003. *Eight Words for the Study of Expressive Culture*. Urbana: University of Illinois Press.

Feldman, Ari. 2020. "Orthodox Jews Under Quarantine Yearn to Reunite, Gather Online in the Meantime." *Forward* (March 10). https://forward.com/news/national/441228/

coronavirus-update-westchester-jewish-orthodox-quarantine/ (accessed May 8, 2020).

Fenster, Mark. 2008. *Conspiracy Theories: Secrecy and Power in American Culture*. Minneapolis: University of Minnesota Press.

Fernandez, Ronald. 2003. *Mappers of Society: The Lives, Times, and Legacies of Great Sociologists*. Westport, CT: Praeger.

Fine, Gary Alan. 1983. *Shared Fantasy: Role-Playing Games as Social Worlds*. Chicago: University of Chicago Press.

———. 1987. "Joseph Jacobs: Sociological Folklorist." *Folklore* 98: 183–93.

Fingeroth, Danny. 2007. *Disguised as Clark Kent: Jews, Comics, and the Creation of the Superhero*. New York: Continuum.

Fink, Carole. 2010. "Jews in Contemporary Europe." In *Ethnic Europe: Mobility, Identity, and Conflict in a Globalized World*, ed. Roland Hsu, 212–40. Stanford, CA: Stanford University Press.

Finkelman, Shimon. 1999. *Lag Ba'omer: Its Observance, Laws, and Significance*. Brooklyn, NY: Mesorah.

Finkelstein, Norman G. 2005. *Beyond Chutzpah: On the Misuse of Anti-Semitism and the Abuse of History*. Berkeley: University of California Press.

Fischman, Fernando. 2011. "Using Yiddish: Language Ideologies, Verbal Art, and Identity Among Argentine Jews." *Journal of Folklore Research* 48: 37–61.

Fishkoff, Sue. 2003. *The Rebbe's Army: Inside the World of Chabad*. New York: Schocken.

———. 2008. "PETA Slams N.Y. Kapparot Ritual." JewishJournal.com, August 25. https://www.jta.org/2008/08/25/united-states/peta-slams-n-y-kapparot-ritual (accessed February 10, 2010).

Fishman, Sylvia Barack. 1989. "The Impact of Feminism on American Jewish Life." *The American Jewish Year Book* 89: 3–62.

Flam, Gila. 1992. *Singing for Survival: Songs of the Lodz Ghetto, 1940–1945*. Urbana: University of Illinois Press.

Foltin, Richard T. 2001. "U.S. National Affairs." In *American Jewish Yearbook 2001*, ed. David Singer and Lawrence Grossman, 145–94. New York: American Jewish Committee.

Fonrobert, Charlotte Elisheva. 2005. "The Political Symbolism of the Eruv." *Jewish Social Studies*, n.s., 11: 9–35.

Foote, Monica. 2007. "Userpicks: Cyber Folk Art in the Early 21st Century." *Folklore Forum* 37: 27–38.

Forman, Ira N. 2001. "The Politics of Minority Consciousness: The Historical Voting Behavior of American Jews." In *Jews in American Politics*, ed. L. Sandy Maisel and Ira N. Forman, 141–60. Lanham, MD: Rowman & Littlefield.

"The *Forward* 50: Making a Difference in a Difficult Year." 2001. *Jewish Forward* (November 9), 15, 19–22.

Forward Staff. 2000. "Gore's Choice for Veep Electrifies American Jews: Lieberman Gets Widespread Praise as Skeptics on Left, Right Emerge." *Jewish Forward* (August 11), 1, 3.

Foster, Derek. 1996. "Community and Identity in the Electronic Village." In *Internet Culture*, ed. David Porter, 23–38. New York: Routledge.

Fox, Marvin. 1978. "Foreword." In *The Minhagim: The Customs and Ceremonies of Judaism, Their Origins, and Rationale,* by Abraham Chill, vii–viii. New York: KTAV.

Fox, William S. 1983. "Computerized Creation and Diffusion of Folkloric Materials." *Folklore Forum* 16: 5–20.

Foxman, Abraham H. 2010. *Jews and Money: The Story of a Stereotype.* New York: Palgrave Macmillan.

Frank, Gelya. 1997. "Jews, Multiculturalism, and Boasian Anthropology." *American Anthropologist* 99: 731–45.

Frank, Russell. 2009. "The *Forward* as Folklore: Studying E-Mailed Humor." In *Folklore and the Internet: Vernacular Expression in a Digital World,* ed. Trevor J. Blank, 98–122. Logan: Utah State University Press.

———. 2011. *Newslore: Contemporary Folklore on the Internet.* Jackson: University Press of Mississippi.

Frankel, Ellen, and Betsy Platkin Teutsch. 1992. *The Encyclopedia of Jewish Symbols.* Northvale, NJ: Jason Aronson.

Frazin, Rachel. 2019. "Lieberman: Democratic Party Is not Anti-Jewish, but Some Members Say Anti-Semitic Things." *The Hill* (March 17). https://thehill.com/homenews/house/434400-lieberman-democratic-party-is-not-anti-jewish-but-some-members-say-anti (accessed June 22, 2019).

Freedman, Jean R. 2011. "The Masquerade of Ideas: The *Purimspil* as Theatre of Conflict." In *Revisioning Ritual: Jewish Traditions in Transition,* ed. Simon J. Bronner, 94–132. Oxford, UK: Littman Library of Jewish Civilization.

Freedman, Samuel G. 2001. *Jew vs. Jew: The Struggle for the Soul of American Jewry.* New York: Touchstone.

———. 2002. Samuel Freedman website, August 2002. http://www.samuelfreedman.com/ (accessed September 1, 2002).

Freud, Sigmund. 1960 [1905]. *Jokes and Their Relation to the Unconscious,* trans. James Strachey. New York: Norton.

Friedlander, Judith. 2011. "Typical Jokes in the Shtetl." On her webpage *Jews and Mexicans: Here and There.* https://tinyurl.com/6y79vfc (accessed October 24, 2017).

Friedman, Lester D. 1987. *The Jewish Image in American Film.* Secaucus, NJ: Citadel Press.

Friedman, Uri. 2010. "People of the E-Book? Observant Jews Struggle with Sabbath in a Digital Age." *Atlantic* (December 21). https://www.theatlantic.com/technology/archive/2010/12/people-of-the-e-book-observant-jews-struggle-with-sabbath-in-a-digital-age/68289/ (accessed October 23, 2017).

Friedman, William S. 1912. "Report of Committee on Church and State." In *Yearbook of the Central Conference of American Rabbis,* vol. 22, ed. Samuel Schulman and Solomon Foster, 101–18. New York: Central Conference of American Rabbis.

Frishman, Judith, and Ido De Haan. 2011. "Introduction." In *Borders and Boundaries in and Around Dutch Jewish History,* ed. Judith Frishman, David J. Wertheim, Ido de Haan, and Joël J. Cahen, 7–18. Amsterdam: Amsterdam University Press.

Fromm, Annette B. 2007. *We Are Few: Folklore and Ethnic Identity of the Jewish Community of Ioannina, Greece.* Lanham, MD: Lexington Books.

Gabler, Neal. 1988. *An Empire of Their Own: How the Jews Invented Hollywood.* New York: Doubleday.

Gans, Herbert. 1957. "Progress of a Suburban Jewish Community." *Commentary* (February), 120–25.

———. 1962. *The Urban Villagers: Group and Class in the Life of Italian-Americans*. New York: Free Press.

———. 1996. "Symbolic Ethnicity: The Future of Ethnic Groups and Cultures in America." In *Theories of Ethnicity: A Classical Reader*, ed. Werner Sollors, 429–59. New York: New York University Press.

Garber, Marjorie. 2012. *Loaded Words*. New York: Fordham University Press.

Gaster, Theodor. 1955. *The Holy and the Profane: Evolution of Jewish Folkways*. New York: W. Sloane.

———. 1961. *Thespis: Ritual, Myth, and Drama in the Ancient Near East*. Garden City, NY: Doubleday.

———. 1978. *Festivals of the Jewish Year: A Modern Interpretation and Guide*. New York: William Morrow.

———. 1980. *The Holy and the Profane: The Evolution of Jewish Folkways*. New York: William Morrow.

Geertz, Clifford. 1973. "Thick Description: Toward an Interpretive Theory of Culture.'" In *The Interpretation of Cultures: Selected Essays*, by Clifford Geertz, 3–32. New York: Basic Books.

Geffen, Rela M., ed. 1993. *Celebration and Renewal: Rites of Passage in Judaism*. Philadelphia: Jewish Publication Society.

Gelbard, Shmuel Pinchas. 1998. *Rite and Reason: 1,050 Jewish Customs and Their Sources*, trans. R. Nachman Bulman. Petach Tikvah, Israel: Mifal Rashi.

Geller, Jay. 1992. "The Unmanning of the Wandering Jews." *American Imago* 49: 227–62.

Gendler, Mary. 1974–1975. "Sarah's Seed: A New Ritual for Women." *Response* 24 (winter): 65–75.

George, Rosemary Marangoly. 2007. "Domestic." In *Keywords for American Cultural Studies*, ed. Bruce Burgett and Glenn Hendler, 88–92. New York: New York University Press.

Georges, Robert A. 1969. "Toward an Understanding of Storytelling Events." *Journal of American Folklore* 82: 313–28.

Georges, Robert A., and Michael Owen Jones. 1995. *Folkloristics: An Introduction*. Bloomington: Indiana University Press.

Gershenson, Olga. 2008. "Ambivalence and Identity in Russian Jewish Cinema." In *Jewishness: Expression, Identity, and Representation*, ed. Simon J. Bronner, 175–94. Oxford, UK: Littman Library of Jewish Civilization.

Gershon, Stuart Weinberg. 1994. *Kol Nidrei: Its Origin, Development, and Significance*. Northvale, NJ: Jason Aronson.

Gilbert, James. 2005. *Men in the Middle: Searching for Masculinity in the 1950s*. Chicago: University of Chicago Press.

Gillis, John R., ed. 1994. *Commemorations: The Politics of National Identity*. Princeton, NJ: Princeton University Press.

Gilman, Sander L. 1990. *Jewish Self-Hatred: Anti-Semitism and the Hidden Language of the Jews*. Baltimore: Johns Hopkins University Press.

———. 1991. *The Jew's Body*. New York: Routledge.

————. 1996. *Smart Jews: The Construction of the Image of Jewish Superior Intelligence*. Lincoln: University of Nebraska Press.

————. 1999. "'The Frontier as a Model for Jewish History." In *Jewries at the Frontier: Accommodation, Identity, Conflict*, ed. Sander L. Gilman and Milton Shain, 1–28. Urbana: University of Illinois Press.

————. 2003. *Jewish Frontiers: Essays on Bodies, Histories, and Identities*. New York: Palgrave Macmillan.

————. 2006. *Multiculturalism and the Jews*. New York: Routledge.

————. 2008. "Are Jews Musical? Historical Notes on the Question of Jewish Musical Modernism." In *Jewish Musical Modernism, Old and New*, ed. Philip V. Bohlman, vii–xvi. Chicago: University of Chicago Press.

Gilman, Sander L., and Milton Shain, eds. 1999. *Jewries at the Frontier: Accommodation, Identity, Conflict*. Urbana: University of Illinois Press.

Ginzberg, Louis. 1955. *Jewish Law and Lore*. Philadelphia: Jewish Publication Society of America.

Girard, René. 1996 [1977]. "Violence and the Sacred: Sacrifice." In *Readings in Ritual Studies*, ed. Ronald L. Grimes, 239–56. Upper Saddle River, NJ: Prentice-Hall.

Gitelman, Zvi. 1998. "The Decline of the Diaspora Jewish Nation: Boundaries, Content, and Jewish Identity." *Jewish Social Studies*, n.s., 4: 112–32.

Gittell, Seth. 1998. "Feinstein Seen as in Running." *Jewish Forward* (January 30), 1.

————. 2000. "Veep Aspirants in Good Stead on Middle East." *Jewish Forward* (March 10), 1.

Glass, Montague. 1911. *Abe and Mawruss: Being Further Adventures of Potash and Perlmutter*. Garden City, NY: Doubleday, Page.

Glassenberg, Sam Z. 2014. "JDate Works for Profit—and the Continuity of the Jewish People." *Forward* (February 10). http://forward.com/opinion/192429/jdate-works -for-profit-and-the-continuity-of-the/.UvpkOwBcc00.facebook (accessed October 24, 2017).

Glassie, Henry. 1968. *Pattern in the Material Folk Culture of the Eastern United States*. Philadelphia: University of Pennsylvania Press.

Glazer, Simon. 1928. *The Bar-Mitzvah Pulpit: Sermonettes for Bar-Mitzvah Boys and Others*. New York: Hebrew Publishing.

Glenn, Susan A., and Naomi B. Sokoloff. 2010. "Introduction: Who and What Is Jewish?" In *Boundaries of Jewish Identity*, ed. Susan A. Glenn and Naomi B. Sokoloff, 3–11. Seattle: University of Washington Press.

Glick, Leonard B. 1982. "Types Distinct from Our Own: Franz Boas on Jewish Identity and Assimilation." *American Anthropologist* 84: 545–65.

————. 2005. *Marked in Your Flesh: Circumcision from Ancient Judea to Modern America*. Oxford, UK: Oxford University Press.

Goffman, Erving. 1959. *The Presentation of Self in Everyday Life*. New York: Doubleday Anchor.

————. 1963. *Stigma: Notes on the Management of Spoiled Identity*. New York: Simon & Schuster.

————. 1967. *Interaction Ritual: Essays in Face-to-Face Behavior*. Garden City, NY: Doubleday.

———. 1974. *Frame Analysis: An Essay on the Organization of Experience*. New York: Harper & Row.

Goffman, Ethan. 2000. *Imagining Each Other: Blacks and Jews in Contemporary American Literature*. Albany: State University of New York Press.

Golan, Oren. 2015. "Legitimation of New Media and Community Building Among Jewish Denominations in the U.S." In *Digital Judaism: Jewish Negotiations with Digital Media and Culture*, ed. Heidi A. Campbell, 125–44. New York: Routledge.

Golany, Gideon S. 1999. *Babylonian Jewish Neighborhood and Home Design*. Lewiston, NJ: Edwin Mellen Press.

Goldberg, Halina. 2016. "Family Pictures at an Exhibition: History, Autobiography, and the Museum Exhibit on Jewish Łodz 'In Mrs. Goldberg's Kitchen.'" In *Going to the People: Jews and the Ethnographic Impulse*, ed. Jeffrey Veidlinger, 256–83. Bloomington: Indiana University Press.

Goldberg, Harvey E. 2003. *Jewish Passages: Cycles of Jewish Life*. Berkeley: University of California Press.

Goldberg, Harvey E., and Hagar Salamon. 2011. "The Riddle of Se'udat Yitro: Interpreting a Celebration Among Tunisia's Jews." In *Revisioning Ritual: Jewish Traditions in Transition*, ed. Simon J. Bronner, 45–67. Oxford, UK: Littman Library of Jewish Civilization.

Goldberger, Frimet, and Shimon Steinmetz. 2014. "The Complete History of the Sheitel." *Forward* (August 13). https://forward.com/sisterhood/203981/the-complete-history -of-the-sheitel/ (accessed July 26, 2020).

Golden, Harry. 1965. "Introduction." In *Röyte Pomerantsen: Jewish Folk Humor*, ed. Immanuel Olsvanger, vii–xv. New York: Schocken.

Goldman, Alex J. 1958. *A Handbook for the Jewish Family: Understanding and Enjoying the Sabbath and Holidays*. New York: Bloch.

Goldman, Ari L. 2000. "Little Fanfare for One of Their Boys." Beliefnet, November 2000. http://www.beliefnet.com/story/36/story_3640_1.html (accessed December 1, 2000).

Goldman, Moshe. 2017. "Is the Internet Evil?" Chabad.org. http://www.chabad.org/ library/article_cdo/aid/675087/jewish/Is-the-Internet-Evil.htm (accessed October 24, 2017).

Goldschmidt, Robert. 2000. "Fervently Orthodox Succeed in America." Letter to the Editor, *Jewish Forward* (August 18), 8.

Goldstein, Andrew. 2000. *My Jewish Home*. Rockville, MD: Kar-Ben.

Goldstein, Elyse. 1991. *Seek Her Out: A Textual Approach to the Study of Women and Judaism*. New York: KTAV.

Goldstein, Eric L. 2006. *The Price of Whiteness: Jews, Race, and American Identity*. Princeton, NJ: Princeton University Press.

Goldstein, Judith S. 2006. *Inventing Great Neck: Jewish Identity and the American Dream*. New Brunswick, NJ: Rutgers University Press.

Goldstein, Sidney. 1992. "Profile of American Jewry: Insights from the 1990 National Jewish Population Survey." In *American Jewish Yearbook 1992*, ed. David Singer, 77–176. New York: American Jewish Committee and Jewish Publication Society.

Goldstein, Sidney, and Alice Goldstein. 1996. *Jews on the Move: Implications for Jewish Identity*. Albany: State University of New York Press.

Gollaher, David L. 2001. *Circumcision: A History of the World's Most Controversial Surgery*. New York: Al Saqi Bookshop.

Gonen, Rivka. 1994. "An-Sky in Jerusalem." In *Back to the Shtetl: An-Sky and the Jewish Ethnographic Expedition, 1912–1915*, ed. Rivka Gonen, viii–xii. Jerusalem: Israel Museum.

Goodman, Martin, ed. 2002. *The Oxford Handbook of Jewish Studies*. Oxford, UK: Oxford University Press.

Goodstein, Laurie. 2000. "Democrats: The Observances; Lieberman Balances Private Faith with Life in the Public Eye." *New York Times* (August 18). https://www.nytimes.com/2000/08/18/us/democrats-observances-lieberman-balances-private-faith-with-life-public-eye.html?searchResultPosition=2 (accessed June 22, 2019).

Gordon, Albert I. 1959. *Jews in Suburbia*. Boston: Beacon Press.

Goren, Arthur A. 1999. *The Politics and Public Culture of American Jews*. Bloomington: Indiana University Press.

Gottesman, Itzik Nakhmen. 2003. *Defining the Yiddish Nation: The Jewish Folklorists of Poland*. Detroit: Wayne State University Press.

Gottlieb, Roger S. 1990. *Thinking the Unthinkable: Meanings of the Holocaust*. New York: Paulist Press.

Gould, Jillian. 2011. "Shiva as Creative Ritual in an Institutional Home." In *Revisioning Ritual: Jewish Traditions in Transition*, ed. Simon J. Bronner, 317–40. Oxford, UK: Littman Library of Jewish Civilization.

———. 2013. "A Nice Piece of Cake and a Kibitz: Reinventing Sabbath Hospitality in an Institutional Home." *Home Cultures: The Journal of Architecture, Design, and Domestic Space* 10: 189–206.

Gray, Herman S. 2005. *Cultural Moves: African Americans and the Politics of Representation*. Berkeley: University of California Press.

Green, Emma. 2015. "Hanukkah, Why?" *Atlantic* (December 9). https://www.theatlantic.com/business/archive/2015/12/hanukkah-sucks-amirite/419649/ (accessed December 25, 2019).

Greenbaum, Avraham. 2010. "Newspapers and Periodicals." In *YIVO Encyclopedia of Jews in Eastern Europe*, ed. Gershon David Hundert. http://www.yivoencyclopedia.org/article.aspx (accessed October 24, 2017).

Greenberg, Betty D., and Althea O. Silverman. 1941. *The Jewish Home Beautiful*. New York: Women's League of the United Synagogue of America.

Greenberg, Blu. 1983. *How to Run a Traditional Jewish Household*. New York: Simon & Schuster.

Greenberg, Eric J. 1998a. "At Last, Kaddish in Auschwitz." *Jewish Week* (June 19), 1, 15.

———. 1998b. "The Politics of Family." *New York Jewish Week* (October 30). https://jewishweek.timesofisrael.com/the-politics-of-family/ (accessed December 25, 2019).

Greenberg, Gail Anthony. 2006. *Mitzvah Chic: How to Host a Meaningful, Fun, Drop-Dead Gorgeous Bar or Bat Mitzvah*. New York: Simon & Schuster.

Greenberg, Steven. 2005. *Wrestling with God and Men: Homosexuality in the Jewish Tradition*. Madison: University of Wisconsin Press.

Greenhouse, Carol J. 2010. "Cultural Subjects and Objects: The Legacy of Franz Boas and Its Futures in Anthropology, Academe, and Human Rights." *Proceedings of the American Philosophical Society* 154: 1–7.

Gregory, R. L. 1970. *The Intelligent Eye*. New York: McGraw-Hill.

Grimes, Ronald L. 1982. *Beginnings in Ritual Studies*. Lanham, MD: University Press of America.

———. 1996. "Introduction." In Ronald L. Grimes, ed., *Readings in Ritual Studies*, xiii–xvi. Upper Saddle River, NJ: Prentice-Hall.

———. 2006. "Performance." In *Theorizing Rituals: Issues, Topics, Approaches, Concepts*, ed. Jens Kreinath, Jan Snoek, and Michael Strausberg, 379–94. Leiden, Netherlands: Brill.

Grimm, Jacob. 2004. *Teutonic Mythology*, 4 vols. Mineola, NY: Dover.

Grinspan, Izzy. 2005. "Blogs Offer Glimpse into Hidden Corners of Orthodox Life." *Forward* (August 26). http://forward.com/articles/2669/blogs-offer-glimpse-into -hidden-corners-of-orthodo/ (accessed October 24, 2017).

Grossberg, Lawrence, Cary Nelson, and Paula Treichler, eds. 1992. *Cultural Studies*. New York: Routledge.

Grossman, Grace Cohen, ed. 2001. *Romance and Ritual: Celebrating the Jewish Wedding*. Los Angeles: Skirball Cultural Center.

Grözinger, Karl E. 2010. "Jewish Legends from Kraków." *Scripta Judaica Racoviensia* 8: 61–67.

Gruber, Ruth Ellen. 1994. *Upon the Doorposts of Thy House: Jewish Life in East-Central Europe, Yesterday and Today*. New York: Wiley.

———. 2002. *Virtually Jewish: Reinventing Jewish Culture in Europe*. Berkeley: University of California Press.

———. 2014. "Beyond Virtually Jewish: Monuments to Jewish Experience in Eastern Europe." In *Framing Jewish Culture: Boundaries and Representations*, ed. Simon J. Bronner, 335–56. Oxford, UK: Littman Library of Jewish Civilization.

Gruber, Samuel D. 2014. "Selective Inclusion: Integration and Isolation of Jews in Medieval Italy." In *Framing Jewish Culture: Boundaries and Representations*, ed. Simon J. Bronner, 97–124. Oxford, UK: Littman Library of Jewish Civilization.

Gruberger, Risa. 1993. "A Mini-Course on Writing a Drash." In *Bar/Bat Mitzvah Education: A Sourcebook*, ed. Helen Leneman, 281–87. Springfield, NJ: A.R.E. Publishing.

Grunwald, Max. 1897. "Zur Volkskunde der Juden." *Israelitische Monatsschrift* 6 (June): 21–22, 7 (July): 25–26, 8 (August): 29–30.

———. 1923a. "Fünfundzwanzig Jahre jüdische Volkskunde." *Mitteilungen zur jüdischen Volkskunde* 25: 1–22.

———. 1923b. "Zur Vorgeschichte des Sukkothrituals und verwandeter Kultformen." In *Jahrbuch für Jüdische Volkskunde*, ed. Max Grunwald, 427–72. Berlin: Benjamin Harz.

Guitierrez, Juan Marcos Bejarano. 2017. *Secret Jews: The Complex Identity of Crypto-Jews and Crypto Judaism*. Grand Prairie, TX: Yaron.

Gurock, Jeffrey S. 1998. *East European Jews in America, 1880–1920: Immigration and Adaptation*. New York: Routledge.

Haas, Kristin Ann. 1998. *Carried to the Wall: American Memory and the Vietnam Veterans Memorial*. Berkeley: University of California Press.

Hagen, Rolf, David Davidovitch, and Ralf Busch. 1984. *Tora-Wimpel: Zeugnisse jüdischer Volkskunst aus dem Braunschweigischen Landesmuseum*. Braunschweig: Braunschweigischen Landesmuseum.

Hall, Stuart, 1992. "Encoding/Decoding." In *Culture, Media, Language: Working Papers in Cultural Studies, 1972–1979*, ed. Stuart Hall, Dorothy Hobson, Andrew Lowe, and Paul Willis, 128–38. London: Routledge.

———, ed. 1997. *Representation: Cultural Representations and Signifying Practices*. London: SAGE.

Hall, Stuart, and Paul Du Gay, eds. 1996. *Questions of Cultural Identity*. London: Sage.

Halloran, Liz. 2000. "Lieberman Shows He's a Real Stand-Up Guy." *Hartford Courant* (September 15). https://www.courant.com/news/connecticut/hc-xpm-2000-09-15 -0009152075-story.html (accessed June 22, 2019).

Hammer, Jill. 2005. "Holle's Cry: Unearthing a Birth Goddess in a German Jewish Naming Ceremony." *Nashim* 9: 62–87.

Handelman, Don. 2006. "Framing." In *Theorizing Rituals: Issues, Topics, Approaches, Concepts*, ed. Jens Kreinath, Jan Snoek, and Michael Strausberg, 413–28. Leiden, Netherlands: Brill.

Handelman, Don, and Elihu Katz. 1990. "State Ceremonies of Israel: Remembrance Day and Independence Day." In *Models and Mirrors: Toward an Anthropology of Public Events*, ed. Don Handelman, 191–233. Cambridge, UK: Cambridge University Press.

Harlow, Ilana. 1993. " 'We Are Bound to Tradition Yet Part of That Tradition Is Change': The Development of the Jewish Prayerbook." *Folklore Forum* 26: 30–41.

Hart, Mitchell Bryan. 2011. *Jews and Race: Writings on Identity and Difference, 1880–1940*. Waltham, MA: Brandeis University Press.

Harth, Dietrich. 2006. "Ritual and Other Forms of Social Action." In *Theorizing Rituals: Issues, Topics, Approaches, Concepts*, ed. Jens Kreinath, Jan Snoek, and Michael Strausberg, 15–36. Leiden, Netherlands: Brill.

Hasan-Rokem, Galit. 2002. "Jewish Folklore and Ethnography." In *Oxford Handbook of Jewish Studies*, ed. Martin Goodman, 956–74. Oxford, UK: Oxford University Press.

Hasan-Rokem, Galit, and Alan Dundes, eds. 1986. *The Wandering Jew: Essays in the Interpretation of a Christian Legend*. Bloomington: Indiana University Press.

Haskell, Guy H. 1996. "Jewish Americans." In *American Folklore: An Encyclopedia*, ed. Jan Harold Brunvand, 409–11. New York: Garland.

Hathaway, Rosemary V. 2005. " 'Life in the TV': The Visual Nature of 9/11 Lore and Its Impact on Vernacular Response." *Journal of Folklore Research* 42: 33–56.

Haugeland, John. 1981. "Analog and Analog." *Philosophical Topics* 12: 213–26.

Heilman, Samuel C. 1987. *The People of the Book: Drama, Fellowship, and Religion*. New York: Routledge.

———. 1992. *Defenders of the Faith: Inside Ultra-Orthodox Jewry*. New York: Schocken.

———. 1998. *Synagogue Life: A Study in Symbolic Interaction*. Chicago: University of Chicago Press.

———. 2006. *Sliding to the Right: The Contest for the Future of American Jewish Orthodoxy*. Berkeley: University of California Press.

Hennenberg, Jacob. 1995. *A Generation of Stones*. Cleveland: Jacob Hennenberg.

Hertz, Joseph H., trans. 1945. *Sayings of the Fathers, or Pirke Aboth*. New York: Behrman House.

———. 1959. *Authorized Daily Prayer Book*. New York: Bloch.

Hertzog, Esther, Orit Abuhav, Harvey E. Goldberg, and Emanual Marx. 2010. "Introduction: Israeli Social Anthropology—Origins, Characteristics, and Contributions." In

Perspectives on Israeli Anthropology, ed. Esther Hertzog, Orit Abuhav, Harvey E. Goldberg, and Emanuel Marx, 1–16. Detroit: Wayne State University Press.

Heskes, Irene. 1997. "Cantors." In *Jewish Women in America: An Historical Encyclopedia*, ed. Paula E. Hyman and Deborah Dash Moore, 202–5. New York: Routledge.

Hill, Logan. 2013. "At ChristianMingle and JDate, God's Your Wingman." *Business Week* (February 25), 1.

Hing, Bill Ong. 2004. *Defining America Through Immigration Policy*. Philadelphia: Temple University Press.

Hirsh, David. 2018. *Contemporary Left Antisemitism*. New York: Routledge.

Hoberman, J., and Jeffrey Shandler. 2003. *Entertaining America: Jews, Movies, and Broadcasting*. New York: Jewish Museum.

Hoberman, Michael. 2011. "Be Worthy of Your Heritage: Jews and Tradition at Two New England Boarding Schools." In *Revisioning Ritual: Jewish Traditions in Transition*, ed. Simon J. Bronner, 133–62. Oxford, UK: Littman Library of Jewish Civilization.

Hödl, Klaus. 2002–2003. "The Viennese Jews' Search for Integration Through the Jewish Museum in the Late 19th Century." *Yearbook of Jewish Studies at the Central European University* 3: 53–65.

Hoffman, Lawrence A., and Janet R. Walton, eds. 1993. *Sacred Sound and Social Change: Liturgical Music in Jewish and Christian Experience*. Notre Dame, IN: University of Notre Dame Press.

Hoffman, Sam. 2010. *Old Jews Telling Jokes*. New York: Villard.

Holzel, David. 2013. "E-Readers to Join Prayer Books at Conservative Convention." *Washington Jewish Week* (17 July). http://washingtonjewishweek.com/3700/e-readers -to-join-prayer-books-at-conservative-convention/news/world-news/ (accessed October 24, 2017).

Holzman, Michael. 2007. "The Reminder on the Doorpost." In *A Kiss for the Mezuzah*, ed. Matthew Singer, 8. Philadelphia: Philadelphia Museum of Jewish Art.

Hornstein, Jonathan. 2019. *Jewish Poverty in the United States: A Summary of Recent Research*. Owing Mills, MD: Harry and Jeanette Weinberg Foundation.

Houseman, Michael. 2006. "Relationality." In *Theorizing Rituals: Issues, Topics, Approaches, Concepts*, ed. Jens Kreinath, Jan Snoek, and Michael Strausberg, 571–82. Leiden, Netherlands: Brill.

Howard, Robert Glenn. 2011. *Digital Jesus: The Making of a New Christian Fundamentalist Community on the Internet*. New York: New York University Press.

Hubka, Thomas C. 2003. *Resplendent Synagogue: Architecture and Worship in an Eighteenth-Century Polish Community*. Hanover, NH: University Press of New England.

Huddart, David. 2006. *Homi K. Bhabha*. New York: Routledge.

Hufford, Mary. 1995. "Context." *Journal of American Folklore* 108: 528–49.

Hürlimann. Martin. 1928. *Indien: Baukunst, Landschaft und Volksleben*. Berlin: E. Wasmuth.

Hutchinson, Ron. 1996. "The Jazz Singer." National Film Preservation Board, Library of Congress. https://www.loc.gov/programs/national-film-preservation-board/film -registry/index-of-essays/ (accessed October 24, 2017).

"Into the Light." 2000. *Jewish Forward* (August 18), 8.

Iny, Julie. 2003. "Ashkenazi Eyes." In *The Flying Camel: Essays on Identity by Women of North African and Middle Eastern Jewish Heritage*, ed. Loolwa Khazzoom, 81–100. New York: Seal Press.

Isaacs, Miriam. 2008. "Yiddish in the Aftermath: Speech Community and Cultural Continuity in Displaced Persons Camps." In *Jewishness: Expression, Identity, and Representation*, ed. Simon J. Bronner, 85–104. Oxford, UK: Littman Library of Jewish Civilization.

Itzkoff, Dave. 2008. "Message to Your Grandma: Vote Obama." *New York Times* (October 6). https://www.nytimes.com/2008/10/07/arts/television/07sara.html (accessed December 25, 2019).

Jacobivici, Simcha, dir. 1998. *Hollywoodism: Jews, Movies, and the American Dream*. Waltham, MA: National Center for Jewish Film, Brandeis University.

Jacobs, Alan. 2011. "Why Bother with Marshall McLuhan?" *New Atlantis* 31: 123–35.

Jacobs, Janet Liebman. 2002. *Hidden Heritage: The Legacy of the Crypto-Jews*. Berkeley: University of California Press.

Jacobs, Joseph. 1886. "The Comparative Distribution of Jewish Ability." *Journal of the Anthropological Institute of Great Britain and Ireland* 15: 351–79.

———. 1890. "Jewish Ideals." *Jewish Quarterly Review* 2: 494–508.

———. 1893. "The Folk." *Folklore* 4: 233–38.

———. 1919. *Jewish Contributions to Civilization: An Estimate*. Philadelphia: Jewish Publication Society.

Jacobs, Joseph, and Lucien Wolf. 1887. *Catalogue of the Anglo-Jewish Historical Exhibition, 1887*. London: W. Clowes.

Jacobs, Louis. 1987. *The Book of Jewish Practice*. West Orange, NJ: Behrman House.

Jacobs, Melville. 1959. "Folklore." In *The Anthropology of Franz Boas: Essays on the Centennial of His Birth*, ed. Walter Goldschmidt, 119–38. American Anthropological Association Memoirs 89. San Francisco: American Anthropological Association and Howard Chandler.

Jacobson, Matthew Frye. 2006. *Roots Too: White Ethnic Revival in Post–Civil Rights America*. Cambridge, MA: Harvard University Press.

Jansen, William Hugh. 1959. "The Esoteric-Exoteric Factor in Folklore." *Fabula: Journal of Folktale Studies* 2: 205–11.

Jason, Heda. 1967. "The Jewish Joke: The Problem of Definition." *Southern Folklore Quarterly* 31: 48–54.

J. Correspondent. 2010. "Public Displays of Chanukah: Community Lightings Arise from Holidays Big Mitzvah." *J.: The Jewish News of Northern California* (December 3). https://www.jweekly.com/2010/12/03/public-displays-of-chanukah-community -lightings-arise-from-holidays-big-mit/ (accessed August 15, 2020).

JDate. 2017. "About JDate." JDate. https://www.jdate.com/help/about/ (accessed October 24, 2017).

Jeffay, Nathan. 2013. "Kosher Smart Phone Arrives as Ultra-Orthodox Tech Taboo Shifts." *Forward* (September 18). http://forward.com/news/184099/kosher-smart -phone-arrives-as-ultra-orthodox-tech/ (accessed October 24, 2017).

———. 2020. "14 Sephardic Orthodox Rabbis Say Passover Seder Can Be Held via Videoconference." *Times of Israel* (March 25). https://www.timesofisrael.com/sephardic -orthodox-rabbis-say-passover-seder-can-be-held-via-videoconference/ (accessed May 9, 2020).

Jenkins, Henry. 2006. *Convergence Culture: Where Old and New Media Collide*. New York: New York University Press.

Jenkins, Henry, Sam Ford, and Joshua Green. 2013. *Spreadable Media: Creating Value and Meaning in a Networked Culture*. New York: New York University Press.

Jennings, Karla. 1990. *The Devouring Fungus: Tales of the Computer Age*. New York: Norton.

Jessel, George. 1928. "Why I Alternate on Stage and Screen: A Player Who Frankly Avows That Only the Big Money Lured Him into Film Acting." *Theatre Magazine* 47, no. 323 (February): 22.

Jews for Morality. 2000a. "Joe Lieberman's Counterfeit Orthodoxy." Jews for Morality, August 30. http://www.jewsformorality.org/joe_liebermans_counterfeit_orthodoxy.htm (URL inactive, accessed November 1, 2000).

———. 2000b. "Rabbinical Court Excommunicates Senator Lieberman." Jews for Morality, October 18. http://www.jewsformorality.org/press_releases/lieberman_excommunicated.htm (URL inactive, accessed November 1, 2000).

Johnson, David E., and Scott Michaelsen. 1997. "Border Secrets: An Introduction." In *Border Theory: The Limits of Cultural Politics*, ed. David E. Johnson and Scott Michaelsen, 1–42. Minneapolis: University of Minnesota Press.

Johnson, Hannah R. 2012. *Blood Libel: The Ritual Murder Accusation at the Limit of Jewish History*. Ann Arbor: University of Michigan Press.

Johnson, Steven. 1999. *Interface Culture: How New Technology Transforms the Way We Create and Communicate*. New York: Basic Books.

Jones, Michael Owen. 1971. "(PC + CB) × SD(R + I + E) = Hero." *New York Folklore Quarterly* 27: 243–60.

Jordan, Michael J. 2000. "Landmark Selection." *Atlanta Jewish Times* (August 11). http://www.atljewishtimes.com/archives/2000/081100cs.htm (URL inactive, accessed November 1, 2000).

Joselit, Jenna Weissman. 1990. "'A Set Table': Jewish Domestic Culture in the New World, 1880–1950." In *Getting Comfortable in New York: The American Jewish Home, 1880–1950*, ed. Susan L. Braunstein and Jenna Weissman Joselit, 19–74. New York: Jewish Museum.

———. 1994. *The Wonders of America: Reinventing Jewish Culture, 1880–1950*. New York: Henry Holt.

———. 2010. "Culture Mavens: Feeling at Home in America." In *Jews at Home: The Domestication of Identity*, ed. Simon J. Bronner, 287–94. Oxford, UK: Littman Library of Jewish Civilization.

Joselit, Jenna Weissman, and Karen S. Mittelman, eds. 1993. *A Worthy Use of Summer: Jewish Summer Camping in America*. Philadelphia: National Museum of American Jewish History.

JTA Staff. 2000. "Poland Allows Shopping Center near Auschwitz." Jewish Telegraphic Agency. https://www.jta.org/2000/08/06/lifestyle/poland-allows-shopping-center-near-auschwitz (accessed June 14, 2019).

Judd, Robin. 2007. *Contested Rituals: Circumcision, Kosher Butchering, and Jewish Political Life in Germany, 1843–1933*. Ithaca, NY: Cornell University Press.

Kalmar, Ivan Davidson, and Derek J. Penslar. 2005. "Orientalism and the Jews: An Introduction." In *Orientalism and the Jews*, ed. Ivan Davidson Kalmar and Derek J. Penslar, xiii–xl. Waltham, MA: Brandeis University Press.

Kampeas, Ron. 2019. "Trump to Sign Order Recognizing Jews as a Nationality, Protected Class." *Forward* (December 10). https://forward.com/news/breaking-news/436256/trump-to-sign-order-recognizing-jews-as-a-nationality-protected-class/ (accessed December 25, 2019).

Kapchan, Deborah A. 2003. "Performance." In *Eight Words for the Study of Expressive Culture*, ed. Burt Feintuch, 121–45. Urbana: University of Illinois Press.

Kaplan, Brett. 2012. "Double-Consciousness and the Jewish Heart of Darkness: *The Counterlife* and *Operation Shylock*." In *Roth and Celebrity*, ed. Aimee Pozorski, 133–54. Lanham, MD: Lexington Books.

Kaplan, Louis. 1997. "On the Border with *The Pilgrim*: Zigzags Across a Chapl(a)in's Signature." In *Border Theory: The Limits of Cultural Politics*, ed. David E. Johnson and Scott Michaelsen, 97–128. Minneapolis: University of Minnesota Press.

Kaplan, Mordecai. 1994 [1934]. *Judaism as a Civilization: Toward a Reconstruction of American-Jewish Life*. Philadelphia: Jewish Publication Society.

Kaplan, Zvi, and Cecil Roth. 1972. "Bar Mitzvah, Bat Mitzvah." In *Encyclopedia Judaica*, ed. Cecil Roth and Geoffrey Wigoder, 4: 244–47. Jerusalem: Keter.

Kaplan-Mayer, Gabrielle. 2004. *The Creative Jewish Wedding Book: A Hands-on Guide to New and Old Traditions, Ceremonies, and Celebrations*. Woodstock, VT: Jewish Lights.

Karppinen, Kari. 2013. *Rethinking Media Pluralism*. New York: Fordham University Press.

Katz, Ethan B., Lisa Moses Leff, and Maud S. Mandel, eds. 2017. *Colonialism and the Jews*. Bloomington: Indiana University Press.

Katz, Jacob. 1931. *Attaining Jewish Manhood: Bar-Mitzvah Addresses*. New York: Bloch.

Katz, Naomi, and Eli Katz. 1971. "Tradition and Adaptation in American Jewish Humor." *Journal of American Folklore* 84: 215–20.

Katz, Steven T. 2007. *The Shtetl: New Evaluations*. New York: New York University Press.

Kauffman, Debra Renee. 1991. *Rachel's Daughters: Newly Orthodox Jewish Women*. New Brunswick, NJ: Rutgers University Press.

Kaufman, Bel. 1964. *Up the Down Staircase*. Englewood Cliffs, NJ: Prentice-Hall.

Kaufman, David. 1999. *Shul with a Pool: The 'Synagogue-Center' in American Jewish History*. Hanover, NH: University Press of New England.

Kelman, Ari Y. 2009. *Station Identification: A Cultural History of Yiddish Radio in the United States*. Berkeley: University of California Press.

———. 2010. *The Reality of the Virtual: Looking for Jewish Leadership Online*. AVI CHAI Foundation. http://www.bjpa.org/Publications/details.cfm?PublicationID=12881 (accessed October 24, 2017).

Kelner, Shaul. 2010. *Tours That Bind: Diaspora, Pilgrimage, and Israeli Birthright Tourism*. New York: New York University Press.

———. 2011. "The Bureaucratization of Ritual Innovation: The Festive Cycle of the American Soviet Jewry Movement." In *Revisioning Ritual: Jewish Traditions in Transition*, ed. Simon J. Bronner, 360–91. Oxford, UK: Littman Library of Jewish Civilization.

Kember, Sarah, and Joanna Zylinska. 2015. *Life After New Media: Mediation as a Vital Process*. Cambridge, MA: MIT Press.

Kennedy, Ellen J. Narotzky. 2005. "Bar Mitzvah and Bat Mitzvah: Rites of Affirmation and Integration." *In Rituals and Patterns in Children's Lives*, ed. Kathy Merlock Jackson, 58–78. Madison, WI: Popular Press.

Kessler, E. J. 1999. "Policy-Makers Scrambling to Identify Right Strategy as Religion, Families Wax: Parley to Hear How 'Personalization' Will Hail a Renaissance in America." *Jewish Forward* (July 2), 1, 17.

Keysar, Ariela, and Barry A. Kosmin. 2020. *The Bar/Bat Mitzvah Class of 5755: Tracking Jewish Connections over Two Decades, 1995–2019.* New York: Jewish Theological Seminary/William Davidson Graduate School of Jewish Education.

Khaimovich, Boris. 2002. "The Characteristic Features of Caucasian Jewish Construction." In *Mountain Jews: Customs and Daily Life in the Caucasus,* ed. Liya Mikdash-Shamailov, 65–77. Jerusalem: Israel Museum.

Khizghilov, Tyilo. 2002. "Jewish Motifs in Caucasian Rugs." In *Mountain Jews: Customs and Daily Life in the Caucasus,* ed. Liya Mikdash-Shamailov, 151–57. Jerusalem: Israel Museum.

Kim, Kwang-Ki. 2002. *Order and Agency in Modernity: Talcott Parsons, Erving Goffman, and Harold Garfinkel.* Albany: State University of New York Press.

Kimmel, Michael. 1996. *Manhood in America: A Cultural History.* New York: Free Press.

Kingsley, John Sterling, ed. 1885. *The Standard Natural History,* vol. 6, *The Natural History of Man.* Boston: S. E. Cassino.

Kiran, Asle H. 2015. "Four Dimensions of Technological Mediation." In *Postphenomenological Investigations: Essays on Human-Technology Relations,* ed. Robert Rosenberger and Peter-Paul Verbeek, 123–40. Lanham, MD: Lexington Books.

Kirschenbaum, Aaron. 1972. "Domicile." In *Encyclopedia Judaica,* 158–59. Jerusalem: Encyclopedia Judaica.

Kirshenblatt-Gimblett, Barbara. 1975. "A Parable in Context: A Social Interactional Analysis of Storytelling Performance." In *Folklore: Performance and Communication,* ed. Dan Ben-Amos and Kenneth S. Goldstein, 105–30. The Hague: Mouton.

———. 1977. *Fabric of Jewish Life: Textiles from the Jewish Museum Collection.* New York: Jewish Museum.

———. 1985. "Di Folkloristik: A Good Yiddish Word." *Journal of American Folklore* 98: 331–34.

———. 1990. "Kitchen Judaism." In *Getting Comfortable in New York: The American Jewish Home, 1880–1950,* ed. Susan L. Braunstein and Jenna Weissman Joselit, 75–105. New York: Jewish Museum.

———. 1998. *Destination Culture: Tourism, Museums, and Heritage.* Berkeley: University of California Press.

Kirshenblatt-Gimblett, Barbara, and Jeffrey Shandler, eds. 2012a. *Anne Frank Unbound: Media, Imagination, Memory.* Bloomington: Indiana University Press.

———. 2012b. "Introduction: Anne Frank, the Phenomenon." In *Anne Frank Unbound: Media, Imagination, Memory,* ed. Barbara Kirshenblatt-Gimblett and Jeffrey Shandler, 1–24. Bloomington: Indiana University Press.

Kitov, A. E. 1963. *The Jew and His Home,* trans. Nathan Bulman. New York: Shengold.

Kleeblatt, Norman L., ed. 1996. *Too Jewish? Challenging Traditional Identities.* New York: Jewish Museum.

Klein, Amy. 2009. "YouTube Jews." *Jewish Chronicle* (March 31). http://thejewishchronicle.net/view/full_story/2210743/article-YouTube-Jews? (accessed August 31, 2017).

Klein, Michele. 1998. *A Time to Be Born: Customs and Folklore of Jewish Birth.* Philadelphia: Jewish Publication Society.

Kline, Kip. 2016. *Baudrillard, Youth, and American Film: Fatal Theory and Education.* Lanham, MD: Lexington Books.

Knecht, Edgar. 1977. *Le Mythe du Juif errant: essai de mythologie littéraire et de sociologie religieuse.* Grenoble: Presses universitaires de Grenoble.

Knott, Blanche. 1982. *Truly Tasteless Jokes.* New York: Ballantine.

Kobre, Eytan. 2000. "Ideology and Senator Lieberman's Observance." Letter to the Editor, *Jewish Forward* (September 8), 8.

Koffman, David S. 2019. *The Jews' Indian: Colonialism, Pluralism, and Belonging in America.* New Brunswick, NJ: Rutgers University Press.

Kolatch, Alfred J. 2005. *A Handbook for the Jewish Home.* Middle Village, NY: Jonathan David.

Koller, Aaron. 2014. *Esther in Ancient Jewish Thought.* Cambridge, UK: Cambridge University Press.

Königseder, Angelika, and Juliane Wetzel. 2001. *Waiting for Hope: Jewish Displaced Persons in Post–World War II Germany*, trans. John A. Broadwin. Evanston, IL: Northwestern University Press.

Konner, Melvin. 2009. *The Jewish Body.* New York: Schocken.

Korazim, Malka, and Esther Katz. 2002. "Patterns of Jewish Identity in Moldova: The Behavioral Dimension." In *New Jewish Identities: Contemporary Europe and Beyond*, ed. Zvi Gitelman, Barry Kosmin, and András Kovács, 159–70. Budapest: Central European University Press.

Kosher Kitchen. 2008. "Kosher Certification." Committee for the Advancement of Torah. http://www.ok.org/Content.asp?ID=115 (URL inactive, accessed August 8, 2008).

Kosmin, Barry A. 2000. "Coming of Age in the Conservative Synagogue: The Bar/Bat Mitzvah Class of 5755." In *Jews in the Center: Conservative Synagogues and Their Members*, ed. Jack Wertheimer, 232–68. New Brunswick, NJ: Rutgers University Press.

Köstlin, Konrad, and Scott M. Shrake. 1997. "The Passion for the Whole: Interpreted Modernity or Modernity as Interpretation." *Journal of American Folklore* 110: 260–76.

Koven, Mikel J. 2000. " 'Have I Got a Monster for You!' Some Thoughts on the Golem, 'The X-Files,' and the Jewish Horror Movie." *Folklore* 111: 217–30.

Kozinski, Alex, and Eugene Volokh. 1993. "Lawsuit, Shmawsuit." *Yale Law Journal* 103: 463–67.

Kram, Mark S. 2003. "Saying Good-Bye at College Time." *Ritualwell* (March 1). https://www.ritualwell.org/ritual/saying-good-bye-college-time (accessed August 4, 2020).

Krasney, Ariela. 2003. "The *Badkhn*: From Wedding Stage to Writing Desk." *Polin* 16: 7–28.

Kraut, Alan M. 1994. *Silent Travelers: Germs, Genes, and the "Immigrant Menace."* Baltimore: Johns Hopkins University Press.

Kravtsov, Sergey R. 2008. "A Synagogue in Olyka: Architecture and Legends." In *Jewishness: Expression, Identity, and Representation*, ed. Simon J. Bronner, 58–84. Oxford, UK: Littman Library of Jewish Civilization.

Krieger, Suri Levow. 2006. "Bar and Bat Mitzvah: History and Practice." Academy for Jewish Religion. http://www.ajrsem.org/index.php?id=85 (accessed December 29, 2008).

Krinsky, Carol Herselle. 1996 [1985]. *Synagogues of Europe: Architecture, History, Meaning.* New York: Architectural History Foundation.

Kristol, Irving. 1951. "Is Jewish Humor Dead? The Rise and Fall of the Jewish Joke." *Commentary* 12 (January 1): 431–36.

Kroeber, A. L. 1917. "The Superorganic." *American Anthropologist*, n.s., 19: 163–213.

Kroyanker, David. 1984. *Jerusalem Architecture: Periods and Styles, The Jewish Quarters, and Public Buildings Outside the Old City Walls, 1860–1914*. Jerusalem: Jerusalem Institute for Israel Studies.

Kugelmass, Jack, ed. 1989. *Going Home: YIVO Annual, Volume 21*. Evanston, IL: Northwestern University Press and the YIVO Institute for Jewish Research.

———. 2006. "The Father of Jewish Ethnography?" In *The Worlds of S. An-Sky: A Russian Jewish Intellectual at the Turn of the Century*, ed. Gabriella Safran and Steven J. Zipperstein, 346–60. Stanford, CA: Stanford University Press.

Kugelmass, Jack, and Jeffrey Shandler. 1989. *Going Home: How American Jews Invent the Old World*. New York: YIVO Institute for Jewish Research.

Kumove, Shirley, ed. 1984. *Words Like Arrows: A Treasury of Yiddish Folk Sayings*. New York: Schocken.

"Lack of Faith." 2001. *Wall Street Journal* (July 25), A16.

Lamm, Maurice. 1969. *The Jewish Way in Death and Mourning*. New York: Jonathan David.

Lancaster, Clay. 1985. *The American Bungalow, 1880–1930*. New York: Abbeville.

Landau, David. 1993. *Piety and Power: The World of Jewish Fundamentalism*. New York: Hill & Wang.

Langer, Lawrence L. 1977. *The Holocaust and the Literary Imagination*. New Haven, CT: Yale University Press.

Lant, Antonia. 1992. "The Curse of the Pharaoh, or How Cinema Contracted Egyptomania." *October* 59: 86–112.

Lavallee, Guillaume. 2020. "Passover on Zoom: Jewish Leaders Split on Digital Seders." *Barron's* (April 2). https://www.barrons.com/news/passover-on-zoom-jewish-leaders-split-on-digital-seders-01585879508 (accessed May 8, 2020).

Lavazzi, Tom. 2001. "Communication On(the)line." *South Atlantic Review* 66: 126–44.

Lazar, Moshe, ed. 1972. *The Sephardic Tradition: Ladino and Spanish-Jewish Literature*. New York: Norton.

Leach, Edmund. 1968. "Ritual." In *International Encyclopedia of the Social Sciences*, ed. David L. Sills, 13: 520–26. New York: Hill & Wang.

———. 1989. *Claude Lévi-Strauss*. Chicago: University of Chicago Press.

Leacock, Stephen Butler. 1938. *Humor and Humanity*. New York: Henry Holt.

Lears, T. J. Jackson. 1985. "The Concept of Cultural Hegemony: Problems and Possibilities." *American Historical Review* 90: 567–93.

Lederhendler, Eli. 1993. "Modern Jewish Politics." In *The Modern Jewish Experience: A Reader's Guide*, ed. Jack Wertheimer, 181–88. New York: New York University Press.

Lehnardt, Andreas. 2014. "'Mazzal Tov': Die Tora-Wimpel aus der Genisa der Synagoge Weisenau." *Mainzer Zeitschrift* 109: 103–12.

Lehrer, Erica T. 2013. *Jewish Poland Revisited: Heritage Tourism in Unquiet Places*. Bloomington: Indiana University Press.

Lehrer, Erica T., and Michael Meng, eds. 2015. *Jewish Space in Contemporary Poland*. Bloomington: Indiana University Press.

Leneman, Helen. 1993. "Survey Results, Implications, and Evaluation." In *Bar/Bat Mitzvah Education: A Sourcebook*, ed. Helen Leneman, 1–29. Springfield, NJ: A.R.E. Publishing.

Lesniewski, Niels. 2019. "Schumer Says Trump 'Redefined Chutzpah' When He Called the Democratic Party 'Anti-Jewish.'" *Roll Call* (March 8). https://www.rollcall .com/news/congress/schumer-trump-redefined-chutzpah (accessed December 25, 2019).

Levine, Ephraim. 1924–1927. "Sir Isidore Spielmann, 1854–1925." *Transactions of the Jewish Historical Society of England* 11: 233–37.

Levine, Joseph A. 1989. *Synagogue Song in America.* Crown Point, IN: White Cliffs Media.

Lévi-Strauss, Claude. 1963. *Totemism,* trans. Rodney Needham. Boston: Beacon Press.

Levitan, M. Y. 1911. *Motke Chabad, Oder Vitse iber Vitse.* Vilna: F.Y.R.

Levitt, Laura. 1997. *Jews and Feminism: The Ambivalent Search for Home.* New York: Routledge.

Lewis, Amanda. 2012. "Texting During Yom Kippur Services? How One L.A. Rabbi Is Bringing Social Media to His Synagogue." *LA Weekly* (October 1). https://www .laweekly.com/texting-during-yom-kippur-services-how-one-l-a-rabbi-is-bringing -social-media-to-his-synagogue/ (accessed October 24, 2017).

Lewis, Herbert. 2001. "The Passion of Franz Boas." *American Anthropologist* 103: 447–67.

Lewis, Jeff. 2002. *Cultural Studies: The Basics.* London: Routledge.

Libo, Kenneth, and Irving Howe. 1984. *We Lived There Too: In Their Own Words and Pictures—Pioneer Jews and the Westward Movement of America, 1630–1930.* New York: St. Martin's Press.

Lieber, Andrea. 2010. "Domesticity and the Home (Page): Blogging and the Blurring of Public and Private Among Orthodox Jewish Women." In *Jews at Home: The Domestication of Identity,* ed. Simon J. Bronner, 257–86. Oxford, UK: Littman Library of Jewish Civilization.

Lieberman, Joseph I. 2000. *In Praise of Public Life.* New York: Simon & Schuster.

———. 2001a. "Introduction." In *Jews in American Politics,* ed. L. Sandy Maisel and Ira N. Forman, xxi–xxiii. Lanham, MD: Rowman & Littlefield.

———. 2001b. "Lieberman Renews Call for Larger, Lawful Space for Faith in American Life." Senator Joseph Lieberman website, December. http://www.senate.gov/~lieberman/ speeches/01/03/2001821610.html (URL inactive; accessed December 30, 2001).

Liebman, Charles S. 1973. *The Ambivalent American Jew: Politics, Religion, and Family in American Jewish Life.* Philadelphia: Jewish Publication Society.

Liebman, Charles S., and Steven M. Cohen. 1990. *The Two Worlds of Judaism: The Israeli and American Experiences.* New Haven, CT: Yale University Press.

Lifshits, Y. 1930. "Badkhonim un letsim bay yidn." In *Arkhiv far der geshikhte fun yidishn teater un drame,* ed. Jacob Shatzky, 38–74. Vilna: Yidisher Visnshaftlekher Institut.

Linke, Stuart. 1999. *Psychological Perspectives on Traditional Jewish Practices.* Northvale, NJ: Jason Aronson.

Lipman, Steve. 2011. "For Many Orthodox Teens, 'Half-Shabbos' Is a Way of Life: Texting on Saturdays Seen as Increasingly Common 'Addiction.'" *New York Jewish Week* (June 22). http://jewishweek.timesofisrael.com/for-many-orthodox-teens-half -shabbos-is-a-way-of-life/ (accessed October 24, 2017).

Lippe, Serge A. 2001. "To Live in Interesting Times." Brooklyn Heights Synagogue (Erev Rosh Hashanah 5761/2000). http://www.bhsbrooklyn.org/sermonrh00.htm (URL inactive, accessed December 1, 2001).

Lipphardt, Anna, Julia Brauch, and Alexandra Nocke. 2008. "Exploring Jewish Space: An Approach." In *Jewish Topographies: Visions of Space, Traditions of Place*, ed. Julia Brauch, Anna Lipphardt, and Alexandra Nocke, 1–26. Aldershot UK: Ashgate.

Liss, Julia. 1995. "Boas, Franz." In *A Companion to American Thought*, ed. Richard Wightman Fox and James T. Kloppenberg, 81–83. Oxford, UK: Basil Blackwell.

List, Edgar A. 1956. "Is Frau Holda the Virgin Mary?" *German Quarterly* 25: 80–84.

———. 1960. "Holda and the Venusberg." *Journal of American Folklore* 73: 307–11.

Loschak, Aharon. 2020. "Prepping for an Out-of-the-Box Lag BaOmer, in Cars and Homes." Chabad.org (May 6). https://www.chabad.org/news/article_cdo/aid/4737182/jewish/Prepping-for-an-Out-of-the-Box-Lag-BaOmer-In-Cars-and-Homes.htm (accessed May 9, 2020).

Lowenstein, Steven M. 2000. *The Jewish Cultural Tapestry: International Jewish Folk Traditions*. New York: Oxford University Press.

Lowitt, Bruce. 2006. "They're for the Shiva." *Jewish Sightseeing* (July 4). http://www.jewishsightseeing.com/jewish_humor/punchlines_and_their_jokes/2006-07-04-Number%2093.htm (URL inactive; accessed October 24, 2017).

Lukin, Benjamin. 1994. "From Folklore to Folk: An-Sky and Jewish Ethnography." In *Back to the Shtetl: An-Sky and the Jewish Ethnographic Expedition, 1912–1915*, ed. Rivka Gonen, xiv. Jerusalem: Israel Museum.

Macaluso, Laura A. 2019. *Monument Culture: International Perspectives on the Future of Monuments in a Changing World*. Lanham, MD: Rowman & Littlefield.

Machin, David, and Andrea Mayr. 2015. *How to Do Critical Discourse Analysis: A Multimodal Introduction*. Los Angeles: SAGE.

Maisel, Grace Ragues, and Samantha Shubert. 2004. *A Year of Jewish Stories: 52 Tales for Young Children and Their Families*. New York: UAHC Press.

Maisel, L. Sandy. 2001. "Preface." In *Jews in American Politics*, ed. L. Sandy Maisel and Ira N. Forman, xi–xii. Lanham, MD: Rowman & Littlefield.

Maley, Corey J. 2011. "Analog and Digital, Continuous and Discrete." *Philosophical Studies* 155: 117–31.

Mann, Reva. 2007. *The Rabbi's Daughter: A Memoir*. New York: Dial Press.

Manor, Ehud. 2009. *Forward: The Jewish Daily Forward (Forverts) Newspaper—Immigrants, Socialism, and Jewish Politics in New York, 1890–1917*. Brighton, UK: Sussex Academic Press.

Maraghy, Mary. 2000. "Lieberman Called 'The Perfect Jew.'" *Florida Times-Union* (Jacksonville) (August 17). http://www.jacksonville.com/tu-online/stories081700/met_3820681.html (November 2000) (URL inactive, accessed April 11, 2020).

Marcus, Ivan G. 1996. *Rituals of Childhood: Jewish Acculturation in Medieval Europe*. New Haven, CT: Yale University Press.

———. 2004. *The Jewish Life Cycle: Rites of Passage from Biblical to Modern Times*. Seattle: University of Washington Press.

Marcus, Jacob Rader. 1990. *To Count a People: American Jewish Population Data, 1585–1984*. Lanham, MD: University Press of America.

Marcus, Kenneth I. 2015. *The Definition of Anti-Semitism*. New York: Oxford University Press.

Marder, Janet R. 1996. "Are Women Changing the Rabbinate? A Reform Perspective." In *Religious Institutions and Women's Leadership: New Roles Inside the Mainstream*, ed. Catherine Wessinger, 271–90. Columbia: University of South Carolina Press.

Marinari, Maddalena. 2019. *Unwanted: Italian and Jewish Mobilization Against Restrictive Immigration Laws, 1882–1965*. Chapel Hill: University of North Carolina Press.

Marinari, Maddalena, Madeline Y. Hsu, and María García, eds. 2019. *A Nation of Immigrants Reconsidered: U.S. Society in an Age of Restriction, 1924–1965*. Urbana: University of Illinois Press.

Mark, Elizabeth Wyner, ed. 2003. *The Covenant of Circumcision: New Perspectives on an Ancient Jewish Rite*. Hanover, NH: Brandeis University Press.

Markel, Howard. 1999. *Quarantine! East European Jewish Immigrants and the New York City Epidemics of 1892*. Baltimore: Johns Hopkins University Press.

Marx, Bill. 2005. "Theater: Queens of Chutzpah." WBUR website. http://www.wbur.org (accessed November 26, 2007).

Mason, Jackie. 1990. *How to Talk Jewish*. New York: St. Martin's Press.

Mason, Jackie, and Raoul Felder. 2000. "Lieber(al)man Creates a New Jewish Denomination." *Jewish World Review* (October 10). http://www.jewishworldreview.com/cols/mason101000.asp (URL inactive; accessed November 1, 2000).

Massa, Mark. 2004. "'As If in Prayer': A Response to 'Catholicism as American Popular Culture.'" In *American Catholics, American Culture: Tradition and Resistance*, ed. Margaret O. Steinfels, 112–18. Lanham, MD: Rowman & Littlefield.

Matts, Abraham. 1968. "Preface." In *Reasons for Jewish Customs and Traditions*, by Rabbi Abraham Isaac Sperling; trans. Abraham Matts, 7. New York: Bloch.

McCain, John, and Mark Salter. 2018. *Restless Wave: Good Times, Just Causes, Great Fights, and Other Appreciations*. New York: Simon & Schuster.

McCurdy, David W., James P. Spradley, and Dianna J. Shandy. 2004. *The Cultural Experience: Ethnography in Complex Society*, 2nd ed. Long Grove, IL: Waveland Press.

McGinley, Brandon. 2017. "Saying 'Merry Christmas' Isn't an Affront, But Trump Is Trying to Make It One." *Denver Post* (December 7). https://www.denverpost.com/2017/12/07/saying-merry-christmas-isnt-an-affront-but-trump-is-trying-to-make-it-one/ (accessed December 25, 2019).

McGowan, Alan H. 2014. "The Lessons of Franz Boas." *Procedia: Social and Behavioral Sciences* 149: 558–64.

McKeever-Furst, Jill Leslie. 1992. "Art and Rites of Passage." In *Rites of Passage in America: Traditions of the Life Cycle*, ed. Pamela B. Nelson, 24–43. Philadelphia: Balch Institute for Ethnic Studies.

McLuhan, Marshall. 1964. *Understanding Media*. New York: McGraw-Hill.

Mead, George Herbert. 1967. *Mind, Self, Society from the Standpoint of a Social Behaviorist*, ed. Charles W. Morris. Chicago: University of Chicago Press.

Mechling, Jay. 1980. "The Magic of the Boy Scout Campfire." *Journal of American Folklore* 93: 35–56.

———. 1983. "Mind, Messages, and Madness: Gregory Bateson Makes a Paradigm for American Culture Studies." In *Prospects 8: An Annual Review of American Cultural Studies*, ed. Jack Salzman, 11–30. New York: Cambridge University Press.

———. 1989. "Richard M. Dorson and the Emergence of the New Class in American Folk Studies." *Journal of Folklore Research* 26: 11–26.

———. 1991. "*Homo Narrans* Across the Disciplines." *Western Folklore* 50: 41–51.

———. 2004. "Picturing Hunting." *Western Folklore* 63: 51–78.

———. 2008. "Gun Play." *American Journal of Play* 1: 192–209.

———. 2009. "Is Hazing Play?" In *Transactions at Play: Play and Culture Studies, Volume 9*, ed. Cindy Dell Clark, 45–62. Lanham, MD: University Press of America.

Medjuck, Sheva. 1988. "From Self-Sacrificing Jewish Mother to Self-Centered Jewish Princess: Is This How Far We've Come?" *Atlantis: A Women's Studies Journal* 14: 90–97.

Medved, Michael. 2000. "The Left Prays, But the Right Pays." *Wall Street Journal* (August 11), A14.

Meikle, Jeffrey. 2018. "Paradigm Dramas Revisited: A Brief History of American Studies as Reflected in *American Quarterly*." *SOAR: Society of Americanists Review* 1: 10–51.

Meiselman, Moshe. 1978. *Jewish Women in Jewish Law*. New York: KTAV.

Merwin, Ted. 2006. *In Their Own Image: New York Jews in Jazz Age Popular Culture*. New Brunswick, NJ: Rutgers University Press.

———. 2015. *Pastrami on Rye: An Overstuffed History of the Jewish Deli*. New York: New York University Press.

Messer, Ellen. 1986. "Franz Boas and Kaufmann Kohler: Anthropology and Reform Judaism." *Jewish Social Studies* 2: 127–40.

Michaels, Ralf. 2006. "Two Economists, Three Opinions? Economic Models for Private International Law: Cross-Border Torts as Example." Duke Law Faculty Scholarship, Paper 1234. http://scholarship.law.duke.edu/faculty_scholarship/1234 (accessed August 31, 2017).

Michaelson, Jay. 2006. "Two Lawyers, Three Opinions: On the Jewishness of Law, and Vice Versa." *Jewish Daily Forward* (November 3). http://www.forward.com/articles/7395/ (URL inactive; accessed August 31, 2017).

Michels, Tony, ed. 2012. *Jewish Radicals: A Documentary History*. New York: New York University Press.

Michelsen, Peter. 1966. "The Origin and Aim of the Open-Air Museum." In *Dansk Folkemuseum and Frilandsmuseet: History and Activities*, ed. Holger Rasmussen, 227–43. Copenhagen: Nationalmuseet.

Mikdash-Shamailov, Liya. 2002. "Daily Life in the Caucasus." In *Mountain Jews: Customs and Daily Life in the Caucasus*, ed. Liya Mikdash-Shamailov, 123–34. Jerusalem: Israel Museum.

Millard, William B. 1997. "I Flamed Freud: A Case Study in Teletextual Incendiarism." In *Internet Culture*, ed. David Porter, 145–60. New York: Routledge.

Millen, Rochelle L. 2004. *Women, Birth, and Death in Jewish Law and Practice*. Waltham, MA: Brandeis University Press.

Miller, Carolyn. 1993. "Are Jews Funnier than Non-Jews?" In *Semites and Stereotypes: Characteristics of Jewish Humor*, ed. Avner Ziv and Anat Zajdman, 13–28. Westport, CT: Greenwood.

Miller, Daniel. 2001. "Behind Closed Doors." In *Home Possessions: Material Culture Behind Closed Doors*, ed. Daniel Miller, 1–19. Oxford, UK: Berg.

Miller, Michael. 2010. "Jokes in Prison." *Old Jews Telling Jokes*, posted March 10. http://www.oldjewstellingjokes.com/2018/11/16/michael-miller-jokes-in-prison-379/ (accessed August 31, 2017).

Milligan, Amy K. 2014. *Hair, Headwear, and Orthodox Jewish Women: Kallah's Choice*. Lanham, MD: Lexington.

———. 2017. "Hair Today, Gone Tomorrow: Upsherin, Alef-Bet, and the Childhood Navigation of Jewish Gender Identity Symbol Sets." *Children's Folklore Review* 38: 7–26.

———. 2018. "Settings of Silver: The Feminization of the Jewish Sabbath, 1920–1945." In *Connected Jews: Expressions of Community in Analogue and Digital Culture*, ed. Simon J. Bronner, 69–88. Oxford, UK: Littman Library of Jewish Civilization.

———. 2019a. "Embodying Herself: A Jewish Feminist Approach to Body Liberation." *AJS Perspectives* (fall), 42–43.

———. 2019b. *Jewish Bodylore: Feminist and Queer Ethnographies of Folk Practices*. Lanham, MD: Lexington Books.

Millman, Joyce. 2000. "The Road to the White House Goes Through Oprah." *Salon* (September 25). https://www.salon.com/2000/09/25/oprah_10/ (accessed June 22, 2019).

Mills, C. Wright. 2000 [1956]. *The Power Elite*. New York: Oxford University Press.

Minkoff, David. 2005. *Oy! The Ultimate Book of Jewish Jokes*. New York: St. Martin's Press.

———. 2008. *Oy Vey: More! The Ultimate Book of Jewish Jokes, Part 2*. New York: St. Martin's Press.

Mintz, Jerome R. 1992. *Hasidic People: A Place in the New World*. Cambridge, MA: Harvard University Press.

Miron, Dan. 2000. *The Image of the Shtetl and Other Studies of Modern Jewish Literary Imagination*. Syracuse, NY: Syracuse University Press.

Mitchell, Carol. 1985. "Some Differences in Male and Female Joke-Telling." In *Women's Folklore, Women's Culture*, ed. Rosan A. Jordan and Susan J. Kalčik, 163–86. Philadelphia: University of Pennsylvania Press.

Mitchell, Harvey. 2008. *Voltaire's Jews and Modern Jewish Identity: Rethinking the Enlightenment*. New York: Routledge.

Mitchell, W. J. T., and Mark B. N. Hansen. 2010. *Critical Terms for Media Studies*. Chicago: University of Chicago Press.

Mocatta, F. D. 1887. "Report to the Members of the General Committee of the Anglo-Jewish Historical Exhibition." In *Papers Read at the Anglo-Jewish Historical Exhibition, Royal Albert Hall, London, 1887*, 289–300. London: Jewish Chronicle.

Moltke, Johannes Von. 1997. "Identities on Display: Jewishness and the Representational Politics of the Museum." In *Jews and Other Differences: The New Jewish Cultural Studies*, ed. Jonathan Boyarin and Daniel Boyarin, 79–107. Minneapolis: University of Minnesota Press.

Moore, Deborah Dash, ed. 1991. *YIVO Annual*, vol. 20, Evanston, IL: Northwestern University Press.

———. 1994. *To the Golden Cities: Pursuing the American Jewish Dream in Miami and L.A.* New York: Free Press.

Moore, R. Laurence. 1994. *Selling God: American Religion in the Marketplace of Culture*. New York: Oxford University Press.

Morahg, Gilead. 1991. "Are Jewish Studies Ethnic Studies?" *Shofar: An Interdisciplinary Journal of Jewish Studies* 9: 110–12.

Morawska, Ewa T. 1996. *Insecure Prosperity: Small-Town Jews in Industrial America, 1890—1940*. Princeton, NJ: Princeton University Press.

Morley, David. 2005. "Media." In *New Keywords: A Revised Vocabulary of Culture and Society*, ed. Tony Bennett, Lawrence Grossberg, and Meaghan Morris, 211–14. Malden, MA: Blackwell.

Morris-Reich, Amos. 2008. *The Quest for Jewish Assimilation in Modern Social Science*. New York: Routledge.

Motz, Lotte. 1984. "The Winter Goddess: Percht, Holda, and Related Figures." *Folklore* 95: 151–66.

Mufti, Aamir R. 2007. *Enlightenment in the Colony: The Jewish Question and the Crisis of Postcolonial Culture*. Princeton, NJ: Princeton University Press.

Müller, Christoph Daxel. 1999. "Hundert Jahre jüdische Volkskunde: Dr. Max (Meïr) Grunwald und die 'Gesellschaft für jüdische Volkskunde.' " *Aschkenas: Zeitschrift für Geschichte und Kultur der Juden* 9: 133–44.

Munro, Patricia Keer. 2016. *Coming of Age in Jewish America: Bar and Bat Mitzvah Reinterpreted*. New Brunswick, NJ: Rutgers University Press.

Murphy, Paul L. 1964. "Sources and Nature of Intolerance in the 1920s." *Journal of American History* 51: 60–76.

Murrells, Joseph. 1978. *The Book of Golden Discs*. London: Barrie & Jenkins.

Musher, Sharon Ann. 2015. "The Closing of the American Studies Association's Mind." In *The Case Against Academic Boycotts of Israel*, ed. Cary Nelson and Gabriel Noah Brahm, 105–18. Detroit: Wayne State University Press.

Musolf, Gil Richard. 2003. *Structure and Agency in Everyday Life: An Introduction to Social Psychology*. Lanham, MD: Rowman & Littlefield.

Musser, Charles. 2011. "Why Did Negroes Love Al Jolson and *The Jazz Singer*? Melodrama, Blackface, and Cosmopolitan Theatrical Culture." *Film History* 23: 196–22.

Myerhoff, Barbara. 1982. "Rites of Passage: Process and Paradox." In *Celebration: Studies in Festivity and Ritual*, ed. Victor Turner, 109–35. Washington, DC: Smithsonian Institution Press.

———. 1992. *Remembered Lives: The Work of Ritual, Storytelling, and Growing Older*. Ann Arbor: University of Michigan Press.

Myrdal, Gunnar. 1944. *An American Dilemma: The Negro Problem and Modern Democracy*. New York: Harper & Brothers.

Nadell, Pamela S. 2019. *America's Jewish Women: A History from Colonial Times to Today*. New York: Norton.

Nathan, Joan. 1994. *Jewish Cooking in America*. New York: Knopf.

———. 2001. *The Foods of Israel Today*. New York: Random House.

———. 2004. *Joan Nathan's Jewish Holiday Cookbook*. New York: Schocken.

National Archives. 2019. " 'A Chicken in Every Pot': Political Ad and Rebuttal Article in New York Times." National Archives Catalog. https://catalog.archives.gov/id/187095 (accessed June 22, 2019).

Nelson, Cary. 2019. *Israel Denial: Anti-Zionism, Anti-Semitism, and the Faculty Campaign Against the Jewish State*. Bloomington: Indiana University Press.

Nelson, Cary, Paula A. Treichler, and Lawrence Grossberg. 1992. "Cultural Studies: An Introduction." In *Cultural Studies*, ed. Lawrence Grossberg, Cary Nelson, and Paula Treichler, 1–16. New York: Routledge.

Nevo, Ofra, and Jacob Levine. 1994. "Jewish Humor Strikes Again: The Outburst of Humor in Israel During the Gulf War." *Western Folklore* 53: 125–45.

Nicolaisen, W. F. H. 1984. "Legends as Narrative Response." In *Perspectives on Contemporary Legend*, ed. Paul Smith, 167–78. Sheffield, UK: Centre for English Cultural Tradition and Language.

———. 2006. "Cultural Register." In *Encyclopedia of American Folklife*, ed. Simon J. Bronner, 255–56. Armonk, NY: M. E. Sharpe.

Nie, Norman H., and Lutz Erbring. 2000. *Internet and Society: A Preliminary Report*. Stanford Institute for the Quantitative Study of Society. http://www2.uca.es/HEURESIS/documentos/Preliminary_Report.pdf (accessed October 24, 2017).

Nierenberg, Amelia, and Emma Goldberg. 2020. "The Passover Rules Bend, if Just for One Pandemic." *New York Times* (April 8). https://www.nytimes.com/2020/04/08/dining/passover-coronavirus.html (accessed May 5, 2020).

Nord, Hans. 2000. "Keep Religion Out of Race." Letter to the Editor, *Jewish Forward* (August 25), 10.

Norris, Pippa. 2004. "The Bridging and Bonding Role of Online Communities." In *Society Online: The Internet in Context*, ed. Philip N. Howard and Steve Jones, 31–42. Thousand Oaks, CA: SAGE.

Noy, Chaim. 2006. *A Narrative Community: Voices of Israeli Backpackers*. Detroit: Wayne State University Press.

Noy, Dov [Neuman]. 1954. "Motif-Index of Talmudic-Midrashic Literature." PhD diss., Indiana University.

———. 1980. "Eighty Years of Jewish Folkloristics: Achievements and Tasks." In *Studies in Jewish Folklore*, ed. Frank Talmage, 1–12. Cambridge, MA: Association for Jewish Studies.

———. 1982. "Dr. Max Grunwald: The Founder of Jewish Folkloristics." *Folklore Research Center Studies* 6: ix–xiv.

———. 1994. "An-Sky the Meshulah: Between the Verbal and the Visual in Jewish Folk Culture." In *Back to the Shtetl: An-Sky and the Jewish Ethnographic Expedition, 1912–1915*, ed. Rivka Gonen, xvii. Jerusalem: Israel Museum.

Nulman, Macy. 1993. *The Encyclopedia of Jewish Prayer: Ashkenazic and Sephardic Rites*. Northvale, NJ: Jason Aronson.

Nusbaum, Philip. 1979. "Some Notes on the Construction of the Jewish American Dialect Story." *Keystone Folklore* 23: 28–52.

Nussbaum Cohen, Debra. 2001. *Celebrating Your New Jewish Daughter: Creating Jewish Ways to Welcome Baby Girls into the Covenant*. Woodstock, VT: Jewish Lights.

Nye, Russel. 1970. *The Unembarrassed Muse: The Popular Arts in America*. New York: Dial Press.

Ochs, Vanessa L. 1999–2000. "What Makes a Jewish Home Jewish?" *Crosscurrents* 49. http://www.crosscurrents.org/ochsv.htm (accessed May 24, 2008).

———. 2007. *Inventing Jewish Ritual*. Philadelphia: Jewish Publication Society.

———. 2011. "Same-Sex Marriage Ceremonies in a Time of Coalescence." In *Revisioning Ritual: Jewish Traditions in Transition*, ed. Simon J. Bronner, 190–210. Oxford, UK: Littman Library of Jewish Civilization.

———. 2020. *The Passover Haggadah: A Biography*. Princeton, NJ: Princeton University Press.

Oinas, Felix J., and Stephen Soudakoff, eds. 1975. *The Study of Russian Folklore*. The Hague: Mouton.

Olitzky, Kerry M., and Ronald H. Isaacs. 1993. *The How-To Handbook for Jewish Living.* Hoboken, NJ: KTAV.

Olitzky, Kerry M., and Rabbi Daniel Judson, eds. 2002. *The Rituals and Practices of a Jewish Life: A Handbook for Personal Spiritual Renewal.* Woodstock, VT: Jewish Lights.

Oliver, Paul, ed. 1997. *Encyclopedia of Vernacular Architecture of the World*, 3 vols. Cambridge, UK: Cambridge University Press.

Olrik, Axel. 1965. "Epic Laws of Folk Narrative." In *The Study of Folklore*, ed. Alan Dundes, 129–41. Englewood Cliffs, NJ: Prentice-Hall.

Olsvanger, Immanuel, ed. 1965. *Röyte Pomerantsen: Jewish Folk Humor.* New York: Schocken.

OPW Interview. 2006. "Spark Networks CEO, David Siminoff—OPW Interview." *Internet Dating Investments* (October 20). http://www.onlinepersonalswatch.com/internetdatinginvestments/2006/10/spark-networks-ceo-david-siminoff-opw-interview.html (accessed September 26, 2017).

Orchowski, Margaret Sands. 2015. *The Law That Changed the Face of America: The Immigration and Nationality Act of 1965.* Lanham, MD: Rowman & Littlefield.

Oring, Elliott. 1975. "Everything Is a Shade of Elephant: An Alternative to a Psychoanalysis of Humor." *New York Folklore* 1: 149–60.

———. 1976. "Three Functions of Folklore: Traditional Functionalism as Explanation in Folkloristics." *Journal of American Folklore* 89: 67–80.

———. 1983. "The People of the Joke: On the Conceptualization of a Jewish Humor." *Western Folklore* 42: 261–71.

———. 1992. *Jokes and Their Relations.* Lexington: University Press of Kentucky.

———. 2003. *Engaging Humor.* Urbana: University of Illinois Press.

———. 2008. "Legendry and the Rhetoric of Truth." *Journal of American Folklore* 121: 127–66.

———. 2016. *Joking Asides: The Theory, Analysis, and Aesthetics of Humor.* Logan: Utah State University Press.

Orla-Bukowska, Annamaria. 2014. "Virtual Transitioning into Real: Jewishness in Central Eastern Europe." In *Framing Jewish Culture: Boundaries and Representations*, ed. Simon J. Bronner, 365–82. Oxford, UK: Littman Library of Jewish Civilization.

Orthodox Union. 2000a. "OU Applauds Vice-President Gore's Decision to Choose Senator Joseph Lieberman as Running Mate." Orthodox Union (August 7). http://www.ou.org/oupr/2000/liebnom00.htm (URL inactive, accessed November 1, 2000).

———. 2000b. "Union of Orthodox Jewish Congregations Condemns Violent Speech Against Senator Lieberman." Orthodox Union (July 25). http://www.ou.org/oupr/2000/liebjol00.htm (URL inactive, accessed November 1, 2000).

Osgerby, Bill. 2001. *Playboys in Paradise: Masculinity, Youth, and Leisure-Style in Modern America.* Oxford, UK: Berg.

Ouaknin, Marc-Alain, and Françoise-Anne Ménager. 2005. *Bar Mitzvah: A Guide to Spiritual Growth.* New York: Assouline.

Packard, Vance. 1972. *A Nation of Strangers.* New York: McKay.

Paradise, Viola. 1913. "The Jewish Immigrant Girl in Chicago." *Survey* 30 (September 6): 700–704.

Paredes, Américo. 2002. "Border Identity: Culture, Conflict, and Convergence Along the Lower Rio Grande." In *Folk Nation: Folklore in the Creation of American Tradition*, ed. Simon J. Bronner, 199–214. Wilmington, DE: SR Books.

Paredes, Américo, and Richard Bauman, eds. 1972. *Toward New Perspectives in Folklore*. Austin: University of Texas Press.

Parry, Marc. 2020. "California State U. Board Approves Ethnic-Studies Requirement That Dismays Ethnic-Studies Professors." *Chronicle of Higher Education* (July 22). https://www.chronicle.com/article/california-state-u-board-approves-ethnic-studies-requirement-that-dismays-ethnic-studies-professors (URL inactive; accessed August 24, 2020).

Patai, Raphael. 1946. "Problems and Tasks of Jewish Folklore and Ethnology." *Journal of American Folklore* 59: 25–39.

———. 1960. "Jewish Folklore and Jewish Tradition." In *Studies in Biblical and Jewish Folklore*, ed. Raphael Patai, Francis Lee Utley, and Dov Noy, 11–28. Bloomington: Indiana University Press.

———. 1983. *On Jewish Folklore*. Detroit: Wayne State University Press.

Patai, Raphael, and Jennifer Patai. 1989. *The Myth of the Jewish Race*. Detroit: Wayne State University Press.

Patai, Raphael, Francis Lee Utley, and Dov Noy, eds. 1960. *Studies in Biblical and Jewish Folklore*. Bloomington: Indiana University Press.

Pearl, Jonathan, and Judith Pearl. 1999. *The Chosen Image: Television's Portrayal of Jewish Themes and Characters*. Jefferson, NC: McFarland.

Pearl, Judea, and Ruth Pearl, eds. 2005. *I Am Jewish: Personal Reflections Inspired by the Last Words of Daniel Pearl*. Woodstock, VT: Jewish Lights.

Pearse, Holly A. 2008. "As *Goyish* as Lime Jell-O? Jack Benny and the American Construction of Jewishness." In *Jewishness: Expression, Identity, and Representation*, ed. Simon J. Bronner, 272–90. Oxford, UK: Littman Library of Jewish Civilization.

———. 2014. "Negative Interfaith Romances and the Reassertion of Jewish Difference in Popular Film." In *Framing Jewish Culture: Boundaries and Representations*, ed. Simon J. Bronner, 217–40. Oxford, UK: Littman Library of Jewish Civilization.

Pelley, Scott. 2019. "Former Starbucks CEO Howard Schultz Says He's Considering Independent Run for President." *60 Minutes* (January 27). https://www.cbsnews.com/news/howard-schultz-starbucks-ceo-considering-independent-run-for-president-60-minutes/ (accessed June 22, 2019).

Pennell, Joseph. 1892. *The Jew at Home: Impressions of a Summer and Autumn Spent with Him*. New York: Appleton.

Pentikäinen, Juha Y. 1997. "Ritual." In *Folklore: An Encyclopedia of Beliefs, Customs, Tales, Music, and Art*, ed. Thomas A. Green, 733–36. Santa Barbara, CA: ABC-CLIO.

Pepperstone, Paula. 2003. "Two-Part Ceremony for a Son or Daughter Leaving for College." *Ritualwell* (March 1). https://www.ritualwell.org/ritual/two-part-ceremony-son-or-daughter-leaving-college (accessed August 4, 2020).

Perlez, Jane. 1993. "Pope Orders Nuns Out of Auschwitz." *New York Times* (April 15). https://www.nytimes.com/1993/04/15/world/pope-orders-nuns-out-of-auschwitz.html (accessed June 14, 2019).

Perz, Sally Anne. 2009. "Are You Forwarding Folklore?" *Family Times* 2 (November–December): 1–2.

Peterson, Richard A., and Paul Di Maggio. 1975. "From Region to Class, the Changing Locus of Country Music: A Test of the Massification Hypothesis." *Social Forces* 53: 497–506.

Pew Research Center. 2012. *Faith on the Move: The Religious Affiliation of International Migrants.* https://www.pewforum.org/2012/03/08/religious-migration-exec/ (accessed June 6, 2019).

———. 2013. *A Portrait of Jewish Americans.* Washington, DC: Pew Research Center.

Pinto, Diana. 2006. "The Jewish Space in Europe." In *Turning the Kaleidoscope: Perspectives on European Jewry*, ed. Sandra Lustig and Ian Leveson, 179–86. Oxford, UK: Berghahn Books.

Pirandello, Luigi. 1974. *On Humor.* Chapel Hill: University of North Carolina Press.

Pitimson, Natalie. 2016. "I've Just Been Verbally Abused—Tell Me Again How Racism Played No Part in Brexit." *The Conversation* (June 28). https://theconversation.com/ive-just-been-verbally-abused-tell-me-again-how-racism-played-no-part-in-brexit-61765 (accessed December 24, 2019).

Plaskow, Judith. 1991. *Standing Again at Sinai: Judaism from a Feminist Perspective.* San Francisco: Harper.

Platt, Roberta. 2011. "Shloime Is Dying." *Old Jews Telling Jokes*, posted May 4. http://www.oldjewstellingjokes.com/?s=shloime+is+dying (accessed August 31, 2017).

Plaut, Joshua Eli. 2012. *A Kosher Christmas: 'Tis the Season to Be Jewish.* New Brunswick, NJ: Rutgers University Press.

Pogrebin, Abigail. 2005. *Stars of David: Prominent Jews Talk About Being Jewish.* New York: Broadway Books.

Poll, Solomon. 1962. *The Hasidic Community of Williamsburg: A Study in the Sociology of Religion.* New York: Free Press of Glencoe.

Pollack, Herman. 1971. *Jewish Folkways in Germanic Lands (1648–1806): Studies in Aspects of Daily Life.* Cambridge, MA: MIT Press.

Polonsky, Antony, ed. 2005. *The Shtetl: Myth and Reality.* Oxford, UK: Littman Library of Jewish Civilization.

Popkin, Henry. 1952. "The Vanishing Jew of Our Popular Culture: The Little Man Who Is No Longer There." *Commentary* 14: 46–55.

Posen, Felix. 2000. "The Secular Silent Majority." *Jewish Forward* (November 24), 9.

Posner, Menachem. 2016. "Multifaceted Montreal Campaign Inspires Jewish Gatherings." Chabad.org (February 25). http://www.chabad.org/news/article_cdo/aid/3240709/jewish/Multifaceted-Montreal-Campaign-Inspires-Jewish-Gatherings.htm (URL inactive; accessed September 19, 2017).

Poster, Mark. 2001. "Cyberdemocracy: The Internet and the Public Sphere." In *Reading Digital Culture*, ed. David Trend, 259–71. Malden, MA: Blackwell.

Potok, Chaim. 1978. *Wanderings: Chaim Potok's History of the Jews.* New York: Alfred A. Knopf.

Pratt, Mary Louise. 1992. *Imperial Eyes: Travel Writing and Transculturation.* London: Routledge.

Prawer, S. S. 2007. *Between Two Worlds: The Jewish Presence in German and Austrian Film, 1910–1933.* New York: Berghahn Books.

Prell, Riv-Ellen. 1989. *Prayer and Community: The Havurah in American Judaism.* Detroit: Wayne State University Press.

———. 2007. "Introduction: Feminism and the Remaking of American Judaism." In *Women Remaking American Judaism*, ed. Riv-Ellen Prell, 1–24. Detroit: Wayne State University Press.

Prensky, Marc. 2010. *Teaching Digital Natives: Partnering for Real Learning*. Thousand Oaks, CA: Corwin.

———. 2012. *From Digital Natives to Digital Wisdom: Hopeful Essays for 21st Century Learning*. Thousand Oaks, CA: Corwin.

Preston, Michael J. 1996. "Computer Folklore." In *American Folklore: An Encyclopedia*, ed. Jan Harold Brunvand, 154–55. New York: Garland.

Prosic, Tamara. 2007. "Kol Nidre: Speaking of the Unspoken (Of)." *Bible and Critical Theory* 3: 1–14.

Puglia, David J. 2019. "Internet and Media in American Folklore and Folklife." In *Oxford Handbook of American Folklore and Folklife Studies*, ed. Simon J. Bronner, 598–624. New York: Oxford University Press.

Rabinovitch, Simon. 2005. "Positivism, Populism, and Politics: The Intellectual Foundations of Jewish Ethnography in Late Imperial Russia." *Ab Imperio* 3: 227–56.

Raisin, J. S. 1907. *Sect, Creed, and Custom in Judaism: A Study in Jewish Nomology*. Philadelphia: J. H. Greenstone.

Rand, Robert. 2001. *My Suburban Shtetl: A Novel About Life in a Twentieth-Century Jewish American Village*. Syracuse, NY: Syracuse University Press.

Raphael, Ray. 1988. *The Men from the Boys: Rites of Passage in Male America*. Lincoln: University of Nebraska Press.

Raphaelson, Samson. 1935. *The Jazz Singer*. New York: S. French.

———. 2003. "How I Came to Write 'The Jazz Singer.'" In *Entertaining America: Jews, Movies, and Broadcasting*, by J. Hoberman and Jeffrey Shandler, 82–83. New York: Jewish Museum.

Rappaport, Ernest A. 1975. *Anti-Judaism: A Psychohistory*. Chicago: Perspective Press.

Rappaport, Roy A. 1992. "Ritual." In *Folklore, Cultural Performances, and Popular Entertainments: A Communications-Centered Handbook*, ed. Richard Bauman, 249–60. New York: Oxford University Press.

———. 1996. [1979]. "The Obvious Aspects of Ritual." In *Readings in Ritual Studies*, ed. Ronald L. Grimes, 427–40. Upper Saddle River, NJ: Prentice-Hall.

Rappoport, Angelo S. 1937. *The Folklore of the Jews*. London: Soncino Press.

Raskin, Richard. 1992. *Life Is Like a Glass of Tea: Studies of Classic Jewish Jokes*. Aarhus, Denmark: Aarhus University Press.

Raspa, Dick. 1991. "A Short History of Giglio's: Occupational Role as Play Frames." *Western Folklore* 50: 201–8.

Ratcliffe, R. G. 2019. "Q & A: Starbucks Cofounder Howard Schultz on Running for President." *Texas Monthly* (March 12). https://www.texasmonthly.com/politics/starbucks-cofounder-howard-schultz-running-president/ (accessed June 22, 2019).

Ravnitzky, J. H. 1922. *Yidishe Vitsn*. New York: Sklarsky.

Rebhun, Uzi, and Eli Lederhendler, eds. 2015. *Research in Jewish Demography and Identity*. Brighton, MA: Academic Studies Press.

Reich, Aaron. 2020. "18,000 Australian Jews to United for '18for18' Online Lag Ba'omer Event." *Jerusalem Post* (May 8). https://www.jpost.com/diaspora/18000-australian-jews-to-unite-for-18for18-online-lag-baomer-event-627357 (accessed May 9, 2020).

Reichard, Gladys. 1943. "Franz Boas and Folklore." *Memoirs of the American Anthropological Association* 61: 52–57.

Reifman, Toby Fishbein, ed. 1978. *Blessing the Birth of a Daughter: Jewish Naming Ceremonies for Girls*. New York: Ezrat Nashim.

Reik, Theodor. 1931. *Ritual: Psycho-Analytic Studies*. London: Hogarth Press.

———. 1962. *Jewish Wit*. New York: Gamut Press.

Reisner, Neil. 2000. "Fate of Free World Resting with *Bubes, Zaydes* as Dems, Republicans Spar over Sunshine State." *Jewish Forward* (November 17), 1, 5.

Religious Action Center of Reform Judaism. 2000. "Nation's Largest Jewish Organization Reacts to Selection of Sen. Joseph Lieberman as Democratic Vice-Presidential Candidate." Religious Action Center of Reform Judaism (August 7). http://www.rac.org/news/080700.html (URL inactive, accessed November 1, 2000).

Reuben, Steven Carr. 1992. *Raising Jewish Children in a Contemporary World: The Modern Parent's Guide to Creating a Jewish Home*. Rocklin, CA: Prima.

Reuters. 2014. "WhatsApp Founder Jan Koum's Jewish Rags-to-Riches Tale." *Forward* (February 20). http://forward.com/news/world/193103/whatsapp-founder-jan-koums-jewish-rags-to-riches-t/ (accessed September 26, 2017).

Richman, Irwin. 1998. *Borscht Belt Bungalows: Memories of Catskill Summers*. Philadelphia: Temple University Press.

Rieder, Jonathan. 1985. *Canarsie: The Jews and Italians of Brooklyn Against Liberalism*. Cambridge, MA: Harvard University Press.

———. 1992. "Placing Canarsie." *Sociological Forum* 7: 337–53.

Rittner, Carol. 1991. *Memory Offended: The Auschwitz Convent Controversy*. New York: Praeger.

Ritzer, George, and Nathan Jurgenson. 2010. "Production, Consumption, Prosumption: The Nature of Capitalism in the Age of the Digital 'Prosumer.'" *Journal of Consumer Culture* 10: 13–36.

Rocker, Simon. 2015. "So What Is 'Cultural' Judaism?" *Jewish Chronicle* (July 16). https://www.thejc.com/lifestyle/features/so-what-is-cultural-judaism-1.67699 (accessed October 24, 2017).

Rogin, Michael. 1996. *Blackface/White Noise: Jewish Immigrants in the Hollywood Melting Pot*. Berkeley: University of California Press.

Roginsky, Dina. 2007. "Folklore, Folklorism, and Synchronization: Preserved-Created Folklore in Israel." *Journal of Folklore Research* 44: 41–66.

Romanian National Committee for the International Council of Museums. 1966. *The Symposium "Organization of Open-Air Ethnographic Museums: Principles and Methods."* Bucharest: Romanian National Committee, International Council of Museums.

Romeyn, Esther. 2008. *Street Scenes: Staging the Self in Immigrant New York, 1880–1924*. Minneapolis: University of Minnesota Press.

Rose, Evelyn. 1992. *The Complete International Jewish Cookbook*. New York: Carroll & Graf.

Rosen, Christine. 2005. "The Image Culture." *New Atlantis* 10: 27–46.

Rosenau, William. 1903. *Jewish Ceremonial Institutions and Customs*. Baltimore: Friedenwald.

Rosenberg, Stuart E. 1965. "The Right Age for Bar Mitzvah." *Religious Education* 60: 298–300.

Rosenfeld, Alvin H. 1980. *A Double Dying: Reflections on Holocaust Literature*. Bloomington: Indiana University Press.

Roskies, David G. 1992. "S. Ansky and the Paradigm of Return." In *The Uses of Tradition: Jewish Continuity in the Modern Era*, ed. Jack Wertheimer, 243–60. New York: Jewish Theological Seminary.

Rosten, Leo. 1936. "The Rather Difficult Case of Mr. K*A*P*L*A*N." *New Yorker* (August 14), 18–20.

———. 1937. "Terrible Vengeance of H*Y*M*A*N K*A*P*L*A*N." *New Yorker* (June 19), 15.

———. 1938. "The Return of H*Y*M*A*N K*A*P*L*A*N." *New Yorker* (September 16), 19.

———. 1946 [1937]. "The Education of H*Y*M*A*N K*A*P*L*A*N." In *Treasury of Laughter*, ed. Louis Untermeyer, 516–20. New York: Simon & Schuster.

———. 1959. *The Return of H*Y*M*A*N K*A*P*L*A*N.* New York: Harper.

———. 1968. *The Joys of Yiddish.* New York: Simon & Schuster.

———. 1976. *O K*A*P*L*A*N! M*Y K*A*P*L*A*N!* New York: Harper and Row.

———. 1982. *Hooray for Yiddish: A Book About English.* New York: Simon & Schuster.

———. 2001. *The New Joys of Yiddish.* New York: Crown.

Roth, Cecil. 1941. *A History of the Marranos*, rev. ed. Philadelphia: Jewish Publication Society of America.

———. 1955. "Bar Mitzvah: Its History and Its Associations." In *Bar Mitzvah Illustrated*, ed. Abraham I. Katsh, 15–22. New York: Shengold.

———, ed. 1959. *The Standard Jewish Encyclopedia.* Garden City, NY: Doubleday.

Roth, Joseph. 2001. *The Wandering Jews*, trans. Michael Hofmann. London: Granta Books.

Roth, Laurence. 2015. "Networks." In *The Routledge Handbook of Contemporary Jewish Cultures*, ed. Laurence Roth and Nadia Valman, 195–210. London: Routledge.

Rothkoff, Aaron. 1972. "[Rachel] In the Aggadah." In *Encyclopedia Judaica*, ed. Cecil Roth and Geoffrey Wigoder, 13: 1487–88. Jerusalem: Keter.

Rothman, Hal. 1989. *America's National Monuments: The Politics of Preservation.* Lawrence: University Press of Kansas.

Rourke, Constance. 1931. *American Humor.* Garden City, NY: Doubleday.

Rozakis, Laurie. 2007. *The Portable Jewish Mother.* Avon, MA: Adams Media.

Rożek, Michał. 1991. *Jewish Monuments of Kraków's Kazimierz.* Kraków: Oficyna Cracovia.

Rubin, Derek, ed. 2005. *Who We Are: On Being (and Not Being) a Jewish American Writer.* New York: Schocken.

Rubin, Louis D., Jr. 1976. "The Great American Joke." In *Humor in America*, ed. Enid Veron, 255–65. New York: Harcourt, Brace & Jovanovich.

Rubin, Nissan. 2009. *New Rituals, Old Societies: Invented Rituals in Contemporary Israel.* Boston: Academic Studies Press.

Rubin, Rachel, and Jeffrey Melnick. 2006. *Immigration and American Popular Culture: An Introduction.* New York: New York University Press.

Rulnick, Arthur D. 2000. "The Lieberman Challenge." *Woodbury Jewish Center* (Rosh Hashanah). http://www.thewjc.org/sermons/lieberman.htm (URL inactive, accessed December 1, 2000).

Russ, Ian. 1993. "The Psychosocial Tasks and Opportunities of Bar/Bat Mitzvah." In *Bar/Bat Mitzvah Education: A Sourcebook*, ed. Helen Leneman, 309–15. Denver: ARE Publishing.

Rutland, Suzanne D. 2010. "Reflections on 'Cultural Mavens' from an Australian Jewish Perspective." In *Jews at Home: The Domestication of Identity*, ed. Simon J. Bronner, 307–15. Oxford, UK: Littman Library of Jewish Civilization.

Ruttenberg, Danya. 2001. *Yentl's Revenge: The Next Wave of Jewish Feminism.* New York: Seal Press.

———. 2009. "Heaven and Earth: Notes on New Jewish Ritual." In *Reinventing Ritual: Contemporary Art and Design for Jewish Life*, ed. Daniel Belasco, 71–93. New Haven, CT: Yale University Press.

Sabar, Shalom. 2000. *Ketubbah: The Art of the Jewish Marriage Contract*. New York: Rizzoli.

———. 2010. "From Sacred Symbol to Key Ring: The *Hamsa* in Jewish and Israeli Societies." In *Jews at Home: The Domestication of Identity*, ed. Simon J. Bronner, 140–62. Oxford, UK: Littman Library of Jewish Civilization.

Sabar, Shalom, Ella Arazi, Avriel Bar-Levav, and Roni Weinstein. 2006. *Ma'agal Ha-Chayim* [The Life Cycle]. Jerusalem: Hebrew University of Jerusalem (Hebrew).

Sachs, Angeli, and Edward van Voolen, eds. 2004. *Jewish Identity in Contemporary Architecture*. Munich: Prestel.

Sacks, Jonathan. 2002. *The Dignity of Difference: How to Avoid the Clash of Civilizations*. London: Continuum.

Safire, William. 2007. "Schlep." *New York Times Magazine* (September 16). https://www.nytimes.com/2007/09/16/magazine/16wwln-safire-t.html (accessed December 23, 2019).

Safran, Gabriella. 2010. *Wandering Soul: The Dybuuk's Creator, S. An-sky*. Cambridge, MA: Belknap Press.

Sagan, Paul, and Tom Leighton. 2010. "The Internet and the Future of News." *Daedalus* 139: 119–25.

Said, Edward. 1993. *Culture and Imperialism*. London: Chatto & Windus.

———. 1994 [1979]. *Orientalism: Western Conceptions of the Orient*, 25th anniversary ed. New York: Vintage.

Sales, Amy L., and Leonard Saxe. 2003. *"How Goodly Are Thy Tents": Summer Camps as Jewish Socializing Experiences*. Hanover, NH: University Press of New England.

Santino, Jack. 2009. "The Ritualesque: Festival, Politics, and Popular Culture." *Western Folklore* 68: 9–26.

Saper, Bernard. 1993. "Since When Is Jewish Humor Not Anti-Semitic?" In *Semites and Stereotypes: Characteristics of Jewish Humor*, ed. Avner Ziv and Anat Zajdman, 71–86. Westport, CT: Greenwood Press.

Sarna, Jonathan D. 2003. "The Question of Music in American Judaism: Reflections at 350 Years." *American Jewish History* 91: 195–203.

Sarna, Nahum M. 1996. *Exploring Exodus: The Origins of Biblical Israel*. New York: Schocken.

Sax, William S. 2006. "Agency." In *Theorizing Rituals: Issues, Topics, Approaches, Concepts*, ed. Jens Kreinath, Jan Snoek, and Michael Strausberg, 473–81. Leiden, Netherlands: Brill.

Saxe, Leonard, and Barry Chazan. 2008. *Ten Days of Birthright Israel: A Journey in Young Adult Identity*. Waltham, MA: Brandeis University Press.

Schachter, Stanley J. 2008. *Laugh for God's Sake: Where Jewish Humor and Jewish Ethics Meet*. Jersey City, NJ: KTAV.

Schaktman, Peter B. 1998. "To See or Not to See." ReformJudaism.org. https://reformjudaism.org/learning/torah-study/torah-commentary/see-or-not-see (accessed May 3, 2020).

Schatzki, Theodore R. 2001. "Introduction: Practice Theory." In *The Practice Turn in Contemporary Theory*, ed. Theodore R. Schatzki, Karin Knorr Cetina, and Eike Von Savigny, 1–14. London: Routledge.

Schauss, Hayyim. 1950. *The Lifetime of a Jew: Throughout the Ages of Jewish History*. New York: Union of American Hebrew Congregations.

Schechter, Ronald. 2003. *Obstinate Hebrews: Representations of Jews in France, 1715–1815*. Berkeley: University of California Press.

Scheff, Thomas J. 2006. *Goffman Unbound: A New Paradigm for Social Science*. Boulder, CO: Paradigm.

Schlör, Joachim. 2014a. "Robert Gilbert (1899–1978): Songwriter and Translator of Musical Comedy." *Transatlantic Perspectives* (February 1). http://www.transatlanticperspectives .org/entry.php?rec=149 (accessed October 24, 2017).

———. 2014b. "Robert Gilbert, Hermann Leopoldi and the Role of Languages Between Exile and Return." *Prezladaniec: A Journal of Translation Studies* 29: 157–78.

———. 2016. "Werner Richard Heymann in Hollywood: A Case Study of German-Jewish Emigration After 1933 as a Transnational Experience." *Jewish Culture and History* 17: 115–32.

Schmalzbauer, John. 2010. "Popular Culture." In *The Blackwell Companion to Religion in America*, ed. Philip Goff, 254–75. Malden, MA: Blackwell.

Schoenfeld, Stuart. 1993a. "Folk Judaism, Elite Judaism, and the Role of Bar Mitzvah in the Development of the Synagogue and Jewish School in America." In *Bar/Bat Mitzvah Education: A Sourcebook*, ed. Helen Leneman, 78–89. Springfield, NJ: A.R.E. Publishing.

———. 1993b. "The Significance of the Social Aspects of Bar/Bat Mitzvah." In *Bar/Bat Mitzvah Education: A Sourcebook*, ed. Helen Leneman, 325–38. Springfield, NJ: A.R.E. Publishing.

Schreiber, Lynne. 2003. *Hide and Seek: Jewish Women and Hair Covering*. New York: Lambda.

Schrire, Dan, and Galit Hasan-Rokem. 2012. "Folklore Studies in Israel." In *A Companion to Folklore*, ed. Regina F. Bendix and Galit Hasan-Rokem, 325–48. Malden, MA: Wiley-Blackwell.

Schuman, Howard, Vered Vinitzky-Seroussi, and Amiram D. Vinokur. 2003. "Keeping the Past Alive: Memories of Israeli Jews at the Turn of the Millennium." *Sociological Forum* 18: 103–36.

Schwartz, Arthur. 2008. *Arthur Schwartz's Jewish Home Cooking: Yiddish Recipes Revisited*. Berkeley, CA: Ten Speed Press.

Schwartzman, Ana, and Zoë Francesca. 2004. *Make Your Own Jewish Wedding: How to Create a Ritual That Expresses Your True Selves*. San Francisco: Jossey-Bass.

Seidman, Naomi. 1997. "Theorizing Jewish Patriarchy *in extremis*." In *Judaism Since Gender*, ed. Miriam Peskowitz and Laura Levitt, 40–48. New York: Routledge.

Seifter, Jacob. 1977. "Die Stadt Ospitsin." In *Sefer Oshpitsin*, ed. Ch. Wolnerman, A. Burstin, and M. S. Geshuri, 355–61. Jerusalem: Irgun Yotzey Oswiecim.

———. 1996. "The Town of Oshpitsin [Oswiecim or Auschwitz]: The Memoirs of Jacob Seifter, Cleveland, Ohio," translated and annotated by Simon J. Bronner and Jacob Hennenberg. *Yiddish* 10: 34–46.

Sennett, Richard. 1977. *The Fall of Public Man*. New York: Vintage.

———. 2012. *Together: The Rituals, Pleasures, and Politics of Cooperation*. New Haven, CT: Yale University Press.

Sered, Susan Starr. 1992. *Women as Ritual Experts: The Religious Lives of Elderly Jewish Women in Jerusalem*. New York: Oxford University Press.

Serracino-Inglott, Peter. 2001. "To Joke or Not to Joke: A Diplomatic Dilemma in the Age of Internet." In *Language and Diplomacy*, ed. Jovan Kurbalija and Hannah Slavik, 21–38. Msida, Malta: DiploProjects.

Shafran, Avi. 2010. "Wings and Prayers." Jewish America 16 (website provided by Am Echad Resources: Information and Opinion from a Traditional Jewish Perspective). http://www.jewishamerica.com/ja/content/amechad/amarch17.cfm#Wings%20and%20Prayers (URL inactive, accessed February 10, 2010).

Shalin, Dmitri. 2009. "Saul Mendlovitz: Erving Was a Jew Acting Like a Canadian Acting Like a Britisher." Remembering Erving Goffman website. http://cdclv.unlv.edu//archives/interactionism/goffman/mendlovitz_08.html (accessed June 6, 2019).

Shandler, Jeffrey. 2009. *Jews, God, and Videotape: Religion and Media in America*. New York: New York University Press.

———. 2014. *Shtetl: A Vernacular Intellectual History*. New Brunswick, NJ: Rutgers University Press.

Shandler, Jeffrey, and Beth S. Wenger, eds. 1997. *Encounters with the "Holy Land": Place, Past, and Future in American Jewish Culture*. Philadelphia: National Museum of American Jewish History.

Shank, Barry. 2001. "Culture and Cultural Studies." In *Encyclopedia of American Studies*, ed. George T. Kurian, Miles Orvell, Johnnella E. Butler, and Jay Mechling, 443–48. New York: Grolier.

Shapiro, Edward. 2001. "Right Turn? Jews and the American Conservative Movement." In *Jews in American Politics*, ed. L. Sandy Maisel and Ira N. Forman, 195–212. Lanham, MD: Rowman & Littlefield.

Sharaby, Rachel. 2011. "Tradition in Intercultural Transition: Marriage Rituals in Ethiopia and Israel." In *Revisioning Ritual: Jewish Traditions in Transition*, ed. Simon J. Bronner, 234–62. Oxford, UK: Littman Library of Jewish Civilization.

Shavit, Yaacov, and Shoshana Sitton. 2004. *Staging and Stagers in Modern Jewish Palestine: The Creation of Festive Lore in a New Culture, 1882–1948*, trans. Chaya Naor. Detroit: Wayne State University Press.

Shelamay, Kay Kaufman. 1998. *Let Jasmine Rain Down: Song and Remembrance Among Syrian Jews*. Chicago: University of Chicago Press.

Shendelman, Sara, and Avram Davis. 1998. *Traditions: The Complete Book of Prayers, Rituals, and Blessings for Every Jewish Home*. New York: Hyperion.

Shepard, Paul. 1973. *The Tender Carnivore and the Sacred Game*. Athens: University of Georgia Press.

Sherman, Josepha. 1992. *A Sampler of Jewish American Folklore*. Little Rock, AR: August House.

Sherwin, Byron L. 1990. *In Partnership with God: Contemporary Jewish Law and Ethics*. Syracuse, NY: Syracuse University Press.

Sherzer, Joel. 1993. "On Puns, Comebacks, Verbal Dueling, and Play Languages: Speech Play in Balinese Verbal Life." *Language in Society* 22: 217–33.

Sheskin, Ira M. 2001. *How Jewish Communities Differ: Variations in the Findings of Local Jewish Population Studies*. New York: Mandell L. Berman Institute–North American Jewish Data Bank.

Shevelev, Raphael. 1996. *Liberating the Ghosts: Photographs and Text from the March of the Living*. Portland, OR: LensWork.

Shiffman, Dan. 1999. "The Ingratiating Humor of Leo Rosten's Hyman Kaplan Stories." *Studies in American Jewish Literature* 18: 93–101.

———. 2000. "The Comedy of Assimilation in Leo Rosten's Hyman Kaplan Stories." *Studies in American Humor*, n.s., 7: 49–58.

Shiloah, Amnon. 1992. *Jewish Musical Traditions*. Detroit: Wayne State University Press.

Shribman, David M. 2001. "The Lieberman Candidacy." In *Jews in American Politics*, ed. L. Sandy Maisel and Ira N. Forman, xxv–xxvii. Lanham, MD: Rowman & Littlefield.

Shuldiner, David P. 1999. *Of Moses and Marx: Folk Ideology and Folk History in the Jewish Labor Movement*. Westport, CT: Bergin & Garvey.

Shulem, Baruch, and David Koenigsberg. 2007. "The Differences Between Jewish Education (Chinuch) and Education That Is Jewish." Shema Yisrael Torah Network. http://www.shemayisrael.co.il/orgs/torahpsychology/chinuch.htm (accessed December 29, 2008).

Shulman, Yaakov David. 1991. *The Rema: The Story of Rabbi Moshe Isserles*. New York: C.I.S. Publishers.

Shwartz-Be'eri, Ora. 2000. *The Jews of Kurdistan: Daily Life, Customs, Arts and Crafts*. Jerusalem: Israel Museum.

Sidlofsky, Paul. 1993. "Life After Bar/Bat Mitzvah: The 'Chai' Program." In *Bar/Bat Mitzvah Education: A Sourcebook*, ed. Helen Leneman, 302–6. Springfield, NJ: A.R.E. Publishing.

Siegel, Richard, Michael Strassfeld, and Sharon Strassfeld, eds. 1973. *The Jewish Catalog: A Do-It-Yourself Kit*. Philadelphia: Jewish Publication Society of America.

Siegel, Sharon R. 2012. "Jewish Welcoming Ceremonies for Newborn Girls: The Modern Development of a Feminist Ritual." *Modern Judaism* 32: 335–58.

———. 2014. *A Jewish Ceremony for Newborn Girls: The Torah's Covenant Affirmed*. Waltham, MA: Brandeis University Press.

Silver, Mitchell. 1998. *Respecting the Wicked Child: A Philosophy of Secular Jewish Identity and Education*. Amherst: University of Massachusetts Press.

Silver, Monroe. 1919. "Cohen at the Picnic, Part l." Record no. Victor 18608-A.

Silverman, Eric Kline. 2006. *From Abraham to America: A History of Jewish Circumcision*. Lanham, MD: University Press of America.

———. 2016. "The Waters of Mendangumeli: A Masculine Psychoanalytic Interpretation of a New Guinea Flood Myth—and Women's Laughter." *Journal of American Folklore* 129: 171–202.

Silverman, Jonathan, and Dean Rader. 2005. *The World Is a Text: Writing, Reading, and Thinking About Culture and Its Contexts*. Upper Saddle River, NJ: Pearson/Prentice-Hall.

Silverman, Morris. 1932. "Report of Survey on Ritual." In *Proceedings of the Rabbinical Assembly of America*, 322–43. New York: Rabbinical Assembly.

Singer, Isaac Bashevis. 1983. *The Penitent*. New York: Farrar, Straus & Giroux.

Singer, Matthew, ed. 2007. *A Kiss for the Mezuzah*. Philadelphia: Philadelphia Museum of Jewish Art.

———. 2009. *Wimpel! Wrapped Wishes*. Philadelphia: Philadelphia Museum of Jewish Art.

Singular, Stephen. 2000. *Joe Lieberman: The Historic Choice*. New York: Kensington.

Siporin, Steve. 2014. " 'The Night of the Ovietani' and the Mediation of Jewish and Italian Identities." In *Framing Jewish Culture: Boundaries and Representations*, ed. Simon J. Bronner, 241–70. Oxford, UK: Littman Library of Jewish Civilization.

Sklare, Marshall. 1979. *Jewish Identity on the Suburban Frontier: A Study of Group Survival in the Open Society*, 2nd ed. Chicago: University of Chicago Press.

———. 1993. *Observing America's Jews*, ed. Jonathan D. Sarna. Hanover, NH: Brandeis University Press.

Sklare, Marshall, and Joseph Greenblum. 1979 [1967]. *Jewish Identity on the Suburban Frontier: A Study of Group Survival in the Open Society*, 2nd ed. Chicago: University of Chicago Press.

Slapak, Orpa. 2003. *The Jews of India: A Story of Three Communities*. Jerusalem: Israel Museum.

Slobin, Mark. 2000. *Fiddler on the Move: Exploring the Klezmer World*. Oxford, UK: Oxford University Press.

———. 2002. *Chosen Voices: The Story of the American Cantorate*. Urbana: University of Illinois Press.

Smason, Rav Ze'ev. 2000. "Lieberman." *Nusach Hari B'nai Zion* (August 12). https://www.nhbz.org/_sermons/sermons_detail.php?sermonid=6 (accessed April 11, 2020).

Smith, Chris. 2000. "The Running Mensch." *New York Magazine* (October 30). http://nymag.com/nymetro/news/politics/national/features/3995/ (accessed June 21, 2019).

Smith, John B. 2004. "Perchta the Belly-Slitter and Her Kin: A View of Some Traditional Threatening Figures, Threats, and Punishments." *Folklore* 115: 167–86.

Smith, M. W. 2001. *Reading Simulacra: Fatal Theories for Postmodernity*. Albany: State University of New York Press.

Smith, Paul. 1991. "The Joke Machine: Communicating Traditional Humour Using Computers." In *Spoken in Jest*, ed. Gillian Bennett, 257–78. Sheffield, UK: Sheffield Academic Press.

Smith, Robert Jerome. 1972. "Festivals and Celebrations." In *Folklore and Folklife: An Introduction*, ed. Richard M. Dorson, 159–72. Chicago: University of Chicago Press.

Smith, W. Robertson. 1907. *Lectures on the Religion of the Semites: First Series, The Fundamental Institutions*. London: Adam and Charles Black.

Snoek, Jan A. M. 2006. "Defining 'Rituals.' " In *Theorizing Rituals: Issues, Topics, Approaches, Concepts*, ed. Jens Kreinath, Jan Snoek, and Michael Strausberg, 3–14. Leiden, Netherlands: Brill.

Sokolov, Y. M. 1971. *Russian Folklore*, trans. Catherine Ruth Smith. Detroit: Folklore Associates.

Sollors, Werner. 1996. "Theories of American Ethnicity." In *Theories of Ethnicity: A Classical Reader*, ed. Werner Sollors, x–xliv. New York: New York University Press.

Solomont, E. B. 2005. "Point, Click, Chuckle: Jewish Humor Goes Online." *Jewish Forward* (February 4). http://www.forward.com/articles/2879/ (URL inactive; accessed August 31, 2017).

Solotaroff, Ted, and Nessa Rapoport. 1992. *Writing Our Way Home: Contemporary Stories by American Jewish Writers*. New York: Schocken.

Spalding, Henry D. 1969. "Preface." In *Encyclopedia of Jewish Humor: From Biblical Times to the Modern Age*, ed. Henry D. Spalding, xiii–xix. New York: Jonathan David.

———. 1976. "Introduction." In *A Treasure-Trove of American Jewish Humor*, ed. Henry D. Spalding, xiii–xvii. Middle Village, NY: Jonathan David.

Spencer, Gary. 1989. "An Analysis of JAP-Baiting Humor on the College Campus." *Humor: International Journal of Humor Research* 2: 329–48.

Sperling, Avraham Yitzchak. 1999 [1890]. *Sefer Tamei Ha-minhagim U'mekorei Ha-dinim*. Jerusalem: Shay Lamora.

Spiegel, Nina S. 2011. "New Israeli Rituals: Inventing a Folk Dance Tradition." In *Revisioning Ritual: Jewish Traditions in Transition*, ed. Simon J. Bronner, 392–418. Oxford, UK: Littman Library of Jewish Civilization.

Spielmann, Isidore. 1902–1905. "South African War Memorial: Unveiling at the Central Synagogue." *Transactions of the Jewish Historical Society of England* 5: 58.

Spiro, Jack D. 1977. "The Educational Significance of the Bar Mitzvah Initiation." *Religious Education* 72: 383–99.

Splansky, Yael. 2012. "Hiddur Mitzvah: The Aesthetics of Mitzvot." *Holy Blossom Temple Bulletin* (December), 4. https://holyblossom.org/wp-content/uploads/2012/12/w1_BulletinDec12.pdf (URL inactive; accessed August 30, 2020).

Stack, Liam. 2020. "'Plague on a Biblical Scale': Hasidic Families Hit Hard by Virus." *New York Times* (April 21). https://www.nytimes.com/2020/04/21/nyregion/coronavirus-jews-hasidic-ny.html (accessed May 9, 2020).

Stavans, Ilan, ed. 1998. *The Oxford Book of Jewish Stories*. New York: Oxford University Press.

Steinhardt, Michael. 2000. "Giving Voice to a Secular Majority." *Jewish Forward* (September 15), 9.

Steinmetz, Sol. 1986. *Yiddish and English: A Century of Yiddish in America*. Tuscaloosa: University of Alabama Press.

Stephens, John Richard. 2001. *Into the Mummy's Tomb*. New York: Berkley.

Stern, J. 1987. "Modes of Reference in the Rituals of Judaism." *Religious Studies* 23: 109–28.

Sternhell, Zeev. 1999. *The Founding Myths of Israel*, trans. David Maisel. Princeton, NJ: Princeton University Press.

Sternlicht, Stanford. 2004. *The Tenement Saga: The Lower East Side and Early Jewish American Writers*. Madison: University of Wisconsin Press.

Stewart, Edward C., and Milton J. Bennett. 1991. *American Cultural Patterns: A Cross-Cultural Perspective*, rev. ed. Yarmouth, ME: Intercultural Press.

Stivale, Charles J. 1997. "Spam: Heteroglossia and Harassment in Cyberspace." In *Internet Culture*, ed. David Porter, 133–44. New York: Routledge.

Stradomski, Wiesław. 1989. "The Jewish Cinema in Inter-War Poland." *Polish Art Studies* 10: 167–77.

Strassfeld, Sharon, and Michael Strassfeld, eds. 1976. *The Second Jewish Catalog: Sources and Resources*. Philadelphia: Jewish Publication Society.

Stratton, Jon. 2009. *Jews, Race, and Popular Music*. Farnham, UK: Ashgate.

Strauss, Susan, and Parastou Feiz. 2013. *Discourse Analysis: Putting Our Worlds into Words*. New York: Routledge.

Sutton, Joseph A. D. 1979. *Magic Carpet: Aleppo in Flatbush. The Story of a Unique Jewish Community*. New York: Thayer-Jacoby.

Sutton-Smith, Brian. 1960. "'Shut Up and Keep Digging': The Cruel Joke Series." *Midwest Folklore* 10: 11–22.

Sweterlitsch, Richard. 1997. "Custom." In *Folklore: An Encyclopedia of Beliefs, Customs, Tales, Music, and Art*, ed. Thomas A. Green, 168–72. Santa Barbara, CA: ABC-CLIO.

Syme, Daniel B. 2004. *The Jewish Home: A Guide for Jewish Living*, rev. ed. New York: URJ Press.

Sztokman, Elana Maryles. 2011. *The Men's Section: Orthodox Jewish Men in an Egalitarian World*. Waltham, MA: Brandeis University Press.

Szurmuk, Mónica. 2010. "Home in the Pampas: Alberto Gerchunoff's Jewish Gauchos." In *Jews at Home: The Domestication of Identity*, ed. Simon J. Bronner, 241–56. Oxford, UK: Littman Library of Jewish Civilization.

Tabory, Ephraim, and Sharon Erez. 2003. "Circumscribed Circumcision: The Motivations and Identities of Israeli Parents Who Choose Not to Circumcise Their Sons." In *The Covenant of Circumcision: New Perspectives on an Ancient Jewish Rite*, ed. Elizabeth Wyner Mark, 161–76. Waltham, MA: Brandeis University Press.

Tabory, Joseph. 1997. "Minhag." In *The Oxford Dictionary of the Jewish Religion*, ed. R. J. Zwi Werblowsky and Geoffrey Wigoder, 496–97. Oxford, UK: Oxford University Press.

Takaki, Ronald. 1993. *A Different Mirror: A History of Multicultural America*, rev. ed. New York: Little, Brown.

Talmage, Frank, ed. 1980. *Studies in Jewish Folklore*. Cambridge, MA: Association for Jewish Studies.

Telushkin, Joseph. 1991. *Jewish Literacy: The Most Important Things to Know About the Jewish Religion, Its People, and Its History*. New York: Morrow.

———. 1992. *Jewish Humor: What the Best Jewish Jokes Say About Jews*. New York: William Morrow.

Teman, Elly. 2008. "The Red String: The Cultural History of a Jewish Folk Symbol." In *Jewishness: Expression, Identity, and Representation*, ed. Simon J. Bronner, 29–57. Oxford, UK: Littman Library of Jewish Civilization.

Teter, Magda. 2020. *Blood Libel: On the Trail of an Antisemitic Myth*. Cambridge, MA: Harvard University Press.

Thomas, James M. 2020. "Du Bois, Double Consciousness, and the 'Jewish Question.'" *Ethnic and Racial Studies* 43: 1333–56.

Thompson, Stith. 1975 [1955–1958]. *Motif-Index of Folk-Literature: A Classification of Narrative Elements in Folktales, Ballads, Myths, Fables, Mediaeval Romances, Exempla, Fabiaux, Jest-books, and Local Legends*, 6 vols., rev. and enlarged ed. Bloomington: Indiana University Press.

Times Wire Services. 1996. "Construction Halted on Auschwitz Mall." *Los Angeles Times* (March 23). https://www.latimes.com/archives/la-xpm-1996-03-23-mn-50392-story.html (accessed June 14, 2019).

Tobin, Jonathan S. 1998. "Getting Lost in History: Museums Are the Latest Jewish Battlegrounds." *New Jersey Standard* (March 13): 5, 49.

Toelken, Barre. 1996. *The Dynamics of Folklore*, rev. and expanded ed. Logan: Utah State University Press.

Trachtenberg, Alan. 1982. *The Incorporation of America: Culture and Society in the Gilded Age*. New York: Hill & Wang.

Trachtenberg, Joshua. 1939. *Jewish Magic and Superstition: A Study in Folk Religion*. New York: Behrman's Jewish Book House.

Traub, James. 2000. "Closing the Piety Gap." Salon.com (August 18). https://www.salon.com/2000/08/16/religion_5/ (accessed November 1, 2000).

———. 2001. "Mildly Ambitious." *New York Times Magazine* (June 10), 58–61.

Traverso, Enzo. 2019. *The Jewish Question: History of a Marxist Debate*, trans. Bernard Gibbons. Leiden, Netherlands: Brill.

Troy, Gil. 2000. "Al and Joe: Multiculturalism-Lite." *Jewish Forward* (October 13), 9.

Tsur, Muky. 2007. "Pesach in the Land of Israel: Kibbutz Haggadot." *Israel Studies* 12: 74–103.

Turkle, Sherry. 2011. *Alone Together: Why We Expect More from Technology and Less from Each Other*. New York: Basic Books.

Turner, Terence. 2006. "Structure, Process, Form." In *Theorizing Rituals: Issues, Topics, Approaches, Concepts*, ed. Jens Kreinath, Jan Snoek, and Michael Strausberg, 207–46. Leiden, Netherlands: Brill.

Turner, Victor W. 1967. *The Forest of Symbols: Aspects of Ndembu Ritual*. Ithaca, NY: Cornell University Press.

———. 1969. *The Ritual Process: Structure and Anti-Structure*. Chicago: Aldine.

———. 1977. "Process, System, and Symbol: A New Anthropological Synthesis." *Daedalus* 106: 61–80.

———. 1979. "Frame, Flow, and Reflection: Ritual and Drama as Public Liminality." *Japanese Journal of Religious Studies* 6: 465–99.

———. 1982. "Introduction." In *Celebration: Studies in Festivity and Ritual*, ed. Victor Turner, 11–32. Washington, DC: Smithsonian Institution Press.

———. 1995. *The Ritual Process: Structure and Anti-Structure*. New York: Aldine de Gruyter.

Ukeles, Jacob B., and Ron Miller. 2004. *Jewish Community Study of New York: 2002*. New York: UJA–Federation of New York.

Umble, Diane Zimmerman, and David Weaver-Zercher, eds. 2008. *The Amish and the Media*. Baltimore: Johns Hopkins University Press.

Union of Orthodox Rabbis. 2000. "UOR Calls on Lieberman to End Support of Homosexual Agenda." Union of Orthodox Rabbis of the United States and Canada (October 5). http://www.orthodoxrabbis.org (URL inactive, accessed November 1, 2000).

Unterman, Alan. 1991. *Dictionary of Jewish Lore and Legend*. London: Thames & Hudson.

———. 1999. *The Jews: Their Religious Beliefs and Practices*. Portland: Sussex Academic Press.

Upton, Dell. 2015. *What Can and Can't Be Said: Race, Uplift, and Monument Building in the Contemporary South*. New Haven: Yale University Press.

Uvezian, Sonia. 1999. *Recipes and Remembrances from an Eastern Mediterranean Kitchen: A Culinary Journey Through Syria, Lebanon, and Jordan*. Austin: University of Texas Press.

Vaitsblit, Hannah. 2015. "JDate Acquires JSwipe." *Tablet* (October 16). https://www.tabletmag.com/sections/news/articles/jdate-aquires-jswipe (accessed August 1, 2020).

Valley, Eli. 2010. "New Jewish Ritual." *Contact* 12 (winter): 2.

Van Gennep, Arnold. 1960. *The Rites of Passage*, trans. Monika B. Vizedom and Gabrielle L. Caffee. Chicago: University of Chicago Press.

Varanda, Fernando. 1997. "San'ā: Jewish Quarter." In *Encyclopedia of Vernacular Architecture of the World*, ed. Paul Oliver, 1458–59. Cambridge, UK: Cambridge University Press.

Verbeek, Peter-Paul. 2005. *What Things Do: Philosophical Reflections on Technology, Agency, and Design*. University Park: Pennsylvania State University Press.

"Vice-Presidential Values." 2000. *Jewish Forward* (August 11), 1, 8.

Vinecour, Earl. 1977. *Polish Jews: The Final Chapter*. New York: New York University Press.

Wagner, Matthew. 2009. "Soldiers Turn to Secret Weapon: Jewish Spirituality." *Jerusalem Post* (January 14). https://www.jpost.com/jewish-world/jewish-features/soldiers-turn-to-secret-weapon-jewish-spirituality (accessed February 9, 2009).

Waligórska, Magdalena. 2013. *Klezmer's Afterlife: An Ethnography of the Jewish Music Revival in Poland and Germany*. Oxford, UK: Oxford University Press.

———. 2014. "The Framing of the Jew: Paradigms of Incorporation and Difference in the Jewish Heritage Revival in Poland." In *Framing Jewish Culture: Boundaries and Representations*, ed. Simon J. Bronner, 313–34. Oxford, UK: Littman Library of Jewish Civilization.

Wallace, Patricia. 1999. *The Psychology of the Internet*. Cambridge, UK: Cambridge University Press.

Ward, Seth. 2011. "Ritual and History: The Order of Prayers for Israel Independence Day (Yom Ha'atsma'ut)." In *Revisioning Ritual: Jewish Traditions in Transition*, ed. Simon J. Bronner, 68–93. Oxford, UK: Littman Library of Jewish Civilization.

Waskow, Arthur O., and Phyllis O. Berman. 2011. *Freedom Journeys: The Tale of Exodus and Wilderness Across Millennia*. Woodstock, VT: Vermont Lights.

Wasserfall, Rahel. 1992. "Menstruation and Identity: The Meaning of Niddah for Moroccan Women Immigrants to Israel." In *People of the Body: Jews and Judaism from an Embodied Perspective*, ed. Howard Eilberg-Schwartz, 309–28. Albany: State University of New York Press.

Weaver, Simon. 2011. "Jokes, Rhetoric, and Embodied Racism: A Rhetorical Discourse Analysis of the Logics of Racist Jokes on the Internet." *Ethnicities* 11: 413–35.

Weaver-Zercher, David. 2001. *The Amish in the American Imagination*. Baltimore: Johns Hopkins University Press.

Webber, Jonathan, ed. 1994. *Jewish Identities in the New Europe*. London: Littman Library of Jewish Civilization.

———. 2002. "Notes Towards the Definition of 'Jewish Culture' in Contemporary Europe." In *New Jewish Identities: Contemporary Europe and Beyond*, ed. Zvi Gitelman, Barry Kosmin, and András Kovács, 317–40. Budapest: Central European University Press.

———. 2014. "Representing Jewish Culture: The Problem of Boundaries." In *Framing Jewish Culture: Boundaries and Representations*, ed. Simon J. Bronner, 33–76. Oxford, UK: Littman Library of Jewish Civilization.

Weber, Bruce E. 2004. "Alan King, Comic with Chutzpah, Dies at 76." *New York Times* (May 9). https://www.nytimes.com/2004/05/09/national/alan-king-comic-with-chutzpah-dies-at-76.html (accessed November 27, 2006).

Weber, Donald. 2003. "Accents of the Future: Jewish American Popular Culture." In *The Cambridge Companion to Jewish American Literature*, ed. Hana Wirth-Nesher and Michael P. Kramer, 129–48. Cambridge, UK: Cambridge University Press.

———. 2005. *Haunted in the New World: Jewish American Culture from Cahan to* The Goldbergs. Bloomington: Indiana University Press.

Weiner, Deborah R. 2006. *Coalfield Jews: An Appalachian History*. Urbana: University of Illinois Press.

Weiner, Melissa F., and Bedelia Nicola Richards. 2008. "Bridging the Theoretical Gap: The Diasporized Hybrid in Sociological Theory." In *Hybrid Identities: Theoretical and Empirical Examinations*, ed. Keri E. Iyall Smith and Patricia Leavy, 101–16. Leiden, Netherlands: Brill.

Weinreich, Beatrice S. 1960. "The Americanization of Passover." In *Studies in Biblical and Jewish Folklore*, ed. Raphael Patai, Francis Lee Utley, and Dov Noy, 329–66. Bloomington: Indiana University Press.

———, ed. 1988. *Yiddish Folktales*, trans. Leonard Wolf. New York: Pantheon.

Weinreich, Uriel. 1968. *Modern English-Yiddish, Yiddish-English Dictionary*. New York: YIVO Institute for Jewish Research.

Weinstein, Simcha. 2008. *Shtick Shift: Jewish Humor in the 21st Century*. Fort Lee, NJ: Barricade.

Weinstein, Valerie. 2005. "Dissolving Boundaries: Assimilation, and Allosemitism in E. A. Dupont's *Das alte Gesetz* (1923) and Veit Harlan's *Jud Süs* (1940)." *German Quarterly* 78: 496–516.

Weisberg, Jennifer. 2008. "The Student Who Wouldn't Go Away." *Tablet* (June 24). https://www.tabletmag.com/jewish-arts-and-culture/books/940/the-student-who-wouldnt-go-away (accessed June 15, 2019).

Weiss, Moshe. 1994. *From Oswiecim to Auschwitz: Poland Revisited*. Oakville, Canada: Mosaic Press.

Weiss, Shayna. 2016. "*Frum* with Benefits: Israeli Television, Globalization, and *Srugim*'s American Appeal." *Jewish Film and New Media: An International Journal* 4: 68–89.

Weissbach, Lee Shai. 2005. *Jewish Life in Small-Town America: A History*. New Haven, CT: Yale University Press.

———. 2015. *The Synagogues of Kentucky: Architecture and History*. Lexington: University Press of Kentucky.

Weissler, Chava. 1992. "*Mitzvot* Built into the Body: *Tkhines* for *Niddah*, Pregnancy, and Childbirth." In *People of the Body: Jews and Judaism from an Embodied Perspective*, ed. Howard Eilberg-Schwartz, 101–15. Albany: State University of New York Press.

Whitfield, Stephen J. 2007. "Between Memory and Messianism: A Brief History of American Jewish Identity." In *The New Authentics: Artists of the Post-Jewish Generation*, ed. Staci Boris, 44–55. Chicago: Spertus Press.

———. 2008. "Black Like Us." *Jewish History* 22: 353–71.

Wildavsky, Aaron B. 1993. *Assimilation vs. Separation: Joseph the Administrator and the Politics of Religion in Biblical Israel*. New Brunswick, NJ: Transaction.

Wilde, Larry. 1974. *The Official Jewish Joke Book*. New York: Pinnacle.

———. 1980. *The Last Official Jewish Joke Book (Maybe Next to the Last)*. Toronto: Bantam.

Williams, Raymond. 1983. *Keywords: A Vocabulary of Culture and Society*, rev. ed. New York: Oxford University Press.

Wilner, Michael. 2019. "Starbucks' Schultz, Raised in Jewish Brooklyn, Mulls Presidential Run." *Jerusalem Post* (January 27). https://www.jpost.com/American-Politics/Starbucks-Schultz-formed-in-Jewish-Brooklyn-mulls-presidential-run-578850 (accessed June 22, 2019).

Wilson, William H. 1994. *The City Beautiful Movement*. Baltimore: Johns Hopkins University Press.

Wisse, Ruth R. 1992. *If I Am Not for Myself . . . : The Liberal Betrayal of the Jews*. New York: Free Press.

———. 2007. *Jews and Power*. New York: Schocken.

———. 2013. *No Joke: Making Jewish Humor*. Princeton, NJ: Princeton University Press.

Wodziński, Marcin. 2014. "The Question of Hasidic Sectarianism." In *Framing Jewish Culture: Boundaries and Representations*, ed. Simon J. Bronner, 125–50. Oxford, UK: Littman Library of Jewish Civilization.

Wolf, Lucien. 1911–1914. "Origin of the Jewish Historical Society of England." *Transactions of the Jewish Historical Society of England* 7: 206–15.

Wolitz, Seth L. 1988. "The Americanization of Tevye or Boarding the Jewish 'Mayflower.'" *American Quarterly* 40: 514–36.

Wolnerman, Ch., A. Burstin, and M. S. Geshuri, eds. 1977. *Oswiecim-Auschwitz Memorial Book*. Jerusalem: Irgun Yotzey Oswiecim, Israel.

Wolowelsky, Joel B. 1997. *Women, Jewish Law, and Modernity: New Opportunities in a Post-Feminist Age*. Hoboken, NJ: KTAV.

Wulf, Christoph. 2006. "Praxis." In *Theorizing Rituals: Issues, Topics, Approaches, Concepts*, ed. Jens Kreinath, Jan Snoek, and Michael Strausberg, 395–411. Leiden, Netherlands: Brill.

Ydit, Meir. 1972. "Mehizah." In *Encyclopedia Judaica*, 11: 1234–35. Jerusalem: Encyclopedia Judaica.

YIVO. 1944. *Muzee fun die alte heimen*. New York: YIVO Institute for Jewish Research.

Yoder, Don. 2001. "Sectarian Costume Research in the United States." In *Discovering American Folklife: Essays on Folk Culture and the Pennsylvania Dutch*, by Don Yoder, 143–72. Mechanicsburg, PA: Stackpole Books.

Yoffie, Leah R. C. 1916. "Present-Day Survivals of Ancient Jewish Customs." *Journal of American Folklore* 29: 412–17.

———. 1918. "Yiddish Proverbs, Sayings, etc., in St. Louis, Mo." *Journal of American Folklore* 33: 134–65.

Young, James E. 1993. *The Texture of Memory: Holocaust Memorials and Meaning*. New Haven, CT: Yale University Press.

———, ed. 1994. *The Art of Memory: Holocaust Memorials in History*. New York: Jewish Museum.

———. 2000. *At Memory's Edge: After-Images of the Holocaust in Contemporary Art and Architecture*. New Haven, CT: Yale University Press.

Young, William K. 2004. *The 1950s*. Westport, CT: Greenwood.

Younger, Aryeh. 2013. "Texting and the Power of 'Half Shabbat.'" *Forward* (June 20). http://forward.com/opinion/178988/texting-and-the-power-of-half-shabbat/ (accessed October 20, 2017).

Yudelson, Larry. 2000. "Pinning the Label on Lieberman." *Jewish Forward* (August 25), 9.

Zangwill, Israel. 1938 [1892]. *Children of the Ghetto: A Study of a Peculiar People*. Philadelphia: Jewish Publication Society of America.

Zauderer, David. 2011. "Two Jews, Three Opinions." *Torah from Dixie*. http://www.tfdixie.com/parshat/korach/013.htm (accessed October 24, 2017).

Zavin, Benjamin Bernard. 1968. *The Education of H*Y*M*A*N K*A*P*L*A*N: A Musical Play in Two Acts*. Music and lyrics by Paul Nassau and Oscar Brand. Based on the stories by Leo Rosten. Woodstock, IL: Dramatic Publishing.

Zeitlin, Steve, ed. 1997. *Because God Loves Stories: An Anthology of Jewish Storytelling*. New York: Touchstone.

Zelinsky, Wilbur. 2001. *The Enigma of Ethnicity: Another American Dilemma*. Iowa City: University of Iowa Press.

Zenner, Walter P. 2000. *A Global Community: The Jews from Aleppo, Syria*. Detroit: Wayne State University Press.

Zerubavel, Yael. 1995. *Recovered Roots: Collective Memory and the Making of Israeli National Tradition*. Chicago: University of Chicago Press.

Ziv, Avner. 1998. "Introduction to the Transaction Edition." In *Jewish Humor*, ed. Avner Ziv, 5–16. New Brunswick, NJ: Transaction.

Zukin, Sharon. 2005. *Point of Purchase: How Shopping Changed American Culture*, rev. ed. New York: Routledge.

Zumwalt, Rosemary Lévy. 2019. *Franz Boas: The Emergence of the Anthropologist*. Lincoln: University of Nebraska Press.

Zurawik, David. 2003. *The Jews of Prime Time*. Hanover, NH: University Press of New England.

Zwiebel, David. 2000. "Getting Beyond Misleading Labels." Letter to the Editor, *Jewish Forward* (August 18), 8.

INDEX

www.ingramcontent.com/pod-product-compliance
Lightning Source LLC
Chambersburg PA
CBHW030855270326
41929CB00008B/426